Prosecution in Common Law Jurisdictions

The International Library of Criminology, Criminal Justice and Penology
Series Editors: Gerald Mars and David Nelken

Titles in the Series:

Prosecution in Common Law Jurisdictions

Edited by

Andrew Sanders

Centre for Criminological Research
University of Oxford, UK

KF
5425
P76
1996

Dartmouth

Aldershot · Brookfield USA · Singapore · Sydney

Published by
Dartmouth Publishing Company Limited
Gower House
Croft Road
Aldershot
Hants GU11 3HR
England

Dartmouth Publishing Company
Old Post Road
Brookfield
Vermont 05036
USA

British Library Cataloguing in Publication Data
Prosecution in common law jurisdictions. – (The
  international library of criminology, criminal justice and
  penology)
  1. Common law 2. Prosecution
  I. Series II. Sanders, Andrew, 1952–
  342.5′5042

Library of Congress Cataloging-in-Publication Data
Prosecution in common law jurisdictions / edited by Andrew Sanders.
       p. cm. — (International library of criminology, criminal
  justice, and penology)
     Includes bibliographical references and index.
     ISBN 1-85521-460-1
       1. Prosecution—Great Britain—Decision making. 2. Police—Great
  Britain. 3. Prosecution—United States—Decision making.
  4. Police—United States. I. Sanders, Andrew, 1952–   .
  II. Series: International library of criminology, criminal justice &
  penology.
  K5425.P76 1996
  345.41′05042—dc20
  [344.1055042]   96-11125
                                                                               CIP

ISBN 1 85521 460 1

Printed in Great Britain by Galliard (Printers) Ltd, Great Yarmouth

Contents

PART IV   NON-POLICE PROSECUTIONS

Acknowledgements

The editor and publishers wish to thank the following for permission to use copyright material.

Academic Press Limited for the essays: Katherine de Gama (1988), 'Police Powers and Public Prosecutions: Winning By Appearing To Lose?', *International Journal of the Sociology of Law*, **16**, pp. 339–57. Copyright © 1988 Academic Press Limited. Andrew Sanders (1988), 'Personal Violence and Public Order: The Prosecution of "Domestic" Violence in England and Wales', *International Journal of the Sociology of Law*, **16**, pp. 359–82. Copyright © 1988 Academic Press Limited.

Blackwell Publishers for the essays: Stewart Field (1994), 'Judicial Supervision and the Pre-Trial Process', *Journal of Law and Society*, **21**, pp. 119–35. Copyright © Basil Blackwell Ltd 1994. Doreen McBarnet (1988), 'Law, Policy, and Legal Avoidance: Can Law Effectively Implement Egalitarian Policies?', *Journal of Law and Society*, **15**, pp. 113–21; Bridget M. Hutter (1989), 'Variations in Regulatory Enforcement Styles', *Law and Policy*, **11**, pp. 153–74. Copyright © 1989 Basil Blackwell.

Douglas Hay (1983), 'Controlling the English Prosecutor', *Osgoode Hall Law Journal*, **21**, pp. 165–86. Copyright © 1983, Douglas Hay. By permission of Osgoode Hall Law Journal.

Law and Society Association for the essays: George F. Cole (1970), 'The Decision to Prosecute', *Law and Society Review*, **4**, pp. 331–43; David A. Ford (1991), 'Prosecution as a Victim Power Resource: A Note on Empowering Women in Violent Conjugal Relationships', *Law and Society Review*, **25**, pp. 313–34; Kitty Calavita and Henry N. Pontell (1994), 'The State and White-Collar Crime: Saving the Savings and Loans', *Law and Society Review*, **28**, pp. 297–324. Copyright © 1994 by The Law and Society Association. All rights reserved. Reprinted by permission of the Law and Society Association.

Macmillan Press Limited for the essay: Roger Leng, Michael McConville and Andrew Sanders (1992), 'Researching the Discretions to Charge and to Prosecute' in D. Downes (ed.), *Unravelling Criminal Justice*, pp. 119–37.

Open University Press for the essay: Dee Cook (1989), 'Fiddling Tax and Benefits: Inculpating the Poor, Exculpating the Rich' in Pat Carlen and Dee Cook (eds), *Paying for Crime*, pp. 109–28.

Oxford University Press for the essays: Peter Duff (1993), 'The Prosecutor Fine and Social Control: The Introduction of the Fiscal Fine to Scotland', *British Journal of Criminology*, **33**, pp. 481–503; John Pratt (1989), 'Corporatism: The Third Model of Juvenile Justice', *British Journal of Criminology*, **29**, pp. 236–54.

Police Review Publishing Company for the essays: Tim Newburn, David Brown, Debbie Crisp and Patricia Dewhurst (1991), 'Increasing Public Order', *Policing*, **7**, pp. 22–41; Andy Layzell (1984), 'Discretion in Traffic Law Enforcement', *Policing*, **1**, pp. 245–53.

Sage Publications, Inc. for the essays: Laureen Snider (1990), 'Cooperative Models and Corporate Crime: Panacea or Cop-Out?', *Crime and Delinquency*, **36**, pp. 373–90. Copyright © 1990 Sage Publications, Inc. Reprinted by permission of Sage Publications Inc. Elizabeth A. Stanko (1981), 'The Arrest Versus the Case: Some Observations on Police/ District Attorney Interaction', *Urban Life*, **9**, pp. 395–414. Copyright © 1981 Sage Publications, Inc. Reprinted by permission of Sage Publications, Inc.

Sage Publications Limited for the essay: Gary Slapper (1993), 'Corporate Manslaughter: An Examination of the Determinants of Prosecutorial Policy', *Social and Legal Studies*, **2**, pp. 423–43.

Every effort has been made to trace all the copyright holders but if any have been inadvertently overlooked, the publishers will be pleased to make the necessary arrangement at the first opportunity.

Series Preface

The International Library of Criminology, Criminal Justice and Penology, represents an important publishing initiative designed to bring together the most significant journal essays in contemporary criminology, criminal justice and penology. The series makes available to researchers, teachers and students an extensive range of essays which are indispensable for obtaining an overview of the latest theories and findings in this fast changing subject.

This series consists of volumes dealing with criminological schools and theories as well as with approaches to particular areas of crime, criminal justice and penology. Each volume is edited by a recognised authority who has selected twenty or so of the best journal articles in the field of their special competence and provided an informative introduction giving a summary of the field and the relevance of the articles chosen. The original pagination is retained for ease of reference.

The difficulties of keeping on top of the steadily growing literature in criminology are complicated by the many disciplines from which its theories and findings are drawn (sociology, law, sociology of law, psychology, psychiatry, philosophy and economics are the most obvious). The development of new specialisms with their own journals (policing, victimology, mediation) as well as the debates between rival schools of thought (feminist criminology, left realism, critical criminology, abolitionism etc.) make necessary overviews that offer syntheses of the state of the art. These problems are addressed by the INTERNATIONAL LIBRARY in making available for research and teaching the key essays from specialist journals.

GERALD MARS
Professor in Applied Anthropology, University of Bradford
School of Management

DAVID NELKEN
Distinguished Research Professor, Cardiff Law School,
University of Wales, Cardiff

Introduction

Although criminology is a relatively new discipline, most of the main areas of criminological inquiry were well established before the study of pre-trial criminal justice emerged as a sub-discipline of criminology. And, within criminal justice, research on prosecutions has only really developed in the last 25 years or so. This is at first sight puzzling. For in order to be defined legally as a criminal one must first be convicted, and in order to be convicted one must first be prosecuted. Prosecution forms the crucial link between law enforcement and penal sanction. And even without a conviction, prosecution has symbolic and practical consequences for the prosecuted and others. If, regardless of outcome, the trial is a status-degradation ceremony, then the State can exert power through prosecution.

This way of conceiving the criminal process is, however, relatively recent in origin. Traditionally, prosecution was seen as largely unproblematic. It used to be assumed that when the police arrested or reported individuals for suspected offences, they would prosecute if there was sufficient evidence to do so, but not otherwise. It must have seemed that there was little worth researching. This is despite the common law tradition of allowing enforcement agencies almost unfettered discretion over whether or not to prosecute, which allows agencies to take account of factors other than evidence in making their decisions. The main area of debate, in Britain at any rate, concerned those few occasions when overt political considerations arose, such as in alleged treason or corruption. Until the establishment of the police in the mid-19th century, this was the only type of circumstance in which the State in England and Wales had a direct interest or in which it took direct control. Prosecution of such offences is still a matter for the Attorney-General, a lawyer-politician who is a member of the government. This aspect of prosecutions has been the subject of extensive research, but it poses different questions from those raised by the majority of offences. The former will not be pursued further in this volume, apart from a brief discussion in Chapter 1 by Hay.

The common law tradition of unfettered discretion is sometimes characterized as an 'opportunity' system. This is in contrast to the 'legality' approach common to many European jurisdictions which deny discretion to enforcement agencies (Sanders and Young, 1994). Although there is a good deal of convergence between these systems (the approach in the Netherlands, for instance, is not really classifiable: see Brants and Field 1995), the different principles underlying them are such that they require separate discussion. This volume will therefore be primarily concerned with common law jurisdictions (largely England/Wales and the US). Other jurisdictions will be discussed either where it is useful to compare common law and European approaches (see Chapter 3 by Field) or where particular developments have wider applications (see Chapter 8 by Duff on prosecutor fines in Scotland).

Historical Development: England and Wales

In Chapter 1, Hay shows that, until the late 19th century in England and Wales, crimes which were not overtly political were largely the concern of the victim (acting alone or in an 'Association for the Prosecution of Felons'). Victims who wished to prosecute did so by bringing an action which, in legal form, was similar to a civil action. As the police became better established and responsible for more and more law enforcement, so they gradually took responsibility for prosecutions. Private prosecutions still take place in England and Wales and, indeed, survive the major changes to the system of the mid-1980s which occurred after Hay wrote his article. But the importance of private prosecutions lies less in their number and more in their legal form. For police prosecutions (and now those by the Crown Prosecution Service) retained the original form of the private prosecution and some of its accompaniments, two of which are of particular importance. The first is the complete discretion as to whether or not to proseute (and what to prosecute for), to which we have already referred.

The second important accompaniment was that, as a party to the proceedings, the police could either undertake the prosecution themselves or instruct lawyers to do so. Either way, the police retained control of the prosecution, except in the few very serious cases handled by the office of the Director of Public Prosecutions (DPP). This public office was created in 1879. As Hay shows, when first established and for over 100 years, the limited scope of the DPP's remit represented a compromise between those who wanted to retain England's traditional unsystematic approach to prosecution and those who wanted prosecutions in general to be structured and controlled, as was believed to happen in most of Europe (and, indeed, in Scotland). For over 100 years the office of the DPP remained small, having fewer professional prosecutors than many police forces.

For most of the 20th century, then, in the overwhelming majority of cases the police alone decided whether or not to prosecute, what to prosecute for, and then either conducted the prosecution themselves or instructed lawyers to do so. This system was widely criticized. First, it was generally believed that the police sometimes pursued broad policing goals through prosecution. Prosecuting lawyers could thus be used as tools for the police to pro- secute cases which were weak or in which malpractice was hidden. The Royal Commission on Criminal Procedure, which in 1981 established the blueprint for what was to become the Crown Prosecution Service (CPS), was set up partly because of concern about the prosecution of weak cases in general and miscarriages of justice in particular (see the discussion of the 'Confait affair' by de Gama in Chapter 2). Second, there was consider- able inconsistency of police prosecution decision making. Third, it was thought that there was scope for more diversion of offenders from prosecution. (All these three issues are discussed further in Chapter 10 by Vennard.)

The Crown Prosecution Service was established in 1986. On the basis of the background given above, it might be thought that the intention was to wrest control of prosecutions from the police. While this was the aim of some of those involved in these changes, de Gama shows in Chapter 2 that one cannot assume that this was its underlying purpose, for the changes it established were actually minimalist. She argues that the establishment of the CPS was a crude trade-off for increased police powers which actually had some hidden benefits for the police. For, as Leng et al. also argue in Chapter 14 (on the basis of empirical research), the police control the CPS, rather than vice versa. This is despite a Code for Crown Prosecutors which proclaims the independence of the CPS. The lack of powers available to the CPS is part of the problem, but the greater difficulty is the adversarial system itself. For in this system the police and the prosecution agencies have broadly similar objectives; they are on the 'same side', allowing the police to appeal to the law enforcement duty of the CPS; the police also control the information available to prosecutors. In Chapter 3 Field argues that this need not be so. He contends that inquisitorial systems are capable of exercising more control over police prosecutions than are common law systems, even though they are not always more effective in practice. The 1993 Royal Commission on Criminal Justice missed a golden opportunity to strengthen judicial control of prosecutions in England and Wales.

Discretion

There is a developing body of work in Britain which argues that prosecution is one way in which policing goals can be achieved. In Chapter 14, for instance, Leng et al. show that decisions to prosecute or not flow from the imperatives of police 'working rules' relating to order, authority, 'suspiciousness' and so forth. Newburn et al. (Chapter 4), researching low-level public disorder, found that many charges are used by the police either to protect themselves or to assert their authority on the street. Similarly, in his study of traffic law enforcement, Layzell (Chapter 5) found that whether or not traffic 'tickets' were issued depended on such things as whether a 'purge' was in operation (as a result of public complaints or traditional Christmas drunkenness, for instance), or whether law enforcement was being subordinated to another goal (such as keeping traffic speeds up and therefore congestion down). Although none of these studies uses the term, it can be seen that, where there is de facto discretion, the reason for prosecuting is often 'contempt of cop' on the part of the offender. This should not be seen as mere officiousness on the part of police officers, but as part of their concern to maintain their authority by any reasonable means available.

Some of the England-based research in this volume was undertaken before the inception of the CPS, and some after. Leng et al. argue that little has changed for, since the police 'construct' the prosecution case for the CPS, prosecutors are rarely in a position to challenge police decisions. Few cases are therefore dropped, although in recent years the CPS has become more assertive (Crisp and Moxon, 1994). The congruence of approach of police officers and prosecutors gives rise, according to Cole's path-breaking American research (Chapter 11), to 'exchange relationships' between them. Later research did not always adopt this explanation, and cooperative relationships were not found to be inevitable (see Chapter 12 by Stanko, but also Chapter 10 by Vennard). What is clear, though, is that formal power and actual power were different, and that the dynamic of power relations between prosecutors and police officers, the courts and the community, is complex. Cole shows that a variety of influences are exerted on prosecutors, which must limit the effectiveness of any one set of rules or guidelines such as the CPS Code in the UK.

The Royal Commission on Criminal Justice, which reported in 1993, did not appreciate these subtleties, as Field shows in Chapter 3. Substantial change in Britain in the near future is therefore unlikely. What if de Gama is right to argue that the intention of the CPS–police structure is to return the police to its original order-maintanance role, with prosecution as a subsidiary element; to allow the police to control prosecutions to whatever extent is required for them to carry out that role? If this is the case (and for as long as it remains the hidden agenda of goverment), then the system will work much as intended and change will be unlikely regardless of any analysis which a Royal Commission might bring to bear on the issue (McConville et al., 1991).

It may be that relationships between police and prosecutors in England and Wales are now displaying more of the conflictual features identified by Stanko in Chapter 12, although she does not argue that these conflicts are common in the US, nor does any evidence suggest that they are in Britain. But more important than knowing the *number*, is identifying the *type* of cases in which there is conflict: how far do prosecution agencies assert their particular goals (e.g. certainty of conviction) above those of the police (e.g. order maintenance) in cases of particular importance to the latter? The answer to this question is not known. It is not even clear how usefully we can generalize across apparently similar jurisdictions for, as Vennard shows in Chapter 10, there are cultural and geographical differences between the various prosecution agencies which influence the exercise of prosecution discretion. Even if prosecution agencies do assert the primacy of probability of conviction, this is no guard against miscarriages of justice, for these generally involve convictions. If the police 'construct' cases to *appear* strong, as Leng et al. argue, police and prosecution goals will coincide and the risk of miscarriage will not be reduced.

It should not be surprising if research reveals prosecution to be the tool of law enforcement, worrying though this may be for traditional constitutionalists on the one hand, and civil libertarians anxious to control the police on the other. Unless prosecution is made automatic, as in 'legality'-based systems, it is impossible to eliminate the discretion that allows prosecution decisions to be manipulated in the interests of broader policing goals. And the ultimate goal of prosecution will always be invoked when judging police action; for unless police detention is to be allowed even when there is no evidence of criminal activity, the test of legality of detention has to be the existence of evidence of a crime which is triable by a court. Furthermore, it is commonplace in the literature on white-collar crime and 'regulation' that prosecution is considered as only part of an armoury of compliance mechanisms. It is only the artificial separation of this criminological literature from that on 'criminal justice' which has obscured the essentially similar relationship between law enforcement and prosecution in both 'regulatory' and 'policing' spheres of activity. Only the most recent British criminal justice texts (e.g. Ashworth, 1994; Sanders and Young, 1994) give substantial treatment to the former. It is precisely the intention of Part IV ('Non-Police Prosecutions') to highlight the parallels between these two subject areas.

We have seen that the CPS was ostensibly established to reduce miscarriages of justice, to reduce inconsistency of decision making and to facilitate more diversion. Doubtless the rationale behind prosecution agencies in other jurisdictions is similar. We have also seen that there is little reason to believe that the CPS or similar agencies succeed in relation to the first objective. What about inconsistency? The reality is that, once again, prosecution agencies are far more controlled by the police than vice versa. That patterns of discretionary decisions which might be perceived as inconsistent from the legal point of view (that is, inconsistently adhering to official guidance) might be entirely consistent applications of working rules is evident from all the research discussed so far (see Chapters 4, 5 and 14).

If, as Layzell observes, some police officers ignore some offences while others are keen to enforce them, thus producing inconsistent patterns, this is something about which courts are generally unconcerned. As long as there is sufficient evidence on which to convict, English courts will not take into account the equity of one person being prosecuted where another is not (Sanders and Young, 1994). Thus the CPS and similar prosecution agencies will not drop such cases (for their concern is also convictability and not fairness); the CPS can, of course, do nothing about cases which the police do not pursue.

Diversion

We have seen that the police role in prosecution has developed in an ad hoc manner, allowing the police almost unfettered discretion. This discretion is as general in relation to diversion as to all other aspects of prosecutions. Since the CPS has been grafted on to the pre-existing system, it can influence cases which were not diverted but which should have been, but has no influence over cases which were diverted but which should not have been. Enquiry into diversion from prosecution in any common law jurisdiction operating the 'opportunity' principle has therefore to focus on the police as much as on the prosecution agency.

The basic idea behind diversion is simple. One of the lessons of the criminological labelling theory which became prominent in the 1960s was that the criminal sanction could do more harm than good, especially in relation to unsophisticated criminals who might not yet have criminal self-identities. It follows that diversion from prosecution should be an option in relatively minor cases involving largely law-abiding offenders. This idea was initially taken up almost exclusively in relation to juveniles in many different countries. In Chapter 6, Hancock discusses her findings which, although Australian, are representative of a considerable amount of research in common law jurisdictions, particularly in her explicit adoption of the labelling perspective. This research illustrates some of the key issues surrounding diversion. Since the main assumption behind diversion is that dispositions should be chosen in order to minimize recidivism, the most influential factors are likely to be 'welfarist' rather than 'legalistic' (the latter according to a 'justice' approach). This, though, involves evaluations of offenders' characters and family environments, and predictions of their future behaviour. Hancock, like Piliavin and Briar in their famous 1964 study, found that this led to stereotyping based on factors related to class. It is generally thought that crime is related to class, age, environment and so forth, a view supported by official statistics and everyday observation of the criminal courts at work. If these facts really are a product, in part, of labelling processes, it would seem from this research (and many similar studies discussed by Sanders and Young, 1994) that welfarist approaches contribute to those labelling processes. Ironically, then, diversion may exacerbate the very problem it is designed to ameliorate.

In Britain the idea of extensive diversion for adults became accepted in the 1980s. Home Office guidance has been issued periodically which encourages the police to caution adults as well as juveniles. It lists the 'public interest' factors of which the police should take account; these also appear in the CPS Code (e.g. seriousness of offence, offender's record, attitude of the victim, subsequent attitude and behaviour of the offender). By 1992, 24 per cent of all adults found guilty or cautioned were in fact cautioned, a rise from 4 per cent in 1978 (the figures for juveniles in 1978 and 1992 were 49 and 78 per cent respectively). Do these remarkable rises indicate that most divertible cases are being diverted? Evans' research on young adults suggests not (Chapter 7). A change in the 'law and order' attitudes fostered by 'cop culture' will be needed before this can happen. The research of Leng et al. (Chapter 14) also suggests that prosecution screening diverts relatively few from prosecution, despite this being a key aim of the CPS. Where all the information on which the diversion decision is based comes from the police, it is not surprising that police attitudes dominate.

It seems that the rise in English diversion rates, for juveniles and adults, could be as much due to offenders being diverted into the system (cautioned rather than NFA) as well as being diverted out (cautioned rather than prosecuted). This is known as 'net widening'. Duff (Chapter 8) describes the 'prosecutor fine' in Scotland, whereby an offender can be asked to pay a fine without a court hearing. He establishes that this has led both to 'net widening' and to diversion from prosecution. Some have argued that the explanation behind net widening is a push to increase discipline and surveillance. For this reason, and because of the labelling processes facilitated by the 'welfarist' position discussed earlier, 'justice' approaches have been gathering momentum in the last 20 years. Duff, though, argues that the prosecutor fine, at any rate, is not an example of the 'dispersal of discipline', but instead part of a developing 'administrative–bureaucratic' style of criminal justice. Pratt, however, sees no contradiction between the 'dispersal of discipline' idea and an 'administrative–bureaucratic' style of criminal justice (Chapter 9). Reviewing juvenile justice as a whole, he argues that these developments can be best understood as 'corporatism'. Whether or not one agrees with this argument, his analysis shows that one should not be misled by the rhetoric of 'welfare' and 'justice' into believing that these ideologies actually drive the system. Cook's discussion of recent non-prosecution policies towards allegedly fraudulent welfare claimants adds further weight to Pratt's thesis, for she argues that this policy is driven by fiscal rather than humane considerations (Chapter 19). The argument between 'welfare' and 'justice', and the appearance of 'diversion' as humane, may in fact obscure a harsher reality.

Non-police Prosecutions

In all common law jurisdictions there are, in addition to the police, many specialist law enforcement agencies for particular types of crime. These agencies (e.g. the Inland Revenue which deals with tax evasion, and the Factory Inspectorate which investigates health and safety at work) decide whether to prosecute, divert or take no action at all. In England and Wales they carry out the prosecution themselves without reference to the CPS. Like the police, then, they have virtually unfettered discretion. Unlike the police, this is usually exercised against prosecuting, although there are exceptions (see Chapters 18 and 19). The Inland Revenue, for instance, prosecutes very few cases (see Chapter 19 by Cook). Moreover, a study of 96 Australian non-police agencies found that, over a three-year period, one-third had launched not one prosecution. This is all despite the tremendous cost in life, health and monetary loss caused by 'white-collar' crime (see Sanders and Young, 1994, and Nelken (ed.), 1995, for detailed discussions). The decision-making structures of these agencies, unlike that of the police, encourages non-prosecution (see Hutter in Chapter 20; Sanders, 1985), but that is probably because prosecution is seen as a last resort as distinct from a normal response. The decision-making structure, then, is the facilitative mechanism for, rather than the cause of, this 'cooperative' or 'compliance' approach (these terms are discussed and elaborated by Snider in Chapter 17 and by Hutter in Chapter 20).

The divergent patterns of these different agencies therefore invite comparison. Slapper's paper is interesting because it draws attention not only to the propensity of non-police agencies not to prosecute, but also to their tendency to prosecute for less serious charges (Chapter 16). Nearly as many people die at work as on the streets, yet corporate manslaughter (let alone corporate murder) charges are almost unknown. It might be argued that this is all due to the non-criminogenic character of non-police crime. Labelling theorists, to return to a theme canvassed earlier, would observe that the causal relationship could equally plausibly be reversed: perhaps it is the lack of enforcement which creates the non-criminogenic image. This is a major part of Snider's argument in Chapter 17, though she goes beyond labelling theory by grounding her analysis in the structural conditions under which corporate crime flourishes in capitalist society.

We saw that the movement to diversion was predicated on the belief that prosecution should be used only where it is considered more effective at minimizing recidivism than other methods. Can it be claimed that 'compliance' approaches to white-collar law enforcement reduce recidivism? This debate, which Slapper refers to in Chapter 16, is explored at length in Nelken's (1995) volume and so will not be pursued here, but the continuing high levels of white-collar crime do not inspire confidence in the efficiency of 'compliance' approaches, just as high levels of 'ordinary' crime do not inspire confidence in the efficiency of 'punitive' approaches. Alternative explanations for these differential patterns include relational factors (advocated by Hutter) and economic factors (propounded by Slapper, Snider and – in Chapter 18 – by Calavita and Pontell).

Economic explanations are given greater credibility when we compare different types of non-police agencies. All of the agencies discussed by Hutter in Chapter 20 are of one type: their 'suspect populations' are businesses, and their crimes are committed in the course of business. While Hutter rightly draws attention to the different enforcement strategies of various non-police agencies (and to differences within geographically dispersed agencies), she does not dispute the fact that *none* of the agencies which she studied adopts the 'deterrence' or 'criminalization' model generally used by the police. We could thus argue that the differences between most non-police agencies are not as great as the similarities.

There are two important exceptions to the general use of the compliance approach by non-police agencies. First, there are those which regulate financial institutions. In Chapter 18, Calavita and Pontell use state theory to explain recent 'crackdowns' on savings and loan fraud. Rather than indicating a move away from compliance approaches in general, thus undermining the economic explanations discussed earlier, the selective approach to these frauds adds weight to those economic explanations. Second, there are the (few) non-police agencies whose 'suspect population' is similar to that of the police. Enormous differences can be observed between the approach of the department of Social Security (DSS) and almost any other non-police body, as Cook shows in Chapter 19. This is important because the DSS is virtually the only non-police agency in England and Wales whose suspect population – like that of the police – is poor. There is no doubt that the pattern of prosecution and diversion in common law jurisdictions is class-biased, although there is no reason to believe that repression of the poor is the underlying motivation. Some form of socioeconomic explanation is needed, based on what Slapper calls 'coherence without conspiracy' (Nelken, 1983). However, even this may be too generous when, as Hutter observes, Conservative-controlled local authorities prosecute white-collar offenders less frequently than do Labour-controlled local authorities.

Reading these chapters may lead us to the conclusion that 'white-collar crime' would be greatly lessened, and its perpetrators more readily brought to justice, if its enforcement were tightened up. McBarnet, in Chapter 21, cautions us against this simplistic conclusion. Although not specifically about prosecutions, this essay is really arguing that a more vigorous prosecution policy might achieve little against those who can afford to manipulate the law and keep one step ahead of the prosecuting authorities. The policies described in Part IV may thus not be so foolish as they appear. That, however, does not make the disparity between the treatment of the rich and of the poor any fairer. It means that, if society itself is unfair, we cannot expect the legal system to be fair either.

Victims

Recently, after years of almost total neglect, victims have come to assume great importance in discussions of criminal justice. In Britain there is now a 'Victims' Charter', which recommends that the views and interests of victims be taken into account when deciding whether to prosecute. This will often be consonant with policing goals (although, if the evidence is weak or the case cautionable, not always with prosecution goals). However, where the interests of the victim clash with other police working rules, the police officers have difficult decisions to make which will not always favour the victim. Nor should they. We have seen that police caution guidelines and the CPS Code list several factors which should influence the prosecution decision, of which the victim is only one. The problem is that these factors are not prioritized. This provides an opportunity for the police to override the victim's views, ostensibly on a legitimate pretext, when the real reason may lie in an illegitimate 'working rule'.

Leng et al. identify the wishes of victims as one of several 'working rules', but this research reveals that some victims carry more weight than others. Shops and businesses, for instance, appear to be more influential than individual victims of violence. In Chapter 13 Sanders compares prosecution decisions in domestic violence cases with those in non-domestic violence cases, finding that while there is less willingness on the part of the police to prosecute in the former than in the latter group, the really determinate factor was whether or not a threat existed to order or police authority. This suggests that 'soft' enforcement of the law in cases of domestic violence (which has given rise to mandatory arrest laws in some American states; see e.g. Sherman and Berk, 1984) has little to do with 'cop culture' or tolerance of violence against women as such. Very recent English research seems to support this view, finding that the police now do usually arrest and prosecute when this is what the victim of domestic violence wants, if she is prepared to testify (Hoyle, 1996). It remains true, though, that in many other crimes – e.g. burglary and public order offences – the views of the victim are not taken into account if the police wish to prosecute. This may in part be because the law makes conviction without the testimony of the victim easier in such cases. But Hoyle found that, in domestic violence cases, the police adopt 'the wishes of the victim' as an invariable working rule even when they do not need their testimony.

An ambiguity here, and at the heart of this whole area of policy, is whether it is the *views* or the *interests* of victims which we believe should be taken into account. The two cannot always be assumed to be the same. Early versions of the CPS Code referred to the 'attitude' of the victim, while the 1994 edition refers to the victim's 'interests'. An 'Explanatory Memorandum' accompanying the Code makes it clear that this is a deliberate change of thinking, and that while the prosecutor should be aware of the views of the victim, it is his/her interests which should have primacy. It is because attitudes and interests cannot be assumed to be consonant that, as Ford discusses in Chapter 15, it is sometimes argued that victims should not be permitted to drop charges. However, both Ford and Hoyle argue that it cannot always (or even usually) be assumed that it is in the interest of victims of domestic violence that offenders be prosecuted. Thus Ford contends that both prosecution and non-prosecution can be used as strategies by victims; removing the right of a domestic violence victim to drop a charge would undermine what little power she has within her abusive relationship. Rather than seeing the dropping of charges as a problem for the criminal justice system we could consider it as, in Ford's words, a 'victim power resource'. At the same time, having this power imposes a responsibility on the victim which can be manipulated by the abusive partner who may intimidate her into dropping charges. Ford leaves unanswered the question how far the *ostensible* views of victims should be heeded when these may not coincide with their interests.

Similar problems can be canvassed in areas of criminal activity regulated by non-police agencies. It is often argued that these agencies rarely prosecute because, among other things, the victims (e.g. factory employees in the case of health and safety legislation) would suffer as much as the criminals (i.e. the companies). Is it the *interests* or the *views* of the employees which are the concern here? How systematically are their views sought? Is the victim invoked in non-police cases because this might seem more acceptable than identifying economic factors? Whose interests is the State protecting or promoting when prosecution decisions are made? Who is the victim anyway? The victims of fraud, pollution and so forth are widely dispersed but rarely recognized as victims, while the victims of minor public order offences often appear (according to the research of Leng et al. and Newburn et al.) to be the police themselves. Protection of police officers from verbal abuse was presumably not the intention of those who framed recent public order law, but its potential in this area was quickly identified by them.

Underlying these questions is the concern which McBarnet articulates: can we expect a criminal justice system to attempt to correct structural inequalities, whether manifested in domestic violence or violence at work? If we juxtapose Part IV with Parts II and III we find that prosecution is the norm where the police are concerned (except in juvenile cases), whereas diversion or no action at all prevails in most non-police agencies. Would this be the pattern if the views or the interests of victims were equally influential across the board? These questions are all implicitly raised by the material in Part IV (and Parts I and II) as well as in Part III, but regrettably it is rare for them to be made explicit in discussions of prosecutions, whether of 'white-collar' or of 'normal' crime. If this collection acts as a spur to inquire and to research these complex matters, it will have served its purpose.

References

Ashworth, A. (1994), *The Criminal Process*, Oxford: OUP.

Brants, C. and Field, S. (1995), 'Discretion and Accountability in Prosecution' in P. Fennell et al., *Criminal Justice in Europe: A Comparative Study*, Oxford: Clarendon.

Crisp, D. and Moxon, D. (1994), *Case Screening by the CPS*, London: HMSO (HORS 137).

Hoyle, C. (1996), *Responding to Domestic Violence: the Role of the Police and the Criminal Justice System* (unpublished D. Phil. thesis, Centre for Criminological Research, University of Oxford).

McConville, M., Sanders, A. and Leng, R. (1991), *The Case for the Prosecution*, London: Routledge.

Nelken, D. (1983), *The Limits of the Legal Process*, London: Academic Press.

Nelken, D. (ed.) (1995), *White Collar Crime*, Aldershot: Dartmouth.

Piliavin, I. and Briar, S. (1964), 'Police Encounters with Juveniles', *American Journal of Sociology*, **70**, 206.

Sanders, A. (1985), 'Class Bias in Prosecutions', *Howard Journal of Criminal Justice*, **24**, 76.

Sanders, A. and Young, R. (1994), *Criminal Justice*, London: Butterworths.

Sherman, L. and Berk, R. (1984), 'The Specific Deterrent Effects of Arrest for Domestic Assault', *American Sociological Review*, **49**.

Part I
Structuring and Controlling
Prosecutions

[1]

CONTROLLING
THE ENGLISH PROSECUTOR

By Douglas Hay*

I. INTRODUCTION

In two 1971 appeals, both the Ontario Court of Appeal and the Supreme Court of Canada affirmed a High Court ruling upholding the Attorney-General's discretion to conduct criminal prosecutions as he saw fit, particularly with respect to the decision to prosecute and the mode of proceeding.[1] In the course of its judgment, the High Court had recapitulated the English history of the Attorney-General's exclusive rights to issue a fiat for a writ of error, to exhibit an *ex officio* criminal information, to enter a *nolle prosequi* or stay of proceedings, and to act in relator actions.[2] Not confining itself to the delineation of these powers, however, the Court expressed some general propositions about the right to prosecute:

> there has existed in the United Kingdom, and thus in Canada, a constitutional discretion in the Attorney-General, which discretion is exercised on behalf of the Crown, to deal with the institution and control of prosecutions. *It therefore follows* that the right of the individual to equality before the law . . . is modified by the *exclusive* constitutional right of the Attorney-General, as the chief law officer of the Crown, to deal with the prosecution of the offences under our law. [Emphasis added.][3]

This says, or appears to say, too much. If "exclusive" means that particular powers of the Attorney-General are not subject to judicial supervision, and that the Attorney-General is answerable for them only to Parliament, it is an unexceptional statement of the law. But it would be a mistake to take this to mean that in England only the Attorney-General or his agents could prosecute,[4] although such an interpretation would be consistent with an at-

---

© Copyright, 1983, Douglas Hay.

* Associate Professor, Law and History, Osgoode Hall Law School and York University. A version of this paper was presented at the Annual Lecture Series, Osgoode Hall Law School, December 2, 1981. The historical research on which it is based was generously supported by the Social Sciences and Humanities Research Council (Canada) and the Social Science Research Council (United Kingdom). Those findings will be published at length elsewhere, with full references. I am grateful to Professors J.M. Beattie, B.M. Dickens and J.Ll.J. Edwards (Toronto), Reuben Hasson (Osgoode) and John Smith (Nottingham) for reading another version of this paper.

[1] *R.* v. *Smythe*, [1971] 2 O.R. 209, 17 D.L.R. (3d) 389, 3 C.C.C. (2d) 97, *aff'd* (1971), 3 C.C.C. (2d) 366 (S.C.C.).

[2] For a full account of the history and powers of the Attorney-General, cited by the court, see Edwards, *The Law Officers of the Crown* (London: Sweet & Maxwell, 1964). The *ex officio* information was abolished by the *Criminal Law Act*, 1967, c. 58, s. 6 (6) (U.K.). The fiat for the writ of error was replaced by judicial certificate in 1960: *Administration of Justice Act*, 1960, 8 Eliz. 2, c. 65, s. 1 (U.K.).

[3] *Supra* note 1, at 222 (O.R.), 402 (D.L.R.), 109-10 (C.C.C.).

[4] A misreading might be fostered by the statement (at 219 (O.R.), 399 (D.L.R.), 107 (C.C.C.)) that "it was the King's constitutional right to prosecute *all* [emphasis added] crimes, and it was on his behalf that the Attorney-General instituted the prosecutions." The reference here is to a paragraph in *Wilkes* v. *The King* (1768), Wilm. 322, 97 E.R. 123, which in fact established only that an *ex officio* information could be exhibited by servants of the King other than the Attorney-General. In any case, it said nothing about any other criminal prosecutions, that is, the vast majority. See text accompanying note 15, *infra*.

titude to prosecutorial powers that can be found in other Canadian cases, which have held that "the State alone can prosecute," that the Attorney-General is the proper representative of the State, and that when a private individual attempts to prosecute any but minor offences, law or policy or both suggest that he or she should not be encouraged to do so.[5] English as well as Canadian authorities have been cited in support.

What follows is not a discussion of the present law of Canada. It is a brief sketch of the origins of a different attitude, in England, to the wider implications of private prosecutions. Much of the emphasis in Canadian cases and comments is on the malignant dangers lurking in private use of the law. Farris C.J. in a decision on an appeal before the British Columbia Supreme Court, said in 1946:

> For individuals who are thinking only of themselves and not of society as a whole to have the right to institute and carry on criminal proceedings would destroy the whole fabric of the recognised fairness of our criminal prosecutions.[6]

Another statement, often quoted, is that of Miller J. of Manitoba in 1964:

> [Greater rights to private prosecutors would] unnecessarily widen the field of prosecution of Her Majesty's subjects to any obsessed, vindictive, unscrupulous, self-styled saviour. Her Majesty's subjects are entitled to freedom from unwarranted prosecution.[7]

And in 1976, Gushue J. of Newfoundland on an appeal from a conviction obtained by a private prosecutor without the knowledge or concurrence of the Attorney-General, declared that without such concurrence the result of private prosecutions "could very well be anarchy."[8] These and other judgments emphasize the beneficent effects of the Crown's quasi-judicial role in protecting the rights of the accused, notably as a shield to unjust and malicious accusations.[9] Almost entirely absent is consideration of two facts of striking significance to an historian of English criminal law: that private prosecution was carefully protected until the recent past, and that it was thought an important constitutional guarantee of civil liberty.[10]

---

[5] *R.* v. *Gilmore* (1903), 6 O.L.R. 286, 7 C.C.C. 219 (H.C.); *Woo Tuck* v. *Scallen* (1928), 46 Que. K.B. 437 at 441, 51 C.C.C. 365 at 368; *R.* v. *Whiteford*, [1947] 1 W.W.R. 903 at 907, 89 C.C.C. 74 at 77-78 (B.C.S.C.); *Campbell* v. *Sumida* (1964), 49 D.L.R. (2d) 263 at 270-71, 50 W.W.R. 16 at 25, [1965] 3 C.C.C. 29 at 38-39 (Man. C.A.); *Mandelbaum* v. *Denstedt* (1968), 66 W.W.R. 636 at 640, [1969] 3 C.C.C. 119 at 128 (Man. C.A.); *R.* v. *Dalton* (1976), 22 A.P.R. 287 at 290, 292-93, 294, 11 N. & P.E.I.R. 287 at 290, 292-93, 294 (Nfld. C.A.). *Supra* note 1, at 370-71.

[6] *Whiteford, supra* note 5, at 906 (W.W.R.), 76 (C.C.C.).

[7] *Campbell, supra* note 5, at 271 (D.L.R.), 25 (W.W.R.), 39 (C.C.C.).

[8] *Dalton, supra* note 5, at 294 (A.P.R.), 294 (N. & P.E.I.R.).

[9] *Campbell, supra* note 5, at 271 (D.L.R.), 25 (W.W.R.), 39 (C.C.C.); *Mandelbaum, supra* note 5, at 638 (W.W.R.), 126 (C.C.C.); and *Dalton, supra* note 5, at 293-94 (A.P.R.), 293-94 (N. & P.E.I.R.).

[10] The fullest account of this "basic right, derived from English Law" is that of Wilson J. in *R.* v. *Schwerdt* (1957), 23 W.W.R. 374, 119 C.C.C. 81 (B.C.S.C.), in which the possibility that an Attorney-General might refuse to prosecute where he should do so is considered at 385 (W.W.R.), 91 (C.C.C.); that possibility is also mentioned in *R.* v. *Weiss* (1915), 8 Sask. L.R. 74 at 76, 23 D.L.R. 710 at 712, 23 C.C.C. 460 at 463 (S.C.C.). See also *Re McMicken* (1912), 22 Man. R. 693 at 701-702, 8 D.L.R. 550 at 556, 20 C.C.C. 334 at 342 (C.A.); and *R. ex rel. McLeod* v. *Boulding* (1920), 53 D.L.R. 657, 33 C.C.C. 227 (Sask. C.A.). The place of private prosecution in Canadian law has arisen recently in two cases, decided in the Ontario Court of Appeal, for which leave to appeal was granted by the Supreme Court of Canada on 17 December, 1981 (*Re*

In the words of Sir James Stephen, writing in 1883, private prosecutions "both in our own days and in earlier times, have given a legal vent to feelings in every way entitled to respect, and have decided peaceably and in an authentic manner many questions of great constitutional importance."[11] Many other commentators in the nineteenth century were more emphatic: they argued that the engrossing of all criminal prosecutions into the hands of the law officers of the Crown, or the police, was to be resisted vigorously. The constitutional history of England suggested to them that, far from being the proper source of protection for the citizen against unjust charges, the executive could well be the most dangerous of oppressors. One of the crucial safeguards of the citizenry against an executive contemptuous of liberty was the right of private prosecution. In the twentieth century that tradition has not been so strongly expressed, but there are signs that it may be reviving.[12] A review of its history suggests that Canadians should be more attentive to it also.

II. THE ENGLISH PRIVATE PROSECUTOR

It invites confusion to suggest that the English Attorney-General since the mid-eighteenth century has held a virtual monopoly "to deal with the prosecution of the offences under our law."[13] Nor is it very helpful to look at the treatises for the evidence: the right of any private citizen to initiate and conduct a prosecution through to conviction, whether he was the victim or not, was so constantly exercised in the eighteenth century that it needed no comment. It was in fact the paradigm of prosecution. More than eighty percent of indictable offences (all of them tried by judge and jury, and constituting about one half of all criminal cases) were prosecuted by the victim of the crime or his agent.[14] Most of the remaining offences were prosecuted by ordinary citizens who happened to occupy the rotating office of parish constable at the time and who had been bound over by magistrates to prosecute because the victim of the crime was too poor or otherwise incapable. A handful of cases were prosecuted by the Treasury Solicitor, acting for the government in coining cases and thus in some sense as a state prosecutor.

Finally, a very small number of cases, fewer than one percent of the total, were prosecuted at the direction of the Attorney-General or his agents. Almost all of these were state trials, usually for treason or seditious libel. The latter,

---

Dowson and The Queen (1981), 62 C.C.C. (2d) 286, 24 C.R. (3d) 139; *Re Inderpaul Candhoke, ex p. Howard Buchbinder* (unreported), decided at the same time for the same reasons). These judgments turned on the question of the point at which the Attorney-General's power to direct a stay may be exercised, but implicitly raise many of the policy issues discussed in this article. See Kopyto, *Dowson/Buchbinder Case Comment* (1982), 25 Crim. L.Q. 66, published after the lecture on which the present article was based, for a discussion of some of the legal and policy issues. Kopyto's *Comment* is unfortunately marred by serious errors in the brief and undocumented historical account he gives at 90-92.

[11] *A History of the Criminal Law in England* (London: Macmillan, 1883) vol. 1 at 496. On the meaning of the term "private prosecution", see *infra* note 35.

[12] *Infra* note 68.

[13] *Smythe, supra* note 3.

[14] The numbers given here and below are those for Staffordshire in the second half of the eighteenth century; it is likely that they are comparable to those for other counties. See Hay, *War, Dearth and Theft in the Eighteenth Century: the Record of the English Courts* (1982), 95 Past and Present 124 at 151. For the nineteenth century *cf.* Philips, *Crime and Authority in Victorian England* (London: Croom Helm, 1977) at 123 *ff.*

which were more numerous, were usually prosecuted in the eighteenth and nineteenth centuries by the Attorney-General, exercising his unique privilege of prosecuting grave misdemeanours by an *ex officio* information in King's Bench. This procedure eliminated the grand jury, could allow the careful packing of a special jury, and saddled the defendant with heavy costs even if the Crown lost. The information was therefore often attacked as the monstrous offspring of Star Chamber, an anomaly of which the constitution should be purged. The courts upheld *ex officio* informations, but they fell into disuse in the latter part of the nineteenth century because of their connotations of political oppression. They were always few in number.[15]

Thus the typical prosecution in England was on indictment at the initiative of a private citizen who was the victim of a crime and who conducted the prosecution in almost all cases. Blackstone's only mention of this most obvious fact of eighteenth-century English criminal law was the remark that "indictments . . . are preferred . . . in the name of the King, but at the suit of any private prosecutor. . . ."[16] Chitty began his account of the criminal law with the observation that "as offenses, for the most part, more immediately affect a particular individual, it is not usual for any other person to interfere."[17]

When he went to law (ninety-four percent of prosecutors were men[18]), the private individual enjoyed discretion at many crucial points. He could often choose the charge on the indictment, either because the recognizance binding him to prosecute did not specify the offence exactly, or because the court did not inquire provided some indictment was preferred, or because he exercised the prerogative of any citizen to charge any other with any offence before the grand jury. Even the indictment, the only formal written record of the charge, could be drawn by his own lawyer on his instructions, rather than by the Clerk of the Court. The effective result was often that the prosecutor could choose among a variety of likely penalties, or do his utmost to ensure that technical drafting problems (a frequent cause of failed prosecutions) were dealt with by his own solicitors. Thus Matthew Boulton, head of the famous engineering firm of Boulton and Watt, was well pleased with the craftsmanship of his lawyers in a difficult burglary prosecution in 1801. Boulton wanted a death sentence, and had high hopes for the trial: the indictment measured two feet by four, contained eight counts, and, according to Boulton's son, "it appears to be formed like a swivel gun and may be directed to all points as circumstances require."[19]

The private prosecutor also had much influence in deciding what witnesses to take before the magistrate for the preliminary hearing (which was

---

[15] Although approximately 6,000 indictments were laid at Quarter Sessions and Assizes in Staffordshire, the Attorney-General exhibited fewer than twenty *ex officio* informations against defendants in the county between 1742 and 1802. About twice that many criminal informations were exhibited by private prosecutors through the Master of the Crown Office (author's unpublished findings).

[16] 4 *Commentaries* 303.

[17] *A Practical Treatise on the Criminal Law* (1816) vol. I at 1.

[18] *Supra* note 14.

[19] Letter (March 8, 1801), Birmingham Reference Library, *Boulton and Watt MSS, Parcel B*; Public Record Office, Assi 5/121 Staffs. Lent 1801. The case is discussed in Hay, *Manufacturers and the Criminal Law in the Later Eighteenth Century: Crime and 'Police' in South Staffordshire* (1983), Past & Present Colloquium, Police and Policing.

not a necessary step), and before the grand jury (which was necessary for the finding of any indictment). The fact that a preliminary hearing was optional, but that it was always followed by a grand jury hearing, increased the discretionary powers of the prosecutor. If he decided to avoid the preliminary hearing and go directly to the grand jury with what came to be called a "voluntary bill", on which only his own witnesses were heard, he could seek an indictment for any offence and construct a case without the accused even being aware that proceedings had begun.[20] If he chose to go before a magistrate first, his evidence was sometimes heard *ex parte*, and it was said in both the eighteenth and nineteenth centuries that lay magistrates were loath to dismiss charges, apparently believing that that was the proper role of the grand jury, and perhaps influenced by clerks with a pecuniary interest in prosecutions.

If, for whatever reasons, the prosecutor decided to drop the charge, he could do so without resulting official inquiry. In the case of a voluntary bill, this could be done at will and without penalty, as there had been no recognizances. On the other hand, a prosecutor bound over in preliminary hearings could drop the charge by forfeiting the recognizance or, with a little care, perhaps at no cost at all. A new witness with contradictory testimony, or hesitation and a contrived appearance of insincerity on the part of the prosecutor, might convince the grand jurors (who had no depositions from the preliminary hearing) to throw out the charge.[21] In the early nineteenth century, critics argued that both the collusive dropping of charges and vexatious or malicious prosecutions were facilitated by the nature of preliminary inquiries and grand jury hearings.[22]

The private prosecutor also strongly influenced the outcome of the trial through the fact that he chose his own solicitor, who instructed counsel (if a barrister was retained) to conduct the case in the manner most likely to yield the outcome he wished. In these circumstances, it was not unknown for the prosecuting lawyer to be unhappy with the result. In one case in 1787 the barrister petitioned for a pardon for a prisoner whom he had just successfully prosecuted, declaring that he:

---

[20] Replaced by "bill of indictment" proceedings since the abolition of the grand jury in 1933: *Administration of Justice (Miscellaneous Provisions) Act*, 1933, 23 & 24 Geo. 5, c. 36, s. 2 (U.K.). Its recent use by the Crown to avoid preliminary hearings in cases in Northern Ireland has drawn criticisms reminiscent of those directed against the *ex officio* information, now defunct, in earlier centuries. See *The Guardian*, Oct. 6, 1982, "Crown Tries to Avoid Supergrass Hearing."

[21] On the other hand, to get a *nolle prosequi* with the consent of the prosecutor or at his request required the fiat of the Attorney-General: *R.* v. *Emlyn* (Trinity 1820; Chitty, *A Practical Treatise on the Criminal Law* (2nd ed., 1826) vol. I at 479); *R.* v. *Cranmer* (1700), 12 Mod. 648, 88 E.R. 1578, 1 Ld. Raym. 721, 91 E.R. 1381. See also Edwards, *supra* note 2, at 238.

[22] For evidence that such practices occurred before some magistrates and grand juries in the 1840s, see the *Appendix to the Royal Commission on Criminal Law, Eighth Report* (c. 656, 1845). A summary of some of the testimony on these points is given in Pue, *The Criminal Twilight Zone: Pre-Trial Procedures in the 1840's* (1983), 21 Alta. L. Rev. 335 at 338-39, 352-53 (*ex parte* or inadequate preliminary hearings), 347-49, 355 (perjury before grand juries), 354 (pecuniary interests of clerks and weak cases going forward), 356 (malicious use of voluntary bill). Widely scattered evidence in other sources supports such assertions. On the *Report* see also Cornish, "Defects in Prosecuting: Professional Views in 1845," in Glazebrook, ed., *Reshaping Criminal Law* (London: Stevens, 1978).

170   OSGOODE HALL LAW JOURNAL   [VOL. 21, NO. 2

was so unfortunate as to be Counsel against the prisoner at his trial, that His prosecutors discovered the most rancorous malice and revenge upon the Occasion, and that there were not wanting circumstances on his trial which rendered him an Object of great Compassion.[23]

Finally, after a conviction, the Government and the King would pay great attention to the wishes of the prosecutor in deciding whether or not to grant a free or conditional pardon, particularly in cases in which the death sentence had resulted.

Small wonder, then, given the range of prosecutorial discretion, that one frequently finds eighteenth-century private prosecutors reflecting gravely on their power. As one observed in 1796 in a theft case:

> [I]f I succeed I shall most certainly hang the culprit. 'It is certainly more honourable to detect felons than it is to committ Felonys. However I wish to hold the scales of justice even and never suffer one's power to border upon Tyranny.[24]

His words betray an acute awareness that he would be the focus of much local attention by both the propertied and the poor. Because his discretion was so wide, the private prosecutor's acts were constantly scrutinized and subjected to the ethical judgments of the community, and of the different classes of which it was composed. Because he might be made to change his course, the pressure could be very great. When the prosecutor was determined to proceed in the face of sharp public criticism, he would commonly defend his actions in the press, as in this appeal published after an execution in 1802:

> Edward Allen, one of the unfortunate Men who suffered on Washwood Heath on Monday last for a Forgery on the Bank of England, having persisted in his Innocence to the last, and accused me of being his Murderer, I think it a Justice due to myself to state to the Public, through the Medium of your Paper, the Circumstances which led to his detection and Conviction. . . .[25]

Such a declaration might help to meet the objections of the propertied and the literate, but prosecutors affronting popular opinion had to decide whether to take the chance (by prosecuting rigorously, or even prosecuting at all) that their hedges would be broken, their saplings slashed or their animals maimed. The danger of anonymous malicious damage to property, particularly in rural parishes, undoubtedly subjected some prosecutors to strong pressure to drop charges, to reduce the charge between the preliminary inquiry and the grand jury hearing, or not to begin at all. Within the community itself this greatly accentuated the pressure to reach accommodations outside the courts. In each case, the pressure exerted on the prosecutor differed according to the norms of the community, the personal reputations of the prosecutor and the accused, and the degree to which the particular offence appeared to threaten others.

For much of the eighteenth century, the disadvantages that resulted — indifferent enforcement, widespread compounding of offences between thieves and victims, fear of retaliation — were not felt to be a serious disadvantage by the political elite that controlled Parliament. Their own property was relatively secure; they rarely used the more severe penal laws against theft; and the

---

[23] Letter of Theophilous Swift (July 31, 1787), Public Record Office, HO42/12 fol. 98.

[24] Mr. Lampton to M. Boulton (June 7, 1796), Birmingham Reference Library, *Boulton and Watt MSS, Parcel D.*

[25] *Swinney's Birmingham Chronicle*, April 22, 1802.

discretion that private prosecution gave them to forgive the offender in the interests of *noblesse oblige* was very useful as a means of maintaining consent to their oligarchic rule.[26] However, as the subsequent history of attempts to develop a state prosecutorial function suggests, their attachment to private prosecution probably derived above all from their abhorrence of the alternative, a state prosecution. The political elite of the eighteenth century were bred in a constitutional tradition that celebrated the recent humbling of tyrannical kings by Parliament. Many came from families in which executive tyranny under the Commonwealth or the Stuarts had caused much personal suffering, and the memory was still sharp. Star Chamber had been abolished in 1641 and the monarchy restored and made beholden to Parliament in 1660 and 1688, and the gentlemen of England were not now going to be party to any increase in the power of the executive to set the criminal law in motion. Even the extant powers of the Attorney-General, such as the ability to proceed by way of *ex officio* informations, were the targets of strong parliamentary criticism as a dangerous inheritance from the past. It was almost inconceivable that the Attorney-General should act as the protector of the ordinary citizen from oppressive prosecutions. The law officers of the Crown knew nothing of the vast majority of prosecutions and there was no administrative machinery to provide that information. The *nolle prosequi* was a practical nullity in day-to-day prosecutions. The protection of the innocent was instead confided in the main to the grand jury, and properly so, in the view of contemporary opinion. Grand juries did indeed throw out twenty-five percent of the bills of indictment (compared to four percent by the late nineteenth century),[27] although what proportion of these was rejected as malicious, or vexatious, or poorly drawn or unsupported by the evidence, one cannot say. It is clear, however, that controlling the abuse of prosecution was, like its use in the first place, principally in the hands of the citizenry rather than the government.

From time to time, and for particular classes of the propertied, the disadvantages of relying on the private prosecutor brought changes that nonetheless never touched the principle. Legislation enacted in the eighteenth and, especially, the nineteenth centuries gradually increased the costs granted to prosecutors, in an effort to spur them on to greater action. It had some unforeseen results (discussed *infra*) in opening the law to more democratic uses. The other expedient was even more typical of the period; it fact, it epitomizes all the assumptions on which the enforcement of the law was based. It was the private "Association for the Prosecution of Felons". There were hundreds of such groups throughout the country — probably about a thousand by the mid-nineteenth century.[28] Their growth is discernable from the middle of the eighteenth century, although some appear as early as the late 1600s.

---

[26] Hay, "Property, Authority and the Criminal Law," in Hay, Linebaugh, Thompson, eds., *Albion's Fatal Tree: Crime and Society in Eighteenth Century England* (London: Allen Lane, 1975).

[27] Hay, *Crime, Authority and the Criminal Law: Staffordshire 1750-1800* (Ph.D. thesis, Univ. of Warwick, 1975) at Table 8.3; Maitland, *Justice and Police* (London: Macmillan, 1885) at 139.

[28] Philips, *Good Men to Associate and Bad Men to Conspire: Associations for the Prosecution of Felons in England 1770-1860*, paper presented at a conference on The History of Law, Labour, and Crime, Univ. of Warwick, School of Law, Sept. 15-18, 1983.

172   OSGOODE HALL LAW JOURNAL   [VOL. 21, NO. 2

In a typical case the members entered into articles of association and agreed to share costs, pool any rewards obtained on convictions, offer rewards to witnesses, and elect a committee to decide which cases to prosecute. Sometimes associations also organized foot and horse patrols, paid retainers to keepers of turnpike gates to watch for stolen horses, and agreed at least to consider undertaking cases on behalf of poorer victims of crime who could not afford to go to law themselves. Such benevolence was not always fully appreciated; in one Birmingham case, in which the association prosecuted for a poor woman and then kept the substantial parliamentary reward for getting a capital conviction, "[t]he poor woman says now with tears, that the society Robbed more than the thief did of what was her due in reason."[29] In most cases, however, associations prosecuted only on behalf of their own members, and only after a committee decision as to which offences to pursue.

These private bodies undoubtedly affected the administration of the criminal law to a considerable extent. Although their members probably constituted fewer than ten percent of the adult male population, they accounted for as much as a quarter or more of prosecutions.[30] Some sought even greater influence. A few of the most active associations attempted to compel their members to surrender the most important discretionary decision of the private prosecutor, the right to forgive the offence entirely. One Midlands association in the 1770s provided that if any members should "screen, forgive, or otherwise overlook any Felony or Felonies" they should pay a healthy fine. Others promised to prosecute their members for compounding offences. Still others provided for expulsion from the association.[31] Such terms were by no means general, probably because insistence on them would diminish memberships in the prosecuting associations, particularly from among the gentry. Prosecutorial discretion was so pervasive, so useful in negotiations between the victim of the crime and the accused, and so coloured with libertarian constitutional meaning, that even wholly voluntary bodies rarely succeeded in curtailing it in the eighteenth century.

This system persisted to some extent throughout the nineteenth century. In particular, the right of the private prosecutor to initiate and conduct proceedings was largely untouched. The private prosecutor remained uncontrolled except by grand and petty juries, to a lesser extent by magistrates, and by the remote possibility of a *nolle prosequi*. There were changes, however. The most significant was the creation of the new-style police forces between 1829 and 1856, beginning with the Metropolitan force in London and gradually extending to boroughs and counties by the enactment of permissive and eventually compulsory legislation. In roughly the same period successive Acts of Parliament, most notably in 1826, provided for ever more generous costs for prosecutors.[32] A major reason for both the new police forces and the more generous costs, and almost certainly a result of them as well, was the phenomenal increase in indictments between 1815 and the late 1840s. At a time

[29] James Murray to Henry Kempson (Sept. 12, 1785), Birmingham Reference Library, 259647.

[30] An estimate based on the activity of 21 Staffordshire associations active in the 1780s: see Hay, *supra* note 27, at Table 7.3.

[31] *Aris' Birmingham Gazette*, Mar. 16 & 30, 1772, Oct. 14 & 19, 1771; Birmingham Reference Library, *Caddick and Yates MSS* (Feb. 1, 1773).

[32] 1826, 7 Geo. 4, c. 64 (U.K.). For a brief outline of the legislation see Philips, *supra* note 14, at 112-13.

when population in England increased by perhaps fifty percent, the number of indictments for felonies and misdemeanours increased seven-fold.[33] Contemporary accounts argued that this massive increase in indicted crime represented to some degree a real increase in crime, and it is likely, in view of widespread destitution in this period, that they were right. One response was to increase the granting of costs to induce more private prosecutors to come forward in the public interest.

The creation of the police had various purposes: preventive surveillance to deter criminals, and espeeially the calculated use of moderate force to deal with political demonstrations and other disorder, in which the use of the army had often proved to be worse than useless. However, when the modern police were invented in the second quarter of the century it was certainly not envisaged that they should come to control the prosecutorial process. The police were regarded at first by the middle and upper classes, as well as the working class, as a potentially dangerous innovation — the creation for the first time since the seventeenth century of an executive force that might be used to subvert political liberty through spying, harassment, and the exercise of arbitrary power. Their powers and their operations, especially in London, were strictly controlled to avoid exacerbating such criticisms, and it was only the level of crime and working-class confrontations with employers and government that convinced Parliament to create the new police.[34] To propose entrusting all prosecution to them was, in the early years, unthinkable. The point is to be emphasized, because by the mid-twentieth century the police prosecuted in eighty-eight percent of indictable cases in England: the proportions of "official" (although not "state") prosecutions compared to those brought by private individuals had been wholly reversed from the eighteenth century.[35]

---

[33] Gatrell and Hadden, "Criminal Statistics and their Interpretation," in Wrigley, ed., *Nineteenth-Century Society* (Cambridge, 1972) at 387 *ff.* is the most convenient summary for this period.

[34] See Philips, " 'A New Engine of Power and Authority': the Institutionalization of Law-enforcement in England 1780-1830," in Gatrell, Parker, Lenman, eds., *Crime and the Law: the Social History of Crime in Western Europe since 1500* (London: Europa, 1980) and (for some of the many other recent studies of the origin of the new police) the references in Hay, "Crime and Justice in Eighteenth and Nineteenth-Century England," in Morris and Tonry, eds., *Crime and Justice: An Annual Review of Research* (Chicago: Univ. of Chicago Press, 1980) ch. III at 45. On police prosecutions see *infra* notes 37, 38 and 41.

[35] Devlin, *The Criminal Prosecution in England* (London: Oxford Univ. Press, 1960) at 20-21. (See also text accompanying note 65, *infra*.) Devlin distinguishes the latter as "unofficial" on the grounds that "to call such prosecutions 'private' would be misleading: the great majority of prosecutions are in theory private. It is true that the proceedings are in the name of the Queen, but then in any *civil* action it is the Queen who issues the writ of summons and in whose name the attendance of the defendant is commanded; in each case the Crown is acting at the request or upon the information of an individual. Again, every *police* prosecution is in theory a private prosecution; the information is laid by the police officer in charge of the case, but in so doing he is acting not by virtue of his office but as a private citizen interested in the maintenance of law and order." (*Id.* at 16-17). Maitland commented on the ambiguities of the term when systems were compared: "To speak of the English system as one of *private* prosecutions is misleading. It is we who have *public* prosecutions, for any one of the public may prosecute; abroad they have *state* prosecutions or *official* prosecutions." (*Supra* note 27, at 141). I have nonetheless used the word *private* to describe what Devlin and Maitland call "unofficial" prosecutions because it accurately describes not only the theory but the practice in England for much of the period under discussion, and because it reflects Canadian usage.

174   OSGOODE HALL LAW JOURNAL   [VOL. 21, NO. 2

How and when that occurred is not yet clear. But most of the change probably occurred in the second half of the nineteenth century, with some further change even in the early twentieth century. The context in which it occurred is important for understanding the second salient feature of the English prosecutorial system that is overlooked by contemporary Canadian courts: the constitutional significance traditionally attached to private prosecution.

III. THE PRIVATE PROSECUTOR'S ROLE PRESERVED

By the 1830s and 1840s, features of private prosecution that had satisfied upper-class political opinion in the 1700s were instead arousing profound concern. It was a period of rapid population increase, urbanization, and momentous economic change such as England had never known. In many areas of English life the classes represented in Parliament and the professions felt a dismaying loss of control. The acute political conflict accompanying these changes had particular significance for the criminal law because it was in part class conflict, at a time of widespread destitution and revolutionary criticism of the political and economic structure. For many propertied Englishmen, the mounting crime rate summarized all these issues. Publication of criminal statistics had begun in 1805, and the data indicated ever-increasing rates of prosecutions and (so it was believed) of crime. In the same period the early Victorian legislature was embarked on a thorough examination of all aspects of the criminal as well as civil law, spurred on in part by the self-interest of the lawyers, whose professional consciousness was developing rapidly in a period of high professional unemployment.

In these circumstances the personal knowledge, local scale, and discretionary accommodations of the eighteenth-century system of private prosecution seemed far less acceptable. Lawyers and magistrates increasingly castigated serious defects: the compounding of offences that should have been prosecuted, the malicious prosecution of innocent individuals by personally interested or blackmailing prosecutors, the inability of grand jurors to sift the evidence when three or four hundred cases now came before them in a week, the blow to the legitimacy of the law when injustices were perpetrated, and the weakening of social and political authority when serious cases were not pursued. Equally distressing, the increased granting of costs had probably admitted more poor prosecutors to the system, and they sometimes used it for their own dubious ends. As a result, critics in Parliament, some of them Chief Justices and Lords Chancellor, attempted in the 1830s, again in the 1850s, and finally in the 1870s, to introduce a system of public prosecution in England.[36] Extensive evidence was gathered from the United States, Scotland, Ireland, and France, where public prosecution was long established. Detailed bills providing for a new system under one form or another were introduced repeatedly in the House of Commons. All of them failed to become law, and when Parliament finally created the office of Director of Public Prosecutions, in 1879, it was hardly what the name implied. Holding a watching brief, with limited powers, the Director of Public Prosecutions until the twentieth century had

---

[36] An outline of the early legislative history is given in Kurland and Waters, *Public Prosecution in England, 1854-79. An Essay in English Legislative History* (1959), 9 Duke L.J. 493. A more detailed account of the period from the 1870s is in Edwards, *supra* note 2, especially chs. 16 and 17.

relatively little power over the course of the vast majority of prosecutions. The private prosecutor continued to reign supreme. It is important to see the reasons for this.

First, however, we should note that by 1879 the private prosecutor had begun, slowly, to turn blue. The police had become convenient substitutes for private prosecutors who would not, or could not, go to the trouble or expense of proceeding. As new police forces were created throughout England, they increasingly shared prosecutorial duties with private citizens, with prosecuting associations, and with a competing group of "official" (in fact semi-official) prosecutors, the magistrates' clerks. In a few towns chief constables, with selected barristers, came to dominate prosecutions. It was partly in response to these developments that some Members of Parliament sought to introduce a professional, lawyerly public prosecutorial system. Parliament was presented with extensive evidence by the 1850s that the police in some parts of the country, attracted by the award of costs, were responsible for a great many malicious and vexatious prosecutions, usually initiated with the assistance of disreputable attorneys. The mover of the abortive legislation of the 1850s gave as one of his most important goals in seeking a public prosecutorial system the removal of policemen from the sphere of prosecution:

> The Crown, indeed, was the nominal prosecutor, but the consequence [of the lack of a public prosecutor] was that we gave to policemen, to a class amongst whom were to be found some of the most hardened and profligate of mankind, and over whom the most incessant vigilance was requisite to prevent flagrant and cruel abuses of their authority, we gave to these men [when they prosecuted] an unlimited power of pardon and connivance; and we entrusted them with an authority which in every country but England was regulated with as much anxiety as the functions of the Judge himself.[37]

Sir Alexander Cockburn, Attorney-General in 1855, probably expressed the Parliamentary consensus about the practical and constitutional implications of police prosecutors:

> I will add another, to my mind, very serious evil which I have observed very often myself, when sitting as recorder, and that is the manner in which policemen mix themselves up with these prosecutions. I must say that I think it is a great scandal (to use no milder term) to see a case brought into court by one of the inferior ministers of the law such as a policeman. I do not think it is consistent with the proper administration of public justice, in a great country like this, that you should have a subordinate officer, who is merely the keeper of the prisoner, clothing himself with the functions of a public prosecutor. I think it has, also, this further mischievous effect. I have observed often, and have had occasion to notice it in court, how policemen become over-zealous in the conduct of prosecutions. I can quite account for it now . . . [that I know] . . . that the promotion of policemen is made to depend upon the prosecutions which they successfully conduct.[38]

The apparently logical solution, a system of professional prosecutors who would wholly replace both the police and unofficial private prosecutors, never came into being. Instead, the police came to dominate what in England remains, in theory, a system of private prosecution. And for that there are three main explanations.

---

[37] 136 *Parl. Deb.*, H.C. (3rd ser.), col. 1651 (1855) (John George Phillimore). For a brief biography of Phillimore, a Liberal jurist and Q.C., see 15 *D.N.B.* 1071.

[38] (1854-55), *12 Parliamentary Papers* at 186. (Question 2396).

One was vested interest: solicitors who were magistrates' clerks, the other main body of semi-official prosecutors, feared that if deprived of their right to prosecute they would suffer a significant loss of income. By the 1850s, solicitors were a formidably organized group. Another explanation for the resistance to a system of public prosecutors was Parliament's concern about the political effects and legal costs of creating more patronage positions. Finally, there was the old eighteenth-century Whig argument, sometimes implicit, sometimes in very clear terms, that the consequences of prosecution were too important for the political liberties of the nation to entrust it to the executive. In 1844 James Paul Cobbett, a London barrister, son of William Cobbett, and a democrat in an age when few men of his class or profession were such, protested to the Criminal Law Commissioners that public prosecution would be a most dangerous innovation.

> In this country [he wrote] any man has a right to indict any other man upon any charge. We are so accustomed to this right, and are so completely free from trammels to interfere with it, that it is no wonder if, having often to consider the unavoidable trouble of the duty, we are not always alive to the advantages of the right. This right, when exercised, is not without its responsibilities; another part of the law has wisely taken care of that; but it is a most valuable right, and perhaps next only to that of being fairly tried when we are ourselves indicted. Set up the "public prosecutor", and then you have, at once, a power of *veto* against every man's prosecution; and the great offender, with great interest, may be allowed to escape by this new fangled authority, without even the intervention of a Grand Jury's *"ignoramus"*. If we absolutely prohibit the common law prosecutor, that is, the party injured or complaining, from taking legal steps, this is the result which will happen to a certainty . . . I repeat that you have no right to deprive the subject of his liberty, so long enjoyed, and with such good effects, by preferring a criminal charge against others who may have at once done him and his country a wrong, to strip him of the power of enforcing that redress, and making that example which the law requires for the good of both.[39]

Cobbett foresaw the corrupt protection of the powerful offender, and a danger of the kind of oppression associated with Star Chamber. The Clerk of the Peace of Wigan was more succinct; a public prosecutor, he said:

> would have the power of refusing to proceed in cases where parties thought there ought to be a prosecution, and this power might (and particularly in cases of political excitement) cause a denial of justice. I think that in all cases any man who has sustained injury, ought to be at liberty to put the law in force, and not be deprived of his remedy through the malice or caprice of a public prosecutor refusing to proceed, and therefore leaving him without remedy. If this power is entrusted to a public prosecutor, it will be a greater encroachment upon the right of a trial by jury than any encroachment there has been, and these are not a few.[40]

By the late 1800s, the mid-century attack on police prosecution and the insistent demand for a professional state prosecution had largely disappeared. The creation and consolidation of the limited powers of the Director of Public Prosecutions after 1879 can be only part of the reason. Other possible influences include the gradual development of a more judicial preliminary procedure (codified in 1848) under more diligent magistrates; the increasing professionalization of the provincial police forces so that they increasingly resembled that of London; and perhaps the absorption of a certain amount of

---

[39] *Royal Commission on Criminal Law, Eighth Report* (c. 656, 1845) at 295-96.
[40] *Id.* at 226.

professional unemployment that had prompted briefless young barristers to campaign for a prosecutorial system. A more general influence may have been the long, largely uninterrupted secular decline in the number of prosecutions from the 1850s to the end of the century. The fears of the early-Victorian middle class that political and social authority was dangerously threatened, and that the criminal law was being abused, yielded to the greater confidence that characterized the second half of the century when the policeman came to epitomize (for much òf the middle class) security and order. Exactly when and why police prosecutions came to predominate is not yet known, but it was probably in this period.[41] The policed society came to be perceived as the normal society and the prosecuting constable as, for many, part of the efficiently functioning modern state, even if the law considered him as simply another private prosecutor.

Nonetheless, few formal and no substantial curbs were put on the private prosecutor before 1900. The 1859 *Vexatious Indictments Act*,[42] introduced by the Government, reflected criticisms made by the Chief Justice in 1854, and was apparently inspired by a few prosecutions for conspiracy launched against respectable solicitors who had acted for less respectable clients. A very limited measure touching only voluntary bills and then only for some misdemeanours,[43] it left the right of private prosecution otherwise unaffected. It nevertheless aroused in some the usual constitutional anxieties: one Member of Parliament protested that although he was concerned to guard against abuses, he doubted that this was the proper way. "The measure was one [he said] which proposed a fundamental change in the constitutional rights of a British subject, and which appeared to him to be totally subversive of his liberty in those matters."[44] In 1879 the Criminal Code Commissioners recommended that the Act be extended to control all voluntary bills[45] and in 1883 Stephen (a member of the Commission) argued that the 1859 legislation imposed wholly inadequate limitations on "a dangerous right":

[41] One study (from imperfect sources) shows that the new police were prosecuting in only a minority of cases at quarter sessions in the Black Country in the 1830s and 1840s (Philips, *supra* note 14, at 101, 124-25). It appears that most associations for the prosecution of felons abandoned their prosecutorial duties to the new police within a period of years, especially after the compulsory establishment of forces throughout the country after 1856 (Philips, *supra* note 28).

[42] 1859, 22 & 23 Vict., c. 17 (U.K.).

[43] Perjury, subordination of perjury, conspiracy, obtaining money or other property by false pretenses, keeping a gambling house, keeping a disorderly house, and any indecent assault.

[44] *Report of the Royal Commission on Criminal Procedure* (Cmnd. 8092, 1981) at 161 para. 7.50-7.51: a private citizen would apply first to the (proposed) Crown prosecutor and, if blocked, would then be allowed to make application to a magistrate's court of two justices and a clerk. The Crown prosecutor would be required to attend the hearing, in private, to explain the decision not to prosecute. If leave were granted the private prosecutor would be allowed to employ his own solicitor and to expect automatic payment of reasonable costs. In its submission to the Commission (no. 161) the Criminal Bar Association recommended (part 4, paras. 36-37) the enactment of some equivalent to the sixth clause of the 1879 Act (*supra* note 36). In 1972 the government rejected an amendment to the Criminal Justice Bill to limit the right: Mr. Mark Carlisle, Minister of State at the Home Office, H.C. Standing Committee G. *Proceedings* 11 April 1972, cols. 1139, 1144. Similar comments were made in the Lords.

[45] *Royal Commission Appointed to Consider the Law Relating to Indictable Offences, Report* (c. 2345, 1879) at 32-33; (1878-79), 20 *Parliamentary Papers* at 200-201.

178   OSGOODE HALL LAW JOURNAL   [VOL. 21, NO. 2

It is a monstrous absurdity that an indictment may be brought against a man secretly and without notice for taking a false oath or committing forgery but not for perjury; for cheating but not for obtaining money by false pretences; and for any crime involving indecency or immorality except the three . . . [of] keeping gambling houses, keeping disorderly houses, and indecent assaults.[46]

Parliament's inaction in the face of such strictures suggests the strength of the reluctance to interfere with the right of private prosecution, even in its most extreme form, except where vexatious and malicious prosecutions were notoriously common. Judges, too, found it useful to cite the possibility of recourse to the voluntary bill when allowing magistrates a wide discretion in refusing to hear an information. In 1849 it was decided that "when an information is laid before justices of the peace for an indictable misdemeanour, it is in the discretion of the justices to hear it, or refuse to hear and leave the complaining party to originate his prosecution before a grand jury."[47] Mr. Justice Coleridge observed, "[t]he refusal of this rule [to compel the justices to hear evidence] does not prevent a trial if the prosecutor chooses to go before a grand jury. We only say that we will not oblige the justices to hear an information."[48] Those words were quoted in 1902, when the Chief Justice remarked that in cases where a wide discretion should be preserved:

I think the magistrate, as was pointed out in *Reg.* v. *Ingham* (*sup.*), is entitled to take into his consideration the fact that his decision is not final, but that a bill can be preferred by any person, and that a private person can present that bill of indictment, if he is disposed to do so.[49]

A reluctance to interfere with the private prosecutor in the nineteenth century can also be inferred from the infrequency of the more important inroads on his discretion, such as the various provisions requiring official consent to prosecute, or the statutory prohibition of private prosecutors. The 1793 *Lottery Act*[50] is apparently the only eighteenth-century legislation. The 1829 *Roman Catholic Relief Act*[51] required that informations to recover penalties be filed in the name of the Attorney-General, and it has been termed the first significant inroad on the rights of private prosecutors — or at least the first to provoke legislative comment.[52] Two statutes of 1839[53] and 1846[54] introduced a

---

[46] *Supra* note 11, at vol. 1, 294.

[47] *R.* v. *Ingham* (1849), 14 Q.B. 396, 117 E.R. 156.

[48] *Id.* at 401 (Q.B.), 158 (E.R.).

[49] *R.* v. *Kennedy* (1902), 20 Cox C.C. 230 at 237, 86 L.T. 753 at 757, 50 W.R. 633 at 636. Alverstone C.J.'s observation that in ordinary criminal prosecutions it was "not convenient" that there should be no preliminary proceedings, is evidence of the increasing distaste for the voluntary bill, and perhaps of its decreasing use. Darling J. mentioned in passing (at 242 (Cox C.C.)) the banal general truth: "The legislation . . . is put in the form of a criminal offence, and as it is put in the form of a criminal offence it appears to me that a private individual is entitled to prosecute for it."

[50] 1793, 33 Geo. 3, c. 62, s. 38 (U.K.). This and following examples are taken from the list of statutes with exclusion clauses or consent provisions that is given in Dickens, *The Discretion to Prosecute (in England and Wales)* (Ph.D. thesis, London, 1971) at 54-59, 69-72.

[51] 1829, 10 Geo. 4, c. 7, s. 38 (U.K.).

[52] Dickens, *supra* note 50, at 54; Edwards, *supra* note 2, at 239. The Parliamentary concern was partly that its enforcement might fall into the hands of a Catholic Attorney-General. The Act was considered in *Kennedy*, *supra* note 49, where Alverstone C.J. and Darling J. (at 238 (Cox C.C.)) gave their opinion that s. 38 in no way prevented a private prosecutor from acting under other sections.

requirement for the consent of the Attorney-General to any penal actions for sedition, or its encouragement, under legislation originally enacted without such provisions in 1799 and 1817. Several statutes put excise prosecutions in the hands of the Commissioners or required that they be in the name of the Attorney-General.[55] Finally, seven other statutes concerning specific offences gave prosecuting powers only to certain inspectors or local authorities, or required the consent of (variously) Police Chiefs or magistrates, a Secretary of State, the Director of Public Prosecutions, or the Attorney-General. (The last three were named respectively in three statutes likely to be used in cases with sensitive domestic or international implications: *Territorial Waters* (1878), *Newspaper Libel* (1881, changed to consent of a judge in chambers in 1888), and *Explosive Substances* (1883)).[56] With these few exceptions (compare the number of current ones[57]), the private individual maintained his full status as a prosecutor in English law into the twentieth century. Moreover, in almost all cases of indictable offences he could bypass the preliminary inquiry and take his accusation directly to a grand jury.

The legislation in fact manifested substantial support for the general right of the private prosecutor to proceed in most cases without any interference from the Attorney-General (apart, of course, from the latter's ancient right to enter a *nolle prosequi*). All the bills for the creation of a public system introduced to Parliament in the nineteenth century specifically protected the right of the private prosecutor, as did the *Prosecution of Offences* Acts of 1879 and 1884.[58] Only in 1908 did it become possible for the Director of Public Prosecutions to assume a private prosecution and then drop it, with no recourse for the private prosecutor.[59] Professor Edwards argued persuasively that this was a significant blow to a constitutionally significant right, and that the right of the original prosecutor, if the Director withdrew a prosecution, to apply to a judge of the High Court to have the prosecution reinstituted and continued either by the Director or by the private prosecutor himself — part of the 1879 Act but abolished in 1908 — should be re-enacted. He has also expressed disquiet, as have others, with the plethora of consent provisions

[53] 1839, 2 & 3 Vict., c. 12, s. 4 (U.K.) (revised as 1859, 32 & 33 Vict., c. 24 (U.K.)).
[54] 1846, 9 & 10 Vict., c. 33, s. 1 (U.K.); the preambles refer to vexatious prosecutions by common informers under 1799, 39 Geo. 3, c. 79 and 1817, 57 Geo. 3, c. 19 (U.K.).
[55] 1827, 7 & 8 Geo. 4, c. 53, s. 61 (U.K.); *Inland Revenue Regulation Act*, 1890, 53 & 54 Vict., c. 21, s. 21(1) (U.K.).
[56] *The Sunday Observation Prosecution Act*, 1871, 34 & 35 Vict., c. 87, s. 1 (U.K.); *Metalliferous Mines Regulation Act*, 1871, 35 & 36 Vict., c. 77, s. 35 (U.K.); *The Public Health Act*, 1875, 38 & 39 Vict., c. 55, s. 253 (U.K.); *The Territorial Waters Jurisdiction Act*, 1878, 41 & 42 Vict., c. 73, s. 3 (U.K.); *Newspaper Libel and Regulation Act*, 1881, 44 & 45 Vict., c. 60, s. 3 (U.K.); *The Explosive Substances Act*, 1883, 46 & 47 Vict., c. 3, s. 7 (U.K.); *Law of Libel Amendment Act*, 1888, 51 & 52 Vict., c. 64, s. 8 (U.K.).
[57] See the list given by the Attorney-General in 1977 of those offences requiring the consent of the Attorney-General or the DPP: 928 *Parl. Deb.*, H.C. (5th ser.), Written Answers, cols. 37-45. The total number was given as 96 in *Home Office Evidence to the Royal Commission on Criminal Procedure: Memorandum No. VIII. The Prosecution Process* (London: Home Office, 1978) at 11. All were under review.
[58] 1879, 42 & 43 Vict., c. 22 (U.K.) and 1884, 47 & 48 Vict., c. 58 (U.K.). The 1879 Act provided that none of its terms should "interfere with the right of any person to institute, undertake, or carry on any criminal proceeding" (s. 7). It also gave the injured party the right to appeal to the High Court if the Director dropped a prosecution (s. 6).
[59] *Prosecution of Offences Act*, 1908, 8 Edw. 7, c. 3, s. 2(3) (U.K.).

that have marked the legislation of the twentieth century.[60] The *Official Secrets Act, 1911,*[61] was of a piece with the few late nineteenth-century statutes with consent provisions, but the great flood of legislation requiring the consent of a variety of public officials for particular prosecutions began during the Second World War. It has been variously explained as the logical outcome of the assumptions of total war and of the welfare state, of a belief that regulatory legislation will be most responsibly enforced by officers who are publicly accountable, and of the rationalizing tendencies of modern government.[62] It has also been argued that consent provisions, particularly those naming the Attorney-General, arise:

> particularly in sensitive areas of public affairs in which law-enforcement would tend to be not simply a matter of routine recourse to criminal courts, such as for the usual property offences and assault cases, but an occasion of public and political significance in which issues of public policy and challenge would be inclined to arise attracting widespread attention and debate and permitting the accused to appear to defend important principles and freedoms.[63]

These conclusions, partly historical generalizations, partly normative judgments, summarize twentieth-century views quite well. However, a full explanation of why modern Parliaments have been so insensitive to the constitutional significance of private prosecutions as it appeared to their predecessors over at least two hundred years would take us far into the history of government and public opinion in this century. In the light of the longer history, the widespread assumption that a criminal trial should not be allowed (without high approval) to be "an occasion of public and political significance" concerning "important principles and freedoms," is a strange one. It marks how far memories of executive tyranny have receded, as well as how far the assumption that a universal franchise ensures benign government has proceeded, in this century.[64]

IV. THE FUTURE ROLE OF THE PRIVATE PROSECUTOR

It might seem that the right of private prosecution is now of little constitutional significance in England. Most prosecutions, although in theory private, are conducted by the police, their solicitors, or other official agents. Fewer than three percent of defendants are prosecuted by private individuals (most such prosecutions are for common assault) and about three times that number are prosecuted for shoplifting by retail stores. Although roughly one quarter of adult prosecutions on non-traffic offences are not brought by the police,

---

[60] Edwards, *supra* note 2, at 364-65, 397-98.

[61] 1911, 1 & 2 Geo. 5, c. 28 (U.K.).

[62] Dickens, *The Attorney-General's Consent to Prosecutions* (1972), 35 Mod. L. Rev. 347 at 345-55; Edwards, *supra* note 2, at 237 *ff.*

[63] Dickens, *supra* note 50, at 338. A more neutral formulation is given by the same author in *The Prosecuting Roles of the Attorney-General and Director of Public Prosecutions* (1974), 51 Public Law 57. *Cf.* the reference of Miller C.J. to "self-styled saviours" prosecuting, *supra* note 7.

[64] Many parliamentarians and other gentlemen who defended private prosecution in the nineteenth century were probably less inclined to trust the intentions of future governments precisely *because* the franchise might become wider; see *supra* note 11 and J.A. Colaiaco, *James Fitzjames Stephen and the Crisis of Victorian Thought* (London: Macmillan, 1983) at 12-13, 23 *ff.*, 35, 49, 132, 147-56.

more than one half of these originate with other official bodies.[65] In light of these facts, and of the expense of prosecution and the legal bars to private initiative enacted by Parliament, there is good reason to doubt the accuracy of judicial and other pronouncements of the importance of private prosecution. However, such pronouncements continue to be made. The most widely quoted in recent years are probably those of Lords Diplock and Wilberforce, in 1977, that the right is "a useful constitutional safeguard against capricious, corrupt or biased failure or refusal of [the prosecuting] authorities," a right that "remains a valuable constitutional safeguard against inertia or partiality on the part of authority."[66] More specific arguments have suggested that private prosecution is less restricted than sometimes thought. In his evidence to the Royal Commission on Criminal Procedure, the Director of Public Prosecutions observed that the 1908 Act explicitly preserved the right, although it allowed the Director to take over at any time. He added:

> With this in mind, I and my predecessors have always considered that taking over a private prosecution with a view to offering no evidence would be an improper exercise of the power to intervene, save in the exceptional circumstances of a case like Turner's. The protection against unjustified prosecution lies, in my view, with the Courts. . . . If process is granted to a private prosecutor, the case should, in my view, be allowed to proceed subject to the normal rules of evidence and procedure.[67]

But about the very extensive consent provisions, and what constituted exceptional circumstances, he had on this occasion little to say.

There is recent evidence, however, that the private prosecutor may still have constitutional significance in England. Accepting the argument of many witnesses before it that private prosecutions should be retained and strengthened "as an effective safeguard against improper inaction by the prosecuting authority," the Royal Commission on Criminal Procedure recommended, as

---

[65] Lidstone, Hogg and Sutcliffe, *Prosecutions by Private Individuals and Non-Police Agencies*, Royal Commission on Criminal Procedure, Research Study No. 10 (London: H.M.S.O., 1980) at 15-33.

[66] *Gouriet* v. *Union of Post Office Workers*, [1978] A.C. 435 at 477, 498, [1977] 3 All E.R. 70 at 79, 97, [1977] 3 W.L.R. 300 at 310, 329. Other frequently quoted statements are those of Glanville Williams in *The Power to Prosecute* (1955), Crim. L.R. 576 at 599; the late Viscount Dilhorne (then Attorney-General) in 604 *Parl. Deb.*, H.C. (5th ser.), col. 840; Wilcox, *The Decision to Prosecute* (London: Butterworths, 1972) at 6; Maitland, *Constitutional History of England* (Cambridge: Univ. Press, 1965) at 481; Stephen, *supra* note 11, at vol. 1, 495-96.

[67] Evidence no. 167, paras. 214, 209, copy deposited in the Library of the Institute of Advanced Legal Studies. Written submissions and Oral Evidence Minutes to the Commission are hereafter cited by number. Turner, convicted of robbery on the evidence of his accomplice Saggs, prosecuted Saggs, to whom the DPP had given an undertaking not to prosecute. The Director subsequently intervened and offered no evidence. See para. 212 and *Turner* v. *DPP* (1979), 68 Cr. App. R. 70. The Attorney-General, Sir Michael Havers, stated to the Commission that he did "not think it right that any attempt to control generally the private prosecutor should be made through the Directors' powers to take over a case and offer no evidence or my power to enter a *nolle prosequi*. Both would smack of interference by the Executive in the citizen's right of free access to the Courts; it is better that the control be by judicial process." (Oral Evidence Minute 16, para. 32). For the power of the Director to intervene with the intention of ending a prosecution see *Raymond* v. *H.M. Attorney-General* (*The Times*, Mar. 15, 1982). The relevant provision of the 1908 Act (*supra* note 59) now appears in the *Prosecution of Offences Act*, 1979, c. 31, s. 4 (U.K.).

part of a new system, an innovation that would allow a private prosecutor to contest the decision of a Crown prosecutor not to proceed.[68]

Of interest, at least to those who are aware that few of our civil liberties were established without strong, sometimes violent, popular support, is the range of lay and legal organizations, as well as officials, who told the Royal Commission that it was important to preserve or strengthen the rights of private individuals to prosecute. A partial list includes Justice, the Association of Liberal Lawyers, the Society of Conservative Lawyers, the Society of Labour Lawyers, the Criminal Bar Association, the British Legal Association, the Law Society, the Council of Her Majesty's Circuit Judges, the British Society of Criminology, the Police Superintendants' Association of England and Wales, the Police Federation of England and Wales, the Association of County Councils, the National Council of Women of Great Britain, the National Federation of Women's Institutes, the National Union of Conservative and Unionist Associations Women's Advisory Committee, the Lambeth Central Constituency Labour Party, the Residential Care Association, the Royal Societies for the Protection of Birds and Animals, Friends of the Earth, the Commons, Open Spaces and Footpaths Preservation Society, and the Automobile Association.[69]

It may be hazarded that they did not all have the same motives. Certainly many of the last-mentioned groups were anxious to preserve or extend their right to bring prosecutions of immediate interest to their own constituencies (although Friends of the Earth understandably interpreted that term widely). Likely concerns of the police were to preserve their current powers in face of a

---

[68] *Report of the Royal Commission on Criminal Procedure* (Cmnd. 8092, 1981) at 161 para. 7.50-7.51: a private citizen would apply first to the (proposed) Crown prosecutor and, if blocked, would then be allowed to make application to a magistrate's court of two justices and a clerk. The Crown prosecutor would be required to attend the hearing, in private, to explain the decision not to prosecute. If leave were granted the private prosecutor would be allowed to employ his own solicitor and to expect automatic payment of reasonable costs. In its submission to the Commission (no. 161) the Criminal Bar Association recommended (part 4, paras. 36-37) the enactment of some equivalent to the sixth clause of the 1879 Act (*supra* note 58). In 1972 the government rejected an amendment to the Criminal Justice Bill to limit further the right of private prosecution: Mr. Mark Carlisle, Minister of State at the Home Office, H.C. Standing Committee G. *Proceedings* April 11, 1972, cols. 1139, 1144.

[69] Evidence nos. 174, 152, 208, 367, 161, 122, 252, 237, 148, 163, 176, 126, 159, 107, 56, 83, 139, 91, 157, 103, 115, 112. The right of private prosecutions was supported also by the Metropolitan Police Commissioner (179), the London Criminal Courts Solicitors' Association (194), the Metropolitan Stipendiary Magistrates (220), the Senate of the Inns of Court and the Bar (Oral Evidence Minute 9) and witnesses from the Home Office (Oral Evidence Minute 4), all explicitly on the constitutional ground, and by the Penal Affairs Committee of the Religious Society of Friends (198), the British Council of Churches and the Free Church Federal Council (218), the Magistrates' Association (231), the London Magistrates' Clerks Association (233), the Greater London Regional Council of the Labour Party (317), the Association of Magisterial Officers (372), and the Nationwide Festival of Light (316). Evidence by individuals, including academic and practising lawyers, was also heavily in favour. All this suggests that if Edmund Davies L.J. was right in saying in 1968, in *R. v. Metropolitan Police Cmnr., ex. p. Blackburn*, [1968] 2 Q.B. 118 at 149, [1968] 1 All E.R. 763 at 777, [1968] 2 W.L.R. 893 at 914, that private prosecution was "a process which . . . is becoming regarded with increasing disfavour in this country," that statement is no longer true today.

reform that would create professional state prosecutors, and to avoid being forced under the existing system to assume prosecutions for minor assaults or other offences that are now only prosecuted privately.[70] A few witnesses were interested only in furthering private prosecutions against pornographers. But most witnesses who gave reasons for supporting the right of private prosecution argued for the general constitutional importance of an ultimate safeguard against official inaction, whether due to corruption, inefficiency, or other causes. Many thought it as much a part of the constitution as had James Paul Cobbett in 1844. Those who knew most about the present state of the law criticized consent provisions and the powers of the DPP to intervene. Only a very small minority argued that the twentieth-century pattern of increasing restrictions was justified and should be carried to its logical conclusion, the abolition of private prosecutions.[71]

A constitution exists not only in law and convention but in the minds and the actions of those who live within it. Much of the English public apparently still values the right to prosecute, either to circumvent a negligent, corrupt, or unwise prosecuting authority, or to bring charges when necessary against the police or other representatives of government. Whether that right will once again be extended will depend upon the evolution of English opinion, and its awareness of the existing state of the law, as much as upon the recommendations of Royal Commissioners and the *dicta* of judges.

It seems more doubtful that Canadians will rediscover an attitude and a right that has a much more attenuated existence in Canada. Nevertheless, some other features of Canadian prosecutorial traditions suggest that what remains of the right of private prosecution in Canada should be cherished rather than scorned. And here one more contrast with England is apposite.

Professor Edwards argued in *The Law Officers of the Crown* that one of the most important constitutional safeguards against abuse of the pros-

---

[70] Chief Constable of Cleveland (evidence no. 147); *cf.* the Home Office Memorandum, *supra* note 57, at para. 61.

[71] The Legal Action Group suggested abolition in a new system of public prosecution, with a right of appeal up the hierarchy (226; in the existing system it has urged the provision of legal aid to private prosecutors in cases of domestic violence and when local authorities fail to enforce the *Public Health Act*; LAG Bulletin, January 1976, at 6). The National Council for Civil Liberties, suggesting a full public scheme, advocated abolition only after proof of the success of a new system, which would include a tribunal with a strong lay element to make final binding decisions on appeals by private individuals against official decisions not to prosecute (250). It has emphasized the importance of the right in the existing system: see Cox, *Civil Liberties in Britain* (Harmondsworth: Penguin, 1975) at 100. New limitations to prevent misuse were suggested by the Association of Metropolitan Authorities (limit to those with a direct interest, especially where a local authority has a licensing or regulating duty, as with films; 185), the Association of Chief Police Officers of England, Wales and Northern Ireland (limit to less important offences; 221), and the London Gay Activist Alliance (limit to prosecutors who are victims; 363). Finally, Lord Lloyd of Hampstead, Q.C. (33) argued that the "so-called right" of private prosecution was "more in the nature of a historic accident stemming from the very early Common Law" and open to abuse because "officious" private individuals might "at their pleasure . . . invoke criminal proceedings. . . ." He therefore advocated abolition as the best course. It seems misleading, however, to describe as an accident the survival of a right explicitly preserved by Parliament over a period of centuries, and with strong academic, professional and lay support to the present day.

184   OSGOODE HALL LAW JOURNAL   [VOL. 21, NO. 2

ecutorial system in England in this century has been the insulation of the
Attorney-General from the more obvious forms of political pressure by the
convention that he cannot sit in the Cabinet, by the fact that responsibility for
the efficiency of the police lies with another minister (the Home Secretary) and
especially by the convention, established only by the fall of the first Labour
government in 1924, that an Attorney-General must be above the suspicion
that narrow political considerations have caused him either to institute or halt
a prosecution. In particular, he must never take direction from the Government in such matters. To further enhance the rule of law over the pressures of
political expediency, Edwards advocated the restoration of the right of the
private prosecutor, taken away in 1908, to ask a judge to re-institute proceedings in a private prosecution that the Attorney-General has assumed only
to drop.[72] In short, the English constitutional convention of a quasi-judicial
Attorney-General kept at a distance from his political colleagues did not appear to the closest student of the subject to offer a sufficient guarantee of un-
tainted and responsive administration of the criminal law. It was necessary to
re-invigorate the older guarantee of the private prosecutor's power.

The contrasts with this approach that are presented by some of the Canadian cases cited at the outset of this article, and by some of the conventions of
our constitution and our political culture, are dismaying.[73] In Canada it has
been common to give both police and prosecutorial supervision to one
minister. The practice was in fact embedded in the earliest post-Confederation
legislation, in 1868, by the provision that the Minister of Justice at the federal
level should also be the Attorney-General,[74] a plan imitated in the provinces.
And in marked contrast to the English convention that the Attorney-General
should be excluded from the Cabinet to help preserve his quasi-judicial state of
mind from the immediate pressures of political colleagues, the Canadian
Attorney-General has typically been a central figure in the Government.
Often, with the advent of responsible government, he was the Prime Minister
himself. Finally, there has been a widespread assumption that private prosecutions are somehow less than legitimate parts of the common law inheritance.

These differences must have historical explanations, some of which are as
yet unclear. One explanation is that the separation of functions represented in
the respective offices of the Home Secretary, Attorney-General, and Lord
Chancellor had no equivalent in Canada from colonial times. In the eighteenth
century, and indeed throughout the period of direct colonial rule, the
Attorneys-General of the several parts of British North America were important instruments of London's rule, and the joining of both political and quasi-

---

[72] Edwards, *supra* note 2, at 36, 37. See also Edwards, "The Integrity of Criminal
Prosecutions — Watergate Echoes Beyond the Shores of the United States," in
Glazebrook, ed., *Reshaping the Criminal Law: Essays in Honour of Glanville Williams*
(London: Stevens, 1978) 364 at 386.

[73] Here again Professor Edwards has done the pioneering work. The comments that
follow are based on information in his study for the Commission of Inquiry Concerning
Certain Activities of the Royal Canadian Mounted Police (the McDonald Commission):
*Ministerial Responsibility for National Security as it Relates to the Offices of Prime
Minister, Attorney-General and Solicitor General of Canada* (Hull: Min. of Supp. and
Serv. Canada, 1980) especially chapters 7, 8, and 10. The conclusions drawn are my
own.

[74] *Department of Justice Act*, 1868, S.C. 31 Vict., c. 39, s. 1.

judicial functions, begun at that early date, has continued to this day. When the English came to elaborate a new constitutional convention, following the Campbell case of 1924,[75] that sought to protect the prosecutorial function from political interference, they had a separation of functions that could be adapted for that purpose and a conception of the Attorney-General that allowed the easy grafting on of a newly-articulated principle of non-interference. In Canada the historical inheritance of an Attorney-General centrally connected with (among other things) the repression of colonial demands for self-government, and then charged later with control of the police forces and their secret services, made such an engrafting of new constitutional convention far less likely, even had events analogous to the Campbell case occurred here.

If private prosecutions have also been less prominent in our constitutional tradition, perhaps it is because they were less important in the daily administration of the law than in England over the last two centuries. The research remains to be done, but it appears likely that the interest of colonial Attorneys-General in fees, and the lineal influences of New France, the Thirteen Colonies, and perhaps Scotland, had that effect.[76] Also relevant is our political tradition, one of strong state activity in many areas, coupled with a pervasive and deep-rooted belief, particularly among politicians, that the governing of Canada is a difficult art precariously achieved. It may well be that the difficulties of maintaining party unity and avoiding explosions of intergovernmental and inter-regional animosity have dulled sensitivity to the very different question of the relationship of government to citizen. A strong state is not an unmixed blessing.

We might, in Canada, ask ourselves about the result of our own peculiar development. Like the English, we have not had in the twentieth century anything resembling the eighteenth- or nineteenth-century liberty of the ordinary citizen in England to put the criminal law in action, if necessary against the authorities themselves. Nor have we developed what perhaps in England became a partial compensation for increasing state control of private prosecution, the principle that control should be in the hands of a minister who is better able to resist party or personal political pressures because he is responsible neither for penal and police policy nor for the administration of the courts, and is even excluded from the Cabinet. Whether such conventions will ever surround the office of Attorney-General in Canada is a moot point. It is unfortunate, however, that we also have a bench, a bar, and a general public that appear to be either unimpressed by, or wholly ignorant of, the argument that private prosecutions, instead of being merely good opportunities for malicious misuse of the criminal law, may sometimes be important means to safeguard crucial rights. Even if, by making private prosecutions easier, we found "some

---

[75] In 1924, the Attorney-General authorized, then withdrew under pressure of the Cabinet, a prosecution under the *Incitement to Mutiny Act* of J.R. Campbell, a Communist leader. The resulting furore led to the downfall of the Labour Government.

[76] In addition to Edwards, *supra* note 73, see the brief outline in *R. v. Hauser*, [1979] 1 S.C.R. 984 at 1028-33, [1979] 5 W.W.R. 1 at 38-43, 8 C.R. (3d) 89 at 129-34. For the wider significance of the issue in Scots law, see the account of the most notorious recent case in Harper and McWhinnie, *The Glasgow Rape Case* (London: Hutchinson, 1983), and also Moody and Tombs, *Prosecution in the Public Interest* (Edinburgh: Scottish Academic Press, 1982).

obsessed . . . self-styled saviours"[77] taking cases before the courts, that might not be a bad thing. It is worth remembering that of those litigants who brought the most important criminal and civil cases of the last three centuries that helped establish what civil liberties we do have, many fit that description perfectly. A number of such cases might make it hard for governments or Attorneys-General to assume that their judgment of the public interest is invariably the right one. In particular, it might be more difficult to stifle with a stay of proceedings politically sensitive prosecutions, at least without arousing public opinion.

Such developments would be healthy ones in our constitution. The responsibility of the Attorney-General to Parliament for prosecutorial decisions, in Canada as in England, is not an impressive safeguard, since a quasi-judicial role can easily become an excuse for the most terse of explanations.[78] Moreover, that the democratic franchise is the only necessary safeguard of civil liberties, and that the Crown will always be vigilant in their protection, are assumptions that have not been tested and that never can be. In the late twentieth century new technologies make misdirected surveillance, misinterpreted intelligence, and covert illegality a standing temptation to governments and to their police forces. It is an unwise person who assumes that the case for criminal proceedings by private citizens, even against agents of the state or against their will, is now wholly irrelevant.

---

[77] *Supra* note 7. Even those few commentators impressed by the potential usefulness of the right of private prosecution in Canada have for the most part ignored the constitutional argument. Thus Burns (*Private Prosecutions in Canada: The Law and a Proposal for Change* (1975), 21 McGill L.J. 269 at 288-91, 297 n. 160) recommends their contribution to the enforcement of environmental regulations, and as a safe outlet for the ineradicable human passion for revenging a wrong. He cites Glanville Williams' statement of the constitutional point (*supra* note 66) but does not explore it.

[78] *E.g.*, the evidence of Professor Michael Zander (249) to the Royal Commission on Criminal Procedure *supra* note 67, at 3: "Even the control of the House of Commons on prosecution decisions of the Attorney-General is more notional than real. MPs can question the Attorney-General as to why he consented or refused consent for a prosecution in a particular case — but it is unlikely that his reply will reveal any significant information." Zander supported the retention of private prosecution, the reporting of such prosecutions to the Director of Public Prosecutions, and the *status quo* with respect to the right of the Attorney-General to intervene.

[2]

International Journal of the Sociology of Law 1988, **16**, 339–357

Police Powers and Public Prosecutions: Winning By Appearing To Lose?

KATHERINE DE GAMA

Department of Law, Keele University, Keele, Staffordshire ST5 5BG, U.K.

> The real art of policing a free society or a democracy is to win by appearing to lose (Sir Robert Mark, former Commissioner of London Metropolitan Police).

Introduction

The civil liberties lobby and the Left have given a warm welcome to the Government's decision to set up a nationwide system of public prosecution, independent from the police. But what they mistake for an unproblematic, progressive reform can be more usefully understood, at best, as sugar on the bitter pill of the Police and Criminal Evidence Act, at worst, as evidence of a definitive shift from the Rule of Law to the ideology of order [1].

As what appears to be an undisguised attack on police autonomy and discretion, the new Crown Prosecution Service stands out as a curious anomaly. Buttressed and sustained by an all-powerful law and order lobby, the Conservative Party remains, in all other areas of legislative activity, committed to the stockpiling of police powers. The question most commentators have failed to ponder is how CPS managed to impose itself upon such a bleak political landscape. Two rather tentative approaches to the problem have begun to emerge: firstly, a 'reformist' view which sees the Prosecution of Offences Act in terms of a great British balancing act, a *quid pro quo* for PACE (Baldwin & Kinsey, 1982; Christian, 1983; Uglow, 1984); secondly, an 'institutional' view which focuses more upon the vested interests of the Home Office and the police and on the disturbingly intimate relationship which has developed between them (Leigh, 1983; Uglow, 1984). The police were certainly willing to pay a price for PACE and, by the same token, were forced to concede that their resistance to CPS was indefensible. This uncharacteristic stoicism in the face of

340   *K. de Gama*

defeat is underpinned by something rather sinister. Prosecution is no longer of
real interest to the police. The passing of the Prosecution of Offences Act is an
expression, in police policy and practice, of a retreat from traditional conceptions of 'crime' and criminal justice. Our uniquely amateurish and ramshackle
approach stands out in contrast to the pivotal role played by prosecution in
other systems of criminal justice. For the British bobby, prosecution has ceased
to mark the locus of power.

Policing and Prosecution in the Nineteenth Century

Policing and prosecution began to assume their present form between 100 and
150 years ago. Policing in the sense of an organised, disciplined force of men,
patrolling and surveying civil society arose within the context of shifting patterns of class division and conflict associated with emergent forces of Capitalism (Mather, 1959; Silver, 1967; Hirst, 1975; Storch, 1975). The criminal
justice system in the eighteenth-century relied on rudimentary concepts of
justice, characterised by the use of crude deterrents and by the primacy of private interest and initiative in prosecution. After many abortive attempts at
legislation, it was the political acumen of Sir Robert Peel which, in the face of
enormous opposition from a gentry and industrial bourgeoisie fearful of the the
spectre of the interventionist State, finally steered the model of the New Police
through Parliament. The Metropolitan Police, as envisaged by the 1829 Act,
was not in essence an investigating and prosecuting agency. The fundamental
principles embodied in Peel's celebrated instructions to the Force remain valid
today.

> It should be understood at the outset that the object to be attained is the
> *prevention* of crime. . . . The security of persons and property and the pre-
> servation of a police establishment *will thus be better effected than by the detec-*
> *tion and punishment* of the offender after he has succeeded in committing
> crime [2]. (Critchley, 1978, p. 52).

The main priority was the policing of public order. Peel's mission was
against the "dangerous classes"; vagabonds, footpads, agitators, gangs, mobs,
and riotous hordes [3]. The popular image of the constable was that of a civil
soldier: ill-educated, large and led by gentlemen. The idea of extensive police
powers and discretion was, in the early days of the Met, unthinkable. The success of the New Police lay both in combatting diffuse criminality and more systematic expressions of political dissent, and in convincing the propertied
classes that the English 'Peeler' neither exercised arbitrary power not threatened individual liberty. The image of a 'neutral' civil force, seen as independent from the State, impartial in social conflict, accountable to law and
democracy, came to impose itself within the context of changing relations of
production. Force became prefixed by 'legitimate', and like law itself, came to
be seen as autonomous, removed from social and political conflict.

Proponents of radical police reform: Colquhoun, Chadwick, Bentham, Peel, saw too the need to set up a parallel system of *public* prosecutions (Radzinowicz, 1956). Peel, however, abandoned the campaign, aware that opposition, underpinned by the fear of central executive power, was sufficiently vigorous to threaten the entire policing enterprise. In the early nineteenth century the public prosecutor, undermining notions of the private, fitted even more problematically than the New Police with emergent liberal accounts of the relationship between the citizen and the State.

England has never had a public official with a *duty* to prosecute. Traditionally law enforcement was a communal responsibility. A local jury presented wrong-doers to mediaeval "Justices on Eyre"; i.e., royal officials who secured the interests of the Crown through the forfeiture, on conviction, of lands and possessions, but were not concerned with the general investigation of crime. In the sixteenth century the Marian Statutes offered the possibility of the Justice of the Peace as both investigator and prosecutor. Magistrates, however, failed to take up the challenge. Until well into the nineteenth century they relied on private citizens to lay informations, produce witnesses and steer proceedings through the Grand Jury and the criminal trial (Langbein, 1974; Uglow, 1984).

Criticism of the prosecution system has a long political history (Philips, 1977; Cornish, 1978). Successive nineteenth-century parliamentary committees produced powerful and compelling evidence that existing arrangements were: firstly, ineffective—criminals went unprosecuted; secondly, corrupt—police and justices' clerks "consorted with low attorneys" to carve up cases and split the fees. Condemnation of police involvement in the prosecution process was unanimous. For example, John George Phillimore, mover of the 1850s abortive legislation:

> 'The Crown, indeed, was the nominal prosecutor, but the consequence was that we gave to policemen, to a class amongst whom were to be found some of the most hardened and profligate of mankind and over whom the most incessant vigilance was requistite to prevent flagrant and cruel abuses of their authority, we gave to these men an unlimited power of pardon and connivance; and we entrusted them with an authority which in every other country but England was regulated with as much anxiety as the functions of the judge himself' (Hay, 1983, p. 169).

The pressure for reform was deflected by the Prosecution of Offences Act 1879 which created the office of Director of Public Prosecutions. The Director, however, was given little more than a watching brief. His function was to institute and supervise the prosecution of particularly important or difficult cases on behalf of the State. The beginnings of the office were inauspicious; successive groups assumed and then devolved themselves of responsibility and Directors displayed a consistent propensity to read relevant statutes restrictively (Edwards, 1964 and 1984). Former DPP, Sir Theobald Mathew, for example,

342   *K. de Gama*

claimed his title was a misnomer. The DPP "can direct nobody and there are no public prosecutions in the ordinary sense of that term" (Edwards, 1964).

Routine prosecutions were handled as inadequately as before. The attacks on police prosecutors and the demands for a professional state prosecutor, however, were conspicuous only by their absence. The policed society came to be seen as necessary and inevitable. From a threatening novelty it became a symbol of national prode. Notions of private vengeance and control became subjugated to an over-arching concept of the 'public interest'.

The police, acting in law as private citizens, slowly came to clothe themselves in the functions of public prosecutors. There is, in England and Wales, no statutory definition of the term 'prosecutor' and no *official* system of public prosecution. But actions brought by the police in pursuance of superior orders, under statutory authority and at public expense can hardly be called 'private'.

The prosecutor is assumed to be the person named as informant in the criminal action (Administration of Justice (Miscellaneous Provisions) Acts, 1933, s.2(1)). In *Webb v. Catchlove* (1886) [4] the High Court stated the view that a police officer should properly act only as a witness and quashed a conviction where a superintendent had acted as an advocate. Conceivably, the decision would have been different had he laid the information. In *Duncan v. Toms* (1887) [5] the High Court held that the informant is entitled, in the lower courts, to conduct the case, examine and cross-examine witnesses. Section 13(1) of the Magistrates' Court Act, 1968 confirms her/his right to address the court. The standard police practice, censured in *Webb v. Catchlove* was finally legitimised by *O'Toole v. Scott* (1965) [6]. Magistrates now have a discretion to allow persons other than counsel or solicitors to conduct the prosecution on behalf of the informant.

The police moved in to fill the gap. Under the fiction of the 'citizen in blue' they expanded their operational autonomy and the State came to dominate the prosecution process without appearing to have taken central control.

Policing and prosecution are inextricably linked. It was only through the unintended consequences of their founding father's political compromise that the early 'Peelers' took the first steps towards assuming the role of public prosecutors. The 'system' was so successful that for almost a century the critics were silent. The quite separate functions of investigation and prosecution became integrated and gradually concentrated within the hands of an increasingly professionalised police force. The failure of the movement for the reform of the prosecution system can be attributed to two major factors: firstly, the emergence in the late nineteenth century and early twentieth century of more profitable forms of law, deflecting the legal profession's economistically based demands for change; secondly, and more importantly, the triumph of the notion of policing by consent. By the late nineteenth century the legitimacy of policing was tacitly acknowledged. It is only over the last 20 years that the capacity of the police to be impartial and dispassionate has been seriously questioned.

The vicissitudes of the movement for reform correspond to the rise and fall of police legitimacy. Paradoxically, the process of de-legitimisation has given rise to a radical change in police powers and prosecutions. PACE and CPS seem strange bedfellows. They share, however, a common source. In June 1977 James Callaghan announced his Government's intention to set up a Royal Commission on Criminal Procedure and defined its scope of inquiry and recommendation in terms of "striking a balance" between the interests of the whole community and the rights and liberties of the individual citizen. "The Government", he added, "consider that the time has come for the whole criminal process, from investigation to trial, to be reviewed". Its terms of reference were later broken down into the investigation and prosecution of offences.

The Liberal Path to the RCCP

Throughout the 1970s the credibility of the police was attacked in three crucial areas. Firstly, allegations of widespread, institutionalised bribery and collusion in the Met's Drugs, Obscene Publications and Robbery Squads were taken sufficiently seriously for Commissioner Sir David McNee to set up "Operation Countryman" to investigate. Secondly, the decade saw a secular increase in the number of deaths in police custody, from eight in 1970 to 48 in 1978. Complaints against the police relating to non-fatal attacks increased correspondingly. Thirdly, following the six-day siege of Saltley Gate by secondary pickets in the 1973 miners' strike, a 'third force', without public debate, began to be developed. By 1974 every force had a Police Support Unit capable of rapid mobilisation and co-ordination to deal with strikes and demonstrations.

Similarly, the Met's Special Patrol Group began to assume an increasingly paramilitary role in the policing of public order and terrorism. Themes of police brutality, corruption and the rejection of strategies of minimal force in favour of more confrontational styles of policing came together in the liberal mind to produce a moral panic over police powers. Within this context it was the Confait case which provided the immediate impetus for the setting of the RCCP. In April 1972 the body of Maxwell Confait was found in a blazing house in Catford. Three boys aged 14, 15 and 18, one of whom was mentally retarded, were on the basis of uncorroborated confession evidence, charged and convicted of a number of criminal offences, including arson and murder. Three years later, on the basis of new scientific evidence, their convictions were quashed. Anxiety surrounding the case led to an official inquiry, chaired by Sir Henry Fisher, which reported in December 1977. The Fisher Report provided authoritative evidence of systematic abuse of suspects' rights. The administrative directions regulating the detention, questioning and general treatment of suspects were found to be routinely breached and police questioning to be unfair and oppressive. Direction no.7, for example, which established the right of a suspect to be informed of her/his right to communicate by telephone with a third party and consult a solicitor in private was, as Fisher con-

344   *K. de Gama*

firms, "unknown to counsel and senior police officers alike". His Report recommended that the Judges' Rules should be backed by exclusionary sanctions but refused to advocate further reform on the basis of only one case. This, he argued, could be done only within the framework of, "something like a Royal Commission". Fisher defined the appropriate context of inquiry a "balance between police effectiveness and individual rights".

Home Secretary, Merlyn Rees, hardly remembered for his innovative approach to criminal justice, anticipated Fisher's conclusions and set up the RCCP in order to placate an increasingly vociferous civil liberties lobby whilst deferring decision-making beyond the parliamentary life of his Government. As A. P. Herbert, doyen of the critics of the Royal Commission technique of government, claims:

> A Royal Commission is generally appointed not so much for digging up the truth as digging it in; and a government department appointing a Royal Commission is like a dog burying a bone, except that the dog does eventually return to the bone (Bulmer, 1983, p. 436).

Labour's classic delaying tactic backfired as the political landscape changed out of all recognition. The RCCP's period of deliberation, 1978–1981, coincided precisely with the rise of Thatcherism as a moral and political force. The economic liberalism of the New Right is necessarily and inevitably paralleled by powerful currents of social control in the areas of family, education, welfare and criminal justice (Hall, 1983).

The dynamic of legal reform operated at an openly political level. The RCCP was rapidly transformed into a battleground in which the civil liberties and police lobbies became locked in combat. The legislation following it its wake, PACE and the Prosecution of Offences Act, originated not in the Final Report but in the evidence submitted by major institutional spokespeople and pressure groups. David Leigh presents a disturbing image:

> The real inside story of the Police Bill is a murky one stretching back almost twenty years that does not show the British political process in a very comforting light. It is a history of secret lobbying, intellectual confusion and vicious infighting, largely conducted behind the public's back (Leigh, 1983).

An understanding of how a Commission so enthusiastically welcomed by civil liberties groups came to be hijacked by a strident law and order lobby, made up of the police, the Home Office and the Conservative Party can only be located in the context of the politics of policing and the politicalisation of the police.

The Law and Order Discourse

The need for review was equally apparent to the law and order lobby, although from a different perspective and institutional basis. Turning it back

Police powers and public prosecutions   345

on a powerful constitutionalist tradition that the police should be clothed in
political purdah, seen but never heard, in 1965, the Police Federations, then a
lowly 'professional association' published a document entitled, 'The Problem'.
Its manifesto stated the need for pay increases, better equipment and more
consultative management structures. Such assertions, now tame and commonplace, shocked 'public opinion'. One member of the Police Council exclaimed,
"I never thought I would see the day when the representatives of law and
order would be advocating anarchy" (Reiner, 1982, p. 469). Today, however,
the police have come to be regarded as authoritative commentators and legitimate opinion-formers and are given a free hand to set the terms of debate on
law and order policy. The New Right's definition of law and order, moreover,
goes beyond a narrow policy area associated with crime and criminal justice.
As Martin Kettle terms it, it is

> A belief in the practice of *discipline* in attitudes, behaviour and choices in
> the home, the streets and the workplace (Kettle, 1983 p. 218).

Stuart Hall similarly describes the law and order society as one, "toned up
for the routinisation of social control" (Hall, 1978, p. 278).

Since 1972 the law and order lobby has been actively encouraged by senior
police officers. This change was facilitated by the amalgamation of forces in
1966, following the 1962 Report of the Royal Commission on the Police and
the 1964 Police Act. A forseeable and perhaps foreseen result of the transition
to fewer but larger forces was the enhanced political power of individual Chief
Constables within their own 'fiefdoms'. The new political profile of the police
was personified by the arrival of Robert Mark as Metropolitan Police Commissioner in 1972. Ironically remembered as a liberal for his attack on the corruption which characterised the 'firm within a firm' in the Met, his
autobiography reveals a deep hostility to the Labour Party and all the traditional institutions of liberal democracy. Mark quickly became accepted as a
major pundit on law and order, particularly in its wider sense of 'moral fibre'.
Arguably, his most important legacy was in his relations with the media. A
new openness was heralded by his first annual report. This was not without its
price. In July 1979 *The Leveller* revealed extraordinary editorial privileges
enjoyed by the Met at the BBC; they were permitted to preview and control
the content of all broadcasting relating to police work. (*The Leveller*, 1979)
Mark's emphasis upon communication and public relations is articulated in
his forward to Critchley's police history.

> The post-war years have seen a gradual change in our role from mere law
> enforcement to participants in the role of social welfare and even more
> importantly, to that of contributors in the moulding of public opinion
> (Critchley, 1978, p. xiii).

He disguises, however, the role of his own organisational ability, political
acumen and public relations skill in the creation of this new model of policing.

346   *K. de Gama*

The intellectual underpinnings of the law and order lobby are provided largely by the analysis and recommendations of the 11th Report of the Criminal Law Revision Committee, 1972. Strongly reflecting Mark's own assertions, the Report was characterised by sweeping and unsupported statements about the inadequacy of the system of criminal procedure. The committee gave majority support to those proposals on the jury system outlined by Mark in 1965 which were not subsequently contained within the 1967 Criminal Justice Act. The solution, to 'The Problem', however, was to undermine the right to silence. The committee's guiding assumption was that the rules of criminal evidence are weighted heavily in favour of the defence. Tellingly, the defence is synonymous with 'the criminal'. Criticised by academics, editorials and Law Lords the Report was hastily shelved. Probably more important than civil liberties protests was the widespread police resistance to the *quid pro quo* of tape-recording of police interrogations.

Mark's controversial Dimbleby Memorial Lecture in November 1973 signified the coming of age of a politically confident police force. Its undisguised political content was justified on the grounds that the police occupy a unique position from which to comment on crime, criminal justice and social policy. Mark used the lecture as a platform from which to launch an attack on the jury system and to introduce the idea of the 'bent lawyer'. His concluding statement was thrown out as a challenge,

> Unwillingness to make the law effective will inevitably produce demands for harsher sentences and will increase the pressures on the police to use more arbitrary methods (Dimbleby Lecture, BBC TV).

Four years later the Fisher Report confirmed that this was more than empty rhetoric. The threads linking the Fisher Report and Sir Robert Mark's campaign for law and order intertwine. Mark, from an entirely different perspective, also affirmed the need for a review of the 'whole system of criminal justice' (Mark, 1978).

Mark prepared the ground for the Police Federation to launch a strident and systematic campaign for Law and order at the end of 1975. Its avowed aim was

> to harness the public's growing concern about the state of crime and public order in Britain into a campaign for positive action. (Reiner, 1985, p. 73).

A recurrent theme in law and order politics is an attempt, on the part of the police, to identify their own views with those of the general public. The rhetoric is exemplified by Thatcher's address to the 1977 Conservative Party Conference.

> People have asked me whether I am going to make the fight against crime an issue at the next election. No I am not going to make it an issue. It is the people of Britain who are going to make it an issue (Kettle, 1983, p. 216).

Although Mark acted as a catalyst the origins of the Police Federation campaign are structured in terms of material concerns. Any attempt at an assessment of the objectives, achievements and current state of play of the law and order lobby needs to relate the micro-factors of why Federation members chose or were constrained to pursue the campaign at a certain juncture in the mid 1970s to the macro-factors of why its demands gained purchase with the State. An analysis of the contradictory class position of the police provides a useful starting point (Reiner, 1978). The Police play a crucial role in the maintenance of the ongoing economic and political system. Very crudely, this role confers upon them a conservative ideology. More importantly, however, the police are wage labourers, subject to discipline and control. It is the dialectic between the functions of the police as part of the ideological and the more pragmatic armoury of the repressive State, and as employees of that self-same State which explains the particular form taken by the law and order lobby. A purely economistic demand for higher wages logically came to be expressed with the terms of reference of their primary task of law enforcement.

If police power was enhanced and consolidated by the manpower shortage and increasing concern about the seemingly inexorable increase in recorded crime, by 1975 rising unemployment began to undermine the Police Federation's bargaining power. The new-found tripartite consensus between police spokesmen, Government and Opposition was rent apart by Home Secretary Roy Jenkins's angry response to the Federation's alarmist propaganda. "You must not make me think I am dealing with the International Marxists", he warned (Reiner, 1982, p. 469).

This marginalisation was short-lived. The underlying trend emphasised increasing involvement and consultation in social policy and legislation. The enhanced political assertiveness of the police came to be expressed in concerns which went beyond their original economistic interests. The Federation began to articulate police frustration with what it perceived to be 'anti-police' elements in society, i.e., demands for more 'lenient' sentences and for a more independent review of complaints against the police.

In 1978 the campaign was relaunched with a vengence, specifically to influence the outcome of the 1979 General Election. Chairman James Jardine promised that the Federation's lobby would be, "strictly non-political and will not become involved in campaigning on behalf of any party" (Reiner, 1982, p. 470). His rhetoric was undermined by the striking parallels between the public statements made by police spokesmen and those of the Conservative Party. In an unprecedented attack, revealing the true nature of the campaign Sir Robert Mark publicly compared the relationship between the Labour Party and the Trade Union Movement to the absolute control of the State exercised to the National Socialist German Workers' Party. The following day the infamous 'law and order' advertisements, funded by the Police Federation, appeared in most national daily newspapers. Shortly afterwards the inauspicious partnership between the Conservative Party, the Police Federation and

348   *K. de Gama*

the more vociferous Chief Constable was again underlined when Shadow
Home Secretary presented a six-point law and order pledge on behalf of his
Party, which corresponded exactly with police demands. Immediately after
the Conservative victory Police Federation representatives were informed of
the Government's decision to implement the pay increase recommended by
the Edmund-Davies Committee. The value of the award greatly exceeded
public sector pay policy and was to be maintained by a series of inflation-
linked increments. The police were better off in real terms than ever before in
their history and were to remain so. At this point the Federation for the first
time since the appointment of a parliamentary adviser in 1955 discarded the
traditional practice of nominating from the Opposition party. Eldon Griffiths,
a Tory MP closely associated with the 'hang 'em and flog 'em' brigade was
duly re-appointed.

The Hijack

The police approach to the RCCP dovetailed neatly into this overt politicalisation of the last ten to fifteen years. The RCCP, placing a high premium on its
acceptability to the forces of law and order, tailored its suit very much according to its political cloth. Its research methods, data analysis and policy prescriptions were all heavily influenced by the intellectual and pragmatic thrust
of the Home Office and the police. The Final Report, published in January,
1981 was presented by Chairman, Sir Cyril Philips as an uncontroversial codi-
fying measure. The press, however, recognised that its authors' recommendations went beyond the bounds of simple rational and technical reform. Banner
headlines announced, "Tough proposals on police powers" (*The Guardian*),
and, "Sweeping new powers" (*The Daily Telegraph*).

The attention of the critics was focused almost exclusively on the proposed
changes in police powers. The prosecution process failed to arouse the same
passions. The RCCP's recommendations on prosecution were widely regarded
as providing that elusive balance between police powers and civil liberties.
That balance was to be statutorily based Crown Prosecution Service in every
police area in England and Wales, independent of the police and accountable
to a joint Police and Prosecutions Authority. Its functions were to comprise:
the decision to proceed after the initial police decision to charge has been
taken; the conduct of all criminal proceedings except those which come under
the category of "Director's cases"; the provision of advocates in the Magistrates' Courts and the briefing of counsel. Interestingly, the Common Law
prerogative of the private citizen, and by logical extension, the police, to lay
the information is left untouched.

The social and political composition of the RCCP had been intended as a
compromise to placate both the law and order and the civil liberties lobbies.
Its membership included representatives from three major camps: police, lawyers and 'liberals'. Any Royal Commission or similar large-scale public

inquiry has structural limits upon its independence. As Dibelius, in the evocatively titled "England" points out,

> The statesman who nominates the commission can almost always determine the course it is going to take since he will have a pretty good knowledge beforehand of the minds of the experts he puts on it while of course avoiding any appearance of packing his team. (Bulmer, 1980, p. 343)

A former Permanent Under Secretary of State at the Home Office, Chief Constable, and Secretary of the Police Federation, flanked by a number of acquiescent, careerist 'liberals', largely uncommitted to the Commission's enterprise, made up a determined and irrepressible caucus of authoritarian power. Paradoxically though, the appointment of three Scots and two members of the legal reform group 'Justice', one of whom the co-author of the 1970 report recommending the establishment of a national prosecution service, along the lines of the Procurator Fiscal system, operated as a 'trigger' to render the questions posed by the Home Office largely tautological. The Commission's 'independence' from the agencies of law and order was further undermined by the dominating influence of its secretariat—a team of civil servants seconded from the Home Office Criminal Policy Department. The secretariat was largely responsible for drafting the RCCP's Final Report. Few members added dissenting comments or even footnotes. One member, Walter Merricks, admitted

> It is quite possible to have a Royal Commission without any members. The secretariat do all the work and the members just sign the report [7].

The now old-fashioned values of balance and consensus were of first importance to Chairman, Sir Cyril Philips. He foresaw, given the terms of reference, the inevitability of major cleavage. It was his astute chairmanship which secured a collective approach. Before the balance between police powers and individual rights had become a contentious and highly charged issue he persuaded the membership of the need for a quorum, designated as five, before a Minority Report could be written. The so-called liberal members of the Commission never managed to disagree or be present to disagree on the same issues at the same time. Similarly, although Part 1 of the Report focuses upon the investigation and Part 2 on the prosecution of offences the latter was, in fact, considered first. He saw it as a useful way of "coasting in", as he put it, to the more disputed terrain of police powers while preventing the membership from becoming "embittered and embattled" from the outset [8]. Members of the Commission speak of two camps rapidly disappearing. Philips's main objective was to "get something down on paper that would work". Publicly, the solution was not to allow competing interest groups to horsetrade new powers for safeguards but to construct a 'factual base' on which a framework of 'first principles' could be built. Thus, the RCCP conflated the analytically distinct

350   *K. de Gama*

categories of factual base and first principles and assumed the relationship between them to be unproblematic. It failed to recognise the importance of knowledge as a source of power. Given the primary aim of finding a solution that would work the police were in an excellent position to define what was practicable, and, furthermore, what were the facts.

The Commission's knowledge of the operation of the criminal justice system was derived from two major sources: firstly, written and oral submissions of evidence from major institutional interests; secondly, a package of twelve studies published in the Commission's research series and available to the reader at a cost of £57.50. Only three months after written evidence had been requested the Metropolitan Police leaked its notorious 'shopping list', drawn up by James Sewell who was later to assist the Home Office in the drafting of the Police Bill, to the Times. Metropolitan Commissioner, Sir David McNee, interested in wholesale rather than marginal change demanded a series of checks on suspects' rights which now seem all too familiar: the abolition of the right to silence; a power to detain suspects for up to 72 hours; general stop and search powers relating to persons and vehicles; wider powers of search and seizure without a warrant; general road block searches; a power to fingerprint anyone within a prescribed area; and easier access to private bank accounts. The Association of Chief Police Oficers (ACPO) threw in its weight: "no further safeguards to the rights of suspects need be given"[9]. The political strategy of the police was to demand over and above what they wanted in order to be guaranteed what they did want. In retrospect, the importance of the police evidence lies not so much in its empirical substance but in its role in setting the Commission's terms of debate.

The emphasis on evidence of 'fact' or informed opinion reflects a British tradition of giving priority to practical experience over systematic investigation. This reinforces the fallacy, as Martin Bulmer puts it, "that he who does, knows" (Bulmer, 1980, p. 343). The RCCP's research programme, however, was underpinned by an equally police orientated approach. It was organised by the Home Office and the vast majority of its authors had some professional involvement in those state agencies concerned with law and order. Its time scale and the belief in co-ordination with the police involved what is accepted as sound research methodology on its head. Rather than collecting data on the ground and examining it later in detachment, Philips revealed at the 1981 Leicester University conference on the work of the Royal Comission that findings had been "checked on the ground," and "tested with the people who have to work with the system"[10]. However, the inescapable conclusion of the RCCP's research studies is that the rights of suspects are in need of greater protection. As academic contributors, John Baldwin and Michael McConville comment from personal experience, "the research is better described as neutered than neutral" (*The Times*, 6 January 1981). Their criticism is equally applicable to the Home Office's restrictive selection of issues in criminal justice to be placed upon the agenda. To a significant extent, the role of the research commissioned by the RCCP was to provide a cloak of respectability for a package of highly contentious proposals.

Within the context of the RCCP's exploration of the prosecution system, factual analysis was replaced by pure speculation. The Commission repeatedly set out the proposition that it was neither proven nor suggested that the existing system of criminal prosecution was fundamentally flawed, but the fact that it could not be proved flawless was sufficient justification for radical change. The sole empirical base to the RCCP's argument for the separation of the functions of investigation and prosecution was the evidence provided by acquittal statistics. What appears to be an alarmingly high proportion of ordered and directed acquittals is explained, however, without challenging the competence or integrity of police, prosecution solicitors or counsel [11]. The decision to set up a statutory prosecution system, independent of the police, was one made *in principle*.

The Commission's starting point was defined by the need to "secure change with the minimum of upheaval and at the lowest possible cost." Although Home Secretary, Leon Brittan, billed the publication of the 1983 White Paper, "An Independent Prosecution Service", as heralding the most important change in criminal procedure for 100 years, its approach is minimalist. There would, in England and Wales, still be no public official with a *duty* to prosecute. The police were to retain the right to initiate proceedings through their monopoly over the decision to charge and therefore will determine the input to the Crown Prosecutor's office. The charge is a purely administrative convenience and has no legal significance. It is the laying of the information which begins criminal proceedings. This probably occurs when the court receives the charge sheet but the situation is by no means unambiguous. It is therefore unclear whether the new Crown Prosecutor initiates proceedings or merely takes over and conducts cases initiated by the police. If the latter is the case, it might be extremely difficult for the Crown Prosecutor to drop charges brought by the police (Sanders, 1985). Even if the issue could be assumed to be unproblematic, the autonomy of the prosecutor remains fettered. In a detailed empirical study of prosecutorial decision-making in Scotland, Moody and Tombs maintain that the Procurator Fiscal operates within strict parameters. They point to the powerful bureaucratic pressures to routinise the handling of cases and shared perceptions of appropriate practice. More importantly, however, they focus upon the critical role of the police as providers of information and, as such, as 'gatekeepers' to the criminal justice system (Moody & Tombs, 1982).

The RCCP's proposals for a Crown Prosecution Service are largely the outcome of a compromise worked out between the police and the 'liberal' members of the Commission. The Commission's primary objective, defined in its terms of reference was to find a 'fundamental balance' between the interests of the community and the rights and liberties of individual citizens. Its conclusion was a system of checks and balances; wider powers perceived as necessary

352   *K. de Gama*

to combat crime would be offset by increased safeguards, such as CPS, against
abuse. Hardly surprisingly, police powers are spelt out in uncompromising detail while safeguards, including the proposed prosecution system, remain baffl-
ingly vague. Moreover, the entire notion of balance is false. The RCCP
assumed that the interests of the community are necessarily at odds with those
of the individual. It elaborated its aims and objectives in terms of two diametrically opposed philosophies; utilitarianism and libertarianism. It chose to
overlook these contradictions and then absurdly went on to posit the existence
of a 'fundamental balance' between two opposing points of view. However, as
David Leigh confirms, this approach was not without its costs.

> Desperate for unanimity, according to its members, the liberal and radical
> members of the Commission started horsetrading with the police, trying to
> sense what compromises would satisfy them (Leigh, 1983)

It is within this context that the Crown Prosecution Service can be understood in terms of a crude trade-off for increased police powers.

From the Rule of Law to the Ideology of Order

Police submission to the RCCP maintained that the removal of the right to
prosecute would be an arbitrary and unjustified expression of a vote of no confidence. What has to be asked, then, is how the demands of the Prosecuting
Solicitors Society, dismissed by the Home Office in subsequent consultations as
an insignificant band of ambulance chasers, came to be accepted over and
above the competing claims of a pressure group as powerful as the police [12].
Although the RCCP's proposals for local accountability and control ultimately proved unacceptable to the police and the Home Office, as the 'independence' of the new prosecution service became re-defined, almost
imperceptibly, in terms of the need to guard against interference from politics
rather than from the police, by the time the White Paper was published in
October 1983 the issue, for police leadership and rank and file alike, was at
most an irrelevance.·

The police had both pragmatic and ideological reasons for giving their
assent to CPS [13]. Firstly, they were sufficiently astute to realise the danger
and futility of opposing the inevitable. After the attempts to tack a new system
of public prosecution onto the coat-tails of the Criminal Justice Act 1982 and
the particular choice of appointments to the RCCP, the police were made
acutely aware of the strength of interest and commitment from the Home
Office. Secondly, although the empirical evidence for the separation of the
functions of investigation and prosecution was neither conclusive nor compelling the police quickly accepted that their initial position was in principle
untenable. Thirdly, the cost to the police of conducting prosecutions is high.
As public attention is focused on this area of activity only when things go
wrong, prosecutions are inevitably a source of complaint rather than con-

gratulation. More economistically, by recruiting civilian lawyers to relieve the administrative workload CPS represents a concealed increase in police manpower. Fourthly, P. A. J. Waddington articulates, in the Police Federation's trade paper, the argument of the positive rewards of CPS. The RCCP's proposed system of accountability through the Crown Prosecutor to the DPP would, he suggested, deflect the growing movement for local democratic control, in such a way that calls for local accountability could be dismissed as illegitimate political interference. In Waddington's words,

> Dual accountability to the Local Authority and a representative of the legal system could allow chief officers valuable room for manoeuvre in protecting the independence of this force." (Christian, 1983, p. 199)

At a less pragmatic level, the key variable is undoubtedly the definitive, yet largely unobserved, shift in the Tory conception of appropriate policing priorities. The 'hang 'em and flog 'em' campaign is, by any objective measure on a hiding to nothing. Since Thatcher came to power in 1979 recorded crime has increased by an unprecedented 40%. The all-too-familiar solutions of more police, increased powers, tougher sentences, have proved useless in the fight against crime. Yet law and order remains, at least publicly, in post. 'Crime' is cynically manipulated to deny civil and political liberties and to fuel the fires of moral indignation in order to separate out, in a Durkheimian sense, those within society from those without. However, Tory thinking has recently undergone a subtle transformation. A growing body of research conducted by the Home Office provides authoritative evidence that there is little the police can do to combat crime. In 1979, for example, Clark and Hough, in a report which lent support for community policing in conjunction with the targetted surveillance of certain types of offences, emphasise than an increase of over 10% in police manpower in the preceding five years had not been accompanied by either a decrease in recorded crime or an increase in the clear-up rate (Clark & Hough, 1979). By 1982 Burrows and Tarling were arguing, "crime detection owes little to investigative skill" (Burrows & Tarling, 1982). The following year, the British Crime Survey provided official sanction to the proposition that recorded crime was no more than the tip of the iceberg, the 'dark figure' of unrecorded crime exceeding recorded crime by a factor of three to four. Similarly, it underlined the fact that only 14% of calls to the police are centrally related to crime (Hough & Mayhew, 1983).

The Home Office solution, in common with other areas of Tory policy, has been to emphasise the need for self-help. The 1983 Report of the Commissioner of Police for the Metropolis was used to lay out the major strands in contemporary police thinking. The concept of an implied contract between the people and the police was introduced. A description of what the police could do was conflated with a prescription for what they should do. The 'notional contract', Commissioner Sir Kenneth Newman explained,

> ... is ... an unwritten, implicit contract obliging each party—the criti-

354   *K. de Gama*

> cism and the police officer—to acknowledge that peace and community
> well-being is the responsibility of everybody ... in discharging the obliga-
> tion of this conceptual agreement, the citizen must be encouraged and
> facilitated to opt into, rather than out of, the prevention of crime (Report
> of the Commissioner of Police for the Metropolis for the Year, 1983, p. 2).

The police have relinquished what is generally seen as their primary role to
the public. By the end of 1985 there were, in the Metropolitan Police District
alone, 3,770 Neighbourhood Watch Schemes and proposals for another 913
(Report of the Commissioner of Police for the Metropolis for the year, 1985,
p. 5).

It is politically expedient for the Government to abandon crime and give
priority to public order. This cue has been taken from James Q. Wilson, whose
work provides the intellectual underpinnings to the Reagan administration's
policies on law and order. Wilson argues that it is not crime which causes our
fear of crime, but *fear* of crime which causes crime. Therefore, the police
should be armed with wide discretionary powers to enable them to maintain
order on the streets and to preserve what he terms 'middle-class values'. The
second British Crime Survey accepts the main thrust of Wilson's argument.

> Fear of crime is triggered by non-criminal disorder on the streets—drunks,
> youths causing disturbances, noisy householders, graffiti, rubbish and
> litter ... these incivilities serve as signs of crime and thus lead to fear
> regardless of actual levels of crime. This can provide a downward spiral of
> fear of crime, neighbourhood decline and increased crime itself (Hough &
> Mayhew, 1985, p. 39)

This conceptual shift in conventional wisdom marks a transformation, and
to some extent, consolidation of police power. Under the new urban policing
strategy the higher echelons of the Met have cast the constable in the role of
repressive social worker.

In October 1982 Sir Kenneth Newman succeeded Sir David McNee as
Commissioner of Police for the Metropolis. Newman has consistently and sym-
pathetically avoided the high-profile public politiking of his predecessors. During the run-up to the 1983 General Election police interventions were
conspicious only by their absence. Voted communicator of the year by the
media in 1983 his influence is arguably more subtle and pervasive than his
more vociferous counterparts. Under a special brief from the Home Office he
was required to create a single, coherent urban policing strategy. His "corporate" or "multi-agency" approach combines elements of fire-brigade, preventive and community policing with new innovations of localised riot squads,
widespread surveillance and community liaison schemes. Although commonly
associated with a quasi-liberal element within the police, the emphasis in
theory as well as in practice in community policing, belies an essential similar-
ity with the more overtly repressive strands of the law and order campaign. Its
most important exponent, ex-Chief Constable of Devon and Cornwall, John

Alderson underlines its distinctive character: it is pro-active, preventive and pre-emptive (Alderson, 1979). Community policing is not an alternative but a compliment to reactive modes of policing. It is an attempt at surveillance and control which centralises the function of different agencies of the State under the over-arching supervision of the police. The Newman strategy retains the iron fist behind a rather threadbare velvet glove. The 1980s approach to public order is characterised by the increasing centralisation, militarisation and stockpiling of police powers. Robert Reiner evokes an appropriate image, "Dixon is out and Darth Vader is in" (Reiner, 1984).

The major focus of the new policing strategy is the production of order in public places. It marks a return to the core values of policing as expounded by Sir Robert Peel; ie the primacy of prevention over detection. Bridges and Bunyan define the essential elements of the corporate approach.

> It merges at the local level the coercive and consensual functions of government, enabling the police to wield a frightening mixture of repressive powers on the one hand and programmes of social intervention on the other, as mutually reinforcing tools in their efforts to control and contain the political struggles of the black and working class communities. It is a model of the local police state that must be resisted. (Bridges & Bunyan, 1985, p. 106) [14]

Against the backdrop of the new urban policing strategy, PACE and the Public Order Act, the police advocate is something of an anachronism.

Notes

1 Paradoxically, the setting up of CPS was result of the operation of forces informed by an ideology of order. However, the idea of a prosecution service independent of the police of course fits unproblematically with notions of the rule of law.
2 My italics.
3 England in the early nineteenth century saw a shift in the meaning of collective disorder from a form of proto-democracy to a serious threat to social and political order (Silver, 1967, n.5, pp. 15-20, Hobsbawn, 1959, p. 116).
4 *Webb v. Catchlove* (1886) 50 Justice of the Peace 795.
5 *Duncan v. Toms* (1887) 51 Justice of the Peace 631.
6 *O'Toole v. Scott* [1965] 2 All E.R. 240.
7 My own interview with Walter Merricks (unpublished) 27 February 1985.
8 My own interview with Sir Cyril Philips (unpublished) 6 March 1985.
9 Written evidence submitted to the RCCP PRO/BS12, Evidence no. 221.
10 Philips, Sir C. (1981) *The Work of the Commission and Policy Problems* (Paper presented at Leicester Conference).
11 The sole empirical plank for the argument for the separation of investigation and prosecution is that of acquittal statistics. In 1978 47% of all defendants pleading not guilty in the Crown Court were acquitted. 19% of these were ordered and 24% directed by the judge. Therefore, 43% of all acquittals can be attributed to the prosecution's failure to establish even a *prima facie* case against the accused. The

356   *K. de Gama*

RCCP, however, cites three studies which suggest that what appears to be an alarmingly high proportion of ordered and directed acquittals is unavoidable to the extent that crucial witnesses, often without warning, fail either to attend court or to come up to proof. (*Final Report*, paras 6.19-6.21).

12 The Prosecuting Solicitors' Society ceased to exist the moment CPS was wheeled into place.

13 Interestingly, today, over two years after the introduction of a severely under-resourced CPS it is the excesses and the omissions of the prosecutor and not the policeman which occupy the attention of the media. The image of the police as an institution has probably not been shinier at any point in the 1980s. Criticism is personalised and thereby depoliticised, restricted in recent months to the unholy alliance between Anderton (the bible-thumping Chief Constable of Manchester) and God.

14 The authors correctly point out that by extending police powers, safeguarding police discretion and undermining the tradition of police accountability before the law, PACE gives legal authority to the very autonomy from democratic control which characterises the "new urban policing strategy".

References

Alderson, J. (1979) *Policing Freedom*. Macdonald and Evans: Plymouth.

Baldwin, R. & Kinsey, R. (1982) *Police Powers and Politics*. Quartet Books: London.

Bridges, L. & Bunyan, T. (1983) Britain's new urban policing strategy: the Police and Criminal Evidence Act in context. *Journal of Law and Society*, **10**(1), 85

Bulmer, M. (Ed.) (1980) *Social Research and Royal Commissions*. Allen & Unwin: London.

Bulmer, M. (1983) Increasing the effectiveness of Royal Commissions: a comment. *Public Administration*, **161**, 436.

Burrows, J. & Tarling, R. (1982) *Clearing Up Crime*. Home Office Research Unit: London.

Christian, L. (1983) *Policing by Coercion*. GLC Police Committee and Pluto Press: London.

Clarke, R. & Hough, M. (1979) *The Effectiveness of Policing*. Home Office Research Unit: London.

Cornish, W. (1978) Defects in prosecuting: professional views in 1845. In *Reshaping the Criminal Law* (Glazebrook, P., Ed.). Stevens: London.

Critchley, T. (1978) *A History of Police in England and Wales*. Constable: London.

Edwards, J. (1964) *The Law Officers of the Crown*. Sweet and Maxwell: London.

Edwards, J. (1984) *The Attorney-General, Politics and the Public Interest*. Sweet and Maxwell: London.

Fisher, Sir H. (1977) *The Confait Case: Report*. HMSO: London.

Hall, S. *et al.* (1978) *Policing the Crisis*. Macmillan: London.

Hall, S. (Ed.) (1983) *The Politics of Thatcherism*. Lawrence and Wishart: London.

Hay, D. (1983) Controlling the English Prosecutor. *Osgoode Hall Law Journal*, **121**, (2), 166-188.

Hirst, P. (1975) Marx and Engels on Law, Crime and Morality. In *Critical Criminology* (Taylor, I., Walton, P. & Young, J., Eds). Routledge & Kegan Paul: London.

Hobsbawn, E. (1959) *Primitive Rebels*. Manchester University Press: Manchester.

Home Office (1983) *An Independent Prosecution Service*. Cmnd 9074. HMSO: London.

Police powers and public prosecutions   357

Hough, M. & Mayhew, P. (1983) *The British Crime Survey*. Home Office Research Unit: London.

Hough, M. & Mayhew, P. (1985) *Taking Account of Crime*. Home Office Research Unit: London.

Kettle, M. (1983) The Drift to Law and order. In *The Politics of Thatcherism* (Hall, S., Ed.). Lawrence & Wishart: London.

Kinsey, R. (1986) Crime in the City. *Marxism Today*, **30**(5), 6–12.

Langbein, J. (1974) *Prosecuting Crime in the Renaissance*. Harvard University Press: Cambridge, MA.

Leigh, D. (1983) The Secret War for Police Powers, *The Observer* 26 March 1983.

The Leveller (1979)

Mark, R. (1973) The Dimbleby Lecture. *The Listener*, **90**, 613–618.

Mark, Sir R. (1978) *In the Office of Constable*. Collins: London.

Mather, F. (1959) *Public Order in the Age of the Chartists*. Manchester University Press: Manchester.

Moody, S. & Tombs, J. (1982) *Prosecution in the Public Interest*. Scottish Academic Press: Edinburgh.

Philips, D. (1977) *Crime and Authority in Victorian England*. Croom Helm: London.

Radzinowicz, L. (1956) *A History of the English Criminal Law*. Vol III. Stevens: London.

Reiner, R. (1978) *The Blue-Coated Worker*. Cambridge University Press: Cambridge.

Reiner, R. (1982) Bobbies Take the Lobby Beat. *New Society*, **59**, 469–71.

Reiner, R. (1984) Is Britain Turning into a Police State? *New Society*, **69**, 51–56.

Reiner, R. (1985) *The Politics of the Police*. Wheatsheaf: Brighton.

Report of the Commissioner of Police for the Metropolis for the Year 1983 (1984) Cmnd 9268, HMSO: London.

Report of the Commissioner of Police for the Metropolis for the Year 1985 (1986) Cmnd 9790. HMSO: London.

Royal Commission on Criminal Procedure (1981) *Report*, Cmnd 8092. HMSO: London.

Sanders, A. (1985) The Uncertain Powers of Crown Prosecutors. *New Law Journal*, **21**, 313.

Silver, A. (1967) The Demand for Order in Civil Society. In *The Police* (Bordua, D., Ed.). Wiley: New York.

Storch, R. (1975) A plague of blue locusts: police reform and popular resistance in northern England 1840-57. *International Review of Social History*, **20**, 61–90.

Uglow, S. (1984) Independent Prosecutions. *Journal of Law and Society*, **11** (2), 233–247.

Wilson, J. (1982) *Thinking About Crime*. Vintage: New York.

[3]

Judicial Supervision and the Pre-Trial Process

STEWART FIELD*

INTRODUCTION

When the Royal Commission on Criminal Justice was appointed, few issues seemed more fundamental than the adversarial character of the pre-trial process. The search for causal common denominators to the series of miscarriages of justice that prompted the Commission led straight to the police's working view of their responsibilities in investigation. Behind the more obvious malpractices – the failures of disclosure, the intimidatory interrogation, the reshaping of witness testimony – was a more general police belief that, once detectives were clear that a suspect was guilty, they were under no moral or legal responsibility to pursue exculpatory lines of inquiry. Academic researchers had long pinned these police attitudes to the logic of an adversarial system.[1] Not surprisingly, therefore, when the immediate air of public scandal seemed to demand fundamental reform, one possible path was seen to lead in an inquisitorial direction and in particular to the unlikely icon of the French *juge d'instruction*.

Two years later and, with very muted adverse media comment, the Runciman Commission was able in short order to reject pre-trial judicial monitoring of the police.[2] Yet, at the same time, some of the Commission's recommendations, if adopted, would signal further moves away from classical adversarial principles in the pre-trial process. In seeking to promote efficiency, the Commission recommends a more developed pre-trial process under judicial supervision, largely based on written submissions and designed to determine, or at least define, many of the key trial issues. We would see fewer expensive and time-consuming trials based on the oral taking and testing of evidence. But in thus seeking to 'minimise the danger of adversarial practices being taken too far',[3] the Commission's proposals may well lead to the marginalization of adversarial trial safeguards without

* *Cardiff Law School, University of Wales, P.O. Box 427, Museum Avenue, Cardiff CF1 1XD, Wales*

The author would like to thank Peter Alldridge for helpful comments on an earlier draft.

the introduction of the strong pre-trial judicial presence that some inquisitorial systems possess. Justice may be sacrificed to efficiency.

JUDICIAL MONITORING OF THE POLICE: THE BACKGROUND

The Commission's terms of reference included, among others, the examination of:

> (ii) the role of the prosecutor in supervising the gathering of evidence and deciding
> whether to proceed with a case . . .
> (vi) the powers of the courts in directing proceedings, [and] the possibility of their having
> an investigative role both before and during the trial . . .

Within the context of the debate at the time, these terms of reference
clearly raised the issue of Continental inquisitorial experience. Many of the
arguments are longstanding,[4] but were given public momentum in the '80s
by the advocacy of Ludovic Kennedy and Lords Scarman and Devlin. Lord
Devlin had argued in his 1979 Hamlyn lectures for the introduction of a
judicial officer to supervise the pre-trial investigative process. Drawing from
his experience of the Virag, Dougherty, and Timothy Evans miscarriages,
he set out the structural problems: a system based on a presumption of
equality of arms in investigation that was now manifestly false, a vague and
rhetorical claim that the police and prosecution should act in a quasi-judicial
manner that was grounded in no detailed statutory or common-law duties,
and the existence of psychological and structural pressures on the police that
made it unlikely that vague injunctions to act quasi-judicially would cut
much ice in the police station. What was needed, Lord Diplock argued, was
a pre-trial judicial officer to supervise investigation. These officers would
stand between the prosecution and the defence with a 'clear and publicly
proclaimed duty to investigate both sides using the police as [their] agents'.[5]
Lord Scarman and Ludovic Kennedy differed from this proposal only at
the level of detail: their underlying analysis and solution ran along the same
broad lines.[6]

The French inquisitorial pre-trial tradition and, in particular, its *juge
d'intruction* were often cited as examples of what was envisaged, but their
recommendation was seldom rooted in detailed examination of the way the
institutions actually worked. Indeed, it was sometimes acknowledged that
what was attractive was the principle, that foreign practice might not
adequately reflect foreign principle.[7] But this left unexamined many key
questions about the way pre-trial judicial figures would interact with existing
prosecutors, police, and defence lawyers in England and Wales, and the way
their presence might change traditional rights, roles, and responsibilities,
both in theory and in practice. For example, Lord Devlin's proposals
envisaged that the accused would talk freely to examining judges. But this
must imply a belief that exculpatory 'leads' could be safely entrusted to
them. But what role would this leave for defence lawyers in such a system?

120

The danger is, of course, that we might give up the (in theory[8]) early intervention and active investigative role of the adversarial defence solicitor, only to get in return a half-hearted, malfunctioning version of the pre-trial judicial fact-finder. This might produce more, rather than fewer, convictions of the innocent.

THE COMMISSION'S APPROACH

The Commission's approach was fatal to an explicit inquisitorial move within the pre-trial process. Nowhere is the report more clear in stating its methods: its proposals were not arrived at by 'a theoretical assessment of the relative merits of the two legal traditions' but by reference to 'practical considerations'.[9] In fact, its reasoning is based on a mixture of influences, some certainly practical, but others based on half-articulated statements of principle and/or rather particular readings of the research evidence. What it did not do was to develop and consider detailed empirical evidence about a range of inquisitorial jurisdictions, using them as a basis for thinking about the ways that underlying processes, structural pressures, and occupational cultures operate, shaped by the varying points of detail within different systems. This meant that it could have no capacity to think creatively about institutions: it needed a perfect working model to borrow. The report complained that no foreign model existed in which the rights and interests of the various parties were so well balanced that it could simply be adopted.[10] This assumes a particular function for foreign experience: that all the Commission could do would be to take a pre-existing system and implant it in its entirety. The idea that foreign experience might cast light on the kind of underlying principles needed for designing systems is not considered by the Commission. And no-one supplied the Commission with a detailed plan.[11]

This left the Commission with the problem with which the previous section of this paper concluded: how would an inquisitorial pre-trial figure fit into the established roles of police, prosecutor, and defence lawyer? With no answers to these questions, the Commission stressed the danger of a cultural transplant that did not 'take'.[12]

There is no doubt that the Commission was hampered by the limitations of the easily available empirical research on the inquisitorial pre-trial process. Systematic observation, interview, and questionnaire research has simply not been published in relation to many inquisitorial jurisdictions – and certainly not translated.[13] The Commission's only research study to give a detailed picture of the workings of such systems was restricted to France and Germany. Even there, time constraints precluded systematic observation work or case file analysis: the study was based on interviews and secondary literature. This suggests the limitations of the Commission's information base.[14]

121

How one reacts to this depends in part on one's view of what can be expected of a Royal Commission. The Commission itself clearly had a very restricted view of its own role and capacities, seeing its agenda as set by the evidence to it and its research programme as a matter of reacting to proposals from the academic community rather than initiating them. An acceptance of a two-year time schedule and the extensive period needed for those lacking familiarity with the existing research base to 'read themselves in' seems to have effectively precluded the commissioning of extensive new empirical research on the particular issues raised by proposals for pre-trial investigative monitoring. This left the Commission, in the absence of perfect models to adopt, wary of innovation.

THE COMMISSION'S (NON)RECOMMENDATIONS

The Commission's salient decisions may be summarized as follows:

(i) the Commission rejected the idea that judges or the Crown Prosecution Service (CPS) should have a power and responsibility to supervise police investigation and preparation of evidence (pp. 3, 22);

(ii) the Commission recommended that the police should consult the CPS at the earliest possible stage in serious and complex cases where sufficiency of evidence was likely to be a problem (p. 22);

(iii) it recommended that the CPS should be free to ask police to seek further evidence before deciding whether to continue the prosecution. It should not have the power to compel the police to do this; rather, a consultations mechanism should be established at the appropriate level to resolve any disputes (p. 69);

(iv) the Commission rejected any idea that the CPS or other body of persons might be given the authority to protect the rights of suspects at police stations. Since they would be unable to maintain their independence, it would be better to leave this role to the custody officer (p. 30).

(v) The Commission did not recommend the imposition of a specific duty on either prosecutor or police to ensure that all relevant evidence be investigated and presented. It appeared to think that such a duty already existed: 'it is the duty of the police to investigate fairly and thoroughly all the relevant evidence, including that which exonerates the suspect'(p. 9).[15] No authority was cited for this proposition. Lord Devlin said almost fifteen years ago: 'if this is part of the duty of the police, it would help them a lot, I think, if they were told so plainly.'[16]

(vii) However, the Commission did make certain recommendations which it suggested could be seen as seeking 'to move the system in an inquisitorial direction' (p. 3). This seems[17] to refer to a number of proposed changes in pre-trial procedure: the introduction of preparatory hearings and sentencing canvassing before a judge, requirements of mutual pre-trial disclosure supervised by pre-trial judges, written procedures for no-case-to-answer applications, and some move to agreed written expert forensic evidence.

'THE INTERESTS OF JUSTICE'

How did the Commission think its way to its conclusions? Despite its shyness in admitting any place for theoretical reasoning, the Commission does support its arguments with more than the purely pragmatic. The report argues that investing prosecutors or pre-trial examining judges with functions of investigation or monitoring of investigation would not just be impracticable but would also be contrary to the 'interests of justice' and mean less effective protection for the innocent defendant. It offered a number of arguments.

First, accountability for investigation most 'naturally' belonged to the police.[18] This may come as a surprise to many readers from the Continental inquisitorial jurisdictions where fundamental legal responsibility and accountability for police investigation rests with the prosecutor or investigating judge. However, they should remember that it has long been a cultural tradition of the British to suppose that the racy Continentals are dangerously attached to unnatural practices.

Secondly, the Commission argues:

> there is no reason to believe that [the CPS], whose members are recruited and promoted for their legal skills and experience, would be proficient at investigating crime or at supervising and monitoring investigation conducted by those specifically trained for that purpose' [that is, the police] (p. 22).

This fails to make some important distinctions. Certainly, it is the police that have the broad investigative skills in both inquisitorial and adversarial traditions.[19] But one of the Commission's most impressive research studies clearly demonstrated that the British police are not well skilled nor trained in supervision.[20] Furthermore, the Commission ignores the point that training typically flows from being given a particular role: Continental investigative judges have some investigative skills because they have investigative responsibilities and are therefore trained to carry them out. The CPS does not have such skills or training because it currently has no investigative role. The Commission's argument is ultimately circular.

Thirdly, the report argues that combining investigating, prosecuting, and judicial functions leads to a confusion and tension in roles. The view seems to be that the nature of these respective roles requires their clear separation and that they be vested in different legal figures.[21] Two reasons are advanced for the need for functional separation: first, that resentment and argument between prosecutor and police are more likely where the prosecutor supervises police inquiries, and secondly, that a combination of roles tends to lead to a loss of objectivity on the part of the prosecutor or supervising officer.[22]

The first argument is wholly spurious. It is based on a very partial reading of the evidence on police/prosecutor relationships within a supervisory constitutional framework. The only evidence in the report is the citing of Leigh and Zedner's comment that in Germany, the 'combination of investigative and evaluative roles, and in particular [the prosecutors'] powers in respect of interviewing witnesses, can produce certain tensions'. They were apparently told that the police sometimes resent direction by the prosecutor.[23] But this confuses a qualification to a general picture with the

123

general picture itself. Despite the odd remark about occasional tensions, the general thrust of Leigh and Zedner's study actually emphasized the close, co-operative nature of the relationships in France and Germany: 'there is close co-operation between the police and the *parquet* [French prosecutor] and obviously good personal relationships. There seems little evidence of tension between the various actors'.[24] And: '[t]he German system is, therefore, marked by a high degree of co-operation and of mutual trust and confidence between police and prosecutors, these being seen as the precondition for effective law enforcement.'[25] The report itself testifies to the existence of friction between the CPS and the police; in part this is said to flow from police refusal to comply with CPS requests to make further inquiries.[26] The evidence adduced to support the view that tensions will be worse where the prosecutor has a legal power of direction and supervision seems extremely weak.

Furthermore, it is arguable that a certain amount of distance and the possibility of occasional conflict is inherent in any effective supervisory relationship. The real question is, surely, whether it would be desirable for prosecutors and police to have a more clearly hierarchical constitutional relationship. Whether the police like the arrangement or not is surely a subsidiary question, influencing how change should be presented and its precise institutional terms rather than the principle.

The point about possible loss of objectivity is more substantial, but it is important to distinguish between different sets of functions. Combining prosecution with supervision of investigation raises different issues to those involved where prosecution is combined with investigation itself, or where functions of prosecution, investigation, and adjudication are all exercised by the same figure. The historical development of the inquisitorial pre-trial process in different Continental jurisdictions has lead to a variety of combinations, not all of them satisfactory.

The report starts by pointing out that it was dissatisfaction with the combination of police investigation and police prosecution in England and Wales that lead to the creation of a separate prosecuting authority.[27] Certainly, one of the arguments revolved around objectivity and impartiality: research – done before the creation of the CPS – suggested some prosecution decisions were made because of the perceived demands of operational policing rather than an assessment of evidential strength, and that public interest was too often a cloak for police interest.[28] But that was in a context where functions of investigation and prosecution were vested in the same body; in the main, the inquisitorial prosecutor has *de facto* functions of prosecution and *supervision* of investigation rather than the function of investigation itself. Supervision is largely office-bound work, a question of assessing dossiers, hearing and deciding on pre-trial representations from defence lawyers and police, and perhaps directing police officers to pursue particular lines of inquiry. Prosecutors do not generally hear witnesses, interrogate suspects or visit scenes of crime. They are one step removed from the pressures and

124

solidarities of front-line policing. True, the role of the investigating judge does, in some inquisitorial jurisdictions, involve a combination of actual investigation, recommendations as to prosecution as well as judgement in relation to pre-trial detention. This has been said, even from within inquisitorial jurisdictions, to undermine impartiality, among other things, because investigation necessitates the development of working hypotheses about the guilt of particular individuals.[29] Specifically, there are allegations that adjudicative powers to remand in custody are sometimes used to further investigative aims, in particular, to coerce confessions.[30] But it is not a necessary feature of the institution of investigating judge that such functions be combined. The Dutch *rechter commisaris* plays no part in decisions as to prosecution. During *instruction*, he or she commissions tests and reports from experts, (re)interviews witnesses and suspects and makes a report upon which prosecutor and trial judge(s) base their decisions. They make no recommendations as to prosecution. Similarly the problems of giving decisions as to remand to the *juge d'instruction* have been recognized in France and reforms were implemented which removed the power. Chiefly because of opposition from *juges d'instruction* themselves, a refusal to finance reform effectively, and a certain institutional conservatism, the reform was controversial and has been repealed.[31] But resistance to change was built on pragmatics rather than principle: it was not regarded as a necessary feature of pre-trial judicial supervision of police investigation that supervision and decisions as to remand be made by the same judicial officer(s).

The more limited combination of supervisory judicial control of investigation with prosecution does not seem to be regarded as a problem on the Continent. In France, the Delmas-Marty report recently recommended a greater role for the public prosecutor in supervision of police investigations (to compensate for the loss of investigative functions vested in the *juge d'instruction*).[32] It remains an intrinsic feature of Dutch and German practice. Maguire and Norris, in their study of supervision within the police of routine CID investigations, argued that frontline solidarities and lack of cultural distance between supervisors and the supervised represented 'weak spots' in the British system of evidence gathering.[33] It would be unfortunate if fears of loss of objectivity amongst prosecutors were to blind us to their current practical dependence on police files generated by relationships even less characterized by distance and independence than those criticized by the Commission.

THE PRACTICE OF JUDICIAL MONITORING

Another major reason advanced for rejecting judicial monitoring was simply that the systems do not work in practice. In Scotland, the Commission pointed out, investigations are conducted almost entirely by the police with little or no direction from the Procurator-fiscal.[34] In most cases in Germany, the prosecutors first deal with a case when the completed police investigation file is turned over to them so that they can make a decision on charge. Much is made of the fact that the French *juge d'instruction* is involved in only 10 per cent of cases. These comments seem to reflect some commonly held assumptions about how judicial monitoring or supervising systems work. First, it is assumed that if they are to be effective, judicial officers must intervene very early in the case and be involved thereafter on a day-to-day basis, assisting in the development of investigative strategy in individual routine cases.[35] Since this is hardly ever true – whether one is talking of the Dutch, French, German or Scottish systems – the assumption leads to a view that supervision is largely rhetorical, a dangerous disguise for untramelled police control of investigations.[36] This is often regarded as particularly worrying in view of the much more limited (and in some cases non-existent) rights to defence counsel during police interrogation.[37] In one sense, the Commission's doubts about file-based, *ex post facto* supervision are understandable. Much research evidence from England and Wales concludes that prosecutors cannot effectively monitor police investigations via police-constructed files.[38] But this need not necessarily be the case in jurisdictions where there is a greater diversity of influences on the file; the difficult trick is to ensure that diversity.[39]

A second assumption implicit in the way that the Commission reasoned, at least about the French system, was that the key figure had to be the *juge d'instruction*. The Commission could then cite figures showing how rare *instruction* is to imply that judicial supervision is peripheral to most cases.[40] But to assess the significance of this, one needs to understand the cultural and institutional position of the inquisitorial prosecutor. In French, Dutch, and German theory they are regarded as judicial figures, trained and educated in the same way as other judges, including investigating judges, with the same duty to seek out inculpatory and exculpatory evidence in search of the truth.[41] If the Commission had evidence that in reality these judicial pretensions are a sham, it should have been presented. The Commission cites the Delmas-Marty report as evidence of the widespread criticism of the role of the *juge d'instruction* in France.[42] It fails, however, to recognize that Delmas-Marty reaffirmed the importance of judicial supervision of the police investigation: it simply argued that this should be entrusted exclusively to the *juge du parquet* (the public prosecutor) rather than to the *juge d'instruction*.[43] The Commission needed to examine much more closely the role of inquisitorial prosecutors and, in particular, their relationships with defence counsel and police to understand the way supervisory relationships operate.

JUDICIAL SUPERVISION: MECHANISMS AND RELATIONSHIPS

One starting point, given the evidence of Leigh and Zedner, should have been closer comparison of the French and German systems. The evidence

126

from Germany certainly confirmed the view that prosecutors' monitoring generally started after preliminary police investigations had been completed.[44] But Leigh and Zedner do not conclude from this that prosecutors always become prisoners of a police-constructed file and their supervision meaningless. Rather, the picture was ambivalent: sometimes defence lawyers, after interviewing their client, could suggest alternative accounts to prosecutors which challenged the police view and opened up new lines of investigations which might produce exculpatory evidence. But defence lawyers differed in their assessment of the effectiveness of this power. The key variable seemed to be the development of mutual trust and confidence between defence lawyer and prosecutor, so that the former trusted the latter to pursue lines of exculpatory inquiry without seeking to neutralize the evidence. Where this trust existed, the defence lawyer played a key role in prompting prosecutors to go beneath the surface of the police account. Where defence lawyers were unhappy with the attitude of prosecutors they tended to do more investigation themselves, to leave questioning of a relevant witness to trial, or get a judge to hear the witness to fix the evidence. But usually the defence lawyer would seek to get the prosecutor involved.[45]

These data confirm the available evidence on the workings of the Dutch system.[46] Defence lawyers there stress that the police cannot be supervised if the only information is the written evidence of the preliminary police investigation which is supplied by the police themselves.[47] Yet, just as in Germany, prosecutorial scrutiny of routine cases almost always occurs after most of the police investigation has been completed. If the case looks unambiguous on the basis of the police report, prosecutors work on the basis that it is in fact straightforward. They do not have time to do more unless they have some reason for thinking there is more to it.[48] They rely on defence lawyers to read the file, consult with their client to get his or her account, and then to suggest alternative lines of inquiry, inconsistencies or lacunae in the evidence, or perhaps police impropriety. If defence lawyers are not satisfied with the prosecution's response to their suggestions, they may demand the opening of an *instruction* and make the same suggestion to the investigating judge. If turned down again they may repeat the request before the trial judge(s). Prosecutors and examining magistrates have incentives to take defence requests seriously as they are charged with the preparation of a dossier which is supposed to contain all relevant evidence both for and against the suspect and which will be the starting point for decision-making at trial.

Both the German and Dutch systems seem to depend on the development of a particular kind of relationship between defence lawyer, prosecutor, and (in the Netherlands) investigating judge in the development of the dossier. Where cultural commitment to teasing out all relevant evidence or basic competence is lacking in a prosecutor or investigating judge, or a defence lawyer lacks the time or inclination to read the file carefully and tease out his/her client's account, or does not trust the prosecutor or investigating judge or have the rights to assert the client's story himself or herself, the system will not work effectively. The prosecutor's assessment of the case will be too dependent on initial police constructed information.

This might suggest reasons as to why the system is less effective in other jurisdictions which the Commission considered. In Scotland, the Procurator has a power to demand that the police investigate a case further but Moody and Tombs found that it was exercised in only 6 per cent of cases. They concluded that, although Procurators-fiscal have extensive powers, they are highly dependent on police information.[49] This is not surprising, given an adversarial context: without a clear institutional duty placed on Procurators to present all relevant evidence,[50] defence lawyers in Scotland are more reluctant to play the prompting role seen in Germany or the Netherlands. Procurators reported suspicions that the defence might have information which they were not revealing that might undermine the straightforward story told by the police reports.[51] While the plea-bargaining process often involved mutual exchange of information, some defence lawyers regarded it as legitimate to withhold information. In theory, in an adversarial system, the only question for the defence lawyer is whether disclosing the information furthers the client's interest.[52] Defence lawyers may well wish to reserve information to provide a surprise for the prosecution at trial so the prosecutor cannot rely on the defence as a ready source of suggestions for reinvestigation.

The system of judicial monitoring in France appears to have other problems. There are claims that defence lawyers, even in middle-ranking cases before the *Tribunal Correctionel*, 'are lucky if they see the day's files in time to grasp their contents'.[53] According to Leigh and Zedner, in these cases, defence lawyers do not ask prosecutors to investigate matters going to innocence. They would be dealt with before the trial court, unless the examining magistrate has been brought in. If unforeseen issues arise at trial, or it becomes clear that facts are at issue which have not been fully investigated, the court would suspend the trial and send it back to prosecutor or examining magistrate for further investigation.[54] But the danger is that, with only limited time for preparation, the defence lawyer may not be able to see the issues that need pursuing. Furthermore, there is a danger that trial judges may take an unduly restrictive view to prevent delays.[55] If the trial judge does not agree that there is an issue requiring suspension of trial for more investigation, the defence lawyer will have to rely on a challenge to the conviction itself on appeal. The same practical opportunities to make requests for investigation to a number of different kinds of judicial officer, such as seem to exist in the Netherlands, do not appear to exist in routine cases in France. Although rights of access are more extensive in cases going to *instruction*, until recently, even in these cases, defence lawyers only had a right of access to the official dossier two working days prior to interrogation by the *juge d'instruction*. The situation has just been improved.[56] There are also allegations of lack of cultural commitment to impartiality amongst some prosecutors and *juges d'instruction* – or at least

128

doubts.[57] It is very difficult to make general assessments but there does seem to be an impressionistic case for thinking that processes of training do not seem to shape cultural attitudes in quite the same way in France as they do in Germany and the Netherlands. Added to fears about police behaviour during the unregulated *garde à vue*, it may be that France has practical problems in enabling the dossier to avoid dominance by police construction.

POSSIBLE PATHS TO CHANGE:
AN INSTITUTIONAL REVOLUTION

There are two ways to see these deficiencies: first, as a reason for avoiding any kind of change in England and Wales, and secondly, as highlighting those features essential to effective judicial supervision. Negative examples can be as revealing as positive blueprints. If the Commission had given more creative thought to the evidence before it, and perhaps commissioned more extensive consideration of the way a variety of systems work in practice, it would have been in a better postion to judge the two main options for reform. The first was the radical option: to place a formal duty on prosecutors and/or a newly created investigating judge to seek out and set down all the relevant evidence both for and against guilt and innocence, using new powers to direct the police investigation. Effective working models for this do exist but are demanding in their requirements: a cultural and institutional commitment by the judicial supervisor to see that all the facts are properly investigated; powers to direct the police within a constitutional relationship that is utimately hierarchical; defence lawyers with early rights of access to the prosecution file, sufficiently well paid, trained, and empowered to spend time discovering from the accused any possible alternative lines of inquiry; sufficient defence confidence in the impartiality and thoroughness of the judicial supervisors for them to entrust the investigation of leads to them (or to the police under their direction); a number of opportunities for defence lawyers to make investigative demands of different judicial figures; perhaps even a fall-back opportunity for defence lawyers to apply for legal aid funding to do investigations themselves where completely unsatisfied by the prosecutors'/investigating judges' response.

This would need an institutional revolution in British criminal justice. We have no ready source for the judicial supervisors: the judges we have are too few, certainly not trained for the job, and probably too old for the demands of it. Given that the Crown Prosecuton Service has neither the status nor the cultural background to play a judicial role, it would certainly require the creation of a career judiciary structure, through which both prosecutors and (at least some) judges could emerge. But this might be no bad thing.[58] It would require powers of direction of the police in individual cases and mechanisms to ensure obedience.[59] Such change would be likely to have strong knock-on effects on other parts of the system. It need not

129

necessarily involve a relatively unregulated police interrogation – the system could operate with strong rights to a lawyer at the police station and an obligation to tape-record interviews. But if a duty were placed on prosecutor or judge to present all germane facts, where would they present them? It would make no sense to wait until trial, given the costs for the state (mainly financial) and the accused (mainly psychological and in deprivation of liberty if on remand). The reports would have to be in an official file. While this need not necessarily lead to a full-blown dossier system with few opportunities for detailed cross-examination at trial, it is inevitable that the status of the information in the file would become much stronger. This would be likely to limit the practical importance of oral presentation of evidence at trial. Indeed, if the objective is to make pre-trial investigation more balanced and thorough, fewer cases would be likely to go to trial, largely those where the credibility of competing witness accounts is still in the balance or where the defence remained dissatisfied with the impartiality of the investigation.

Change in this form would be both extremely risky and politically controversial. Risky because much would depend on new ethical and constitutional demands on police, prosecutor, and defence lawyer, and the creation of cultural attitudes through training and recruitment to reinforce those demands. Politically controversial because it would involve the overt subordination of police officers to the public prosecutor (and perhaps to a pre-trial examining magistrate). Recently, senior police officers have argued passionately for a system that entrenches the search for the truth rather than adversarial 'games'.[60] But their ardour would be likely to cool once it was appreciated that this involved taking directions from the CPS (or its successor). Given the political power of the police, any government is likely to hesitate. But if the Commission's recommendations as to developing pre-trial procedures are accepted, we will in any case end up with a pre-trial bargaining judge and even more limited use of formal trial based on traditional oral principles.[61] Perhaps the more obvious response at the moment is to defend the traditional adversarial system from drift and to argue for the extension of defence rights and resources in the pre-trial process to produce the equality of arms in investigation that the adversarial system requires. But long-term questions would remain: is a society that is not prepared to maintain the living standards of its 'deserving poor' likely to fund properly two full investigations of incidents in the defence of those labelled as the 'undeserving poor'? Any effective adversarial system will always be dependent on fairly generous legal aid funding and organization of defence services: imagine a legally aided criminal justice system where cases were prepared and investigated as thoroughly on both sides as civil cases currently are in the name of adversarial justice. Such systems also require a strong ethical commitment by defence lawyers, either to their clients' interests or to the ideal of adversarial justice and their role within it. The research evidence is that most of these conditions either do not exist or do so with great fragility.[62] The task of making the adversarial system work may look less daunting in the short term, but if Runciman's recommendations on pre-trial procedures are adopted, a further incremental drift from a classical version of the system is probably inevitable. We may find ourselves looking again at the requirements for institutional revolution.

REFORM

A more limited option and one that might allow subsequent incremental growth, would have been to introduce pre-trial judicial officers to do a number of relatively limited, discrete tasks within the pre-trial process, to establish certain pieces of evidence authoritatively at an early stage or to supervise particular points in it. This would involve a delicate task of integration between an inquisitorial point and the surrounding adversarial process. One possibility mooted, but not discussed in the Commission's report, was a system whereby either side could request that a pre-trial judge should interview a particular witness.[63] The advantage would be that the defence could bring forward exculpatory evidence and 'establish' it without giving the opportunity to the prosecution to neutralize it.[64] This will become more important if the Commission's recommendations on defence disclosure are implemented. Another suggestion would be a power for such judges to reinterview – at the request of CPS or defence – suspects or other witnesses who have already been questioned but where the integrity of police questioning is disputed or where the witness is thought to have given an incomplete account. They would need powers of access to all the records of the police investigation to preserve evidence of the circumstances surrounding the interview, and the power to follow up new evidence brought to light in order to draw up a report for the guidance of the CPS and perhaps the trial court. In our context, such a figure would represent something grafted onto the basic adversarial structure, activated only when one side or the other was unhappy with the integrity of existing evidence or investigation. Given the basic premise, unhappiness with police investigation, the procedures would be more likely to be used by the defence, but it would also give the CPS access to an investigative power. It would be a more limited version of the role played by the Dutch *rechter commisaris*, who prepares and/or commissions factual reports for the guidance of the prosecutor and trial court without drawing any conclusions himself or herself.[65] A further function that such a figure might perform would be to commission neutral expert reports at the request of either defence or prosecution.[66] The system would have to be well-organized and resourced if it were not to cause undue delay. There would need to be a defined path into a career on the bench and specialized recruitment and training. There might be a need for a corps of investigators at their command, given that the basic pressures on the police would remain overtly adversarial.[67]

131

© Basil Blackwell Ltd. 1994

CONCLUSION

Professor Zander has said that judicial/prosecutorial supervision did not, in fact, emerge as a serious proposition.[68] Had it done so, the Commission would have had to examine seriously what the essentials of an effective system are, where its weak spots are likely to be found, and what could be done to address them. Evidence of bad practice might have been taken to suggest vital elements in an effective supervisory framework that were missing in a particular criminal justice culture or set of institutions. In fact, evidence of bad practice was used to bury the idea.

Arguments about the merits or demerits of the adversarial and the inquisitorial must start from analysis of the kind of structural, institutional, and cultural forces that need to be created if they are to work and the specific mechanisms needed to create and sustain those forces. Clear decisions need to be made about how to define the function and division of labour as between police, prosecutor, defence counsel, and pre-trial and trial judge. The Royal Commission seems to have decided there are no fundamental structural problems in the way these relationships are constructed in our adversarial system. But even if one accepts this, rejecting the doubts expressed in this paper, more than coherence in structure is required. There needs to be the political will to provide the material resources to finance the system and the ideological resources to protect the system values involved. Here, the Royal Commission, with its narrow pragmatic focus and its ultimately complacent conclusions, has provided no pressure upon the Government to take seriously either the ideology or the financing of the existing structures of adversarial justice. It may be that we will come this way again looking for alternative models, for new ways of reconciling the interests of efficiency in early pre-trial resolution of most cases with a rigorous and just accumulation and assessment of evidence. For those concerned about the institutional processes of criminal justice and disappointed by the absence of radical or even systematically theoretical thought in the report, perhaps the lesson is that Royal Commissions need such thinking done for them in the years leading up to their creation. This should be a spur for more comparative empirical and theoretical work.

NOTES AND REFERENCES

1 See A. Sanders, 'Constructing the Case for the Prosecution' (1987) 14 *J. of Law and Society* 229 at 230–4, and D. McBarnet, *Conviction* (1981).
2 *Report of the Royal Commission on Criminal Justice* ('RCCJ') (1993; Cm. 2263; Chair, Lord Runciman). In this article, judicial supervision will be taken to include scrutiny by prosecutors where they are, within the tradition of the jurisdiction, recruited, trained, and regarded as judges.
3 id.
4 A. Stein, 'A Political-Analysis of Procedural Law' (1988) 51 *Modern Law Rev.* 659; J. Jackson, 'Two Methods of Proof in Criminal Procedure' (1988) 51 *Modern Law Rev.* 549.

5 Lord Devlin, *The Judge* (1979) ch. 3.
6 Lord Scarman, 'The system must change' *Times*, 19 November 1991; L. Kennedy, 'Wrong Arm of the Law' *Guardian*, 16 November 1989.
7 Scarman, id.
8 See M. McConville, J. Hodgson, L. Bridges, and A. Pavolvic, *Standing Accused: The Organisation and Practices of Criminal Defence Lawyers in Britain* (1994, forthcoming) for evidence of the distance between theory and practice.
9 RCCJ, op. cit., n. 2, p. 3, para. 12.
10 id., p. 4, para. 13.
11 id.
12 id., p. 83. Fear of cultural transplants does not prevent the Commission recommending, after very little argument, the Scottish and Continental practice of prosecutor fines, despite the major constitutional shift this would signal.
13 Witness the formalism of the Commission's survey, N. Osner, A. Quinn, and G. Crown (eds.), *Criminal Justice Systems in Other Jurisdictions* (1993).
14 L. Leigh and L. Zedner, *A Report on the administration of criminal justice in France and Germany*, RCCJ research study no. 1 (1992). The researchers describe their review as 'inevitably impressionistic'.
15 The Commission also stated that it is the duty of the police 'to discover the facts relevant to an alleged or reported criminal offence, including those which may tend to exonerate the suspect' (RCCJ, op. cit., n. 2, p. 69). Again, it cited no statute or case in support of this proposition.
16 Devlin, op. cit., n. 5, p. 77. Presumably he also meant authoritatively by statute or case-law.
17 The report cites its recommendations in relation to forensic science evidence as an example. But we are left to guess what other recommendations are intended to have this effect. RCCJ, op. cit., n. 2, at p. 3, para. 12.
18 id., at pp. 22–3, para. 67.
19 Inquisitorial investigating judges usually have expertise in questioning suspects and witnesses.
20 M. Maguire and C. Norris, *The Conduct and Supervision of Criminal Investigations*, RCCJ research study no. 5 (1993).
21 RCCJ, op. cit., n. 2, p. 22, para. 67.
22 id., p. 72, paras. 15–16.
23 id.
24 Leigh and Zedner, op. cit., n. 14, p. 4. See, also, pp. 17–18.
25 id., at p. 26.
26 RCCJ, op. cit., n. 2, pp. 73–4, paras. 23–6.
27 id., p. 69, para. 2.
28 A. Sanders, 'Prosecution Decisions and the Attorney-General's Guidelines' [1985] *Crim. Law Rev.* 4.
29 *Commission justice pénale et droits de l'homme* (Chair: M. Delmas-Marty), *La Mise en Etat des Affaires Pénales* (1991) at pp. 129, 134. The anxiety about combining investigation and judgement has been a point of criticism for inquisitorial systems since the nineteenth century. See Jackson, op. cit., n. 4, at p. 559.
30 For Italy, see T. Erikson, 'Confessions in evidence: a look at the inquisitorial system' [1990] *New Law J.* 884; for France, see M. Dorwling-Carter, '*Faut-il supprimer le juge d'instruction?*' (1990) *Juris Classeur Périodique*. 1.3458 (*La Semaine Juridique*); see, for complaints from *avocats* about *detentions-pressions*, Anne Chemin, '*Magistrats, avocats et policiers dressent un premier bilan de la réforme de la procedure pénale*' *Le Monde*, 29 September 1993, and G. Flécheux, '*Pour un compromis*' *Le Monde*, 27 May 1993.
31 *Mise à Jour 1993 du Code de Procédure Pénale* (Litec 1993), arts. 122, 135, 137.
32 Delmas-Marty, op. cit., n. 29.
33 Maguire and Norris, op. cit., n. 20, p. 23 onwards.

34 RCCJ, op. cit., n. 2, p. 71, para. 14.
35 A view reflected in Leigh and Zedner, op. cit., n. 14, p. 69.
36 For discusssion of the Dutch system, see S. Field, N. Jörg, and P. Alldridge, 'Prosecutors, Examining Judges and Control of Police Investigations' in *Europeanization of Criminal Justice*, eds. C. Harding, P. Fennell, N. Jörg, and B. Swart (forthcoming, 1994).
37 For critical comment on the French situation, see R. Vogler, 'France: an unsuitable model?' *Legal Action*, January 1992, 7 at 8; for the Netherlands, see Field et al., id.
38 M. McConville, A. Sanders, and R. Leng, *The Case for the Prosecution* (1991) 201.
39 I will argue below that there is evidence that systems in the Netherlands and in Germany do achieve this – at least most of the time.
40 Around 10 per cent of cases in France and 3 per cent in the Netherlands go to *instruction*, Delmas-Marty, op. cit., n. 29, p. 130 and Field et al., op. cit., n. 36.
41 Delmas-Marty, id., p. 13, For a detailed observation-based study of Dutch prosecutors that stresses their self-image as magistrate, see H.G. Van de Bunt, '*Officieren van Justitie: verslag van een participerend observatieonderzoek*' (doctoral thesis, University of Utrecht, 1985).
42 RCCJ, op. cit., n. 2, p. 4, para. 14.
43 Delmas-Marty, op. cit., n. 29, p. 134.
44 Leigh and Zedner, op. cit., n. 14, p. 72.
45 id., pp. 36–7, 40.
46 Generally, L. Leigh and J. Hall Williams, *The Prosecution Process in Denmark, Sweden and the Netherlands* (1981); Field et al., op. cit., n. 36.
47 Leigh and Hall Williams, id., pp. 59–60.
48 Field et al., op. cit., n. 36. See, also, H.G. Van de Bunt, op. cit., n. 41.
49 S. Moody and J. Tombs, *Prosecution in the Public Interest* (1982) 44–8.
50 Witness their suggestion that the ideological stance of the Procurator-fiscal is pro-police rather than neutral, id., pp. 47–8, 120.
51 This would provide Procurators with a motive for bargaining: id., p. 121.
52 Studies suggest that that other personal and occupational factors are in play that sometimes bring about greater co-operation, see M. McConville and J. Baldwin, *Negotiated Justice* (1977) and McConville et al., op. cit., n. 38, pp. 165–70.
53 J. Monahan, 'Sanctioning Injustice' (1991) *New Law J.* 679. Leigh and Zedner suggest that sometimes defence may get access 'no more than four days before trial', op. cit., n. 14, p. 14.
54 Leigh and Zedner, id., at pp. 13–14.
55 J. Pradel, *Procédure Pénale* (1989) 523: '*Le régime appliqué est restrictif car ces incidents retardent la solution du procès*'.
56 Art. 114, *Code du Procédure Pénale* now gives defence counsel the right to consult the dossier four days before the first interrogation and from then on at any point during *instruction. Mise à Jour 1993 du Code de Procédure Pénale*, op. cit., n. 31. For the difficulties posed by the former situation, see M Dorwling-Carter, op. cit., n. 30.
57 Vogler, op. cit., n. 37, p. 8; Leigh and Zedner, op. cit., n. 14, p. 23.
58 See the arguments of T. Gifford, *Where's the Justice* (1986) 32-3.
59 Two spring to mind: first, regular reports by prosecutors on the work of the police under their direction which would feed into an appraisal process and secondly, in cases of neglect of duty, a system of complaint to a truly independent Police Complaints Authority.
60 C. Pollard, 'The view from the iceberg' *Guardian*, 24 July 1993.
61 See, in this issue, S. Field and P.A. Thomas, pp. 1–19, and L. Bridges, pp. 20-38.
62 J. Baldwin, *The Role of Legal Representatives at the Police Station*, RCCJ research study no. 3 (1993); M. McConville and J. Hodgson, *Custodial Legal Advice and the Right to Silence*, RCCJ research study no. 16 (1993); McConville, Hodgson, Bridges, and Pavolvic, op cit., n. 8; Justice, *A Public Defender* (1987) 6–17.
63 See Leigh and Zedner, op. cit., n. 14, pp. 69, 72-3.

64 This happened in both the Confait and Carole Richardson (one of the Guildford Four) cases.
65 See S. Field et al., op. cit., n. 36.
66 See, in this issue, the arguments of P. Alldridge, pp. 136–50.
67 District Attorneys in the United States of America have a specialist corps of investigators and can initiate inquiries. See L. Lustgarten, *The Governance of Police* (1986) 6–7.
68 M. Zander, 'Where the critics got it wrong' (1993) *New Law J.* 1338, 1341.

Part II
Discretion and Diversion

[4]

TIM NEWBURN, DAVID BROWN, DEBBIE CRISP AND PATRICIA DEWHURST

INCREASING PUBLIC ORDER

The 1986 Act is being increasingly used by the police to deal with behaviour previously penalised under other legislation

The authors completed this research while attached to the Home Office Research and Planning Unit

IN 1986, the Public Order Act introduced a structure of new offences to replace the old common law offences of riot, rout, affray and unlawful assembly. The new offences in the 1986 Act are riot (s.1), violent disorder (s.2), affray (s.3), threatening behaviour (s.4) and disorderly conduct (s.5). Here we consider the use of sections 2-5 of the new Act by two police forces. (Riot is used infrequently; no cases were encountered in the areas studied during the period covered by the research.) The data on which it is based are derived primarily from case records from five police stations in these two force areas.

The stimulus for the research was the large increase in the number of public order offences being recorded by the police and the corresponding rise in prosecutions following the changes in the law made by the new Act. During the period 1986-88 the number of prosecutions for public order offences more than doubled, with the greatest proportional increase being for indictable offences. In

all police areas but one, this pattern of a rise in public order prosecutions was repeated. The major question for the research was that
of how the rise in offences could be explained. Does it merely
reflect that a growing number of disorderly incidents are being
encountered or is it more closely related to the nature of the new
legislation and current police practice with regard to its use? If it is
the latter, further questions arise about the possible advantages of
the legislation and why it might be being used by the police more
frequently.

In considering these questions the study sought first of all to
identify and describe the kinds of situation in which the different
sections of the Act are used. A total of 470 cases were examined.
These were all ones in which some action was taken by the police
and, more particularly, where at least one person arrested was
charged with an offence under the Public Order Act. The cases
were drawn from 1988 records at the five police stations involved
in the study, and the analysis of these cases was backed up with
semi-structured interviews with custody officers.

Disorderly incidents: an outline

Unsurprisingly, a large proportion of disorderly incidents
occurred late at night. Of the 470 incidents in the sample over one-
third (164) happened during the late evening between 9pm and
midnight. A further 18 per cent (86) occurred between midnight
and 3am. Approximately 53 per cent of incidents therefore
occurred during this one six-hour period. It is also not surprising to
find that 40 per cent of incidents occurred on a Friday and
Saturday and a further 17 per cent on a Sunday.

Over half of all the incidents in the sample were classified as
occurring on the street. This proportion would in fact increase
markedly if it included those incidents connected with licensed
premises that also occurred on the street. However, these incidents
were included in a general category of those that occurred in or
were connected with licensed premises, since these were of particular interest. Altogether, 20 per cent of cases fell into this group.
Drink had a significance beyond those cases closely connected
with licensed premises: altogether, of the 381 cases for which
information was available, 195 (51 per cent) were drink-related. A
further 14 per cent were suspected to be drink-related and only 120
cases (31 per cent) did not involve drink or drugs.

In a quarter of the cases for which information was available the
police were the sole victims of the incident. (Technically, there

23

need be no victim in cases of riot or violent disorder since the violence used or threatened may be against property. In fact, there is
usually an identifiable victim.) In almost half the cases the victims
were members of the public and in a further 18 per cent of cases
they were a mixture of both police and public. It is worth remark-
ing on the number of cases in which police officers were the victims of public order offences. In all, 194 cases (42 per cent)
involved police officers as victims, though they were proportionately more likely to be victims of incidents that gave rise to
charges under ss.4 or 5 than under ss.2 or 3.

Charges and court proceedings

The 470 cases in the study involved a total of 760 offenders
who were charged with public order offences. Because the more
serious incidents tended to involve a greater number of suspects
(indeed for a charge under s.2 to be brought there has to be a minimum of three persons involved in the incident) this greatly
increased the number of more serious charges in the sample. In
total, the 470 incidents gave rise to to 334 charges under s.5, 175
under s.4, 128 under s.3 and 123 under s.2.

Out of a total of 597 cases which had been finalised at the time
data were collected, defendants were found guilty in 342 (57 per
cent) and not guilty in only 33 (6 per cent). A summary of the
main outcomes is contained in Table 1. The number of cases that
were dismissed, withdrawn, discontinued or discharged is included
and these exercise quite a degree of influence on the overall picture. Quite high proportions of s.2 and s.4 cases were dismissed at
court: the proportions were, respectively, 21 per cent and 18 per
cent. In all offence groups, but particularly in relation to affray
(s.3), quite high numbers of cases were discontinued or withdrawn
or the defendant discharged. It was unusual in the less serious
cases for the outcome in court to be a not guilty verdict: only four
s.4 cases and one s.5 case ended in this way. A much higher proportion of s.2 and s.3 cases ended with a not guilty verdict (15 per
cent and 13 per cent respectively) and, if coupled with the proportions of such cases that were dismissed, provides a fairly high
'failure' rate.

There was little indication from the police files as to why so
many cases were being dismissed, discontinued or withdrawn.
Occasionally there was a note on the file about lack of evidence,
but nothing in most cases that would explain what happened in
court. Interestingly, however, of those who had public order

Table 1: Public Order Charge by Court Outcome

Charge	Outcome					
	Guilty n (%)	Not guilty n (%)	Bound over n (%)	Dismissed n (%)	Discharged, Discontinued or Withdrawn n (%)	Total
s.2	41 (45)	14 (15)	11 (12)	19 (21)	7 (8)	92
s.3	40 (37)	14 (13)	12 (11)	9 (8)	17 (16)	109
s.4	84 (60)	4 (3)	14 (10)	25 (18)	14 (10)	141
s.5	177 (69)	1	25 (10)	30 (12)	24 (9)	257

charges against them dropped, 74 had also been charged with other offences. Over half of these had been charged with offences of violence and, indeed, those who had public order charges dropped were somewhat more likely also to have been charged with violence than were the defendants in the sample generally. Some officers interviewed suggested that they would sometimes cover themselves by charging both a public order offence and violence, although they anticipated that the CPS would decide to proceed with one or the other, depending on the nature of the evidence.

Information was available on the sentencing of 363 defendants who were found guilty of public order offences. Of these, 46 were charged with violent disorder (s.2). Half of this group were sentenced to immediate custody, while five had part of their sentence suspended. Of the remainder, 11 received a community service order, four were fined, one was sentenced to probation, six were conditionally discharged and one received an absolute discharge. A further 44 defendants were found guilty of affray (s.3). Eleven of these received custodial sentences and six suspended custody. The bulk of the rest were fined. Fines were also the most common sentences received by those found guilty under s.4 (56 of 89 - 63 per cent) or s.5 (138 of 184 - 75 per cent). Approximately 15 per cent of those found guilty under these two sections received conditional discharges.

Threatening behaviour and disorderly conduct

S.4 of the 1986 Act ('threatening behaviour'), which replaces s.5 of the 1936 Public Order Act, provides that:
(1) A person is guilty of an offence if he -
(a) uses towards another person threatening, abusive or insulting words or behaviour, or
(b) distributes or displays to another person any writing, sign or other visible representation which is threatening, abusive or insulting, with intent to cause that person to believe that immediate unlawful violence will be used against him or another by any person, or to provoke the immediate use of unlawful violence by that person or another, or whereby that person is likely to believe that such violence will be used or it is likely that such violence will be provoked.

The offence is very similar to that contained in the 1936 Act, with two exceptions: it also applies to conduct in private places and catches behaviour that might not formerly have been covered because the victim (for example, a policeman or old lady) was someone who was not likely to be provoked into violence (Card, 1987).

S.5 of the new Act is in some ways of more interest than s.4, in that it creates a new offence ('disorderly conduct'). Partly for this reason and partly because this section was found to be used in such a wide variety of contexts, its use is discussed more fully than that of s.4. The purpose of s.5 was to cover minor acts of hooliganism or other anti-social behaviour, which are of particular concern where they affect vulnerable groups such as the elderly. Many such acts may not formerly have been covered by the criminal law (Card, *ibid*) and this section therefore effectively has a 'net-widening' effect. Section 5 provides that:

(1) A person is guilty of an offence if he -

(a) uses threatening, abusive or insulting words or behaviour, or disorderly behaviour, or

(b) displays any writing, sign or other visible representation which is threatening, abusive or insulting, within the hearing or sight of a person likely to be caused harassment, alarm or distress thereby.

Generally speaking, the incidents that resulted in s.4 and s.5 charges tended to occur in broadly similar contexts. However, the officers that were interviewed argued that they were able fairly easily to distinguish which section to use when deciding on charges. The clearest explanation offered was that s.5 incidents were more likely to involve just one person, whereas s.4 offences almost always involved two or more. The data from the cases examined tend to support this general distinction.

Conduct covered by ss. 4 and 5. Of the 470 cases in the sample, 113 (24 per cent) resulted in charges under s.4 and 263 (56 per cent) under s.5. Section 5 is in fact the most common charge under the 1986 Public Order Act as well as the least serious. The varied nature of offences resulting in charges under s.5 reflect the very general nature of the powers given to the police under the Act. Thus, it was suggested by some officers interviewed that certain acts that would not previously have resulted in an arrest are now subject to arrest and proceedings under s.5, and that this section of the Act is flexible enough to allow charges to be brought where evidence might not support other, perhaps more serious, charges. For example, there were cases where a member of the public had been sexually harassed in a public place but it had been difficult for the police to secure sufficient evidence to support a charge of indecent assault because evidence from a victim or wit-

27

ness was not available. As a result the offender was arrested under
s.5 for disorderly conduct. This is a good example of one of the
ways in which the legislation is viewed as a helpful tool by police
officers. Prior to the 1986 Act, they argue, it would been much
more difficult to put a stop to the behaviour that was causing
someone distress.

It is often the case, of course, that although some distress may
be caused, the victim may not wish to press charges. The police
may still make an arrest under the new Act once an offender persists with his or her threatening or disorderly behaviour, having
being warned to desist. Thus, in one case the offender, who was
attending a major sporting event, was described as 'rubbing up
against the backsides of women members of the audience'. A complaint was made to a steward who called the police. The officers
who arrived observed the behaviour of the man in question and,
after he had failed to heed a warning to desist, they made an arrest
under s.5. In this case the arresting officer suggested that there was
insufficient evidence for a charge of indecent assault or exposure
but the suspect was, in their view, using disorderly behaviour in
the vicinity of the person likely to be caused harrassment, alarm or
distress.

'Net-widening'. One concern about the new Act which has been
voiced is that it might potentially 'widen the net' by criminalising
behaviour previously outside the scope of the law. Interestingly, a
guide to the Act produced for training purposes by one of the
forces studied itself implies exactly this. Its introduction states
that 'the scope of behaviour covered by [the Act] is particularly
wide, even extending... to conduct thought by some to be anti-
social. Indeed under this new provision (s.5) behaviour previously
thought of as "high spirits" may become an offence'. It was, of
course, one of the aims of the Act to criminalise some low-level
nuisances that the police had inadequate powers to deal with
before.

Extension of police powers. There are two specific areas in
which ss.4 and 5 extend police powers. Firstly, powers of arrest
are extended by making it an offence under s.4 to use words,
behaviour etc with the intention of causing a 'person to believe
that immediate unlawful violence will be used against him or
another by any person, or to provoke the immediate use of unlawful violence by that person or another'. The effect of this reformu-
lation has been to overturn earlier court decisions that there could

be no likelihood of a breach of the peace when the only people present were police officers. Now, although it would still be expected that an officer would not be 'likely' to react by using unlawful violence, the fact that the officer is likely to believe that unlawful violence might be used against him or her would mean that an offence had been committed and that an arrest could be made.

Secondly, one major benefit of the new Act, this time under s.5, is that police officers may now be regarded as people who can be distressed, alarmed or harrassed. While there was initially some doubt about whether this interpretation of the Act was correct (Smith, 1988), the decision of the Divisional Court in *DPP v Orum* (*The Times*, 25 July, 1988) confirms the view of many officers interviewed that s.5 did provide them with a protection against public abuse. This was perceived as a major advance on the previous situation in which they were dependent, at least to a degree, on the presence of a member of the public who was harmed or threatened with harm. The high proportion of cases in the sample in which the incident resulting in an arrest being made was witnessed by the police during the course of their duty, rather than as a result of a complaint from a member of the public, together with the fact that in almost 30 per cent of s.5 cases police officers were the sole victims, illustrate the effect of this change in the legislation.

One feature of s.5 cases was the large number in which the process leading towards arrest was begun by the police rather than a member of the public. Some involved a lone offender and the victim or victims were either members of the public who were peripheral to the incident, or one or more police officers. In such cases, of which there were quite a large number (approximately 15 per cent of s.5 cases), the single offender was often allegedly drunk, and staggering about in public, and using abusive language. The offender would be given one or more warning about his behaviour and, if he refused to desist, would be arrested. In such cases the officer would note, where appropriate, that there were members of the public nearby who appeared to be distressed in some way by the person's behaviour. For example, one arresting officer simply noted that 'there were several people nearby, including young children and some middle-aged women' and another that 'there were small children playing nearby and there were also two elderly ladies who appeared to hear and shook their heads'. In this general way, arresting officers showed that the disorderly behaviour was within the hearing or sight of a person likely to be caused harass-

ment, alarm or distress. In fact, in some cases the disorderly conduct was not actually directed at a particular person but was merely a public outburst. In such cases, as was suggested above, it is
arresting officers who actually become the 'victim' of the offence.
For, having warned offenders about their behaviour, officers make
arrests on the basis that they were alarmed or distressed by the
conduct or that they believed that it was likely that violence might
be used against them. It is not always clear in such cases why the
offender is charged with a public order offence rather than with
being 'drunk and disorderly'. Custody officers, when asked about
the difference between s.5 and the 'drunk and disorderly' offence
were often unable to differentiate the two. Some suggested that
they relied on the arresting officer's view when considering
charges, while others felt that it had something to do with the
'degree of disorderliness' involved.

Breach of the peace. Custody officers also suggested that there
may be a tendency to use s.5 of the Act in preference to common
law breach of the peace. One important respect in which, from the
police officer's point of view, s.5 is comparatively advantageous is
that it removes the need to establish that the *locus in quo* was a
public place. This has been replaced with what Smith (1987) has
called a 'domestic dwelling exemption'. Thus, a public order
offence may now be committed both in public and in private,
although there must either be someone outside the private dwelling
at whom the offensive behaviour is directed or who is likely to be
caused alarm or distress by that behaviour. Consequently, s.5 was
often viewed by officers as constituting a helpful advance on previous arrangements in relation to 'domestic' cases. The fact that
public order offences could now occur 'in private' meant, it was
argued, that it was easier for officers to make arrests in cases in
which the victim did not wish to press charges. Formerly, it was
suggested, the police would have been limited to arresting the
offender for breach of the peace. Again it was argued that it was
dispiriting for police officers, and generally unhelpful for the victim, to be faced with the prospect of being unable to press charges
when an offence had clearly been committed. Thus, in the current
climate, in which there is a much greater emphasis on making
arrests in 'domestic' cases, the new Public Order Act provides a
particularly useful tool for the police.
    Those interviewed also suggested to us that an arrest under the
Public Order Act was sometimes preferred to arrest for breach of
the peace because the former would result in the offender being

charged and tried by a court, whereas the latter would result merely in the offender being 'bound over'. Officers argued that it was demoralising to make arrests only to find that the suspect merely spent an hour or two at the station. The ability to use s.5 was viewed as important by the officers interviewd. Indeed, some suggested that those offenders who were charged under s.5 were much less likely to be found reoffending than those arrested for breach of the peace.

'Victimless' offences. One type of incident which illustrates two further aspects of current practice, mainly in relation to s.4 of the Public Order Act, although s.5 charges may sometimes be used, is the public fight which has no obvious 'victims'. The bestowal of the label 'victim' on one or more parties to an offence is generally dependent upon their having either some degree of innocence (they were, for example, subject to an unprovoked attack), or simply due to the fact that they were not present. A number of cases in the sample involved a public fight in which two or more people were not distinguishable by their degree of participation. In such cases it is not generally possible for officers to separate 'offenders' from 'victims' nor is it usually realistic for them to consider charging any of those involved with assault since participants are unlikely to be interested in pressing charges or making statements. A s.4 (or s.5) charge, even when there are no members of the public around, is now the most obvious possibility.

Affray

Section 3 of the Act covers affray. Some 14 per cent of cases examined involved charges under this section. The new definition of affray provides that:

(1) A person is guilty of affray if he uses or threatens unlawful violence towards another and his conduct is such as would cause a person of reasonable firmness present at the scene to fear for his personal safety.

One difference from the old common law offence of affray is that the offence is no longer one of group disorder and may be committed by one person attacking another. It is not necessary for there to be a bystander, actual or likely, in order for an offence to have been committed, nor need the offence occur in public. Theoretically, therefore, an affray may occur between two people in their own home. It is fairly widely accepted that the offence of affray has been downgraded and seems now, as Thomas (1987) has suggested, to be appropriate only for relatively small-scale incidents. The data from the study appear to confirm this assertion. Even so, despite this downgrading, some of the offences that the police charge as affray are eventually prosecuted under the less serious s.4 by the Crown Prosecution Service.

Offences giving rise to charges under s.3 involved violence or the threat of it, but injuries did not often occur and, when they did, were not severe. The cases that resulted in the worst injuries tended to be incidents such as gang fights that involved several people, in which all those involved were potential or actual guilty parties. The majority of incidents which contained more obviously 'innocent' and 'guilty' parties frequently involved only the threat of violence, even if this was of a potentially very serious nature.

The following are two fairly typical examples. In the first, four youths were seen chasing two others. The one person who was eventually charged was heard to shout 'kill the bastards' and was also seen carrying a knife. He was caught by the police before any violence occurred and was charged with affray. In the second case a man was asked to leave a pub by the landlord because he had been barred on a previous occasion. He threatened the barman, who called the police, and then threw a bar stool through one of the windows. He ran away when the police arrived and was chased to his home. He threatened the police officers who chased him and, when arrested, was charged with affray. If anything, these offences were somewhat more serious than many of the affrays that occurred at other stations. The data regarding police use of 'affray' would not appear to point to a rise in the level of serious disorder. As has been argued, the vast majority of incidents that gave rise to charges of affray were generally relatively minor in character, seldom involving violence and usually only the threat of violence.

Violent disorder

Violent disorder is covered by s.2 of the 1986 Public Order Act. This offence replaces the old one of unlawful assembly, as well as covering some public disturbances involving fewer than 12 people, which used to be covered by the offence of riot (Card, 1987). Roughly 6 per cent of the cases studied involved charges under this section. S.2 states that:

(1) Where 3 or more persons who are present together use or threaten unlawful violence and the conduct of them (taken together) is such as would cause a person of reasonable firmness present

32

at the scene to fear for his personal safety, each of the persons using or threatening unlawful violence is guilty of violent disorder.

There are a number of distinctions between the types of offences that result in charges brought under s.3 and those which become defined as 'violent disorder'. Perhaps the most straight-forward is that the violence used or threatened may be against people or property. In fact, in the cases studied it was invariably other people.

The second distinction relates to the number of people involved in the incident, or at least the number of people arrested and charged as a result of the incident. The new s.2 offence requires that there be three or more persons present together using or threatening unlawful violence, though it is not necessary for all three to be prosecuted for an offence to be deemed to have occurred. Of the 26 incidents in the sample that gave rise to charges under s.2, eight involved 11 or more people and a further five involved between six and ten. In fact, as a general rule, the higher the charge the greater the number of people that was likely to be involved and *vice versa*. On average, court cases involving s.2 charges had five defendants compared with only two in affray cases.

The third difference relates to the level of violence involved. While there were many affray cases in which there was only the threat of violence, albeit sometimes serious, this was extremely unusual in cases of violent disorder. Most of the incidents involved fights between groups of youths and, on occasion, result-ed in quite serious injuries. The following two cases are illustra-tive of 'violent disorder'. The first occurred at a birthday party at a Day Centre. As the party ended one youth shouted 'riot!' and a large number of young men started throwing chairs at the disco equipment. When someone tried to intervene he was beaten up. Upon the arrival of the police a group of about 50 youths started throwing bricks and bottles at the police vehicles. Extensive dam-age was caused to cars and local property. Eventually 13 men aged between 16 and 21 were arrested and charged under s.2.

The second case occurred on the street outside a take-away food shop. A large group of youths - approximately 100 - were general-ly behaving in a rowdy manner and sporadic scuffles were break-ing out from time to time. In one of these, a young man was being badly beaten and a passing PC who noticed this ran to the scene and grabbed hold of the most violent person. As he did this he was attacked by a group of youths who shouted 'kill the pigs, kill the pigs'. He was severely beaten and was eventually rescued by

33

other officers who attended the disturbance. Six arrests were made, all defendants were charged under s.2, and three were found guilty and given custodial sentences.

A final possible distinction between 'violent disorder' and 'affray' was suggested by one custody officer. In his view, an incident which he felt had involved 'spontaneous violence' would be likely, depending on its extent, to result in s.3 charges, whereas anything premeditated or planned, as long as sufficient numbers were involved, would be charged under s.2.

A typology of public disorder

To divide incidents of disorder according to offence categories creates artificial distinctions. The difference between one offence and another may be more a question of degree than of kind. It was therefore felt that it would be useful to construct a typology of public disorder that cuts across legal definitions. Incidents were classified either according to their essential 'nature' or location. Most of the classifications are fairly self-explanatory, but perhaps a word of clarification may be necessary on the distinction between what has been termed 'street disorder involving the public', and incidents which are directed at the police. The distinction relates to the identity of the original victims caught up in the incident. Thus, although the police may eventually have been victims in incidents categorised as 'street disorders', the initial incident that led to police attendance involved only members of the public. In contrast, incidents (threats/abuse or violence) classified as directed against the police did not involve members of the public as initial victims. Table 2 shows the breakdown of incidents according to this typology.

Street disorder. The two categories of 'street disorder' together represent the greatest number of incidents in the sample: 145 in total or 31 per cent of all incidents. Of these, 80 actually involved physical violence, while 65 involved only abuse or threats. Not surprisingly, the relative seriousness of these incidents is reflected in the charges eventually brought. Of the 80 street disorder cases which involved violence, 45 resulted in s.4 or s.5 charges and 35 in s.3 or s.2 charges. Over half of the violent disorder (s.2) cases in the sample arose out of this category of incident. Conversely, of the 65 incidents which did not involve violence, all but five resulted in charges of threatening behaviour (s.4) or disorderly conduct (s.5), the majority (41) being s.5 charges.

34

Prosecution in Common Law Jurisdictions

Table 2: Frequency of Different Types of Public Disorder

Type of incident	Number	%
Street disorder involving public (i) violence	80	17
(ii) threats/abuse	65	14
Threats/abuse at police	81	17
Violence against police	22	5
Fights in pubs, clubs, discos	44	9
Drunk & disorderly	37	8
Domestic dispute	32	7
Indecency	24	5
Disorder at restaurant/fast food shop	20	5
Football-related	17	4
Miscellaneous	42	9
Total	464	100

In the less serious, non-violent incidents the police would typically notice groups of youths shouting and swearing at each other and move in to calm the situation down. Arrests would follow when members of the group refused to desist. In the more serious cases, varying degrees of violence were involved. Some involved small numbers of people and would probably best be described as minor brawls. The larger public fights, generally ending with charges of affray or violent disorder, frequently involved large groups of people and occasionally the use of weapons.

35

Threats, abuse at police/violence against the police. There was a total of 103 cases in which the principal victims were the police. Most involved only threats or abuse, although in 22 some violence was used. The great majority of the threats/abuse cases resulted in s.4 or s.5 charges, although two ended with a charge of affray. Of the 22 cases involving violence, 13 resulted in s.4 or s.5 charges, five in charges of affray and four in charges of violent disorder.

The cases examined in the study suggested that s.5 charges in particular are often used by the police as a method of 'street clearance'. The cases that involved threats or abuse against the police were generally illustrative of this point. 'Street clearance' was employed for a number of reasons: typically, to prevent the escalation of existing disorder or to prevent further trouble at a later date. On occasion, perhaps, the aim was to exert or demonstrate police authority and to ensure a certain level of respect for the police - or as Smith and Gray (1985) describe it, to prevent being 'had over'.

Although there were relatively few cases of violence against the police, a few were quite serious. Some started off not unlike the cases described above but escalated into violent scuffles before an arrest could be made. Others involved serious assaults on officers. In such cases, although assault charges were brought, it was not uncommon to prosecute the offenders for violent disorder or affray as well. Custody officers suggested that charges under the Public Order Act would often be kept in reserve in case there were any difficulties with the major charges.

Fights in pubs, clubs or discos. Almost 10 per cent of the public order cases in this study resulted from incidents in pubs, clubs, discos or other licensed premises. There was considerable variation in the nature of the incidents, some being little more than disorderly behaviour on the part of one or two drunken customers, others being quite extensive fights between large numbers of people. Suspects in roughly three-quarters of these cases (32 of 44) were eventually charged under s.4 or s.5. In nine they were charged with affray and in three with violent disorder.

Drunk and disorderly. There were a number of cases in the sample in which the behaviour of the offender could best be described as 'drunk and disorderly', although the legislation used to effect an arrest was the Public Order Act rather than the Criminal Justice Act 1967. In these cases the offenders were commonly on their own and the behaviour which brought them to the attention of the police usually involved shouting and swearing, sometimes at a particular individual, often at anyone who happened to be passing, and occasionally, seemingly at no-one at all. They would be approached by a police officer who would either suggest that they went home quietly or merely desisted in their behaviour. In the cases in which an arrest was eventually made, the arresting officer often stated that the first and any subsequent warnings either failed to have the desired effect or only served further to antagonise the offender.

It was often unclear in these cases why public order charges were used rather than 'drunk and disorderly'. Some of the officers interviewed suggested that there was a qualitative difference between the offences, but different distinctions were drawn by different officers, and by and large the reasons for using one piece of legislation rather than another appeared to be fairly arbitrary.

Domestic disputes. A further 32 cases in the sample (7 per cent of the total) were classified as 'domestic disputes': these involved related parties inside or in the vicinity of a domestic dwelling. The Public Order Act was used to some extent in such cases at all the five stations. The cases varied in character, but generally they centred on a fight or potential violence between members of a family - usually partners. The 32 incidents gave rise to nine cases involving charges of disorderly conduct, 13 of threatening behaviour and ten cases resulting in charges of affray. The following case is an example of affray. A man arrived home from the pub after a 'drinking spree' and had a row with his girlfriend. A neighbour from the flat above intervened and tried to calm them down. The man then ran off and returned carrying an axe. He threatened both his girlfriend and the neighbour and proceeded to smash the fridge in the kitchen. The argument developed into a fight, spilling into the street, where the man was eventually overpowered and relieved of the axe. When arrested he was still trying to attack his girlfriend.

Indecency. One characteristic of the 1986 Act is its apparent adaptability. It is used in a variety of different contexts in order to deal with incidents that may prove difficult to tackle using different charges. 'Indecency' cases provide an example of this versatility. There were 24 cases that were allocated to this category in the sample - roughly 5 per cent of the total. Of these, 18 led to charges under s.5 of the Act and six to s.4 charges. The circumstances of the cases varied considerably. Several incidents occurred at public

37

sporting events where men were arrested for offences that might best be described as sexual harassment. A number of other arrests resulted from incidents in public toilets. These cases generally involved men openly masturbating in public urinals and arrests were often the result of planned police operations rather than complaints from members of the public.

Disorder at restaurants/fast food shops. There were 20 incidents leading to arrests under the Act which occurred at restaurants or fast food outlets. Typically, these occurred late at night and were drink related (or suspected to be so). Disputes flared up fairly readily over alleged queue-jumping, for example, sometimes involving the parties concerned coming to blows, but more frequently only the exchange of abuse. In many respects these incidents were similar in character to those occurring in the street. Most led to charges under s.5 (11 cases), but there also five cases of affray, and two each of violent disorder and threatening behaviour.

Football-related disorder. There were just 17 incidents in the sample (about 4 per cent of the total) that could be described as football-related. Of these, 13 resulted in a s.5 charge, three in a s.4 charge and one in a charge of violent disorder under s.2. The majority of these incidents were fairly minor in character, consisting of little more than the offenders swearing at opposing supporters or at police officers who had requested that the swearing cease. Most of such cases did not occur at football grounds, but were merely fairly typical disorderly incidents which happened to involve football supporters. One of the police areas studied was an exception to this general rule in that officers made use of the Act inside the local ground against spectators using bad language.

Conclusions

Sections 2 to 5 of the Public Order Act 1986 were viewed unanimously, by the police officers that were interviewed, as a useful resource. In the main this was because these sections of the Act made certain of their powers clearer or more explicit, but also because they extended their powers and gave officers greater protection against abuse and attack. The view was expressed that the Act is flexible, adaptable and structured. It is flexible because it can be used either as the main charge or as a supporting charge in cases where there is some doubt about the adequacy of the evidence for the principal offence. It is also flexible because in cases where there is some doubt about what the constituent elements of an offence are, or whether they are satisfied in a particular case, an officer has a general resource with which he can restore order.

The Act is viewed as adaptable because the charges may be used in a variety of different contexts. This is particularly true of ss.4 and 5: charges were brought under these sections in circumstances as wide-ranging as minor football holliganism, domestic disputes, cases of indecency and obstruction. Furthermore, the Act is seen in a postive light because of its structured character. The available charges, ranging from the most serious offence of riot (s.1) down to disorderly conduct (s.5), were viewed by officers as providing them with a coherent and easily explicable set of guidelines with which to intervene and deal with breaches of public order.

The offences that gave rise to charges under the Public Order Act ranged from very serious assaults involving large groups of people (although no cases of riot were encountered) down to the comparatively minor - swearing at or showing a lack of respect towards a police officer. The fact that the police had powers to deal with the more minor incidents and, in particular, the fact that they themselves now came within the definition of potential victims of abuse or harassment, were seen by them as being crucially important.

Further up the scale it appears to be the case that the offence of affray has been downgraded. Not only, as was intended, is a charge under s.3 of the 1986 Act less serious than a charge of affray under the 1936 Act, but it also appears possible that the police are using s.3 charges for less serious offences than was actually intended by the new Act. This section is now being used to deal with incidents which often only involve the threat of violence, but are nevertheless deemed by the police to be too serious to be dealt with under s.4 of the Act. However, the distinction between s.3 and s.4 was not always clear, whereas the boundary between incidents classified as affray and those defined as violent disorder did appear to be distinct. Firstly, cases of violent disorder generally involved a greater number of protagonists than did affrays, and resulted in a greater number of arrests. In addition to this, violent disorder tended to involve actual violence - often considerable. The distinction between s.4 and s.5 also appeared to relate to the number of people involved in the disorderly incident. The police argued that incidents resulting in s.5 charges would usually involve only one offender, whereas there would generally be more than one if s.4 charges were being used. Some also suggested that they knew

39

'instinctively' what was a s.4 and what was a s.5 offence but were unable to rationalise the basis for their instinctive judgements.

We have earlier noted that there is some uncertainty as to why there has been a substantial rise in the number of recorded public order offences and in prosecutions. The possibility that this was simply a reflection of the growing disorderliness of the streets was rejected by all the officers that were interviewed. If anything, a few felt the opposite to be the case. All agreed, to some extent, that it was the flexible and adaptable nature of the legislation itself which underlay the rise in the figures. The data collected in this study tend to support this general view. For example, the charge of affray appears to be more accessible than it used to be, and is being used for relatively minor offences which involve the threat of violence more often than actual violence. Furthermore, it appears likely that the increase in the number of s.2 offences may in part be attributable to the flexibility of the legislation. Many of the custody officers interviewed suggested that a public order charge (s.2 if there were three or more involved, s.3 if not) would often be used either as an alternative to an ABH, or GBH charge if there was insufficient evidence for the latter, or in conjunction with such charges if there was any doubt as to how the CPS would wish to proceed.

The other facet of the Act which should also be mentioned at this point is that the new s.5 has had the effect of redefining as criminal certain forms of misbehaviour which would previously have been viewed merely as rowdy, boisterous or, at worst, anti-social. This 'net-widening' attribute appears from the cases in this study to result in a relatively large number of arrests for ostensibly minor misbehaviour. It is difficult to gauge from the data how many cases in the study might not have resulted in criminal pro-ceedings (or at least would not have been classified as public order offences) before the 1986 Act. However, the cases which are the most likely source of 'new' public order offences are among those which have been classified in this study as 'drunk and disorderly', 'indecency', 'threats/abuse against the police' and 'domestic dis-putes'. Together, these categories represent almost 40 per cent of the total sample. Part of the impetus for the use of s.5 in these cir-cumstances may have stemmed from the desire of the police to protect themselves from abuse from the public. Additionally, pub-lic and media concern may have contributed to an increase in police action against rowdy behaviour and domestic disturbances.

Only a larger and more specific research project could provide more reliable estimates of changes in arrest and charging practices, but it would appear that the Public Order Act 1986 has opened up a whole area of behaviour to criminal proceedings. By doing so it has met with a very positive response from the police and has become a favourite tool for the officer tasked with policing public places. As a result of this it appears likely not only that more offenders are coming before the courts charged with public order offences but also that other charges are being used less frequently.

References

Card, R (1987).*Public Order: the new law.* London: Butterworths.

Smith, A T H (1987). The Public Order Act 1986. (1) The New Offences. *Criminal Law Review*, March, p156-67.

Smith, A T H (1988). Assaulting and Abusing the Police. *Criminal Law Review*, September, p600-3.

Smith, D J and Gray, J (1985). *Police and People in London.* London: Policy Studies Institute.

Thomas, D A (1987). The Public Order Act 1986. (4) The Sentencing Implications. *Criminal Law Review*, March, p191-3.

[5]

ANDY LAYZELL

Discretion in traffic law enforcement

Andy Layzell, of the Transport Studies Unit,
Oxford University, examines the reasons for and
the variations in, the discretion employed by
police officers dealing with offending motorists.
He also comments on the pressure on young
officers to report offenders, and the effects on the
public of what appears to be inconsistent
enforcement of the law.

IN THE FIELD of law enforcement there is perhaps no area where police officers exercise a wider discretion than that of road traffic law. In all areas of legal decision-making those called upon to exercise discretion have a wide margin or freedom for decision . . . "Sometimes the decision-making margin is so great . . . that more of the person than the law determines the decisions made." (Black, 1980.)

For the police and in particular for individual, lower-ranking officers, discretion in decision-making is a particularly important principle. Previous examinations, however, have centred largely upon two particular aspects of police discretion.

Discretion as selective enforcement. Davis has argued strongly that the police maintain a pretence of enforcing all laws. In practice, the number of laws and offences makes this impossible, with the result that the police have to make policies about what law to enforce, how much to enforce it, against whom and on what occasions. This policy, Davis argues, is determined by the accumulated actions of individual officers at the bottom of the police hierarchy.

Discretion as 'an officer's ability to choose between two or more mutually exclusive dispositional alternatives.' This approach (see for example Lundman) assumes an encounter between the police and an offending member of the public and examines the most likely outcome of that encounter in terms of whether it results in the offender being warned or prosecuted.

An alternative to these more specific approaches, however, is to see discretion in the legal process as existing at any point where the outcome of a given action by a member of the public is uncertain, and dependent upon the judgement of a 'legal agent.' With this approach, and it is the one used in this paper, discretion can be defined as the public's perception of variability in police practice.

The exercise of discretion can work to the public's advantage in several ways. It does, for example, allow the particular circumstances of any offence to be taken into consideration (and there will be some situations in which sanctions would be entirely inappropriate). Alternatively, police discretion may result in some offenders receiving friendly advice or an informal caution, rather than being reported for prosecution. In both these cases discretion effectively acts to filter trivial offences from the legal process. At the same time it is more likely to benefit than harm police-public relations.

In other situations, however, the public may feel less enthusiastic about the powers of discretion available to the police, and it is with some of these areas that this paper is largely concerned. Discretion, to the public, may simply appear to be inconsistency as between individual officers, or between one encounter with the police and the next. This is not to suggest that inconsistency is incorrect (in the sense that it has resulted from the mis-use of discretion), but rather that it may be incomprehensible. Additionally, it is necessary to note that, in extreme cases, discretion may seem to be (and indeed be) little more than an expression of the prejudices of individual officers.

If any progress is to be made in improving the public's perception of police work (or some of the public's perception of some police work), then it is likely to be important to distinguish between these forms of police discretion which are, or are not, legitimate. The following analysis is intended to contribute to such a discussion by *identifying* some of the forms of discretion which are apparent in the area of traffic policing.

Identification of discretion in traffic-law enforcement
Perhaps more than in any other area of police work, traffic-law enforcement offers opportunities to examine processes of discretion. These derive from the sheer scale of contact between police and the public (Griffiths *et al* found that 43 per cent of male drivers had been spoken to by the police in connection with a traffic offence within the last five years); the range of offences encountered (from parking to causing death by dangerous driving); and the specialisation of the police in traffic duties.

Recent research by Dix and Layzell, upon which this paper is based, examined the attitudes of road-users and the police towards each other and towards the law which brings them into contact and occasional conflict. It was commissioned by the Police Foundation as an essentially exploratory study, intended to generate hypotheses rather than provide policy options or quantitative analysis, and any results or conclusions in this paper should be viewed in that context. Fieldwork consisted of approximately 100 tape-recorded, unstructured interviews with members of the public and police officers. Roughly half of these were conducted in homes or police stations and half during tours of duty in patrol cars with officers and with offenders who had been stopped. All interviews were transcribed verbatim and analysed.

By interviewing both police and public it was possible to register public perceptions of variability in police practice and also to look for explanations of such variations from the viewpoint of individual officers. Starting with an initial (traffic-related) action by a member of the public in the presence of a police officer, it is suggested that two main forms of discretion can be identified:

The degree to which individual officers want to perceive traffic-law violations (and in certain cases the degree to which they are able to perceive violations).

A key distinction here exists between traffic and divisional officers. Traffic officers have typically elected for that area of specialism and are more knowledgeable, more interested, and more highly motivated in the detection of traffic offences. As with any other specialism, constant acquaintance with one area of legislation results in a knowledge of, and familiarity with, legislation which will not be obtained by other officers. Consequently it is highly likely that there will be traffic offences (detailed construction and use offences, for example), or changes in legislation, of which divisional officers are simply not aware. Alternatively, they may be aware of the legislation but not know it well enough to be able to enforce it.

> 'One of the good reasons that I don't ever stop them is that there are about 22 documents you can check on a heavy goods vehicle. I can get up to about five I should think and after that I would be struggling. Leave that to traffic division . . . *(Divisional officer)*

Not only will there be a different awareness of traffic offences as between traffic and divisional officers, there is also likely to be a difference in their *motivation*. Many divisional officers are simply *not interested* in traffic offences and so are not on the lookout for them.

> 'Let's put it this way. If I was extra extra keen on traffic, I'd probably see a lot more traffic offences than I see now.'
> 'Traffic isn't really my line . . . There's times when it's unavoidable but I certainly don't go out with the intention of getting any. I'm not really interested in it . . . I can't remember the last time I did any traffic process.'

In contrast, even within specialist traffic departments there is a tendency for individual officers to become even more specialised in one particular area of legislation:

> 'My pet is "construction and use" offences . . . It's useful to have a field that you are better at than anyone else . . . people come to you for advice . . . It's a good way of getting yourself noticed. People certainly don't know about trailer's brakes and wings, and they certainly don't know the speed limits (for trailers)." *(Traffic officer)*

The public are unlikely to be able to distinguish between variations in police reactions which result from the non-perception of certain offences, and those which result from officers perceiving, but not intervening with, an offence.

There is a second important form of discretion the degree to which individual officers are willing to intervene once an offence has been detected.

Decisions are also taken by individual officers as to whether or not they will intervene once a traffic violation has been perceived. In general the more serious the offence, the greater the probability that intervention will occur. However, three other specific influences can be identified. The first of these is the motivation and specialism of the officer. Thus divisional officers, in general, are less likely to become involved with traffic offences (with the possible exception of parking offences), and all officers will tend to be influenced by their own particular area of specialism.

> '. . . you can always pick and choose what you want to deal with. And you can sit still and let the stuff come past you until something of interest comes past — and go and stop it . . . trailers are my forte. If I see a trailer I normally stop it. *(Traffic officer)*

The question that arises where discretion in intervention occurs, is whether or not it results in certain offences (perhaps even the more obscure ones) receiving an amount of attention which is unwarranted by their prevalence or 'seriousness', and other offences receiving correspondingly less attention. If, for example, older cars ('a rough car with a London registration, invariably there'll be offences on it') or particular types of car ('the majority of cars stolen are Ford Cortinas'), are more likely to result in interventions, then comparably less resources will be available for intervening where HGV or speeding offences are concerned.

Given the vast number of traffic rules and regulations in existence, discretion in intervention permits all offences to be policed, although not necessarily in the right proportions (according to the number of transgressions or the 'seriousness' of the offence). In other words it may not result in the most beneficial use of resources.

The public perception of this form of discretion should not be ignored. In the absence of information to the contrary, road users are likely to assume that all police officers have uniform knowledge of the law which they apply in a consistent way. To them, discretion in intervention may simply appear as inconsistent police behaviour, prompting queries as to why an offence which is not noticed or is ignored by one officer, occasions an informal warning or a report by another.

A second major influence upon an officer's decision to intervene is the existence of current force directives or campaigns. The effect of these is to override an officer's use of discretion (frequently only for a short period). Thus one divisional officer who claimed to have little or no interest in traffic process, and who was unable to remember the last time that she had reported a traffic offender, explained how a bicycle lighting campaign affected her use of discretion:

> '. . . cyclists with no lights blasted all over the *Oxford Mail and Journal*, and then for two weeks all we do is go out and book pedal cycles with no lights, and at the end it's "How many have you done?" *(Divisional officer)*

Although specific campaigns are a useful tactic for the police, allowing them to publicise and focus attention upon one particular offence, it would also appear that they may be particularly resented by some members of the public because they are the most obvious examples of inconsistent police reaction to a given situation. Particularly if an offender is not aware that a campaign is in effect, he may well question why he is being prosecuted this time and wasn't last time. One householder described the impact of a particular campaign:

'. . . because of the nature of this road being narrow, and the car ownership rate, you tend to find that people had to park on both sides of the road and it developed that (households on) . . . the other side tended to park with one wheel on the pavement. One night . . . the police came and booked everyone who was parking half on and half off and also for failure to display lights and also parking facing the wrong direction . . . I understand that the police were having a purge throughout the city, trying to regularise the parking.'

Such a campaign is obviously defensible but, given its short-lived impact upon parking behaviour and the grievances felt by some of the householders, it would be appropriate to question whether this type of police activity is either effective or beneficial to public-police relations.

Perhaps in contrast to this situation, campaigns which the public perceive as being conducted regularly and consistently such as the Christmas drinking and driving campaigns may be more readily understood, accepted and effective. This argument is developed more fully in Dix and Layzell.

An officer's decision to intervene may also be influenced by a third phenomenon, that of consensus offending. This is, in effect, an implicit agreement between motorists and the police that certain regulations, at certain locations or times, will not be enforced. On certain sections of road, for example, an offence such as speeding may have become so rife that the police no longer enforce, or are no longer able to enforce, the law.

Consensus offending seems to have evolved in three particular situations:

Police and road-users acknowledge that the existing regulations are unrealistic. (This most frequently applies to speed limits on a given road and may result in the police applying to have the limit raised);

Police consider the offence is of low priority. (For example illegal parking in residential roads);

Police consider enforcement of one regulation is of lower priority than some other goal. (For example, breaking speed limits in some areas of London may be a subordinate goal to maintaining traffic flow).

Again, a fuller discussion of consensus offending is available in Dix and Layzell.

The type of sanction which the individual officer imposes.

The major dispositional alternatives open to an officer are to issue a verbal warning or to report (for probable prosecution) the offender. Again there is a tendency for less experienced officers to resort immediately to reporting an offence which would be dealt with differently by other officers. The apparent emphasis of much police training is to concentrate on booking practice, rather than upon the greater personal skills which are required if an informal caution is to be administered.

249

'When you come out of training school you're so conditioned to nick. They don't tell you to use your discretion.' *(Divisional Officer)*

This tendency is exaggerated by pressure which probationary officers experience from both tutor constables and from supervisory officers. Tutor constables, for example, who are initially responsible for instructing officers in process work and patrol skills may use traffic offences as examples of easy process.

'I remember my first (report) . . . the PC said, "There's a defective light ahead — we'll report this person, won't we?" I had to do it because, you know, my tutor constable was there, making me do it. I felt really awful. His (the motorist's) attitude was right. He didn't know his light was out,' *(Divisional officer)*

Supervisory officers also expect probationary officers to produce a certain volume of process. There is no suggestion here that officers compete with one another in the number of reports which they produce, but it is clear (Jones has reached a similar conclusion) that the volume of work (as measured by the number of reports) undertaken by officers is seen as an important indication of their alertness and efficiency. This is acknowledged by probationary officers themselves:

'The first two years as a probationer, I know it shouldn't really, but quite a bit goes on the amount of process you've put in. Once you get your two years in, you can relax a bit . . . Then, they (supervisory officers) aren't so fussy. But the first two years, the more you can get — I know it sounds a bit harsh — the better. I want to get on, so I want a lot. *(Probationary officer)*

and by supervisory officers:

'We don't set down any quotas . . . some officers will put in a lot more (reports) than others. At the end of the year, the sergeants will say, "You know, this fellow really works hard, he put a lot of work in", or "This fellow doesn't put in as much, he could be more productive, he could be more observant", or whatever. So whilst we don't lay down any particular figures, I expect the chaps to justify their existence as traffic officers by putting in a certain amount of reports." *(Senior Traffic officer)*

As officers become more experienced, there is less requirement for them to have to 'justify their existence'. They also tend to develop the more advanced skills of personal communication (and the confidence to use such skills). Consequently, once an offence has been detected and the offender stopped, more experienced officers have the wider choice between administering an informal warning or reporting the offender. The two main influences upon this decision again appear to be the disposition of the individual officer towards certain offences, and any local or national force policies or directives.

A further factor which can play an important part in the decision of an officer to warn or report an offender is the attitude of the motorist. In our interviews there was considerable disagreement amongst the officers as to whether decisions to prosecute are taken before or after an officer has spoken to the offender. Where the decision was taken prior

250

to any communication, it is more likely that the judgement will depend solely upon the nature of the offence. A decision which is reached after such communication will allow the offender to offer a defence of, or extenuating circumstances for, his behaviour (some examples are given in Dix and Layzell). On the other hand, an unfortunate exchange between the two parties may result in the officer punishing the offender's attitude, rather than the offence itself. This may be defensible if the offender does not acknowledge the seriousness of the offence itself, but may prove counterproductive if the offender is instead displaying general antipathy towards the police, or is, in turn, reacting to the attitude of the officer.

In addition to warning or reporting or warning an offender, a third option is open to more experienced officers in the form of *informal sanctions*. At the time that a driver is stopped by the police, many may feel an immediate sense of embarrassment or shock at being stopped and, in effect, isolated from the stream of road users. They may also be uncertain as to why they have been stopped or as to what is going to happen, and they will almost certainly be inconvenienced, even if no further action is taken. Actions by the police which unnecessarily prolong any of these feelings of embarrassment, shock, uncertainty or inconvenience, can be identified as informal sanctions. Some such sanctions are merely the unnecessarily punctilious or prolonged application of standard police procedures, such as document or vehicle checks. Others, such as the repeated questioning of the driver as to his name and destination or vehicle radio checks within his hearing, are likely to have a much more unsettling effect.

The essential characteristic of informal sanctions is that they are usually superfluous to the outcome of any encounter between the police and the road user. They can, however, be used positively, *in addition* to an informal warning (to strengthen the impact of the warning), or *instead* of a report. Delay as a sanction in itself can also be used to quieten or reassure an otherwise excited offender. Excepting this last situation, however, it would seem harder to justify the use of informal sanctions in addition to reporting an offender.

Discretion in later stages of the legal process

Two other types of discretion were also identified during the research, although these did not relate directly to encounters between an officer and a member of the public, and so were not examined in such detail:
The recommendations of supervisory officers, and the final decision (taken by the Prosecutions Department) as to whether or not an offender will be prosecuted.

It is at this stage that the decision is taken as to whether an offender will be dealt with by prosecution through the courts or by warning letter. As an example of the discrepancies which exist as between different forces, it can be noted that, for example, in 1982, 97 per cent of offenders were prosecuted in Norfolk and Hampshire, compared with 76 per cent in Nottinghamshire, Lincolnshire and West Yorkshire.
The decision taken by the Magistrates.

251

The majority of traffic offences are dealt with by the Magistrates' Courts. Indeed, some 60per cent of Magistrates' Court time is allotted to driving offences (Evidence provided by the Magistrates' Association before the House of Commons Transport Committee). Paradoxically, although Magistrates are commonly considered to have quite wide ranging powers of discretion, these are not normally exercised for the vast majority of traffic offences. This is because the sheer volume of offences and the rate at which they are processed precludes much consideration of individual cases. The court decision is, for example, required by statute to make allowance for individual circumstances, but, in practice, Hood has reported that many Magistrates think that this is improper. (Interestingly, some variations do now seem to occur, but according to the economic prosperity of the region, rather than the individual; again see the Evidence provided by the Magistrates' Association).

Discretion and the legitimacy of police action

Increasingly, as the police service is subject to more detailed and critical scrutiny, inconsistent policies and practices are likely to be highlighted, both as between individual officers and as between different police forces. Some of these inconsistencies will reflect the legitimate decision-taking strategies of individuals who are concerned with the equitable administration of the law, or with the effectiveness (in terms of recidivism) of their judgement. In these situations discretion is likely to be comprehensible to the public (particularly if it is explained to them) and appreciated by them. Other inconsistencies in police practice, however, may reflect the whims and prejudices of individual officers or basic differences in the philosophies of different forces. It is in these situations that the police can have less to respond to their critics. By identifying the forms which discretion can take in the comparatively less contentious area of traffic policing, this paper has attempted some initial steps towards allowing the legitimacy of various actions to be discussed.

Initially, however, for more progress to be made, further questions need to be addressed concerning the scope and quality of police discretion. It is appropriate to divide these into three areas:

The exercise of discretion by the individual officer. What are the limits of discretion for officers and what are the goals and principles which guide their actions within these limits? How are such limits initially formulated and to what degree are they consistent between different officers? To what extent do these limits become artificially restricted either by discretion 'hardening' to reflect personal prejudices, or by pressure of work from senior officers?

The impact upon police discretion of the police hierarchy. If, as Davis argues, discretion results in force policy being determined 'from the bottom of the hierarchy upwards', to what extent is this policy in accordance with that of, or even recognised by, senior officers? Similarly, when policy is issued by senior officers, what are the implications for individual officers who will be required to adjust their use of discretion?

Consistency between different police forces. How consistent are practices of discretion between different police forces, both at the level of individual officers and, particularly, at the level of senior and prosecuting officers? How far are recommendations of the Association of Chief Police Officers capable of creating consistent enforcement policies?

Ultimately, it is necessary to determine whether or not it would be desirable deliberately to bring variations in police practice to the public's attention. It seems likely, however, that by eroding the myth that the police are able to enforce all of the law all of the time, and by explaining the nature of police discretion, traffic policing might become more comprehensible to the public with commensurate gains in public sympathy and support.

References
Black, D. (1980) *The Manners and Customs of the Police,* Academic Press.
Davis, K. C. (1975) *Police Discretion,* West Publishing Company.
Dix, M. C. & Layzell, A. D. (1983) *Road Users and the Police,* Croom Helm.
Griffiths, R., Davies, R. F., Henderson, R. & Sheppard, D. (1980) *Incidence and Effects of police action on motoring Offences as described by Drivers,* TRRL Supplementary report 543
Hood, R. (1972) *Sentencing the Motoring Offender,* Heinemann
House of Commons Transport Committee (1984) Minutes of evidence taken before the Road Safety Committee. Evidence from the Association of Chief Police Officers and The Magistrates' Association, HMSO 286-i
Jones, J. M. (1980) *Operational Aspects of Police Behaviour,* Gower
Lundman, R. J. (1980) *Police and Policing,* Holt, Rinehart & Winston

[6]

Police Discretion in Victoria: The Police Decision to Prosecute

Linda Hancock
Swinburne College of Technology
Hawthorn
Victoria

Progression of a juvenile offender through the different stages of the juvenile justice system is dependent on the discretionary decisions of various functionaries such as police and magistrates. However, little substantive evidence is available, especially in Australia, on the way that discretionary power is used and the sorts of criteria on which such decisions are based.

As part of a larger study including court dispositions and the female offender, the data discussed in this paper focuses on one stage of the juvenile offender processing system—the police decision to recommend an official police warning or to prosecute and thus refer the child to court. Unofficial warnings are not recorded and are therefore not included. From studying these decisions, it is hoped that some insight can be gained into police decision-making and the stereotypes of juvenile offenders which operate at the level of police-juvenile contact.

The theoretical framework adopted in this paper is primarily that of the interactionist or labelling perspective, which stresses the need for a critical appraisal of the agents involved in defining deviance. (See for example, Lemert (1972), Becker (1966), Lofland (1969), Cicourel (1968)). Such an approach steers attention away from a causal emphasis on the personal and social characteristics of the individual rule-breaker and focuses on the influence of social reaction processes in defining and processing deviants. Schur summarises this position when he says that 'A societal reaction perspective is more concerned with what is made of an act socially than with the factors that may have led particular individuals to behave in the first place' (1973: 119). Following this approach, this study was designed to investigate aspects of the 'rate-producing processes' (Kitsuse and Cicourel, 1963) and specifically, the role of the police in juvenile delinquency. The primary objective was to demonstrate how

considerations of police discretion and criteria used in decision-making can increase our understanding of police 'working rules', of police stereotypes and typifications of 'juvenile delinquents', and the nature of police organisation and police-court interdependence.

Legalistic or Welfare Model?

Asking questions about police use of discretionary power, whether their use of discretion reflects bias and on what criteria such decisions are based, inevitably raises more questions. Are police decisions based mainly on considerations of legalistic variables, like seriousness of offence, number and seriousness of prior offences—a 'legalistic' model—or do their decisions reflect a 'welfare' model, where other considerations related to family, parents, peers, socioeconomic status, neighbourhood, the perceived needs of the child and community, are viewed as equivalent or of greater importance than legalistic ones?

Any suggestion that the 'principle of offence' (or the 'rule of law'—Skolnick's (1966) term) should prevail, is confused in a consideration of juvenile offenders and the Childrens' Court. A separate court jurisdiction for juveniles is the result of a movement to separate children from the processes of the ordinary criminal law, so that the main task of the juvenile court is not to determine criminal responsibility, but to adjudicate according to the needs of the child and community.

The 'principle of offence' or legalistic model is not appropriate to the juvenile court because of the commitment to a welfare and treatment philosophy and a focus on the 'whole offender', or what Matza (1964) calls 'the principle of individualised justice'. This means that the needs of each child will be considered by giving attention to a wide range of criteria, including family, social, individual and offence-related factors. In Victoria, the Childrens' Court combines a legal and welfare approach, characteristic of a 'welfare model', defined in two separate acts: the Childrens' Court Act, 1958 and 1973, and the Social Welfare Act, 1970. The emphasis on a welfare approach is exemplified in section 27 (3) of the Childrens' Court Act (1958) which states 'the court shall firstly have regard to the welfare of the child'.

Considerations of bias and stereotyping become more complex when a welfare model, involving dual legal and treatment functions, prevails. Schur comments that 'the philosophy of the juvenile court—with its thorough-going social investigation of the alleged delinquent, and its relative lack of concern with the particular offence—virtually ensures that stereotypes will influence judicial dispositions' (Schur, 1973: 121).

The purpose of the part of the study reported here was to investigate, through an analysis of police reports, whether legalistic or welfare criteria are more closely associated with the decision to prosecute rather than to warn juveniles.

Methods

The data used in this study were based on a content analysis of the Police Form 276,[1] a social investigation report which is made out for all juvenile offenders, whether warned or prosecuted, by the police who, it must be remembered, act also as the informant if the case is taken to court. The final sample comprised 300 male and 141 female court appearances (C/A's) and 151 male and 130 female warnings. All cases which involved police contact[2] between 1 January, 1975 and 30 June 1975 were selected, but prior to sampling, some cases were excluded (principally young children involved in protection applications where no illegal or offensive behaviour on the part of the child was mentioned). A sample of 722 reports was chosen (from the 5,846 police contacts remaining after exclusions), by a stratified systematic sample from alphabetical files of male and female warnings and C/A's. In this report male and female offender categories are combined and comparisons are made between C/A's and warnings as total groups.

Sample Description

Prior to more detailed analysis, the characteristics of offenders in the sample were compared, where possible, with Victorian base population figures to determine any differences between the two groups. These comparisons will only be reported briefly here, to make the point that, as with the findings of many other studies, this group of officially contacted juveniles is atypical compared with the Victorian population, especially on indices related to socio-economic status and sex.

Males, 14-16 year olds, Australian born and juveniles attending government (especially junior technical) schools, are over-represented in comparison with Victorian figures. Juveniles in the sample were more likely (i) to have left school earlier, (ii) not to have achieved as high a standard at school, (iii) to have left school earlier than their age-matched peers, and (iv) if employed, were predominantly working in 'blue-collar' occupations and if they were not working, higher proportions than would be expected were unemployed.

In terms of living situation, only 67 per cent of the sample were recorded as living at home with both parents and 23 per cent lived with one (natural) parent, most often the mother. Although no appropriate Victorian figures are available for comparison, it seems that a high proportion of offenders live in situations which diverge from the two (natural) parent families.

On various measures of S.E.S.,[3] high proportions of the sample juveniles came from lower S.E.S. families and tended to be over-represented in 'blue-collar' and under represented in 'white-collar' occupational categories in comparison with Victorian figures.

Many other studies reveal similar profiles of officially contacted juvenile offenders on the factors discussed above, like sex, age, S.E.S., school performance, truancy, and living situation; for example, studies in Victoria (Challinger, 1974; Leaper 1974), in New Zealand (Hampton, 1975) and in South Australia (Jamrozik, 1974; Meschemberg, 1974).

Having established that the sample of officially contacted juveniles differs from the Victorian population, the important question to ask is whether these differences and any differences which emerge between the warnings and court appearance groups reflect a legalistic or a welfare decision-making model and hence imply a selective emphasis on some criteria in deciding whether to warn or prosecute.

The principal statistical measure employed in establishing the relationships between these decisions and the criteria used is Kendall's Tau b and c. Tau was chosen as an appropriate measure of association for ordinal level data and has a magnitude from 1.00 to -1.00 (Blalock, 1972: 418-23). Any relationship is considered substantial if tau equals or exceeds $\pm.10$. Where tau was inappropriate, chi-square was used, though this measure was less preferable since it cannot indicate the strength of any association.

Findings

Variables related to the police decision to warn or to prosecute are organised into four sections:

(1) Legalistic variables;
(2) Juveniles' behaviour and character;
(3) Parents' behaviour and character;
(4) Social location and environment.

I. Legalistic Variables—Consideration of legalistic variables is the most obvious starting point for seeing how important legal criteria are in decision-making. Type and seriousness of offence precipitating current police contact, number and seriousness of prior offences and dispositions of any past offences are legalistic variables most pertinent to the police decision to warn or prosecute.

(i) Number of Prior Offences—As one would expect from the spirit of Police Standing Orders, most of the Warnings group (99%) were first offenders. However, a fairly high proportion of the C/A group (54%) were also first offenders. Among the remaining cases, 1 per cent of the warnings and 17 per cent of C/A's had one prior offence, 16 per cent of C/A's had two or three, and 13 per cent had four or more. This seems to indicate that past offences, though significant (see tau values given in Table 3), were only one consideration in the highly subjective decision-making process.

(ii) Type of Offence—Offences were coded into 4 grades of seriousness (taking the most serious where there was more than one charge). From least to most serious these

were protection applications or juvenile 'status' offences. offences not in the Victoria Police major crime index, property offences (other than those in the preceding group) and offences against persons.[4]

The type of offence was significantly related to the police decision to warn or prosecute (see Table 3). However, the apparent significance of this general relationship is in fact due to the presence of group 1 offences (protection applications), as can be seen from Table 1 in which these offences have been omitted. It is also the case that some referrals to court involve rather trivial offences. Such data indicate that perhaps other non-legal criteria were important to the decision and/or that offending (irrespective of seriousness) was the criterion used to justify a court appearance: i.e., some police may merely refer all offenders to court.

Most studies relating past offence to police and court decisions have taken the number of prior offences as an index of the seriousness of the record (e.g., Terry (1967), Werthman and Piliavin (1967), Sieverdes (1973), Cohen (1974), Cohn (1970)). However, the number of prior offences recorded gives no indication of the severity of past offences and decisions. A summary score on a variable called 'legal' was compiled for each offender, taking into account the seriousness of offence, number of prior offences, seriousness of prior offences (as for offence) and type of dispositions for any such offences.[5] This variable, 'legal', was highly correlated with the number of prior offences and was similarly significant (tau= $.42$: p. $<.0000$) to the police decision to warn or prosecute.

II. Juveniles' Behaviour and Character— Considered under this heading are comments about truancy, the offender's school performance. school attendance and employment, character evaluation and comments on likely recidivism.

(i) Truancy and School Performance— Reported truancy was higher for the C/A group than the warnings group (tau = $.21$: p. $<.0000$) and was still significant in a sub-sample of first offenders (tau = $.17$:

Table 1—Type of Offence for Warnings and Court Appearances—Excluding Protection Applications

Type of Offence	Warnings	Court Appearances	Total (N = 610)
Non Index Offences	19.2% (54)	24.6% (81)	22.1%
Against Property	78.6% (221)	62.9% (207)	70.2%
Against Person	2.1% (6)	12.5% (41)	7.7%
Total	99.9% (281)	100.0% (329)	100.0%

Tau value = —.03 at .2086 (not significant).

p. = < .0000) indicating that even for first offenders, truancy was more likely to be associated with a C/A than with a warning. Any additional comments on school performance indicated again that negative attributes were more prevalent for the C/A group (such as bad attitudes, always 'in trouble', bad performance) and that the warnings group was said to be 'coping well'. Although this information was mentioned for only 16 per cent of the sample, a tau value of .31: p. = .0000 is indicative of a trend.

(ii) School Attendance and Employment— Offenders in the warnings group were more likely to be still attending school (no doubt this reflects their younger age). More importantly, when juveniles attending school or employed were compared with those who were unemployed, a tau value of .25: p. = < .0000 was obtained, indicating that the warnings group were more likely to be either at school or employed, and that higher proportions of C/A's were likely to be unemployed.

(iii) Character Evaluation and Estimated Recidivism—Piliavin and Briar (1964) in their classic study of police-juvenile interactions, found that arrests of suspect youths were more common for youths who showed lack of respect, displayed uncooperative behaviour and lacked the 'proper' demeanour. Their study suggested that attitudinal and interactional variables are more important than 'legalistic' ones.

Character evaluations and comments on likely recidivism were found to be related to type of police decision. Character evaluations (mentioned in 54 per cent of cases) of the warnings group were overwhelmingly positive—87 per cent mentioned the child's 'good character', cooperation and genuine regret and contrition at the experience of being caught. Allusions to 'bad attitude towards authority', 'poor character', 'non-cooperative', 'lies', were more common for the C/A group (30 per cent compared with 5.2 per cent for warnings). A chi-square value of 67 with 3 d.f. (p. < .0000) indicates that a systematic relationship exists between positive character evaluations for warnings and positive or negative evaluations for court appearances.

Similarly, police assessment of likely recidivism was related to whether police warned or prosecuted the juvenile. Although likely recidivism was mentioned in only 37 per cent of cases, the results still show more positive evaluations for the warnings (93%),

and positive (65%), indecisive (10%) or negative evaluations (25%) for the C/A group. This relationship was significant (χ^2 = 49.02 with 3 d.f.: p. = < .0000) and remained significant (although reduced) for the sample of first offenders.

III. Parents' Behaviour and Character— Included under this heading is information on parents' marital status, evaluations of parents' characters, 'family background' and whether the parents are seen as exercising control, contributing to the child's lapse and showing interest in the child's future.

The extent to which 'broken homes' and 'single parents' are associated with stereotypes of delinquency is an important question. Perhaps deviation from the ideal standard of the two-parent family can be seen as a risk factor in the decision to prosecute rather than as a causative factor. Goldman (1963: 123), in interviews, found that the police felt that children could not receive proper home supervision in homes broken by desertion, separation and divorce.

Parents of warnings group juveniles in this study were more likely to be married and living together (80%) than those of the C/A group, (65%); (tau = .7: p. < .0000 and is still significant in the first offender subsample).

When police assessments of parents' characters (these were made in over 70 per cent of cases) were categorised into positive (for example 'good', 'reputable'), average and negative (for example 'poor', 'known criminal', 'doesn't care about children'), higher proportions of the warnings group (93%) were assessed in positive terms, compared with 69 per cent of C/A parents. Also, over 90 per cent of the negative character evaluations were made about the C/A parents. Tau is .21 for mother's character and .26 for father's (p. = < .0000), indicating a significant relationship between type of character evaluation and police decision (see Table 3).

Comments relating to parental supervision and concern and 'home conditions', were also significantly related to police decisions (tau = .37: p. < .0000), in that the C/A group in 60 per cent of cases was coded as 'poor', including lack of sufficient supervision or interest in the child, lack of care, domestic disputes, and poor relationship with the child. Only 21 per cent of comments about the warnings group fitted into this category.

The answers to three questions were strongly inter-related (i.e., whether parents control the child, contribute to the child's lapse and show interest in the child's future) and were all significantly related to police decision group (see Table 3). Thus, it appears that a negative impression on parental variables was more likely to be conveyed for C/A's than for warnings and that evaluations were more uniformly positive for warnings. Goldman found that police tended to see juvenile delinquency as 'a reflection of disturbed home conditions or lack of training in the home' and 'parents not taking proper interest in what their children are doing' (1963: 120).

IV. Social Location and Environment— Under this heading, variables like character of companions, character of siblings, living situation, home appearance, character of neighbourhood and socio-economic status are considered.

Again, positive evaluations were more likely to be made of warnings group juveniles than for C/A's. For example, companions were seen as poor or bad (exemplified by comments like 'thief', 'have prior convictions', 'known to police', 'often come under police notice') in 71 per cent of C/A's and only 29 per cent of warnings and a most significant tau value of .43 (p. = < .0000) was obtained.

It seems, then, that associations with friends with 'bad reputations' for delinquent and trouble-making behaviour probably renders a juvenile more 'delinquent' in the eyes of the policeman.

One of the most interesting findings was the correlation between police decision group and the evaluation of the home appearance: 80 per cent of descriptions of home appearance for the warnings group were positive and 13 per cent negative, compared with 61 per cent positive and 27 per cent negative for the C/A group (tau = .13: p. = < .0000).[6]

Remembering that such information is presented to the court, one can question the necessity of such highly subjective information which is likely to reflect conservative middle-class standards of cleanliness and home quality and which, it seems, is consistent with the informant presenting C/A cases in consistently more negative terms than warnings, perhaps as part of a stereotype of the delinquent. So, it seems that an unsatisfactory 'home situation' may constitute part of the justification for prosecution.

There is surely justification for arguing that evaluations of the character of a neighbourhood are linked to police conceptions of 'high' and 'low' delinquency-rate areas which in turn has a self-fulfilling effect on the rates, through differential surveillance and arrest rates. Arnold (1972: 221) argued that coming from a high delinquency-rate area could become a partial justification for the need for treatment. In this study it was found that neighbourhood evaluations were significantly linked to type of police decision (tau = .24: p. < .0000) and were positive about 75 per cent of the time for warnings and about 50 per cent of the time for C/A's. Correspondingly, negative evaluations were more common for C/A's than for warnings.

Socio-Economic Status (S.E.S.)

Congalton's (1969) four-point scale was used to classify the occupational status of heads of households, as an indicator of S.E.S. Fathers' occupations were coded into 4 groups and the results are presented in Table 2.

Table 2 reflects the tendency for officially contacted juvenile offenders to come from lower socio-economic strata (tau = .18: p. = < .0000) and was still significant for first offenders (tau = .11: p. = < .0000). This indicates that juveniles (even first offenders) from lower S.E.S. families were more likely to progress further through the processing system than juveniles from higher S.E.S. families.

Consideration of social location and environmental variables has indicated that even for first offenders, more negative

Table 2—Occupational Status and Police Decision to Warn or Prosecute

Congalton's Groups*	Warnings	Court Appearances	Total (N = 579)
1.	3.3% (8)	1.8% (6)	2.4%
2	15.8% (38)	9.4% (32)	12.1%
3	52.5% (126)	44.2% (150)	47.7%
4	28.4% (68)	44.5% (151)	37.8%
Total	100.0% (240)	100.0% (339)	100.0%

*Groups are ranked from highest status (group 1) to lowest (group 4).

Table 3—Summary of Tau Scores for Total Sample and First Offenders

Variable	Total Sample		First Offenders	
	Tau value	Significance	Tau value	Significance
I Legalistic				
Type of offence	.22	.0000	.32	.0000
Number of priors	.43	.0000	—	—
'Legal'	.42	.0000	—	—
II Juvenile Behaviour and Character				
Age	.35	.0000	.37	.0000
Truancy	.21	.0000	.17	.0000
School Adjustment	.23	.0000	.25	.0000
Employment	.25	.0000	.24	.0000
III Parents' Behaviour and Character				
Marital status	.17	.0000	.12	.0000
Mother's character	.21	.0000	.16	.0000
Father's character	.26	.0000	.21	.0000
Parental/home conditions	.37	.0000	.28	.0000
Parents' control	.47	.0000	.41	.0000
Contribution to Lapse	.29	.0000	.21	.0000
Show Interest	.25	.0000	.19	.0000
IV Social Location and Environment				
Character of Companions	.43	.0000	.38	.0000
Character of Siblings	.25	.0000	.21	.0000
Living situation	.20	.0000	.08	.0000
Home Appearance	.13	.0000	.12	.0000
Character of Neighbourhood	.24	.0000	.14	.0000
Congalton Score	.19	.0000	.11	.0000

aspects on all variables were associated with the police decision to prosecute and refer to court, and that positive or favourable elements were more uniformly associated with the decision to warn.

To summarise the results discussed in the four sections above, Table 3 presents the tau values for the total sample and for a sub-sample of first offenders.

From Table 3, it can be seen that all variables except living situation remain significant, although usually reduced for the sub-sample of first offenders. The tau value for type of offence increased in the first offender sub-sample, indicating that prosecution of first offenders was related to the more serious nature of the offence. Also, age was still strongly related to the decision to warn or prosecute first offenders.

Conclusions

The results of this study are consistent with those of Emerson (1968), Cohn (1970), Box and Ford (1971) and Goldman (1963), which indicate that non-legal variables are significantly associated, sometimes more strongly than legalistic ones, with the police decision to warn or prosecute juvenile offenders. However, the data are at variance with those of other writers, such as Black and Reiss (1970), Hirschi (1975) and Meade (1974). These authors suggest that a legalistic model is most important to understanding the criteria on which police and court decisions are made. For example

Terry (1967), found no class or race discrimination when controls for seriousness of offence were applied.

The data in this study indicate that not only was a welfare model of decision-making more evident from police officers' decisions to warn or prosecute, but also, sometimes, legalistic variables were not as important as other non-legal variables. Groups of characteristics were related to police decisions: those in the warnings group were more consistently positively evaluated, were more likely to come from an 'intact' home, in a 'good' neighbourhood, with caring and competent parents of 'good' character and of higher S.E.S. Negative assessments were consistently associated with the C/A group who were more likely than the warnings group to come from single parent homes, to be of lower S.E.S., and to live in an average or low status neighbourhood with parents who did not control their child.

It is not possible to tell whether police assessments of juveniles precede decisions or follow as justifications for action. However, what does appear relevant is that the judgements discussed in the above 'fit' lay and sociological stereotyped notions of delinquents—i.e., broken homes, peers of poor character, low S.E.S., parents of questionable character, from high delinquency-rate areas. To use Emerson's (1968: 190) comparison of 'routine' and 'trouble' cases, 'routine' cases are more likely to receive a warning, but those involving 'trouble' encompass factors more far reaching than offence type or prior offences and are related to general misbehaviour in the attempt to assess the probability of future offending. This often involves assessment of patterns of behaviour which are trivial but seen as part of a progression towards a delinquent career, and which also happen to fit with accepted notions of delinquency. Cicourel points out how 'commonsense or lay theories are transformed into semi-professional interpretations' by probation officers in their decisions. He states 'the officers invoked negative comments about the home, peers, etc. when justifying placements in juvenile hall, a country boy's ranch or a foster home 'for his own good' ' (1968: 36).

A remarkable feature of the results is the agreement between police officers on criteria and the highly significant associations between the various factors mentioned and police decisions. In selecting between alternatives, the statements made are surprisingly uniform, especially in the absence of officially stated criteria. Such uniformity suggests that police 'delinquency theories in the mind' (Cicourel) are shared. Cicourel writes how members develop their own theories, recipes and shortcuts for meeting general requirements acceptable to themselves and tacitly or explicitly acceptable to other members acting as 'superiors' (1968: 1).

A latent function of shared public and police stereotypes is the imposition of harsher penalties on the more powerless and disadvantaged groups in society, and, in doing so, the completion of the circle of an elaborate 'self-fulfilling prophecy', where the characteristics of apprehended and prosecuted juveniles serve to support widely held notions of 'delinquent types' and delinquency causation. Box and Ford state 'the bias is there, both in the institutional method of suspicion and in the normal recipes for categorising suspects' (1971: 46). Goldman suggests that factors frequently considered causal with regard to juvenile delinquency should rather be viewed in terms of risk or liability of court referral (1963: 7).

Since the data discussed in this report suggest that social background reports prepared by police reflect highly subjective, discretionary judgements indicative of well accepted stereotypes of delinquency, an important question is whether these reports, which include recommendations to the court, should be tendered by persons other than police informants, as is the practice in other countries such as the U.K. and New Zealand, and in other States in Australia such as South Australia and Tasmania.

A focus on police decision-making criteria also raises questions related to police jurisdiction; whether the decision to warn or prosecute should be made by a non-police, non-judicial body like the Juvenile Aid Panel in South Australia; and the more general question of police-court interdependence within the juvenile processing system.

FOOTNOTES

1. The Police Form No. 276 is set out in standardised form and requests both descriptive and evaluative information. The nature of this information is indicated by the sub-heading used in the presentation of results section of this paper.
2. Police behaviour is regulated by Police Standing Orders. Paragraphs 310 and 311 (which were amended in March, 1977) set out the circumstances relating to cautioning or prosecuting a juvenile offender. They essentially recommend a court referral in cases where the offence is of a serious nature, where the child is alleged to be in need of care and protection, where the child or parents desire a court hearing or where the facts of innocence or guilt are in dispute. Police warnings, appropriate for first offenders and juveniles commiting minor offences, are aimed at diverting the child from the stigma and formal sanction of a court proceeding.
3. Measures of S.E.S. included parents' job descriptions, a classification of occupations according to Congalton's Scale (1969) and a classification of home addresses according to Jones' status ranking scale of Melbourne suburbs (1967).
4. This classification into seriousness categories accords with that used by Sieverdes (1973: 43) and also with the Victorian Police major crime index.
5. Disposal of past offences was coded into Police Warnings, Court dismissal, adjournments, fine or bond, probation and institutionalisation. Scoring on the scale gave a lowest score of 1 and a possible highest score of 80. The scores on 'legal' were then divided into 3 groups so that group 1 referred mostly to 1st offenders, group 2 to offenders with 1 or 2 prior offences, and group 3 to offenders with mostly 3, 4 or 5.
6. Positive included general positive words 'good', 'nice', 'excellent', positive structural descriptions 'nice brick', 'neat weatherboard' and references to cleanliness or tidiness; 'very neat and tidy', 'clean and well kept', etc. Middle-range evaluations referred to descriptions like 'fair', 'average', etc., and negative evaluations included words like 'bad', 'poor', 'sub-standard'; structural descriptions, 'rotting weatherboard', 'delapidated shack', and references to the state of the home — 'dirty', 'filthy', 'untidy', 'scruffy', etc. References to 'housing commission' dwellings were also included in this category, due to the association between public housing and 'social problems'. At least one such description was provided in over 60 per cent of cases.

REFERENCES

Arnold, William R.
1972 'Race and Ethnicity Relative to other factors in Juvenile Court Dispositions'. *American Journal of Sociology*, 77 (2): 211-227.

Becker, Howard S.
1966 **Outsiders: Studies in the Sociology of Deviance.** New York: Free Press.
Black, Donald J. and Albert J. Reiss
1970 'Police Control of Juveniles'. **American Sociological Review,** 35 (2): 63-72.
Blalock, H.
1972 **Social Statistics.** (2nd ed.). Tokyo: McGraw-Hill, Kogakusha.
Box, Stephen and Julienne Ford
1971 'The facts don't fit: On the relationship between social class and criminal behaviour'. **Sociological Review,** 19: 31.
Challinger, Dennis
1974 'The Juvenile Offender in Victoria'. Criminology Dept.: University of Melbourne.
Cicourel, Aaron V.
1968 **The Social Organisation of Juvenile Justice.** New York: Wiley.
Coher., Lawrence E.
1974 'Conferring the delinquent label: The relative importance of social characteristics and legal factors in the processing of juvenile offenders'. Ph.D, University of Washington: Xerox University Microfilm.
Cohn, Yona
1970 'Criteria for the probation officer's recommendation to the juvenile court'. In P. G. Garabedian and D. C. Gibbons (eds.), **Becoming Delinquent.** Chicago: Aldine Press.
Congalton, A. A.
1969 **Status and Prestige in Australia.** Melbourne: Cheshire.
Emerson, R. M.
1968 'The Juvenile Court: Labelling and Institutional Careers'. Xerox University Microfilm.
Goldman, Nathan
1963 'The Differential Selection of Juvenile Offenders for Court Appearance'. New York: National Council on Crime and Delinquency.
Hampton, Ross E.
1975 **Sentencing in a Childrens' Court and Labelling Theory.** New Zealand Research Series No. 5. Research Section Dept. of Justice. Wellington: Government Printer.
Hirschi, Travis
1975 'Labelling Theory and Juvenile Delinquency: An Assessment of the Evidence'. In W. Gove (ed.), **The Labelling of Deviance: Evaluating a Perspective.** New York: John Wiley & Sons.
Jamrozik, Adam
1974 **The Delinquent and the Law: Trends and Patterns in Juvenile Delinquency: South Australia 1954-1977.** South Australia: Flinders University of Australia Press.

Jones, F. Lancaster
1967 'A social ranking of Melbourne suburbs'. **Australian and New Zealand Journal of Sociology,** 3 (2): 93-110.
Kitsuse, John I. and Aaron V. Cicourel
1963 'A note on the Use of Official Statistics'. **Social Problems,** 11: 131-139.
Leaper, Patricia M.
1974 'Children in need of Care and Protection: A Study of Children brought before Victorian Children's Courts'. Criminology Department, University of Melbourne.
Lemert, Edwin McCarthy
1972 **Human Deviance, Social Problems and Social Control.** Englewood Cliffs, N.J.: Prentice Hall.
Lofland, John
1969 **Deviance and Identity.** Englewood Cliffs, N. J.: Prentice Hall.
Matza, David
1964 **Delinquency and Drift.** New York: Wiley.
Meade, Anthony
1974 'The Labelling Approach to Delinquency: State of the theory as a function of Method'. **Social Forces,** 53 (September): 83-91.
Meschemberg, H.
1974 'Juvenile Offenders in South Australia: A Sociological Pilot Study'. Unpublished report, Adelaide Research Unit, South Australia Department of Community Welfare.
Piliavin, Irving and Scott Briar
1964 'Police encounters with juveniles'. **American Journal of Sociology,** 70 (September): 206-214.
Schur, Edwin
1973 **Radical Non-Intervention: Re-thinking the Delinquency Problem.** Englewood Cliffs N.J.: Prentice Hall.
Sieverdes, Christopher Michael
1973 'The Differential Disposition of Juvenile Offenders: A Study of Juvenile Court Labelling'. Ann Arbor, Michigan: University Microfilm.
Skolnick, Jerome H.
1966 **Justice Without Trial: Law Enforcement in Democratic Society.** New York: Wiley.
Terry, Robert M.
1967 'Discrimination in the handling of juvenile offenders by Social Control Agencies'. **Journal of Research on Crime and Delinquency,** 4: 218-230.
Werthman, Carl and Irving Piliavin.
1967 'Gang members and the Police'. In David Joseph Bordua (ed.), **The Police: Six Sociological Essays.** New York: John Wiley.

[7]

[1993]

Evaluating Young Adult Diversion Schemes in the Metropolitan Police District

By Roger Evans

Professor and Director of the School of Law, Social Work and Social Policy, Liverpool John Moores University*

Summary: *This research study found only a slight increase in cautioning rates after two young adult diversion pilot schemes were established by the Metropolitan Police. The small change in rate is attributable to the negative attitudes of custody officers towards cautioning. The implications for the workload of the Youth Courts are considered and the alternatives open to forces, which aspire to increase their young adult cautioning rate, are discussed.*

Once offenders reach the age of 17 their chances of receiving a police caution are significantly reduced. For example in 1991 the cautioning rate for indictable offences for 17-year-old males was 35 per cent. whilst that for 16-year-olds was 62 per cent. This may be of considerable significance for the work of the Youth Courts following the implementation of the Criminal Justice Act 1991. If in future 17-year-olds are treated as juveniles for the purposes of police cautioning then the workload of the Youth Court may be not much greater than the juvenile courts which they replace. Alternatively if current cautioning practice with the young adult age group is maintained then the Youth Courts will have to deal with a considerable volume of work as the majority of 17-year-olds will not be diverted from court.

Few commentators appear to have realised that the work of the Youth Courts will be directly affected by whether or not police forces implement new guidance on cautioning issued to Chief Constables by the Home Office in 1990.[1] The circular was drawn up in the light of research findings on the impact of previous guidance on cautioning and sets out national standards for cautioning applicable to juveniles and adults alike.[2] The clear intention of Home Office Circular 59/1990 is that diversion from court, which so far has been used mainly with juveniles, should be extended to all age groups.

Despite an upward trend cautioning rates for young adults remain considerably lower than those for juveniles. In 1991 the average cautioning rates for all

* The research referred to in this paper was funded by the Home Office Research and Planning Unit. I am grateful to my colleagues in the Department of Social Policy and Social Work at The University of Birmingham for their support during this project and to Roger Leng of the Law Faculty for comments on earlier versions of this paper.
[1] Home Office, *The Cautioning of Offenders* (1990) Home Office Circular 59/1990.
[2] Evans, R. and Wilkinson, C., *The Impact of Home Office Circular 14/1985 on Police Cautioning Policy and Practice in England and Wales* (1988) Report to the Home Office Research and Planning Unit.

Crim.L.R.   EVALUATING YOUNG ADULT DIVERSION SCHEMES   491

England and Wales forces, for 14–16-year-old males and females, were 71 per cent. and 87 per cent. respectively whilst those for 17–20-year-olds were 26 per cent. and 45 per cent. For young adult males the cautioning rate ranged from 5 per cent. in South Wales to 44·per cent. in Kent. For females it ranged from 17 per cent. in South Wales to 70 per cent. in Kent.

This article presents research findings from an evaluation of two young adult diversion schemes set up in the Bromley and Westminster Divisions of the Metropolitan Police.[3] The research provides an opportunity to assess the likely impact of Home Office Circular 59/1990 by examining pilot projects specifically designed to achieve its aims. It also provides an opportunity to assess the effect of police cautioning practice with 17-year-olds on the work of the Youth Courts in areas which are arguably at the cutting edge of good practice.

The Bromley and Westminster schemes

The Bromley and Westminster-Harrow Road young adult diversion schemes are inter-agency initiatives and commenced in July and October 1991 respectively. The main aim of both schemes is to divert as many young adults from court as possible and to bring young adult cautioning rates into line with those for juveniles. In the adult criminal justice system decisions to charge or caution are usually made at the police station by custody officers under the supervision of more senior officers. The schemes aim to encourage custody officers to have a more positive attitude to cautioning young adults; to filter out inappropriate charges; to increase the consistency of decision making; and to enable senior officers more closely to supervise cases and monitor decisions.

The key instrument devised to achieve these aims is a "caution consideration chart" which focuses custody officers' attention on the factors to take into account when deciding to charge, caution or take no further action. The criteria for decision making are drawn from the Attorney-General's prosecution guidelines and the Code for Crown Prosecutors. Consistent with the sentencing aims of the Criminal Justice Act 1991 the focus is on the offence rather than the offender. The decision making criteria also take account of Home Office Circular 59/1990 and the Victim's Charter.

In addition to introducing the caution consideration chart the Bromley scheme have set up an inter-agency young adult diversion panel. Young adults, who are not suitable for immediate charge or caution, who live in the borough, who admit the offence, and who agree to be referred are passed to the panel for a decision to be taken on their case.

Cautioning rates before and after the schemes

Randomly selected samples of 100 juveniles and 300 17 to 20-year-olds, arrested in the same six-month periods before and after the implementation of the schemes, are used to measure any changes in cautioning rates. These samples consist of one in three of all arrests in the relevant age groups in Bromley and two in three in Westminster. The change in rate for young adults in Bromley, in the period before and after the start of the scheme, is from 27.6 per

---

[3] Evans, R., *Evaluating and Comparing Young Adult Diversion Schemes in the Metropolitan Police Area* (1992) Report to the Home Office Research and Planning Unit.

cent. to 32.6 per cent. The change for Westminster is from 13.4 per cent. to 20.7 per cent. This rate slightly underestimates the "official" cautioning rate because of the way in which it is calculated. In both divisions no further action, as a proportion of all decisions, remains roughly the same. If cautions substitute for no further action rather than prosecutions then it could be argued that "net-widening" has occurred.

The differences in cautioning rates before and after the schemes and between the two divisions can be accounted for in a number of ways. Previous research has found that the main factors affecting cautioning rates are the proportion of first offenders and force policy.[4] Other legal variables may have an influence, for example offence patterns, as may non-legal variables including age, sex, race and employment status. Whilst the changes in the caution rates between the study periods are not statistically significant the data were never the less analysed to assess if any change could be accounted for in these terms.

The only statistically significant difference between the samples is that the proportion unemployed increased from 38.3 per cent. to 53.2 per cent. in Bromley and from 67.5 per cent. to 76.1 per cent. in Westminster. In both areas there is a statistically significant relationship between employment status and the likelihood of receiving a caution. Table 1 shows that non-manual workers are more likely to be cautioned than manual workers and the unemployed. One explanation could be that "recidivists" are more likely to be unemployed and less likely to be cautioned but the relationship holds for first offenders. Since the proportion unemployed increases in both areas, between the before and after periods, this cannot account for any increase in the young adult cautioning rate. Indeed on this evidence this ought to have had the opposite effect.

Table 1—Young adult caution rate by employment status for Bromley and Westminster during the first six months of the scheme

Employment Status	Bromley		Westminster	
	Caution rate %	No. of individuals	Caution rate %	No. of individuals
Unemployed	34.3	131	19.2	161
Manual	50.0	76	16.7	25
Non manual	75.0	44	37.5	26
Totals		251		212

The difference between the cautioning rate in Bromley and Westminster is statistically significant. The data analysis suggests that the only factor which might contribute to this difference is that the proportion of unemployed is significantly higher in Westminster. In all other respects the Bromley and Westminster samples are similar. Since cautions are less likely to be used for the

---

[4] Laycock, G. and Tarling, R., "Police force cautioning: policy and practice" (1985) 24 *Howard Journal of Criminal Justice* 81. Evans, R. and Wilkinson, C., "Variations in police cautioning policy and practice in England and Wales" (1990) 29 *Howard Journal of Criminal Justice* 155.

unemployed this may contribute to the lower young adult cautioning rate in Westminster. The inescapable conclusion is that the lower rate in Westminster is a result of the way in which officers interpret and implement cautioning policy in this area.

These data can also be used to test the claim that there is a drop in the use of cautions once offenders reach 17. In the Bromley after sample for example, the cautioning rate for 16-year-old juveniles is 68.6 per cent. whilst that for 17-year-old young adults is 44.3 per cent. In all other respects the characteristics of the two age groups are similar. The fall off in the use of cautions appears to be a direct result of the different presumptions which are applied to juveniles and adults. The presumption for juveniles is that they will be cautioned whenever possible but that for adults is that they will be charged unless there are special reasons not to do so. The interviews with custody officers hold the key to understanding why the young adult diversion schemes had less of an impact than was hoped for or expected.

The custody officer interviews

In many juvenile cautioning systems, including in the Metropolitan Police, all but the most serious cases are bailed awaiting a decision to be made at "arm's length." In this instance these decisions are taken by officers in the Youth and Community Section. The young adult diversion schemes are different from the juvenile system because decisions are left in the hands of the custody officers after consultation with senior officers when necessary. A principal aim of the schemes is to encourage a more positive attitude towards cautioning and to filter out inappropriate charges. The attitudes of the custody officers are therefore crucial to the success or failure of the schemes.

In contrast to previous research the majority of custody sergeants (14/20) do not believe there are any general differences between juveniles and young adults.[5] First, age is not a good guide. "It's more a question of maturity. You can have street wise twelve year olds and immature young adults." Secondly the distinction between juveniles and young adults is less important than that between the "one off" offender and the "regulars."

> "I know ninety per cent of the faces that come into this station. On this ground youngsters make a decision early on about whether they are going to get involved in crime or not. Then it is a matter of progression. It's not that young adults are different from juveniles. They are mostly the same people that we used to see as juveniles."

The custody officers' attitude to the caution consideration chart and their use of it is crucial to the success of the scheme as this is the main instrument for increasing diversion. All the officers had experience of using the chart and were asked what they saw as its advantages and disadvantages. Eight of the sample of 20 could see advantages in using it which included that: "it prompts you to think of why someone shouldn't be charged"; "it helps you make your mind up—it's an idiot's guide"; "it should lead to consistency." Fifteen of the officers thought

---

[5] Evans, R., "Police Cautioning and the Young Adult Offender" [1991] Crim.L.R. 598 *et seq.*

there were disadvantages which included that: "it does not take account of the attitude of the prisoner"; "it puts you in a straight jacket—every case ought to be decided on its merits"; "it makes me accountable—it's another thing to be pulled up on"; "it takes time"; "you know whether you are going to caution without using the chart."

The most common use of the chart was not as an aid to decision making but as a written justification of a decision that had already been made. After all "you know as soon as they come in through the door what you are going to do. It all depends on their attitude and whether they are genuinely remorseful." Some officers stated that they had used the chart in the early stages of the pilot scheme but once they had memorised the cautioning criteria they tended to fill it in after they had made a decision. "The chart was another piece of paperwork that tends to get overlooked in the heat of the moment. In a busy custody suite your priority is to look after the prisoners within the framework of PACE." During the interviews the chart was frequently referred to as a "justification to charge sheet" which is indicative of the stance of the majority of officers towards it.

The custody officers fall into three distinct groups, of roughly equal size, in terms of their general attitude to cautioning. There are those who believe cautioning is a waste of time, an insufficient reward for officers' investigative efforts, a usurpation of the powers of the court, and a financial expedient. "Police officers get frustrated—they work hard to catch people and at the end of the day we end up cautioning them. Not many officers see this as a satisfactory result for their labours." These views correspond with the findings of a national survey of police cautioning policy and practice and suggests that they may be indicative of more general police attitudes towards cautioning.[6]

A second group consists of those officers for whom cautioning "goes against the grain" but who can nevertheless see a role for it with first offenders committing minor offences. Whilst they might not like "the system" they claim to be able to put their personal beliefs aside and comply with institutional rules and policy. Typical comments include "my views on cautioning are one thing—but I try to apply the guidelines however unwillingly" or "I am not against cautioning whole-heartedly—it is suitable for the one off offender." The final group have a good understanding of the concept of diversion, accept the young adult diversion policy, and implement it willingly.

All three groups think that young adults should only be given one chance or that a maximum of two cautions should be given but only if the offences are not alike and there is a reasonable time lapse. "Everyone should be given one chance. You've got to give people the benefit of the doubt when it is a first offence" or "It should be extended to the whole adult group. I don't see why anyone should be treated differently just because of their age."

Officers were asked whether they thought that the presumption which currently applies to juveniles, that they should only be prosecuted as a last resort and cautioned whenever possible, should also apply to adults. Fifteen replied no, four yes, and one did not know. The majority of those who thought that the principles of current cautioning practice with juveniles should not be extended

---

[6] Evans, R. and Wilkinson, C. (1990) *op. cit.*

Crim.L.R.   EVALUATING YOUNG ADULT DIVERSION SCHEMES   495

for use with adults gave as their reason different versions of the observation that "you've got to draw the line somewhere."

The Bromley young adult inter-agency panel

In Bromley a second mechanism for achieving diversion is the inter-agency panel. Cases are referred to the panel if the custody officer is not sure what decision to take. This is either when the offence was minor but there was a previous caution or conviction or when there are "social or domestic problems." The proportion of cases referred to the panel was relatively small at 5.8 per cent. of all those arrested ($N=809$). Twenty-eight of the 38 cases referred to the panel were recommended for a caution which represents a "diversion" rate of 73.7 per cent.

When the panel recommended prosecution it was usually because of the number of previous cautions or convictions. Prosecution was also recommended if the offender was already subject to a court order such as a conditional discharge or probation order. There is a statistically significant relationship between the number of previous cautions or convictions and the panel's recommendation. Like the custody officers the rule of thumb for the panel appeared to be one, or exceptionally, a maximum of two cautions. Twenty of the 41 referrals had no previous criminal histories but were nonetheless referred to the panel.

Discussion

Young adult cautioning rates have increased slightly following the implementation of the diversion schemes although the rate in Westminster is significantly lower than that in Bromley. Whether the increase is a direct result of the schemes or the continuation of an already upward trend, is difficult to assess. In any case the increase is disappointedly small given the expectations of the members of the inter-agency working parties that initiated the schemes and the commitment of senior officers in the police. The difference between the rates in Bromley and Westminster confirms the finding from previous research that differences in cautioning rates within forces may be as great as those between them.[7] Evans and Wilkinson suggested that this is a relatively neglected aspect of police cautioning practice.

In this study 17-year-olds are much less likely to be cautioned than 16-year-olds. This cannot be accounted for in terms of any of the factors which previous research suggests are relevant to understanding differences in cautioning rates. It would appear that this is largely due to the different attitudes of custody officers towards cautioning juveniles and young adults. Some juvenile justice systems have used the establishment of Youth Courts as an opportunity to include 17-year-olds in the juvenile cautioning structure so bringing the age range of court and pre-court decision making into line. It would be interesting to compare cautioning rates for 17-year-olds processed within juvenile and adult systems. It might be expected that a much higher proportion of those processed in juvenile systems would be cautioned. On the evidence of this study, if 17-year-olds are dealt with within the adult pre-court system, and Home Office Circular

---

[7] Evans, R. and Wilkinson, C. (1991) *op. cit.*

59/1990 fails to have an impact here, then the Youth Courts may be faced with a larger volume of work than that anticipated.

The relatively small increase in cautioning rates is attributed, by some of the key players involved in setting up the schemes, to the failure of senior officers to exercise close case supervision and to monitor decisions. It can be argued that there are inherent limitations to the extent to which line managers can be expected routinely to reverse decisions of their immediate subordinates and yet sustain workable relationships. But given the scale of the problem this is what might be expected.

In the absence of close case supervision the caution consideration chart may have encouraged some custody officers to think about what they were doing but it did no more than that. If they did not accept the diversionary policy they were free to get around it or positively subvert it. Given some of the negative attitudes towards cautioning expressed during the interviews it is likely that this is what happened in practice.

As an instrument of diversion the panel appears to have been effective as approximately 70 per cent. of the cases referred to them were eventually cautioned. This is perhaps not surprising as panel members agreed that their mission was to try to caution whenever possible. The overwhelming majority of cases were decided by the custody officers alone and clearly the use of the caution consideration chart had only a limited impact in terms of increasing the rate of diversion. This brings us to the question of how a police force, which has aspirations to increase its rate of diversion with young adults, can best achieve this.

Sanders[8] points to what he claims is a curious anomaly in the prosecution process. He argues that it is anomalous that prosecution decisions have been taken out of the hands of the police but that all non-prosecution decisions on case disposal are under their sole control. In some areas, including those in this study, the CPS contribute to the formulation of cautioning policy but Sanders suggests that they might also play a role in decisions on the disposal of individual cases. Given the state of the resources of the CPS, however, it is simply unrealistic to anticipate that they will take any major role at this level in the foreseeable future.

Some juvenile justice workers believe that the increase in juvenile cautioning rates is a direct result of the widespread use of inter-agency consultation.[9] In inter-agency consultation decisions are not the responsibility of the police alone. In this sense consultation plays a role similar to that which could be played by the CPS. It puts distance between the investigative and case disposal phases of the prosecution process. Indeed there is some evidence from this study that this is exactly what the young adult diversion panel achieved, albeit in a very limited way.

The major limit on the panel's diversionary ambitions stemmed from the decision to only refer "problematic" or "ambiguous" cases to it. As instant

---

[8] Sanders, A., "The limits to diversion from prosecution" (1988) 28 *British Journal of Criminology* 513.
[9] Blagg, H. and Smith, D., *Crime, Penal Policy and Social Work* (London, Longman, 1989).

charges were not scrutinised by the panel its diversionary potential was inherently limited. The cases that were referred were usually the cases where custody officers said they thought that they would not "*get away*" with charging. In juvenile systems the usual role of the inter-agency panel is to scrutinise those cases that are recommended for prosecution. It is considered crucial to see if these can be diverted from court. The only exceptions would be cases that are so obviously serious, (for example, rape or murder, where there is no alternative to instantly charging), instant cautions, or those cases which the police intend to take no further action on. Given the rate of "diversion" achieved by the panel, in contrast to the custody officers left to their own devices, it is interesting to speculate what would happen if all charges were scrutinised. One might expect this significantly to increase the rate of diversion.

One obvious objection to this, which was voiced by panel members, is that it might result in undue delay in decision making. But it is precisely the element of delay that takes the decision away from investigating officers. As we have seen they may not have the desire let alone the capability of arriving at consistent decisions in line with force cautioning policy. Another objection concerns cost. It is argued that the juvenile system requires dedicated officers placed in the Youth and Community Section and that this is expensive in terms of human resources. In spite of the fact that many police officers believe cautioning to be a low cost expedient there appears to be little research on the comparative costs of cautioning and prosecution attributable to the different agencies involved. The argument that the widespread introduction of young adult panels must be ruled out on the grounds of cost rests on a set of, as yet, untested assumptions.

[8]

THE BRITISH JOURNAL

OF

CRIMINOLOGY

Vol. 33   Autumn 1993   No. 4

THE PROSECUTOR FINE AND SOCIAL CONTROL

The Introduction of the Fiscal Fine to Scotland

PETER DUFF*

The 'dispersal of discipline thesis' is tested against the introduction to Scotland of the prosecutor fine, a diversionary mechanism used in several European jurisdictions. The prosecutor fine does not represent the therapeutic type of measure around which the 'dispersal of discipline thesis' is usually constructed. The growth of mundane monetary sanctions, including attempts at diversion through the use of fixed penalties and prosecutor fines, has largely been ignored. In Scotland, the introduction of the prosecutor fine has led to considerable 'net-widening' and the reasons for this are suggested. Nevertheless, rather than providing evidence of the 'dispersal of discipline', the prosecutor fine appears to represent a move towards a more administrative–bureaucratic style of criminal justice.

Diversion and 'the Dispersal of Discipline'

In recent years, there has been much talk of 'diverting' offenders from the criminal justice system or of finding 'alternatives' to traditional criminal justice processes. Initiatives with this aim in mind have been implemented in many countries. After the initial burst of enthusiasm which inevitably surrounds any apparently progressive trend in criminal justice, the move towards diversion has been assessed with a more jaundiced eye. The resulting critical literature has been described, by Bottoms (1983), as advancing the 'dispersal of discipline thesis' (the use and meaning of the term 'discipline' in this context deriving from the writings of Foucault). More recently, McMahon (1990) has argued that the growing disenchantment of criminologists with the idea of 'diversion' or 'alternatives' is based upon their use of 'the concept of net-widening'.

These phrases—'net-widening' and 'dispersal of discipline'—are commonly used as a

* Faculty of Law, Aberdeen University. I am grateful to Kenneth Meechan, Michael Christie, and David Lessels who participated in the research upon which this paper is based. I should also like to thank Crown Office for the grant which made the research possible and their subsequent ready co-operation.

PETER DUFF

form of shorthand to summarize the following argument: diversionary mechanisms tend to be counter-productive because, in practice, they operate as an addition to existing penal measures rather than as a replacement ('net-widening'); further, they are usually more intrusive than the measures they were designed to replace and often involve welfare agencies ('dispersal of discipline'); hence, the movement towards diversion tends inadvertently to strengthen the state's network of social control. In the classic account of this type, Cohen (1985: 44) observes that 'destructuring movements were aimed at decreasing the size, scope and intensity of the formal deviancy control system'. Paradoxically, he argues, they usually have the following effects: (1) the number of deviants entering the system increases, i.e. 'wider nets'; (2) the overall intensity of intervention increases, i.e. 'denser nets'; and (3) new agencies supplement the original mechanisms of control, i.e. 'different nets' (see also Austin and Krisberg 1981: 169).

It was 'critical' criminologists, such as Cohen, who first identified the failure of diversion to reduce the activity of the criminal justice system. As McMahon (1990: 125) comments, there is a certain irony to their conclusion that the attempt to reform the repressive tendencies of the criminal justice system is doomed to failure:

critical criminologists substituted the recalcitrant criminal justice system for the recalcitrant offender of the positivist criminology which they sought to critique.

The principal worry of the critics of diversion was that, as a result of the phenomenon of net-widening, the state's mechanisms of social control were actually becoming more powerful while this process remained disguised by a humanitarian or welfare ideology (with concomitant misleading terminology). More recently, some commentators have suggested that this vision of an increasingly powerful, therapeutic state, penetrating ever more deeply the lives of its wayward citizens, may have been overstated (Bottoms 1983; Rodger 1988; McMahon 1990). Indeed, Cohen (1987) himself appears to have admitted that his earlier pessimism was perhaps exaggerated (see also Matthews 1987).

Many attempts to implement 'alternatives' have involved either the diversion of juvenile offenders from the criminal justice process or decarceration, usually through the use of 'community corrections'. Partly as a result of this, the academic literature has tended to revolve around these aspects of diversion.[1] The focus on these areas has tended to obscure the fact that there exists a much wider range of diversionary strategies.[2] In his discussion of decarceration and social control, Matthews (1987: 340) warns of the dangers of 'globalism', by which he means the tendency of the theorist to over-generalize from the examination of an individual diversion scheme. Similarly, there is an obvious danger of arriving at misleading conclusions about the trend towards diversion if the focus of attention is limited solely to the areas of the criminal justice system outlined above.

This weakness in the literature lies at the heart of Bottoms's (1983) criticism of the 'dispersal of discipline thesis'. He argues that its proponents have ignored the growing

[1] For summaries of the literature, see Austin and Krisberg 1981; Blomberg 1977; Cohen 1985; Lowman *et al.* 1987; Jones 1990; McIvor 1990; McMahon 1990.

[2] It must also be noted that the attempt to divert can take place at various stages in the criminal justice process. Some commentators have distinguished three stages of diversion: 'primary'—i.e. before a criminal prosecution is commenced; 'secondary'—at some stage during the prosecution process; or 'tertiary'—after conviction, usually in an effort to avoid incarcerating the offender (see Stewart Committee 1983: para. 2.21; Stedward and Millar 1989: 2).

THE PROSECUTOR FINE AND SOCIAL CONTROL

use of the fine and the corresponding decrease, in proportionate terms, in the use of imprisonment and probation. Bottoms observes that the fine does not involve control or supervision by a penal agent and that it clearly represents 'more of a classical than a disciplinary punishment' (p. 178). Hence, in his view, the increasing use of the fine does not 'look remotely congruent' with the claims of Cohen and others that the criminal justice system is currently expanding its network of social control. Young makes a similar point when he observes that the criminal justice system uses monetary sanctions far more often than anything else, yet these are little studied in comparison with imprisonment which represents 'a point of focus where liberal fears come together' (1992: 435).

In her recent critical analysis of the 'concept of net-widening', McMahon (1990: 142) comments that Bottoms's argument has been dealt with cursorily by advocates of the 'dispersal of discipline thesis'. She further observes that 'the theme of expansion overshadows mundane but important penal developments'. The gist of these complaints is that apparently unexciting initiatives which may be taking place at the 'soft end' of the criminal justice system may tell us as much, if not more, about what is going on in the system than more striking developments taking place at the 'hard end'.[3] This is particularly so if, as is likely, the former type of strategy affects a much larger number of offenders than the latter.

Against this theoretical background, the introduction of the prosecutor fine to Scotland ought to be of particular interest. The prosecutor fine is a diversionary measure used in various continental jurisdictions whereby the public prosecutor offers an alleged offender the chance of avoiding prosecution by paying an immediate financial penalty. In other words, it works in a roughly similar manner to the 'fixed penalty' system for road traffic offences—the operation of which will be familiar to most readers—but it covers a much wider range of offences and is administered by the prosecutor. It is significant that the theoretical debate about diversion has virtually ignored the advent of the fixed penalty system despite the vast number of cases involved.[4] Similarly, the widespread use of the prosecutor fine in continental jurisdictions passes without comment. Yet, where it exists, far more offenders are diverted from the criminal justice process through this mechanism than through the therapeutic-type measures around which the 'dispersal of discipline thesis' is constructed.

It is worth emphasizing the reasons for the neglect of the prosecutor fine. First, it tends to operate at the 'soft' end of the criminal justice process and to involve the run-of-the-mill adult offender. Thus, it involves neither juvenile justice nor decarceration and is obscured by other aspects of diversion. Secondly, it is, of course, a *fine* and, hence, it does not lend itself to sweeping claims about the 'dispersal of discipline', the 'surveillance society' etc. Thirdly, with one or two notable exceptions,[5] the literature in this area tends to be dominated by commentators from English speaking, common law jurisdictions. It sometimes seems that reference is more likely to be made to tribal or socialist legal systems than to those of other western European countries. Fourthly, the structure of the criminal justice system in common law jurisdictions does not facilitate

---

[3] For a comment on the frequent use of this type of imagery, see McMahon (1990: 123).

[4] The honourable exception to this complaint is Bottoms (1983: 185 ff.). I shall return to his analysis below.

[5] There have been some important continental contributions to theorizing in this area, for example, that made by Mathieson. Nevertheless, such commentators have tended to adhere to the traditional agenda: decarceration; juvenile justice; the growth of therapeutic disposals, etc.

PETER DUFF

an understanding—far less an adoption—of the prosecutor fine. The mechanism is better suited to the civilian tradition of the continent, with its inquisitorial approach and, in particular, its powerful public prosecutor.

Nevertheless, in an attempt to divert cases from the criminal courts, the prosecutor fine was recently introduced to Scotland.[6] One aim of this article is simply to discuss the impact of this measure upon the process of criminal justice in Scotland. In particular, it is important to assess whether the prosecutor fine has actually succeeded in diverting offenders from the more formal mechanisms of the criminal justice process or whether it has simply had a net-widening effect. The other purpose of the article is to contribute some comments towards the debate over the 'dispersal of discipline thesis' in the light of the evidence described below.

The Fiscal Fine

The Stewart Committee was set up in 1977 in Scotland to study alternatives to the prosecution of minor offences in an attempt to ease the pressure of work upon both the prosecution service and the court system.[7] The Committee published two reports, the first of which recommended extending the use of the existing fixed penalty system for road traffic offences (Stewart Committee 1980). In its second report (Stewart Committee 1983), the Committee discussed various methods of 'primary diversion' (para. 2.21) for a much wider set of offences, both statutory and at common law. It considered possibilities ranging from informal verbal warnings by the investigating police officer (para. 3.04) to a variety of more sophisticated disposals instigated by the public prosecutor, including psychiatric treatment (paras. 3.23–28), social work intervention (paras. 3.29–30), and the 'prosecutor fine' (ch. 4). The latter option was regarded as the most promising and hence was discussed at the greatest length.[8]

At this stage, it is necessary to explain that the Scottish prosecution process is rather different from its English counterpart, although with the arrival of the Crown Prosecution Service the differences may decrease. Virtually all criminal prosecutions in Scotland have long been undertaken by an independent public prosecution service to whom the police report possible cases of criminal conduct. This service is headed by the Lord Advocate who, in the great majority of cases, acts through local prosecutors, known as procurators fiscal. There are 49 such local prosecutors, running offices of varying sizes. Several offices process fewer than 1,000 police reports per year and in these the legally qualified staff comprises the procurator fiscal alone. At the other extreme, the busiest office deals with an annual workload of around 80,000 cases. The procurator fiscal here is supported by around 60 other legally qualified prosecutors—known as assistant fiscals and depute fiscals—and nearly 400 administrative staff. The prosecution service as a whole is administered by the Crown Office in Edinburgh and headed by the Crown Agent who is accountable to the Lord Advocate. It must be

---

[6] This is a result of the fact that, for historical reasons, the Scottish legal system is more receptive to imports from the continent than its Anglo-American counterparts. It is a 'mixed' system, incorporating elements of both common law and civilian systems. Although the criminal justice process is largely adversarial, traces of the inquisitorial system can be found (Sheehan 1990: 43).

[7] The significance of this motivation will be discussed below.

[8] 'Diversion' for psychiatric treatment, social work intervention or mediation was introduced at around the same time as the prosecutor fine. This enables a useful comparison to be drawn between the impact of the two types of measure upon the Scottish penal process. For this, and a comment upon the terminology, see below.

THE PROSECUTOR FINE AND SOCIAL CONTROL

stressed that the procurator fiscal service has long emphasized the considerable discretion possessed by each local procurator fiscal and, in particular, his or her independence from the police. (For a description of the fiscal service and its work, see Moody and Tombs 1982.)

It was against this background that the majority of the Stewart Committee recommended that the prosecutor fine should be adopted 'as an expedient and efficient method of removing a substantial number of cases from the courts' (1983: para. 4.38). The government subsequently implemented this recommendation through section 56 of the Criminal Justice (Scotland) Act 1987, which empowers a procurator fiscal to make a 'conditional offer' to an alleged offender as regards any offence which could competently be tried in the district court (excluding those traffic offences already covered by the 'fixed penalty' scheme).[9] Thus a conditional offer may be issued for various common law offences—such as assault, breach of the peace, and theft—and for a variety of statutory offences—such as being drunk and incapable and urinating in public.

The conditional offer has come to be known as the 'fiscal fine' in order to differentiate it from the 'fixed penalty' levied for road traffic offences. The substance of a conditional offer is that if the alleged offender accepts, by paying a specified amount to the clerk of the relevant district court within a certain time (invariably 28 days), criminal proceedings shall not be brought. The specified sum is presently set at £25.[10] An alleged offender may opt to pay either in a lump sum or in five instalments of £5. In the latter eventuality, payment of the first instalment within the specified period constitutes acceptance of the offer and, thereafter, payments must be made on a fortnightly basis. Outstanding instalments may be enforced only through civil debt procedure rather than through the mechanisms used for recovering fines imposed by the criminal courts. In essence, failure to pay the outstanding instalments of a fiscal fine cannot lead to imprisonment. Finally, it is crucial to note that the acceptance of a conditional offer does not amount to a criminal conviction.

A major research exercise into the operation of the fiscal fine was carried out shortly after its introduction.[11] Various methods of enquiry were adopted. First, the Annual Statistical Returns compiled by the Crown Office were analysed. These figures provide a numerical breakdown of the way in which each of the 49 procurator fiscal offices disposes of crime reports received. Secondly, a questionnaire was circulated by post to all 255 fiscals. Of these, 176 completed questionnaires were returned—a response rate of 69 per cent. Thirdly, a series of semi-structured interviews was carried out with various procurators fiscal and district court clerks. Finally, in several offices the research team collected a sample of cases in respect of which a fiscal fine had been offered and followed these to their conclusion. In three large offices, all such offers

[9] The district court is the lowest in the hierarchy of criminal courts in Scotland. Under the District Courts (Scotland) Act 1975, its jurisdiction covers both a variety of minor common law offences and also statutory offences for which the prescribed penalty does not exceed 60 days imprisonment or a £2,500 fine, unless the statute dictates otherwise. For both types of offence, the justices are empowered to impose imprisonment for a period not exceeding 60 days or a fine not exceeding £2,500.

[10] The Stewart Committee (1983) favoured empowering fiscals to operate with a sliding scale, similar to the model used in the Netherlands, rather than being confined to a fixed sum. This recommendation was not adopted because it was thought to involve too great a usurpation of the judicial function.

[11] The research was funded by the Crown Office and carried out between 1 April 1989 and 31 March 1991 by a team from the Faculty of Law, Aberdeen University.

PETER DUFF

made within a one-month period were monitored. This produced the following numbers of cases: Office A—201; Office B—89; Office C—57. Further, in one large office and two medium-sized offices, cases were collected over a three-month period, resulting in samples of: Office D—193; Office E—31; and Office F—10.

Is the Net Becoming Wider?

Table 1 illustrates the use made of the fiscal fine since its introduction on 1 January 1988. Clearly, the fiscal fine has become established as 'an important weapon in the fiscal's armoury' (in the words of one interviewee).[12] It is interesting to note that the number of cases disposed of by fiscal fine is roughly equivalent to the number of cases where a custodial sentence—prison or Young Offenders Institution—is the outcome (Scottish Office 1992). Yet, as noted above, attention will tend to focus on the latter sanction.

TABLE 1   *Fiscal Fine Use*

Year	No. of fiscal fines	Percentage of all reports	Percentage of appropriate reports[a]
1988	9,304	2.7	5.6
1989	15,556	4.2	9.8
1990	16,985	4.5	10.5
1991	15,599	4.4	10.1

[a] This figure represents the percentage in which a fiscal fine might *possibly* have been offered. It excludes from the calculation those cases which were prosecuted in the High Court or Sheriff Court and those which were disposed of by the fixed penalty scheme for road traffic offences.

It must be emphasized that there are considerable variations in the use of the fiscal fine from office to office.[13] For example, in 1990 the proportion of all crime reports disposed of by fiscal fine in the ten largest offices—all dealing with over 10,000 cases annually—ranged from 2.2 per cent up to 12.3 per cent. The latter rate was not exceeded by any of the other 39 offices while, at the other end of the scale, one medium-sized office—dealing with around 5,000 cases annually—offered only five fiscal fines (a usage rate of 0.1 per cent). Indeed, in 1991, this office did not use the fiscal fine at all.[14]

---

[12] Table 1 gives the impression that the fiscal fine, as presently constituted, may have reached the limit of its use. Obviously, only a certain proportion of cases is suitable for a fixed penalty of £25, especially when one bears in mind the fact that over this period the average district court fine has been higher. It is perhaps significant that the apparent ceiling which has been reached—around 16,000 or 17,000 cases—tallies roughly with the Government's estimate of the potential: during the debate over the legislation, the Solicitor-General told the First Scottish Standing Committee that it was thought that 18,000 to 19,000 cases might benefit from the new procedure (HC Deb. 1986–7: vol. 6, col. 186). The effect of monetary inflation since these figures were calculated is likely to have reduced slightly the number of cases which can appropriately be disposed of with a £25 fixed penalty. Nevertheless, given the wide variations in the use of the fiscal fine in different offices (see below), further expansion may yet take place. Clearly, if the Stewart Committee's recommendation of a sliding scale were to be adopted, the potential would be increased greatly.

[13] It must be noted that the use of several disposals, including the fiscal fine, varies greatly between offices. There are a number of possible reasons for such differences, for example: differing police policy on what is reported to the fiscal; regional variations in the public concern raised by particular offences; the relevant fiscal's attitude to particular offences and disposals; changes in personnel in fiscals' offices; and waiting lists for the various courts in the area.

[14] The procurator fiscal in question commented that he did not approve of fiscal fines as a method of disposing of cases, preferring to leave the question of the appropriate punishment of offenders to the courts.

THE PROSECUTOR FINE AND SOCIAL CONTROL

Thus, it must be noted that the range of fiscal fine use is sufficiently great to mean that the national figures provide no more than a crude indication of what is happening across the country.[15]

More important, for the purposes of this article, is the pattern of use. In order to elaborate upon this point, it is necessary to explain that a fiscal has various options for the disposal of minor cases. Specifically, a file may be 'marked' for any of the following disposals: no further proceedings—known as a 'no pro'; a warning letter from the fiscal; 'diversion', for treatment by psychiatric or social work services or for reparation to take place; a conditional offer—a 'fiscal fine'; or prosecution in the district court. Guidelines issued by the Crown Office make it very clear that a fiscal fine should only be issued in a case which would otherwise merit prosecution. This approach follows logically from the fiscal fine's *raison d'être* of reducing the number of prosecutions in the district court.

Figure 1 illustrates the proportionate use made nationally of the relevant disposals for the three years before and after the introduction of the fiscal fine—i.e. from 1985 to 1990 inclusively. If the fiscal fine were working as intended, the level of district court prosecutions should have fallen by the amount of fiscal fine usage and, in contrast, the use of the 'no pro' and the warning letter should have remained unaffected (assuming for the time being that all other factors are constant). However, as a glance at Figure 1 reveals, this possibility can be discounted ($p < 0.01$).[16] On the contrary, it is the use of the 'no pro' and the warning letter which has dropped, instead of the rate of prosecution in the district court. This appears to indicate that the effect of the fiscal fine has been to draw alleged offenders further into the criminal justice process, in that many of those now receiving a fiscal fine would previously have escaped with a 'no pro' or, at worst, a warning letter.

Despite this evidence that the national picture is one of net-widening, the pattern of fiscal fine usage varies considerably between different offices. In order to assess the position in each office, it is necessary to identify which other disposals are being replaced by fiscal fines. This poses difficulties because it is inherently unlikely that offices will simply fall into two clear-cut categories: those where all fiscal fine cases would previously have received a 'no pro' or a warning letter (i.e. pure net-widening); and those where, as intended, all fiscal fine cases would previously have been prosecuted in the district court (i.e. no net-widening). In practice, most offices fall between these two extremes: fiscal fines are drawn from a number of other disposals. A further analytical difficulty is that over the period examined other factors were undoubtedly causing movements of cases from one disposal to another. In particular, for reasons which will be discussed below, there was a general decline in the 'no pro' rate, as can be seen from Figure 1.

Despite the difficulties involved in interpreting the data, it is clear that there has

---

[15] The Crown Office is shortly to issue guidelines upon the use of the fiscal fine in an effort to achieve a more consistent pattern of use.

[16] This and the further statistical tests referred to below were carried out by Mark Brewer, of the Department of Mathematical Sciences, Aberdeen University, to whom I am grateful. These tests looked at contingency tables of proportions of disposals before and after the introduction of the fiscal fine, with the null hypothesis 'no change in proportion'. The significance probability in rejecting the null hypothesis (shown by 'p') was less than 0.01 in this case. This shows strong evidence that the proportion of disposals changed after the introduction of fiscal fines. For recent discussion of the use of statistical methods—and problems thereof—for assessing the impact of net-widening, see Jones 1990; McIvor 1990; McMahon 1990.

PETER DUFF

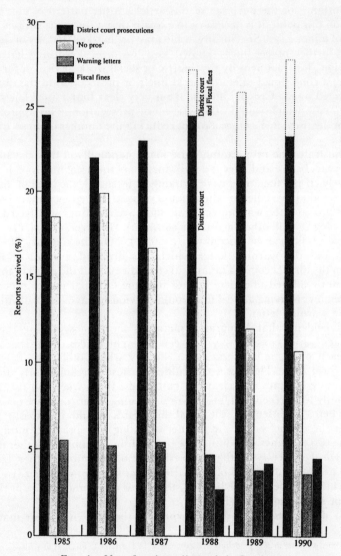

FIG. 1   Use of various disposals in Scotland

THE PROSECUTOR FINE AND SOCIAL CONTROL

been a great deal of net-widening. The movement of cases from the 'no pro' disposal to the fiscal fine has taken place, to differing degrees, in 24 of the 49 procurator fiscal offices ($p < 0.05$). In two of these offices, this is combined with a switch from warning letters to fiscal fines. In a further two offices, there was a movement from warning letters to fiscal fines ($p < 0.05$). In summary, therefore, in just over one-half of procurator fiscal offices (26 out of 49), fiscal fine cases appear to be replacing warning letters and/or 'no pro' cases. The pattern in Office C—one of the four large offices from which a sample was taken—provides a good example of this phenomenon. It is clear from Figure 2 that despite increasing use being made of the fiscal fine, the district court prosecution rate has remained relatively unchanged and it is the 'no pro' rate which has dropped. This office has a high fiscal fine usage rate but the same pattern occurs in Office D where the rate is around the average.

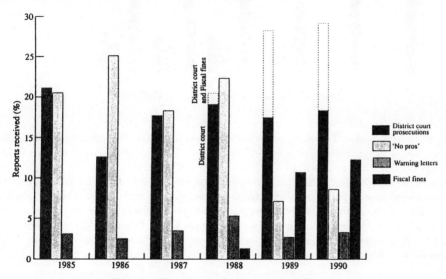

FIG. 2   Use of various disposals in Office C

On the other hand, in ten offices there are varying degrees of movement of cases from district court prosecution to the fiscal fine ($p < 0.05$). In other words, it appears that in these offices the fiscal fine is being used, to some extent, as was intended. In six of these offices, however, this phenomenon is combined with a movement from 'no pro' cases to fiscal fines and in one further office with a switch from warning letters to fiscal fines. Thus, in seven of the ten offices where the fiscal fine is operating to some extent as a direct replacement for district court prosecution, a degree of net-widening is also taking place.[17] A good example of the fiscal fine operating as intended is provided by Office B. It is clear from Figure 3 that the district court prosecution rate has dropped by roughly the same proportion as the fiscal fine rate has risen, while the 'no pro' rate has remained relatively stable and the use of warning letters has actually increased.

---

[17] Consequently, these seven offices are also included in the figures cited above.

PETER DUFF

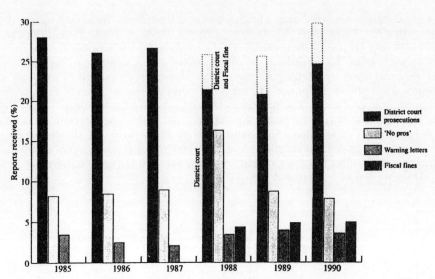

FIG. 3   Use of various disposals in Office B

Nevertheless, and still working on the assumption that other factors are constant, the general trend appears to be that of net-widening.[18] This is confirmed to an extent by findings which emerge from two other avenues of research. First, in the general questionnaire circulated to all fiscals, respondents were asked: 'In approximately what percentage of cases where you offer a fiscal fine would you have marked such cases for prosecution if the option of a fiscal fine had not been available?' The responses of the 165 fiscals who answered this question appear in Table 2 which demonstrates that many fiscals are prepared to admit, to varying degrees, to the issue of fiscal fines in cases where they would not have prosecuted.

TABLE 2   *Proportion of Fiscal Fine Cases which Fiscals*
would otherwise have Prosecuted

Percentage of cases prosecuted	No. of fiscals	Percentage of fiscals
100	69	41.8
90–9	41	24.6
80–9	25	15.6
70–9	13	7.9
60–9	17	10.3

[18] In eight offices, the only statistically significant movement of cases involved disposals other than the fiscal fine—for example, from 'no pro' to district court prosecution—and in 12 offices, all with low fiscal fine usage rates, there was no statistically significant movement of cases at all.

THE PROSECUTOR FINE AND SOCIAL CONTROL

Secondly, as regards each of the 578 cases gathered from the six separate samples, fiscals were asked (through the use of a pro forma) how they would have marked the case if the fiscal fine had not been available. The majority of responses indicated that, in such circumstances, the case would have been prosecuted in the district court. The apparent rate of prosecution in the four large offices ranged from 62.9 per cent in Office B to 93.3 per cent in Office D (and was 90 per cent and 100 per cent in the two smaller offices). Again, fiscals were clearly acknowledging that some net-widening was taking place.

It is obvious, however, that there is a discrepancy between the picture presented by the analysis of the official figures and fiscals' own accounts. The extent to which fiscals are prepared to admit to net-widening is insufficient to account for the degree to which this phenomenon has occurred according to the Crown Office Annual Statistical Returns.[19] How can one explain this discrepancy? One simple possibility runs as follows: fiscals are well aware of the purpose of the fiscal fine; in practice, however, the fiscal fine is used to some extent to drive down 'no pro' rates (for reasons which will be discussed below); fiscals are reluctant to admit to this explicitly; and, hence, it is understandable that fiscals will tend to claim that they are using the fiscal fine in the officially approved manner. Informal discussion with individual fiscals indicated that this explanation had some validity.

Another possible factor might be that fiscals were talking about the world as they would like it to be, not as it is. A fiscal who claims that he or she would have prosecuted an offender if the option of a fiscal fine had not been available, might simply mean that, ideally, he or she would like to have prosecuted that offender whereas, in reality, that course of action would have been unlikely because of the workload in his or her office or the district court waiting list. Thus, the high 'prosecution rates' might result from wishful thinking as well as a reluctance to admit to the reality of fiscal fine usage.

In summary, a considerable degree of net-widening is taking place. The calculations portrayed in Figure 1 lead to the conclusion that the majority of offenders who now receive a fiscal fine would previously have found their cases disposed of by a 'no pro' or a warning letter. Beyond that it is not safe to go; it is simply not possible to arrive at a reliable estimate of the proportion of cases in which a fiscal fine replaces prosecution. First, the variation between offices in the pattern of fiscal fine use renders any such attempt highly problematic. Secondly, the claims of fiscals cannot be taken at face value so it is impossible to arrive at reliable figures via this alternative route. Finally, as we shall see below, other factors have impinged to such an extent upon the movement of cases from one disposal to another that the best one can hope for is to identify the broad trends.

Possible Reasons for Net-widening

As we have seen, the official aim of the fiscal fine was to reduce the number of cases prosecuted in the district court, and the Crown Office guidelines on its use clearly reflect this policy. It would be naive, however, to assume that every initiative aimed at reforming or adjusting the operation of the criminal justice process works precisely as

---

[19] For example, Offices D and E claimed that, respectively, 93.3 per cent and 100 per cent of fiscal fine cases would previously have been prosecuted. These figures are inconsistent with the fact that in both offices, following the introduction of the fiscal fine, the district court prosecution rate remained at much the same level and the 'no pro' rate dropped substantially.

PETER DUFF

envisaged. The formal goal(s) and rules comprise only one set of factors that influence what happens in practice. All such initiatives are mediated and negotiated by the bureaucracies affected and by the individuals within such bureaucracies. Other relevant factors might include, for example: any ambiguity in the goals of the reform; the organizational aims of the agencies involved; conflict between the demands of production and of quality; the scarcity and uncertainty of resources; internal relationships with other criminal justice agencies; and external political relationships, both with government and the general community (see Blomberg 1977: 275). Thus, it is inevitable that various unofficial and, for this reason, relatively unacknowledged factors have contributed to the fact that many of those now receiving a fiscal fine would not previously have been prosecuted. What are these?

First, and probably most influential, there has recently been considerable political pressure upon procurators fiscal to attain 'no pro' rates which are consistent with those in other offices. In practice, greater emphasis has been placed upon the reduction of high 'no pro' rates. This demand originated in a parliamentary inquiry into the fiscal service by the Committee of Public Accounts (1989) and, in particular, a somewhat critical report by the National Audit Office (1989) commissioned for the inquiry. The report revealed *inter alia* that the 'no pro' rate varied widely between offices, ranging from 2.5 per cent in Forfar to 25.5 per cent in Edinburgh in 1987. As a result, the Committee of Public Accounts criticized the fiscal service in fairly strong terms and gave a particularly rough ride to the Crown Agent when he gave evidence before it. Concern centred around the following points: no explanation could be provided for the variation in 'no pro' rates; the Crown Office made no attempt to identify or monitor the reasons for 'no pro' cases; and, quite simply, the 'no pro' rates were much too high in many offices.

The effect of this concern was to produce widespread pressure upon the Crown Office and, consequently, upon many individual procurators fiscal to lower 'no pro' rates. Whatever influence this political pressure has had, there has certainly been a steady decline in the 'no pro' rate since such criticisms first surfaced. On a national basis, the rate has declined from 16.7 per cent in 1987, through 15.0 per cent in 1988 and 12.0 per cent in 1989, to 10.7 per cent in 1990.[20] In purely numerical terms, 59,019 cases were disposed of through the use of a 'no pro' in 1987, whereas by 1990 this figure had fallen to 40,813 cases. During this period, the 'no pro' rate fell in 31 of the 49 procurator fiscal offices, whereas it rose in only three offices, all of which had very low 'no pro' rates in the first place ($p < 0.05$).

The pressure to reduce 'no pro' rates arose shortly after the introduction of the fiscal fine. Against such a background, it is an obvious bureaucratic gambit to use the fiscal fine to drive down the 'no pro' rate rather than to reduce the number of district court prosecutions. This is likely to have proved a particularly attractive course of action in those offices with high 'no pro' rates; certainly, the nine offices in which the only discernible movement of cases was from 'no pro' to fiscal fine all had higher than average 'no pro' rates.[21]

[20] It is interesting to note that a 'no pro' rate of around 10 per cent was the historical norm until it began rising in the late 1970s.
[21] In the other 15 offices where there was a movement of cases from 'no pro' to fiscal fine, this was combined with other statistically significant trends, for example, 'no pro' to district court prosecution or district court prosecution to fiscal fine.

THE PROSECUTOR FINE AND SOCIAL CONTROL

Thus, while the decline in the 'no pro' rate is steeper than can be accounted for by the introduction of the fiscal fine, it is likely that the decrease has been achieved partially by marking cases for fiscal fines rather than for no proceedings. Ironically, it is possible that the existence of the fiscal fine served to mitigate the inevitable net-widening effect of the pressure to reduce 'no pro' rates. In short, the demand to reduce 'no pro' rates might well have been sufficiently strong to ensure that the present reduction would have been achieved whatever the available options. If this were so, it might be that the movement from 'no pro' to fiscal fine replaced a potential movement from 'no pro' to prosecution. In other words, perhaps many of those offenders affected by the pressure to reduce 'no pro' rates were given fiscal fines rather than being prosecuted. This can remain only in the realms of speculation but it does demonstrate the considerable difficulties involved in interpreting the raw data in this type of exercise.

A second factor which has probably contributed to the existence of net-widening is the creative use by fiscals of the fiscal fine. From the perspective of the fiscal engaged in marking cases, there is an obvious temptation to use the fiscal fine as an intermediate step between district court prosecution and the various alternatives thereto. Many fiscals emphasize that their attitude towards the disposal of cases is flexible and this claim is supported by the fact that prosecution now occurs in only around one-half of the cases reported to them.[22] Fiscals see themselves as skilled professionals, accustomed to acting creatively and responsibly, adept at assessing cases and disposing of them appropriately against a background of the demands made by the 'public interest' (see Moody and Tombs 1982). Throughout the marking process, the fiscal operates with a notional tariff of the various disposals according to their perceived level of severity. In finding the appropriate disposal for a case, the factor which is most influential upon a fiscal tends to be the perceived seriousness of the offence although the nature of the offender can also be influential.

It is natural, therefore, that the fiscal fine should appear to be the appropriate disposal for a borderline case where previously the fiscal would have had difficulty in deciding whether a prosecution was necessary or not. It represents a response which is seen to be more severe than a 'no pro' or a warning letter but which is not as severe as a prosecution. Striking evidence that this is the way in which the fiscal fine is sometimes perceived emerges from an important, recent text on criminal procedure:

It is envisaged that fiscal fines will be a half-way house to be used in cases which merit more than simply a warning but yet do not merit the full paraphernalia of prosecution . . . (Sheehan 1990: 73)

The statement is inaccurate but extremely illuminating. As we have seen, the fiscal fine was not intended to act as a 'half-way house' but that particular metaphor might well represent the way in which it has come to be used.

Further confirmation of this creative use of the fiscal fine emerged from the answers to the general questionnaire. Fiscals were asked whether they thought it worthwhile to offer a fiscal fine in a case which was so trivial that prosecution was not justified.

---

[22] In the only major piece of research into the fiscal service, Moody and Tombs (1982: 62) observed that fiscals were extremely prosecution minded. At that time, the relevant figures bore out this claim. Fiscals' attitudes appear to have changed in the interim and, indeed, many fiscals explicitly assert that the findings of Moody and Tombs would not be replicated today. In my view, their claim is credible.

PETER DUFF

Eighty-five fiscals (53.1 per cent) responded in the affirmative, yet the officially 'correct' answer would have been that a fiscal fine was not appropriate in such circumstances.[23] Of the 83 respondents who gave reasons for this stance, most felt that offenders should be 'punished' in some way or should not 'get away with it' or that society should 'mark its disapproval' of the offender's actions. Clearly such respondents thought that the fiscal fine was an appropriate disposal in cases where prosecution was too severe but other alternatives were too lenient.

A third factor was anticipated to some extent by the Stewart Committee itself. It expressed concern that cases were being marked 'no pro' as a result of a lack of resources and emphasized that it was important to introduce the prosecutor fine in order to maintain an acceptable level of enforcement within the current resources of the criminal justice system (1983: paras. 2.08, 4.38). It seems, therefore, that in the view of the Stewart Committee, some cases for which prosecution was the appropriate response were being marked 'no pro' purely as a result of pressure of work. This point was also acknowledged in the Scottish Standing Committee by the Solicitor-General in the debate over the legislation which introduced the fiscal fine (HC Deb. 1986-7: vol. 6, cols. 180-1, 198) and by the Crown Agent before the Committee of Public Accounts (1989: Minutes of Evidence, Q. 2073). Finally, in the general questionnaire circulated to all fiscals, ten of the 85 respondents who indicated that they would use a fiscal fine where prosecution was not justified commented that the impetus towards non-prosecution stems from excessive workloads and not from any feeling that offenders do not deserve to be punished.

It must be emphasized, however, that even if this factor were present, the movement of cases from 'no pro' to the fiscal fine would still amount to net-widening. It may be that the fiscal fine is serving to bring back into the criminal justice process some cases which, in an ideal world, would never have left it, but the inescapable fact is that they have left the system. It is impossible to assess the influence of this factor. The difficulties are exacerbated by the fact that its impact is likely to vary from office to office depending upon workloads and court waiting-times. Thus, in some offices the majority of fiscal fines might represent cases which previously would have been marked 'no pro' purely as a result of excessive workloads; in other offices, however, most fiscal fines might represent cases which previously would have escaped prosecution as the result of an unfettered decision that the case was too trivial to prosecute—albeit with a hint of prosecutorial regret that the offender was escaping rather lightly.

Is the Net Becoming Denser?

It would seem that with the introduction of the fiscal fine the net of the criminal justice process has spread itself wider. It must be emphasized, however, that only a partial account of the impact of the fiscal fine is provided by the quantitative assessment carried out above. The story can only be completed by a qualitative assessment and, thus, it is necessary to attempt to estimate the intensity of this apparent increase in activity by the criminal justice process. This can best be achieved by beginning with a

---

[23] Of the 75 fiscals who answered this question in the negative, only 28 noted that a fiscal fine should be offered solely in cases which would otherwise have been marked for prosecution. This represents the expected response and, in terms of the Crown Office guidelines, the correct response. Thus, of the 160 fiscals who answered this question, only 17.5 per cent explicitly echoed the 'official line'.

THE PROSECUTOR FINE AND SOCIAL CONTROL

description of what happened to the offenders in our samples who were offered a fiscal fine.

In each of the six samples, a high proportion of those offered a fiscal fine accepted. The take-up rate in the four large offices was remarkably consistent, ranging from 65.7 per cent in Office A (132 of 201 cases) to 73.3 per cent in Office B (63 out of 86 cases). (In Office E, 28 out of 31 alleged offenders accepted the offer, as did all ten in Office F.) Broadly speaking, it is the minority, namely those who do not accept the offer, who are sucked deeper into the criminal justice process. Before describing their fate, it is useful to outline what happened to those who accepted the offer.

What happened to those who accepted the fiscal fine?

Undoubtedly the most important point to emphasize is that payment of a fiscal fine does not amount to a criminal conviction. Thus, acceptance of a conditional offer does not affect an alleged offender's criminal record. In most procurator fiscal offices, an informal register of fiscal fines is kept but that is generally as far as the information goes. It is extremely rare—although not illegitimate—for the fact that someone has paid a fiscal fine to be made public. In essence, a fiscal fine is regarded as a private matter between the procurator fiscal and alleged offender. Thus, for those who previously would have escaped prosecution, there is virtually no chance of stigmatization while, for those who previously would have been prosecuted, the associated consequences are avoided.

In the majority of cases, alleged offenders paid their fiscal fines as a lump sum (i.e. £25) and this immediately ended their contact with the criminal justice system. A substantial minority, however, chose to pay by means of instalment (five payments of £5 at fortnightly intervals). In Office D, 23.5 per cent—27 of the 132 who accepted the offer—opted to pay in this way.[24] The proportion of those paying by instalment in Offices B and C was higher: respectively, 33.3 per cent—21 out of 63, and 46.2 per cent—18 out of 39. This was probably because these offices were situated in economically depressed areas of the country.[25] In Office E, eight out of 27—29.6 per cent—chose to pay by instalment while, in Office F, none of the ten offenders opted for this method. Both these offices were in economically healthy regions. (The relevant information as to the method of payment was unobtainable for Office A.)

In all areas, the pattern of payment by instalment was extremely irregular. Consequently, district court clerks were required to cite a number of alleged offenders to a Means Enquiry Court (MEC). From Office B, nine (of 21 paying by instalment) were cited to the MEC and from Office D, the equivalent figure was 13 (of 27). As regards Office C, a new computer at the relevant district court did not yet check that fines were being paid on time. However, 12 (of 18) alleged offenders were in arrears— by between five and eight months—by the end of the research period and would

---

[24] In 17 of the 132 cases, the record of the method of payment had been deleted at the district court before there was time to examine it. The speed of these deletions indicates that the alleged offenders had almost certainly paid their fines as lump sums.

[25] This interpretation is supported by the fact that in Office D, only one-fifth of the sample was unemployed whereas in Offices B and C, the relevant proportions were, respectively, well over one-third and over one-half. It is worth noting that unemployed persons were less likely to accept the offer of a fiscal fine in the first place and, where they did, less likely to pay it as a lump sum.

PETER DUFF

normally have been cited to the MEC. In Office E, three (of eight) were so far in arrears with their instalments that the clerk assured us that they would be taken before the next sitting of the MEC—this was a rural district where a MEC was only held occasionally.

An important aspect of the legislation is that enforcement lies through the civil law rather than through criminal procedure. Thus, the MEC may not impose imprisonment as an alternative to payment. In fact, the only reason that district court clerks call offenders to the MEC is that mere citation usually produces payment.[26] The ultimate sanction for the tardy payment of instalments is civil diligence which, in most cases, would involve a warrant sale (a compulsory sale of the person's goods). None of our informants had taken this step nor had they heard of it being carried out elsewhere. This was for two reasons. First, given the small amounts of money involved—£20 at the most (i.e. £25 minus the first instalment of £5)—a warrant sale would be uneconomic. Secondly, the controversy over the poll tax was at its height around the time of the research and the ultimate method for its enforcement was also civil diligence. Consequently, warrant sales were extremely unpopular. Several district court clerks commented that their 'political masters'—the various district councils—would not allow them to use this procedure. Thus, those offenders who accept a conditional offer cannot become further involved in the *criminal* justice process and, in practice, do not become further enmeshed in the *civil* justice process.

What happened to those who refused a fiscal fine?

What of those who did not take up the offer of a fiscal fine? The proportion prosecuted was high at around three-quarters. In the four large offices it was as follows: 72.5 per cent in Office A (49 out of 69); 77.8 per cent in Office C (14 out of 18); 79.3 per cent in Office D (46 out of 58); and 87.0 per cent in Office B (20 out of 23).[27] The logic of the process dictates this outcome: a fiscal fine should be offered only in cases which merit prosecution; thus, where the offer is refused, prosecution should automatically follow. Responses to the general questionnaire confirmed that prosecution was the normal response to failure to take up the offer of a fiscal fine. Of the 167 fiscals (from the sample of 176) who answered the relevant question, just over one-third (39.5 per cent) claimed that they would mark 100 per cent of such cases for prosecution, and a further half (49.1 per cent) indicated that they would pursue the same course of action in 90–9 per cent of such cases.

Respondents were asked to consider what the main reason(s) might be for not prosecuting in such cases. The most commonly cited factors were that the offender had absconded, mentioned by 90 of the 132 respondents to this question (68.2 per cent), and the operation of time-bars, referred to by 32 fiscals (24.2 per cent). The latter problem is likely to be exacerbated by the fact that delays are common at all stages in the process: receipt of the crime report from the police; initial marking for a fiscal fine;

---

[26] At the time the research was conducted, there was some legal debate as to whether it was competent to cite alleged offenders to the MEC for non-payment of the outstanding instalments of a fiscal fine. It now seems to be generally accepted that citation is competent, albeit that the MEC has no power to impose the alternative of imprisonment or even vary the time-scale for payment.

[27] In Office E, only one of the three non-acceptors was prosecuted and, in Office F, the question did not arise because everyone paid the fiscal fine.

THE PROSECUTOR FINE AND SOCIAL CONTROL

return of the file from the district court if the offer is not accepted; re-marking of the case. The logic of the process is not upset by non-prosecution for either of the above reasons; prosecution would take place were it not for supervening events.

Returning to the sampling exercise, it is interesting to note that it was relatively rare for an alleged offender to have refused the offer of a fiscal fine in order to deny the charges.[28] Overall, 80 persons pled guilty compared with 21 who entered pleas of not guilty.[29] Virtually all of the latter group were subsequently convicted: overall, only two out of the seventeen trials which had taken place by the end of the research period resulted in acquittal.[30]

Of the 94 offenders who were convicted, only 30 had no previous convictions. The proportion of those with no previous convictions in the total sample was significantly higher—at around one-half. Thus, as one might anticipate, people with no previous convictions were more likely to accept the offer of a fiscal fine than those with a criminal record. Clearly, the incentive to avoid a criminal conviction was greater in the case of those with a clean record.

A fine was the almost invariable outcome of a district court appearance. From Office A, 22 persons were fined and two had their sentences deferred. Fines ranged from £25 to £100, with an average of £59. From Office B, 17 offenders were fined sums ranging from £10 to £100—the average was around £40—and one sentence was deferred.[31] From Office C, seven offenders were fined, one was admonished and one had his sentence deferred (and two were acquitted). The average fine was around £46, the range running from £25 to £80. Finally, the sample from Office D produced 40 fines, one admonition and two deferred sentences. The average fine was around £42. This office covers two district court jurisdictions and the busier court was responsible for 33 fines at an average of around £39.

For comparative purposes, a sample of 161 district court cases was taken from the latter court, excluding traffic offences and cases where there was a prior offer of a fiscal fine. The 'district court' sample produced: 111 fines; 42 admonitions; three acquittals; three absolute discharges and two jail sentences. The average fine was around £43. When the different types of offence were analysed separately, the fine levels in each sample remained very similar. The most striking difference between the two samples was that around a quarter of the cases in the district court sample resulted in admonition compared with only one of the 34 cases in the fiscal fine sample. If those cases where the offender was merely admonished are deemed to represent a fine of £0, the average fine drops to just over £31 for the district court sample compared with

[28] Virtually everyone cited to court appeared. Two offenders from Office A, two from Office B, and one from Office C did not. Warrants were issued in these cases and, hence, the offenders were becoming increasingly enmeshed in the criminal justice process.
[29] The numbers pleading guilty were as follows: Office A—20 out of 28; Office B—18 out of 18; Office C—seven out of 11; Office D—34 out of 43; and Office E—one out of one.
[30] Both of these were from Office C. It is striking that of 578 persons offered a fiscal fine only two were ultimately found not guilty. It must be remembered, however, that four of the eight not guilty pleas from Office A had not come to trial by the conclusion of the research. Whatever the outcome in these cases, it is clear that only a tiny proportion of those offered a fiscal fine eventually secured an acquittal. This has interesting implications which I hope to develop elsewhere.
[31] It must be noted that fine levels varied over the three district courts within Office B's jurisdiction: in one court, six offenders were fined an average of around £25; in another, ten were fined an average of £49; and in the third court, the remaining offender was fined £45. These figures were consistent with the experience of local fiscals. Despite fiscals' fears that the reduced fine level in the first court would lead to a low fiscal fine take-up rate, this did not appear to be the case.

PETER DUFF

£38 for the fiscal fine sample. The harsher treatment of the fiscal fine sample might, at first, seem odd because it is those cases which have been deemed by the fiscal to be the more trivial. The explanation, we were informed, lies in the attitude of the justices in the district court: apparently, it is felt that, first, those refusing a fiscal fine have missed their opportunity to be dealt with lightly and, secondly, if an incentive to accept the fiscal fine is to be maintained, those who refuse the offer must be fined more than £25. In such cases, therefore, it would seem that offenders are dealt with more severely than if they had not been offered a fiscal fine in the first place.

Summary of outcomes

At this point, it is helpful to summarize the experiences, first, of those persons who accepted the conditional offer and, secondly, of those who did not.

1. Over two-thirds of those offered a fiscal fine accepted the opportunity to avoid prosecution and a possible criminal conviction (404 out of 578). The majority paid by lump sum (£25), immediately ending their involvement with the criminal justice system. A minority paid by instalment. Enforcement proceedings were taken against a few of the latter group but the effects of this step were minimal.

2. Around one-third of the sample did not take up the offer of a fiscal fine. Of these, a narrow majority (94 out of 174) were ultimately convicted in the district court. This represented around one-sixth of *all* those offered a fiscal fine. While the majority of this sub-group had prior criminal convictions, around one-third did not. Finally, in cases where the offer of a fiscal fine was rejected, offenders appear to have been fined a slightly higher sum in the district court than would have been the case if their files had simply been marked for prosecution in the first instance.

The Fiscal Fine and Social Control

At this stage, it is essential to make a fundamental point which is often ignored by proponents of the 'dispersal of discipline thesis'. The fact that a degree of net-widening is taking place does not automatically lead to the conclusion that the state is thereby intruding further into the life of its citizens. The evidence shows that while many diversionary schemes result in some offenders becoming more deeply entangled in the state's network of social control, most such initiatives do succeed to some extent in reducing the involvement of other offenders. As McMahon (1990: 141) notes, much of the research on 'community corrections' has emphasized the former process and ignored the latter:

Identification of the negative consequences of penal reform has been given priority over identifying more beneficial ones.

Cohen makes a similar point in his more recent writings, claiming that it is only 'the dark side' of diversion that is exposed and that 'a sensitivity to success' should be cultivated (1987: 36). In short, much of the literature glosses over the fact that diversionary measures are rarely a complete failure.

498

THE PROSECUTOR FINE AND SOCIAL CONTROL

Thus, while it appears likely that the introduction of the fiscal fine has led to some degree of net-widening by the Scottish criminal justice process, that does not, of itself, prove that the measure has led to an overall increase in state intervention into offenders' lives. Certainly, some offenders are now faced with a fiscal fine rather than simply receiving a warning letter or discovering that no proceedings are to be taken, but it has to be recognized that other offenders now receive a fiscal fine instead of being prosecuted in the district court. Obviously, the extent to which state intervention is increasing or decreasing depends upon the balance between these two processes. This is not simply a question of quantitative assessment, as is often assumed, but of qualitative assessment too. For example, the subjects of a diversion scheme may comprise 50 per cent 'new' cases and 50 per cent 'genuinely diverted' cases. That does not mean to say that the overall effect of the scheme upon the state's network of social control is neutral. Obviously, any accurate assessment of the impact of a diversionary initiative involves comparing the extent to which state intervention is increased in the 'new' cases as against the extent to which it is decreased in the 'genuinely diverted' cases.

From this perspective, it is apparent that the advent of the fiscal fine does not seem to strengthen the state's network of social control in Scotland. As we saw above, around two-thirds of those given a fiscal fine accepted the offer. Of this group, those who were 'genuinely diverted' avoided criminal conviction (and the various consequences thereof), whereas those who represented 'new' cases were simply £25 out of pocket.[32] Viewed qualitatively, the reduction in social control in the former type of case is likely to outweigh the increased intervention in the latter type of case. (The quantitative imbalance between 'new' cases and 'genuinely diverted' cases would need to be great in order for an overall increase in social control to have taken place.) The picture is the same as regards the one-third of alleged offenders who did not take up the offer of a fiscal fine. Ultimately, only about one-half of these were convicted in the district court, that is one-sixth of all of those originally offered a fiscal fine. Most of this group were unlikely to be significantly affected by another conviction for a minor criminal offence. Thus, unless there were almost no 'genuinely diverted' offenders in the other five-sixths of cases, there is unlikely to have been an overall increase in social control.

In theoretical terms, the introduction of the fiscal fine does not support the darker forebodings of those devotees of conspiracy who see net-widening as a deliberate ploy by the state to strengthen surreptitiously its network of social control. The alleged transformation to a 'disciplinary' society has not been advanced by the advent of the fiscal fine. On the contrary, as we saw above, the ordinary court fine is recognized as being one of the least invasive sanctions exercised by the criminal justice process (see Bottoms 1983). Both Matthews (1987) and Rodger (1988) have claimed that Bottoms underestimates the 'disciplinary' aspect of the fine, primarily because it is underpinned by the threat of imprisonment, but this point does not apply to the fiscal fine which involves neither imprisonment for failure to pay nor criminal conviction.

At this point, it is useful to return to the Stewart Committee's (1983) report. It will be remembered that as well as recommending the adoption of the fiscal fine, the Committee also suggested that other alternatives to prosecution be implemented,

---

[32] As explained above, it was impossible either to distinguish the 'genuinely diverted' cases from the 'new' cases in the sample or to arrive at the precise proportion of each via any other route, for instance, by using the Crown Office Annual Statistical Returns.

including: medical or psychiatric treatment; social work intervention; and reparation (paras. 3.23–32). These disposals were recognized[33] at around the same time as the fiscal fine was introduced. It is significant that these alternatives to prosecution have come to be known by those involved in the Scottish criminal justice process as 'diversion'.[34] The terminology betrays a similar preconception to that held by the criminological theorists who have constructed the 'dispersal of discipline thesis' around the introduction of therapeutic-type disposals. Both groups view the prosecutor fine as something rather different from 'diversion'. Yet the fiscal fine clearly represents a form of diversion in that, quite simply, it diverts offenders from the normal process of prosecution.[35]

The respective fortunes of each of these alternatives to prosecution are interesting. In 1991, there were 1,400 cases of 'diversion' compared with 15,599 fiscal fines; in 1990, the respective figures were 1,403 and 16,985; in 1989, they were 1,175 and 15,556; and, in 1988, they were 1,014 and 9,304. Thus, the fiscal fine is used in around ten times more cases than 'diversion'. In short, this mundane, administrative form of diversion affects far more people than the more dramatic, therapeutic-type measures to which many criminological theorists attach such significance.

Rather than illustrating the 'dispersal of discipline' thesis or bearing out fears about 'net-widening', the advent of the fiscal fine seems to exemplify a rather different trend in criminal justice systems. This has recently been identified by a number of commentators. Peters (1986), in perhaps the best exposition, labels the new approach as the 'Social Control School of Criminal Law'—as opposed to the 'Classical School' or the 'Modern or Criminological School'. In brief, he argues that exponents of this new school of thought tend to view the criminal law simply as one method of social control. Whether the criminal law is used or not thus becomes a matter of policy, governed primarily by issues of cost, efficiency, and ease of management. Accordingly, the legal, moral, and humanitarian considerations which influence the other two schools of thought assume less importance. In Peters' words, 'Strategic thought has thus taken over from normative thought' (1986: 33–4). Bottoms, in his critique of the 'dispersal of discipline thesis' makes essentially the same point when he talks of a current trend towards an 'essentially bureaucratic–administrative law-enforcement system' (1983: 185–7).[36] Analysis of this development in penal theory is beyond the scope of the present article but it does appear to provide a useful framework for locating the fiscal fine in terms of penal policy.

[33] It would be inaccurate to state that these disposals were *introduced* following the deliberations of the Stewart Committee. Such measures were already used informally by procurators fiscal for it has always been within their discretion not to proceed with a case on the basis that the offender is receiving the appropriate help or has made reparation to the victim of his crime. The Stewart Committee's recommendations simply provided official encouragement to use this type of disposal and led to the Crown Office attempting to formalize existing practices.

[34] For example, the Crown Office Annual Statistical Returns have separate columns for recording the numbers of 'fiscal fines' and 'diversions'.

[35] The fact that 'diversion' may have a number of legitimate goals is often passed over in the criminological literature. There is often an assumption that the aim of diversion is primarily therapeutic. As Palmer points out, a diversion scheme may be set up with any one of the following goals, or combination thereof, in mind: avoidance of stigmatization; provision of assistance to the needy; prevention of recidivism; reduction of unneccessary social control; and cutting expenditure on the criminal justice system (quoted in Decker 1985: 208).

[36] Young also arrives at similar conclusions when he identifies a new approach which he characterizes as 'administrative criminology' (1986: 9–12).

The introduction and operation of the fiscal fine illustrates nicely an increasingly bureaucratic and administrative approach to crime, criminals, and the criminal law. As we have seen, the Stewart Committee was set up to consider how to reduce the pressure, which was resulting from the volume of summary prosecution, upon the courts and the fiscal service. It was thus concerned with diversion primarily as a method of facilitating the efficient and cost-effective management of cases rather than for any other reasons. Its principal recommendation, namely the introduction of the prosecutor fine, betrays a preconception that the major problem presented by minor crime is essentially administrative. Consequently, the solution is the introduction of a measure which enables a range of petty offences to be dealt with by straightforward, bureaucratic procedures. Broadly speaking, the functionaries who operate the system adopt a similar perspective. Consequently, the discourse surrounding the fiscal fine attaches little importance either to the legal and moral content of the criminal law (the main concern of the 'Classical School') or to the appropriate treatment of offenders (the main concern of the 'Criminological School'). Such issues are simply not regarded as central.

The above argument must not be overstated however. As various commentators have observed (Bottoms 1983; Cohen 1987; Matthews 1987), the criminal justice process is not a unified, coherent whole. It comprises a variety of agencies with differing interests and embodies several competing strands of thought. Each element of the criminal justice process represents a different balance between these competing ideologies and interests. It may be possible to identify an overall current of change within the system but individual developments are not all moving in the same direction or at the same speed.

This is demonstrated by the fact that the Stewart Committee did not adopt exclusively the 'Social Control School' of thought. For example, in considering the possible justifications for diversion, it made the following points as regards minor cases: prosecution may be an over-reaction; it is potentially stigmatising; and it may be unsuitable for offenders in need of help (1983: para. 2.22). Further, as we saw above, the Committee did recommend the introduction of diversion for psychiatric treatment or social work intervention. The motive here was purely humanitarian; the Committee did not envisage that such measures would divert significant numbers of cases and thus conserve resources (paras. 3.23–30). Similarly, fiscals adopt perspectives other than that of 'Social Control'. For example, some were concerned that use of the fiscal fine ought not to be increased lest fiscals stray too far upon judicial territory, thus breaching constitutional convention. Others favoured expansion of the system because it would better enable them to deal humanely with petty offenders. On a practical level, many fiscals noted that the fiscal fine allowed them to 'mark society's disapproval' of the offender's behaviour in a more meaningful way than issuing a warning letter, whereas others commented that the fiscal fine enabled them to fire a 'warning shot' at the first-time offender without having to saddle him with a criminal conviction.

Nevertheless, it does appear that the primary effect of the introduction of the fiscal fine is to advance the 'bureaucratic–administrative' approach which has previously applied only to offences which are obviously regulatory in nature, such as illegal parking and minor road traffic offences. What is significant is that the operation of this approach now extends well beyond what might conventionally be regarded as regulatory crimes. It is interesting that the sample of 578 cases included 40 assaults, 76

PETER DUFF

thefts and 172 breaches of the peace.[37] The change in approach to such offences has interesting implications, even more so if the fiscal fine system is eventually expanded by enabling fiscals to operate a sliding scale of penalties as the Stewart Committee recommended (1983: paras. 4.34–6).[38] As Garland has recently emphasized, an important aspect of any penal disposal is the meaning that is ascribed to it. Punishment is a complex social and cultural institution, comprising *inter alia* 'a statement of collective morality, a vehicle of emotional expression, an embodiment of current sensibilities and a set of symbols which display a cultural ethos and help create a social identity' (1990: 287). The 'Social Control School' tends to ignore the meaning(s) of punishment. Yet the offer of a fiscal fine—or any other administrative penalty—might be seen to say something about society's attitude to the offence in respect of which it is offered. The consequences of the change of approach described above are potentially far-reaching but it is beyond the scope of this article even to attempt to grapple with these.

REFERENCES

AUSTIN, J., and KRISBERG, B. (1981), 'Wider, Stronger and Different Nets: The Dialectics of Criminal Justice Reform', *Journal of Research in Crime and Delinquency*, 18: 165–196.
BLOMBERG, T. (1977), 'Diversion and Accelerated Social Control', *Journal of Criminal Law and Criminology*, 68: 274–82.
BOTTOMS, A. E. (1983), 'Neglected Features of Contemporary Penal Systems', in D. Garland and P. Young, eds., *The Power to Punish*: 166–202. London: Heinemann.
COHEN, S. (1985), *Visions of Social Control*. Cambridge: Polity.
—— (1987), 'Taking Decentralization Seriously: Values, Visions and Policies', in J. Lowman *et al.*, eds, *Transcarceration: Essays in the Sociology of Social Control*: 358–79. Aldershot: Gower.
COMMITTEE of PUBLIC ACCOUNTS (1989), *Prosecution of Crime in Scotland*, 35th Report, House of Commons 1988–9. London: HMSO.
DECKER, S. (1985), 'A Systemic Analysis of Diversion: Net Widening and Beyond', *Journal of Criminal Justice*, 13: 207–16.
GARLAND, D. (1990), *Punishment and Modern Society*. Oxford: Oxford University Press.
HC DEB. (1986–7), vol. 6: cols. 180–1, 198.
JONES, P. (1990), 'Expanding the Use of Non-Custodial Sentencing Options: An Evaluation of the Kansas Community Corrections Act', *Howard Journal*, 29: 114–29.
LOWMAN, J., MENZIES, R. J., and PALYS, T. S., eds. (1987), *Transcarceration: Essays in the Sociology of Social Control*. Aldershot: Gower.
McIVOR, G. (1990), 'Community Service and Custody in Scotland', *Howard Journal*, 29: 101–13.
McMAHON, M. (1990), 'Net-widening: Vagaries in the Use of a Concept', *British Journal of Criminology*, 30: 121–49.

[37] These are common law offences. The other offences which occurred frequently were statutory and primarily regulatory in nature: 144 cases of urinating to the public annoyance (contrary to s. 47 of the Civic Government (Scotland) Act 1982); 63 offences of drunkenness (contrary to s. 50(1) of the Civic Government (Scotland) Act 1982 or s. 74 of the Criminal Justice (Scotland) Act 1980; and 54 offences under various Railways Acts (primarily involving trespass on railway lines).
[38] It is interesting to note that much more extensive use is made of the prosecutor fine in the Netherlands where prosecutors are empowered to use a sliding scale. This enables the mechanism to be used for a much wider range of offences—many fairly serious—than is the case in Scotland.

THE PROSECUTOR FINE AND SOCIAL CONTROL

MATTHEWS, R. (1987), 'Decarceration and Social Control: Fantasies and Realities', in J. Lowman *et al.*, eds., *Transcarceration: Essays in the Sociology of Social Control*: 338–57. Aldershot: Gower.

MOODY, S. R., and TOMBS, J. (1982), *Prosecution: In the Public Interest.* Edinburgh: Scottish Academic Press.

NATIONAL AUDIT OFFICE (1989), *Prosecution of Crime in Scotland: Review of the Procurator Fiscal Service.* London: HMSO.

PETERS, A. A. G. (1986), 'Main Currents in Criminal Law Theory', in J. van Dijk, C. Haffmans, F. Ruter, J. Schutte, and S. Stolwijk, eds., *Criminal Law in Action*, 19–36. Deventer: Kluwer.

RODGER, J. J. (1988), 'Social Work as Social Control Re-examined: Beyond the Dispersal of Discipline Thesis', *Sociology*, 22: 563–81.

SHEEHAN, A. V. (1990), *Criminal Procedure.* Edinburgh: Butterworths.

SCOTTISH OFFICE (1992), *Statistical Bulletin*, Criminal Justice Series CRJ/1992/6. Edinburgh: Scottish Office.

STEDWARD, G., and MILLAR, A. (1989), *Diversion from Prosecution: Diversion to Social Work.* Edinburgh: Scottish Office Central Research Unit Paper.

STEWART COMMITTEE (1980), *The Motorist and Fixed Penalties*, 1st Report, Cmnd. 8027. Edinburgh: HMSO.

——— (1983), *Keeping Offenders Out of Court: Further Alternatives to Prosecution*, 2nd Report, Cmnd. 8958. Edinburgh: HMSO.

YOUNG, P. (1992), 'The Importance of Utopias in Criminological Thinking', *British Journal of Criminology*, 32: 423–37.

[9]

BRIT. J. CRIMINOL. Vol. 29 No. 3 SUMMER 1989

CORPORATISM: THE THIRD MODEL OF JUVENILE JUSTICE

JOHN PRATT (*Wellington*)*

Juvenile justice developments tend to be conceptualized and explained in terms of their accommodation within the respective parameters of the welfare and justice models. Historically, the welfare era in England and Wales reached its peak in the early 1970s. Since then, the justice model has assumed ideological dominance. However, the reality of juvenile justice policies and practices would seem to be more closely in line with a third model, that of corporatism. The paper sets out its form and terms, arguing that it is a more appropriate description of the contemporary Anglo-Welsh juvenile justice system.

Since the 1908 Children Act, the framework of juvenile justice of England and Wales has been periodically redrawn and refurbished to take account of shifts in the prevailing ideological balance. For example, in the 1920s attempts to take the juvenile justice system further along a welfare trajectory by abolishing corporal punishment and raising the age of criminal responsibility were rejected (Departmental Committee on the Treatment of Young Offenders 1927; see also Bailey 1987). On the other hand, the 1933 Children and Young Persons Act prescribed that the welfare of the child would be paramount in juvenile court proceedings. Post-1945, there were attempts to reconstruct juvenile justice in just the same way that there were attempts to reconstruct social policy in general in this area (Taylor 1981).

If, though, there has been no unilinear path to policy development, for much of this century the path that reform *should* take was much clearer. The virtues of the welfare model came to be the taken for granted way forward: each step away from formal procedures, courtroom procedures, and so on was seen as a step in the direction of progress. Hence the consensus on the need for informal proceedings in the juvenile court. As far as possible, lawyers should have a reduced role, if they were to have a role at all, while that of child care experts would be enhanced. Legal discourse should give way to a professional language with psychodynamic rather than juridical roots—hence the subsequent proliferation, in the 1960s and 1970s, of keywords such as 'needs', 'treatment', 'assessment', and so on.

Who were the experts? For the most part they were not analysts and psychologists, but rather probation and child care officers and eventually social workers, the mundane representatives of a diverse group of people trained to varying levels of intensity in the pedagogy of human relationships. Social workers and the like would suffice for the run-of-the-mill case: the more refined, it was thought, the more exotic or inexplicable the behaviour, the greater degree of expertise that was needed. The more

* LLB, MA, PhD, Senior Lecturer in Criminology, Institute of Criminology, Victoria University of Wellington, New Zealand.

I should like to thank Dr Pat O'Malley, Department of Legal Studies, Latrobe University, for helpful comments made during the preparation of this paper; and to acknowledge the suggestions of anonymous reviewers.

CORPORATISM: THE THIRD MODEL OF JUVENILE JUSTICE

unusual it was, the more skilled the expert, and the rarer their appearance in court (as in the case of psychiatrists).

Even so, social workers in particular among this group were unhappy with their courtroom role, accepting this feature of their occupation very begrudgingly—it went against the trend towards preventive social work in the 1950s and 1960s. This helps to explain the ambivalent position taken by many social workers in the aftermath of the 1969 Children and Young Persons Act, which had further enhanced their courtroom space (e.g. the provision for social enquiry reports on all juvenile offenders). On the one hand the court provided them with power and authority; on the other it was best if they maintained a 'casual approach' (e.g. in terms of dress, manner, and attitude in court, and so on) so as to reassure their clients as to whose side they were supposed to be on.

What other dimensions were there to the reform trajectory? One such was individualized sentencing—that 'dominating principle of modern penology' (Mannheim 1946: 228). This would be paramount, whether or not a courtroom setting was retained for the dispensation of juvenile justice. It was as if there should be a symbiosis between diagnosis and sentence, as indicated in the following prescription:

It is necessary to develop further our facilities for observation and assessment, and to increase the variety of facilities for continuing treatment, both residential and non-residential. Increased flexibility is needed so as to make it easier to vary the treatment when changed circumstances or fuller diagnosis suggest the need for a different approach. (Home Office 1968: 20)

Such ideas helped to provide the justification for quasi-indeterminate sentences (e.g. approved school orders, Borstal training orders), or dispositions which would be left to the discretion of social workers to administer (such as care orders and intermediate treatment). Need for and response to treatment, rather than exactitude between punishment and offence, should organize social work intervention. Thus West (1967: 215), writing at the highpoint of welfare thought, claimed that 'the juvenile courts *are meant to be* welfare agencies as well as dispensers of punishment, and they do in fact take into account a great deal more than just the nature of the offence that has brought a child before trial' (emphasis added). Accordingly, social workers and welfare experts would have an entire tradition of penal reform on their side—'the great movement from the doctrines of the classical school to those of the sociological school . . . has first and foremost meant the replacement of the aim of retribution by that of reformation'—the inference being that this would lead to 'the more scientific and humane treatment of the juvenile' (Mannheim 1946: 1). Glueck and Glueck (1960: 1) classified among 'all the reform devices of the present century' various forms of welfare disposition—'the juvenile court, probation, the indeterminate sentence, classifications without institutions . . .'. For Radzinowicz (1966: 115), the progression of penal history had been shaped by two competing forces—'the backward looking elements of retribution may clash with the forward looking object of reform'. The latter, of course, was associated with the evolution of the welfare model.

However, we know that from the mid-1970s the march of history ceased to be on the side of welfare. The 'new orthodoxy' (Jones 1984) of the emergent 'justice model' took policy off at a different tangent and reversed many of the previous taken-for-granted assumptions about 'the way forward'. I will argue, though, that the welfare–justice dichotomy should not be seen as forming the analytical parameters of juvenile justice

237

JOHN PRATT

debate. Instead, this simply laid the foundation stones on which a third model—that of *corporatism*[1]—has been built. Let us now examine why this should be so.

Back to Justice

A number of criticisms of welfare began to emerge in the 1970s which undercut its dominance:

1. *The ineffectiveness of treatment-type intervention* (which the welfare model encouraged) in preventing recidivism (Brody 1976).

2. *Evidence of the inhumanity of welfare:* care that could be more coercive than punishment, the injustices and disparities of individual sentencing, particularly in relation to group offenders, and so on (Taylor *et al.*, 1978).

3. *The critique of the status of expert:* a number of studies began to point to the way in which common sense, agency structure, and routine rather than unique professional knowledge informed the practices of child care experts and such like (Giller and Morris 1981).

4. *The ineffectiveness of welfare in controlling delinquency:* magistrates expressed concern about delinquents being 'set free' by their social workers, or being provided with 'treats' rather than punishment, after court orders had been made (see House of Commons 1975; Morgan 1978).

It was out of such critiques that an alternative juvenile justice discourse—justice itself—began to emerge. This stipulated first that the *process* of juvenile justice should be reorganized. This would mean the abandonment of the 'closed, informal and non-adversarial proceedings in the juvenile courts' (Morris 1978) and its replacement by due process, right to counsel, visible and accountable decision-making, and so on (Morris *et al.* 1980). In effect, such ideas necessitate a return to a *Gesellschaft* legal process if they are to be implemented. This

emphasizes formal procedure, impartiality, adjudicative justice, precise legal provisions and definitions and the rationality and predictability of legal administration. It distinguishes sharply between law and administration, between the public and the private, the legal and the moral, between the civil obligation and the criminal offence. (Kamenka and Tay 1975: 137)

Second, after adjudication of guilt, the court should then impose *punishment:* this 'gets rid of individualized penalties, indefinite periods of control and wide discretion' (Morris and McIsaac 1978: 155).[2] Here was a reform movement, then, that instead of being forward looking, delved into the past and resurrected the long since discarded ideas of classical penology, such as the moral obligation to inflict punishment and the right to receive it (Kant 1929), the need for certainty in punishment delivery, and approximation of punishment content to the degree of harm done (Beccaria [1764], 1963).

Although in the USA the 'back to justice' ideas have been influential in both adult and juvenile penal systems (von Hirsch 1976, 1986), in England and Wales it has been more the juvenile justice system that has become their receptacle, where indeed

---

[1] It is interesting that some of the few exceptions to the welfare/justice dichotomy refer to 'the corporate approach', e.g. Tutt (1984), Bowden and Stevens (1986).
[2] Morris and McIsaac were referring to the Scottish Children's Hearing process.

CORPORATISM: THE THIRD MODEL OF JUVENILE JUSTICE

welfare traditions were most pronounced and thus most vulnerable to the justice critique.

For the justice movement there is thus a necessity to impose punishment. This would constitute *retribution*,[3] but in a precise and restricted form: least restrictive intervention; minimum programmes rather than maximum; community-based rather than custodial sentences. Moreover, such punishment is to be worked out in accordance with a penological mathematics.

We propose that there should be a tripartite division of sanctions: nominal, custodial and non custodial . . . We have set an upper limit of 12 months for custodial sanctions and of 18 months for non custodial sanctions. (Morris *et al.* 1980: 72)

There is thus no scope for open-ended and indefinite social work intervention. At the same time, the specificity of the offence rather than a generic set of problems determines the form and mode of administration of punishment. Supervision, for example,

becomes a method of controlling the offender within the community. The question for the sentencer who is considering a supervision order is not 'Does this offender need help?' but rather 'How much control does this offender deserve in the light of the nature and circumstances of the offence he has committed?' (ibid. 76)

This in turn necessitates important changes in the available written and spoken language to express the major conceptual shift from treatment to punishment.

Social enquiry reports, though retained, would have a fundamentally different role and character. These reports are traditionally based on opinion rather than on scientifically based fact, and their current use is premised on the mistaken belief that we know what the needs of a particular child are and what the appropriate disposition to meet those 'needs' is. We do not know, and we should not pretend otherwise. (ibid.)

Similarly, in relation to programme content: exit the welfare-oriented 'continuum of care' into which any child could be accommodated depending on his or her needs (Paley and Thorpe 1974); enter, in its place, the 'correctional curriculum', a programme related 'specifically to the delinquent actions of individuals' (Denman 1982: 43).

The translation of justice-model ideas into penal practice also demands a new technology of social work. 'Gatekeepers' (Thorpe *et al.* 1980), for example, must filter and assess referrals to ensure that alternatives to custody do actually operate as such. It becomes necessary to undertake such tasks as checking social enquiry reports to ensure that there are no incorrect recommendations, and to negotiate with magistrates and other agencies to convince them of the value of these new policies and the role all

[3] It is recognized, of course, that there are tensions and differences between the various proponents of justice. Generally, it could be argued that the right-wing, 'punishing criminals' movement (e.g. Wilson 1975; Morgan 1978) sees itself as 'just' by so doing; against this the liberal 'back to justice' movement, which had the ideological ascendancy in the late 1970s, tended to argue for due process and rights, *within which framework* convicted offenders would be legitimately punished. At the same time, there are some important distinctions in the liberal camp between the North American and British justice theorists   most significantly, perhaps, over the issue of deterrence —one of the cornerstones of classical penology (Beccaria [1764] 1963). Although this is inscribed in von Hirsch's (1976) framework, it is rejected by Morris *et al.* (1980: 50–1) on ethical grounds ('Is *any* punishment justifiable to deter this offender or potential offender?'); and on the basis of dubious effectiveness ('Research suggests that the criminal justice system has at best an indirect effect on general socialisation rather than an impact on each crime instance in which pros and cons are weighed in a rational manner').

JOHN PRATT

concerned have to play in their implementation. It becomes important, then, to develop an *information base*. Tutt, for example, speaks of the need for

a strategy for community-based programmes for managing juvenile offending and offenders . . . a co-ordinated approach involving several formal and informal agencies and methods, and based on *specific information of where delinquency occurs, at what times, both of the day and year, and who are the delinquents* . . . (1979: 5, emphasis added)

In these respects we see a greater degree of specialization within social work organizations. In place of the child care experts with their too broad and too ill defined generic interests, the *juvenile justice specialist* steps forward (Kerslake 1984). He or she is required to demonstrate capabilities and skills as detailed in the following advertisement for the position of Principal Assistant (Intermediate Treatment):

This post is responsible for developing and monitoring controlled treatment programmes in the community and is particularly suitable for an enthusiastic person who is committed to the policy of reducing the numbers of young children and young persons referred to the courts for institutional care.

The [person] will be accountable . . . for the further development of new forms of I.T. which are changing the emphasis locally from general preventative to activities intensive, specialization in dealing with delinquents and for the monitoring and co-ordination of procedures and practices used by the Department and other agencies in dealing with delinquency. Only persons with a social work qualification, extensive experience in working on programmes designed to deal with delinquency and a detailed knowledge of the juvenile court systems need apply. (*Social Work Today*, 17 Dec. 1984: 35)

For these specialists, courtwork is no longer the most unpopular aspect of the social work repertoire. On the contrary, it becomes one of the most important: social workers abandon their diagnostic heritage and instead become *quasi-advocates*—almost as if they are *de facto* lawyers, but with a guaranteed social conscience. One of the best illustrations of this is the way in which juvenile justice specialists have, with considerable success, become involved in appeals against sentence, particularly custodial sentences (see Johnson and Green 1985). Similarly, Johnson and Holt (1986), as representatives of the Association for Juvenile Justice, argue for alliances not with the child care experts of generic social work but, *inter alia*, with lawyers and law-oriented pressure groups ('the Haldane Society of Socialist Lawyers, . . . the Law Society . . . the Children's Legal Centre . . .', ibid. 3).

In addition, we can see the development of a number of local policies and initiatives which correspond, at least on a prima facie basis, to various principles of the justice model, while at the same time appearing to confirm its ideological hegemony. Thus, the separate tiers of intermediate treatment orders that are now available to the court in many local authority areas seem to speak to (*a*) the least restrictive intervention principle—they are designed as alternatives to custody (non-custody presumed to be a lesser punishment than custody) and (*b*) the necessity for an exactitude between punishment and offence—each tier is designed to cater for different kinds of offence and offending behaviour: 'the intensity and duration of each programme can be varied to meet the severity of each case. Thus a scale of sentencing options is available, providing alternatives to detention centre and to youth custody' (Bowden and Stevens 1986: 328).

CORPORATISM: THE THIRD MODEL OF JUVENILE JUSTICE

Meanwhile, in the custodial sector there has been a marked shift away from the concept of the 'therapeutic community', associated with earlier possibilities of Borstal training; indeed, this is replaced by the determinate sentence of youth custody, under s. 6 of the 1982 Criminal Justice Act. Thus we see the development of institutional regimes (detention centre *or* youth custody), whose primary purpose is to inflict or enforce punishment, to the effect that '*once the term of the sentence has been set*, the institution in which it is to be served should follow'. Indeed, it seems that the logic of these initiatives will be to merge the hitherto separate institutions (the one for punishment, the other for treatment): thus the 1987 Criminal Justice Bill, part VII, provided that young offenders who were sentenced to youth custody could in some circumstances be accommodated in detention centres.

Furthermore, it can be said that other features of the 1982 Act seem to embody justice-model principles, such as the restriction on the availability to implement quasi-indeterminate care orders for criminal offence (s.23); and various prescriptions to be followed prior to the imposition of a custodial sentence, e.g. the need to make available legal representation (s. 4).

Overall, then, the impression is that 'welfare', with its long tradition and history, has come to be superseded by 'justice'—making for a radical detour in the form and practice of juvenile justice.

Current Trends in Juvenile Justice in England and Wales

Do the major trends and developments really correspond to this major shift from welfare to justice that is supposed to have taken place?

An increase in cautioning and pre-court disposal of cases

The police caution has now become the most predominant sanction for juvenile offenders, rising from 33,702 in 1968 to 99,000 in 1984; when, in contrast there were 70,100 court-based findings of guilt (for indictable offences) against young people under seventeen. Indeed, some local authority areas have now developed their own pre-court administrative tariff.

In straightforward cases, a file is closed when confirmation of the disposal is received from the Police. When there is some further involvement this may range from supervising an apology, administering voluntary agreements to pay compensation, organising reparation, referring cases to other agencies, getting youngsters involved in community activities or undertaking to visit a family periodically for a length of time to monitor a child's progress. (Northampton Juvenile Liaison Bureau 1985: 25)

In this particular local authority area, pre-court decision-making and adjudication has almost replaced that of the juvenile court: of 1,087 referrals of juvenile offenders in 1985 by the police to the inter-agency Juvenile Liaison Bureau, only 101 were referred on to court (Bowden and Stevens 1986).

The growth of inter-agency co-operation

This has become a regular feature of most local juvenile justice systems (see e.g. Kenny 1981), with a view to ensuring unified local policy and better understanding between the respective agencies and organizations. Although *not* a new phenomenon (Rose 1968), particular emphasis has been given to it in the last decade (see e.g. LAC 78/26, 80/3; Home Office 1980; Parliamentary All-Party Penal Affairs Group 1981). In effect, such co-operation has a two-fold purpose: (*a*) more efficient and effective sentencing policies (cf. Tutt 1982); (*b*) the development of crime prevention programmes: 'every individual citizen and all those agencies whose policies and practices can influence the extent of crime should make their contribution. Preventing crime is a task for the whole community' (HOC 84/8).

The development of alternative to care/custody programmes

Intermediate treatment has become the vehicle for much of the debate, discussion, and development of such projects, now to be found in most local authority areas (Bottoms *et al.* 1985). Clearly, Thorpe *et al.* (1980) was of great importance in reorientating intermediate treatment (as indeed, have been the subsequent contributions of these authors and their respective colleagues) away from associations with Outward Bound-type activities for delinquent and deprived children. At the same time, it is clear from the range of projects that is now available (e.g. tracking programmes in Leeds, a behaviourist approach which includes residential placements in Coventry; the Norfolk 'wagon train'; a community service type of format in Newcastle) that local factors still play a signficant role in shaping programme content. There are thus a whole range of alternative to custody *programmes* rather than one set model.

A decline in personal autonomy

Notwithstanding the *increase* in administrative discretion that some of the above trends indicate, commitment to wider policy objectives, such as a reduction of custodial sentences, has led to a general decline in personal autonomy, both of the judiciary and social work professionals. The sphere of action of the former has primarily been reduced by the growth of diversion projects, which restrict the flow of cases to it. And then, for the cases which jump the diversion hurdle, there have been increasing attempts in the 1980s to contain the discretionary powers of sentences, so that, now, prior to making a custodial sentence on a young offender, the court must be satisfied (*a*) as to 'the nature and gravity of the offence', and (*b*) that the offender 'qualifies' for a custodial sentence by reason of past 'failure to respond to non custodial penalties', or because custody is needed 'to protect the public from serious harm', or because the offence 'was so serious that a non-custodial sentence for it cannot be justified'; further-more, such a disposition must be for an offence that would have resulted in a custody in the case of an adult offender (see Criminal Justice Act 1988, s. 123 (3)).[4]

Alternative-to-custody projects are designed as a *restricted service*—for those who would otherwise have received a custodial sentence on the grounds of their offence/offending record. This necessarily curtails the professional autonomy of criminal justice social workers: they will no longer be able to refer whomever they want to these programmes. Criteria for referral should specify, for example:

[4] This subsection of the 1988 Act represents a more detailed attempt to prevent the judiciary making unnecessary custodial sentences, in the aftermath of the apparent failure of s.1 (4) of the Criminal Justice Act 1982 to achieve this (see Burney 1985).

242

CORPORATISM: THE THIRD MODEL OF JUVENILE JUSTICE

* whether the project is for boys and/or girls.
* the age of those for whom the project is intended.
* the geographical catchment areas of the project.
* any offence criteria (e.g., particular types of offences or frequency of offending).
* whether court proceedings are pending and the likelihood of removal from home. (NACRO 1985: 13–14)

The gatekeeping role of juvenile justice specialists further entails restrictions in respect of report writing.

Recent research has shown that in many cases the SERS have handicapped a young person appearing in court by including much irrelevant information about the family background. The aim . . . is to shift the emphasis of reports so that *all social workers produce SERS which have the following objectives*. Firstly, to be effective negotiating documents which secure the best possible deal for the offender (i.e., minimum intervention) and second, to supply the court only with information which is relevant to the offence. (DHSS 1981: 48, emphasis added)

In this respect, social workers 'should not be able to write their own individual social enquiry reports' (Professor Tutt, as reported in *Community Care*, 25 Sept. 1986).

The centralization of policy dictates the erosion of discretion in some areas and its increase in others, where this is functional to the development and successful implementation of policy.

An increase in the role of the voluntary sector

Voluntary organizations have always had a role in the provision of intermediate treatment, but this has been enhanced and extended in recent years—particularly in the aftermath of LAC 83/3. This provided (initially) £15 million for the development of alternative to custody projects in this sector, radically redrawing the map of juvenile justice and formalizing collaboration with the statutory sector: '110 grant approvals have been made, providing 3,389 official places at a cost of £13,009,826. Of the total grants allocated, 52% went to local voluntary bodies and 48% to national organizations. Grants were made to bodies situated in 62 English local authorities, of which 21% were London Boroughs, 31% were Metropolitan Boroughs and 48% were Shire Counties' (NACRO 1986: 3).

The development of a juvenile justice technology

By using computer technology it becomes possible to collate the information necessary for planning policies, providing flow charts, drawing maps of local systems of justice, and so on. David Thorpe (1981a: 13) describes some pioneering work.

The results, arrived at in a matter of days, were amazing. We suddenly had information on SER recommendations and results on different types of offences committed before and after the care orders were made and we were able to cross tabulate these with different types of placements, the lengths of time spent in the placements and whether or not the delinquents were absconding at the time the offences were committed. We were able to observe the differential effectiveness of social workers and probation officers . . .

243

JOHN PRATT

(And see subsequently Redmond-Pyle 1983.) There are two particular features to be noted here. First, much of the impetus for the development of this technology has come from the private sector,[5] which represents another aspect of the diversification of interests now taking place in the administration of juvenile justice. Second, the 'delinquency management' approach that this technology facilitates signifies a major shift in the constitution of social work expertise: that is, from working exclusively with individual clients to providing analyses and profiles of local decision-making processes.

Bifurcation

This has been recognized as a major trend in penal policy for over a decade now (see Bottoms 1977; Matthews 1979; Chan and Ericson 1981). That is, there is an official and recognized separation between serious/violent/dangerous/'*hard core*' offenders, for whom custody is thought essential, and '*the rest*'/non-violent/minor offenders, and so on, for whom non-custody is thought to be appropriate (see e.g. Home Office 1976; DHSS 1980). As such, the growth of the 'alternative to custody' movement must be understood in symbiosis with this tendency. Government and policy-makers are only prepared to sanction non-custodial alternatives on the basis that custody will be *retained* for particular segments of the offender population. Consequently the male custodial population has remained from 1979 to 1986 at 12 per cent of the total population sentenced in the *juvenile court* (14–17), notwithstanding increasing use of youth custody sentences (growing from 2 to 4 per cent of court sentences between 1983 and 1986), apparently at the expense of detention centres (a decline from 10 to 8 per cent of court sentences between 1982 and 1986).[6] Meanwhile, alternatives to custody have proliferated over the same period. Hence the careful detailing of the assessment criteria for admission to them: sufficiently wide to include a large catchment population (so as to ensure reasonably full occupancy), sufficiently vague so as to be able to exclude the 'hard core' and thereby not damage credibility with the local magistrates and judges. Thus the following example from Nottinghamshire (Nottinghamshire Social Services 1983: 2):

For acceptance on to the scheme each referral . . . must fulfil the first two criteria and any three of the criteria 3–8:

1. The child is likely to receive a Care or Custody sentence at his next court appearance for offending.
2. The child must have at least two court appearances already.
3. There are sibling/family offences.
4. The child has identified behaviour problems.
5. The child has offended under the age of criminal responsibility.
6. The child's family has experienced marital difficulties.
7. The child has a large and/or extended family.
8. The child has experienced a deprived environment, either within the family or locality.

---

[5] e.g. Information Systems (Lancaster) and Management Data Systems, Ltd.
[6] If we include the cautioning figures, then of course the percentage of all known offenders sent to custody in the 1980s has decreased.

CORPORATISM: THE THIRD MODEL OF JUVENILE JUSTICE

However, we can also see secondary forms of bifurcation: the ideological distinction between the hard core and the rest seems to translate in practice to a disproportionate use of custody for black offenders (Pitts 1986), placing them firmly in the former category. Meanwhile, at the other end of the spectrum, a whole range of minor delinquents, children with welfare-type problems, and most girls are likely to be excluded from this specialized juvenile justice services. 'Community-based facilities should consist of high, medium and low-intensity programmes designed to provide services for clearly defined categories of juvenile offenders. *The high and medium-intensity programmes should rigidly exclude all non-offenders.*' (Thorpe *et al.* 1980: 163, emphasis added; see also Roach 1983).

Corporatism

What conclusions can we draw from these developments? There can be no denying that justice-model talk and ideas have assumed an *ideological* dominance over those of welfare. However, there has been no corresponding shift towards a fully blown justice-model legal form which puts into operation all this talk and these ideas. Against some of the prerequisites of this model, such as certainty, due process, visibility, accountability, least restrictive intervention, we see instead an increase in administrative decision-making, greater sentencing diversity, centralization of authority and co-ordination of policy, growing involvement of non-juridical agencies, and high levels of containment and control in some sentencing programmes.

For the proponents of justice, such features will no doubt be written off as unintended consequences of their ideas, or as ironic anomalies: Conservative governments provide LAC3 monies to encourage private and voluntary sector initiatives, which has the effect of feeding money to social work activities with offenders despite the suspicions and hostilities that government representatives had expressed in relation to this (see Holt 1984).

However, these trends can also be seen as *necessary* and *essential* features of a third model of juvenile justice: *corporatism.* This sociological concept refers to the tendencies to be found in advanced welfare societies whereby the capacity for conflict and disruption is reduced by means of the centralization of policy, increased government intervention, and the co-operation of various professional and interest groups into a collective whole with homogeneous aims and objectives (Unger 1976). Corporatist tendencies must be understood as part of a historical process. The shift away from a nineteenth-century state form (where a free market economy and *Gesellschaft* legal process were essential and complementary features) to a welfare state pattern of intervention, regulation, and planning also saw crucial changes in the legal form.

The first type of effect is the rapid expansion of the use of open ended standards and general clauses in legislation, administration and adjudication . . .

The second major impact of the welfare state on law is the turn from formalistic to purposive or policy oriented styles of legal reasoning and from concerns with formal justice to an interest in procedural and substantive justice. (ibid. 194; see also Prosser 1982)

In effect, this constitutes a major shift from uniformity and general rules with universal validity to policy-ordered decision-making and legal reasoning. But of course, the welfare state itself is not a static entity (Mishra 1984). These trends come to be

JOHN PRATT

exemplified in the advanced form of the welfare state, which takes on the characteristics of corporatism. This entails

the effacement both in organisation and in consciousness of the boundary between state and society and therefore between the public and the private realm. As the state reaches into society, society itself generates institutions that rival the state in their power and take on many attributes formerly associated with public bodies. (Unger 1976: 201)

And in contrast to the typology of *Gesellschaft* law, the legal process now assumes the form of *bureaucratic–administrative* law, where

the presupposition and concern is neither an organic human community nor an atomic individual; the pre-supposition and concern is a non-human abstracted ruling interest, public policy or on-going activity of which human beings and individuals are subordinates, functionaries or carriers ... [such] regulations ... take for their object ... the efficient execution of tasks and attainment of goals and norms ... which are set by the authorities, or the 'community', or the bureaucracy as its representative. (Kamenka and Tay 1975: 138)

   This is not to say that corporatism is an *exclusive* phenomenon. Some of the features of this model have been in existence during the hegemony of different legal forms. It should thus be of no surprise that some developments *do* correspond to features of the *Gesellschaft* ideal type (see Garland and Young 1983). Futhermore, corporatism in the juvenile justice section is not reflective of a general phenomenon now taking place in civil society. In this respect, I am following Panitch's (1980: 161) argument that corporatism in a 'partial structure', as opposed to the 'increasingly common tendency to see these particular corporatist structures not as representing new *partial* elements *within* the existing economic and political system, but as corporatist ideologues once claimed they would be, new political and/or economic systems in their own right' (emphasis in original).

   Indeed, given that most analyses of corporatism have been set at the level of changes in the state formation and have usually drawn empirically on economic and industrial relations policies (Winckler 1975; Panitch 1981), it would seem to be a highly problematic concept to apply right across British society post-1979 with the advent of Thatcherism. The subsequent break-up of the political consensus of the post-war years, the commitment, in varying degrees to free-market rather than state-managed economic policies, the reduction of union power, the willingness to tolerate high levels of unemployment—all seem to be pointing the way to or are features of a 'post-corporate' state formation (Lewis and Wiles 1984). As part of this process, it may be that these same shifts away from corporatism in the areas of industrial relations, economic policy, and so on necessitate a shift *towards* corporatist intervention and regulation in the penal spectrum (see also Bottoms 1983; O'Malley 1983). More starkly, free-market economic policies that generate high levels of unemployment, *particularly among the young*, necessitate extended and increased forms of social policing. Corporatism provides the mechanics and machinery for this. However, the detail of such a hypothesis must be the matter of a separate paper. The task here, and to which I shall now turn, is to sustain the argument that corporatism has become the predominant trend in juvenile justice.

   In this respect, let us first consider the increase in administrative discretion that diversion programmes and the like have encouraged. As argued earlier, the pre-court

CORPORATISM: THE THIRD MODEL OF JUVENILE JUSTICE

tribunal has replaced the juvenile court as the main site for the dispensation of juvenile justice. In addition, referral to programmes (diversion from court or alternative to custody) is likely to be subject to the discretion of some other decision-making committee. For example:

Prior to the preparation of the Social Enquiry Report the Social Worker or Probation Officer would negotiate with the young person, his parents, with [the project] and with other involved parties.

Subsequently the applications would be brought before an Admission Panel consisting of Programme Workers, [the project] Manager, and an independent permanent Chair Person. The School will be asked to send a representative if appropriate.

For the successful applicant a contract will be drawn up. This will identify a programme of Intermediate Treatment and will also include details about what will be expected of the young person . . . (Halton Intermediate Treatment Scheme, n.d.: 2)

If such developments contradict the dictates of the justice model, they none the less support the corporatist argument. Reliance on the formal processes of law and due process can lead to inefficiency and delay, which hinders policy implementation— hence the *importance* of administrative decision-making to this model (Winckler 1975). The increase in discretion is not just an unintended consequence of the supposed move 'back to justice', but is *central to the functioning of the corporatist model*. Delays and costs can be avoided in this way. Equally, instead of relying on breach procedures for every failure to report to the alternative-to-custody intermediate treatment centre, let power be given to social workers to impose sanctions. If not, cases might be brought back into the formal legal system, resulting in a sanction (custody) that the state is anxious to avoid wherever possible. Consequently, many projects now have their own built-in sanctions, which can be applied and administered without recourse to courtroom approval, as in the following example:

Minor breaches or problems will be dealt with by counselling and/or restriction of privileges etc. If these should continue, or when serious violations occur, the young person will be recalled to the residential unit and a conference held, in order to discuss reasons for the action, and to outline new objectives as necessary, with return to the community in mind. (Coventry PACE, n.d.: 3)

The 'hard core' will still be locked up: but a delinquency management service is now provided in the community for that troublesome segment of the youth population not dangerous enough to lock away but too disruptive to ignore. Hence the concentration of resources here to the exclusion of those with more welfare-based problems: so long as the latter remain just a threat to themselves they do not warrant further attention. But social workers are not merely co-opted into the adjudication and decision-making processes: they may be involved in constructing and devising the penalty itself. Raynor (1985: 204) describes a sanction put together by a probation officer, made up of a number of smaller penalties and administrative dictates, the intention being that it would then operate as an alternative to custody:

This programme . . . involved the active participation of the defendant: the court, his parents, the other members of the intermediate treatment group; the beneficiaries of the community service work; the victim; the volunteers who supervised the work; the police, the Careers Officer;

JOHN PRATT

and the psychiatrist, in addition of course to the [Probation] Officer himself . . . it offers an interesting illustration, not of some vague notion of 'community involvement' but of the purposeful mobilisation of community resources to resolve a criminal justice problem in a fair and helpful way.

Second, in place of a reassertion of the *judicial* determination of crime and punishment (which the justice model requires) we find the 'blurring of the boundaries' (Unger 1976; Cohen 1979) between the private and public realm, as with the LAC3 initiative; between the courts and other decision-making bodies, and between various criminal justice agencies whose positions and responsibilities become increasingly amorphous in the inter-agency co-operation ventures, whether this be to administer punishment or prevent crime (HOC 8/84). The blurring of the boundaries at an agency level is taken to its ultimate form in the model of the Northampton Juvenile Liaison Bureau. Designed to act as a body that will divert cases from court and deliver a form of administrative justice, it was constituted by a wholesale merger of the various juvenile justice agencies and

employs full time a social worker, probation officer, youth worker, teacher and police officer and is administered by a management team consisting of local managers of the represented agencies [who] undertake the consultation process involving all the parent agencies . . . and possibly some others as well, for example, the education welfare service and child guidance clinic. (Northamptonshire CC 1982)

Such developments are again essential to the corporatist model of juvenile justice. Importantly, they allow potential conflict to be negotiated, managed, and thus diffused: adversarial proceedings may again be expensive and inefficient, and may ultimately hinder the implementation of policy. Far better to work out in advance what kind of penalty will be acceptable in each case.

Magistrates need to be satisfied that each youth will receive proper supervision from social workers or probation officers and that a programme of school attendance, youth training or work experience is available. Some of the young people attend day centres where they receive special training. In addition, more intensive levels of community service work are often prescribed such as helping with meals on wheels, running youth clubs, or repairing toys for the children's ward of a local hospital. (Tutt 1984)

Furthermore, a recourse to privatization does not mean that the government is contracting out of or giving up on its responsibilities, For reasons of fiscal policy, the government *does* have a vested interest in ensuring that the LAC3 initiative, like other aspects of its deinstitutionalization programme, is successful. As such, privatization enables central government to intervene *much more directly* in the framework of local policy. Recourse to the private sector ensures that social service bureaucracies (which might be able to subvert policy) are bypassed, and that negotiations take place with individuals who are likely to have a commitment to the success of the policy.

Third, instead of an emphasis on 'rights', what we find in practice at nearly all levels of decison-making is this overarching emphasis on policy. To ensure policy objectives, the personal autonomy of social workers and the judiciary is reduced. Furthermore, the rights of the client come to be conflated with the objectives of policy. This can be seen in the justification for the introduction of the Northampton Juvenile Liaison Bureau:

CORPORATISM: THE THIRD MODEL OF JUVENILE JUSTICE

The delays inherent in the [previous] system which lacked a co-ordinated approach by the various agencies, together with the enormous number of cases being processed through the courts, meant that the juvenile court was extremely busy sitting some six half-day courts each week, with all the attendant costs and problems that this entailed. (Bowden and Stevens 1986: 326)

Fourth, the issue of punishment. The justice model maintains a philosophical commitment to the imposition of punishment, alongside its administrative principles of due process and so on. However, although many alternatives to custody projects do maintain high levels of punishment, they do *not* represent a return to the punishment principles of classicism (and as re-presented in the justice model). Outside of the custodial sector, we are not seeing a resurgence of a kind of retributive moral enforcement wherein punishment is measured in exactitude to the amount of harm done, is awarded exclusively by the judiciary for a set and known period, and so on. Instead, what we find is an emphasis on the development of penalties that provide for a form of behavioural containment (O'Malley 1983). This can be behaviour *modification* in the community, as with the Church of England PACE project:

Its prime objective is to enable the young person to learn to live within his family and community without major conflict or risk to himself or others and without needing to resort to delinquent or other forms of anti-social behaviour. This will be achieved by working to a plan tailored to each individual need and circumstance, in order to help the young person to recognise and accept responsibility for himself and his own actions, as well as to acknowledge and deal with the reality of his everyday situation . . .

The underlying philosophy of the scheme is the conviction that to establish an intense, positive supportive one to one relationship and to provide a powerful alternative adult model is the most effective means of producing positive changes in behaviour and attitudes. (Coventry PACE, n.d.: 2)

Alternatively, there is behaviour *surveillance*: schemes such as 'tracking', which offer precisely this. Thus the Nottinghamshire 'linking' programme:

In one scheme the linker lived with the family every weekend for a month and was responsible for the linkee from Friday at 4.30 p.m. until Monday at 8.30 a.m. The linkee in question had been involved in the commission of offences during the weekend period for some considerable time and this input over a relatively short period is effective and gives time for other less intensive alternatives to be worked out between the linkee, his/her family and the linker and caseholder. (A. Thorpe 1983: 2)

This 'new behaviourism' (Cohen 1985) is more in keeping with the objectives of corporatism than the justice model in that it provides a logical response to the aims of keeping offenders out of courts and institutions. Restriction of behaviour opportunities, or programmes that induce changes in behaviour, clearly offers far more in terms of policy implementation than the punishment 'pure and simple' of the justice model (unlikely to have any consequences on future behaviour); and offers more than the treatment-based practices of the welfare model (ineffective and inefficient).

A fifth factor is the expanding dialogue on delinquency that emanates from all the inter-agency meetings and discussions. It had been the hope that the justice model would minimize the delinquency problem, after the excesses of welfare. Yet we now

JOHN PRATT

find the maximization of delinquency as a crucial social issue, magnified by the production of more flow charts, community profiles, and so on, which become the products of each new inter-agency venture. For example:

Local authority departments in particular are likely to be useful sources both of information directly about crime, such as vandalism of school buildings and on housing estates, and of the social and demographic data necessary to place crime in its local context. Such data might, for example include information about housing stock, population characteristics, and perhaps transport and recreational facilities in areas noted for high levels of crime. (HOC 8/84: 3)

This, again, is essential to corporatism: the increasing range of agencies involved in the administration of juvenile justice necessitates more efficient and detailed use of resources. 'What is being proposed is not additional, unproductive work, but a more systematic use of available statistics' (ibid.).

As such, the juvenile justice specialists have a far more enlarged role than would have been possible under the strict application of a justice model format which minimized such social work intervention. Instead, the specialists are at the hub of the juvenile justice system itself; they have become the socio-technical experts of corporatism—instrumental in policy implementation within their own organizations, crucial figures in promoting inter-agency dialogue. In effect, the post-war social democratic faith in social planning (the subject of so much criticism in areas such as health, social security, and housing in the political climate of the 1970s and 1980s) has been given a fresh lease of life in this particular sector of the welfare state.

There is an opportunity here for social workers and their managers to get away from the generally *ad hoc* planning decisions of the 1970s and use the new technology not to replace case files and administrative registers, but to provide a detailed analysis of local policy and practices which will enable the broadest discussion of policy objectives and more rational and economic deployment of resources to meet those objectives. (D. Thorpe 1981*b*: 21)

A Reconsideration of the Welfare–Justice Argument

The specific characteristics and attributes of the corporatist model of juvenile justice can now be seen in contrast to those of welfare and justice (see Table 1). If, then, the whole debate about welfare and justice has been something of a sideshow while centre stage a very different play has been performed, why is it that this has not been recognized? Why is it that the emergence of corporatism has gone largely unnoticed?

Certainly, the justice critique repudiated many of the previous ideas that had informed the history of juvenile justice; and in its rise to ideological dominance contributed a new form of penological language that has been popularized among social work professionals. Phrases such as 'least restrictive intervention', 'diversion from court', and 'alternatives to custody' have become part of the contemporary discourse of juvenile justice specialists, as indeed they have become signifiers of government policy (Hudson 1987). However, there simply has not been a shift towards the exclusively adversarial process that the justice model dictates: indeed, most trends are away from this. Meanwhile, support for other justice objectives in relation to sentencing and punishment initiatives has come mainly from members of social work organizations, whose administrative powers over the offending population have increased during the

CORPORATISM: THE THIRD MODEL OF JUVENILE JUSTICE.

TABLE 1 *Three Models of Juvenile Justice*

Parameter	Welfare	Justice	Corporatism
Characteristics	Informality	Due process	Administrative decision-making
	Generic referrals	Offending	Offending
	Individualized sentencing	Least restrictive alternative	Diversion from court/custody
	Indeterminate sentencing	Determinate sentences	Alternative to care/custody programmes
Key personnel	Child care experts	Lawyers	Juvenile justice specialists
Key agency	Social work	Law	Inter-agency structure
Tasks	Diagnosis	Punishment	Systems intervention
Understanding of client behaviour	Pathological	Individual responsibility	Unsocialized
Purpose of intervention	Provide treatment	Sanction behaviour	Retrain
Objectives	Respond to individual needs	Respect individual rights	Implementation of policy

course of their espousal of the justice model, and about whom its initial architects had been so critical.

Thus, notwithstanding the commitment to these new objectives and new ventures in social work with offenders, it is clear that much of the ideology and discourse of social work in the welfare era has not disappeared—not that it ever could have been simply effaced from memory. Instead, it has been refurbished, brought up to date, remodelled—and then set down in new domains and locations. Here a link is maintained with the helping and caring tradition of social work intervention. The new programmes are not so far removed from social work that they will alienate and deter support from within the profession. Indeed, they are seen as new steps in social work, an innovative way forward. For example, 'an appropriate definition of [intermediate treatment] might be "A method of social work with children which adds a new dimension to improve the quality of life through community based opportunities for personal growth and development"' (East Sussex County Council, n.d.: 3). In this way support for these policies can' be galvanized and sustained from *within* social work and traditional oppositions maintained (for example, to Conservative governments), while at the same time ensuring effective alliances with welfare critics and the policy objectives of governments.

What we find, then, is a replication of some of the mistakes made during the welfare era. The 'best interests' tradition facilitates the growth and extension of new control systems. Yet the apparatus of these systems, their technology, their talk, and so on, are indicators of future developments and trends. There can be 'no return to rehabilitation' (Hudson 1987; Matthews 1987), as if all that we now see represents some kind of temporary aberration, ready to be swept aside. Not only is this to misunderstand the reality of power and its operation, but the concept of rehabilitation has anyway been updated and informs the 'new behaviourism'. At the same time, there can be no going back to a non-technologized past. It will be within this sytem of the future that we will variously find advantages and disadvantages, points of resistance and new initiatives of control.

Having said this, then clearly one of the main functions of the justice rhetoric and the

251

JOHN PRATT

humanitarian ideals it is intended to address has been to mask, disguise, and/or justify developments that seem to be the opposite of its rubric (Cohen 1984, 1985). Instead of a concern for the protection of individual rights, we find instead an emphasis on efficiency and the primacy of policy objectives. Instead of a shift from the inhumanities and injustices of the institution, we find these features of the carceral system now being reproduced in the community—in those projects that are supposed to be *alternatives* to the institution. *This is not to say that such developments are inevitably and always unhealthy.* But what we should try to separate out are humane objectives from their inhumane effects—which, in the current context, allegiance to justice-model rhetoric helps to obscure.

REFERENCES

BAILEY, V. (1987), *Delinquency and Citizenship*. Oxford: Clarendon Press.

BECCARIA, C. [1764] (1963), *On Crimes and Punishment*. Indianapolis: Bobbs-Merrill.

BOTTOMS, A. E. (1977), 'Reflections on the Renaissance of Dangerousness', *Howard Journal of Penology and Crime Prevention*, 16: 70–96.

—— (1983), 'Neglected Features of Contemporary Penal Systems', in *The Power to Punish*, D. Garland and P. Young, eds., 166–202. London: Heinemann.

BOTTOMS, A. E., BROWN, P., McWILLIAMS, B., McWILLIAMS, W., and PRATT, J. (1985), *The National IT Survey: Some Preliminary Findings*. Sheffield: NITFED Annual Conference.

BOWDEN, J., and STEVENS, M. (1986), 'Justice for Juveniles: A Corporate Strategy in Northampton', *Justice of the Peace*, 326–9, 345–7.

BRODY, S. (1976), *The Effectiveness of Sentencing*. London: HMSO.

BURNEY, E. (1985), *Sentencing Young People*. Aldershot: Gower.

CHAN, J., and ERICSON, R. (1981), *Decarceration and the Economy of Penal Reform*. Toronto: University of Toronto.

COHEN, S. (1979), 'The Punitive City: Notes on the Dispersal of Social Control', *Contemporary Crises*, 3: 339–64.

—— (1984), 'The Deeper Structures of the Law, or "Beware of the Rulers Bearing Justice": A Review Essay', *Contemporary Crises*, 8: 83–93.

—— (1985), *Visions of Social Control*. Cambridge: Polity Press.

COVENTRY, PACE (n.d.), *Intensive Intermediate Treatment Project*. Church of England Children's Society.

DENMAN, G. (1982), *Intensive Intermediate Treatment with Juvenile Offenders*, Centre of Youth, Crime and Community, University of Lancaster.

DEPARTMENTAL COMMITTEE ON THE TREATMENT OF YOUNG OFFENDERS (1927), *Molony Report*, London: HMSO.

DHSS (Department of Health and Social Security) (1980), *Getting on with IT*. London: HMSO.

—— (1981), *Community Provision for Young Offenders*. London: HMSO.

EAST SUSSEX COUNTY COUNCIL (n.d.), *Intensive Intermediate Treatment Report*.

GARLAND, D., and YOUNG, P. (1983), 'Towards a Social Analysis of Penalty', in D. Garland and P. Young, eds., *The Power to Punish*, 1–36. London: Heinemann.

GILLER, H., and MORRIS, A. (1981), *Care and Discretion: Social Work Decisions with Delinquents*. London: Burnett Books.

GLUECK, S., and GLUECK, E. (1960), *Predicting Delinquency in Crime*. New York: Harvard University Press.

CORPORATISM: THE THIRD MODEL OF JUVENILE JUSTICE

HALTON INTERMEDIATE TREATMENT SCHEME (n.d.), *Alternatives to Care and Custody Programme*. Cheshire Social Services.
HOLT, J. (1984), *No Holiday Camps*. Leicester: Association of Juvenile Justice.
HOME OFFICE (1968), *Children in Trouble*, Cmnd 3601. London: HMSO.
—— (1976), *CYPA 1969: Observations on the 11th Report from the Expenditure Committee*, Cmnd 6494. London: HMSO.
—— (1980), *Young Offenders*, Cmnd 8045. London: HMSO.
HOUSE OF COMMONS (1975), *11th Report from the Expenditure Committee*. London.
HUDSON, B. (1987), *Justice through Punishment*. London: Macmillan.
JOHNSON, T., and GREEN, C. (1985), 'Appeals and the Social Work Ethos', *Yorkshire and Humberside I.T. Association Training Anthrology*, 40–7. North Humberside Social Services.
JOHNSON, T., and HOLT, J. (1986), 'Future Directions for the AJJ: A Discussion Paper', *Association of Juvenile Justice*, 8: 3–5.
JONES, R. (1984), 'Questioning the New Orthodoxy', *Community Care*, 11 Oct.
KAMENKA, E., and TAY, A. E-S. (1975), 'Beyond Bourgeois Individualism', in E. Kamenka and R. Neale, eds., *Feudalism, Capitalism and Beyond*, 126–44. London: Edward Arnold.
KANT, I. (1929), *Critique of Pure Reason*. New York: Macmillan.
KENNY, D. (1981), *Intermediate Treatment: Review of Practices and Policies in the Central London Boroughs*. London: Central Policy Unit, GLC.
KERSLAKE, A. (1984), 'IT: Caught in the Policy Crossfire', *Youth in Society*, Sept., 14–15.
LEWIS, N., and WILES, P. (1984), 'The Post-Corporatist State', *Journal of Law and Society*, 11: 65–89.
MANNHEIM, H. (1946), *Criminal Justice and Social Reconstruction*. London: Routledge and Kegan Paul.
MATTHEWS, R. (1979), 'Decarceration and the Fiscal Crisis', in NDC–CSE, eds., *Capitalism and the Rule of Law*. London: Hutchinson.
—— (1987), 'Taking Realist Criminology Seriously', *Contemporary Crises*, 11: 371–402.
MISHRA, R. (1984), *The Welfare State in Crisis*. Brighton: Wheatsheaf.
MORGAN, P. (1987), *Delinquent Fantasies*. London: Croom Helm.
MORRIS, A. (1978), 'Revolution in the Juvenile Court', *Criminal Law Review*, 529–39.
MORRIS, A., and McISAAC, M. (1978), *Juvenile Justice?* London: Heinemann.
MORRIS, A., GEACH, H., GILLER, H., and SZWED, E. (1980), *Justice for Children*. London: Macmillan.
NACRO (1985), *Project Development Survey: DHSS IT Initiatives*. London.
—— (1986), *Findings From The Second Census of Projects Funded Under the DHSS IT Initiative*. London.
NORTHAMPTONSHIRE COUNTY COUNCIL (1982), *Juvenile Liaison Bureau Information Handout*. Wellingborough.
NORTHAMPTON JUVENILE LIAISON BUREAU (1985), *First Annual Report*. Northampton.
NOTTINGHAM SOCIAL SERVICES (1983), *Bassetlaw Intermediate Treatment Scheme*. Nottingham.
O'MALLEY, P. (1983), *Law, Capitalism and Democracy*. Sydney: Allen and Unwin.
PALEY, J., and THORPE, D. (1974), *Children: Handle with Care*. Leicester: National Youth Bureau.
PANITCH, L. (1980), 'Recent Theorization of Corporatism', *British Journal of Sociology*, 31: 159–87.
—— (1981), 'Trade Unions and the Capitalist State', *New Left Review*, 125: 23–41.
PARLIAMENTARY ALL-PARTY PENAL AFFAIRS GROUP (1981), *Young Offenders: A Strategy for the Future*. Chichester: Barry Rose.

JOHN PRATT

PITTS, J. (1986), 'Black Young People and Juvenile Crime: Some Unanswered Questions', in R. Matthews and J. Young, eds., *Confronting Crime*. London: Sage.

PROSSER, T. (1982), 'Towards a Critical Public Law', *Journal of Law and Society*, 5: 1–11.

RADZINOWICZ, L. (1966), *Ideology and Crime*. London: Heinemann.

RAYNOR, P. (1985), *Social Work, Justice and Control*. Oxford: Basil Blackwell.

REDMOND-PYLE, D. (1983), *Investigating the Local Juvenile Criminal Justice System*. University of Lancaster, Centre of Youth, Crime and Community.

ROACH, P. (1983), 'Where Have all the Young Girls Gone?', *Eureka*, 4: 9–11.

ROSE, G. (1968), 'Preventing Delinquency by Committee', *British Journal of Criminology*, 8: 300–8.

TAYLOR, I. (1981), *Law and Order: Arguments for Socialism*. London: Macmillan.

TAYLOR, L., LACEY, R., and BRACKEN, D. (1978), *In Whose Best Interests*. London: Cobden Trust.

THORPE, A. (1983), *Linking: One Year Review*. Leicester: National Youth Bureau.

THORPE, D. (1981*a*), 'Juvenile Justice and the Computer', *Community Care*, 18 June.

—— (1981*b*), 'Diverting Delinquents', *Community Care*, 25 June.

THORPE, D., GREEN, C., PALEY, J., and SMITH, D. (1980), *Out of Care*. London: Allen and Unwin.

TUTT, N. (1979), 'Some Aspects of Interdisciplinary Co-operation in IT', in *Working Together in IT*. Cardiff: Welsh Office.

—— (1982), 'Justice or Welfare', *Social Work Today*, 19 Oct.

—— (1984), 'Short, Sharp and Ineffective', *Observer*, 7 Oct.

UNGER, R. (1976), *Law and Modern Society*. London: Macmillan.

VON HIRSCH, A. (1976). *Doing Justice*. New York: Hill and Wang.

—— (1986), *Past or Future Crimes*. Manchester: Manchester University Press.

WEST, D. (1967), *The Young Offender*. Harmondsworth, Middx.: Penguin.

WINCKLER, J. (1975), 'Law, State and Economy: The Industry Act 1975 in Context', *British Journal of Law and Society*, 2: 103–28.

WILSON, J. (1975), *Thinking about Crime*. New York: Basic Books.

Part III
Relationships and Objectives:
Police, Prosecutors and Victims

[10]

[1985]

Decisions to Prosecute: Screening Policies and Practices in the United States

By Julie Vennard
Home Office Research and Planning Unit

By what criteria should decisions to prosecute be assessed? In their 1981 review of present arrangements for the prosecution of criminal offences in England and Wales, the Royal Commission on Criminal Procedure assessed the adequacy of those arrangements "on the broad standards of fairness, openness and accountability, and efficiency."[1] The Commission based their assessment of the fairness of the system on two key measures. First, is the system fair in the sense that the prosecution brings to trial only those against whom there is an adequate and properly prepared case, and whom it is in the public interest to prosecute? Secondly, is there consistency in the criteria applied by police forces throughout the country to the decision whether or not to prosecute? Evidence of arbitrary variation in prosecution policy and practice would be reason for doubts about the working of the present system.

These criteria are as relevant to questions concerning the efficiency of present prosecution arrangements as to the issue of fairness. Arguing in favour of the establishment of an independent prosecution service, comprising legally qualified Crown prosecutors, the Royal Commission observed that the police not infrequently bring cases to trial where the evidence is weak, or include more charges in an indictment than is warranted by the evidence. These practices create unnecessary work for the courts and waste the resources of the criminal justice system. It is widely felt that the high proportion of cases which result in acquittal because the prosecution either offer no evidence or fail to make out a prima facie case against the defendant, is a measure of the failure of the system in this respect. The annual Judicial Statistics indicate that in the Crown Court roughly a fifth of contested cases result in either ordered acquittal (before the jury is empanelled), or acquittal by direction of the judge.

Caution is needed in drawing conclusions from these figures regarding the efficacy of the prosecution system in screening out weak cases before they come to court. As a proportion of all cases committed for trial at the Crown Court, ordered and directed acquittals are relatively few (some 7 per cent.). Moreover, the prosecutor's decision to offer no evidence may be based on factors other than the sufficiency of the evidence (such as the triviality of the incident). Directed acquittals are the result of evidentiary weaknesses in the prosecution case, although it cannot be inferred that all such cases are intrinsically weak. McConville and Baldwin (1981) have shown that the

---

[1] Royal Commission on Criminal Procedure Report (1981).

Crim.L.R.   DECISIONS TO PROSECUTE: POLICIES IN THE U.S.   21

failure of cases in the Crown Court—for example where witnesses do not "come up to proof"—is frequently, though not necessarily, forseeable.[2] The authors estimated that about half of their ordered and directed acquittals were predictably weak. This picture was supported by a small scale study undertaken for the Royal Commission by the Prosecuting Solicitors' Department of Greater Manchester. And in a study of contested trials in the magistrates' courts, Vennard (1980) estimated that while in two-thirds of the cases in which the bench did not find a case for the defence to answer, the evidence was manifestly weak, in the remainder of cases the outcome probably could not have been foreseen.[3] It will not automatically follow, therefore, that the establishment of an independent prosecution service will ensure that the system entirely avoids prosecution failure. The expectation is, however, that the new service will reduce the number of cases brought on manifestly unsatisfactory evidence.

It was against this background that a Home Office memorandum was circulated to existing prosecutors in 1983, containing guidelines commended by the Attorney General regarding the standards and criteria they should aim to bring to their decisions whether to institute or continue criminal proceedings. The guidelines amount to a checklist of broadly defined criteria for judging the sufficiency of the evidence (such as availability and credibility of witnesses), and whether it is in the public interest to prosecute. Their object is to foster a higher standard of proof than the bare prima facie case, by encouraging prosecutors to apply the test of whether there is a "reasonable prospect of a conviction."

It is obviously hoped that the adoption of the guidelines will increase the effectiveness of the system in preventing weak and trivial cases from going to court and minimise local disparity. Evidence received by the Royal Commission suggested that variation between Crown Court Circuits in the proportion of cases dismissed by the judge may reflect regional differences in the extent to which the police accept the advice of the lawyer who has conduct of the prosecution. Questions are likely to remain however under an integrated prosecution service, of how to put into operation throughout the country the "reasonable prospect of conviction" standard favoured by the Attorney General. The police will continue to exercise a general discretion over the initial decision whether or not to prefer charges, and a more rigorous arrest and charging policy may result in a fall in subsequent prosecutorial filtering and charge amendment. But as observed in an editorial in this *Review*, many of the substantive issues about the way in which the system will operate—such as the standards for deciding whether to drop or alter charges—have not been fully discussed.[4] Consistency of practice is unlikely to be achieved unless the criteria for prosecution are articulated in such a way that they have practical utility in relation to different types of offence.

---

[2] M. McConville and J. Baldwin *Prosecution, Courts and Conviction* (1981).
[3] J. Vennard, *Contested Trials in Magistrates' Courts* (1980), Royal Commission on Criminal Procedure, Research Study No. 6, HMSO.
[4] [1984] Crim.L.R. 1.

Given the forthcoming reorganisation of the prosecution system, there is some merit in examining the findings of research in the United States, where the role of the police is confined to investigation, and authority to charge defendants rests with the prosecutor. The paucity of official data on the reasons why so many cases are filtered out of the American prosecution system, and the standards prosecutors and police bring to their decisions, have given rise to a number of major empirical studies which have sought to explain the statistics on so called "case attrition"—or arrests which do not result in conviction. A central issue addressed in several recent studies is whether attrition should be interpreted as a measure of police failure to supply sufficient evidence to support their arrests; a reflection of prosecutorial failure to follow up arrests properly brought by the police; or an inevitable process of screening in which progressively higher standards of proof are applied. Those who have focused on the third interpretation point to the fact that the standard of "probable cause," required to justify arrest, calls for considerably less evidence than that adopted by the prosecutor when filing charges (e.g. Feeney, 1982).[5] It is instructive to consider the contribution of this body of research in furthering understanding of the reasons why decisions are taken not to prosecute, and in developing consistent prosecution policies and practices.

Reducing the extent of non-conviction following arrest

Over the last decade the Vera Institute of Justice has undertaken detailed empirical investigation of patterns of disposition in felony arrest cases in New York. Their research was largely prompted by the knowledge that across jurisdictions, and over several years, some 45 per cent. of felony arrests were dropped by the police, not proceeded with by prosecutors, or dismissed by the courts. Their object was to attempt to understand how and why "case deterioration" takes place. Is it, for example, because most cases are inherently weak, or is there evidence of "laxness on the part of prosecutors and judges?" What role is played by the often cited factors of pre-trial delay and inadequate resources in the decision not to proceed to trial? In their widely acclaimed monograph Vera (1977) provided a systematic description of events that follow arrest and an explanation for the "deterioration" of cases at an early stage in proceedings.[6] The two factors most strongly related to case dismissal were the prior relationship between defendant and victim, and the defendant's criminal history.

Prior relationships were found in over half of all felonies involving victims, and lack of victim co-operation was the reason most commonly cited by the prosecution for case dismissal. This explanation was given in 87 per cent. of such dismissals. The researchers raised the question whether this deterioration is to society's detriment or benefit. They suggested that in some cases

---

[5] F. Feeney, *Arrests Without Conviction: How Often They Occur and Why,* National Institute of Justice, Washington D.C. (1982).
[6] Vera Institute of Justice, *Felony Arrests: Their Prosecution and Disposition in New York City's Courts* (1977), The Vera Institute, New York. See also Vera Institute of Justice, *Felony Case Preparation: Quality Counts* (1981) The Vera Institute, New York.

informal efforts at diversion and mediation might be used more widely. In other personal relationship cases the harm to the victims, their sense of grievance, and concerns for public safety are such that court adjudication is the most appropriate course.

Less important than the prior relationship factor, but nonetheless a major determinant of disposition, was prior record. Whereas over half of cases in which defendants had no prior record were dismissed, this was the outcome in only a third of cases in which defendants had previous convictions. And of those with prior records who were convicted, over four-fifths were sent to prison, compared with a fifth of the defendants with no prior record. The authors raised the question whether, for first offenders, more consideration needs to be given to the use of alternatives to formal court proceedings.

Where nonconviction was attributed to factors other than prior relationship or prior record, the Vera study concluded that efforts were needed to ensure the timely investigation and preparation of felony cases so as to improve the standard of evidence from which prosecutors make their decisions. Evidence of overcharging and evidentiary weaknesses indicated that prosecutors with more experience should be given greater decision-making authority earlier in the process, so that they could screen out cases that eventually result in dismissal.

Studies undertaken in other jurisdictions in the United States tend to confirm the high rates of attrition found in New York (notably Brosi, 1979[7]; and Forst, 1983[8]). Comparative studies also support the Vera Institute's finding that the vast majority of cases are rejected due to victim reluctance to prosecute or the insufficiency of the physical evidence or testimonial evidence from victims or witnesses. Forst (1981), for example, reported that convictions were systematically more likely to follow when the police produced physical evidence and information from two or more witnesses, than where such evidence was lacking.[9] Feeney's (1982) study of arrests without conviction also strongly emphasised that measures of evidentiary strength—such as the availability of a confession, and eyewitness evidence—were by far the most important indicators of case outcome. By quantifying measures of evidentiary strength and weakness more systematically than hitherto, Feeney discovered major differences between offences in the kinds of evidence associated with conviction, which earlier studies had obscured.

Though not surprising, such findings highlight the fact that case acceptance and rejection policies and practices are not random but, rather, are driven primarily by the strength of the evidence as presented by the police officer. One of the central policy implications drawn from American studies in this field is therefore that better documentation and follow-up procedures can produce higher conviction rates and less recourse to the dropping of charges or their downward adjustment as part of plea negotiation. An example of the

---

[7] K. Brosi, *A Cross City Comparison of Felony Case Processing* (1979) INSLAW, Washington D.C.

[8] B. Forst, "Prosecution and Sentencing," in *Crime and Public Policy* (ed. J. Wilson, Institute for Contemporary Studies, 1984).

[9] B. Forst *et al.*, *Arrest Convictability as a Measure of Police Performance* (1981) INSLAW, Washington D.C.

way in which research has aided in reducing case attrition is the exercise undertaken by the New York police department, drawing on the Vera Institute's study of "Felony Arrests." Between 1979–1981 the department undertook an experiment which introduced new procedures to secure immediate post-arrest investigation by detectives and earlier reporting of the facts to prosecutors. Evaluation of the impact of the experiment by Vera indicated a substantial improvement in the indictment and conviction rates, and an increase in the proportion of cases screened out before reaching the courts.

Comparison of the outcomes of prosecution before and after the programme was implemented showed that the proportion of felony arrests "voided" (that is dismissed) by the police increased significantly from 3·4 per cent. to 13·2 per cent. This increase in the efficiency of police screening resulted in a fall in the proportion of cases that were declined for prosecution by the District Attorney (from 7·4 per cent. to 5·1 per cent.), and a decline in the court dismissal rate (from 40 per cent. to 30 per cent. of arrests carried forward). In a matched control precinct, screening rates and court dismissal rates remained relatively stable over the experimental period. Moreover, the project also had clear impact on the sentence inasmuch as prosecutors were less likely to reduce the original charge once they were assured of the strength of the evidence in their case. This meant that, for those cases not filtered out at the pre-trial stages the gravity of charges at conviction was higher than in the pre-programme period. These results strongly suggested that the experimental case preparation procedures helped to capture at the earliest moment all the evidence needed by the prosecutor, either for pressing cases forward, or identifying and dropping those where the requisite evidence was unobtainable.

Feeney (1982) drew a number of implications for police administrators and prosecutors from his study of case attrition which accord with the Vera findings. He commented that, because the police are geared more to arrest than conviction, and initiate proceedings at a lower ("probable cause") standard of evidence than prosecutors, there should be more effective communication between police and prosecutors concerning what evidence is required for conviction, and the best techniques for building strong cases. Early decisions about case strength and appropriate charge(s) are viewed as crucial. Moreover, since the types of evidence which are associated with conviction differ according to offence—for example, relationships between victims and witnesses in robbery cases were particularly problematic—more attention should be given by police and prosecutors to the factors associated with conviction which are "crime-specific."

Variation in prosecutors' screening decisions

Though confirming the central role of evidence in prosecutorial screening practices, at the same time American research indicates that other considerations influence the way cases are handled. One of the objectives of Feeney's research was to learn whether high attrition rates are an inevitable, perhaps even a desirable feature of the prosecution process. Systematic comparison between jurisdictions with differing attrition rates pointed to the conclusion that the best test of efficiency was not the rate itself but the kinds of charges filed and dropped by the prosecution. Feeney found marked differences between the jurisdictions he examined in prosecutorial charging policies and practices, and concluded that a high prosecutorial conviction rate may indicate either an effective performance or a conservative charging policy. Conversely, a high attrition rate may reflect inefficiency in the prosecution process, or effective procedures which filter out at an early stage cases which are evidentially weak and would be unlikely to result in conviction. Indeed, Feeney reported that the single most important factor in determining whether a prosecutor's office had a high or low conviction rate was the policy that the office followed with regard to screening cases. He also warned that the validity of comparative research in this area of .decision-making may be seriously undercut by differences in defining and measuring case attrition, for example, where defendants are convicted on one charge but have other charges dropped by the prosecutor.

Other American studies have also illustrated marked variation in prosecution screening and charging decisions. Jacoby, for example, (1982b) sought to measure levels of disparity, and determine the relative importance of a variety of legal and extra-legal factors which an earlier (1982a) study has shown to be influential.[10] Using a so-called "case set," consisting of simulated cases of varying offence type and seriousness, an attempt was made to hold constant the effects on the character of the prosecutor's operations of external factors such as patterns of criminal activity, local court procedures and court backlog. The study in fact reports a high level of consistency in the criteria applied. As anticipated, offence severity, defendant's criminal record and strength of evidence were the major criteria influencing acceptance/rejection decisions. However, prosecutors differed in their views on whether cases should be disposed of through negotiation with the defence, the dropping or reduction of charges, or by trial. This was seen as reflecting large jurisdictional differences in reliance on plea negotiation and willingness to reduce charges.

Church (1978) used a similar technique to explore differences in disposition patterns across several courts.[11] Use of a "hypothetical case" questionnaire enabled him to investigate norms regarding appropriate mode of disposition, including negotiated plea (*i.e.* charge reduction or sentence concession), dismissal and jury trial. Substantial differences were apparent in practitioners' beliefs about the way the same cases should be handled. When Church compared the hypothetical case data with actual disposition patterns he found overall congruence. For example, where local norms supported trial rather than a negotiated plea this was reflected in the proportion of cases disposed of by a guilty plea. McDonald's (1982) study of plea bargaining practices similarly revealed major differences in charging policies among six jurisdictions visited, including the number of charges brought, the standard of proof required by the prosecutor before filing charges, and the extent of charge

---

[10] J. Jacoby *et al.*, (1982a): *Policy and Prosecution*, National Institute of Justice, Washington D.C.; and J. Jacoby *et al.* (1982b): *Prosecutorial Decisionmaking: A National Study*, National Institute of Justice.

[11] T. W. Church Jr., *Examining Local Legal Culture: Practitioner Attitudes in Four Criminal Courts* (1982), U.S. Dept. of Justice, NIJ.

bargaining.[12] Mcdonald concluded from his results that there should be a greater degree of formalisation and standardisation in prosecution screening procedures, though implicit in his discussion is a recognition that some flexibility must remain.

Conclusions

When considering what lessons might be learnt from this brief discussion of recent studies of prosecutorial decision-making in the United States, it must be borne in mind that in a number of important respects the American prosecution process differs from the independent system of prosecution proposed in the 1983 White Paper, *An Independent Prosecution Service for England and Wales*.[13] The prevalence of plea bargaining in the United States affects every stage of the process, as does the historical lack of involvement of the police in case preparation and presentation. The fact that the American District Attorney is elected to office may also influence local arrest and prosecution policies. He is responsible for the decision whether or not to prefer charges following arrest, and frequently plays a major part in the investigative function. In the proposed English prosecution service, generally speaking the police will continue to make the initial decision to proceed.

On the other hand, it is expected that the new prosecutor will liaise closely with the police, and his approach to cases may affect arrest and charging decisions. Like his American counterpart, moreover, the independent prosecutor working within the proposed new system would decide whether to proceed with, amend or drop charges. Given the common concerns here and in the United States about how to measure and improve efficiency and consistency within the system, research and policy developments in America have some bearing on forthcoming reforms in our own prosecutorial system.

Research in the United States is beginning to play a part not only in articulating prosecution policies and exposing the nature of variation in local attitudes and practices, but in suggesting how efficiency and fairness might be increased. Concern about the abuse of discretionary power in the hands of the American prosecutor is not new, but past efforts to provide standards and minimise diversity of practice are reported to have had little success. In her study of prosecutorial decision-making, Jacoby (1982) accounts for this failure in terms of the difficulties that have been experienced in attempting to translate broad standards into working models. This is largely because differences in volume and type of caseload, and in prosecution and court systems, can radically influence the way cases are handled. The simulation "case set" devised by Jacoby was intended essentially as a research tool. Simultaneously, it has been found to have practical utility in reducing disparities. Some prosecutors have used it as an instrument for articulating policies currently in use, for measuring levels of consistency within their offices, and identifying areas where there is a need to clarify, and communicate new policy or shifts in emphasis. In Brooklyn, for instance, it was discovered

---

[12] W. McDonald, *Plea Bargaining: Critical Issues and Common Practices* (1982), National Institute of Justice.

[13] White Paper, *An Independent Prosecution Service for England and Wales* (1983), HMSO.

that some prosecutors were not complying with current policies with regard to case acceptance, charge reduction, etc. Acting upon this information, the District Attorney investigated the reasons for these differences and instituted new procedures to promote more efficient communication of policy. As Jacoby herself notes, however, such exercises are at an experimental stage and caution is needed in endorsing the case set as a method of reducing charging disparities. Responses to the simulation exercise need to be rigorously validated against actual operating conditions, caseloads, charging practices and dispositions.

The American research material illustrates that prosecution of weak cases, and variation in screening and charging decisions, is not necessarily eliminated when responsibility for prosecution rests with trained lawyers. In the reorganisation of the prosecution system in England and Wales, therefore, research may be valuable in identifying the standards and criteria prosecutors currently bring to their decisions, developing techniques for translating into practice the standard policymakers wish to promote, and monitoring the working of the new system. Comparative studies in America indicate, for example, that with greater investigative effort on the part of the police at the early post-arrest stage, many cases which are dropped for evidentiary reasons could be salvaged. To be effective these efforts need to be informed by fuller knowledge of the kinds of evidence associated with conviction for particular types of offence. Here research can play an important part in making explicit the relationship between type of offence and evidentiary requirements (*e.g.* Feeney 1982).

Studies of the American prosecutorial system strongly suggest that closer scrutiny of cases by the prosecutor in the initial post-arrest stage enhances the chances that the requisite evidence will be produced, or that cases which would eventually end in dismissal are screened out of the system at the earliest possible stage. The setting up of an independent prosecution service in this country will bring to an end the existing solicitor-client relationship between prosecutors and the police, and this will doubtless have implications for the working relationship between local police and prosecutors. However, information from police sources indicates that, while under present arrangements some forces do in fact seek the advice of prosecuting solicitors on the level and number' of charges or on the sufficiency of the available evidence, most take these decisions unaided (Royal Commission Report 1981). Weatheritt and McNaughton's (1980) study of prosecuting solicitors' departments indicated that only two of the 30 police forces with such departments sought their advice on the decision whether or not to prosecute.[14] Sanders and Cole (1983) similarly report that under the existing structure police forces who seek advice on the desirability of prosecution are the exception rather than the rule.[15] They comment that early case assessment is central to the decision to prosecute, yet information from police forces

---

[14] M. Weatheritt and J. McNaughton, *The Prosecution System: Survey of Prosecuting Solicitors' Departments* (1980), Royal Commission on Criminal Procedure, Research Study No. 6, HMSO.

[15] A. Sanders and G. F. Cole, "The Prosecution of Weak Cases in England and Wales" (1982) 7 *Criminal Justice Review* 23.

indicates that this seldom occurs; "prosecuting solicitors everywhere used the term 'fait accompli' to describe the effect of a charge on the decision to prosecute." Separation between the role of the investigator and prosecutor under the new procedures will mean that initial screening and charging decisions will remain with the police, albeit that the latter will have authority to amend or drop charges. It is all the more important therefore that if a "reasonable prospect of conviction" is to be achieved, an effective machinery should be established for communicating the standards of proof required when instituting proceedings and the types of evidence needed to sustain conviction, and for enabling early intervention by the prosecutor.

For those seeking to formulate valid measures of the efficiency of the prosecutorial system, studies of case attrition stress that the crude statistics on the numbers of cases proceeded with and dropped following arrest may be misleading. More reliable indices of performance are the nature and strength of the evidence in cases which are either filtered out of the system or proceeded with. As research indicates, some offices are more conservative than others in their charging policies, and may decline to prosecute on what would generally be regarded as sufficient evidence. Studies must therefore look at the criteria and evidentiary standards applied by the police and prosecutors when screening cases, particularly when comparing jurisdictions.

Finally, it is important to bear in mind that changes in prosecution screening policies impinge on aspects of court procedure in a number of important ways. Notably, rigorous screening procedures, and explicit policies regarding the standard of proof required before charges are brought, provide less opportunity for "overcharging" (a criticism sometimes levelled at prosecutors in this country). Improved case screening may also reduce the extent of reliance on the practice whereby defendants plead guilty in exchange for the dropping or reduction of charges. While not suggesting that pre-trial negotiation between the parties plays such an important part in the English judicial system as in the American trial courts, the limited empirical information on plea bargaining in this country indicates that prosecutors not infrequently agree to drop or reduce charges in exchange for a guilty plea (Bottoms and McClean, 1976[16]; Baldwin and McConville, 1978[17]). More rigorous arrest and charging policies are in turn likely to reduce congestion in the criminal justice system and may affect waiting time in bringing cases to trial. Research undertaken in America indicates, for example, that more accurate charging and less plea bargaining means that in general, cases are disposed of more expeditiously (McDonald, 1982; Jacoby, 1982). Similar benefits may derive in this country from improved screening procedures and a higher standard of prosecution.

---

[16] A. E. Bottoms and J. D. McClean, *Defendants in the Criminal Process* (1976).
[17] J. Baldwin and M. McConville, "Sentencing Problems Raised by Guilty Pleas: An Analysis of Negotiated Pleas in the Birmingham Crown Court" (1978) 41 M.L.R. 544.

[11]

The Decision to Prosecute

This paper is based on an exploratory study of the Office of Prosecuting Attorney, King County (Seattle), Washington. The lack of social scientific knowledge about the prosecutor dictated the choice of this approach. An open-ended interview was administered to one-third of the former deputy prosecutors who had worked in the office during the ten year period 1955-1965. In addition, interviews were conducted with court employees, members of the bench, law enforcement officials, and others having reputations for participation in legal decision-making. Over fifty respondents were contacted during this phase. A final portion of the research placed the author in the role of observer in the prosecutor's office. This experience allowed for direct observation of all phases of the decision to prosecute so that the informal processes of the office could be noted. Discussions with the prosecutor's staff, judges, defendant's attorneys, and the police were held so that the interview data could be placed within an organizational context.

The primary goal of this investigation was to examine the role of the prosecuting attorney as an officer of the legal process within the context of the local political system. The analysis is therefore based on two assumptions. First, that the legal process is best understood as a subsystem of the larger political system. Because of this choice, emphasis is placed upon the interaction and goals of the individuals involved in decision-making. Second, and closely related to the first point, it is assumed that broadly conceived political considerations explained to a large extent "who gets or does not get—in what amount—and how, the good (justice) that is hopefully produced by the legal system" (Klonski and Mendelsohn, 1965: 323). By focusing upon the political and social linkages between these systems, it is expected that decision-making in the prosecutor's office will be viewed as a principal ingredient in the authoritative allocation of values.

[332] LAW AND SOCIETY REVIEW

THE PROSECUTOR'S OFFICE IN AN EXCHANGE SYSTEM

While observing the interrelated activities of the organizations in the legal process, one might ask, "Why do these agencies cooperate?" If the police refuse to transfer information to the prosecutor concerning the commission of a crime, what are the rewards or sanctions which might be brought against them? Is it possible that organizations maintain a form of "bureaucratic accounting" which, in a sense, keeps track of the resources allocated to an agency and the support returned? How are cues transmitted from one agency to another to influence decision-making? These are some of the questions which must be asked when decisions are viewed as an output of an exchange system.

The major findings of this study are placed within the context of an exchange system (Evan, 1965: 218).[1] This serves the heuristic purpose of focusing attention upon the linkages found between actors in the decision-making process. In place of the traditional assumptions that the agency is supported solely by statutory authority, this view recognizes that an organization has many clients with which it interacts and upon whom it is dependent for certain resources. As interdependent subunits of a system, then, the organization and its clients are engaged in a set of exchanges across their boundaries. These will involve a transfer of resources between the organizations which will affect the mutual achievement of goals.

The legal system may be viewed as a set of interorganizational exchange relationships analogous to what Long (1962: 142) has called a community game. The participants in the legal system (game) share a common territorial field and collaborate for different and particular ends. They interact on a continuing basis as their responsibilities demand contact with other participants in the process. Thus, the need for the cooperation of other participants can have a bearing on the decision to prosecute. A decision not to prosecute a narcotics offender may be a move to pressure the United States' Attorney's Office to cooperate on another case. It is obvious that bargaining occurs not only between the major actors in a case—the prosecutor and the defense attorney—but also between the clientele groups that are influential in structuring the actions of the prosecuting attorney.

Exchanges do not simply "sail" from one system to another, but take place in an institutionalized setting which may be compared to a market. In the market, decisions are made between individuals who occupy boundary-spanning roles, and who set the conditions under which the exchange will occur. In the legal system, this may merely mean that a representative of the parole board agrees to forward a recommendation to the prosecutor, or it could mean that there is extended bargaining between a deputy prosecutor and a defense attorney. In the study of the King County Prosecutor's Office,

THE DECISION TO PROSECUTE [333]

it was found that most decisions resulted from some type of exchange relationship. The deputies interacted almost constantly with the police and criminal lawyers, while the prosecutor was more closely linked to exchange relations with the courts, community leaders, and the county commissioners.

THE PROSECUTOR'S CLIENTELE

In an exchange system, power is largely dependent upon the ability of an organization to create clientele relationships which will support and enhance the needs of the agency. For, although interdependence is characteristic of the legal system, competition with other public agencies for support also exists.

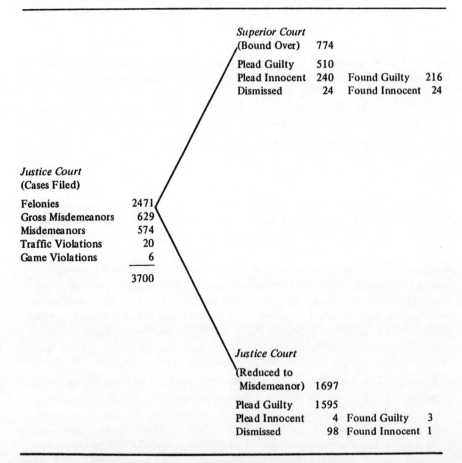

Superior Court
(Bound Over)   774

Plead Guilty   510
Plead Innocent   240   Found Guilty   216
Dismissed   24   Found Innocent   24

Justice Court
(Cases Filed)

Felonies   2471
Gross Misdemeanors   629
Misdemeanors   574
Traffic Violations   20
Game Violations   6
                                        ————
                                        3700

Justice Court
(Reduced to
Misdemeanor)   1697

Plead Guilty   1595
Plead Innocent   4   Found Guilty   3
Dismissed   98   Found Innocent 1

Figure 1. DISPOSITION OF FELONY CASES—KING COUNTY, 1964

[334] LAW AND SOCIETY REVIEW

Since organizations operate in an economy of scarcity, the organization must exist in a favorable power position in relation to its clientele. Reciprocal and unique claims are made by the organization and its clients. Thus, rather than being oriented toward only one public, an organization is beholden to several publics, some visible and others seen clearly only from the pinnacle of leadership. As Gore (1964: 23) notes, when these claims are "firmly anchored inside the organization and the lines drawn taut, the tensions between conflicting claims form a net serving as the institutional base for the organization."

An indication of the stresses within the judicial system may be obtained by analyzing its outputs. It has been suggested that the administration of justice is a selective process in which only those cases which do not create strains in the organization will ultimately reach the courtroom (Chambliss, 1969: 84). As noted in Figure 1, the system operates so that only a small number of cases arrive for trial, the rest being disposed of through reduced charges, *nolle pros.*, and guilty pleas.[2] Not indicated are those cases removed by the police and prosecutor prior to the filing of charges. As the focal organization in an exchange system, the office of prosecuting attorney makes decisions which reflect the influence of its clientele. Because of the scarcity of resources, marketlike relationships, and the organizational needs of the system, prosecutorial decision-making emphasizes the accommodations which are made to the needs of participants in the process.

Police

Although the prosecuting attorney has discretionary power to determine the disposition of cases, this power is limited by the fact that usually he is dependent upon the police for inputs to the system of cases and evidence. The prosecutor does not have the investigative resources necessary to exercise the kind of affirmative control over the types of cases that are brought to him. In this relationship, the prosecutor is not without countervailing power. His main check on the police is his ability to return cases to them for further investigation and to refuse to approve arrest warrants. By maintaining cordial relations with the press, a prosecutor is often able to focus attention on the police when the public becomes aroused by incidents of crime. As the King County prosecutor emphasized, "That [investigation] is the job for the sheriff and police. It's their job to bring me the charges." As noted by many respondents, the police, in turn, are dependent upon the prosecutor to accept the output of their system; rejection of too many cases can have serious repercussions affecting the morale, discipline, and workload of the force.

A request for prosecution may be rejected for a number of reasons relating to questions of evidence. Not only must the prosecutor believe that the

THE DECISION TO PROSECUTE [335]

evidence will secure a conviction, but he must also be aware of community norms relating to the type of acts that should be prosecuted. King County deputy prosecutors noted that charges were never filed when a case involved attempted suicide or fornication. In other actions, the heinous nature of the crime, together with the expected public reaction, may force both the police and prosecutor to press for conviction when evidence is less than satisfactory. As one deputy noted, "In that case [murder and molestation of a six-year-old girl] there was nothing that we could do. As you know the press was on our back and every parent was concerned. Politically, the prosecutor had to seek an information."

Factors other than those relating to evidence may require that the prosecutor refuse to accept a case from the police. First, the prosecuting attorney serves as a regulator of case loads not only for his own office, but for the rest of the legal system. Constitutional and statutory time limits prevent him and the courts from building a backlog of untried cases. In King County, when the system reached the "overload point," there was a tendency to be more selective in choosing the cases to be accepted. A second reason for rejecting prosecution requests may stem from the fact that the prosecutor is thinking of his public exposure in the courtroom. He does not want to take forward cases which will place him in an embarrassing position. Finally, the prosecutor may return cases to check the quality of police work. As a former chief criminal deputy said, "You have to keep them on their toes, otherwise they get lazy. If they aren't doing their job, send the case back and then leak the situation to the newspapers." Rather than spend the resources necessary to find additional evidence, the police may dispose of a case by sending it back to the prosecutor on a lesser charge, implement the "copping out" machinery leading to a guilty plea, drop the case, or in some instances send it to the city prosecutor for action in municipal court.

In most instances, a deputy prosecutor and the police officer assigned to the case occupy the boundary-spanning roles in this exchange relationship. Prosecutors reported that after repeated contacts they got to know the policemen whom they could trust. As one female deputy commented, "There are some you can trust, others you have to watch because they are trying to get rid of cases on you." Deputies may be influenced by the police officer's attitude on a case. One officer noted to a prosecutor that he knew he had a weak case, but mumbled, "I didn't want to bring it up here, but that's what they [his superiors] wanted." As might be expected, the deputy turned down prosecution.

Sometimes the police perform the ritual of "shopping around," seeking to find a deputy prosecutor who, on the basis of past experience, is liable to be sympathetic to their view on a case. At one time, deputies were given complete authority to make the crucial decisions without coordinating their

[336] LAW AND SOCIETY REVIEW

activities with other staff members. In this way the arresting officer would
search the prosecutor's office to find a deputy he thought would be sympathetic to the police attitude. As a former deputy noted, "This meant that
there were no departmental policies concerning the treatment to be accorded
various types of cases. It pretty much depended upon the police and their
luck in finding the deputy they wanted." Prosecutors are now instructed to
ascertain from the police officer if he has seen another deputy on the case.
Even under this more centralized system, it is still possible for the police to
request a specific deputy or delay presentation of the case until the "correct"
prosecutor is available. Often a prosecutor will gain a reputation for specializ-
ing in one type of case. This may mean that the police will assume he will get
the case anyway, so they skirt the formal procedure and bring it to him
directly.

An exchange relationship between a deputy prosecutor and a police officer
may be influenced by the type of crime committed by the defendant. The
prototype of a criminal is one who violates person and property. However, a
large number of cases involve "crimes without victims" (Schur, 1965). This
term refers to those crimes generally involving violations of moral codes,
where the general public is theoretically the complainant. In violations of laws
against bookmaking, prostitution, and narcotics, neither actor in the transaction is interested in having an arrest made. Hence, vice control men must
drum up their own business. Without a civilian complainant, victimless crimes
give the police and prosecutor greater leeway in determining the charges to be
filed.

One area of exchange involving a victimless crime is that of narcotics
control. As Skolnick (1966: 120) notes, "The major organizational requirement of narcotics policing is the presence of an informational system."
Without a network of informers, it is impossible to capture addicts and
peddlers with evidence that can bring about convictions. One source of
informers is among those arrested for narcotics violations. Through promises
to reduce charges or even to *nolle pros.*, arrangements can be made so that
the accused will return to the narcotics community and gather information for
the police. Bargaining observed between the head of the narcotics squad of
the Seattle Police and the deputy prosecutor who specialized in drug cases
involved the question of charges, promises, and the release of an arrested
narcotics pusher.

In the course of postarrest questioning by the police, a well-known drug
peddler intimated that he could provide evidence against a pharmacist
suspected by the police of illegally selling narcotics. Not only did the police
representative want to transfer the case to the friendlier hands of this deputy,
but he also wanted to arrange for a reduction of charges and bail. The police
officer believed that it was important that the accused be let out in such a

THE DECISION TO PROSECUTE [337]

way that the narcotics community would not realize that he had become an informer. He also wanted to be sure that the reduced charges would be processed so that the informer could be kept on the string, thus allowing the narcotics squad to maintain control over him. The deputy prosecutor, on the other hand, said that he wanted to make sure that procedures were followed so that the action would not bring discredit on his office. He also suggested that the narcotics squad "work a little harder" on a pending case as a means of returning the favor.

Courts

The ways used by the court to dispose of cases is a vital influence in the system. The court's actions effect pressures upon the prison, the conviction rate of the prosecutor, and the work of probation agencies. The judge's decisions act as clues to other parts of the system, indicating the type of action likely to be taken in future cases. As noted by a King County judge, "When the number of prisoners gets to the 'riot point,' the warden puts pressure on us to slow down the flow. This often means that men are let out on parole and the number of people given probation and suspended sentences increases." Under such conditions, it would be expected that the prosecutor would respond to the judge's actions by reducing the inputs to the court either by not preferring charges or by increasing the pressure for guilty pleas through bargaining. The adjustments of other parts of the system could be expected to follow. For instance, the police might sense the lack of interest of the prosecutor in accepting charges, hence they will send only airtight cases to him for indictment.

The influence of the court on the decision to prosecute is very real. The sentencing history of each judge gives the prosecutor, as well as other law enforcement officials, an indication of the treatment a case may receive in the courtroom. The prosecutor's expectation as to whether the court will convict may limit his discretion over the decisions on whether to prosecute. "There is great concern as to whose court a case will be assigned. After Judge _____ threw out three cases in a row in which entrapment was involved, the police did not want us to take any cases to him." Since the prosecutor depends upon the plea-bargaining machinery to maintain the flow of cases from his office, the sentencing actions of judges must be predictable. If the defendant and his lawyer are to be influenced to accept a lesser charge or the promise of a lighter sentence in exchange for a plea of guilty, there must be some basis for belief that the judge will fulfill his part of the arrangement. Because judges are unable formally to announce their agreement with the details of the bargain, their past performance acts as a guide.

[338] LAW AND SOCIETY REVIEW

Within the limits imposed by law and the demands of the system, the prosecutor is able to regulate the flow of cases to the court. He may control the length of time between accusation and trial; hence he may hold cases until he has the evidence which will convict. Alternatively, he may seek repeated adjournment and continuances until the public's interest dies; problems such as witnesses becoming unavailable and similar difficulties make his request for dismissal of prosecution more justifiable. Further, he may determine the type of court to receive the case and the judge who will hear it. Many misdemeanors covered by state law are also violations of a city ordinance. It is a common practice for the prosecutor to send a misdemeanor case to the city prosecutor for processing in the municipal court when it is believed that a conviction may not be secured in justice court. As a deputy said, "If there is no case—send it over to the city court. Things are speedier, less formal, over there."

In the state of Washington, a person arrested on a felony charge must be given a preliminary hearing in a justice court within ten days. For the prosecutor, the preliminary hearing is an opportunity to evaluate the testimony of witnesses, assess the strength of the evidence, and try to predict the outcome of the case if it is sent to trial. On the basis of this evaluation, the prosecutor has several options: he may bind over the case for trial in Superior Court; he may reduce the charges to those of a misdemeanor for trial in Justice Court; or he may conclude that he has no case and drop the charges. The President Judge of the Justice Courts of King County estimated that about seventy percent of the felonies are reduced to misdemeanors after the preliminary hearing.

Besides having some leeway in determining the type of court in which to file a case, the prosecutor also has some flexibility in selecting the judge to receive the case. Until recently the prosecutor could file a case with a specific judge. "The trouble was that Judge_____was erratic and independent, [so] no one would file with him. The other judges objected that they were handling the entire workload, so a central filing system was devised." Under this procedure cases are assigned to the judges in rotation. However, as the chief criminal deputy noted, "the prosecutor can hold a case until the 'correct' judge came up."

Defense Attorneys

With the increased specialization and institutionalization of the bar, it would seem that those individuals engaged in the practice of criminal law have been relegated, both by their profession and by the community, to a low status. The urban bar appears to be divided into three parts. First, there is an inner circle which handles the work of banks, utilities, and commercial

THE DECISION TO PROSECUTE [339]

concerns; second, another circle includes plaintiff's lawyers representing interests opposed to those of the inner circle; and finally, an outer group scrapes out an existence by "haunting the courts in hope of picking up crumbs from the judicial table" (Ladinsky, 1963: 128). With the exception of a few highly proficient lawyers who have made a reputation by winning acquittal for their clients in difficult, highly publicized cases, most of the lawyers dealing with the King County Prosecutor's Office belong to this outer ring.

In this study, respondents were asked to identify those attorneys considered to be specialists in criminal law. Of the nearly 1,600 lawyers practicing in King County only eight can be placed in this category. Of this group, six were reported to enjoy the respect of the legal community, while the others were accused by many respondents of being involved in shady deals. A larger group of King County attorneys will accept criminal cases, but these lawyers do not consider themselves specialists. Several respondents noted that many lawyers, because of inexperience or age, were required to hang around the courthouse searching for clients. One Seattle attorney described the quality of legal talent available for criminal cases as "a few good criminal lawyers and a lot of young kids and old men. The good lawyers I can count on my fingers."

In a legal system where bargaining is a primary method of decision-making, it is not surprising that criminal lawyers find it essential to maintain close personal ties with the prosecutor and his staff. Respondents were quite open in revealing their dependence upon this close relationship to successfully pursue their careers. The nature of the criminal lawyer's work is such that his saleable product or service appears to be influence rather than technical proficiency in the law. Respondents hold the belief that clients are attracted partially on the basis of the attorney's reputation as a fixer, or as a shrewd bargainer.

There is a tendency for ex-deputy prosecutors in King County to enter the practice of criminal law. Because of his inside knowledge of the prosecutor's office and friendships made with court officials, the former deputy feels that he has an advantage over other criminal law practitioners. All of the former deputies interviewed said that they took criminal cases. Of the eight criminal law specialists, seven previously served as deputy prosecutors in King County, while the other was once prosecuting attorney in a rural county.

Because of the financial problems of the criminal lawyer's practice, it is necessary that he handle cases on an assembly-line basis, hoping to make a living from a large number of small fees. Referring to a fellow lawyer, one attorney said, "You should see_____. He goes up there to Carroll's office with a whole fist full of cases. He trades on some, bargains on others and never goes to court. It's amazing but it's the way he makes his living." There are incentives, therefore, to bargain with the prosecutor and otlier decision-

[340] LAW AND SOCIETY REVIEW

makers. The primary aim of the attorney in such circumstances is to reach an accommodation so that the time-consuming formal proceedings need not be implemented. As a Seattle attorney noted, "I can't make any money if I spend my time in a courtroom. I make mine on the telephone or in the prosecutor's office." One of the disturbing results of this arrangement is that instances were reported in which a bargain was reached between the attorney and deputy prosecutor on a "package deal." In this situation, an attorney's clients are treated as a group; the outcome of the bargaining is often an agreement whereby reduced charges will be achieved for some, in exchange for the unspoken assent by the lawyer that the prosecutor may proceed as he desires with the other cases. One member of the King County Bar has developed this practice to such a fine art that a deputy prosecutor said, "When you saw him coming into the office, you knew that he would be pleading guilty." At one time this situation was so widespread that the "prisoners up in the jail had a rating list which graded the attorneys as either 'good guys' or 'sell outs.' "

The exchange relationship between the defense attorney and the prosecutor is based on their need for cooperation in the discharge of their responsibilities. Most criminal lawyers are interested primarily in the speedy solution of cases because of their precarious financial situation. Since they must protect their professional reputations with their colleagues, judicial personnel, and potential clientele, however, they are not completely free to bargain solely with this objective. As one attorney noted, "You can't afford to let it get out that you are selling out your cases."

The prosecutor is also interested in the speedy processing of cases. This can only be achieved if the formal processes are not implemented. Not only does the pressure of his caseload influence bargaining, but also the legal process with its potential for delay and appeal, creates a degree of uncertainty which is not present in an exchange relationship with an attorney with whom you have dealt for a number of years. As the Presiding Judge of the Seattle District Court said, "Lawyers are helpful to the system. They are able to pull things together, work out a deal, keep the system moving."

Community Influentials

As part of the political system, the judicial process responds to the community environment. The King County study indicated that there are differential levels of influence within the community and that some people had a greater interest in the politics of prosecution than others. First, the general public is able to have its values translated into policies followed by law enforcement officers. The public's influence is particularly acute in those

THE DECISION TO PROSECUTE [341]

gray areas of the law where full enforcement is not expected. Statutes may be enacted by legislatures defining the outer limits of criminal conduct, but they do not necessarily mean that laws are to be fully enforced to these limits. There are some laws defining behavior which the community no longer considers criminal. It can be expected that a prosecutor's charging policies will reflect this attitude. He may not prosecute violations of laws regulating some forms of gambling, certain sexual practices, or violations of Sunday Blue Laws.

Because the general public· is a potential threat to the prosecutor, staff members take measures to protect him from criticism. Respondents agreed that decision-making occurs with the public in mind—"will a course of action arouse antipathy towards the prosecutor rather than the accused?" Several deputies mentioned what they called the "aggravation level" of a crime. This is a recognition that the commission of certain crimes, within a specific context, will bring about a vocal public reaction. "If a little girl, walking home from the grocery store, is pulled into the bushes and indecent liberties taken, this is more disturbing to the public's conscience than a case where the father of the girl takes indecent liberties with her at home." The office of King County Prosecuting Attorney has a policy requiring that deputies file all cases involving sexual molestation in which the police believe the girl's story is credible. The office also prefers charges in all negligent homicide cases where there is the least possibility of guilt. In such types of cases the public may respond to the emotional context of the case and demand prosecution. To cover the prosecutor from criticism, it is believed that the safest measure is to prosecute.

The bail system is also used to protect the prosecutor from criticism. Thus it is the policy to set bail at a high level with the expectation that the court will reduce the amount. "This looks good for Prosecutor Carroll. Takes the heat off of him, especially in morals cases. If the accused doesn't appear in court the prosecutor can't be blamed. The public gets upset when they know these types are out free." This is an example of exchange where one actor is shifting the responsibility and potential onus onto another. In turn, the court is under pressure from county jail officials to keep the prison population down.

A second community group having contact with the prosecutor is composed of those leaders who have a continuing or potential interest in the politics of prosecution. This group, analogous to the players in one of Long's community games, are linked to the prosecutor because his actions affect their success in playing another game. Hence community boosters want either a crackdown or a hands-off policy towards gambling, political leaders want the prosecutor to remember the interests of the party, and business leaders want policies which will not interfere with their own game.

Community leaders may receive special treatment by the prosecutor if they run afoul of the law. A policy of the King County Office requires that cases involving prominent members of the community be referred immediately to the chief criminal deputy and the prosecutor for their disposition. As one deputy noted, "These cases can be pretty touchy. It's important that the boss knows immediately about this type of case so that he is not caught 'flat footed' when asked about it by the press."

Pressure by an interest group was evidenced during a strike by drug store employees in 1964. The striking unions urged Prosecutor Carroll to invoke a state law which requires the presence of a licensed pharmacist if the drug store is open. Not only did union representatives meet with Carroll, but picket lines were set up outside the courthouse protesting his refusal to act. The prosecutor resisted the union's pressure tactics.

In recent years, the prosecutor's tolerance policy toward minor forms of gambling led to a number of conflicts with Seattle's mayor, the sheriff, and church organizations. After a decision was made to prohibit all forms of public gaming, the prosecutor was criticized by groups representing the tourist industry and such affected groups as the bartenders' union which thought the decision would have an adverse economic effect. As Prosecutor Carroll said, "I am always getting pressures from different interests—business, the Chamber of Commerce, and labor. I have to try and maintain a balance between them." In exchange for these considerations, the prosecutor may gain prestige, political support, and admission into the leadership groups of the community.

Summary

By viewing the King County Office of Prosecuting Attorney as the focal organization in an exchange system, data from this exploratory study suggests the market-like relationships which exist between actors in the system. Since prosecution operates in an environment of scarce resources and since the decisions have potential political ramifications, a variety of officials influence the allocation of justice. The decision to prosecute is not made at one point, but rather the prosecuting attorney has a number of options which he may employ during various stages of the proceedings. But the prosecutor is able to exercise his discretionary powers only within the network of exchange relationships. The police, court congestion, organizational strains, and community pressures are among the factors which influence prosecutorial behavior.

THE DECISION TO PROSECUTE [343]

NOTES

1. See also Levine and White (1961: 583) and Blau (1955).
2. The lack of reliable criminal statistics is well known. These data were gathered from a number of sources, including King County (1964).

REFERENCES

BLAU, P. M. (1955) The Dynamics of Bureaucracy. Chicago: Univ. of Chicago Press.
CHAMBLISS, W. J. (1969) Crime and the Legal Process. New York: McGraw-Hill.
EVAN, W. M. (1965) "Towards a theory of inter-organizational relations." Management Sci. 11 (August): 218-230.
GORE, W. J. (1964) Administrative Decision Making. New York: John Wiley.
King County (1964) Annual Report of the Prosecuting Attorney. Seattle: State of Washington.
KLONSKI, J. R. and R. I. MENDELSOHN (1965) "The allocation of justice: a political analysis." J. of Public Law 14 (May): 323-342.
LADINSKY, J. (1963) "The impact of social backgrounds of lawyers on law practice and the law." J. of Legal Education 16, 2: 128-144.
LEVINE, S. and P. E. WHITE (1961) "Exchange as a conceptual framework for the study of inter-organizational relationships." Administrative Sci. Q. 5 (March): 583-601.
LONG, N. (1962) The Polity. Chicago: Rand McNally.
SCHUR, E. M. (1965) Crimes Without Victims. Englewood Cliffs, N.J.: Prentice-Hall.
SKOLNICK, J. E. (1966) Justice Without Trial. New York: John Wiley.

[12]

THE ARREST VERSUS THE CASE
Some Observations on
Police/District Attorney Interaction

ELIZABETH A. STANKO

THE ALL TOO FAMILIAR organizational flowchart may represent the smooth step-by-step process of the criminal justice system, but it is the employees of that system, engaged in complex bureaucratically and organizationally structured human interactions, who actually determine the work that gets accomplished. Each employee's role within the criminal justice system is often described as if it were a position covered by a player on some sort of sporting team. While each player does contribute one specialized skill to the collective effort of the criminal justice team, the actual contribution which that player makes can only be understood within the context of the particular game he or she is playing.

It is this "game context" played between police officers and assistant prosecutors that is the concern of this article.

AUTHOR'S NOTE: My thanks to Michael Brown and Lindsey Churchill for keeping alive these thoughts, and for their helpful criticisms of earlier versions. I would like to express my appreciation to Tom Ewart for his editing and unquestioned support. An earlier version of this article was presented at the Society for the Study of Social Problems Meeting, Chicago, 1977. My sincere appreciation is extended to the anonymous Urban Life reviewers whose comments aided my own clarification of this work.

URBAN LIFE, Vol. 9 No. 4, January 1981 395-414
© 1981 Sage Publications, Inc.

396   URBAN LIFE   January 1981

While these individuals are equipped with the entire criminal justice system's rules, each actor must additionally satisfy the organizational demands of his or her particular employer, i.e., the police department or the prosecutor's office. Thus, any complete description of the criminal justice system will include not only an account of the actor's "flowchart" activities, i.e., the external rules, but also an account of the actor's everyday activities that are governed by each individual's organizational demands, i.e., internal rules. The existence of two sets of rules, the external set for the entire system's operations and the internal set for the individual's specific organizational operations, creates the potential for contradictory expectations, goals, and outcomes for these actors.

Conflict between police and prosecutors is readily acknowledged in both popular and sociological arenas. Neubauer (1974) speaks of the police/prosecutor relationship as one embedded in the potentials for conflict. He notes three primary factors for this conflict:

(1) the varying social backgrounds of both actors
(2) the different views of law held by each actor
(3) the different pressures and goals produced by their work environments

Thus, while the police officer and the prosecutor both are guided by the same penal statutes, each of these individuals will apply those statutes differently through his or her specific job demands which reflect the internal mandates, policies, and procedures of that organization. Neubauer sees the police/prosecutor relationship as one in which

---

EDITOR'S NOTE: The term "criminal justice system" may be a misnomer, insofar as it does not always reflect the integration, cohesiveness, and operational interdependence conveyed by the term "system." Elizabeth Stanko's article reveals the conflict stemming from antagonistic structural and interactional features of the criminal justice process by describing the tensions embedded in the police-prosecutor relationship. Her study contributes both to the understanding of the prosecution process as an interaction process, as well as to the recognition of the tacit rules and often discretionary character of the prosecution process.

conflict is always present. Any contact between the two organizations is confined almost exclusively to formal interchanges.

In contrast, Carter (1974) views the police/prosecutor relationship as one that encourages accommodation and compromise. The important distinction here is that police/prosecutor interaction occurs informally, with both sides pursuing a smooth working relationship. He cites factors such as the prosecutors' empathy toward the police job, the necessity of maintaining trust and the fear of criticism as the reasons why prosecutors become, essentially, advocates for the police. This advocacy role, in turn, discourages the prosecutors from screening out cases they know to have defects. However, if a jurisdiction is involved with a considerably larger number of police and prosecutors, the informal working relationship is not likely to exist. Therefore, a more formal relationship may contribute to the potential conflict that arises within the everyday encounters of police and prosecutors.

Skolnick (1966) further alerts us to possible conflict between the police and prosecutor by noting the police officer's craftsmanlike judgments of the guilt or innocence of a suspect. A potential conflict would arise if the officer's decision to arrest is not treated seriously by a prosecuting attorney in his decision to charge.

The above studies set the stage for potential police/prosecutor conflicts. This paper provides conversational accounts of this conflict as it occurs during the routine processing of felony arrests. Through an examination of the routine operations of the criminal justice system, the potentially contradictory components of the system are illustrated along with the various strategies utilized by each party to transform or mute this conflict. The discussion focuses on how the divergent work routines of the police and the prosecutor may lead to the conflicting goals and expectations of the criminal justice system itself, generating conflicts through a variety of interaction processes.

398   URBAN LIFE   January 1981

WORK ENVIRONMENTS

This study takes place within a densely populated urban center on the East Coast. During 1975, over 100,000 arrests were processed through the halls of its criminal court. Of those arrests, over 31,000 were for felony offenses.

In order to more efficiently handle the influx of felony offenses in 1975, the district attorney established a bureau staffed primarily with senior assistant prosecutors (ADAs) to screen all incoming felony offenses. This screening process involves both the review of the arrest charges and the selection of the more serious felony offenses for immediate action in superior court. All other felony arrests which, during subsequent plea negotiations are likely to be reduced below the felony level, are handled in the lower courts.

For the purposes of examining police officer/ADA interactions, this screening bureau, known as the Early Case Assessment Bureau (ECAB), provides a unique setting which allows the viewer a glimpse at both the police officer and ADA's work contexts. Here, seven days a week, eight hours a day, the ADAs encounter the police officers immediately following an arrest in this first step of the criminal court process.

For approximately thirteen months, I observed felony arrest screening, and recorded descriptive accounts of the interactions among the assistant prosecutor, arresting police officer and complaining witness(es). During the last five months of observation, I was able to transcribe the dialogue among these actors. Although I witnessed over 1000 felony screenings, I transcribed over 100 conversational exchanges of felony case assessment, limiting my data collection to assault, rape and robbery offenses. Additionally, I conducted intensive interviews with the assistant prosecutors of ECAB and some administrative prosecutors.

THE ASSISTANT DISTRICT ATTORNEY

During the arrest screening, the ADA interviews the arresting officer and the complainant, if any. With these individuals, the ADA reviews the circumstances of the arrest, assesses the evidence against the individual who has been arrested, and draws up an affidavit that reflects the actions of that individual. Then, the ADA assigns the case a disposition category which determines the boundaries for the final resolution of the felony arrest charges. While the choice of dispositional boundaries for the ADA anticipates the plea bargaining process, the essential decision rests upon whether or not the arrest is a prosecutable felony case. All other case determinations, i.e., the actual charges after a plea bargain are left to the ADA staffing the subsequent stages of the criminal processing. Thus, the ADA has the following choices for that category of disposition: s/he may

(1) decline prosecution (dismiss the charges)
(2) file a misdemeanor complaint (reduce the charges)
(3) file a felony complaint (with instructions to dispose the case in the lower court—de facto reduction of charges)
(4) file a felony complaint (with instructions for further investigation prior to a final determination)
(5) file a felony complaint recommending the immediate presentation of the case to the grand jury (retain felony charges)

Early case screening exemplifies one instance of prosecutorial discretion. Experienced trial attorneys staff the screening bureau, drawing on their competence to know when a felony arrest is likely to be prosecuted successfully. Similar to Sudnow's (1967) defense attorneys, this competence is based upon the ADA's ability to typify arrests in terms of normally prosecutable serious offenses.

For the ADAs, then, the screening function of the ECAB serves as the gate-keeping mechanism for all cases handled

400   URBAN LIFE   January 1981

by the district attorney's office. More importantly, the activity of the screening bureau reduces the workload of the ADAs in superior court. During felony screening, the ADA chooses cases which are most likely to result in the conviction of the defendant. Reducing the court's case backlog is a mandate for this bureau. Thus, the ECAB ADA will determine the seriousness of a case not only through a variety of legal and extra-legal criteria, but with an eye to the total organizational context of workload and the desire for a high conviction rate.

Furthermore, the criterion of convictability is based upon perceived probability of conviction at trial, a much more rigid requirement of felony cases. For the ADAs, trials introduce an element of uncertainty due to the unpredictable jury verdict. Therefore, the ADAs prefer to select only cases that meet optimal conditions of "guilt," easily recognized by any potential juror. Because of the uncertainty of the jury factor, the ADAs will eliminate cases whose extra-legal criteria, i.e., credibility questions raised by the complainant's character, present commonsensically recognized problems for the prosecution.

Thus, through the "common" knowledge of what constitutes a typical convictable case, this gatekeeping function is accomplished as an internal organizational work task for the prosecutor within the context of reducing the growing backlog of felony cases entering superior court. Screening felony arrests, while normally understood as an intake procedure for the entire criminal justice system, may also be viewed as the intake procedure for the work of the district attorney's office.

THE POLICE OFFICER

Turning to the activities of the police, we can see that an arrest is only one activity of police work. In the course of an average tour of duty, a police officer is called upon to settle disputes, assist in medical emergencies, give directions to lost tourists, answer complaints and occasionally arrest a violator of the law. All are routine police activities. Hence, the overall police purpose is constabulatory, commonly referred to as "maintaining the peace" (Bittner, 1967; Banton, 1964).

Further, within this jurisdiction, the police respond to one of the highest workloads in the country. Similar to Bittner's (1967) police on skid row, this police force exercises discretionary decisions with concern to the continuous condition of crime in their own precincts, rather than to that of the city or to society in general. For Bittner, the decision to arrest is the result of a complex and varied set of circumstances, ranging from the prospect of overtime pay to the situational demands of an incident. Thus, when an arrest is made, there exists a certain set of optimal criteria by which that arrest can be judged as having been made properly or improperly. The criteria for that arrest, while guided by the penal law, are based in the everyday organizational context of the police officer (e.g., Skolnick, 1966).

Thus, in the handling of any given incident involving a possible violation of the law, the police officer may or may not make an arrest. Once an arrest is made, however, it normally constitutes a break from the routine activities of that police officer, and that arrest decision, as Bittner states, is governed by an individual police officer's personal wisdom, integrity, altruism and discretionary options.

In the application of the penal code to an incident, the police officer utilizes his/her own interpretations and recipes for categorizing offenses. The determination of harm, and to a certain extent, of fault, is thus entirely a discretionary matter, and made within the organization context which itself recognizes harm and fault. The ability of the police officer to attribute meaning to a variety of activities involves a certain competence. However, this competence is as much the common sense of the lay person as it is a professional competence (Sachs, 1972).

Once an arrest is made, the police officer begins the processing of the accused individual through the criminal justice system. In arrests involving felony offenses, the first

402   URBAN LIFE   January 1981

step is the screening of that arrest by an ADA. During arrest screening, the prosecutor is deemed the responsible agent for selecting a felony case. The police officer essentially loses control over the final outcome of the matter initiated by his or her original arrest. It is at this point that the seriousness of the arrest charges, as defined by the police officer in the context of his or her work contingencies, may diverge from the potential felony case as defined by the ADA in his or her work context.

THE FELONY ARREST VERSUS THE FELONY CASE

Both the police officer and the ADA exercise their professional discretion with respect to distinct work environments and the assumptions each calls for—the potential jury trial for the ADA and street contingencies for the police officer. Those very environments provide the considerations to which each participant responds.

The ADA's task during casework is to select those felony arrests which can be successfully presented as felony cases.[1] ADAs speak of those cases not afforded felony status as "garbage cases." However, the ADAs must rely upon the police to supply them with felony arrests for assessment. Thus, many arrests which are made during routine policework are treated by the ADAs as garbage cases. The struggle of authority between the ADA and the arresting officer during casework becomes one of the good felony arrest (represented by the rationale of the arresting officer) versus the felony case (as predicted by the ADA during casework).

Often the police officers do not question the ADA's ability to assess the arrest and determine the disposition of the case. In discussions with the police, many indicate that their job is satisfied upon the arrest of a suspect. It is then "up to the court" to decide how it is going to process that suspect. At times, as is the situation with arrests accompanied by civilian complainants, the police officer acts as the agent of the criminal justice system who introduces the matter into that system. In these instances, e.g., robbery and assault arrests, the arresting officer accompanies the case through disposition but is not the primary witness. Unless the arresting officer takes a personal interest in a civilian's complaint, he or she will not be particularly concerned about what the ADA does with the arrest. However, to the arresting police officer involved, the ADA's decisions during arrest screening are now a visible and immediate assessment of the arrest charges as made by that officer. Therefore, the arresting officer now confronts the ADA head-on and witnesses the evaluation of his or her arrest in terms of a case.

Although the work of the ADAs depends on street activity as represented by street arrests, it systematically ignores the character of policework, including the judgments and practices involved in meting out justice on the street. During casework, the legal judgment of the police officer by which he or she categorizes an incident as an offense is replaced by judgment of the prosecutor. This replacement shows quite clearly the confrontation of authorities endemic to a criminal justice system that separates the constabulary from the prosecutory practices.

While the assessments of illegal activity made by the ADA and the police officer occupationally contradict each other, justification for the felony charge variance is sometimes negotiated between the two. But in instances where a police officer determines an act to be more serious than the ADA defines it to be, the ADAs unleash their frustration at police officers who make what they believe to be incompetent interpretations of the law. Occasionally, police officers will file felony charges that "stretch" the penal code's definition of felonious activity. There is a fine line between "overcharging" by a police officer—defining the act as more serious than it is or appears to be—and establishing the correct degree of seriousness of the crime. The significance of overcharging is that its use can be understood as a part of the police occupation. As Bittner (1967) states, the law is merely a resource with which to solve practical problems when "keeping the peace." During

404   URBAN LIFE   January 1981

my observations in the precinct, justification for stretching
the law ranged from the arresting officer's desire for court
overtime pay to the demeanor of the arrested individual.

The following examples illustrate police/ADA interaction
during the screening of felony arrests.

Example 1

> ADA What was the argument about?
>
> A/O (Shrugs his shoulders.) They said they were coming in
> [to the ADA's office] this morning. I said, "make sure."
>
> ADA Hit her in the head and arm?
>
> A/O Nose and face.
>
> ADA Where did he hit the other one?
>
> A/O Right forearm.
>
> ADA Any cuts?
>
> A/O No.
>
> ADA Bruises?
>
> A/O Looked like there was a lump on her face.
>
> ADA No cuts?
>
> A/O No.
>
> ADA Change the charge from felonious assault to misdemean-
> or assault.
>
> A/O (Leans over and sees the ADA reducing the charge to a
> misdemeanor.) I was going to do that last night but I de-
> cided to let you do it instead [A-27].[2]

The ADA's outrage is exacerbated by the police officer's
admission to charging the defendant with a felony rather
than a misdemeanor. The ADA turned to me and complained
about those officers wasting their time with "garbage
cases."

Example 2

> ADA Where's the burglary here?
>
> A/O Entering the building for the purposes of committing a
> crime.

ADA Uh-huh, not an abandoned apartment. The statute refers
to the crimes of larceny, assault, sex crimes, [but] a junkie
in an abandoned building shooting up is not [a crime].
May be criminal mischief, so that's out the window. But
it looks good on the felony rolls in the [precinct] [M-2].

This example of moralizing shows again that the ADA and
the police officer are not simply functionally related in this
performance of parts of an overall task, but are engaged in
different and antagonistic tasks. The ADA indicates his
assessment of why nonfelony cases are brought in as felony
arrests by the police: to increase the number of felony
arrests made in the precinct. Here, the work concerns for
each organization are clearly displayed. For the police, the
increase in the number of felony arrests means a higher
clearance for crimes committed in their precinct. While on
the other hand, the ADA is not interested in wasting his
time on the police officer's organizational needs. Unlike the
prosecutors in Carter's (1974) study, the ADAs do not
hesitate to increase the antagonism between themselves
and the police. At times, the police are viewed as flagrantly
misusing the penal law.

Example 3

An individual was arrested in a fight involving a corrections
officer. The arresting officer was concerned that the corrections officer was injured. He took photographs of the complainant before he entered the hospital for treatment. The
charges against the defendant were attempted murder,
assault in the second degree, attempted robbery, and possession of a controlled substance. The charges were reduced
by the ADA to assault in the third degree [misdemeanor] and
possession of a controlled substance as a misdemeanor.
After the arresting officer had left the room, the ADA
remarked: "Doesn't hold water; he had him charged with
attempted murder, robbery in the first degree, assault in the
second degree—no weapon!! Said that he tried to rob his
gun. These goddamn cops" [A-21].

Charging an arrested individual with an offense is one
power available to the police, as is the power to arrest, and

406   URBAN LIFE   January 1981

either can reflect the officer's perception of the seriousness of a particular situation. Whatever the general reasons for the felony charges, particular charges are often made by the officer for reasons other than the actions of the individual defendant. These charging decisions can be understood within the context and meaning of policework to the officer.

The officer, as a necessary part of his routine work in a particular precinct, often conducts his work in a manner that would not be considered legal by the ADA. For example, in questioning an officer's arrest for the possession of a controlled substance, the ADA asked if the officer had "just routinely searched the jacket before he actually saw the heroin in the pocket." The arresting officer replied that in this case, he had not. "Good," remarked the ADA, "usually cops search without provocation." The arresting officer smiled at the ADA, commenting; "I would have searched without provocation. Listen, when you work in that neighborhood, you protect yourself on all ends." Thus, the officer recognizes that in order to do his work, he may have to conduct his inquiry in a manner that is "not quite legal." Overall, the practical situation plays a more important part in a police officer's actions than the requirements of law.

During casework, the ADA cannot address an officer's attempt to mediate a situation that exists within the precinct unless the arrest results in a felony case.

Example 4

One young male has been arrested for the robbery of another young male. The complainant in the case has been interviewed by the ADA and has just been asked to wait outside while the ADA and the arresting officer finish drawing up the papers:

ADA You've got a bullshit case.

A/O In one respect—you see what the outcome is, so, in a sense, it's not bullshit. They call him [the defendant] "Truck." He's 185 pounds, 6'1"

ADA The thing about him is, though . . . there's got to be more to it than that. They might be shaking the kid [the complainant] down . . .

A/O That's what I think it is.

ADA How are you going to prove it?

A/O I know what you are writing down. You have all of the elements for a 160 [penal law statute for robbery] here. You have fear. . . . I know what you're speaking about. But if this guy gets out, this kid will be DOA tomorrow . . . in St. Luke's.

ADA What do you want to do?

A/O You want me to lock up the third guy [the defendant's partner, who escaped]? I'd like to speak to this. Let me explain what is going on. On 90th street is all muggers. They walk up to people on the street. Two black guys walk up to two white kids and start patting them down . . . and they threaten them. If they find some money on them, they will be in trouble.

ADA This is not a mugging.

A/O I witnessed the kid. My partner, just speak to my partner.

ADA Do whatever you want. That's the police department's problem, whether or not to pick up the third guy. I'm writing this up as a robbery 2 [second degree]. If this ever went to trial, it would be a disaster. The only thing we have is extortion [R-32].

In this instance, the arresting officer attempts to convince the ADA that this arrest is a felony case by explaining his work context. The arresting officer wants the cooperation of the ADA in the mediation of a particular street activity in his jurisdiction. However, the ADA addresses himself to the problems of the arrest as a felony case. The conversation between the ADA and the arresting officer continues with each actor operating within the realm of his occupational demands: casework versus policework. The arresting officer is concerned with the situation as it exists in his precinct. The ADA is unable to respond to the call for higher court intervention and reaffirms his task of forwarding only convictable cases.

The ADA did file the charges against the defendant as a robbery offense. However, he did not determine the case to be a felony case and offered the following explanation: "If this ever went to trial, it would be a disaster." After the arresting officer left the room, I asked the ADA about the case. The ADA seemed concerned, yet replied, "This is what I think: I think the defendant is a bad guy. Possibly shaking down the whole community. But there's nothing I can do with this case."

Occasionally, an arresting officer will go to great lengths to retain the arrest charges that he or she chooses. In the following example, the arresting officer discussed the arrest with two ADAs. After the first encounter with the junior ECAB ADA, the arresting officer stormed out of the room to speak to the desk sergeant. He stopped to talk to the ADA as he was leaving and the discussion turned into an argument. The ADA told the officer to speak to the senior ADA on duty. As the ADA returned to the room, he remarked to the senior ADA: "I think we're going to get regurgitations on this case. . . . The arresting officer wants to go higher. I said to go to you. He said that you're an asshole too." About five minutes later, the arresting officer returned to ECAB and spoke to the senior ADA. The arresting officer insisted that the charges were correct and demanded an explanation for the reductions.

Example 5

ADA What's the problem here?

A/O The problem is what the ADA is doing to the case . . .

ADA (Takes the arrest sheets and looks them over.) Looks like two misdemeanors here.

A/O Why misdemeanors?

ADA Let's start with the gun—it's in his place of work. It's a misdemeanor unless he has a conviction.

A/O He has a conviction, on a weapons charge.

ADA OK, it's an A [misdemeanor] raised to a D felony on a technical felony [level].

A/O What's reckless endangerment?

ADA Not on those grounds.

A/O If I fired one shot within five feet of people on the street, they would charge me with reckless endangerment.

ADA It's got to be risk of death. Firing a gun into the ground is not serious endangerment. The three other people, I assume, were not caught.

A/O I have a witness. . . . I didn't charge him with attempted murder; the problem is with what the charges are.

ADA OK, reckless endangerment in the second degree.

A/O So, it is correct.

ADA We are going to charge it, but we'll never prove it. It's very difficult to prove reckless endangerment.

A/O How's that not reckless endangerment if he fired shots into the ground?

ADA You have to assume that firing into the ground. . . . You can't ask the jury to assume; you have to prove it beyond a reasonable doubt.

A/O But you can charge him.

ADA But we'll never convict him of it.

A/O I don't get involved with convictions.

ADA But that's our job [M-1].

Not only does the above exchange capture the differing organizational perspectives, but it illustrates the strategies used by each party to justify his actions. The ADA's job is to assure convictions from the selected felony cases. On the other hand, the arresting officer does not concern himself with convictions, even though he must concern himself with the formulations of the arrest charges in order to make an arrest. These participants, whose "system" goal is the meting out of "justice," confront each other through the differing organizational interpretations of that goal. Subsequently, the occupational environment for justice differs: the street for the police officer and the court for the ADA.

410   URBAN LIFE   January 1981

As the discussion continues, the ADA and the arresting officer speak as organizational representatives who are vying for authority in mediating criminal matters:

A/O My whole contention here is that I never charged him with attempted murder.

ADA The reckless endangerment is not important.

A/O I charged him with the aspect of reckless endangerment as a felony.

ADA It's an irrelevant charge. If we charged him. . . . We don't need it.

A/O The case also won't go to the grand jury.

ADA You know what happens in the grand jury. We often have to take these cases to the grand jury. Here's the problem. You have a witness that sees three people get out of a cab. We don't know why the shooting started. We give him [defendant] a chance to plea to an A misdemeanor. He gets his shot and we get ours . . . OK, all set. If the guy pleads, we won't see it again [M-1].

After the arresting officer left the room, the ADA remarked: "He's excited about an A misdemeanor." During the discussion, both the ADA and the officer converse in the language of their organization. Further, the logic of either party's argument does not receive legitimacy by the other. As the arresting officer does not concern himself with convictions, the ADA does not concern himself with the arresting officer's reasons for charging as he did, unless it can be useful in the determination of a felony case. The ADA's concern is a felony case, not mediating community matters (unless those matters are determined to be felony cases). I asked the arresting officer a few months later what the disposition of the case was. The officer replied, "$150 fine and he [the defendant] walked out that day."

SUMMARY AND DISCUSSION

The interactional work between the ADA and the police officer during the arrest screening process is characterized here as that of antagonistic cooperation. This strained interaction often is created by the police officer and the ADA as a result of their different and divergent views—views of what a case, in fact, is; of what, according to each participant's knowledge of typical arrests and typical cases, a felony arrest looks like; and of what the appropriate grounds are upon which arrests are selected as cases for the felony category in criminal court. Each view is grounded in the occupational perspective that emerges from the routinization of the employee's daily work activities, and that view is oriented to the specific needs and demands of the particular organization within the criminal justice system which employs that individual.

For the ADA, an arrest represents the raw data from which to select felony cases. Although the ADAs are dependent upon the police to supply them with this data, they do not hesitate to criticize the police for the poor quality of the data. Because an arrest is only one aspect of policework, the arrest can have a variety of meanings for the officer: keeping the peace, protecting the neighborhood, placating an insistent complainant, and so on. The officers feel that the ADAs do not know "what it is like on the street" and therefore cannot appreciate why the police make the particular arrest. The contingencies presented in every arrest decision can seldom be articulated to or appreciated by the ADAs.

Thus, in the exercise of the system's discretion, each actor brings to ECAB his or her particular organizational objectives. While the divergence of these organizational objectives has been noted within the criminal justice system (Skolnick, 1966; Carter, 1974; Neubauer, 1974; Mather,

1974), an actual illustration of such divergence has not, until now, been displayed as a feature of the everyday social interactions found in the daily routine of the arrest screening process.

Given the backlog problems of today's urban courts, felony arrest screening serves theoretical and practical gatekeeping functions for the caseloads entering criminal court. However, this gatekeeping function is one which operates according to the interests, and therefore control, of the district attorney's office. Thus, conflict which arises during this gatekeeping function cannot be understood without recognizing the diverse organizational interests of the two negotiating parties (the police officer and the ADA) that confront each other during the initial stages of criminal court processing. For the police officer and the ADA, the encounter in ECAB is such that neither participant can know the real demands and limitations of the other's work. Thus, many incidents of conflict arise because each participant is unaccountable for and ignorant of the other's work, and, to some extent, even considers it irrelevant to his or her own work.

Unlike the prosecutors in Carter's (1974) study, these ADAs do not empathize with the police officers. Perhaps the antagonistic encounters result from the work overload or the formal relationship between the police department and the district attorney's office. But, this remains an empirical question. Both organizations have liaison offices which conduct regular meetings to iron out problems between them. However, these offices have never seemed to alleviate the everyday conflict that occurs interpersonally between individual ADAs and police officers, and this interpersonal conflict, so engrained within the different demands of each party's organizations, continues to erupt. Just before I completed my series of observations, I witnessed a scuffle between a police officer and an ADA. Both the ADA and the police officer were loudly arguing, then pushing and shoving. Although this incident did not result in a physical contest, the discussion ended with both parties squared off. I could not help thinking that perhaps this represented a continuous stance between the police and prosecutorial organizations as well.

NOTES

1. I have termed casework the process whereby the ADA, in the course of screening felony arrests, selects prosecutable cases from those arrests. Thus, the ADA establishes and maintains, in the course of routinely working, the criteria for a prosecutable case.

2. The data presented are conversational accounts transcribed during the arrest screening process in the Criminal Complaint Room. The assigned symbols represent case numbers (ADA = Assistant District Attorney; A/O = Arresting Officer.)

REFERENCES

BANTON, M. (1964) The Policeman in the Community. New York: Basic Books.

BITTNER, E. (1967) "The police on skid row: a study of peace keeping." Amer. Soc. Rev. 32: 699-715.

CARTER, L. (1974) The Limits of Order. Lexington, MA: D. C. Heath.

COLE, G. F. (1975) The American System of Criminal Justice. Belmont, CA: Wadsworth.

GOLDSTEIN, J. (1960) "Police discretion not to invoke the criminal process." Yale Law J. 69: 543-594.

MATHER, L. (1974) "Some determinants of the method of case disposition: decision making by public defenders in Los Angeles." Law and Society Rev. 8: 187-216.

MILLER, F. W. (1969) Prosecution: The Decision to Charge a Suspect with a Crime. Boston: Little, Brown.

MYER, M. and J. HAGAN (1978) "Private and public trouble: prosecutors and the allocation of court resources." Presented at the annual meetings of the American Society of Criminology, Dallas.

NEUBAUER, D. W. (1974) Criminal Justice in Middle America. Morristown, NJ: General Learing Press.

SACHS, H. (1972) "Notes on police assessment of moral character," pp. 280-293
    in D. Sudnow (ed.) Studies in Social Interaction. New York: Free Press.
SKOLNICK, J. (1966) Justice Without Trial. New York: John Wiley.
STANKO, E. A. (1977) "These are the cases that try themselves." Ph.D. disserta-
    tion, City University of New York.
SUDNOW, D. (1967) "Normal crimes: sociological features of the penal code."
    Social Problems, 12: 255-276.

ELIZABETH A. STANKO is an Assistant Professor of Sociology at Clark University.
Her research focuses upon prosecutorial decision making in everyday settings.
She is currently expanding her interests in the area of the victimology of women.

[13]

International Journal of the Sociology of Law 1988, **16**, 359–382

Personal Violence and Public Order: The Prosecution of 'Domestic' Violence in England and Wales

ANDREW SANDERS

Faculty of Law, Birmingham University, PO Box 363, Birmingham B15 2TT, U.K.

1. Introduction

The scale and seriousness of domestic violence has been, traditionally, grossly underestimated. Recent research has begun to redress the balance, but problems of classification and comparison and the 'dark figure' of unreported and unrecorded crime remain. The 'dark figure' is partly due to under-reporting by victims, itself partly due to their lack of confidence in the criminal justice system (Pahl, 1985). It is also a product of under-recording, such as when the police 'no crime' assaults upon which they do not wish to take action (Edwards, unpublished; Stanko, 1985, ch. 9) [1]. The *particular* problems of domestic violence are highlighted when these findings are contrasted with the way other crime is treated, for the dark figure of domestic violence appears to be greater than that of other crime (Dobash & Dobash, 1980; Hanmer & Stanko, 1985; Worrall & Pease, 1986). But the attitudes, experiences, and processes leading to under-reporting and under-recording are not confined to *domestic* violence (Jones *et al.*, 1986, p. 85).

Criminal justice research on domestic violence has focused on arrest rates. In the U.S.A. the police appear to arrest for domestic assault relatively less frequently than for other assault (Dobash & Dobash, 1980, pp.207–9), although Smith and Klein (1984) did not find this. English arrest rates in domestic cases are around 15–20% (Faragher, 1985). Even in a special initiative in Bedfordshire in 1976, there were arrests in only 36% of cases because in the majority of cases the victim did not wish to pursue the matter and "any injuries visible did not justify police intervention" (quoted in Freeman, 1979, p. 190). It seems that domestic victims' lack of confidence in the police is often justified. But non-domestic violence is also frequently 'no crimed' and dealt with other than

0194–6595/88/030359 + 25 $03.00/0

360   *A. Sanders*

by arrest (Bottomly & Coleman, 1976; Chatterton, 1983, pp. 203–7), justifying the lack of confidence which non-domestic victims also have (according to the Islington Crime Survey: Jones *et al.*, 1986, p. 85). No British research has yet compared domestic and non-domestic violence arrest rates. Given the ambiguity of the American results, differential arrest rates in Britain would not be inevitable, the scale of difference might not be great, and—most important, as we shall see—the difference may not hinge on the domestic/non-domestic dimension.

Comparison raises the question of relevant comparators. Walmsley's recent study of personal violence used offical statistics to discuss different types, circumstances and victims of violence. Male/female and domestic/non-domestic dimensions were among the comparisons made (Walmsley, 1986, p. 28 and Appendix C). Walmsley acknowledged that since the dark figures of different types of violence may vary, comparisons based on official statistics are of limited value. But it is equally problematic to accept police offence classification. Walmsley claims that he specifically excludes offences in which the victim is not "directly and personally invloved" (1986, p. 1) by excluding public order offences (such as threatening behaviour, riot, possession of an offensive weapon) and including (for instance) wounding. This assumes that personal violence does not give rise to public order charges alone and that personal violence charges (such as assault) do not arise out of riotous (i.e., public order) incidents.

In this paper I shall argue that this type of misconception runs through both the 'official' and the 'radical' literature, and produces apparently irreconcilable findings which become comprehensible only when the public order dimension is confronted. I shall draw upon research, carried out in 1981–3, on prosecution decisions in three English police force areas. Police and prosecutors provided full access to all personnel and the papers on 1200 cases (which were followed, where applicable, to court). Unlike most domestic violence research, these cases constituted a completely random sample of adult non-motoring offences [2].

2. The Decision To Prosecute

The research samples were a mixture of cases reported for summons (i.e. prior to the decision whether or not to prosecute) and cases which were already charged (i.e. after the decision to prosecute). It was therefore not possible to identify the overall proportions of domestic violence cases (or any other categories of offence) not prosecuted, although comparisons between offence types are possible.

Table 1 shows that male domestic violence constituted 16.5% of the total violence (15.5% of the violence prosecutions). Yet in the Islington Crime Survey domestic violence constituted 22% of all the violence reported to the police (Jones *et al.*, 1986, p. 63). If my samples and the Crime Survey are both

Table 1. Male violence: prosecutions and non-prosecutions

Cases	Domestic	Non-domestic	Total
Prosecuted	35 (87·5%)	190 (94·1%)	225 (93%)
Not prosecuted	5 (12·5%)	12 (5·9%)	17 (7%)
Total	40	202	242

representative then there is indeed a disproportionately low arrest, charge and prosecution rate in domestic violence cases as compared to other violence. In Table 1, it can be seen that twice as many male domestic violence cases as other male violence cases were not prosecuted, and between all 'domestics' and all other offences there is the same ratio (15% and 7% not prosecuted respectively).

The Association of Chief Police Officers (ACPO) provided the Select Committee on Violence in Marriage with its criteria for deciding whether or not to prosecute domestic assaults (Select Committee, 1975, pp. 367–8). These criteria—offence seriousness, the wishes and availability of the victim and other witnesses, the character of the parties, and so forth—are similar to those applied to 'normal' offences (Sanders, 1985a; DPP, 1986). Although interconnected, these criteria are analytically distinct and their use can therefore be examined separately, with the warning that my material primarily deals with decisions following arrest and charge.

(i) Victim Withdrawal and Unreliability

The police claim that victim withdrawal and unreliability is the usual reason for non-prosecution, as in the Bedfordshire initiative referred to above (Freeman, 1979) and in their evidence to the Select Committee (1975, pp. 361–5). But this begs several questions. First, how true is this in relation to other crime? Second, why are victims unreliable? Third, does this really preclude prosecution?

Stanko (1985) characterises victim unreliability as a "myth". Her view is supported by Faragher, who found few unreliable victims, although his sample was very small. However, in my own (also small) sample, victim withdrawal was the reason for non-prosecution in four of the five 'domestic' cases not prosecuted, and unreliability was feared by the police in many others. Complaints were often made and then withdrawn several days later. In Edward's study of the Metropolitan police (unpublished p. 40), the same was true. The domestic withdrawal rate in my sample (10%) is in fact lower than in McLeod's more extensive American survey in which 7% of female spousal vic-

362   *A. Sanders*

tims declined to prosecute intitially, and a further 40% refused to sign a formal complaint (McLeod, 1983, Table 3).

The important point, so frequently missed, is that *non-domestic cases are similar in these respects to domestic cases*. Although only one non-domestic violence case (WNO54, in *iv* below) was not prosecuted because of victim withdrawal, many were initially prosecuted and then dropped (discussed in Section 3 below). The police appear to believe that victims of domestic violence (but not, by implication, of other violence) are *fundamentally* unreliable and unpredictable, and they therefore approach domestic violence with "caution" (Select Committee, 1975).

> (WN005) D hit V several times on the head, face, body and limbs. She suffered severe bruising and a fractured thumb. D made a partial confession. He was reported for S.47 assault. The Inspector concurred: "No more than a domestic situation . . . she will not make a very good witness. However, the offence is made out . . .". The Chief Inspector agreed to prosecute, but only if V confirmed that she still wished to prosecute, which she did [3].

Similar unjustified concern over the reliability of the victim was expressed in WN134 (3.*iv* below). This is commonplace in the United States (Field & Field, 1973) and Scotland (Dobash & Dobash, 1980, p. 218; Moody & Tombs, 1982, p. 68) as well as in England. Both Faragher and Edwards note that victims are repeatedly asked if they *really* wish to go to court, and/or are provided with 'cooling-off time'. The DPP is similarly concerned, at least in domestic theft and damage cases (which are referred to him automatically) (Mansfield & Peay, 1987, pp. 75–7). Similarly, Steer found some domestic assaults cautioned simply because "the police had anticipated difficulties of this sort" (1970, p. 27).

Similar worries did not influence 'normal' violence cases even when the police had good reason to worry, as in WS070 and WS088 (*ii* and *iii* below respectively). Similarly, the concern revealed by the DPP about reliability in domestic cases was not apparent in other cases (Mansfield & Peay, 1987, pp. 75–7). When the police did worry they prosecuted anyway, and so no non-domestic violence cases were not prosecuted because of fears of victim unreliability. Not surprisingly, there were more prosecuted non-domestic cases with victims who withdrew their complaints or who did not appear in court (8) than prosecuted domestic cases (4). General victim 'unreliability' (insofar as this can be estimated) occurred in 13 and six cases respectively. MC022 (3.*ii* below) is one such case, and here is another:

> (MB047) D and his wife took V into their home. The next day V claimed that D kicked her. She was bruised, but D said that this occurred during a fight between V and his wife. He was arrested and charged with S.47. The charge was dropped several weeks later (although D was bound over) as V was "known to the police" as unreliable, and—according to the

prosecutor—it was "not worth it . . . the assault charge is using a sledge hammer to crack a nut."

Although there were proportionately fewer non-domestic cases of this type, we shall see that many non-domestic cases did not require victim testimony because they concerned public order.

Withdrawal of the complaint secured non-prosecution in all domestic violence cases regardless of the suspect's character or the seriousness of the offence, despite the ACPO guidelines which do not preclude prosecution when complaints are withdrawn. It is difficult to say whether similar cases would have been prosecuted had they not been 'domestic', but the following, although not quite a violence case, is suggestive:

> (WS021) D smashed a window at the house of his co-habitee's parents (V). D resisted arrest and V withdrew their complaint. D was charged with drunk and disorderly (denied by D), and was reported for damage. The arresting officer urged that "consideration be given to summonsing him (V) to give evidence in view of the amount of trouble that was caused". The sergeant agreed with both charges: "Quite simply it is not acceptable for a complainant, after action by the police has had the desired effect, to . . . refuse to substantiate the initial complaint". However, when the police heard that D had just been imprisoned for other matters they dropped both charges.

If the police wish to pursue a case they do not let a withdrawal of complaint stop them if they can avoid it. Since arrest often takes place against the victim's will (albeit proportionately less often than when the victim does desire arrest: Black, 1980, ch. 4), it is not surprising that the next step—the decision to prosecute—is also not determined by victim's wishes. This is particularly evident in public order cases (Section 4 below).

The police are not passive observers here, for they often influence whether a complaint is withdrawn (Ericson, 1981, p. 10 and 1982, p. 169; Chambers & Millar, 1983, p. 41; Faragher, 1985, p. 117; Edwards, unpublished, p. 33; Sanders, 1985a). Moreover, unreliability is a matter of construction and anticipation by decision makers (Stanko, 1982; Chambers & Millar, 1986). Selection and interpretation is an inevitable part of the construction of *all* police decisions, and so police preconceptions must influence judgments about withdrawal and reliability. Preconceptions about domestics generally— "rubbish" cases (Smith & Gray, 1983)—and the types of participants in them (Black, 1980; Ericson, 1981 and 1982) will thus be influential. But their (less stereotypical) preconceptions in other violence cases will be equally influential in those cases too.

Victim withdrawal and unreliability in domestic violence is not the myth that Stanko claims. But it is equally problematic in other types of crime, albeit rarely received as such by the police. Moreover, it is a partial product of police behaviour and it does not preclude prosecution when it occurs in non-domestic cases.

364   *A. Sanders*

(*ii*) *Trivial Cases*

Much domestic violence is regarded by police and prosecutors as trivial (Pahl, 1982; Borkowski *et al.*, 1983, p. 21; McCabe & Sutcliffe, 1978, ch 4; Stanko, 1985, ch. 9), but it is not clear whether this influences the formal decision to prosecute. Only one domestic case (out of 40 in all) was not prosecuted for this reason, although at least one other non-prosecuted case was also regarded as trivial:

> (WN037) V and D were separated. D went to V's new home and assaulted her, causing bruising. D claimed that V hit him first, and there were witnesses to support both sides. V insisted on prosecution. The Inspector recommended summons for s.47 and a bind over: "even if we accept the defendant's account . . . reasonable force to evict a trespasser". The Chief Inspector over-ruled this, and the incident was "no-crimed": "domestic situation in which the injuries were trivial . . . 3 days for (V) to make up her mind about proceedings . . . injury sustained is really only a common assault".

Although trivia was the reason for not prosecuting two non-domestic violence cases, the important point in this context is that many equally trivial non-domestic cases were also prosecuted.

> (EC127) D went to his ex-wife's house, where he broke into the meter and allegedly assaulted her co-habitee (V), bruising and grazing V's back. He was arrested, charged with two burglaries and one s.47 assault, and kept in custody overnight. D admitted the burglaries but not the assault, saying that he and V simply wrestled with each other. V withdrew his complaint about the assault, concurring with D's account, the next day. The arresting officer described it as a "slight injury which (V) complained of on the spur of the moment".

Other cases, such as WS088 (*iii* below) and WS070, were even more similar to WN037: the injuries were similar, there were similar (justified) doubts about the prosecution witnesses, and there were no other suspected offences.

Domestic cases are generally regarded as trivial *per se*. They are therefore presumed to be unsuitable for prosecution. The character of the suspect is therefore ignored, despite the ACPO guidelines:

> (WS183) D and V had been going out together. D pushed her over, causing bruising. She made a complaint and then withdrew it. The detective inspector recommended caution, despite D's criminal record: "(D) is not the type of individual one would normally wish to caution. However, the circumstances are of a domestic nature".

In non-domestic situations there is no lack of concern with defendants' character.

> (WS152/3) D1 and D2 broke a window playing football. D1 phoned the police who arrested D1 and D2. D2 became annoyed, kicking the police

car (£8 damage) and hitting an officer (no injuries, but contrary to s.51
Police Act). The Inspector recommended caution since the police had
provoked D2, but he was summonsed for both offences: provocation was
considered by the Chief Inspector to be no justification. Moreover, "(D) is
on record" (sergeant). He had one drunk and disorderly conviction.

This irrelevance of offence triviality in certain types of non-domestic cases wil
be seen again later. However, 'triviality'—like victim reliability—is not a clear
objective fact capable of being simply reported by investigating officers. Since
facts and impressions have to be selected and interpreted, police officers can
portray offence seriousness in many ways (Ericson, 1981 and 1982; Sanders,
1987).

In most cases there are numerous factors—triviality, character of the suspect, attitude of the victim and so forth—which could influence the decision.
Almost any decision can be justified by reference to the appropriate criterion,
which is a problem with all lists of "public interest factors" that are capable of
pulling in different directions (Sanders, 1985a). In ED045 (non-domestic) D
threatened V with an imitation gun. To the original threatening behaviour
charge was added "indictable common assault" on the grounds that V was
"petrified". This prevented the 'trivial' label from being pinned to the case.
Yet in no domestic cases was the victim's fear even noted, let alone allowed to
influence the charges. Were none of these victims petrified?

(iii) "Deserving" Victims and Suspects

According to Dobash and Dobash the onus is on the woman to "demonstrate
that she did not 'deserve' to be attacked" (1980, p. 218) (4). Two non-
domestic cases were, for this reason, not prosecuted (eg. WN133: "Probably
little to choose between either party", said the DI). Although no domestic
cases were not prosecuted for this reason, this is doubtless because domestics
with 'undeserving' victims—such as with 'trivial' injuries—are rarely followed
up by the police beyond the initial visit to the incident. Edwards discusses
police attitudes to women who had injunctions against their men: "Where
women were considered to have allowed men to return, for whatever reason,
they then forfeited their right to protection when the men became violent."
(unpublished p. 38). Chatterton (1983), Smith and Gray (1983) and Stanko
(1985a) also discuss cases where judgments about desert determined the arrest/
report decision. Thus the question of whether to prosecute only arises in
'domestics' in the first place if the investigating officer deems the victim both
deserving and significantly injured.

There was only one domestic prosecution with an 'undeserving' victim
(MB182, Section 3 below), and this may not have been the police perception
at the time. By contrast, there were several non-domestics with 'undeserving'
victims such as MB047 (*i* above), EC199/200, where the victim was, according

366   *A. Sanders*

to the police, "in a provocative mood . . . looking for trouble . . . who got what he deserved", and the following:

> (WS088) D1 kicked his ex-co-habitee's new co-habitee (V) several times, although D1 claimed this was part of a general fight. D1 was backed up by his friend (D2), against whom no action was taken. D1 was arrested and then reported for s.47 assault. The arresting officer said that it was "hard to say just where the truth lies. (V) is a devious liar . . . (D1) and (D2) appeared the most forthcoming". His sergeant agreed that "(V) is a most untrustworthy complainant", and although the Inspector did not agree he did think that "the evidence is conflicting and unlikely to stand up for a conviction for assault". Despite all this, D1 was prosecuted and (not unusually) convicted following a guilty plea.

As will become clear, if the victim is perceived to have no right to redress the police do not necessarily lose interest. The problem with domestics is that the police have little interest in them, as prosecutable cases, in the first place. Chatterton (1983) notes that police classify cases as either 'legally' or 'morally' deserving, and that the former need not imply the latter. Overcoming this attitudinal hurdle requires a clearly 'deserving' victim at least. Battered women find the police more helpful when contacted after a stay in a refuge than before (Pahl, 1985, p. 89). This suggests that an objective criterion of desert (and, perhaps, perceived seriousness of injury and intent) influences police action.

Unlike the character of the victim, the character and record of the suspect is officially recognised as relevant by both the ACPO and DPP guidelines (DPP, 1986). Since the police regard most domestic violence as an extension of 'normal' behaviour, the suspect is not generally regarded as criminal and hence is not deserving of arrest, let alone prosecution (Edwards; Stanko, 1985). The same is true in many 'normal' violent situations, so where the suspect is not a stereotypical criminal, police attitudes in both non-domestics and domestics are similar. Examples of the former include WS170 (D bruised V's neck—'no crimed'), WS129 (V attacked D, who "may have gone a little beyond self-defence" (sergeant) causing V to spend a night in hospital—cautioned) and EC070 (D bruised V's hand. He "appeared genuinely sorry . . . very slight injury"—cautioned). Thus the police are not prejudiced against domestics *as such*, but they do dichotomise people into 'criminal' and 'non-criminal'. Only if they go right "over the top" are violent spouses perceived by the police as criminal (Edwards, unpublished p. 36).

Like triviality, 'deservedness' is a construction rather than an objective fact (Chambers & Millar, 1986). If a victim is perceived by the investigating officer to be undeserving, then his perception will structure the case to make it unprosecutable.

(iv) Will Prosecution Help?

The police openly state that, in domestic cases, they ask whether prosecution is necessary to resolve the situation (Select Committee, 1975). In both the United States and Britain they usually decide that it is not. The DPP also has "regard in appropriate cases to the prospects of reconciliation being damaged by the institution of proceedings" (Mansfield & Peay, 1987, p. 75). Yet neither the ACPO guidelines nor the DPP's Code (1986) include this consideration. Although Wasoff reports "no evidence of any common practice (among Scottish prosecutors) not to initiate proceedings out of a concern for what was imagined to be the impact on the family" (1982, p. 193), Moody and Tombs (1982, pp. 68–9) found the opposite to be true. There is, in any case, evidence that the police simply do not take official action if they consider that it would be of no value (Johnson, 1985; Ericson, 1982, p. 121). So few cases of this type reach prosecutors or are reported for a summons decision. It is therefore not surprising that no domestic cases were not prosecuted for this reason in my sample or Wasoff's although Steer (1970) found that some domestic cases were cautioned because prosecution was regarded as of no value.

The police sometimes apply this consideration in non-domestic cases.

> (WN054) D attacked 2 fellow members of a club, causing cuts and bruises. Both victims made, and then withdrew, complaints. One was suicidal as a result of "division in the family (he was an in-law of D) and division about the village". D was cautioned. Proceeding without the consent of the victims was regarded as possible but "it does not appear that anything would be gained by doing so. In fact it may cause a worsening of the situation (sgt)".

And in two 'peeping toms' cases no action was taken (despite the 'victim's' wishes in one) because "police action has had the desired effect" (EC146) and "I do not think there will be any repetition" (EC147)—although there were other factors in both cases.

According to Edwards "nearly all officers saw their role in domestic incidents as of crisis intervention . . . officers rarely arrested, felt arrest was inappropriate in such cases and where appropriate still did not arrest" (unpublished, pp. 36–7). The police attitude in domestics is encapsulated by the senior officer who said that arrest "is not going to answer the problem" (Select Committee, 1975, p. 276). As if it resolves 'the problem' in most areas of crime, where arrest, charge and prosecution is routine! The 'usefulness' criterion is routinely applied to 'white collar' crime alone, producing a similarly low prosecution rate in crimes of the powerful and a similar disparity (Sanders, 1985b).

3. Later Prosecution Decisions

We have seen that fear of the victim withdrawing her complaint, and the case therefore collapsing, deters the police from prosecuting domestic cases. How justified are police fears, and how different are domestic and non-domestic cases? First, though, what of case failure itself?

368 *A. Sanders*

Table 2. Male violence: court results*

	Domestic	Non-domestic	Total
G (includes mixed results)	21 (61·8%)	151 (80·3%)	172 (77·5%
NG	13 (38·2%)	37 (19·7%)	50 (22·5%)
Total	34	188	222

* Excludes cases not prosecuted and prosecuted with no result.

(*i*) *Acquittals*

Table 2 shows that a higher proportion of domestics than non-domestics ended in acquittal. Wasoff (1982) found the opposite, but she excluded public order cases.

We should not assume that likely failure makes a case necessarily not worth pursuing. The police do not assume this:

> (WN143) D, a school caretaker, claimed that he hit V when V threatened him on being asked by D to leave the premises. The police claimed not to care about the outcome in court. They prosecuted because of pressure on them not to do so, and because of D's position of authority. D was acquitted of s.47 assault.

The point here is that the prosecution perceives public policy considerations that go beyond the final result in court. Although contrary to the official guidelines (DPP, 1986) this position is both legally tenable and actually influential in murder and in far more trivial cases (Sanders, 1985a; Mansfield & Peay, 1987). It would certainly be appropriate in domestic disputes if women were to be regarded as sufficiently deserving or as being in sufficient danger from their husbands/co-habitees. Although there is plenty of evidence to substantiate this postition (Dobash & Dobash, 1980; Borkowski *et al.*, 1983; Hanmer & Stanko, 1985) it is not widely held among decision makers despite the Select Committee's view that it should be (1975, p. xvii).

(*ii*) *Withdrawal of Complaint*

This was a factor in at least 4 of the 13 domestic acquittals—around 12% of all the domestic violence prosecutions. This is comparable with Dawson and Faragher's 10% (Faragher, 1985, p. 117), but is twice Dobash and Dobash's figure (1980, p. 222), more than Wasoff apparently found (no figures are given), and more than in a study in Stoke (8%) (Maidment, 1985). In the Bedfordshire intiative the victim withdrew her complaint in 17% of the prosecutions, but this must be partly due to the peculiarities of that initiative.

Finally, in McLeod's large scale American research half of all the prosecuted cases (i.e., those which had preliminary hearings) were dismissed for this reason (1983, figure 1). Although a significant minority of domestic violence victims withdraw their complaints after proceedings begin, the same is true of other victims too: at least five of my 37 non-domestic violence acquittals (around 2.5% of non-domestic violence prosecutions) [5]. These figures partially confirm police stereotypes, but many of the non-domestic violence cases included public order charges in which the wishes of the victim were unimportant (See Section 4 below).

But how fatal to the prosecution case is victim withdrawal? As Moody and Tombs (1982) found, the police and prosecution often attempt to pursue the case regardless. This is true of both domestic and non-domestic cases:

> (MC022) (non-domestic) Here there was "A very reluctant IP (victim) who quite frankly does not want to pursue the matter. However, there is a public duty element and I feel we should at least seek a bind over ... (Inspector). The injuries were not serious. The case was pursued, and D pleaded guilty.

> (EC160) (Non-domestic) D, who was summonsed for s.47 assault, had "many convictions for assault" (sergeant). The police rejected D's offer of a bind over despite V withdrawing the complaint, but abandoned the case when V failed to appear for the second time. The prosecutor said that he would have been willing to continue without any witnesses had the interrogation and admissions been better:
> AS: "Can you do it without direct evidence of assault?"
> Prosecutor: "Oh, yes, if the officer saw the injuries. We do it sometimes in domestics ..."

It was, in fact, only *non*-domestic cases which the police actually pursued without witnesses. In ED157 and MC175 (the only domestic cases which the prosecution definitely attempted to continue after the victims withdrew their complaints) the fact that the officer did see the injuries and secured fairly unequivocal confessions did not prevent the prosecution dropping those cases after unsuccessfully remonstrating with the victims. It seems that those domestics were treated seriously by the prosecution—but not as seriously as comparable non-domestics.

The prosecutor's reiteration of the classic 'it's only a domestic' in ED157 marked a limit beyond which he would not venture. Thus in MB182 no attempt was made to find V at the date set for trial and so the case was abandoned, despite D's admission that "I went over the top". Perhaps this was because, unlike in the other cases, there were no witnesses. Or perhaps it was because "(V) is a bit of a toe rag" (prosecutor). Nevertheless, the prosecution dropped charges without any hesitation in most of the non-domestic withdrawals of complaint, too—even when it suspected that money changed hands (MC134). But this, as we shall see, was only where public order and police authority were not at stake.

370   *A. Sanders*

(iii) Other Reasons for Acquittal

These were often not ascertainable, but no domestic cases could be identified as failing through intrinsic weakness (subject to the qualification below). Weak domestics were presumably weeded out prior to the decision to prosecute. Non-domestic cases (especially assaults on police, like WS168, discussed in Section 4 below) were frequently acknowledged by the police to be "a bit thin", but they were prosecuted anyway. If weakness does not deter the prosecution of non-domestic cases, why should possible victim withdrawal deter the prosecution of domestics? The reason is that weakness is irrelevant when the police have more at stake than mere conviction—in other words, in "policy prosecutions" (Sanders 1985a). Domestic incidents rarely create policy prosecutions.

'Weakness' and 'strength' are *constructions* in which the police play a major role (Ericson, 1981 and 1982; McConville, 1984; Sanders, 1987). Acquittals must be interpreted in this context. Two domestic cases were dropped because there was no doctor's report, despite this being inessential (see EC160 in (*ii* above) and despite there being no indication that the victims were unwilling to testify. Moreover the victims could have been told to seek medical evidence at the time of the assaults. The lack of urgency (and consequent acquittal rate) in domestics is well illustrated by the following, albeit non-violent, case:

> (MB101) V's ex-husband (D) broke into her home. D admitted criminal damage and was charged accordingly. After approaches from the defence the prosecutor asked the police if they would drop the case in exchange for a bind over and D compensating V even though he felt the case was properly brought and D had no defence. The police agreed.
> AS: "Would you have advised the same course of action if he had put a brick through a window and then offered to pay?"
> PS: "No, it's a totally different situation ... The one's a domestic, the other's—well—it's crime really."

Compare this with a non domestic neighbour dispute. The defendants in both cases had previous convictions:

> (WS098) D rented a shed from his local authority. He replaced its broken window with one from a neighbour's shed (value £5). He was summonsed for theft despite replacing the window.

Police officers and prosecutors are right to believe that domestic cases fail more often than do other cases. But the prosecution itself produces this differential acquittal rate. There seems to be no greater intrinsic difficulty in obtaining convictions in domestic cases than in other cases, except that (as we shall see) most public order offences have less stringent evidential requirements.

(iv) Choice of Charge and Charge Reduction

Wasoff (1982) and Stanko (1985, ch. 9) found that domestic violence tends to

Table 3. Male violence: original offences charged*

	Domestic	Non-domestic	Total
s.18	4 (11·4%)	10 (5·3%)	14 (6·2%)
s.20	11 (31·4%)	24 (12·6%)	35 (15·6%)
s.47	16 (45·7%)	38 (20%)	54 (24%)
Other (including public order)	4 (11·4%)	118 (62·1%)	122 (54·2%)
Total	35	190	225

* Excludes cases not prosecuted.

be subject to lower charges and brought into lower courts than non-domestic violence of equal severity. I did not find this.

The only difference was in the urban police force (URBAN), where 30% (6) of the non-domestic assault charges were under section 18 (grievous bodily harm (GBH)/wounding), as compared to only 15% (2) of the domestic charges (excluding assaulting police).

The mere fact of similar charges does not mean that domestics and non-domestics were treated similarly if the charges in one category were originally too high. Overcharging is a well known plea bargaining ploy. Assault charges are sometimes used as a lever to secure a guilty plea to lesser charges (e.g., EC110/111 in Section 4 below) and so the extent of charge reduction can provide some idea of how far the original level of charge was justified. Again, although overall charge reductions in domestic and non-domestic cases were similar, in URBAN they were more common in the latter (40% as compared to 23%), although the numbers are very small. Here is a classic encounter:

> (MC021) D, a prisoner, kicked a prison officer (V), breaking his finger and straining his neck. He was charged with S.20 GBH.
> AS: "You wouldn't normally charge a S.20 where the GBH is only technical like this, would you?"
> DS: "Haven't you ever heard of plea bargaining? ... We always charge the top offence. But if he's willing to accept the next one down that's another matter."
> In the event he did plead to S.47.

Yet in domestic URBAN cases S.20 (instead of s.18) was charged where ribs had been broken (MB042/3), and only the lesser charge under S.47 (instead of s.20 or s.18) where there were bad cuts (MC012). The problem was not confined to URBAN:

> (WN134) V left D for another man. A few days later D threw V to the

372   *A. Sanders*

ground and grabbed her throat. The investigating officer (PCx) stated that V could have been strangled had D not been stopped. D admitted the attack. The DCI argued that the charge should be grievous bodily harm or attempted murder. The Superintendant disagreed: "We appear to be a hair's breadth away from a murder but the injuries received only support a charge of s.47". D was reported for a summons decision (not arrested and charged) for s.47 assault "if only to bind him over". PCx did "not forsee it (V's complaint) being withdrawn".

Compare this non-domestic case from the same Force:

(WS003) V suffered cuts and bruises which did not require hospital treatment. D, who had several previous convictions, was arrested and charged with s.20 GBH and s.47 assault. The prosecution inspector said that the former charge was "technically" correct, but "if we wanted to get a S.20 home we'd charge S.18 as well". A guilty plea to the S.47 alone was accepted.

Chatterton (1983) has also observed that levels of violence charges bear little relation to actual harm and culpability. Assault charges have indistinct boundaries, which provides scope for over charging whenever the police particularly want a conviction. This is by no means inevitable in non-domestic violence cases, but it is very rare indeed in domestics.

4. Order, Authority and Violence

Domestic and non-domestic violence appear to be treated differently. A domestic victim's desire to withdraw her complaint, unlike that of other victims, generally decides the issue. Domestic complaints which are not withdrawn are treated warily, domestic prosecutions (when they do take place) are pursued less zealously, and it seems that the victim of domestic violence is regarded as less deserving or less seriously harmed. These findings are not easily reconcilable with the genuine concern, often acted upon, expressed for domestic victims by police (McCabe & Sutcliffe, 1978, ch. 4; Dobash & Dobash, 1980) and prosecutors (Moody & Tombs, 1982). In MC174, for instance, the police arrested and kept D in custody for criminal damage because they feared he would assault his wife. And in ED157 the prosecutor adjourned the case twice and tried hard to locate the victim.

Wasoff (1982) claims that the "myth" of victim withdrawal in domestics provides a neat escape from a dilemma of competing principles: the punishment of violence, and non-intervention in family matters. Dobash and Dobash (1980) have a similar explanation: since marital violence was historically not criminal, and its character is still partially civil, it is qualitatively distinct (in legal and perceptual terms) from violence between strangers (see also McCabe & Sutcliffe, 1978, p 44). Yet Faragher (1985), found that non-domestic public violence between strangers was often treated by the police as dismissively as most domestic violence. Ericson produces similar material (1981, pp. 107–10, and 1982 pp. 119–20). Faragher explains this by reference to police notions of 'private' and 'public', and argues that only a victim complaint transforms private trouble into public trouble. However, this also misreads the situation, for it ignores the presence or absense of public *disorder*.

Order maintenance is "the core of the police mandate" (Reiner, 1985, pp. 111–16). It has been since the early days of the police, when even the CID was created as an afterthought (Brogden, 1982). To help the police to carry out their mandate relatively easily, public order offences are made easier to prove than other violence offences. First, to determine whether behaviour was "threatening" and "likely to cause a breach of the peace", as required by s.5 of the Public Order Act 1936, no victim testimony is needed: " . . . it is the police officer's characterisation of the defendant's behaviour that becomes determinative of guilt" (Lustgarten, 1987, p. 30). Second, little by way of *mens rea* (intent) is required on the part of the suspect. Third, the judiciary has "stretched" public order charges to situations where they had previously been inapplicable (Trivizas, 1984; Salter, 1986). Public order offences are, finally, triable summarily only. Simple violence charges like assault, by contrast, are triable on indictment, which subjects police evidence to scrutiny by the jury, and police procedures to rules of due process, which are largely absent in magistrates courts (McBarnet, 1981, ch. 7).

Prosecutions arising from the policing of the miners' strike in 1984-5 (Fine & Millar, 1985) were therefore predominantly on public order charges in which no actual violence (just the threat of violence) needed to be proved (Percy-Smith & Hilliard, 1986). This was despite the alleged violence which, the police claimed, justified their interventions in the dispute. The same is true of prosecutions arising from the inner city 'riots' of the late 1970s and early 1980s (Trivizas, 1984). In the recent trials arising from the Broadwater Farm disturbances of October 1985, 63 of the 69 defendants were charged with public order offences (riot and/or affray). In only three cases were there witnesses, and in six there was photographic evidence. Otherwise the "evidence depended largely or entirely upon suspects' confessions". (*Guardian* October 1987). Where assault charges are possible the police often use public order charges anyway, because convictions are easier to obtain (Ericson, 1982, pp. 172–3). Thus both arrest (Black, 1980, ch. 4) and conviction (McBarnet, 1981) are facilitated by the less stringent evidential requirements of public order offences. The Public Order Act 1986 now gives the police more flexibility than ever (Dixon, 1987). As the editor of the Criminal Law Review puts it, "there is little doubt that the (new) public order and public nuisance offences have been defined so as to favour the convenience of prosecutors" (Ashworth, 1987, p. 17).

Most of the non-domestic cases which were prosecuted in my sample, but which would probably not have been prosecuted had they been domestic, contained a public order element. Public violence is therefore treated more seriously than private violence. This is, however, not just police policy, but a

374   *A. Sanders*

structural feature of substantive law and criminal procedure. The case referred to earlier with the 'provocative' victim was an example:

> (EC199/200) In a general fight D1 and D2 hit V, who got bruised. D1 and D2 had no previous convictions. They were reported for s.47 assault, but the prosecutors advised that "we lack any independent evidence. If for whatever reason you feel that the matter must go to court then bind-overs are the obvious solution". The police response was to ascertain if they were willing to be bound over "as opposed to being prosecuted for assault" (DCI).

The police were clearly prepared to prosecute for s.47 despite the 'undeserving' victim and trivial injury. The use of assault charges as a threat in general is not unusual. In MC165, the police added assault charges merely to obtain guilty pleas for criminal damage, and then dropped them when those pleas were obtained (further discussed in Sanders, 1986). Assault charges are particularly useful in obtaining bind overs:

> (EC110/111) D1 and D2 had a fight, inflicting cuts and bruises on each other, but finishing as friends. Both were reported for s.47 and s.5. The DC argued that because D2's father insisted on him complaining against D1, and on continuing to press the complaint, "I don't see there is much alternative to putting the matter before the court", albeit only for a bind over application. The DI asked for more information with a view to prosecuting the substantive offences: ". . . offenders have to agree to a bind over and usually have to be charged with a more substantial offence to push them into agreeing." Although D1 refused to provide more information the police still prosecuted both suspects for s.5, despite or perhaps because "As per usual we cannot really establish who started it" (prosecutor).

Witnesses are less common at domestic incidents than at public incidents. The police will therefore be naturally reluctant to prosecute the former unless the one witness—the victim—wholeheartedly co-operates. This case, though, shows that the absence of witnesses—indeed, the absence of any useful evidence at all—does not deter the police where public order offences can be charged. The evidence of non-police witnesses would be superfluous, so the uncooperativeness of the 'victim' in EC110/111 was irrelevant. This is why the police were able to continue prosecuting in WS021 (2.*i* above). Yet another public order case illustrates the same point:

> (WN137–141) Blows and threats were exchanged between two groups of young men at a police station. Members of both sides were arrested, including WN138 and WN139. WN138 was seen to kick WN139 several times, but he (along with all the others) was only charged with s.5 because WN139 refused to make a complaint against WN138.

If a breach of the peace is anticipated or in progress a bind-over can be sought regardless of whether s.5 can be charged. Prosecution can be initiated with less fear of the whole case collapsing than in a domestic situation, for which bind overs are rarely possible. Thus in the non-domestic MC023-5 affray was charged but on the day of the first court appearance the arresting officer was already saying that the case "might end up as a bind-over". This it did—a good example of the initial overcharging and subsequent charge reduction discussed earlier. It follows that when officers do want to arrest violent spouses a public order element can sometimes provide the excuse, as in one of Chatterton's examples when the officer later saw the violent spouse in the street (1983, pp. 214–15), and as Edwards also notes (unpublished, p. 37).

The disparity between the treatment of domestic and public order violence is most striking where police are assaulted:

> (MC064) D hit a WPC in the street after a "routine stop check". She suffered "minor bruising and tenderness". D, an "illiterate mute" who had recently been released from a mental hospital, was charged with s.47. He pleaded not guilty and the case was dropped (9 months later) in exchange for a bind over. The prosecutor considered it not worth the time and trouble pursuing the case in view of the minor injuries.

The weakness of this case was characteristic of assault police cases (WS168, discussed in Sanders [1987] is another example). Yet, as we have seen, weak *domestic* cases are ruthlessly weeded out before proceedings even begin. The trivial injuries in MC064 were typical of assault police cases. WS153 (2.*ii* above), where the Inspector who wanted to caution was overruled, and WN185, where the injury produced "slight soreness and redness" (for two days), are further examples. Injuries like these on wives would never be the subject of prosecution, but since S.51 of the Police Act does not require bodily harm the police are entitled to prosecute cases that would be too trivial in other contexts. Similarly, offers of compensation frequently persuade the police to drop (MB101, in 3.*iii* above), or not to initiate, prosecution (Sanders, 1988.) However, WS153 shows that this is not so in assault police cases.

The public character of trivial attacks on the police and of public violence arguably makes it more serious than other violence. But there is less chance of assistance for victims of private violence than of public violence. Consequently, criminal justice processes prioritise considerations of public order and police authority over personal considerations. The protection given to domestic victims, and the retribution and stigma applied to violent spouses, is less than that which applies to public violence. The values and priorities chosen by those who make and enforce the law are clear. Public order laws are designed to assist the police in what they perceive to be their primary task.

Since public violence usually threatens order it is presumed to be serious by the police and is therefore readily prosecuted. However, if public violence arises and ebbs without disorder the police are unconcerned as in WN054 (2.*iv* above) where D was reported for summons/caution, rather than arrested.

376   *A. Sanders*

Smith and Gray (1983, pp. 100–1) provide other good examples. The situation is different if police authority is successfully challenged. Such challenges sometimes occur when the police attend domestic situations, which might explain the arrests for drunkenness and breach of the peace observed by Chatterton and Edwards. So, returning to Faragher's examples of non-domestic public violence which were treated as dismissively by police officers as domestic violence, the crucial issue is the element of public *disorder* or challenge to authority—not whether the victim wished to press charges. To return also to Wasoff and to Dobash and Dobash, the issue is not *whether* strangers are assaulted; but *when and in what circumstances*. Thus as Dobash and Dobash themselves observe (1980, pp. 214–5), domestic assaulters who are belligerent to the police are usually arrested, regardless of the efficacy of arrest in resolving 'the problem'. Continued belligerance to the woman is, of course, another matter entirely (where the main issue is 'resolving the problem' by supporting the family entity). But where order is threatened or police authority is jeopordised nothing is left to chance.

The dismissive treatment of much (non domestic) sexual assault by police officers and prosecutors is comparable with their treatment of domestic assault (Chambers & Millar, 1983 and 1986). This appears to support the 'police are sexist' theory of domestic assaults, although not the 'family is sacred' theory. However, it also supports the argument that violence receives sustained attention only when it is perceived as particularly serious or when it is accompanied by disorder. The distinction is important. In an influential American study Myers and Hagan (1979) concluded that legal factors (evidence and offence seriousness) were the most important determinants of prosecutors' decisions. Victims' prior relationships with suspects were not found to be significant. This appears either to contradict Dobash and Dobash's view or to confine it to initial police decisions alone, for it suggests that domestic and public violence are treated equally by prosecutors [7]. But this would be an eroneous conclusion, for their sample may have included few violence cases involving public order; or alternatively, they may have had large numbers of public order charges (in which evidence and/or offence seriousness are automatically stronger and greater respectively). Myers and Hagan did not control for public order, wrongly assuming that violence between strangers is perceived as a homogeneous category by law enforcers.

5. New Developments

Two major developments which could influence the prosecution of domestic violence have taken place since 1983 (when my fieldwork was completed). First, the Metropolitan Police now have new guidelines which stress the criminal character of domestic violence. They encourage arrest and charge even when victims wish to withdraw their complaints. (*Observer*, 12 April 1987). The problem with using guidelines to control police, especially in non-prosecutions, is that the incident cannot be scrutinized by supervisors to assess conformity with the guidelines. Only the officer being scrutinized knows about that. What is scrutinized is his *report of the incident*. This is a different matter entirely, for reports are constructed precisely to fit the guidelines, no matter what the nature of the incident (Ericson, 1981 and 1982; Sanders, 1987). According to Chatterton, officers constantly expect criticism from superiors anyway. They therefore

> had to protect themselves, anticipate criticism, and take the necessary precautions. The safest gambit was to control information about the incidents they dealt with, contain it within the boundaries of the situation or, failing that, to construct an account that provided a justification for the action they had reported taking. PCs referred to their reports as pieces of "defensive writing" (Chatterton, 1983, p. 201).

Changes to guidelines are ineffective if the legal and institutional structures in which they operate do not also change. After all, if criteria used outside the DPP and ACPO guidelines have been used until now (see e.g., 2.*iii* and 2.*iv* above) we can anticipate that criteria will continue to be used which are outside the Metropolitan guidelines.

The introduction of the Crown Prosecution Service (CPS) in 1986 is the second major development. The key feature of the old system was the complete discretion wielded by the police. If they did not wish to prosecute they did not do so. But the same is true under the CPS. For while the CPS has complete discretion over cases which the police have decided to prosecute (those discussed in Section 3), the CPS NEVER SEES those which the police decide to not prosecute (which are no crimed or cautioned—discussed in Section 2). It follows that the police will rarely need to justify the non-prosecution of domestics to the CPS, and the CPS will have little effect other than to encourage the more effective concealing of weaknesses in public order cases (Sanders, 1987).

6. Conclusion

There are two standard explanations for the differential treatment of domestic and non-domestic violence. The 'official' explanation favoured by the police and by writers like Myers and Hagan is that domestic cases are more prone to failure and are more trivial. The 'radical' explanation of writers like Dobash and Dobash is that sexist institutions elevate family unity over female safety. The first draft of this paper attempted to 'test' these explanations by comparing the treatment of domestic and non-domestic violence cases, but this proved difficult. Police attitudes, and their consequences, in the two types of cases were often identical. For instance, 'criminal' and 'non-criminal' dichotomies and the 'will prosecution help?' criterion were not confined to domestic cases. On victim withdrawal and triviality there was some differential treatment but it was not overwhelming.

378   *A. Sanders*

Formal attempts at comparison were abandoned because of the problems discussed in the introduction above. If public order is included in the 'non-domestic violence' category then the 'objective' evidential reasons for fewer domestic prosecutions (and, doubtless, fewer arrests) are clear. But the result is misleading, for it is *the law*, rather than the victim, that makes domestic prosecutions more vulnerable than prosecutions with a public order element. On the other hand, if public order is not included than the sample of non-domestic violence would not include cases which the police *could* have charged as simple violence. The comparison would not capture the reality perceived by the officers whose behaviour we are trying to explain. Gregory, in a slightly different context, comes to a similar conclusion about the problems of comparison, and argues that there is

> no simple method of stripping away the gender bias to uncover the true picture ... the activities of women are sexualized at the same moment that they are criminalized, so that the statistics produce the very differences that they are supposed to demonstrate (Gregory, 1986, p. 57).

Most victims of domestic violence are women. Most 'victims' of public order violence (and assaults against police) are men. Arguably this is a function of the greater aggressiveness of men in industrial society, unless there is a significant amount of public violence involving women which (because of gendered perceptions) is not regarded as 'disorderly'. So, this research, in common with other research, shows that—insofar as prosecutions can protect victims—male victims are more protected by the criminal justice system than are women. There is gender bias in prosecutions. However, this is not a product, primarily, of sexist attitudes, just as class bias in prosecutions is not a product of class prejudice (Sanders, 1985*b*). Instead there is structural bias, in the law itself, against the prosecution of personal violence. This is consistent with Gelsthorpe's similar conclusion regarding female suspects:

> Whereas some writers have inferred that criminal justice agencies impose and promote fixed and pervasive sexist assumptions about females as an expression of unalloyed sexism, I found them sustaining assumptions for different reasons ... I found that ideas were affected by the meaning of 'trouble' for the agency, by the micropolitics of institutions, so to speak. Thus 'sexist' beliefs, where they existed, were mediated by administrative and organisational factors (Gelsthorpe, 1986, p. 144).

Consider also the insignificant role given to victims of violence which is well documented by Shapland *et al.* (1985) and Chambers and Millar (1983 and 1986). Research on domestic violence alone which reveals the systematic disregarding of the wishes of victims is misleading, for the same is true of the wishes of victims of non-domestic violence, including violent sexual assault. Victims of property crime, where compensation is a major consideration (Sanders, 1988) are, significantly, treated very differently. But when violence is prosecuted it is to secure order and police authority rather than to satisfy the

Personal violence and public order 379

victim. Indeed, public order considerations often produce prosecutions that are positively contrary to the views of victims of violence[8]. Whilst this is in part a response to legal structures and rules that facillitate conviction for public order charges, those structures and rules simply mediate the State's overwhelming concern for Order. This means that, to Gelsthorpe's "administrative and organisational factors", we have to add external socio-political factors.

It is not so much the sanctity of the family that is being protected as personal safety—for all—that is neglected. This is also true in less obvious contexts of violence, such as causing death on the roads (Spencer, 1985) and hazards in the work-place (Sanders, 1985*b*). These incredibly dangerous phenomena do not threaten order. On the contrary, they are 'natural' products of advanced industrial capitalism. Modern policing, like old fashioned policing, prioritises order and authority first, and property second. Personal safety comes a poor third. Until the conditions which shape public policy are transformed, women, along with all othe other under-privileged of Britain, will continue to suffer at the hands of those more powerful than themselves.

Acknowledgments

Earlier versions of this paper were presented to the Home Office Research and Planning Unit, the Oxford Centre for Criminology, and the British Criminology Conference. Thanks to everyone (especially Nicola Lacey and Elaine Player) for their constructive criticisms, to the ESRC for funding, and to innumerable police officers and prosecutors for their co-operation.

Notes

1 'No Criming' is the classification by police of alleged crimes as non-criminal acts (see Bottomley & Coleman, 1976).
2 The research, which is discussed in more detail in Sanders (1958*a* and *b*), was generously funded by ESRC (Grant No E0023/0050/1). 'Domestic violence' is taken here to include only male violence against females, occurring in the home of one or other member of a spousal or quasi-spousal relationship.
3 All case examples are taken from the project discussed in Note 2. Minor details have been changed to ensure anonymity.
4 Chambers and Miller (1983 and 1986) found similar attitudes among police and prosecutors in connection with (non-domestic) sexual assault.
5 Although difficult to interpret, because domestic and non-domestic assaults are not compared, Shapland *et al.*'s (1985) study of victims of violence also seems to indicate more frequent withdrawals or "some unwillingness to prosecute the offender" (p. 46–7) in domestic cases (see pp. 46–8). Unfortunately the most thorough research on victim withdrawal, which shows a continual drop out of cases for this reason (McLeod, 1983, Table 3), did not include non-domestic cases and so comparison is again not possible.
6 Violence offences are specified by the Offences Against the Person Act 1861, as follows:

380   *A. Sanders*

S.18: Wounding or causing grievous bodily harm (GBH) (i.e. substantial cuts, broken bones, and so forth) with intent so to do

S.20: Wounding or causing grievous bodily harm (GBH) with intent to commit only lesser injury

S.47: Causing actual bodily harm (i.e., any injury causing at least cuts or bruising which is less than wounding or GBH) with intent so to do.

7 If their general results hold good for the violence cases in their sample. Unfortunately Myers and Hagan do not provide results for different offence categories. Smith and Klein (1984), however, found that the police generally avoided arrest in all "interpersonal" disputes, adding weight to the argument that the domestic/non domestic dimension is of secondary importance.

8 Shapland *et al.* (1985) report more dissatisfaction from violence victims over the police insisting on the continuance of prosecution than she does from victims whose cases were dropped against their wills. Again, there is no indication of the type or context of violence in these cases.

References

Ashworth, A. (1987) Defining Criminal Offences without harm. In *Essays In Honour of J. C. Smith* (Smith, P., Ed.). Butterworths: London.

Black, D. (1980) *The Manners and Customs of the Police*. Academic Press; London.

Borkowski, M. *et al.* (1983) *Marital Violence: The Community Response*. Tavistock: London.

Bottomley, A. & Coleman, C. (1976) Police conceptions of crime and no crime. *Criminal Law Review*, 344.

Brogden, M. (1982) *The Police: Autonomy and Consent*. Academic Press: London.

Chambers, G. & Millar, A. (1983) *Investigating Sexual Assault*. HMSO: Edinburgh.

Chambers, G. & Millar, A. (1986) *Prosecuting Sexual Assault*. HMSO: Edinburgh.

Chatterton, M. (1983) Police work and assault charges. In *Control in the Police Organisation* (Punch, M., Ed.). MIT Press: Cambridge, MA.

Director of Public Prosecutions (1986) *Code for Crown Prosecutors*. HMSO: London.

Dixon, D. (1987) Protest and disorder: the Public Order Act 1986. *Critical Social Policy* **7**, 90.

Dobash, R. & R. (1980) *Violence Against Wives*. Open Books: London.

Ericson, R. (1981) *Reproducting Order*. University of Toronto Press: Toronto.

Ericson, R. (1982) *Making Crime*. Butterworths:

Faragher, T. (1985) The police response to violence against women in the home. In *Private Violence and Public Policy* (Pahl, J., Ed.). Routledge & Kegan Paul: London.

Field, M. & H. (1973) Marital violence and the criminal process. *Social Service Review* **47**, 221.

Fine, B. & Millar R. (1985) *Policing the Miners Strike*. Lawrence and Wishart: London.

Freeman, M. (1979) *Violence in the Home*. Saxon House: Farnborough.

Gelsthorpe, L. (1986) Towards a sceptical look at sexism. *International Journal of the Sociology of Law* **14**, 125.

Gregory, J. (1986) Sex, class and crime: towards a non-sexist criminology. In *Confronting Crime* (Mathews, R. & Young, J., Eds). Sage: London.

Hanmer, J. & Stanko, E. (1985) Stripping away the rhetoric of protection: violence to women, law and the state in Britain and the USA. *International Journal of the Sociology of Law* 13, 357.

Johnson, N. (1985) Police, social work and medical responses to battered women. In *Marital Violence* (Johnson, N., Ed.). Soc. Review Monograph: Keele.

Jones, T. *et al.* (1986) *The Islington Crime Survey.* Gower: Farnborough.

Lustgarten, L. (1987) The Police and Substantive Criminal Law. *British Journal of Criminology* 27, 23.

Maidment, S. (1985) Domestic Violence and the Law. In *Marital Violence* (Johnson, N., Ed.). *Soc. Review Monograph:* Keele.

Mansfield, G. & Peay, J. (1987) *The DPP: Principles and Practise for the Crown Prosecutor.* Tavistock: London.

McBarnet, D. (1981) *Conviction.* Macmillan: London.

McCabe, S. & Sutcliffe, F. (1978) *Defining Crime.* Oxford Penal Research Unit, Paper No. 9.

McConville, M. (1984) Prosecuting criminal cases: reflection of an inquisitorial adversary. *Liverpool Law Review* 6, 15.

McLeod, L. (1983) Victim non-cooperation in domestic disputes. *Criminology* 21, 395.

Moody, S. & Tombs, J. (1982) *Prosecution in the Public Interest.* Scottish Academic Press: Edinburgh.

Myers, M. & Hagan, J. (1979) Public and Private Trouble. *Social Problems* 26, 439.

Pahl, J. (1982) Police response to battered women. *Journal of Social Welfare Law,* 337.

Pahl, J. (Ed.) (1985) *Private Violence and Public Policy.* Routledge & Kegan Paul: London.

Percy-Smith, J. & Hilliard, P. (1985) Miners in the arms of the law: a statistical analysis *Journal of Law and Society* 12, 345.

Reiner, R. (1985) *The Politics of the Police.* Wheatsheaf: London.

Salter, M. (1986) Judicial responses to football hooliganism. *Northern Ireland Legal Quarterly* 37, 280.

Sanders, A. (1985*a*) Prosecution decisions and the Attorney General's guidelines. *Criminal Law Review,* 5.

Sanders, A. (1985*b*) Class bias in prosecutions. *Howard Journal* 24, 76.

Sanders, A. (1986) An independent Crown Prosecution service? *Criminal Law Review,* 16.

Sanders, A. (1987) Constructing the case for the prosecution. *Journal of Law and Society* 14, 229.

Sanders, A. (1988) The Limits to diversion from prosecution. *British Journal of Criminology* (forthcoming).

Select Committee on Violence in Marriage (1975) *Report* (HCP 5531, Vol. II), HMSO: London.

Shapland, J. *et al.* (1985) *The Victim in the Criminal Justice System.* Gower: Aldershot.

Smith, D. & Klein, J. (1984) Police control of interpersonal disputes. *Social Problems* 31, 468.

Smith, D. & Gray, J. (1983) *The Police in Action.* PSI: London.

Spencer, J. (1985) Motor vehicles as weapons of offence. *Criminal Law Review,* 29.

Stanko, E. (1985) *Intimate Intrusions.* Routledge & Kegan Paul: London.

Steer, D. (1970) *Police Cautions.* Basil Blackwell: Oxford.

Trivizas, E. (1984) Public order in the 20th century—a study in the exercise of police prosecutorial discretion *British Journal of Criminology* 24, 361.

382   *A. Sanders*

Walmsley, R. (1986) *Personal Violence*. HMSO: London.
Wasoff, F. (1982) Legal protection from wifebeating: the processing of domestic assaults by Scottish prosecutors and criminal courts. *International Journal of the Sociology of Law* **10**, 187.
Worral, A. & Pease, K. (1986) Personal crime against women: evidence from the 1982 British Crime Survey. *Howard Journal* **25**, 118.

Date received: December 1987

[14]

Researching the Discretions to Charge and to Prosecute

ROGER LENG, MICHAEL McCONVILLE and
ANDREW SANDERS

Prominent miscarriages of justice such as the Confait affair and the cases of the 'Guildford Four' and the 'Maguire Seven' have focused public attention on the processes by which alleged offences are investigated and alleged offenders prosecuted. These cases raise serious doubts about the ability of the criminal trial to expose the faults and errors which may be built into a case by the very processes of investigation and prosecution. They further suggest that the problem is not generated simply by corrupt or illegal practices of police and prosecutors, but rather that miscarriages of justice may arise also through currently *lawful* practices. Miscarriage of justice thus may be seen as an inherent feature of our present adversarial system, in which control of a case in its early stages is vested in well-resourced state agencies whose function is to prepare and present a case for the prosecution.

This point was recognised by both the Inquiry under Sir Henry Fisher which considered the Confait case and the Royal Commission on Criminal Procedure which followed in 1981. The reforms inspired by the Royal Commission's Report – the Police and Criminal Evidence Act 1984 (PACE) and the Prosecution of Offences Act 1985 (POOA) – were presented as introducing fairness, openness and accountability and as strengthening the rights of suspects whilst at the same time enhancing police powers of arrest, detention, search and seizure. The underlying assumption was that criminal justice personnel, and the process itself, would be responsive to changes in the law. The system, it was thought, could be changed by legal reform.

As well as seeking to minimise future miscarriages of justice, the reforms of the 1980s sought to address two other major concerns. First, that prosecutions were instituted too readily. This led to weak cases reaching court and forced many people to undergo trial on insufficient evidence, wasting the time of police, lawyers and courts, and having knock-on effects such as increasing pre-trial delays. Secondly, that the police rarely consider alternatives to prosecution even though prosecution might have adverse consequences in starting an offender on a criminal career, and even though the objectives of deterrence and rehabilitation might be achieved by other measures, such as cautioning.

120   *Unravelling Criminal Justice*

The principle that an individual should be prosecuted only where it is in the public interest to do so (that is, where there is no acceptable alternative) was expressed in guidelines issued by the Attorney General in 1983, and repeated in guidelines on cautioning issued by the Home Office in 1985 and in the Code for Crown Prosecutors issued by the Director of Public Prosecutions in 1986. The responsibility for not prosecuting weak cases and for operating the public-interest criterion is shared between the police and the Crown Prosecution Service (CPS), with the CPS acting as ultimate gatekeeper by virtue of its power to veto any prosecution.

THE RESEARCH

A full assessment of the prosecution process would focus on whether or not its checks and balances are effective to avoid miscarriages of justice; on whether weak cases are weeded out before trial; and on whether cases are diverted where there is no public interest in pursuing a prosecution. The more general theoretical question concerns the relationship between legal rules and the behaviour of officials to whom those rules relate: specifically, how far police discretion is, and can be, constrained by legal and other rules (for instance, on the prosecution of weak or cautionable cases); and how far police control of the prosecution process can be attenuated by creating institutions like the CPS. This was the policy and theoretical context for our study.

It built on earlier research which indicates that prosecution decision-making is largely determined by 'working rules' of the police which are geared towards particular policing goals. Cases are constructed by the police, in the sense that the police choose their suspects, choose to collect certain evidence and have choice over the questions asked at interview. The police then have control over the way the resulting evidence is presented and interpreted (McBarnet, 1981). This measure of control allows the police to anticipate and determine later decisions by prosecutors (McConville and Baldwin, 1981; Sanders, 1985). McBarnet (1981) has argued that if this degree of police control is unhealthy, then it is the permissive structure of legal rules that is at fault, rather than police policies as such: the police, she argued, only do what the law allows them to do. The specific aims of our research were to assess: the actual 'working rules' (Smith and Gray, 1983) which guide the police, and their relationship to legal rules; how far the new guidelines on evidential standards and cautioning policy changed police charging practices; and how far the CPS is independent of the police.

Researching Discretions to Charge and Prosecute 121

The fieldwork began in 1986. With the co-operation of three English police forces and the CPS we took random samples of non-motoring arrests and reports for summons in six police stations until a total of 120 adult and 60 juvenile cases per station was reached (producing a total sample of 1080 cases). We had access to the case files at every stage, and also interviewed all the officers involved where possible (achieving success rates of 91.4 per cent for arresting officers and 48.4 per cent for custody officers). Where cases went to court or were otherwise dealt with by the CPS we interviewed all prosecutors handling the case. This research methodology enabled us to test official accounts against those which police and prosecutors gave us in interview and to uncover the motivations of the various actors and the process of case construction.

WORKING RULES AND LEGAL RULES

The law does not tell the police which criminal laws to enforce, which people are suspects, which areas to patrol, which citizen complaints and reports to act upon or which alleged offences to prosecute. In relation to each of these matters the police have broad discretion with which the courts have declined to interfere on the principle of 'constabulary independence'. Research on police discretion (for example, Smith and Gray, 1983; Dixon *et al.*, 1989) shows that the result is the opportunity for the police to set their own priorities and follow their own hunches. The legal limits on discretion are vague. Stop and search on the streets, and arrest, for example, may be done only on the basis of 'reasonable suspicion' (PACE, ss. 1, 24). This concept is so notoriously vague that even the Royal Commission, which commended it, could not define it (para. 3.25).

Similarly broad discretion is conferred upon the police and CPS in relation to prosecution decision-making. The official guidelines provide two main criteria. The first is evidential sufficiency: prosecution should only take place when there is a 'realistic prospect of conviction'. The second is that, even if there is sufficient evidence, there is no presumption in favour of prosecution: it should only take place when in the 'public interest'. This is indicated by various criteria, including seriousness of offence, previous record, interests of the victim and particular characteristics of the offender such as age or illness (Sanders, 1985).

Because the discretion allowed to the police within the law is so broad, we were aware of the pitfalls of seeking to explain police behaviour purely in terms of the legal rules and official criteria, despite McBarnet's (1981) argument (to which we shall return in the Conclusion). Instead, by analys-

122   *Unravelling Criminal Justice*

ing officers' own accounts of their actions and decisions, we attempted to discover the social or working rules which routinely inform their decisions without dismissing the influence of legal rules and official guidelines. It was the *relationships* between official rules and police working rules which particularly interested us.

Other research has suggested that police discretion is substantially influenced by the demands of citizens. Thus, police work is seen as being essentially 'reactive' to citizens' complaints, rather than being 'proactive' in the sense of self-motivated work to seek out crime and criminals (Shapland and Vagg, 1988). However, our research demonstrates that the fact that a lot of police work is reactive does not prevent the operation of police working rules: even where the police react by attending an incident at the behest of a citizen, their freedom of action thereafter is unfettered. For example, it is well documented that where the police are called to incidents of 'domestic' violence, they reserve the right to make decisions about arrest and prosecution according to particular values and standards of their own (Hanmer *et al.*, 1989).

Since we discuss working rules systematically elsewhere (McConville *et al.*, 1991), our purpose here is to set out some major determinants of police behaviour, their consequences for prosecution decisions, and their relationship with legal and other official rules. One major working rule was expressed by an officer in this way: 'When you get to know an area, and see a villain about at 2.00 am in the morning, you will always stop him to see what he is about' (Case AH-A115). 'Previous' is sometimes all the police have as the basis for a stop or arrest. In other cases, the knowledge of 'previous' makes the officer follow the suspect to see if crime or suspicious acts are committed. In Case AT-A047, for instance, the police were in a street market looking for pickpockets when 'up walks this chap who we knew was one of the suspects . . . you tend to follow the ones you know'. In very serious cases, such as a rape investigation taking place in Area AT (one of our six police stations) many suspects were arrested purely on the basis of 'previous' in order to verify alibis and take blood samples.

Another important working rule is that order and authority be maintained. This has been documented in earlier research (Sanders, 1985), but our research shows that the power of this working rule has not been diminished by official guidelines. Thus the arresting officer in Case AT-A053 said of the defendant:

> He had to be Jack the Lad and wanted to be put down. So I put him down. . . . I grabbed him and arrested him.
>
> RES: On what basis?"

Researching Discretions to Charge and Prosecute 123

AO: Well, it's hard to explain. . . . You get him off the streets and make the residents happy.

There are numerous similar examples from other areas: 'We can't have people going around pushing police officers when they feel like it' (Case CC-A085); '. . . refused his details and challenged me to arrest him, so I did' (Case CE-A983).

Victims play an important role in relation to the citizen initiation of crime detection which we discussed earlier. However, police working rules distinguish influential from non-influential victims, and the concept of the victim is itself often a matter of police construction (McConville *et al.*, 1991, ch. 2). The more powerful and 'respectable' the victim, the more likely it is that his or her interests will be reflected in the action taken by the police. Quite minor cases of disorder or alleged dishonesty would result in arrest and charge where they concerned powerful victims, typically businesses. Purely inter-personal disputes not involving influential victims, typically cases of domestic violence, would be far less likely to result in arrest and charge. The differential treatment of these two categories of case could not be justified either on grounds of seriousness or of evidential sufficiency. Consider the following two cases, the first of which resulted in a prosecution, the second in a decision to take no further action.

Three youths were involved in a dispute about the size of their bill in a restaurant. The manager summoned a police constable who arrested the youths after they refused to pay the sum demanded by the restaurant. The youths were prosecuted but the case was later dropped because of lack of evidence of dishonesty. Commenting on the case the arresting officer said that: 'I feel that this matter would not have gone this far if [the defendants'] attitudes towards Pizza Hut staff and the police had been different.' (Case CC-A074/75/76)

A man had been drinking and was threatening his girlfriend in public. He had already struck her and, said the arresting officer: 'She had a swollen face, I believe she had a black eye, and she was in a very distressed situation.' As the officer explained, when the officer arrived, the man ignored police advice, became 'threatening towards the police . . . abusive and started fighting with police officers and had to be arrested for his behaviour (including damage to the police car)'. He had an extensive criminal record for assault, among other matters. (Case CC-A052)

This officer's account in the second case implies that the man would not have been arrested merely for the assault on his girl friend had he not behaved badly towards the police. Moreover, the custody officer did not feel that he should have been arrested anyway. He decided within 20 minutes that no further action would be taken against the man on the basis that this was a domestic incident which was 'just a flash in the pan . . . would have calmed down on its own . . . . When he stood in front of me [he] was quite reasonable.'

As Case CC-A052 shows, prosecution decisions do not automatically follow on from arrest decisions. In fact, around half of all arrested persons are not prosecuted (40 per cent of adults, and 65 per cent of juveniles). Some – juveniles in particular – are cautioned, but in many cases there is a formal police decision to take no further action (nfa). The evidential threshold for arrest – reasonable suspicion – is less stringent than that for prosecution (the 'realistic prospect of conviction'). Thus, even where there are real grounds for suspicion justifying the arrest, further evidence may be required before a prosecution can be brought. As our research discloses, many arrests are made on hardly any evidence at all, for example, all of the arrests made in the rape inquiry in Area AT. In many such cases no further action is the expected and inevitable outcome. In many instances the police are sure of the suspect's innocence, the arrest being only a convenient way of holding the suspect whilst verifying this.

There are other reasons, though, for non-prosecution. Where suspects are arrested because they are 'known' to the police, 'deals' are particularly important. The police frequently allow 'little fish' to escape prosecution in order to catch 'big fish'. In Case BK-A114, for instance, D, who was an informant, admitted stealing from a fellow lodger. According to the officer in charge, no further action was taken 'in view of the fact that he could be useful to us' in the future. This was revealed to us in interview, but was not the 'official' reason recorded on the file. This case well demonstrates the need to look beyond the official guidelines and the official record in order to discover the reasons for police action.

The irrelevance of official rules also becomes apparent in this context. Many suspects who escape prosecution through 'deals' are cautioned instead, particularly for drugs offences. When the police raid premises looking for drugs they seek the conviction of 'dealers' rather than mere 'buyers'. In both Areas AT and CE, those buyers who were prepared to give evidence against the 'dealers' were cautioned or nfa'd. Yet the cautions did not fit the official guidelines in any way, for the police did not consider offence seriousness, previous record or other personal characteristics. Cautions were used as bargaining counters. Also, in these and other cases, the police did not secure confessions to the offences cautioned despite very clear preconditions in the guidelines to this effect. Sanders and Bridges

Researching Discretions to Charge and Prosecute   125

(1990) found a similar example of a youth accused of deception who had 'form as long as your arm' who was cautioned in exchange for information. Again, these reasons were rarely recorded on paper, and could only be ascertained through interview with the officers involved.

A reason for non-prosecution in many other cases is that prosecution serves no police interest. Sometimes this is because the arrest was made simply to mollify the victim (especially in 'domestics'), and sometimes because a suspect who failed to respect authority on the street became more contrite as a result of arrest. Thus in Case CC-A052 (above) the domestic violence was not considered to warrant prosecution, and the suspect's disrespectful street behaviour was overborne by his later co-operative attitude to the custody officer. The suspect was therefore nfa'd. When arrests are made to satisfy entrepreneur-victims, the 'need' to prosecute is reduced if the suspect pays the victim back. Thus in Case BK-A014, the arresting officer said: 'We did a deal. He had £10 in his possession and agreed to take it down to the garage', hence there was nfa. And when arrests are made to mollify domestic victims, cautions are given for injuries which would, in other circumstances, lead to prosecution.

The same is true for positive prosecution decisions. Rather than systematically applying the tests set out earlier, in adult cases the police simply operate a presumption in favour of prosecution, despite the official guidelines' presumption against it. Thus both evidentially weak and policy-weak cases are frequently prosecuted. This can be demonstrated in many ways. For current purposes one illustration of each must suffice.

First, well over half of the cases dropped by the CPS were identified first as weak by senior police officers reviewing the case after the custody officer charged; these cases were, in other words, weak from the start. Prosecutors were frequently scathing about police standards in this respect (McConville *et al.*, 1991, ch. 8). Thus in Case CC-A118 the prosecutor expressed regret to the police at dropping the case. He explained: 'It's all PR. It's another way of saying "You should never have charged this man in the first place".' While the charging of some of these cases was simply error, some cases were prosecuted in full knowledge of the evidential weakness. This was occasionally done to punish the 'criminal'. In an alleged unlawful sexual intercourse case where the evidence was very weak but where the defendant had been in custody for several months, the officer in charge said: 'If he did it he's had some punishment. If he did it, of course, it's not enough. But it's some.' More often it is done in the hope of securing a guilty plea to the original or lesser offence.

Secondly, the Code for Crown Prosecutors suggests that cases in which absolute or conditional discharges are likely are, *prima facie*, suitable for

126   *Unravelling Criminal Justice*

caution. A total of 31 out of 288 sentenced adults (10.8 per cent) were so sentenced. Over half of these were judged by us to be cautionable. Yet we found that police officers rarely considered cautioning adults. When they did, it was usually in the types of circumstance discussed earlier which are not envisaged by the guidelines. The inconsistent applications of the 'public interest' guidelines are only inconsistent in terms of official criteria. In terms of police values there is no inconsistency.

At first glance it might appear that the presumption in favour of prosecution does not operate in juvenile cases: 37.8 per cent of our juvenile sample were cautioned or warned, as against 35 per cent who were prosecuted. However, the police operate an informal tariff by which prosecution normally follows for juvenile suspects who have previously been cautioned either once or twice. The power of the tariff is demonstrated by the fact that for more than one-third of the juveniles who were prosecuted, the decision to charge was made without any reference to special juvenile liaison procedures. Home Office guidelines encourage consultation with other agencies and consideration of personal factors in all juvenile cases, but the police regard all this as irrelevant in cases where *they consider* prosecution to be the only option. Thus, high rates of cautioning do not indicate that presumptive prosecution has been displaced in favour of individualised discretionary decision-making. Rather, the presumption in favour of prosecution is simply deferred rather than being abandoned.

THE ELEMENTS OF THE CONSTRUCTED CASE

The discussion so far has treated as unproblematic the notion that cases may be 'evidentially weak' or 'cautionable'. But this is not the case. Neither the strength of the evidence nor factors indicative of caution are inherent, objectively ascertainable features of a case which wait to be revealed by either prosecution or defence. Rather, both the evidence and the existence (or not) of factors indicative of caution are products of police work in constructing the case. The techniques of case construction include seeking out (or not) particular types of evidence, accepting or rejecting evidence which is offered to the police by suspect or witness, the generation of evidence by asking particular questions in interview, and the evaluation of facts. These techniques apply equally to evidence which tends to prove an offence and evidence which relates to the issues of whether or not it is in the public interest to prosecute.

To describe a case as a 'construction' is not pejorative and does not imply criticism. Case construction is not peculiar to the police and is

Researching Discretions to Charge and Prosecute 127

necessarily a feature of a system for adjudicating or resolving disputes (Nelken, 1983). In an adversary system in which each side must pursue just one side of the story, case construction inevitably becomes a partial and partisan process. In what follows we seek to describe and illustrate some of the techniques of case construction which we observed.

Confession Evidence

Interrogation is the principal investigative strategy employed by the police (McConville and Baldwin, 1981). In order to maximise confessions, the police seek to control both interrogations *per se* and the broad environment in which interrogations take place. This means securing automatic detention following arrest, control over access to solicitors, control over written records of custody and interrogation, and manipulating unsupervised interrogation – in the car, in the cell and so forth – rather than relying upon the formal recorded interrogation (McConville *et al.*, 1991, chs 3 and 4; Sanders and Bridges, 1990). Interrogation takes place on police territory, on police terms, and at the pace of the police. As the PACE Code of Practice governing detention states, a police officer is 'entitled to question any person from whom he thinks useful information can be obtained. . . . A person's declaration that he is unwilling to reply does not alter this entitlement' (Code C, Note 1B).

The police use many different 'tactics' to ensure confessions (Irving, 1980). Trickery, deception, fear, 'Nice-Guy/Nasty-Guy' methods and so forth are all common. Even where the interrogation is not 'oppressive', so as to render any confession inadmissible (PACE, s. 76), the conditions are created for directly pressuring suspects into speaking. Thus the Royal Commission accepted that the concept of the 'voluntary' confession was meaningless. Very large numbers of suspects are either silent or deny the alleged offence(s) initially, but then make partial or complete confessions. Pressure is inevitable, for the essence of interrogation is to overcome the suspect's unwillingness to speak. Some officers accept this: 'Sometimes it's necessary to shout at people, especially the ones who are abusive and you know are restless, and the heat's on and you have to keep up the pressure' (Case CC-A003). The primary purpose of police tactics of pressure and trickery in interrogation is to induce true confessions. However, precisely these tactics may also generate false confessions (as in the Confait and Guildford cases) or, more commonly, statements which are misleading in that they reflect a prior police view of what happened rather than the suspect's own recollections.

128   *Unravelling Criminal Justice*

Psychologists have distinguished two types of false confession. A 'coerced-compliant' confession occurs where the suspect confesses for some instrumental purpose such as obtaining bail or to relieve the pressure upon him or her, but knows throughout the falsity of the confession. A 'coerced-internalised' confession occurs where the suspect confesses because he has been persuaded that he really is guilty of the crime (Gudjonsson and Mackeith, 1988). But our research suggests an important third category: the 'coerced-passive' confession. Here police questioning induces suspects to adopt the confession form without necessarily understanding the legal significance of what they are saying or accepting. The police rarely ask simple information-seeking questions; rather, questioning is usually directive in nature, and aimed at proving the case. For example, 'the suspect was alleged to have damaged a car windscreen. He had been drinking heavily. He said that in the course of a row, he had swung his arm out "and hit the windscreen and it broke" ' (Case CC-A002).

POLICE: Did you intend to smash the windscreen?
SUSPECT: No.
POLICE: So you just swung your hand out in a *reckless* manner? [emphasis supplied]
SUSPECT: yes, that's it, just arguing.
POLICE: Why did you hit the window in the first place?
SUSPECT: Just arguing, *reckless*, it wasn't intentional to break it . . . [emphasis supplied]

The suggestion of recklessness is first implanted by the police as a favourable, exculpatory alternative to the defendant, who accepts it as such and then adopts it. However, recklessness is a term of art. It is part of the definition of the offence with which the man was charged (criminal damage), which is why the police sought the defendant's acceptance of this description of his actions, even though he was not using the term in the technical sense, but rather was using the term colloquially to support a plea that the breakage was accidental. In providing him with the terminology in which to press his 'excuse', the police constructed a key element of the case. Having made this key strategic gain, the officer does not explore the matter further, for to do so would be to run the risk of showing that the man had used the term 'reckless' in a sense quite different from that contemplated in law. Here is another example:

POLICE: How did you take it?
SUSPECT: I just put it in my shopping bag.

POLICE: Then what did you do?
SUSPECT: Walked out of the store.
POLICE: So you stole the bag. Is that correct?
SUSPECT: Yes!

Again, once the suspect has agreed to some act or acts, the police attribute the necessary state of mind and any other legal requirements of guilt by a 'question' which purports to *summarise* the legal effect of what the suspect has related: '*So* you stole . . . '.

There are many other examples which we could give (McConville *et al.*, 1991, ch. 4). The point, though, is that the 'facts' which supply 'strength' or 'weakness' are themselves created by questioning. This is recognised by official actors, as in this request from the CPS to the police: 'Please proceed as charged – theft. But could someone please advise [the store detective] not to say "I believe you forgot to pay" when apprehending shoplifters' (Case CC-A069). Such questions from store detectives create weak facts (the defence that the theft was not deliberate), rather than evidential strength. The choice of what types of fact to create lies with the police and other enforcement agencies.

Exculpatory Evidence

Many suspects deny allegations and provide an alternative story. The police sometimes check these stories, but usually only when they are genuinely undecided about whether to arrest and charge in the first place. The purpose of interrogation is to provide support for the police case, not to elicit the suspect's side of the story. Thus lines of defence provided by suspects are considered irrelevant and are ignored or argued away.

> The suspect was named as a person who was involved in disorder in a town centre on a Saturday evening following a football match. When arrested he told the police that he had spent the evening in a neighbouring town, had gone to the cinema and then returned home. He also named two people who were visiting his mother who could vouch for the fact that he had returned home at 9.50 pm and he also offered to describe what both films were about. The interviewer ignored his offer to describe the two films. The man was charged with threatening behaviour. At trial no evidence was offered after it became apparent that the two named alibi witnesses would support his story.   (Case CCA-A043)

In several acquittals the weakness in the case related to evidence initially offered by the suspect in interrogation but which was not followed up by the

130   *Unravelling Criminal Justice*

police. So not only do the police create strength in cases, they also (by omission through laziness, overconfidence or whatever) create weakness. The resources of the defence are, however, limited. Defendants cannot always follow up their alibis. Some leads are therefore just not checked out. So in one case where the suspect claimed that he did not take part in the offence, and cited two onlookers who could back him up, no one produced the onlookers and the defendant was convicted.

Frequently there is no clear line to be drawn between exculpatory and mitigatory statements. The claim that damage was accidental or that articles were taken when under stress could be both exculpatory (denial of criminal intent) or mitigatory (excuses provided but no legal justification). The latter often provide the basis for cautioning on 'public interest' grounds. Consequently, police interrogation methods which aim to create the strongest possible police case, and to avoid encouraging or checking up on excuses, create not just confessions but also negative any public interest in non-prosecution. Thus in most minor prosecutions it is impossible to judge the cautionability or otherwise of the case because the relevant information is simply not provided in the file. Prosecution becomes inevitable in such cases.

Unverified Police Evidence

Verifiability has been central to many of the problems of criminal justice. Prior to PACE, the police were not required to record interrogation precisely, and confessions were usually contained in the form of written statements by suspects. Allegations of fabrication were frequent. In an attempt to reduce both fabrication and the allegations, PACE and the Code now require contemporaneous recording (by hand or tape) of formal police station interrogations. However, the Code does not forbid 'questioning' in certain informal settings (at time of arrest; in the police car, and so on) and our research found that many conversations with accused persons in the police station are not recorded because the police choose not to characterise them as formal interviews.

Because the police may still rely in evidence on things said by a suspect in an informal setting, the scope for 'verballing' the suspect (attributing to him or her an admission which was not actually made) remains. It is notable that in our research sample the police often alleged that admissions had been made at the time of arrest where the suspect either completely denied the offence in formal interview or said nothing.

A further means of ensuring the creation of evidence favourable to the police case is the practice of using informal 'chats' with a suspect as a

Researching Discretions to Charge and Prosecute 131

means of structuring the interview in advance. Such 'off-the-record' meetings between police and suspect are restricted by PACE, which requires the custody officer to refuse informal access to the suspect and to record all meetings which do take place. However, officers whom we interviewed indicated that such informal contacts were a regular part of police work and a vital tool in the interrogation process. This is confirmed by Sanders and Bridges (1990). The significance of these informal chats is that inducements and deals may be made which could not be made on the record or perhaps with a solicitor present, and that by preparing the way for the formal interrogation, the officer can anticipate and avoid the possibility of the suspect suggesting any form of defence on the record.

There are many other opportunities which the police have to construct evidence. Some were given to us in this interview:

> The officer told us that for threatening behaviour the police would always say that women and children were present, as someone had to be likely to be afraid for the charge to succeed. He said: 'If we know they're guilty we make sure they are.' If he saw a car with a smashed window and a man walking down the road ahead with a radio which he dropped when he saw the police, and if he also denied carrying the radio when apprehended, he (the officer) would say in his evidence that he saw the man break into the car and take the radio. The man, he said, would inevitably say that he had found the radio on the street: 'That might be true but it would be 99 per cent certain that he'd broken in and taken it.' (Case AT-A107).

Implications

When we use terms like 'weak' and 'strong' we generally accept that there is a subjective element in these evaluations. However, it is not just evaluation of evidence that is subjective, but its very creation. Confessions and incriminating statements are created through questions aimed at those results. Exculpatory and mitigatory statements are not created, or are undermined, with the same sense of purpose. And when no confessions are made, or they are unsatisfactory in some way, the police can 'verbal' suspects to fill the gaps. When other evidence is needed the police can often provide that too.

The Royal Commission hoped to deal with these problems by requiring the police to record everything they did. However, it is the police who record everything that the police do. This is fraught with danger, and the written record takes on an existence and evidential quality of its own. If a defendant says he was visited in a cell by an officer, this is hard enough to prove in the face of denials from the officer. If the custody record does not record such a visit, proof is made harder still. Similarly, police statements about what they claimed to see suspects do, whether they were drunk or not, or insolent or not, all have stronger evidential value when written at the time the events in question allegedly occurred.

If weakness and strength are created by the police through written files there is a further implication: later decision-makers vetting those files for weakness and strength, and cautionability or otherwise, will have to do so on the basis of the evidence which has already been constructed for specific purposes by the officers in the case. Cases which fall at later hurdles would, then, be expected to be not those which are intrinsically weak or cautionable (if we can talk in such terms); rather, they would be cases which are constructed poorly. In our research we looked at the work of senior officers who reviewed cases, juvenile liaison bureaux who decide whether or not to caution, and the CPS who decide whether or not to continue prosecutions initiated by the police. Here there is only space to discuss the CPS, but the first two are discussed elsewhere (McConville *et al.*, 1991, ch. 7).

THE ROLE OF THE CROWN PROSECUTION SERVICE (CPS)

The CPS possesses the power to veto any prosecution and is, therefore, the ultimate gatekeeper of the criminal courts. The CPS is formally independent of the police, but is completely dependent in the senses that the police are its sole client and are its only source of information about a case.

The CPS can seek to justify its existence by pointing to the large number of cases which are dropped on the basis of evidential weakness. However, it is in fact rare for the CPS to drop a case following their initial review where the police wish to prosecute. Thus, in many dropped cases the evidential weakness had already been signalled by the earlier review by the police. In Case CC-A085/6/7, for instance, the police reviewer commented: 'I cannot see how the theft charge can be pursued'; and in Case CC-A074/7/6: 'I am not happy with the evidence.' A reluctance to drop cases with which the police wished to proceed was apparent in many cases. Thus, in Case BW-A013 following the defendant's acquittal the prosecutor admitted to us that this was not unexpected because the evidence was a bit 'thin' although there was a case to answer. Here is a similar case:

> The CPS reviewer described the evidence in a public order case as a 'bit thin'. He speculated that the defendant was arrested just to get him off the

street, and expressed sympathy for the police in difficult public-order situations. He prosecuted, but the defendant, not surprisingly, was acquitted. (Case CC-A027)

There are several reasons why the CPS is willing to prosecute cases it perceives to be weak. One, revealed in the case above, is that the CPS empathises with police working rules and therefore avoids undermining them. The CPS also pursues weak cases because, while weak cases which are contested *may* end in failure, *all* dropped cases by definition end in failure. Thus in Case AH-A020 the prosecutor complained bitterly to us about poor police investigation. He expected to lose the case, but in fact the defendant was convicted.

Another reason is that so many defendants plead guilty. Rather than dropping *weak* cases, the CPS drops cases that are likely to *fail*:

The CPS reviewer wrote that the charge was very weak. He advised that the case be dropped if the defendant pleaded not guilty. (Case AT-A109)

The CPS suggested that if the defendant pleaded not guilty, they bargain over compensation instead of proceeding with prosecution. (Case BW-A083)

No cases in our research sample were dropped on public-interest grounds alone, apart from those in which the defendants were already being prosecuted for more serious offences or were already in prison. Yet, even according to the Code's own indicator of cautionability – a nominal court penalty – many cases should have been so dropped. Most of the time it did not occur to prosecutors to drop cases on the grounds of cautionability. One prosecutor explained that prosecutors start from the position that people should be prosecuted if there is sufficient evidence. Thus, the pro-prosecution presumption of the police is maintained by the CPS. On one very rare occasion when a prosecutor did suggest dropping such a case the police objected so strongly that that prosecutor's senior overruled him and personally decided that the case should be prosecuted.

The police anticipate and control review by the CPS by the control which they exercise over case construction. Thus, as discussed above, the police routinely regard exculpatory evidence as irrelevant and rarely follow up defences suggested in interviews or by other evidence. A consequence of this is that at the time when the prosecutor determines whether there is a realistic prospect of conviction it may not be apparent that a defence may be

134 *Unravelling Criminal Justice*

raised. Similarly, with the question of public interest: the Code requires prosecutors to consider such matters as the defendant's attitude to the offence, whether he or she was ill or under stress, or was provoked. But in terms of police objectives there is no reason to collect this information, or, if known, to include it in the file. In many cases in the research, information relevant to cautionability was known to the police but not recorded, and the CPS approved of the decision to prosecute in total ignorance of it.

Since the CPS tends to identify with police values, as embodied in police working rules, the police rarely find it difficult to persuade CPS to prosecute cases which may be otherwise dubious. Here is another example:

> An 18-year-old took a bulb from the civic Christmas tree. He was charged with theft. The police told CPS that 'It would be nice if publicity could be given to the matter with a view to deterring others from acting in the same manner.' This told the CPS that what might, in normal circumstances, be too trivial to prosecute was, in its context, relatively serious. The CPS prosecuted.   (Case BW-A083)

The CPS is essentially reactive. Rather than setting its own prosecution policy, it sees its job as to carry out efficiently police prosecution policy. Thus, in Case CC-A108 a woman was charged with criminal damage for smashing a social services office window. She explained to the police that she did this because they would not find her a new home. She had left her former home as a result of being raped by her landlord. Not only did the CPS not regard this as an extenuating circumstance justifying dropping the case on 'public interest' grounds, but the reviewer did not consider asking the police to investigate the rape allegation. In this case, as in many others, the reviewer – when asked – assumed that the police had good reasons for acting in the way they did. In reality it does not matter to the CPS what the police's reasons are. As long as there is sufficient evidence, a conviction can be recorded.

CONCLUSION

The assumption underlying the reforms of the 1980s is that police and prosecutors are susceptible to control by law and administrative guidelines, and that the practices of these agencies may be changed by tightening the law and increasing the scope of administrative guidance. Thus, it has been assumed that national policies on diverting offenders from prosecution and not prosecuting weak cases can be operationalised by Home Office caution-

Researching Discretions to Charge and Prosecute 135

ing guidelines and the Code for Crown Prosecutors. Similarly, it is assumed that the problem of miscarriages of justice can be addressed by tightening the legal regulation of police investigation and by requiring the police to respect and enforce certain protective rights conferred on suspects.

Our major finding is that these assumptions are wrong. Legislators and government policy-makers have ignored the powerful working rules, linked to the particular goals of the police, which shape police conduct and decision-making. Where legal rules and working rules conflict, the latter will prevail unless there is both a real possibility of being discovered and effective sanctions for breach of those legal rules (Smith and Gray, 1983). Without these possibilities, legal rules become merely presentational devices which inform the police how their decisions must be presented in order to be in apparent conformity with the law.

The law therefore facilitates police conduct and decision-making according to police working rules, by providing a means of both obscuring what actually occurred and of justifying police action. Thus, the working rule that all arrestees may be detained for interview is facilitated by the legal rule which tells the police that detention is lawful provided that the custody officer writes a certain verbal formula on the custody record. The conflict between the legal rule that all interviews with a suspect must be recorded and the working rule that interviews should be preceded by an informal chat is similarly resolved. The informal chat is simply not noted on the custody record as having taken place. This bypasses the need to record what was said. Custody officers are willing to break the law routinely in these ways because the power to make these decisions is conferred on them by law, with no system of effective review and no sanction for abuse of the discretion which they exercise.

As it is assumed that the police will respect the laws which regulate them, so it is assumed that the conduct of prosecutors will be governed by the principles laid out in their Code. This ignores both the relative dependence of the CPS on the police and the influence of the prosecutors' own working rules. Decisions about evidential sufficiency and public interest can be anticipated and controlled by the way in which the case presented to the CPS is constructed by the police. Thus, the evidence of witnesses which contradicts the police case *may never be seen* by the prosecutor. Where the police have decided that a prosecution is appropriate they have no motivation to seek or include information which might support caution or non-prosecution.

For prosecutors the primary working rule is a presumption in favour of prosecution, at least in those cases in which the police have indicated that they wish to proceed. They are content to proceed with weak cases unless the weakness is so blatant that there would be absolutely no question of a conviction, and questions of public interest rarely intrude on their decision-making. This failure rigorously to apply criteria of evidential sufficiency and public interest arises from the absence of any incentive to do so, or sanction for failure to do so. For a service which judges itself, and expects to be judged by others, according to its conviction rate (Crown Prosecution Service, 1989; National Audit Office, 1989) there is no reason to drop provable cases simply on public-interest grounds. In relation to evidentially weak cases, again there is no incentive to drop on that ground alone. It is the experience of prosecutors that weak cases commonly produce a guilty plea. Where a guilty plea is not offered spontaneously, it may often be procured by offering inducements such as a reduction in the number of charges or agreeing to proceed on a less-serious charge. Because weak cases may produce convictions, there is no reason to drop a case when it is first reviewed purely on grounds of weakness. It pays the prosecutor to bide his or her time, and to consider dropping the case only if it appears that the defendant intends to plead not guilty and is not willing to bargain.

Ten years ago, Doreen McBarnet analysed the detailed rules and practices of the criminal justice system to determine how the state obtained convictions (McBarnet, 1981). Her conclusion was that the law did not live up to its rhetoric of 'due process': rules and procedures which were presented as protecting standards of proof, in fact operated in the service of crime control to ease the functions of investigation and prosecution and deliver convictions. She argued that because the law itself facilitated crime control there was little need for police illegality to secure convictions.

Our research supports McBarnet's view that the legal environment in which the police operate facilitates crime control. However, she draws the focus of enquiry away from police practices and towards an examination of what the law permits; and away from the motivations of institutions and individuals towards the structure of the law. We have shown that successful pursuit of crime-control objectives depends upon a variety of police practices. Even when these practices are not illegal or contrary to official guidelines they are not *prescribed by* the law; rather, they are *allowed by* it. The role of law is not to prevent illegality, but to obscure and validate it. Equally, we argue, the key to understanding the criminal process does not lie in the extent to which the law facilitates crime-control practices, but rather in the working rules of the individuals and institutions involved in crime control. To understand why the criminal justice system works in the way it does we need to give equal emphasis to the behaviour of officials and to the legal framework in which they operate.

Researching Discretions to Charge and Prosecute 137

This research illustrates how meaningless it is to pass laws without attending to the goals and occupational culture of those whom these laws are supposed to control. Dixon *et al.* (1989) reached similar conclusions in relation to stop-and-search powers. The research also suggests that review bodies cannot effectively review earlier decisions or processes of other agencies without access to the raw material which those agencies considered, or – at least – submissions from agencies other than those which they are reviewing. This is why the CPS finds its role so difficult to fulfil, and raises similar questions about similar bodies (for example, the Police Complaints Authority). This also means that any expectation we may hold about the role of the CPS or custody officer in reducing miscarriages of justice will have to be radically revised.

REFERENCES

Crown Prosecution Service (1989), *Annual Report 1988/89* (London: Her Majesty's Stationery Office).

Dixon, D. *et al.* (1989), 'Reality and rules in the construction and regulation of police suspicion', *International Journal of the Sociology of Law*, **17**, 185.

Gudjonsson, G. H. and MacKeith, J. (1988), 'Retracted confessions', *Medicine, Science and the Law*, **28**(3), 187–94.

Hanmer, J. *et al.* (1989), *Women, Policing and Male Violence* (London: Routledge).

Irving, B. (1980), *Police Interrogation* (London: Her Majesty's Stationery Office).

McBarnet, D. (1981), *Conviction* (London: Macmillan).

McConville, M. and Baldwin, J. (1981), *Courts, Prosecution and Conviction* (Oxford: Oxford University Press).

McConville, M., Sanders, A. and Leng, R. (1991), *The Case for the Prosecution* (London: Routledge).

National Audit Office (1989), *Review of the Crown Prosecution Service* (London: Her Majesty's Stationery Office).

Nelken, D. (1983), *The Limits of the Legal Process* (London: Macmillan).

Sanders, A. (1985), 'Prosecution decisions and the Attorney-General's guidelines', *Criminal Law Review*, 4–19.

Sanders, A. and Bridges, L. (1990), 'Access to legal advice and police malpractice', *Criminal Law Review*, 494.

Shapland, J. and Vagg, J. (1988), *Policing by the Public* (London: Routledge).

Smith, D. and Gray, J. (1983), *Police and People in London* (London: Policy Studies Institute).

[15]

PROSECUTION AS A VICTIM POWER RESOURCE: A NOTE ON EMPOWERING WOMEN IN VIOLENT CONJUGAL RELATIONSHIPS

DAVID A. FORD

Criminal prosecution of abusive men is described here as a power resource used by battered women to help bring about satisfactory arrangements for managing conjugal violence. This article examines relevant theory on exchange and power processes to explain the conditions of victim empowerment. It then describes cases of women who filed charges against their conjugal partners to show how victims may file, but later drop, charges as a rational power strategy for determining the future course of their relationships. The article concludes with a discussion of the implications of prosecutorial policies that limit battered women's control over criminal justice processes.

I. INTRODUCTION

Men who dominate their conjugal partners through violence are said to use force as an "ultimate power resource" to control women (Allen and Straus 1980; see also Goode 1971; Gelles and Straus 1988; Pagelow 1984). Violence persists, in part, because victimized women are powerless relative to their abusive partners and thus can neither escape nor prevent the violent behavior (Gelles 1983). But powerlessness does not necessarily imply helplessness. Studies of nonclinical samples have shown that victimized women can be active help seekers (Bowker 1983; Gelles and Straus 1988). They are most likely to seek outside intervention when the violence is severe—the point at which it is most difficult to control.[1] Gelles and Straus (1988:159) report that "a firm, emphatic,

---

I appreciate the critical comments offered by Fred DuBow, Wendy Ford, David Funk, Linda Haas, and Charles Jeffords on earlier drafts of this article and revisions suggested by participants in the 1989–90 Family Research Laboratory Seminar at the University of New Hampshire. This article was completed with support of the Family Research Laboratory under a NIMH Postdoctoral Fellowship, grant MH15161-13. I am especially grateful to former Marion County Prosecutor Stephen Goldsmith for his cooperation and support of this research, to Eugenia Smith for her assistance, and to the battered women who graciously shared their experiences.
[1] Accounts of women who kill violent partners suggest, in the extreme, action predicated on powerlessness rather than helplessness, irrespective of whether or not they sought outside help. See Schneider (1986) for a discussion

314   PROSECUTION AS A VICTIM POWER RESOURCE

and rational approach appears to be the most effective personal strategy a woman can use to prevent future violence." Law enforcement agencies, by virtue of their capacity for coercion, offer victims hope for protection in pursuing such a strategy (Bowker 1986).

Intervention by the criminal justice system has the potential to empower victims by providing criminal sanctions as leverage to prevent further abuse (e.g., Bowker 1986; Dutton 1988; Field and Field 1973; Ford 1983; Ford and Burke 1987; Hall 1975; Lerman 1981). In particular, a woman may be able to use the threat of arrest and prosecution to deter her partner from repeated violence (cf. Goode 1971). However, criminal justice agencies have traditionally been unresponsive to the needs of battered women. Battered wives who sought protection through criminal justice were likely, instead, to find themselves further victimized by the system (e.g., Field and Field 1973; Ford 1983; Gayford 1977; Schneider and Jordan 1978). Even with recent advocacy for rigorous law enforcement, prosecutors in some jurisdictions still impose barriers to a woman's use of the criminal justice system.[2] Criminal justice is of questionable value if it creates greater hardship for victims than doing nothing. But do system reforms for a more certain response necessarily empower battered women?

This article explores the idea that victims of violent conjugal relationships use criminal justice as a resource to increase their relative power and to arrange circumstances in a way they perceive as satisfactory for managing conjugal abuse. Prosecution, in particular, is treated as a resource susceptible to control by a victim to determine her own fate. The article studies the manipulation of prosecution as a resource within the general framework of exchange and power in conjugal relations. Illustrating the possibilities for victim empowerment through prosecution, it also examines suggestive data from a study of women seeking to prosecute their partners for acts of violence. Although the ideas presented are derived from established theories, they are not meant to constitute a coherent theory. Rather, they outline an apparently rational strategy of victim action consistent with victim accounts. The article concludes by questioning the wisdom of those prosecution policies that are inconsistent with power resource utilization and that may actually disempower battered wives.

of the problems in formulating a self-defense strategy that characterizes killing as a reasonable action for self-preservation when victims are stereotyped by the label of "learned helplessness."

[2] For example, Dunford et al. (1989) report that in Omaha, victims are required to pay a fee in order to make a criminal complaint directly to the prosecutor's office. More typical, perhaps, is the situation in such cities as Washington, D.C., where in 1989 fewer than 5 percent of victim complaints result in warrants after victims are subjected to multiple interviews, including a nonjudicial probable cause hearing (Naomi Cahn and Joan Meier, personal communication).

II. ADVOCACY FOR THE PROSECUTION OF BATTERERS

Professionals working with battered women disagree over the value of prosecuting abusive conjugal partners. Field and Field (1973:236) state that criminal justice systems are largely "irrelevant" to the solution of domestic violence cases. They note: "There exists an unequivocal mandate for change, and we must look away from the criminal process for remedies" (ibid.). Maidment (1978: 110), noting society's responsibility to provide a variety of services to victims of conjugal violence, describes legal remedies as problematic:

> The law . . . must be seen as just one of these other available services. It is a mistake to see resort to the law as a panacea. One does not have to accept the ultra-cynical view . . . that lawyers have an "interest" in defining events as "legal problems" to realize that the legal remedy is just one of a number of ways of providing a solution for preventing intrafamily violence. It is for the victim and the non-legal experts to decide when and whether the legal solution is appropriate to prevent the recurrence of violence.

She argues further that the law may even exacerbate a woman's relationship and result in further violence, especially retaliatory violence against her for having sought legal help, "a factor which may explain only too well her reluctance to pursue a legal remedy which she has already initiated" (Maidment 1978:111; see also Bard 1980; Field and Field 1973; Finesmith 1983; Gayford 1977).

But other women's advocates, among them many social service providers, call for vigorously imposing criminal sanctions (e.g., Fromson 1977; Walker 1979). Lerman (1981) offers three reasons for prosecuting. First, prosecution demonstrates that spouse abuse is more than an individual problem; it deters battery against women in general by demonstrating society's intolerance of such violence. Second, the combined policies of prosecutors and courts can be used to protect victims and to reduce the violent behavior of abusers, thus functioning as a specific deterrent to conjugal battery. Third, a demonstrable prosecutorial policy toward such abuse may induce concurrent reform of police policies in the interest of victims of conjugal violence.

Prior to Lerman's report, principal demands for the criminalization of spouse abuse called for agents of criminal justice to be more responsive to the interests of victims. These demands assume that an effective criminal justice response exists, so that cases of conjugal violence can and will be readily handled just like any other battery (e.g., Gregory 1976). What has traditionally been seen as a problem is the prejudice and insensitivity of the agents rather than the structure of their activities. A victim's unwillingness to pursue prosecution reflects those problems, and she carries no individual responsibility for creating them. Current advocacy, represented by Lerman (1981) and echoed by Goolkasian (1986),

316   PROSECUTION AS A VICTIM POWER RESOURCE

proposes policy changes designed to force not only agent responsiveness but also victim cooperation. Lerman (1981) describes several of the difficulties posed for effective prosecution, including,
from a prosecutor's perspective, the "problem" of victim noncooperation.

There is ample evidence from jurisdictions around the United
States that high percentages of women who file charges do, in fact,
drop them prior to adjudication. Parnas (1970) found that battered
women either requested dismissal of charges or failed to appear in
court in over half of the cases he studied in Chicago. Ford (1983)
found that over 70 percent of conjugal violence cases in Indianapolis were dismissed at victims' requests under less stringent screening procedures. Bannon (1975:3) discovered what he termed an
"unbelievable" attrition rate for domestic violence cases in Detroit
in 1972—more than 90 percent. Field and Field (1973) reported
that about 80 percent of the marital violence cases in the District
of Columbia in 1967 had charges dropped, presumably by the victim.[3]

To "solve" the problem, Lerman (1981) advocates the prosecutorial policy of not permitting victims to drop charges. But is
noncooperation necessarily a problem? It is conceivable that, from
a victim's perspective, filing and then dropping charges is a useful
strategy for managing her situation. What is troublesome to prosecutors may be a rational use of criminal justice by victims. At issue
is whether or not policies meant to reduce case attrition by depriving battered women of control over prosecution processes can be
said to aid otherwise powerless victims (see Pagelow 1984:333–34).
That is, do such policies *empower* battered women? Or do they *disempower* them by depriving them of control?

The history of criminal prosecution in the United States suggests that victims are disempowered when prosecutors take *complete* control of the process. Criminal prosecution has shifted from
a concern for victim restitution to the primacy of legal representatives, whose interests sometimes limit the gains a victim might expect to achieve through use of legal processes. DuBow and Becker
(1976) characterized the change in terms of a bifurcation of civil
and criminal proceedings.[4] The emergence of a dominant public

---

[3] A notable exception to this pattern of dropped charges is the remarkably low figure of 6 percent reported by Dobash and Dobash (1979:222) for cases
in two Scottish cities in 1974.

[4] The distinction between civil and criminal proceedings has created legal
debate over the propriety of lawyers using the threat of criminal action to extract civil gains. It raises an interesting issue for prosecutors who may be
aware of extralegal civil agreements arranged under threat of criminal prosecution. Disciplinary Rule 7-105(A) of the 1969 ABA Code of Professional Responsibility state: "A lawyer shall not . . . participate in presenting . . . criminal
charges solely to obtain an advantage in a civil matter." However, DR 7-105(A)
was omitted from the 1983 ABA Model Rules of Professional Conduct, thereby
leaving the issue subject to debate, as Wolfram (1986:718) notes:
Thus, abusively harassing another with threats of a well-founded

prosecutor role has cost the victim opportunities for control of a case and restitution: The principal form of power left to the victim is the negative one of not reporting the crime or not cooperating in its prosecution (DuBow and Becker 1976).

In sum, we have two competing views of advocacy relevant to the prosecution of misdemeanor battery cases: One, in support of a no drop policy, calls for the vigorous use of criminal justice in ways consistent with official prosecutorial interest, albeit with concern for victim welfare (e.g., Purdy 1985). The other calls for the use of criminal prosecution in ways defined as appropriate by the victim based on her own assessment of her needs (e.g., Elliott et al. 1985).

III. A THEORETICAL PERSPECTIVE ON POWER AND PROSECUTION

Exchange theorists argue that interpersonal power and dependence are a function of the exchange processes governing social interaction. Each party in a dyad participates in the relationship with the understanding that it will be favorable to his/her reward/cost position, that is, his/her outcomes or profits. A has power over B if, by varying her behavior, A can cause B to vary his behavior. This capability derives from one's dependence on the other for gaining rewards or avoiding costs in their exchange relationship. Those rewards and costs can be manipulated by one person to influence the behavior of another (Blau 1964; Emerson 1962, 1972; Homans 1961; Thibaut and Kelley 1959).

Power theorists in this tradition use the term "resources" to describe whatever may have significance in creating rewards and costs in the relationship, that is, whatever is used by one person to influence another. Gamson (1968:73), for example, characterizes influence in terms of the control of resources, for which he cites Dahl (1957:203): The "base of an actor's power consists of all the *resources*—opportunities, acts, objects, etc.—that he can exploit in order to effect the behavior of another." Goode (1971) groups all such resources into four major sets: economic variables; prestige or respect; force and its threat; and likability, attractiveness, friendship, or love. Any element of these sets can be made available or withheld by one person, under certain conditions, to alter the re-

---

criminal complaint may be permissible under the Model Rules—a clear, and unfortunate, diminution of the protections afforded by the Code. The behavior permitted by the Model Rules, if engaged in by a client legally in some states, is sufficiently close to the edge of legality and so unappealing a tactic in general that it would better have been prohibited outright in the Model Rules.
In cases such as those described in this article, a prosecutor has accepted a case for prosecution based on the state's interest in acting against domestic violence, given probable cause, regardless of victim motivations. In Indiana, a victim may legally file a criminal complaint, provided the charge is well founded, even if solely motivated by an interest in gaining leverage in a civil matter.

318   PROSECUTION AS A VICTIM POWER RESOURCE

ward/cost position of another person (Gelles and Straus 1988; Levinger 1959).

What makes such an element a resource in one circumstance and not in another? Gamson (1968)[5] argues that for a person to use it as a power resource s/he must both control it and bring it to bear on others (cf. Emerson 1972). Power, then, entails more than the possession of resources, it also requires a capacity for manipulating those resources under a power strategy appropriate to a particular interpersonal situation. When A uses a resource as a threat to demand B's compliance, A must convince B of her capability and willingness to use it (cf. Wrong 1980).

Power in conjugal relationships rests with the resources possessed by the partners (Blood and Wolfe 1960; Goode 1971; Rodman 1972; Scanzoni 1982; Scanzoni and Szinovacz 1980; Straus et al. 1980; Wolfe 1959). The *threat* of force, in particular, has been a significant power resource for maintaining traditional patterns of male domination in the family (Goode 1971; Yllo and Straus 1990). Violence is an "ultimate" power resource "invoked when individuals lack other legitimate resources to serve as bases for their power" (Allen and Straus 1980:189; cf. Blau 1964). Prosecution is likewise a potential power resource, one available to the *victim* in a violent relationship. For a woman, it may be an effective means of deterring her partner's violence when invoked in alliance with committed agents of criminal justice.

A battered woman can draw on the "superior force" (Goode 1971:626) wielded by agents of criminal justice as her own power resource. However, following an exchange and power perspective, criminal justice options are victim power resources only if *she* can control the manner in which they are brought to bear on her mate. Thus, victims can be empowered by controlling prosecution as a resource for managing conjugal violence. As a power resource, the *threat* of prosecution, like the threat of violence, may be more significant than actual prosecution in the strategy of managing conflict. Theoretically, a victim could use the threat of prosecution to bargain for arrangements satisfactory to her wishes. Indeed, such informal negotiation may help her attain outcomes that would be impossible through criminal processing.[6]

To be successful as a power strategy, the victim must demonstrate some degree of commitment to prosecuting so that it appears a highly likely outcome if the man does not comply with her

---

5 In his essay on power and discontent, Gamson's discussion of the means whereby "potential partisans" influence "authorities" suggests this general perspective on how an individual can exercise power over, that is, influence, another. For present purposes, his terms "potential partisans" and "authorities" are avoided to facilitate discussion of general principles.

6 For example, she may bargain for a divorce using the threat of invoking criminal sanctions. By analogy to bargaining in civil disputes, "negotiating in the shadow of the court" may allow for broader solutions than would be possible if imposed by court order (Menkel-Meadow 1984:789).

interests (see Schelling 1960:24). Particularly if she wants to stop further violence, deterrence may operate when she can demonstrate the credibility of a threat (Schelling 1960). Ultimately, however, she must be able to withdraw the threat if she secures a favorable settlement. In other words, the effective use of prosecution as a power resource is premised on the victim's ability both to demonstrate a significant threat *and* to control activities relevant to the threat, including its withdrawal.

There are several notable problems (from a victim's perspective) with the use of prosecution as a power resource. First, and most obvious, the batterer may not fear prosecution. If criminal sanctioning has no prospect for deterring, its threat has no value as a power resource. Second, prosecution can be costly to the victim as well as to her abuser (Elliott 1989). She stands to lose whatever he provides in the way of economic security, child care, or even emotional support should he leave or be imprisoned (e.g., Sprey 1971). Indeed, a woman's felt dependence on her partner for such resources prevents her from acting in her own interest (Walker 1979). Moreover, the batterer may cause her or her children more harm in reaction to threatened or actual criminal sanctions (Field and Field 1973; Maidment 1978). If a victim threatens prosecution, she must be prepared to demonstrate her commitment to taking the man to court despite the possible costs to her. The battered woman who initially files charges may be tentative in her resolve to prosecute until she learns enough about the process to evaluate such costs. Only after she has weighed the outcomes and found them relatively favorable will she employ the threat of prosecution as a bargaining strategy. Presumably, many will find it too costly a strategy.

A third problem with using prosecution as a power resource is that victims can never fully control its course. That is, prosecution is a "secondary resource" under ultimate control of another party necessarily more powerful than a victim. Battered wives have long benefitted from the intervention of others on behalf of their interests (Pleck 1979). But with the historical shift toward state intervention in place of traditional informal sanctions, women's personal interests have been displaced by legal interests, resulting in diminished victim self-determination in appeals to others for security. As noted above, victim control is limited to noncooperation (DuBow and Becker 1976), the very behavior which incurs hostility from the agents of criminal justice whose help the victim seeks.[7]

---

[7] Cannavale and Falcon (1976:72) found that a prosecutor's label of "noncooperative" is more likely to be applied to cases in which a witness is known to the defendant. Although perhaps not applicable to a sample of misdemeanor wife-battery victims, it is a relevant observation that "relationship" may say more about a prosecutor's motivation to pursue a case than it says about victim motivations.

320   PROSECUTION AS A VICTIM POWER RESOURCE

Finally, effective bargaining for security requires that the victim's threat be maintained for a period of time sufficient to ensure that the violence will not recur. A man's simple promise to reform should not be cause for dropping charges, for it may be a premature relinquishment of the resource that offers protection. It is common for a victim who is eager to end a relationship, or to put a violent incident behind her, to drop charges before her security is assured. By contrast, the victim who bargains for concrete structural arrangements likely to reduce the chance of violence (e.g., treatment for the batterer or permanent separation) can see the bargain fulfilled before she gives up her resource.

IV. POWER AND THE DROPPED CHARGE SYNDROME

Understanding prosecution as a power resource helps to account for why, in seeking some form of negotiated order, some battered women drop charges. Not every woman approaches the prosecutor with the intent of gaining leverage in her relationship with a violent man. For example, victims of conjugal violence in Indianapolis have previously been described as motivated by curiosity, by confirmation of their victim status, by a desire to affirm a matter of principle, by a need to demonstrate a genuine threat, and by revenge (Ford 1983). This article focuses on cases where the victim seeks to pressure the man into some form of settlement. The victims' aims are reflected not only in their reasons for prosecuting but also in their reasons for dropping charges.

What little is known about why victims drop charges centers on three lines of thought. One points to problems with the criminal justice system's lack of responsiveness, which renders it useless to victims seeking its services (Field and Field 1973; Ford 1983; Truninger 1971). Another argues that victims are intimidated into dropping charges by threats of retaliatory violence from their men if they pursue prosecution (Ford 1983; Maidment 1978; Paterson 1979; Truninger 1971). (This may also be seen as a problem with the criminal justice system's response, as above.) A third idea is that estranged victims and offenders reconcile and perhaps fall back in love (Bard 1980; Hall 1975; Parnas 1970; Walker 1979).[8] Their reconciliation need not mean that they have returned to the status quo of a previously violent relationship. They may, in fact, have found what the victim considers a resolution to the violence (including, for example, permanent separation[9]) and no longer need a criminal justice solution (Ford 1983).

---

[8] It may be that a woman never stopped loving her violent partner. Littleton (1989) argues that a battered woman's love for her abuser and her hope that he will reform give her understandable reason for staying with him. Perhaps, too, they give her reason to reconsider the wisdom of pursuing criminal charges.

[9] Even permanent separation may not free a woman from continuing violence. Many women are terrorized long after their relationship has formally

This view of reconciliation is directly relevant to evaluating prosecution as a power resource. It suggests that instrumental motives for prosecuting have been satisfied in interpersonal conflict resolution, thereby nullifying the need for further criminal justice intervention. In other words, criminal justice is used as part of a strategy for securing outcomes, rather than for catharsis or punishment as an end in itself. To illustrate, if events were consistent with theory and previous empirical indications, we would expect the following sequence of activities: A battered woman threatens to prosecute if her mate does not desist; her threat is made credible by filing charges; the threat succeeds in securing favorable outcomes; and thus prosecution is abandoned as part of the bargain. The remainder of this article describes empirical evidence of such a strategy as reported by women initiating prosecution procedures against their abusers.

V. USING PROSECUTION AS A POWER RESOURCE

This study is grounded in several years of participant observation of battered women in interaction with various criminal justice agencies. Specific data reported here were obtained through interviews with twenty-five women seeking to file charges against their mates for misdemeanor battery or recklessness in Marion County, Indiana. Each woman had, at some time, cohabited with the man in a conjugal relationship. The researcher worked as a volunteer in the prosecutor's office for five hours each Monday morning for nine weeks during the summer of 1981. The project was designed to provide the prosecutor with information on case attrition in conjugal cases.

The Marion County Prosecutor's Office served a population of about 766,000 in 1981, including Indianapolis (701,000) and several small towns. Sixty-eight percent of adults in Marion County had graduated from high school. The median family income was $20,819; 6.9 percent of the work force was unemployed (U.S. Department of Commerce 1983). Twenty percent of the population was black, while blacks constituted 28 percent the defendants in conjugal battery cases studied here. Other minorities made up 1 percent of the total population and were not represented in the study sample.

At the time of this research, the prosecutor's policy on domestic violence was in transition. The prosecutor advocated using his official capacity to protect victims. He had abandoned the "three-day hold" policy of his predecessor[10] but had done so with the un-

---

ended. But the chance of violence is considerably lower when couples cease to cohabit.

[10] The three-day hold policy required a victim who wished to have charges filed against a conjugal partner to complete a probable cause affidavit for tentative approval by a deputy prosecutor. If approved, the victim was told to return three days later to sign her complaint for issuance to a judge. The

322   PROSECUTION AS A VICTIM POWER RESOURCE

derstanding that cases might be more closely scrutinized for prospects of victim cooperation later. The prosecutor's office had a
fledgling domestic violence program under which one deputy prosecutor screened cases, among other responsibilities. There was no
special court for domestic violence cases, and the deputy prosecutor who screened a case was unlikely to deal with it again, as it
would be assigned to one of six municipal courts for approval and
trial.

In 1981, misdemeanor battery charges in Indiana had to be
filed by the victim.[11] Thus, the burden of prosecution, at least in
the initial stages of the process, fell on the victim's shoulders. Such
cases provide an opportunity to explore victim behavior for motivations that are irrelevant in warrantless misdemeanor arrests and
arrests for felony assaults.

For this study, each battered woman asking to file charges was
directed to the researcher who screened the case and asked if she
would mind being interviewed for the project (only one refused).
The prosecutor instructed his deputies to approve all requests for
warrants unless there was no legal foundation for prosecution.[12]
Thus, virtually all cases were admitted to the system.[13] Each woman interviewed gave permission for a follow-up telephone interview. Her case was then tracked through the system until it was
dismissed or adjudicated. Interviews were attempted with women
who dropped charges.[14]

All interviews were conducted under a variation of reason
analysis (Ford 1974; Kadushin 1968; Lazarsfeld 1972; Zeisel 1968).
Preliminary interviews at the prosecutor's office focused on the
basic question, "Why did you come to the prosecutor's office?"
Most women gave such reasons as having been told to prosecute by
the police, wanting the man arrested, or needing information
about prosecution and alternative courses of action. Subsequent
questioning sought clarification of those factors that influenced
each woman's decision to initiate prosecution procedures. Re-

rationale for this "cooling-off" period was to insure that complainants were
committed to following through to adjudication once the prosecution process
was initiated (see Ford 1983).

[11] Effective 1 September 1985, Indiana law provides for warrantless arrests in cases of battery with injury (Indiana Code § 35-33-1-1(a) (1986)).

[12] Deputy prosecutors commonly exercised their discretion to reject cases
for prosecution on grounds unrelated to the alleged crime. For example, they
might not accept charges from a woman who still lived with a suspect or who
had not filed for divorce. Similarly, they might send the victim to a civil court
for a peace bond in lieu of filing criminal charges (Ford 1983).

[13] The present study eliminated the effects of discriminatory processing
(see Ford 1983) by insuring that all victims with demonstrable probable cause
were given the opportunity to prosecute. All but one of their complaints were
accepted for prosecution. One case was excluded by a supervisor who chose to
ignore the prosecutor's request to cooperate.

[14] The research was intended simply to learn why women dropped
charges. Resources were unavailable for interviewing those who followed
through with prosecution.

sponses were probed to discern underlying motives such as wanting the man punished, wanting protection and security, wanting the man to stay away (by frightening him), and trying to exert pressure on him so that other victim interests might be realized (divorce, child protection and support, property settlement).[15] What is presented below focuses on the basic "why" question.

Follow-up telephone interviews with women who dropped charges or allowed charges to be dismissed centered on the question, "Why did you choose *not* to prosecute?" Probes sought evidence of intimidation or threats of force, of impatience with the criminal justice system, and of victims having resolved their relationships so that further intervention would be unnecessary or undesirable. If a woman had previously reported instrumental reasons for prosecuting, she was given an opportunity to volunteer corollary reasons indicating the success or failure of prosecution as a power resource in a bargaining strategy. In every such case, bargaining outcomes were elicited without direct or leading questions; that is, respondents simply volunteered that their influence on the case outcome followed a relevant promise or agreement struck with the defendant.

Figure 1 presents the dispositions of the twenty-five cases processed for this study. Twenty-four had warrants issued from the prosecutor's office for a judge's approval; twenty-three were approved; and twenty-two resulted in a man being arrested on a warrant or summoned to court. In thirteen of the cases resolved in court, a victim "dropped charges" either by failing to appear in court (generally after at least one continuance was granted to locate her) or by appearing in court and requesting dismissal. Each of the nine defendants subjected to full adjudication was found guilty.

There was considerable variation in the time between filing charges and final case outcome. It took between 1 and 324 days for women to drop charges, and although three women dropped within 3 days, the median time to dismissal was 104 days. The time to adjudication was much longer. The median time from filing to determination of guilt was 203 days, with a range of from 1 to 777 days.

Table 1 summarizes the reasons battered women gave for wanting to prosecute their partners. Each reason is followed by figures indicating the number of victims mentioning it for the cases dismissed, for those judged guilty, and for the total sample.

---

[15] The interview sought detailed responses on why a woman wanted her partner prosecuted. In most cases, women also gave information on what they expected to happen during and as a result of prosecution, including their expectations for arrest and jail. Most gave an assessment of the risks they might incur by prosecuting. Finally, they were asked whether they had sought alternative sources of help. However, given constraints of time and opportunity, unless such information figured as reasons for prosecuting, it was not pursued for analysis here.

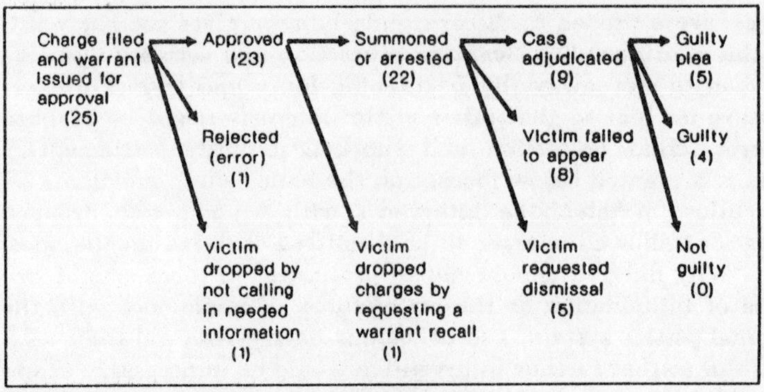

324 PROSECUTION AS A VICTIM POWER RESOURCE

Figure 1. Summary of Case Dispositions

Table 1. Reasons for Prosecuting and Case Outcomes

Reason for Prosecuting	Case Dismissed	Defendant Found Guilty	All Cases
Police advised prosecution	13	9	22
Afraid of abuse/for protection (by scaring him)	6	6	12
Previously warned him/to teach him a lesson	3	6	9
Tired of abuse/will not take it anymore	4	3	7
Need information on what to do about abuse	4	2	6
Want him jailed/want to punish him	3	2	5
To get man needed help (alcohol, psychological)	3	1	4
Attorney advised prosecution	2	1	3
To deter him from hitting others	1	2	3
To get support payments	2	—	2
Want to recover property from residence	2	—	2
Want to punish him for mistreating baby	1	—	1
No alternative/cannot afford divorce	1	—	1
Doctor advised prosecution	—	1	1

Most notable (and perhaps surprising, given the reputation of police for their lack of concern) is the top ranking of police advice as a stated reason for prosecuting. Most women considered the police an important factor in their efforts; they were eager to cite the police as legitimizing their complaints. Other reasons were more significant as motives for prosecuting and have been cited in previous studies (Ford 1983; Ford and Burke 1987; Hall 1975).

Not all these motives are relevant to prosecution as a power resource. Only the following reasons were found, through interviews, to be instrumental factors relevant to power strategies in bargaining for immediate, concrete ends:[16]

---

[16] Other reasons might be classified as "instrumental" to a bargaining strategy, but associated outcomes could not be demonstrated. For example, a woman might have filed to prevent the man from hitting other women, but the victim would not know if that goal was realized.

for protection
to get him help (e.g., counseling)
to get support payments
to recover property from residence

Each of these implies a potential for bargaining toward an expected outcome following the initiation of prosecution procedures, that is, following a significant threat to prosecute if favorable outcomes are not secured.[17] In the event that any woman drops charges after reporting one of these motives, power resource theory predicts that she will subsequently report a satisfactory (to her) resolution of her relationship.[18]

Another motive—that she *previously* warned him but he did not comply—predicts completed prosecution under an earlier-initiated power strategy. The woman is expected to follow through on her threat. This is the only factor on which the relationship between the victims' reporting the factor as a reason and the case dispositions approached statistical significance.[19] As expected, cases involving previous threats were more likely to be adjudicated.

Fifteen of the victims either dropped charges or failed to show for court in the course of the prosecution process. Twelve of these women were contacted by phone after dismissal of the cases to check on their welfare and to elicit their reasons for dropping charges (see Table 2). Three victims could not be located.

The reasons for dropping charges shown in Table 2 are consistent with the reasons originally given for prosecuting. The first three indicate possible favorable outcomes to the threat of prosecution as demonstrated in filing charges. Two instances of retaliatory threats of violence were reported, both of which were made in the context of arranging for reconciliation on terms previously described as acceptable to the victim. In four cases, the victims were persuaded to drop charges by others whom they viewed as having influence over their mates—attorneys and judges. In each case, the woman's decision to accede to their advice was under conditions viewed as consistent with her definition of a satisfactory outcome.

In all, eleven of the twelve victims contacted after dropping charges had previously stated an instrumental factor as a motive for prosecuting. The twelfth victim had originally filed charges to

---

[17] Simply stating an instrumental motive does not necessarily imply a bargaining strategy. Rather, it implies the potential for bargaining as described by power resource theory. Some women may feel that instrumental outcomes will automatically follow court proceedings. For example, a woman who wants a man to stay away may believe that prosecution will deter him. One victim in this study simply hoped that the judge could somehow make the man stay away.

[18] Note that while all of these women want to be free of violence, what they consider "satisfactory" may be outcomes only indirectly related to violence. Such outcomes represent steps toward altering the batterer or structuring the relationship to enhance the likelihood of long-term desistance.

[19] By Fisher's exact test for independence, $p = .03$.

326   PROSECUTION AS A VICTIM POWER RESOURCE

Table 2. Reasons for Dropping Charges

Reason	No. Giving
He has stayed away/left her alone	9
He has agreed to get help/counseling	3
He has agreed to divorce/other settlement	3
Abuser's attorney convinced her to drop	3
Victim does not want more hassles/still uncertain	3
Victim does not want him jailed	3
Man threatened her	2
Victim does not want him to lose job	2
Judge reprimanded/scared him	2
Victim felt prosecutor did not care	1
Learned lesson: "he can't walk over me"	1
No subpoena*	1

* In at least three cases the victims did not receive subpoenas, either because of computer error or because they had moved and mail was not forwarded. Only one case can be documented in which the woman had not appeared in court because she was not aware of the trial date.

show the man she would not take any more abuse. She claimed she would have prosecuted except that she was never subpoenaed. In nine of the remaining eleven cases, women gave reasons for dropping charges consistent with a specific desired outcome previously expressed as a reason for filing (i.e., instrumental motive) and consistent with an implied bargaining strategy. One cannot say, based on these data, that instrumental factors consistent with power resource theory were the principal determinants of dropped charges.[20] However, their coverage in interviews gives credence to theoretical representations of prosecution as a power resource. The next section describes case studies of victim reports on how they manipulated the threat of prosecution as a power resource.

VI. SELECTED CASE STUDIES

The summary data indicate that many women used the criminal justice process for reasons other than simply punishing their mates. Their various instrumental motives suggest that victims who are otherwise powerless in the face of violence seek to use prosecution for leverage in managing conjugal conflict or arranging favorable settlements. The cases discussed in this section demonstrate some of the ways in which prosecution is used as a power resource consistent with theoretical expectations. The first two cases describe women who approached the prosecutor's office seeking to have specific needs satisfied through criminal justice intervention. They show how some battered women may purpose-

[20] Obtaining reasons for filing from all victims would have allowed use of standard statistical procedures for assessing the relationship between those reasons and whether a victim dropped charges. But having only obtained data on reasons for dropping charges from those who did drop them, one cannot use comparable analytic procedures to determine whether hoped-for outcomes expressed at the time of filing were realized and therefore related to case dismissal.

fully bargain for security using the threat of prosecution as a power resource. When they achieved success they abandoned the prosecution process. A third case demonstrates an instance where a woman reported she had *previously* bargained for protection under threat of prosecution, then was victimized in violation of the agreement, and later prosecuted to show the man that she meant business—that she was fulfilling the threat.

In the first case, a 33-year-old man battered his wife and threatened to kill her and their three children. A police dispatcher advised the woman to go to the prosecutor's office to file charges. The victim did not know what to expect, except that she hoped a warrant would force him to get psychiatric help. She was not prepared to divorce him, although she claimed she would if she could afford it. At the very least, she hoped that by filing charges she would be able to get her things from their house so she and her children could live apart from him. One month after filing, she appeared at her husband's arraignment to request that charges be dropped. When interviewed a week later, she said that they were separated (she was able to get her belongings with help from the police) and that he was voluntarily receiving counseling. She reported that she had "worked it out with him." She agreed to drop charges if he continued counseling. She also agreed to give him visitation rights. She felt that she had taken a useful first step, although she was still fearful.

This case illustrates a resolution through bargaining: a deal was struck under threat of invoking the negative sanctions incurred through prosecution. The victim believed that sufficient time had passed between filing and dismissing charges to force the man to fulfill at least part of his agreement.

The next case is typical of victims who express additional, noninstrumental, reasons for filing but find those factors to be less important with the passage of time and apparently successful bargaining outcomes. It also illustrates, incidentally, a type of situation misunderstood by criminal justice personnel who resent women who drop charges after promising to follow through to adjudication.

A 17-year-old woman had left her 21-year-old husband after he assaulted her and "mistreated" their 17-month-old son. She filed charges on the advice of police officers. She believed that "he ain't never going to learn unless it's the hard way" and vowed not to drop charges under any circumstance: "He's got to be punished." However, she had a special interest she thought might be realized through filing charges: she wanted him to get treatment for his alcohol problem. She did not want him to serve time in jail or to lose his job. She was confident that she could have him found guilty without him being sentenced to jail. Almost four months after initiating prosecution procedures, she let charges be dismissed by not appearing in court. Her husband had asked her to drop charges

328   PROSECUTION AS A VICTIM POWER RESOURCE

earlier, but she refused. She had appeared for an earlier trial only
to be informed of a defense continuance. By this time, she may
have been cool to the idea of prolonging the process. Most important to her was that he had agreed to enter an alcohol treatment
program, and she was satisfied with his behavior by the time she
decided not to testify against him.

   Both of these cases demonstrate ways in which the threat of
prosecution was seen by victims as serving their interests in attain-
ing a state of affairs reasonably consistent with their wishes. This
is not to say that each picked the best course of action, or that each
played the strategy to its best advantage, or that each found a long-
term solution to violence. What matters here is that the victims
felt that they had controlled events in their relationships—that
they were *empowered* by having filed charges and having secured
satisfactory short-run arrangements.

   Further evidence of victim empowerment through prosecution, even when outcomes are unsatisfactory, can be found in cases
that were adjudicated. Victims' stated intentions at the time they
filed charges reveal that several of the women had *previously*
threatened their mates with prosecution if they did not leave them
alone. The men persisted in abusing the women, so the women
were carrying out their threatened punishment.

   A 31-year-old woman had lived with a 37-year-old man for
over a year until they broke up a few weeks before she filed battery charges against him. He had gone to her house to talk about
getting back together. They ended up arguing, and he hit her in
the face several times. The police responded to her call for help
and advised her to prosecute. She had good reason to fear the man.
He had an extensive police record, including arrests for armed robbery and two felony assaults. He had served two years in prison
for assault with a deadly weapon ten years before the incident reported here. Her main interest was for him to leave her alone. She
believed that if she did not prosecute, he would do something more
harmful to her: "Plus, I feel better," she said. "If somebody hurts
you they shouldn't get away with it." In their case they "had an
understanding" that he would not hit her. If he did, he would be
punished. This was, according to the victim, the first time he violated that understanding, and she was fulfilling her threat by prosecuting.

   In all, seven of the nine cases that were *not* dropped involved
victims who indicated either that a man had violated a prior agreement or that he had previously harmed her and now she was demonstrating that she meant business. In an eighth case, the victim
was committed to prosecuting with the hope that the judge "would
put something on him" so he wouldn't bother her.

DAVID A. FORD   329

VII. DISCUSSION AND IMPLICATIONS FOR THEORY AND POLICY

The data on reasons demonstrate that instrumental factors are to be counted among the motives leading battered women to prosecute their partners. The high consistency between original intentions and reasons for dropping charges suggests the effectiveness of threatening to invoke criminal justice sanctions in securing outcomes satisfactory to victims. Victim accounts, as exemplified in the case studies reported above, leave little doubt that *some* battered women intentionally use the threat of prosecution as a power resource to pressure their mates into agreements the women consider satisfactory. It is for future research to say how many.

Nevertheless, the contribution of these findings to the confirmation status of theoretical propositions on prosecution as a power resource is limited. One cannot say that fulfilled prosecution is necessarily evidence of a failed bargaining strategy. Cases from this study illustrate that some victims prosecute in fulfillment of a threat over an unsatisfactory or unfulfilled agreement for their partners' behaviors. Research needs to demonstrate further that women who file charges under apparently instrumental motives follow through with prosecution when bargaining yields unsatisfactory outcomes or violated agreements. But even in the absence of theoretical confirmation, the findings of this study should caution against implementing policies for criminal justice that may inadvertently disempower victims.

Lerman (1981) first recommended a set of innovative prosecutorial guidelines based on previously published reports about the effects of alternative policies and on interviews with prosecutors in five jurisdictions around the United States. Her ideas have been widely embraced by policymakers and more recent advocates (Goolkasian 1986). Most of the thirteen recommendations propose changes in administrative procedures for the obvious advantage of victims. For example, the interests and wishes of victims are to be recognized in the decision to file charges, in sentencing recommendations, and in the use of advocates to keep victims informed of legal proceedings. Two of the recommendations, however, are controversial insofar as they reflect prosecutors' concerns with case attrition without demonstrably advancing victim interests in the criminal justice process:

> To reduce case attrition, prosecutors should adopt a policy that once charges have been filed in spouse abuse cases, a victim's request for dismissal will be denied unless there are exceptional circumstances.
>
> Prosecutors should relieve battered women of responsibility for prosecution of charges by signing complaints filed against batterers instead of asking victims to sign, and by sending subpoenas to victims prior to trial. (Lerman 1981:19)

330   PROSECUTION AS A VICTIM POWER RESOURCE

What these arguments and policies fail to consider is the
powerlessness of battered women (which is known to keep them
in violent relationships), their apparent quest for empowerment
through manipulation of criminal justice processes, and the impact
of criminal justice policies on the power of those victims. Coercing
victims to pursue prosecution to settlement presumes that the system can ultimately offer them some protection. The present research argues against completed prosecution as a necessary condition for victim security.

One cannot generalize from this study to conclude that battered women in other circumstances would use prosecution as a
power resource. The battered women I have discussed here acted
within a system amenable to, if not fully supportive of, their efforts to prosecute abusive men. Would they be similarly motivated
to manipulate the prosecution process under a system with greater
support or a fuller range of services? Only future research can say.
The model system response recommended by the Attorney General's Task Force on Family Violence (1984) might, if implemented, offer victims opportunities for satisfactory outcomes so
that they would not be inclined to bargain with charges as a protective strategy. For example, court-mandated batterer counseling
may be a welcome remedy, provided, of course, that charges are
not dismissed (e.g., Dutton 1988; Ganley 1981).

The increasing use of warrantless, on-scene police arrests
poses a similar question. If arrest has a deterrent impact,[21] or if
arrest and rigorous prosecution prevent continuing violence, does
prosecution lose its potential as a power resource? By the arguments presented above, prosecution is a power resource so long as
the victim has some control over it. But its impact may be diminished in an effective, victim-oriented system to the point where,
despite her wishes, a woman's security would be compromised by
granting her control over dropping charges.

Questions of how policy serves to empower victims should not
obscure another important point: Some victims who describe using
prosecution for leverage in their relationships seek more than a
cessation of violence under threat of formal sanctions. Some seek
to restructure life events in the apparent belief that individual preventive measures and informal controls will be at least as effective
as the criminal justice system in stopping habitual violence.

Ideally, a woman should not need to manipulate a system to
achieve ends that would normally be expected if the system func-
tioned in her interest. Victim requests to drop charges may indicate that the criminal justice system cannot accommodate the arrangements needed for security, including any civil remedies

---

[21] Sherman and Berk (1984) found arrest to be effective in preventing
continuing violence in Minneapolis. However, there was no such effect in the
Omaha replication (Dunford et al. 1989).

DAVID A. FORD   331

directed toward that end. Some may argue that it is inappropriate for the criminal justice system to concern itself with civil matters. Indeed, advocacy for specialized treatment of domestic violence in criminal courts (e.g., Friedman and Shulman 1990) may raise legal and ethical issues pertaining to the use of criminal proceedings to enforce traditional civil remedies. Nevertheless, following the recommendations of the Attorney General's Task Force (1984:34–36), judicial systems are expected to protect and support victims through criminal sanctions with a wide range of "civil" dispositional alternatives.

VIII. CONCLUSION

For many battered women prosecution is one of the few resources they have to gain control over their own circumstances. In making a significant threat to prosecute by initiating steps to invoke the process, a battered woman is able to exercise power that was previously missing in her relationship. She uses that power in the hope of gaining security by demonstrating that *she* is the one in charge and that only *she* can alter events which are destined to bring a man to court and possibly to jail. Thus, she gains leverage for managing the conflicts in her relationship. The typical victim in this study uses such leverage in hope of either controlling the violence so that she can remain in the relationship or freeing herself on terms more acceptable to her than had she not threatened to prosecute. In short, actual prosecution of the criminal act is probably less important to such victims than the power they gain through bargaining with significant threats of prosecution and punishment.

Recognizing this can help explain and perhaps alleviate problems that arise between victims and service providers. For example, the frustrations that agents of the criminal justice system experience in working with battered women commonly arise from feelings of being used by or merely wasting time in trying to assist victims who ultimately seem to reject efforts to help. Such feelings stem from a narrow definition of "assistance" denoted in terms of the helper's role rather than victim needs. Battered women are considered irrational when they seek help only to reject it later.

However, if one focuses on victims' needs, their attempts to prosecute can be seen as rational acts consistent with other behaviors meant to alter the balance of power in a conjugal relationship. From this perspective, one can understand seemingly paradoxical behavior of battered women—that a woman who is not divorced (and shows no sign of wanting a divorce) would ask to have her husband jailed; or that a woman who is already using alternative, apparently constructive, resources to free herself from violence would also want to prosecute, even if a successful outcome could be detrimental to her other efforts. It is the threat, coupled with

332   PROSECUTION AS A VICTIM POWER RESOURCE

her ability to control the process, that can be used to her advantage. If women are forced into prosecuting, or if the state takes steps to reduce victim discretion in the prosecution process, then victims of conjugal abuse may be disempowered as they are denied what leverage they command when the choice rests with them.

REFERENCES

ALLEN, Craig M., and Murray A. STRAUS (1980) "Resources, Power, and Husband-Wife Violence," in M. A. Straus and G. T. Hotaling (eds.), *The Social Causes of Husband-Wife Violence*. Minneapolis: University of Minnesota Press.
AMERICAN BAR ASSOCIATION (1969) *Code of Professional Responsibility*. Chicago: American Bar Association.
—— (1983) *Model Rules of Professional Conduct*. Chicago: American Bar Association.
ATTORNEY GENERAL'S TASK FORCE ON FAMILY VIOLENCE (1984) *Final Report*. Washington, DC: U.S. Department of Justice.
BANNON, James (1975) "Law Enforcement Problems with Intra-Family Violence." Presented at the annual meeting of the American Bar Association, Montreal, Canada, 12 August.
BARD, Morton (1980) "Functions of the Police and the Justice System in Family Violence," in M. R. Green (ed.), *Violence and the Family*. Boulder, CO: Westview Press.
BLAU, Peter M. (1964) *Exchange and Power in Social Life*. New York: John Wiley & Sons.
BLOOD, Robert O., Jr., and Donald M. WOLFE (1960) *Husbands and Wives*. New York: Free Press.
BOWKER, Lee H. (1983) *Beating Wife-Beating*. Lexington, MA: Lexington Books.
—— (1986) *Ending the Violence*. Holmes Beach, FL: Learning Publications.
CANNAVALE, Frank J., Jr., and William D. FALCON (1976) *Witness Cooperation*. Lexington, MA: Lexington Books.
DAHL, Robert A. (1957) "The Concept of Power," 2 *Behavioral Science* 201.
DOBASH, R. Emerson, and Russell DOBASH (1979) *Violence Against Wives: A Case Against the Patriarchy*. New York: Free Press.
DuBOW, Frederic L., and Theodore M. BECKER (1976) "Patterns of Victim Advocacy," in W. F. McDonald (ed.), *Criminal Justice and the Victim*. Beverly Hills, CA: Sage Publications.
DUNFORD, Frank W., David HUIZINGA, and Delbert S. ELLIOTT (1989) "The Omaha Domestic Violence Police Experiment, Final Report." Submitted to the National Institute of Justice.
DUTTON, Donald G. (1988) *The Domestic Assault of Women*. Boston: Allyn & Bacon.
ELLIOTT, Catherine, Linda GIDDINGS, and Avreayl JACOBSON (1985) "Against No-Drop Policies," *NCADV Voice*, Summer.
ELLIOTT, Delbert S. (1989) "Criminal Justice Procedures in Family Violence Crimes," in L. Ohlin and M. Tonry (eds.), *Family Violence*. Chicago: University of Chicago Press.
EMERSON, Richard M. (1962) "Power-Dependence Relations," 27 *American Sociological Review* 31.
—— (1972) "Exchange Theory, Part II: Exchange Relations and Network Structures," in J. Berger, M. Zelditch, Jr., and B. Anderson (eds.), 2 *Sociological Theories in Progress*. Boston: Houghton Mifflin.
FIELD, Martha H., and Henry F. FIELD (1973) "Marital Violence and the Criminal Process: Neither Justice nor Peace," 47 *Social Service Review* 221.
FINESMITH, Barbara K. (1983) "Police Response to Battered Women: A Critique and Proposals for Reform," 14 *Seton Hall Law Review* 74.
FORD, David A. (1974) "Reason Analysis: An Expository Review," in the Fi-

DAVID A. FORD   333

nal Report of the Multi-disciplinary Graduate Training Program of the Learning Research and Development Center, University of Pittsburgh. Submitted to the National Institute of Education.

—— (1983) "Wife Battery and Criminal Justice: A Study of Victim Decision-making," 32 *Family Relations* 463.

FORD, David A., and Mary Jean BURKE (1987) "Victim-initiated Criminal Complaints for Wife Battery: An Assessment of Motives." Presented at the Third National Conference for Family Violence Researchers, University of New Hampshire, Durham.

FRIEDMAN, Lucy N., and Minna SHULMAN (1990) "Domestic Violence: The Criminal Justice Response," in A. J. Lurigio, W. G. Skogan, and R. C. Davis (eds.), *Victims of Crime: Problems, Policies, and Programs.* Newbury Park, CA: Sage Publications.

FROMSON, Terry L. (1977) "The Case for Legal Remedies for Abused Women," 6 *N.Y.U. Review of Law and Social Change* 135.

GAMSON, William A. (1968) *Power and Discontent.* Homewood, IL: Dorsey Press.

GANLEY, Anne L. (1981) *Court Mandated Therapy for Men Who Batter: A Three-Day Workshop.* Washington: Center for Women Policy Studies.

GAYFORD, J. J. (1977) "The Plight of the Battered Wife," 10 *International Journal of Environmental Studies* 283.

GELLES, Richard J. (1976) "Abused Wives: Why Do They Stay?" 38 *Journal of Marriage and the Family* 659.

—— (1983) "An Exchange/Social Control Theory," in D. Finkelhor et al. (eds.), *The Dark Side of Families: Current Family Violence Research.* Beverly Hills, CA: Sage Publications.

GELLES, Richard J., and Murray A. STRAUS (1988) *Intimate Violence.* New York: Simon & Schuster.

GOODE, William J. (1971) "Force and Violence in the Family," 33 *Journal of Marriage and the Family* 624.

GOOLKASIAN, Gail A. (1986) *Confronting Domestic Violence: A Guide for Criminal Justice Agencies.* Washington, DC: National Institute of Justice.

GREGORY, Margaret (1976) "Battered Wives," in M. Borland (ed.), *Violence in the Family.* Atlantic Highlands, NJ: Humanities Press.

HALL, Donald J. (1975) "The Role of the Victim in the Prosecution and Disposition of a Criminal Case," 28 *Vanderbilt Law Review* 931.

HOMANS, George Caspar (1961) *Social Behavior: Its Elementary Forms.* London: Routledge & Kegan Paul.

KADUSHIN, Charles (1968) "Reason Analysis," in D. L. Sills (ed.), 13 *International Encyclopedia of the Social Sciences.* New York: Crowell, Collier & Macmillan.

LAZARSFELD, Paul F. (1972) "The Art of Asking Why," in P. F. Lazarsfeld (ed.), *Qualitative Analysis: Historical and Critical Essays.* Boston: Allyn & Bacon.

LERMAN, Lisa G. (1981) "Criminal Prosecution of Wife Beaters," 4 *Response to Violence in the Family*, No. 3, p. 1.

LEVINGER, George (1959) "The Development of Perceptions and Behavior in Newly Formed Social Power Relationships," in D. Cartwright (ed.), *Studies in Social Power.* Ann Arbor, MI: Institute for Social Research.

LITTLETON, Christine A. (1989) "Women's Experience and the Problem of Transition: Perspectives on Male Battering of Women," 1989 *University of Chicago Legal Forum* 23.

MAIDMENT, Susan (1978) "The Law's Response to Marital Violence: A Comparison Between England and the U.S.A.," in J. M. Eekelaar and S. N. Katz (eds.), *Family Violence: An International and Interdisciplinary Study.* Toronto: Butterworths.

MENKEL-MEADOW, Carrie (1984) "Toward Another View of Legal Negotiation: The Structure of Problem Solving," 31 *UCLA Law Review* 754.

PAGELOW, Mildred Daley (1984) *Family Violence.* New York: Praeger.

PARNAS, Raymond I. (1970) "Judicial Response to Intra-Family Violence," 54 *Minnesota Law Review* 585.

PATERSON, Eva J. (1979) "How the Legal System Responds to Battered Women," in D. M. Moore (ed.), *Battered Women.* Beverly Hills, CA: Sage Publications.

334   PROSECUTION AS A VICTIM POWER RESOURCE

PLECK, Elizabeth H. (1979) "Wife Beating in Nineteenth-Century America,"
4 *Victimology* 60.
PURDY, Frances (1985) "Pro-No-Drop Policy," *NCADV Voice*, Summer.
RODMAN, Hyman (1972) "Marital Power and the Theory of Resources in
Cultural Context," 3 *Journal of Comparative Family Studies* 50.
SCANZONI, John H. (1982) *Sexual Bargaining.* 2d ed. Chicago: University of
Chicago Press.
SCANZONI, John H., and Maximiliane SZINOVACZ (1980) *Family Decision-
making: A Developmental Sex Role Model.* Beverly Hills,'CA: Sage Publi-
cations.
SCHELLING, Thomas C. (1960) *The Strategy of Conflict.* Cambridge, MA:
Harvard University Press.
SCHNEIDER, Elizabeth M. (1986) "Describing and Changing: Women's Self-
Defense Work and the Problem of Expert Testimony on Battering," 9 *Wo-
men's Rights Law Reporter* 195.
SCHNEIDER, Elizabeth M., and Susan B. JORDAN (1978) "Representation of
Women Who Defend Themselves in Response to Physical or Sexual As-
sault," 4 *Women's Rights Law Reporter* 149.
SHERMAN, Lawrence W., and Richard A. BERK (1984) "The Specific Deter-
rent Effects of Arrest for Domestic Violence," 49 *American Sociological
Review* 261.
SPREY, Jetse (1971) "On the Management of Conflict in Families," 33 *Journal
of Marriage and the Family* 722.
STRAUS, Murray A., Richard J. GELLES, and Suzanne K. STEINMETZ
(1980) *Behind Closed Doors: Violence in the American Family.* Garden
City, NY: Anchor Press.
THIBAUT, John W., and Harold H. KELLEY (1959) *The Social Psychology of
Groups.* New York: John Wiley & Sons.
TRUNINGER, Elizabeth (1971) "Marital Violence: The Legal Solutions," 23
Hastings Law Journal 259.
U.S. BUREAU OF THE CENSUS (1983) *1980 Census of the Population: Ad-
vance Estimates of Social Economic, and Housing Characteristics,* Part 16:
Indiana. Supplementary Report PHC80-S2-16. Washington, DC: Govern-
ment Printing Office.
WALKER, Lenore E. (1979) *The Battered Woman.* New York: Harper & Row.
WOLFE, Donald M. (1959) "Power and Authority in the Family," in D. Cart-
wright (ed.), *Studies in Social Power.* Ann Arbor, MI: Institute for Social
Research.
WOLFRAM, Charles W. (1986) *Modern Legal Ethics.* St. Paul, MN: West Pub-
lishing.
WRONG, Dennis H. (1980) *Power: Its Forms, Bases and Uses.* New York:
Harper & Row.
YLLO, Kersti A., and Murray A. STRAUS (1990) "Patriarchy and Violence
against Wives: The Impact of Structural and Normative Factors," in M. A.
Straus and R. J. Gelles (eds.), *Physical Violence in American Families:
Risk Factors and Adaptations to Violence in 8,145 Families.* New Bruns-
wick, NJ: Transaction Publishers.
ZEISEL, Hans (1968) *Say It with Figures.* 5th ed. rev. New York: Harper &
Row.

STATUTE CITED

Indiana Code § 35-33-1-1(a) (West 1986).

Part IV
Non-Police Prosecutions

[16]

CORPORATE MANSLAUGHTER: AN EXAMINATION OF THE DETERMINANTS OF PROSECUTORIAL POLICY

GARY SLAPPER

Staffordshire University, UK

INTRODUCTION

THERE ARE over 7000 different criminal offences under current law (Seighart, 1980: 15). In some cases it is perhaps not surprising to learn that the offences are only nominally so. It is, for example, still an offence of treason (and therefore punishable by death) under the Treason Act 1351 for someone to 'violate the King's companion [wife] or the King's eldest daughter unmarried . . .' although the Crown Prosecution Service, is not, of course, overworked by this sort of offender. By contrast, however, between 500 and 600 people are killed at work or through the operation of commerce each year,[1] more than twice the number who fall victim to personal reckless manslaughter.[2]

A case at Glamorgan Assizes in 1965 demonstrated the validity of the indictment for corporate manslaughter. In the unreported case of *R* v *Northern Strip Mining Construction Co. Ltd* (*The Times*, 2, 4, 5 February 1965) a welder-burner, Glanville Evans, was drowned when a railway bridge which the company was demolishing collapsed and threw men working on it into the Wye. Workmen had been instructed to burn down sections of the bridge, starting in its middle, which prosecuting counsel asserted was as ludicrous as telling a man sitting on the branch of a tree to saw that branch. The defendant company was acquitted on the facts of the case but neither eminent counsel appearing in the

SOCIAL & LEGAL STUDIES (SAGE, London, Newbury Park and New Delhi), Vol. 2 (1993), 423–443 case (Mr Philip Wien QC for the Crown; Mr W. L. Mars-Jones for the Defendant company) nor the very experienced presiding judge, Mr Justice Streatfeild appeared to have any doubt about the validity of the indictment. Indeed, Mr Mars-Jones for the defendant directly conceded the propriety of such an indictment when he said:

> it is the prosecution's task to show that the defendant company, in the person of Mr. Camm, managing director, was guilty of such a degree of negligence that amounted to a reckless disregard for the life and limb of his workmen.

February 1965, therefore, has some claim to be the first judicial recognition of the validity of the indictment for corporate manslaughter. Leigh, writing in 1969, accepted that the indictment had been established: 'it now seems clear that corporations may be liable for manslaughter' (Leigh, 1969: 59). Yet since that time 18,151 people have been killed at work without a single company having been convicted for homicide.

Prosecutions have followed against culpable employers in some of these cases but they have been for regulatory offences under legislation like the Health and Safety at Work Act, 1974, rather than for offences of homicide. The sanctions here are almost invariably low fines which carry no stigma and are, in the context of the wealth of many companies, the equivalent financial penalty of a parking fine for an individual (Carson, 1981: 269–89; Ermann and Lundman, 1982: 148). The result of this is that neither social consciousness nor the annual Criminal Statistics register any serious homicide committed by companies although there is much *prima facie* evidence to suggest that many people are killed each year as the result of the criminal recklessness of corporations.

Apart from these deaths, companies have also been implicated in causing death in 'disaster' scenarios like that of Zeebrugge, where 193 people died in March 1987. A catalogue of some other recent incidents clarifies the scale of the problem and in all the following cases the relevant companies have been inculpated by the evidence (and with some an official enquiry report) in contributing in some significant way to the cause of death: the King's Cross fire, 31 deaths in November 1987; the Piper Alpha oil rig fire, 167 deaths in July 1988; the Clapham train crash, 35 deaths in December 1988; the Purley train crash, 5 deaths in March 1989; and the sinking of the *Marchioness*, 51 deaths in August 1989.

Why has there been only a single charge of corporate manslaughter (against P & O European Ferries [Dover] Ltd)[3] brought since the validity of such an indictment was clearly established in 1965? A number of explanations immediately present themselves but none are entirely convincing. The idea that companies have simply not come within the *actus reus* and *mens rea* of this crime during a 25-year period is implausible considering the very high number of deaths and the great diversity of situations from which they resulted. Alternatively, it could be submitted that the reason for the absence of prosecutions for manslaughter is that the HSE has prosecuted for other regulatory crimes. This explanation, however, seems only partly to demystify the issue because it leaves unanswered the question as to why it was thought appropriate for these incidents to result in regulatory offences and for only one of them to involve police action and prosecution for manslaughter. Lacey et al. (1990: 243) have characterized the causational problem:

> It is not always easy to say which comes first – the reluctance to use criminal law which leads to specific regulation, or the existence of specific regulation which diverts attention from the possibility of prosecution for offences such as manslaughter, murder or assault.

Some forceful argument has been advanced recently on the theme of the most effective response to corporate violation of safety law (Pearce and Tombs, 1990, 1991; Hawkins, 1990, 1991; Bergman, 1992). Pearce and Tombs have argued that 'a punitive policing strategy is necessary, desirable and practicable' (1990: 440), whereas Hawkins has argued that although 'stricter enforcement and harsher penalties for regulatory violations are in many instances necessary' (1990: 444), punitive enforcement should be used discriminately. As Wells has argued, however, in much of her pioneering work in this area (1988, 1989, 1990), the significance of the omission to prosecute companies for serious crime is that it perpetuates the social perception that companies do not commit serious violent crime.

CRIME IN THE SUITES

THE EVIDENCE OF CORPORATE MANSLAUGHTER

There is much evidence to suggest that a very high number of the 18,151 deaths occurring within a commercial setting during the last twenty-seven years were classifiable, at least *prima facie*, as instances of reckless manslaughter. It is also possible that some deaths could have entailed prosecutions for 'unlawful act' or 'constructive' manslaughter. This crime occurs where death results from the defendant's unlawful and dangerous act, dangerous in the sense that it is likely to cause direct personal injury, though not necessarily serious injury (Smith and Hogan, 1992: 366). For a conviction here, it is necessary that the unlawfulness of the act the defendant (D) does arises other than by negligent performance. So an act which has become criminally unlawful simply because it was negligently performed, for example, negligent driving, does not constitute an unlawful act for the purposes of 'constructive' manslaughter, the name given to the crime in the first category. Because almost all of the corporate conduct which results in death is intrinsically lawful this charge is largely inappropriate. However, as Wells has argued (Lacey et al., 1990: 243) unlawful act manslaughter could be used in some cases 'to combine the conduct-based regulatory offence [e.g. under the Health and Safety at Work Act, 1974] with the result-based common law'.

The crime of reckless manslaughter is committed where a defendant (D) does an act which creates an obvious and serious risk of causing physical injury to another by: (a) not giving thought to the possibility of there being such a risk; or

(b) having recognized that there was some risk involved, going on to take it (Smith and Hogan, 1992:372–5). For a corporate defendant to be convicted it must be proven beyond a reasonable doubt that the *mens rea* for the offence existed in at least one 'controlling mind' of the company.[4]

The *mens rea* for this offence is largely governed by a principle of *objective* culpability. So a defendant may be convicted for an offence requiring *Caldwell* recklessness (i.e. objective recklessness; Mr Caldwell was the eponymous defendant in a case of 1981)[5] even if he or she did not personally appreciate a risk that would have been recognized by an ordinarily prudent person. This departs from the principle normally applicable for serious offences – that the defendant must have been individually wicked or culpable, e.g. by consciously taking an unjustified risk. Against this, however, it may be recalled that *mens rea* as an element of crime is not quite as traditional as is sometimes assumed, because it has only applied in today's subjective form since 1898 when an accused was permitted to give evidence in his or her own trial. The justification for the objectification of guilt in some areas of criminal law is the imposition of basic standards of care for life, limb and property (Smith and Hogan, 1992: 60–9). This concept is not quite as severe as the imposition of guilt for criminal negligence. This is because for recklessness, D may not be liable if he or she *has* considered whether or not there is a risk and concluded wrongly and unreasonably that there was no risk, or so small a risk that it would have been justifiable to take it.[6] There has recently been a slight alteration in this 'recklessness' formula although the new 'gross negligence' test is still objective.[7]

There are many cases where surgeons and anaesthetists have been prosecuted for reckless manslaughter in circumstances where they were engaged in trying to save or improve a patient's life.[8] However, while the prosecuting authorities have been so conscientious in the prosecution of individuals in what might be termed 'ordinary' manslaughter cases and also many arising from some quite unusual circumstances, they have not been especially concerned to prosecute companies for the equivalent crime.

THE SCALE OF THE PROBLEM

It is appropriate to consider the scale of the problem. If there is a fault or anomaly in the state's prosecutorial policy it is not one which affects only a small, peripheral group of cases. The evidence suggests that there are *hundreds* of cases appearing suitable to attract charges of corporate manslaughter each year which are not treated as such by the police, CPS and DPP. Over any 12-month period, the number of deaths at work is, on average, about three times the number of cases resulting in convictions for manslaughter (excluding 'diminished responsibility' cases – those under s. 2 of the Homicide Act, 1957). Over the decade 1979–89, the number of annual convictions for manslaughter (excluding s. 2 cases) fluctuated between 99 (1989) and 192 (1987). The number of people killed at work over a 12-month period is notably higher, for example: 558 during 1987/88, 730 during 1988/89 and 681 during 1989/90 (Health and Safety Executive, 1987/88; 1988/89; 1989/90). Examining the same problem in the

USA, Reiman has given the issue a particularly dramatic perspective. He estimates that in 1972 the number of people in the USA dying from occupational hazards (diseases and accidents) was 114,000, whereas only 20,600 died as victims of personal homicide. Represented on a time clock for murder there would be one personal killing every 26 minutes but:

> If a similar clock for industrial deaths were constructed . . . and recalling that this clock ticks only for that half of the population that is the labour force – this clock would show an industrial death about every four and a half minutes! In other words in the time it takes for one murder on the time clock, six workers have died just trying to make a living! (Reiman, 1979, cited in Box, 1983: 26)

The grisly figures of death at work represent the number of people who have been crushed, electrocuted, asphyxiated, burnt, drowned, impaled and so forth. What is the evidence that any significant number of them could be regarded, *prima facie*, as instances of corporate manslaughter? Reports of the Health and Safety Executive (HSE) have consistently demonstrated that most of these occupational deaths were avoidable and could have been prevented by the management of the companies concerned. *Blackspot Construction* is an HSE report which analyses the circumstances of 739 deaths in the construction industry between 1981 and 1985. Referring to these deaths, J. D. Rimington, the Director-General of the HSE said: 'They represent a very saddening loss of life, particularly *because most of the deaths could have been prevented*' (Health and Safety Executive, 1988: 1, emphasis added). The report shows that the immediate reasons for most deaths were lack of supervision, inadequate training and lack of attention to detail:

> The figures in this report clearly show that the basic causes of the deaths of 739 people from 1981–1985 have not changed over the last ten years. There were, on average, two deaths every week on construction sites. 90% of these could have been prevented. *In 70% of cases, positive action by management could have saved lives.* (Health and Safety Executive, 1988: 4, emphasis added)

In another report, *Agricultural Blackspot*, a study of 296 deaths between 1981–4 the HSE concluded that in 62 percent of cases 'responsibility rested with management' (HSE, 1986: 12). Again, in *Deadly Maintenance*, a study into deaths at work in a range of industries, the HSE concluded that 'management were primarily responsible in 54% of cases' (1985: 8). According to the law stated in *R* v. *Northern Strip Mining Construction Co. Ltd* (1965) and the preliminary ruling of Mr Justice Turner in *R* v. *P & O European Ferries (Dover) Ltd* (1990)[9] it is possible for a company to be convicted of manslaughter if it can be proven beyond reasonable doubt that: (1) a victim who died had been subjected to an 'obvious and serious risk' of some physical injury prior to death and (2) that a senior manager or director of the company who was a 'controlling mind' of the company was responsible for an act or omission which lead to the death and (3) that when the relevant director(s) committed the *actus reus* he or she had the appropriate *mens rea*, i.e. that they behaved as they did having (a) given no thought to the possibility that a worker would be put in danger of physical injury or (b) having recognized there was such a risk, to have allowed it to continue. It is also necessary to prove (4) that the relevant conduct of the company directors was at least a 'substantial cause' of the death, i.e. that they 'contributed significantly' to the death.[10]

In English criminal law there are important doctrinal barriers to convictions for corporate manslaughter, in particular there is the courts' rejection of the principle of 'aggregated fault' by which the partial fault of several company directors might be combined to incriminate the corporation. This issue is addressed later (p. 434), but here it is relevant to note that such a principle does operate in some systems like the Dutch Criminal Code and could be introduced to English criminal law without significant repercussions in other parts of the law (Field and Jorg, 1991: 163).

The principle of 'identification', by which a conviction is only possible where someone sufficiently senior in the company as to be identified *as* the company acted with the necessary *mens rea* (blameworthy mind), is difficult to apply, especially in large companies (see later, p. 435). Again, however, there are legal systems, like that of the Netherlands, which work without such a rule (Field and Jorg, 1991: 167) and the rules could be adopted in other countries.

These principles, while quite established, are not lapidary. They are arguably no more resistant to change than the ancient rules of law that a 'husband cannot commit rape against his wife' and that '*Hansard* cannot be referred to in a law court to ascertain the meaning of legislation', both of which rules have recently been abolished by the House of Lords.[11] If the law were to be changed to facilitate prosecutions for corporate manslaughter a notable consequence would be the high number of incidents which could be processed as serious crimes; the necessary proofs in respect of legal 'recklessness' and causation would not be significantly more challenging than in normal cases of personal manslaughter.

From the evidence available from transcripts of proceedings in Coroners' Courts and from HSE reports it seems clear that there would be a reasonable probability of proving these matters to the required standard in many cases. It is important to recall that many of the deaths in particular industries result from distinctly repetitive causes. The crux of the Crown's failure to prove its case in the *Herald of Free Enterprise* prosecution was that similar ships in the past had worked without any mishap for seven years during which time there had been more than 60,000 sailings of this class of vessel. It was argued that there was nothing to alert the defendants to the danger presented by their system of ensuring the bow doors were closed before the vessel left port. To people in the position of the defendants, it was argued, the risk was not 'obvious'. This, however could not be said about the risk of physical injury or death in other corporate undertakings which have resulted in major disasters or workplace fatalities. As Bergman has commented:

> Last year alone there were 147 fatalities and 4010 serious injuries on construction sites – 3 deaths and 80 injuries a week – many resulting from identical causes for example dangerous scaffolds or collapsing trenches. It would be much easier to prove that the risk of injury to the person(s) who subsequently died was, in many cases, 'perfectly evident' [Mr Justice Turner's preferred phrase in the P & O case]

and 'immediately apparent' to any reasonable director of a construction company. (Bergman, 1990b: 1501)

The HSE's case reports and allocation of responsibility in studies like *Blackspot Construction* further demonstrate that the criteria for reckless manslaughter appear, *prima facie*, to be present in many of the cases which, if they are prosecuted, are only charged as regulatory offences under the Health and Safety at Work Act, 1974. For example, in the HSE's study of roofwork deaths we learn that: 'In the vast majority of fatal accidents on roofs, management and those in charge of the work did not exercise sufficient control to ensure that relatively simple precautions were taken' (HSE, 1988: 27). Looking at 'Demolition and Dismantling', the HSE note that 95 people died doing this type of work during the period under review and says 'of the 95 accidents, 67 were caused by management allowing unsafe systems of work to be used' (HSE, 1988: 31). It is worthy of note that in both of these HSE statements the word 'accidents' is used to describe deaths for which there are, on the HSE's own admission, identifiable persons who have played a substantial part in causing the deaths. In other contexts it would seem quite improper to refer to such cases as 'accidents'. Even if the word 'accidents' is used to convey the meaning of 'unintentional killing' this is unhelpful. On 30 April 1981, Edward Seymour knocked down Iris Burrows with his lorry and killed her. In one sense this was an 'accident' because it was not an intentional killing. However, Mr Seymour was convicted of the serious crime of reckless manslaughter for this incident and was sentenced to five years imprisonment.[12] This use of the term 'accident' (and its grammatical variants) proliferates through the HSE literature and is very misleading. The point is of more than linguistic significance. The use of such terminology reflects a tacit assumption about the nature of these deaths (even when HSE evidence in the same sentence contradicts the suitability of such a word) and helps promote such an image in the public perception.

Most prosecutions arising from commercially caused deaths are brought in the Magistrates' Court where the maximum fine is £5000. Imprisonment is an available sentence but a custodial sentence has only been given once since the Act's commencement on 1 January 1975, and that was a 12-month suspended sentence imposed on the director of a small construction company in 1987 for failing to have an asbestos licence and ignoring a prohibition notice. In 1988/89, of those cases of fatalities at work which resulted in prosecutions, only 3 percent resulted in prosecutions in the Crown Court, where the average fine was £2145. The remaining 97 percent were taken to the Magistrates' Court where fines averaged £505 (Labour Research, 1990: 13). Nevertheless, even when the prosecution goes to the Crown Court, where the fine is unlimited, the fines, which sometimes appear high compared to personal penalties, are still quite meagre when measured against the net income of the relevant companies. For example the HSE *Annual Report* 1987/88 boasts:

> The fine of £750,000 imposed in March on British Petroleum Ltd in the Scottish Courts for the failure of safety precautions at Grangemouth resulting in the loss of three lives represents a landmark in the application of safety law, and marks the

seriousness with which the judiciary are prepared to regard serious breaches by firms with the heaviest responsibilities and where there is the potential for disaster. (HSE, 1987/8: 30)

But this fine should be evaluated in its proper context. When we turn from the HSE's *Annual Report* for 1987 to that of BP for the same year, we see that the £750,000 fine should be judged against BP's profit (after taxation but before extraordinary items) which was £1,391,000,000 (British Petroleum, 1987: 53). The fine therefore amounts to 0.05 percent of the company's profit after taxation. This is the equivalent of a £7.50 fine for a person whose net earnings are £15,000, an unlikely disposal for someone whose culpable conduct has resulted in three deaths.

It can therefore be argued that many thousands of one of the most serious crimes on the criminal calendar are not being prosecuted as such. Some are left as 'accidents' while others are dealt with as administrative offences. The fact that there is no intention to kill in these cases should not lessen the aversion with which they are treated. In orthodox morality intention to do wrong is regarded with greater abhorrence than recklessness as to whether or not harm occurs, but as Reiman has argued (1979: 60), a reverse formula can be just as cogent: if a person intends doing *someone* harm there is no reason to assume that he or she poses a wider social threat or will manifest a contempt for the community at large, whereas if indifference or recklessness characterizes the attitude a person has towards the consequences of his or her actions then he or she can be seen as having a serious contempt for society at large.

CORPORATE LIABILITY

For the early part of its history, the corporation lay outside the criminal law. 'It had a soul to damn and no body to kick' (cited in Leigh, 1969: 4). If a crime were committed by the orders of a corporation, criminal proceedings for having thus instigated an offence could only be taken against the separate members in their personal capacities and not against the corporation itself (Stephen, 1883, II: 61). In 1701 Lord Holt CJ is reported as having said that 'A corporation is not indictable but the particular members are.'[13] This was a consequence of the technical rule that criminal courts expected the prisoner to 'stand at the bar' and did not permit 'appearance by attorney'.[14] This idea was supported by Roman law. It was argued that, as it did not have an actual existence, a corporation could not be guilty of a crime because it could not have a guilty will. Further, it was said that even if the legal fiction which gives to a corporation an imaginary existence could be stretched so as to give it an imaginary will, yet the only activities that could be consistently ascribed to the fictions thus created, must be such as are connected with the purposes which the corporation was created to accomplish. A corporation, the argument ran, could not, therefore, commit a crime because any crime would necessarily be *ultra vires* the corporation. Moreover a corporation is devoid not only of mind but also of body and therefore incapable of receiving the usual punishments: 'What? Must they hang up the common seal?' asked an advocate in 1682.[15]

The proliferation of companies in modern times and the extent of their influence in social life has necessitated accountability within the criminal law. The legal question arose as to how a company's guilt could be determined. The doctrine of 'identification', by which a corporation can be found criminally liable through the conduct and mental state of certain of its personnel was recognized by Mr Justice Streatfeild in *R* v. *Northern Strip Mining Construction Co.* (1965). It was later given express approval by Mr Justice Turner in his preliminary ruling, in 1990, on whether a corporation could be properly indicted for manslaughter (arising from the charges brought against P & O European Ferries for the sinking of the *Herald of Free Enterprise*). Mr Justice Turner said:

> . . . where a corporation, through the controlling mind of one of its agents, does an act which fulfils the prerequisites of the crime of manslaughter . . . it as well as its controlling mind or minds, is properly indictable for the crime of manslaughter.

Who are the people representing the 'controlling minds' of the corporation? Denning LJ, as he then was, has answered in an anthropomorphic metaphor by saying that it was not those who represented the 'hands which hold the tools' but those 'who represent the directing mind and will of the company and control what it does. The state of mind of these managers is the state of mind of the company and it is treated by the law as such.'[16] A variety of criteria and phrases for determining who in a company thinks and acts *as* that company have been suggested in the leading case of *Tesco Supermarkets Ltd* v. *Nattrass* (1972). Viscount Dilhorne, for example, thought that it would have to be someone:

> . . . who is in actual control of the operations of a company or of part of them and who is not responsible to another person in the company for the manner in which he discharges his duties in the sense of being under his orders. ([1972], AC 153)

In any event, it is a question of *law* whether a person, in doing particular things, is to be regarded as the company or merely as the company's servant or agent.

A CRIME WITHOUT CONVICTION

In seeking to explain prosecutorial policy in respect of commercially caused deaths it is helpful to examine the matter from three points of view. First we can examine the operation of the *mechanics* of the criminal justice system in this area, looking at what part the procedures of the police, the HSE inspectors, the Coroners' Courts and the Crown Prosecution Service (CPS) play in precluding the prosecution of companies for manslaughter. Second, the role of *public perception* in influencing the judgments of the actors in the criminal justice system is evaluated. What tacit assumptions, if any, inform the personnel whose decisions have resulted in the current prosecutorial policy? Finally, we can examine the broader context of the *political economy* to discover what factors may help to explain the development of the axioms which produce the public perception which in turn influences the way that decision-makers in the criminal justice system choose to act.

THE MECHANICS OF THE SYSTEM

In brief, the main procedural reason why there are no prosecutions for corporate manslaughter is that after a workplace death the police arrive and take usually only short statements from a company spokesperson, as responsibility for investigating these deaths lies with the HSE. These deaths are alone in being regarded by the legal system as properly investigated by a body other than the police. Even other areas of non-conventional crime, for example Road Traffic Act offences, are regarded as sufficiently serious to be dealt with by the police. Yet the HSE is only concerned with violations of the Health and Safety at Work Act 1974 etc., *not* with serious crimes like manslaughter. In these circumstances, therefore, consideration of manslaughter is systematically excluded. As Wells has explained (Lacey et al., 1990: 243), regulatory schemes are seen as quasi-criminal and

> tend to be couched in terms of failure to follow a prescribed process rather than being directed towards results. So that whereas conventional crime prohibits causing grievous bodily harm, safety regulations are concerned with failure to fence dangerous machinery.

There is, therefore, behind the annual figures for Health and Safety at Work Act convictions, a catalogue of injuries and deaths which do not feature as part of any official crime statistics. The HSE has severely restricted resources (Foley, 1990: 8) and is mainly concerned, according to its Director-General, John Rimington, to 'negotiate compliance' with employers; the 'primary effort' of the Executive is 'of assisting and advising the generality of well-conducted companies' (Bergman, 1990a: 1108). For these reasons the HSE is not as tenacious in pressing for a manslaughter charge as it might be. There is no legal reason why the police should not investigate a company and its directors after a workplace death. The HSE and CPS have responded to criticism by arguing that it is unnecessary for the police to be involved in the full investigation since the HSE will itself refer suitable cases to the CPS for its consideration. John Rimington has said 'Discussions between the HSE inspector and the police will take place if the most appropriate charge is one not available to an HSE inspector' (Bergman, 1991: 27). There is, however, little evidence of such a procedure having been put into effect. Since 1974, when the HSE was established, there have been 9050 deaths at work yet the HSE has evidently referred only three cases to the CPS. The one prosecution for manslaughter for a workplace death which was taken against a director in the last sixteen years was referred to the CPS by the police not the HSE.[17]

There are other procedural obstacles and caveats which lie on the path to a prosecution for corporate manslaughter. The almost invariable pattern of events at the inquest following a workplace death is for the coroner to direct the jury to a verdict of 'accidental death'. Only if a verdict of 'unlawful killing' is returned would the case be referred to the DPP for his consideration as a possible case of manslaughter. In order, though, for a jury to be able to decide that there had been an 'unlawful killing' by a company, it would be necessary to initially recognize the *mens rea* in at least one director or someone who was a 'controlling mind' of the company. Yet directors and senior managers are almost never called to give evidence at these inquests. The coroner has the sole right to summon witnesses to an inquest so he or she must bear the main responsibility for their absence from these proceedings, but it should be noted that, in deciding who should be called to give evidence, the coroner relies on the statements collected by the police and the HSE inspector who visited the scene of the death. However, neither the police nor the HSE inspectors are disposed to take statements from such senior people.

It is also important to appreciate the role of lawyers at the inquests. Because of the difficulties, outlined above, in relying on coroners to call directors as witnesses so that the jury may properly consider a verdict of 'unlawful killing', the availability at the inquests of lawyers who have the aim of guiding the court in that direction becomes imperative if there is to be a proper hearing of all matters. There are, however, very few attempts by lawyers to intervene at inquests with the aim of encouraging an 'unlawful killing' verdict. There is no legal aid awardable for proceedings in a coroner's court[18] so bereaved families either have to pay for these services themselves or rely on the support of the victim's trade union if he or she belonged to one. In fact, many families are not in a position to pay for representation at the inquest. Even many of those who could pay must fail to see any point in taking such action. They may wish to try and pursue civil litigation to receive compensation, but often the solicitor they consult about that matter will not wish to tackle the 'controlling minds' of the employing company at the inquest because to do so would be seen as hostile and adversarial (part of the criminal law process) and not conducive to a negotiated settlement (the civil law process).[19]

Trade unions can pay for legal representation at an inquest but, by the nature of the work in which many of the victims have been engaged, there is low union membership and relatively few such sponsorships are made. Between 31 March 1989 and 1 April 1990, 427 people were killed at work of whom 139 (over one-third) were working in the construction industry. Most of these victims were not trade union members but were working 'on the lump'. According to Foley:

> By 1990, over 1.5 million people were employed in the building industry; six per cent of the country's total work force. . . . In London and the South East . . . lump workers accounted for 80 per cent of the labour force on many sites. (Foley, 1990:6)

The discretion of the coroner himself cannot generally be relied upon to facilitate the discussion of an 'unlawful killing' verdict in cases involving corporations. For example, the coroner for East Kent, Mr Richard Sturt, had ruled at the Zeebrugge inquest on 19 September 1987 that, as a matter of law, a corporate body could not

be guilty of manslaughter. On an application for judicial review by members of
the victims' families, a Divisional Court held that a corporate body could be
liable for manslaughter. Even so, the coroner had guarded himself by stating that
if he was wrong about the capacity of a corporation, nevertheless there was
insufficient evidence to support a conclusion that those who represented the
directing mind and will of the company had been guilty of conduct amounting to
manslaughter. The jurors did not accept the advice of Mr Sturt and returned a
verdict of 'unlawful killing'. Because of the publicity surrounding the sinking of
the *Herald of Free Enterprise*, the very high number of deaths (192) and the
particularly damning Judicial Inquiry Report (Sheen, 1988) the jury would have
felt emboldened to defy the advice of the coroner in a way which may well not
apply in most cases.

Mr Sturt, by virtue of being HM Coroner for East Kent has also presided over
all the inquests (seven) into the deaths arising from work on the Channel Tunnel.
In each case he has withdrawn the option of an unlawful killing verdict from the
jury leaving them with no alternative but to return a verdict of 'accidental death'.
In the last three inquests he told the jury that they did not even need to leave the
courtroom to discuss the case among themselves.

Prosecutions for manslaughter are made especially difficult by the legal refusal
to adopt a principle of 'aggregated fault'. The point was argued in the judicial
review brought by members of the *Herald* Families Association. They sought to
establish that the instances of fault among several people acting for P & O could
be combined so as to show that the company itself had been reckless. John
Alcindor was deputy chief superintendent of P & O's marine department. He
had received a suggestion that indicator lights showing the state of the loading
doors be fitted to the bridge. He did nothing to implement that suggestion.
Jeffrey Develin, chief superintendent of the marine department and a director of
the company bore a major responsibility for the safety of the fleet and the
systems in operation on board vessels. It was Mr Develin's department which
failed to install the indictor lights and instead passed the matter on to the technical
department. Wallace Ayres, a director and head of the technical department
failed to respond to two requests for indicator lights to be fitted to the bridges of
vessels.

On this matter, Bingham LJ ruled that:

> Whether the defendant is a corporation or a personal defendant, the ingredients of
> manslaughter must be established by proving the necessary *mens rea* and *actus reus*
> against it or him by evidence properly to be relied on against it or him. A case
> against a personal defendant cannot be fortified by evidence against another
> defendant. The case against a corporation can only be made by evidence properly
> addressed to showing guilt on the part of the corporation as such.[20]

This principle here has been endorsed elsewhere. It is adopted, for example, in
Clause 30(2) of the Law Commission's Draft Criminal Code Bill (Law
Commission, 1989: 76) and David Willcox, a solicitor with Partner, Beaumont &
Son, who act for a range of airline companies has argued[21] that this position is
necessary to prevent a company being convicted on too low a threshold of

evidence. Wells has eloquently shown (1988, 1989) how notions of personal responsibility in criminal law are unsuitable when applied to corporations. She has noted (1989: 932) that

> The concept of atomistic actors deviating from the 'norm' of conformity is commonly invoked in the language of the criminal justice system and in the media and other areas of social control such as schools. This image is particularly inappropriate for a large corporation. How would this help in a company which devolved its centres of power to semi-autonomous regional managers? How would this help us to a legal response to a car manufacturer which, by a series of cost cutting policies, allowed its robots to be programmed to observe a lower degree of safety on the installation of brakes.

The Bingham LJ ruling appears to make it virtually impossible for a company to be convicted for manslaughter because the way that responsibilities are distributed through a corporate body makes it extremely unlikely that the necessary fault will ever reside entirely in a single identifiable individual. The analogy with a personal defendant used by Bingham LJ seems inappropriate. Companies gain many benefits from the principle of aggregation. Indeed, the very notion of a separate legal personality being accorded to a group of people *qua* a company is founded upon the principle of aggregation. With benefit comes responsibility. *Qui sensit commodum debet sentire et onus* (he who has obtained an advantage ought to bear the disadvantage as well). It is perverse to dispense with the principle of aggregation just at the point when its application would implicate the company in a serious crime. This apparent perversity, however, becomes more intelligible in the context of a political economy which accords priority to the commercial goal of profit and which is thus loathe to render seriously criminal conduct which can be seen as simply as commercial impetuosity.

We have looked at how, through the *mechanics* of the criminal justice system there are intrinsic obstacles to a conviction for corporate manslaughter. The cursory investigations by the police and HSE inspectors; company directors being left uninvestigated; the unwillingness of coroners to facilitate proper consideration of unlawful killing verdicts; the CPS's misguided reliance on the HSE to refer suitable cases of suspected manslaughter and the HSE's image of itself as an advisory adjunct to industry. The operation of much of this system is perpetuated because of the social perceptions of the people who operate it. It is appropriate to look at this in some detail.

SOCIAL PERCEPTIONS

Owing to various factors of social and historical development it is very common for deaths at work to be perceived as 'accidents' or, in any event, if they are wrongs, they are seen as wrongs which are suitably dealt with as infringements of regulatory legislation.

So popular ideas and implicit assumptions play a part in determining how the criminal justice system operates. In discussing the law which prevents sleeping in public transport facilities in many states of the USA, Chambliss and Seidman point out (1971:82) that the conduct at which the law is aimed is clearly defined but in practice certain types of people sleeping in the stations will be treated differently from others. A homeless, unwashed vagrant will be treated differently from a neat executive who has nodded off while waiting for a commuter train, even though both people are asleep at a station. The reason why the HSE inspectors do not investigate directors after someone has been killed at work is partly because of limited time and resources but also because of commonly held notions about the nature of serious crime. As Quinney has observed: 'Crime is not inherent in behaviour but it is a judgement made by someone about the actions and characteristics of others' (1970:16). Coroners may be seen to share the same sort of assumptions as police officers and HSE inspectors. Such an outlook is the product of the axioms arising from the society we inhabit.

Swigert and Farrell have stated:

> Culturally implicit parameters of law are also evident in the case of homicide. A fatal argument between friends following a Saturday evening of drinking, for example, would leave little doubt as to the applicability of the criminal statutes. Fatal bodily harm, however, may just as easily be the product of dangerous factory conditions, polluted air or unsafe motor vehicles as it is of bullet wounds, knifings or beatings. The latter clearly fall within the meaning of homicide; the former do not. The distinction is an implicit one. (1980–1:163)

In the same vein, Wells has argued that:

> Sandwiched between the Zeebrugge tragedy and the King's Cross disaster came the Hungerford shootings. Nearly 200 people drowned off Zeebrugge in March, 31 died at the Kings Cross fire in November and 16 were fatally shot by a gunman who ran amok in Hungerford in August, 1987. The deaths there were immediately seen as *criminal*. The Prime Minister in a widely reported remark, said that it was so much more shocking than other tragedies *because* it was not an accident but a crime. (1988:791)

So the social perceptions of the actors in the criminal justice system (police officers, HSE inspectors, coroners, lawyers and CPS officers) can help to explain why the system works in the way that it does.

The mechanics of the criminal justice system have worked to preclude prosecutions for corporate manslaughter. Nonetheless, there are ways in which the system could have been made to work so as to allow for such indictments to have been made. It is largely due to the interpretations of circumstances made by the *dramatis personae* that the system is not made to operate in a way which would indict companies for manslaughter. It thus becomes necessary to ask why and how these people come to acquire these precepts. To do so it is helpful to consider the historical and economic factors which have engendered certain ideas.

HISTORICAL AND ECONOMIC INFLUENCES

The regularity of such a high number of occupational deaths each year (often more than the annual number of reported personal homicides; see note 2) suggests that the propensity for companies to conduct their affairs in ways that result in death is not attributable to erratic influences like the occasional enterprise of a few extraordinarily careless or unscrupulous firms. In looking at the operation of the 1833 Factory Act, which set out to 'regulate the Labour of Children and Young Persons in the Mills and Factories of the United Kingdom', Carson sought to explain why factory inspection, despite its operation under the criminal law, came 'to accept violation of the law as a conventional feature of industrial production, only meriting prosecution under the most unusual circumstances' (1979: 51). Thus Alexander Redgrave, a Factory Inspector, could openly state in 1876 that:

> In the inspection of factories it has been my view always that we are not acting as policemen . . . that in enforcing this Factory Act, we do not enforce it as policemen would check an offence which he is told to detect.

Carson concluded that the operation of the law developed in this way in order not to constrain the economic development taking place in the nineteenth century.

In his later study of the high death rate in the North Sea oil fields, Carson notes that by the middle of the 1970s the rate of 'accidental' death in the oil industry was eleven times higher than that for construction, nine times higher than that for mining and six times higher than that for quarrying. His evidence indicates that the accidents were not simply what is only to be expected when an industry undertakes hazardous operations at the very frontiers of technology, but rather the result of factors like poor communication, failure of equipment, poor working practices and lack of safety precautions. Throughout the 1970s the British government was under considerable pressure to extract North Sea oil as rapidly as possible for economic reasons, including a pressing balance of payments problem. The government was heavily dependent on the expertise and resources of the major transnational oil companies who would only act quickly if they were left relatively unhampered by any requirement for costly and time-consuming safety precautions. The government eventually acceded to their demands about the legislative framework in which the companies were to operate. Carson concludes that most of the 106 deaths which had occurred up to December 1980 (which deaths he analyses in great detail) could have been avoided if the 'political economy of speed' had not been allowed to prevail over the 'political economy of employee's lives'. Carson cites the words of an American oil man calling the square dance moves from a *ceilidh* play by John McGrath (Carson, 1981: 46),

> Pipe that oil in from the sea
> Pipe those profits – home to me
> I'll bring work that's hard and good –
> A little oil costs a lot of blood.

Concluding this study, Carson notes that he was struck by the parallels between the history of North Sea oil safety and that of the earliest efforts to impose statutory controls upon the operations of the 'dark satanic mills' of the nineteenth century. In both periods: 'there were immutable laws of capital which rendered it "imperative" that regulation should be minimized. Then, as now, it was constantly threatened that capital would flee if subjected to any more constraints' (1981:302). The paramount economic priority of companies in capitalism is to be profitable concerns. It is their essential purpose. Scruples, moral considerations and legal restraint, in different measure for different people, restrict injurious conduct in the quest for profit. During a recent drought when water supplies were simply exhausted in some parts of England, at least two groups of young men were discovered trying to *sell* buckets of water to old, housebound people. Their conduct may be regarded as morally repugnant but it was not illegal and it was, in a strict sense, within the province of what has been described as 'enterprise culture'.

The economic environment exerts a strong pressure on companies to take risks. This was directly conceded by Dr John Cullen, the Chairman of the Health and Safety Executive, when he stated:

> The enterprise culture, the opening up of markets, and the need to survive competition place businesses under unprecedented pressure . . . the scale and pace of technological change means that increasing numbers of people – the public as well as employees – are potentially at risk. (*Guardian*, 4 March, 1989)

Indeed, as many business people often claim, from the launching of a company onwards the process of running a company is constantly beset with a variety of risks. Companies are relentlessly having to remain 'competitive' by keeping their expenditure as low as possible. Clearly, most companies will not knowingly jeopardize the lives of their customers or the general public but there are enough documented instances of such risks apparently being taken to demonstrate the compelling pressure of commercial competition.

On 13 September 1978, Ford Motor Company was indicted in Indiana, USA, for reckless homicide. A Grand Jury decided after three days of deliberation that Ford was to be tried as a responsible party for the deaths of three teenagers, who were burnt to death when their Ford Pinto burst into flames following a low-speed, rear-end collision. Many people had died in similar incidents all over the USA. Dowie has stated that 'by conservative estimates Pinto crashes have caused more than 500 deaths' (1987:14). Wells has argued (Lacey et al., 1990:245) that the significance of the case is not its result (the company was acquitted) but that a company was considered to be triable for homicide and that 'a grand jury were prepared to apply the vocabulary of criminal liability to corporate harm'. She has cautioned, however, that an important part of this process of extending the 'cultural parameters' of homicide in the Ford Pinto case was the extent to which the harm resulting from the defective fuel tank design could be personalized and characterized in the same way as an incident of conventional crime (Lacey et al., 1990:246).

The actual trial resulted in the company being acquitted but evidence was led in the case which demonstrated that Ford was aware of the danger posed by the Pinto but had used a cost–benefit calculation to decide that the cars should be left, unaltered, with their owners. It would have cost less than $11 per car to remedy the defect but calculations had shown that subsequent insurance claims resulting from the number of people predicted to be killed and maimed would be $47.5 million whereas it would cost $137 million to recall and alter all the Pintos it had sold. This sort of cost–benefit analysis, which relegates human life below the considerations of profit, is not peculiar to Ford Motor Company or to recent developments. It is a feature endemic to the system of commerce.

Max Weber commented on this issue in relation to its implications for capitalism in American cities. In 1904 he observed that:

> After their work . . . [Chicago] workers often have to travel for hours in order to reach their homes. The tramway company has been bankrupt for years. As usual, a receiver who has no interest in speeding up the liquidation, manages its affairs; therefore, new tramcars are not purchased. The old cars constantly break down, and about four hundred people a year are thus killed or crippled. According to the law, each death costs the company about $5,000 which is paid to the widow or heirs, and each cripple costs $10,000, paid to the casualty himself. These compensations are due so long as the company does not introduce certain precautionary measures. But they have calculated that the four hundred casualties a year cost less than would the necessary precautions. The company therefore does not introduce them. (Swigert and Farrell, 1980–81: 166)

A society in which the social production of goods and services is dominated by commercial considerations will necessarily generate a certain human sacrifice. These are portrayed as people who die for the greater good of the majority. What originates as a necessary consequence of the economic structure is translated into a social axiom. This accords with the view expressed by Marx in 1859 when he wrote:

> In the social production of their existence, men inevitably enter into definite relations that are independent of their will, namely relations of production appropriate to a given stage in the development of their material forces of production. The totality of these relations of production constitutes the economic structure of society, the real foundation on which arises a legal and political superstructure and to which correspond definite forms of social consciousness. The mode of production of material life conditions the general process of social, political and intellectual life. It is not the consciousness of men that determines their existence, but their social existence determines their consciousness. (1970: 20–1)

To properly examine why there has not been a single successful prosecution for corporate manslaughter we need to examine (a) the *modus operandi* and perceptions of the police, HSE inspectors, lawyers, coroners and CPS officers and (b) the historical and economic environment which develops and influences those perceptions. The illumination afforded by such a combination of interpretative, phenomenological and structural analyses has been demonstrated by Nelken in his detailed study of the restricted effects of the 1965 Rent

Act. Examining why the legislation, which had been hailed as a great reform, was in fact of very little use, Nelken argued

> ... [the] necessity to draw on both structural and interpretative approaches in order to provide a convincing account of the emergence and implementation of law. Proponents of structural approaches now readily admit that any examination of the structural constellation of forces cannot be used to read out the emergence or content of a given piece of legislation ... whilst those who adopt an interpretative perspective are obliged to concede that the negotiation of meaning is biased in favour of structurally powerful groups. (1983:211)

If this approach, which allows us to see a 'coherence without conspiracy' (1983:212) is taken to the issue of corporate manslaughter we can see how a combination of 'negotiated meaning' and the 'structural constellation of forces' produce a systematic reluctance to convict companies of manslaughter.

CONCLUSIONS

> In a grotesque footnote to a story on the report, one newspaper noted that 30 corpses have still not been recovered from the wreckage of Piper Alpha under the North Sea because the oil company thinks it would be too expensive to retrieve them. (Foley, 1990:25)

The factors which emerge from this study as most clearly instrumental in shaping the operation of policy are the economic pressures and imperatives of the commercial world. If law is regarded as a phenomenon separate from its social object and detachable from its historical development, then an optimistic view may be taken as to how instrumental the criminal law can be in dealing with corporate manslaughter. Conversely, if law is seen as a *product* of social relations, not something *extrinsic* to them, then it is less likely that any significant change to the extent of corporate manslaughter can be wrought by the criminal law while the social relations and pressures from which the crime arises remain in place. Warrington has observed that: 'Law merely attempts to make what is legitimate (i.e. socially accepted relationships) operate smoothly. Its legitimacy cannot depend upon itself (the law) but on what makes law what it is (society)' (1977:29).

The state's prosecutorial policy in respect of corporate manslaughter can be thus regarded as originating in the economic structure and operating precepts of the commercial system. However, the matter is not presented as such but assumes the image of either an independently arrived at legal stance or an accidental cluster of mechanisms and rules. As Engels wrote in 1886:

> But once the state has become an independent power *vis-a-vis* society, it produces forthwith a further ideology. It is indeed among professional politicians, theorists of public law and jurists of private law that the connection with economic fact gets lost for fair. Since in each particular case the economic facts must assume the form of juristic motives in order to receive legal sanctioning and since in so doing, consideration of course has to be given to the whole legal system already in

operation, the juristic form is, in consequence, made everything, and the economic fact nothing. (1973: 5)

In seeking to explain the development of legal phenomena like prosecutorial policy in *prima facie* cases of corporate manslaughter, materialist analysis, in contradistinction to idealistic or autopoietic theory, is relatively compelling. A view of society as 'a recursively *closed system* which can neither derive its operations from its environment nor pass them on to that environment' (Luhmann, 1988: 18) is one which leaves odd but clearly patterned legal phenomena (like the corporate manslaughter problem) in the realm of the inexplicable. A serious problem for those postulating material analyses, however, is the need to be able to clearly expose the precise mechanisms by which 'the economic facts . . . assume the form of juristic motives'. There is a great deal of research still to be done into the role of the 'economic fact' in the emergence and operation of law.

NOTES

I am grateful to Robert Reiner, David Nelken and Elaine Genders for helpful comments on an earlier draft of this paper.

1.   Health and Safety Executive *Annual Reports* 1977–92. This is a problematic category as the figures exclude the thousands of people who die at home or in hospitals from work-related conditions (asbestosis, mesothelioma, etc.) and from other long-term factors with an arguably commercial impetus like smoking-related diseases. Deaths of people in the course of their work, like police officers, are within the scope of this enquiry although I recognize the existence of factors in such cases which might not be present in most work-related deaths.

2.   Over the decade 1979–89, for example, the number of annual convictions for manslaughter, excluding cases of 'diminished reponsibility' fluctuated between 99 (1989) and 192 (1987). Even these figures are higher than the real figures for 'reckless manslaughter' because they include s.3 killings as the result of provocation, and constructive manslaughter killings, i.e. where the defendant has killed unintentionally in the course of committing an unlawful act which a reasonable person would foresee as liable to cause some injury (a category which can be regarded as necessarily involving a form of recklessness). The Home Office does not publish statistics which differentiate 'reckless manslaughter' homicides but see Gibson (1975).

3.   *DPP* v. *P & O European Ferries (Dover) Ltd* (1991) 93 Cr. App. R. 72.

4.   Turner J., *DPP* v. *P & O European Ferries (Dover) Ltd*, supra, p. 84.

5.   *R* v. *Caldwell* [1981] 1 All ER 961.

6.   *Chief Constable of Avon and Somerset Constabulary* v. *Shimmen* (1986) 84 Cr. App. R. 7.

7.   *R* v. *Prentice* [1993] NLJ 850; see Slapper (1993: 897).

8.   See e.g. *Guardian*, 13 March 1991; *Guardian*, 2 November 1991; *The Times*, 11 September 1990.

9.   (1991) 93 Cr. App. R. 72 at pp. 84, 88–89.

10. 'In cases of homicide it is rarely necessary to give the jury any direction on causation as such. . . . Even when it is necessary to direct the jury's minds to the question it is usually enough to direct them that in law the accused's act need not be

442   GARY SLAPPER

the sole cause or even the main cause of the victim's death, it being enough that his act contributed significantly to that result'. *Per* Goff LJ in *R* v. *Pagett* (1983) 76 Cr. App. R. 279.

11.   *R* v. *R* [1991] 4 All ER, 481; *Pepper (HMI Taxes)* v. *Hart* [1993] 1 All ER, 42.
12.   *R* v. *Seymour* [1983] 2 All ER 1058.
13.   Holt LCJ, 12 Mod, p. 559.
14.   This problem was eventually overcome by S. 33 of the Criminal Justice Act, 1925, which allowed for a company to appear by representative.
15.   *R* v. *City of London* (1882) St. Tr. 1039 at 1138.
16.   Denning LJ, *H.L. Bolton (Engineering) Co. Ltd* v. *T.J. Graham & Sons Ltd* [1957] 1QB 159 at 172.
17.   *R* v. *Holt*, HSE *Information Bulletin*, January 1990.
18.   Legal Aid Act, 1988, Part 1, Schedule 2 (by omission).
19.   I am obliged to the following solicitors who gave me the benefit of their experience in these matters: Patrick Whight of Winckworth & Pemberton, Kenneth Shaw of Kenneth Shaw & Co., and Peter Jordan in private practice but formerly with the Legal Aid Board.
20.   *R* v. *HM Coroner for East Kent ex parte* Spooner (1989) 88 Cr. App. R. 10 at 17.
21.   This argument was given in a Law Society Lecture on 'Corporate Manslaughter', London, 20 March 1991.

REFERENCES

Bergman, D. (1990a) 'Manslaughter in the Tunnel', *New Law Journal*, 140(6467): 1108.
Bergman, D. (1990b) 'Recklessness in the Boardroom', *New Law Journal*, 140(6477): 1501.
Bergman, D. (1991) *Deaths at Work: Accidents or Corporate Crime?* London: WEA.
Bergman, D. (1992) 'Corporate Sanctions and Corporate Probation', *New Law Journal*, 25 September: 1312.
Box, S. (1983) *Power, Crime and Mystification*. London: Routledge.
British Petroleum (1987) *Annual Report*. London: BP.
Carson, W. (1979) 'The Conventionalization of Early Factory Crime', *International Journal for the Sociology of Law* 1: 37.
Carson, W. (1981) *The Other Price of Britain's Oil*. Edinburgh: Martin Robinson.
Chambliss, W. and B. Seidman (1971) *Law, Order and Power*. New York:
Dowie, M. (1987) 'Pinto Madness', in S. Hills (ed.), *Corporate Violence: Injury and Death for Profit*. Totowa, NJ: Rowan & Littlefield.
Engels, F. (1973) *Ludwig Feuerbach and the End of Classical German Philosophy*. Progress Press. (Orig. 1886.)
Ermann, M. R. and R. Lundman (eds) (1982) *Corporate and Government Deviance*. Oxford: Oxford University Press.
Field, S. and N. Jorg (1991) 'Corporate Liability and Manslaughter: Should We Be Going Dutch?' *Criminal Law Review* 156–71.
Foley, C. (1990) *Slaughter on Britain's Building Sites*. London: Connolly Publications.
Gibson, E. (1975) *Homicide in England and Wales, 1967*, Home Office Research Study No. 31. London: HMSO.
Hawkins, K. (1990) 'Compliance Strategy, Prosecution Policy and Aunt Sally', *British Journal of Criminology* 30(4): 444.
Hawkins, K. (1991) 'Enforcing Regulation', *British Journal of Criminology* 31(4): 427.
Health and Safety Executive (1985) *Deadly Maintenance*. London: HMSO.
Health and Safety Executive (1986) *Agricultural Blackspot*. London: HMSO.
Health and Safety Executive (1987/8) *Annual Report*. London: HMSO.

Health and Safety Executive (1988) *Blackspot Construction*. London: HMSO.
Health and Safety Executive (1988/89) *Annual Report*. London: HMSO.
Health and Safety Executive (1989/90) *Annual Report*. London: HMSO.
Labour Research (1990) 'Workplace Death: Who to Blame?' 79(9): 13.
Law Commission (1989) *Criminal Law, A Criminal Code for England and Wales*, Law Comm. No. 177. London: HMSO.
Lacey, N., C. Wells and D. Meure (1990) *Reconstructing Criminal Law*. London: Weidenfeld.
Leigh, L. H. (1969) *The Criminal Liability of Corporations in English Law*. London: Weidenfeld & Nicolson.
Luhmann, N. (1988) 'The Unity of the Legal System', pp. 12–35 in G. Teubner (ed.), *Autopoietic Law: A New Approach to Law and Society*. Berlin: de Gruyter. (Orig. 1859.)
Marx, K. (1970) *Contribution to a Critique of Political Economy*. New York: International Publishers.
Nelken, D. (1983) *The Limits of the Legal Process*. London: Academic Press.
Pearce, F. and S. Tombs (1990) 'Ideology, Hegemony and Empiricism', *British Journal of Criminology* 30(4): 423.
Pearce, F. and S. Tombs (1991) 'Policing Corporate Skid Rows', *British Journal of Criminology* 31(4): 415.
Quinney, R. (1970) *The Social Reality of Crime*. Boston: Little Brown.
Reiman, J. (1979) *The Rich Get Rich and the Poor Get Prison*. New York: Wiley.
Seighart, P. (1980) *Breaking the Rules*. London: Justice.
Sheen, J. (1988) *MV Herald of Free Enterprise, Report 8074, D.O.T.* London: HMSO.
Slapper, G. (1993) 'Prosecuting Professionals for Manslaughter', *New Law Journal* 143(6605): 897.
Smith, J. C. and B. Hogan (1992) *Criminal Law*, Butterworths.
Stephen, J. F. (1883) *A History of the Criminal Law of England*, Vol. II.
Swigert, V. and R. Farrell (1980–81) 'Corporate Homicide: Definitional Processes in the Creation of Deviance', *Law and Society Review* 15(1): 163.
Warrington, R. (1977) 'Law – Its Image or Its Reality', *City of London Law Review* 29–52.
Wells, C. (1988) 'The Decline and Rise of English Murder: Corporate Crime and Individual Responsibility', *Criminal Law Review* 788.
Wells, C. (1989) 'Manslaughter and Corporate Crime', *New Law Journal*, 7 July: 931.

[17]

Cooperative Models and Corporate Crime:
Panacea or Cop-Out?

Laureen Snider

This article critiques the new "cooperative" models of regulatory reform, arguing that they will weaken the process of regulation. After documenting some of the problems of criminalization models, the article describes the major cooperative schemes that have been offered. The roots of their current popularity are examined and traced to the fiscal and ideological crises that beset capitalist economies in the 1980s. The consequences of adopting a cooperative model are set out. Last, the unlikely prospects for achieving more effective enforcement by cooperative regulation are discussed.

"The harsh fact of life is that nobody does anything until a lot of lives are lost."[1]

— Dr. Dan Kirkwood

"I have been in all cases cordially received by employers, who . . . show every disposition to conform to the requirements of the Factories' Act, so long as no great outlay of money is involved in making the changes necessary to accomplish that object."[2]

— Report by R. Barber

The orientation that regulatory agencies should adopt and the weapons they should use have become central issues in the policy literature on corporate crime. The debate has come to revolve around a basic disagreement over control strategies. Whereas many continue to argue for more intense regulation and more severe sanctions, others call for "realistic" measures that take into account the powers and the limitations of regulatory regimes in the industrialized democracies as well as the problems of the corporate sector in complying with regulatory law. Such "cooperative models" argue against the use of criminal law, which advocates see as an inappropriate and ineffective tool against corporate crime, and in favor of a combination of persuasion, education, and civil/administrative remedies to secure compliance (Bardach

LAUREEN SNIDER: Associate Professor of Sociology and Associate Dean of the Faculty of Arts and Science, Queen's University in Kingston, Ontario.

CRIME & DELINQUENCY, Vol. 36 No. 3, July 1990 373-390

and Kagan 1982; Jamieson 1985; Kagan 1978; Peltzman 1976; Scholz 1984a, 1984b).

This article traces, first, the history and development of cooperative models in the academic literature, their pitfalls, and their appeal. The article argues that cooperative models have become popular politically because they recognize and legitimate the existing relations of power, the status quo under which regulatory forces are outmatched by the powerful corporate sector. The result of enshrining this disparity in official policy is to stabilize it, weakening thereby the forces that seek to strengthen regulation. By ignoring the corporate political, ideological, and economic dominance that creates regulatory ineffectiveness in the first place, cooperative models set themselves up to be the victims of this dominance. Finally, the article examines the implications of this critique for efforts to increase regulatory effectiveness.

MODELS OF REGULATION

Corporate crimes are white-collar crimes committed with the encouragement and support of a formal organization, and intended at least in part to advance the goals of that organization (Coleman 1985, p. 8; Edelhertz 1970, p. 3; Meier and Short 1982, p. 24). In the majority of Western democracies, corporate crime has been regulated by some combination of civil, administrative, and criminal procedures, enforced by special regulatory agencies acting under federal, state/provincial, or municipal law. Regulatory enforcement is the consistent application of formal rules and sanctions to secure compliance with the enabling legislation and promulgated regulations. Corporate crime includes the vast majority of regulatory offenses subsumed under regulatory law.

Criminalization

From Sutherland in 1938 to Clinard and Yeager in the late 1970s, investigators have documented the minuscule role criminal sanctions play in the control of corporate criminality and called for an increase in their frequency and severity. To summarize this literature: Full enforcement is neither the goal of regulatory agencies nor the reality; penalties are handed out in inverse proportion to offending firms' size and power; and sanctions are so small that they hardly qualify as licensing fees, let alone as deterrents. Regulators prefer persuasion and education to laying charges; often their official mandate directs them to balance the benefits of enforcement against the drawbacks, assessing whether or not enforcement is in "the public interest." (For example, will it have negative consequences such as loss of jobs in a community, or loss of votes for a particular incumbent or party?) Dozens of studies, in Canada, Britain, Australia, United States, and elsewhere, document this reluctance to invoke formal procedures against corporate offenders (e.g., Carson 1970; Clinard and Yeager 1980; Downing and Hanf 1983; Goff and Reasons 1978; Grabosky and Braithwaite 1986; Gunningham 1974, 1984; Hawkins 1984; Morgenstern 1982; Shover, Clelland, and Lynxwiler 1986.).

The tendency to focus on offenders who do the least amount of damage also has been documented. The largest and most powerful organizations are the least sanctioned; the smallest and most peripheral are treated most severely, in both quantitative (number of visits, summonses) and qualitative (criminal versus civil law sanctions) terms. Evidence comes from a number of areas: Food and Drug Laws, False Advertising and Anti-combines in Canada (Snider 1978; Snider and West 1980); tax violations in the United States (Long 1979); coal mining violations in United States (Lynxwiler, Shover, and Clelland 1984); and assorted other countries and fields (for example, Fellmeth 1973; Fisse and Braithwaite 1983; Reasons, Ross, and Patterson 1981; Thomas 1982).

The paucity of sanctions is similarly well established empirically. Civil and criminal fines, for large organizations, typically represent a fraction of the profits made in 1 hour of operation, and imprisonment is virtually unknown (with the exception of American antitrust and securities laws, where short-term sentences for a handful of the less powerful offenders have recently been secured) (Carson 1982; Clinard and Yeager 1980; Levi 1984, 1981; Lynxwiler et al. 1984; Shapiro 1985; Snider 1978).

Identifying this reluctance to "get tough" with corporate offenders as the problem, many scholars see increased use of imprisonment and higher criminal fines as the remedy. They argue that the stigma of criminality is the heaviest moral sanction a society can employ, and the only one that the corporate sector will take seriously (Hawkins 1984; Levi 1984). Criminalization has practical advantages as well. Laws against corporate crime have to be struggled for, and are typically passed only after an environmental crisis or major disaster has aroused public outrage (Snider 1987). In this situation, with the pressure on politicians to take immediate remedial action, criminalizing techniques represent the perfect response. They are visible, they appear tough, and they symbolize moral opprobrium. The fact that increasing the number and severity of criminal laws has not provided better control over corporate crime is explained by focusing on insufficient utilization. If criminal sanctions were to be deployed regularly, if corporations knew that their chances of escaping criminal conviction were slight, if fines commensurate with the size of the firm and the profitability of the crime were imposed, if jail sentences were given, if these procedures were coupled with more enforcement personnel and more punitive laws, backed by civil and administrative remedies where appropriate, then criminalization and deterrence would be effective (Coffee 1984; Elkins 1976; Watkins 1977).

In recent years, however, the results of increasingly sophisticated studies of regulatory agencies have subjected criminalization models to heavy attack. The first and most serious charge has been simply that criminal law does not work against corporate offenders. Regulatory law is different from traditional criminal law because its goal is not to punish, but to secure compliance and educate. Corporate offenders may lack the technical competence required for compliance, they may be ignorant of the law, or unintentional organizational (system) failures may lead them to offend. Moreover, charging corporations and executives and pursuing them through the criminal courts creates antagonism, threatening the cooperation and goodwill that are crucial to the effectiveness of regulation because so many areas of corporate misbehavior are beyond the purview of law (Stone 1975).

A second charge is that criminalization actually increases the amount of harm produced by corporate crime. The strict evidentiary requirements of the criminal courts mean that a regulatory agency, rather than stepping in when it first hears of an offense, has to allow it to continue long enough to gather evidence. The high cost of using criminal justice procedures is also an issue. Because there is by all accounts even more corporate crime than traditional crime, and its damage to the society in lives taken and money lost is much higher (see summary in Braithwaite 1985a, pp. 12-13), reliance on the criminal justice system to control corporate crime, if anything close to full enforcement were attempted, would be fiscally impossible. The result would leave the poor not better off, but worse, "in more dangerous factories, marketplaces, and environments" (Braithwaite 1985a, p. 11; see also Fisse and Braithwaite 1983; Shapiro 1985; Smith 1976; Thomas 1982, p. 100).

Empirical studies show the merit of these criticisms. For example, Shapiro's (1985) examination of the Securities and Exchange Commission in United States, argues that: "Criminal prosecution is associated with regulatory failure. It is a response to offenses that are discovered too late to prevent substantial harm" (p. 199). It is used only when the SEC has failed to discover an offense in its initial stages, when the damage has become significant, and when the administrative or civil remedies that would have contained the offense at an earlier stage are no longer practical. Or it is used on individuals or small "fly-by-night" firms that cannot be punished any other way because they lack corporate connections and ongoing relationships with the agency. Shapiro also pointed out that the success rate is much higher for civil and administrative actions, and that the fines assessed under criminal law are consistently lower than administrative or civil fines, not higher (Shapiro 1985, p. 202; see also Hopkins 1978; King 1985, pp. 15-16; Levi 1984).

Rankin and Brown (1988) compared two agencies in the province of British Columbia, one using administrative penalties and the other criminal sanctions. The Waste Management Branch, using criminal law, filed an average of 44 charges annually from 1984 to 1986, and convicted an average of 16 per year, with an average fine of $565 each. The Workman's Compensation Board, by contrast, issued 300 administrative penalties and a mean fine of $5000 in the first half of 1986 and $3100 in 1985 (p. 6). Jamieson's study (1985) of British factory regulation identified four components of inspectors' beliefs that make them unlikely to use punitive measures: (a) industry is powerful enough to resist regulations it defines as overly restrictive; (b) regulations that threaten economic viability will not be passed in the first place; (c) society only wants the harmful side effects of industry restricted, as it approves of the corporate sector in general; and (d) societal consent for the regulatory function would be withdrawn if policing were seen as overzealous.

Increasingly detailed knowledge about the nature of regulatory agencies also weakens the case for criminalization. The factors that create and nourish regulatory agencies (theories of origins), their advantages and disadvantages, and their various constituencies (from the general public to producers, competitors, and government itself), all have been studied now (Fels 1982, p. 32; Kagan 1978, pp. 13-15; Mitnick 1980). And the more we find out, the more limited the ability of the typical regulatory agency to employ a criminalization strategy appears to be. Consider, for example, the phenomenon of "capture," the process whereby the regulatory agency takes on the perspective of the industry it is supposed to regulate. Capture is thought to be both recurring and inevitable. Regulatory agencies historically have displayed a pattern of long-term growth that has outstripped growth in the industry they were set up to regulate (Noll 1978; Meier and Plumlee 1978; Stigler 1975). This growth is associated not with more efficient control of corporate crime, however, but with greater rigidity of decision making. An agency's creative youth is no defense against a rigid and captured old age (Anderson 1975; Cobb and Elder 1972; Sabatier 1975, 1977).

378   CRIME & DELINQUENCY / JULY 1990

Cooperation

In light of such studies, cooperative models begin to look appealing, and they have come to dominate discussions of policy and reform in popular and business forums. We will look at two proposals typifying this genre, both of which rely predominantly on noncriminal measures. Braithwaite's cooperative proposals represent his continuing efforts to surmount the weaknesses of criminalization models and to find an effective sanctioning mechanism for corporate crime. In 1982 he suggested government enforced self-regulation, whereby all organizations would be required to file, and have approved, their own proposals for policing potentially troublesome areas of operation. Such areas include the control of pollution, standards for worker safety, and provisions for the legal distribution of company shares. There would be strict minimum standards and criteria for each organization, and each plan would be monitored periodically even after approval. This cooperative system, Braithwaite argued, would have several advantages. Inspectors hired by the corporation to enforce the industry-generated standards would be insiders, not outsiders as regulatory agency employees are, and would therefore have access to all kinds of formal and informal sources of information presently denied to outsiders. Also they would have the technical knowledge effective regulation requires, and would be less likely to be seen by fellow employees as "the enemy." The regulated organization would pay most of the costs of the scheme, and each firm could make sure that the rules it drew up fitted its organizational structure. Moreover, standards and procedures could be tightened as technical advances allowed. Braithwaite conceded that company inspectors would be even more subject to capture than state-employed inspectors are, but thinks this could be overcome by laws requiring a public report if management overruled its inspectors (Braithwaite 1982).

Braithwaite and Fisse (1983) next developed a model of "informal social control," defined as "behavioral restraint by means other than those formally directed by a court or administrative agency" (p. 1). Informal social control relies heavily on stigma and adverse publicity as disincentives to antisocial corporate conduct. Provided there were mechanisms to increase public access to and knowledge of corporate crimes, it could be, they argued, a useful deterrent. As evidence, they cited the complete about-face on the asbestos issue that characterized James Hardie, formerly a major asbestos manufacturer in Australia. They do recognize its limitations, however, admitting at one stage: "Perhaps the real lesson . . . is that informal social control can work when structural realities make it possible" (Braithwaite and Fisse 1983, p. 76).

Snider / COOPERATIVE MODELS AND CORPORATE CRIME 379

Building on these schemes, Braithwaite (1988, 1985b) more recently suggested a pyramid approach based on a hierarchy of penalties. Assuming that industrial self-regulation is absent or has failed, the regulatory agency would be required to pursue a fixed sequence of options when it suspects laws have been breached: (a) attempts would be made to persuade the organization to comply; (b) official warnings would be delivered; (c) compulsory civil charges leading to monetary penalties would be assessed; and (d) criminal prosecution would be accompanied by mandatory sanctions ranging from prison sentences for executives to removal of the operating license and plant shutdown. The system is intended to overcome problems which have been caused, Braithwaite argued, by exclusive reliance on either civil/administrative penalties or criminal sanctions (or, indeed, problems caused by using persuasion/education as exclusive strategies).

A political scientist has developed another variation of cooperative regulation. Based on the "prisoner's dilemma" logic game, Scholz (1984a, 1984b) demonstrated, mathematically and logically, that cooperative strategies are advantageous to both regulators and regulated. He assumed that both sides have a common interest in minimizing costs, and the regulated corporation seeks also to minimize sanctions. Cooperative strategies are normally best for both, but only if both sides adhere to this policy. When one player abandons it, the other, to maximize benefits, must defect immediately as well. Thus, if the defector is a firm, the regulatory agency should instantly abandon persuasion/education and move to a deterrence strategy through the appropriate legal mechanisms. (If it is the regulatory agency that abandons the cooperative mode, the firm should immediately, according to this model, adopt avoidance/evasion strategies.) With such a model, the firm derives minimum benefit from cheating, and the regulators are caught out or "suckered" only once before moving to more punitive rules of play. A strategy whereby regulatory agencies use only the criminal law/deterrence orientation, Scholz argued, makes law evasion on the part of the regulated a rational strategy. Illustrative of the increasingly powerful law and economics movement, this scheme appeals for two reasons: (a) it is grounded in mathematical symbols rather than words, and (b) it demonstrates that cooperation represents a sensible economic strategy, a rationale much more persuasive than "soft" concepts such as values and morality.

Comparing this model with his pyramid proposal, Braithwaite (1988) pointed to advantages and disadvantages. On the plus side, Scholz's model has a political advantage for regulatory agencies, as it allows them the moral upper hand—they do not opt for punitive methods until the regulated organization has demonstrated bad faith. Thus they are responding to antisocial

380   CRIME & DELINQUENCY / JULY 1990

corporate behavior that has already occurred, not singling out for special treatment "law-abiding corporations which are minding their own business." It also has the virtues of simplicity and flexibility, in that the agency can revert to cooperative strategies once the industry signals its desire to do so by complying with the law. The negatives are that it cannot easily be used with individuals and organizations that are "one-shotters" as opposed to "repeat players" (Galanter 1974); and it provides no comparable way of dealing with situations where cooperation cannot ever be expected to develop.

Cooperative models, then, try to get around the demonstrated pitfalls of criminalization by putting in place flexible schemes that are purportedly in the interests of both the regulated and the regulators. They have been received with considerable enthusiasm and are said to embody philosophical change that has occurred in regulatory law, especially in United States and Great Britain, in the 1980s.

PITFALLS OF COOPERATIVE REGULATION

Both criminalization and cooperative models can be faulted for recommending remedies without fully taking into account the broader socioeconomic realities of life in a capitalist system. Advocates of criminalization call for stricter enforcement, higher fines, and prison sentences. However, since regulators choose not to use the considerable arsenal of sanctions they already possess, getting even more punitive laws on the books is surely not the answer.

Advocates of cooperative models, on the other hand, fail to deal with the implications of class-based power. They recognize that the overwhelming opposition of the corporate sector has invitiated efforts at criminalization, but they ignore its potential effect on cooperative regulation. It is corporate power that makes regulatory agencies and remedial measures ineffective, not the measures themselves; and corporate power will make cooperative models at least equally futile. In fact, I argue that these models will be much less effective than criminalization in controlling corporate crime (though they may well be more efficient in the sense that the gap between what they attempt and what they achieve is less). Indeed, it is this increased potential to make regulation ineffective that has caused corporate analysts, the business press, and allied politicians to embrace cooperative models with such enthusiasm.

To understand where cooperative models go wrong, one must start by examining their origins. Like criminalization models, they are deeply rooted in mainstream Western thought, part of a pluralist tradition that has championed the continuing extension of social control through the institution of law. Dominant ideology stresses that law is a universalistic instrument that treats all classes, gender, races, and religions alike, and looks with the same disfavor on predatory acts of the rich as those of the poor. Under these circumstances, the virtual exemption corporations and the rich originally enjoyed from coercive legal regulation became a threat to the legitimation and consent essential for the operation of the modern state. Discipline and legal regulation, used originally to transform a pre-industrial peasant class into a functional working class, soon spread to encompass virtually all classes and behaviors (Cohen 1979, 1985; Foucault 1979; Melossi 1980). Once the antisocial acts of the upper classes and corporate elites became visible (with the development of mass media and literacy), and once the lower and working classes gained power (through the universal franchise and working-class organizations), it was inevitable that the former would be called to account. From the 19th century on, reformers, working-class groups and, later, scholars called for greater control over corporate misconduct.

Scholars advocating cooperative models are well grounded in the discourse of increased social control, but here it becomes regulatory and not criminal law that is advocated. And a new twist has been put on the concept of universalism with the argument that treating corporate criminals the same as traditional ones is not necessary, as long as the end result is to produce more and not less control over the wrongdoers. They are not, then, arguing for increased tolerance. Criminal law is rejected by cooperative models not because it is too punitive or controls too heavily, but because it controls too little. Criminalization models are punitive only in theory, only in the law books, because laws are not enforced. Indeed, they cannot be enforced because criminal law itself is seen as a flawed technique. Cooperative models, then, are philosophically very much in tune with dominant ideological currents of the 1980s wherein moves towards "liberalization" or "permissiveness" are greeted with horror (Snider 1985), and moves to "clamp down" are hailed.

However, the reception accorded cooperative models in the public arena in the 1980s must be understood not in the context of scholars' intentions, but in the declining light of liberalism and the dramatic rise of the New Right. These conservative forces, quiescent during the prosperous 1960s and 1970s, came into their own during the 1980s with the election of Ronald Reagan in the United States and Margaret Thatcher in Britain and the advent of fiscal crises in both countries. The capitalist class and its allies in government have promoted an economic agenda that favors austerity capitalism and monetarist policies. The goal, to legitimate a smaller share of national wealth for the working and lower classes and a larger one for the corporate sector, is sold by reason-based appeals to remain competitive combined with emotional appeals to religion and nationalism. In the area of crime, this means a law-and-order agenda attacking Blacks, feminists, homosexuals, and any other group that can be used to symbolize decline, decay, and the loss of traditional White male authority (Comack 1988; Horton 1981).

Corporate crime, however, is treated differently. Here, the New Right advocates deregulation, the removal of government "fetters" over business. Neoconservatives see the shortcomings of criminalization as confirmation of their position. They argue that the arguments favoring cooperative models put forth by the Law and Economics groups (Lewis-Beck and Alford 1980; Smith 1976, 1979; Whiting 1980) confer scholarly blessings on their ideologically motivated attempts to represent the corporate sector as the beleaguered scapegoat of social democracy in the postwar period. They contend that respectable business people do not commit crimes intentionally, that their crimes are victimless bookkeeping errors too trivial to merit criminal prosecution, and that the importance of business to the development of the capitalist economy warrants overlooking any minor excesses that might occur. The movement, then, seeks to rescue capitalism from the ideological and financial threats represented by the 1960s, Watergate-type scandals, and looming fiscal crises.

Scholars supporting cooperative models may have no desire to convey such a message, and may disapprove of the political uses to which their work is put. However, neoconservative use of the movement to cooperative regulation was not foreseen and its implications are still not recognized. Given that the original purpose of cooperative reforms was to increase control over the corporate sector, not decrease it, such a reception should have been a dramatic signal that something was wrong. Scholarship is neither produced nor received in a political and economic vacuum. This is not to say that scholars are unconscious tools of an all-powerful ruling class; merely that, out of all the ideas produced in a given time period, those consonant with and useful to powerful groups will be the ones most likely to be heralded as significant, and incorporated into the commonsense notions by which people make sense of the social world. The popularity of cooperative models does not surprise those who have studied the social diffusion and transmission of ideas. At particular ideological junctures, ideas are seized upon, disseminated, popularized, and thereby transformed into instruments that increase the power of the dominant class.

Dominant ideological currents are continuously being disseminated in this way, though they are met in democratic societies by dissenting groups that oppose them. This is an ongoing but unequal struggle because antithetical ideologies are simultaneously created out of the same contradictory processes as dominant ones. Such opposing ideas, supported by groups outside the hegemonic consensus (such as labor unions, feminist groups, or environmental lobbies), meet with heavy resistance, and have a much more difficult time commanding a mass audience and securing acceptance.

Examples of the speed and enthusiasm with which ideas consonant with dominant ideological currents are adopted would include, in the area of criminal law, the reception and distortion of Martinson's critique of offender rehabilitation programs, commonly and erroneously summed up in the phrase "nothing works." This came along just when the public sector was feeling the fiscal crunch associated with changes in the structure of monopoly capitalism, and was consonant with a hardening of attitudes toward traditional crime (Walker 1985; Martinson 1974).[3] In a field like corporate crime, in which the ideological and financial implications of ideas and the social policies they spawn directly affect the profitability of major corporate actors, the significance of a shift in the assumptions underlying social policy can be enormous. Changes directly affect the interests of the most powerful groups in the society, the corporate elites and the two main levels of the state (federal and provincial/state). When Yeager (1986) said that calling corporate misbehavior criminal was resorting to an unnecessary "linguistic flag," he was forgetting all that we know about the political economy of regulation and enforcement. Obscuring the link between corporate crime and traditional crime may have a profound and deleterious impact on the already weak structure of regulation.

It should also be clear that the emphasis these models place on cooperation with the targets of regulatory law is nothing new—it has always been the dominant strategy regulators actually employed. In fact, it plays a major role in all law enforcement, since every law requires those who would control to negotiate some minimal level of consent from the targets of the law. The limits of this negotiation are set by a constellation of factors: (a) the enabling legislation and precedents; (b) the power of targeted groups; (c) and the subjective and objective relevance of structural variables (such as the interests affected, national policies, and the like). Obviously, this process grants considerably more leverage to the corporate executive than to the armed robber. As we noted previously, cooperative regulators in the area of corporate crime have been the rule not the exception, even where legislation

specifically directs enforcers to the contrary. If there is evidence that criminalization does not work, there is equally compelling evidence that cooperation does not either.

It may be, then, that even the best of the cooperative schemes, such as
Braithwaite's, do no more than describe the operational procedure that good
regulatory agencies generally follow. A sequence from persuasion to civil to
criminal sanctions is common (Rankin and Brown 1988; Shapiro 1985;
Shover et al. 1986; Tucker 1987). Regulatory ineffectiveness was — and is —
the result of agencies being hemmed in by structural factors, and the ideological, political, and economic consequences of this. One result of this
power is that regulators themselves often "buy" the dominant ideology and
see corporations and their executives as non-criminal entities who offend
through ignorance rather than design.[4] But even with zealous regulators, the
typical disparity in resources between them and the regulated means it often
is more efficient, in the narrow sense of the word, for regulators to choose
strategies that gain them the support and trust of the more powerful group (as
all supplicants must do). Because they lack anything approaching equal
power, this is one of the few ways that regulators can influence corporate
behavior. From the regulators' point of view, these tactics make good sense.
However, to persuade scholars that the stratagems regulators have developed
to survive in a hostile regulatory climate are actually and intrinsically the best
ones is a surprising development.

The acceptance of this conclusion comes directly out of the aforemen-
tioned academic failure to recognize the implications of this overwhelming
disparity in power for cooperative models. Class power has shaped the laws
that regulate corporate crime; it has a major impact on the behavior of state
officials; and it is responsible for most of the difficulties they face in
regulating effectively. At the risk of oversimplification, the entire agenda of
regulation is the result of a struggle between the corporate sector opposing
regulation and the much weaker forces supporting it. Cooperative models
allow scholars to conceptualize the existing balance of power between
regulators and the corporate sector as a fundamental and acceptable con-
straint on the state's ability to regulate corporate crime. The acceptance of
"the hegemony of corporate ideology" (Pearce and Tombs 1988, p. 8) makes
this dominance the starting point for regulators rather than a barrier that must
be challenged and overcome. This in turn sets very low limits for regulators,
and signifies an acceptance by scholars of the position that really effective
regulation of corporate crime is not possible.

IMPLICATIONS

It must be clear by now that securing effective regulatory enforcement is going to be very difficult. If this analysis is correct, change will require strategies that weaken the economic and ideological power of the corporate sector while simultaneously strengthening that of oppositional forces. Given present-day economic exigencies and the antiregulatory climate still dominant in the major Western democracies, this will be a major challenge.

It should also be clear, however, that repealing criminal law and substituting the goal of cooperation with regulators can only weaken further proregulatory forces. Some of the reasons for this are symbolic. Criminal law is universalistic and absolute, and those who offend against it are *criminals*, a term fraught with connotations of evil. Transforming corporate criminals into regulatory evaders who have failed to "cooperate" makes their transgressions seem pale by comparison. We know also that publicity has been an important tool in securing action against corporate crime. The difference between pressing a case against an uncooperative executive versus a corporate criminal is the difference between a story which makes the news and one which is buried in the business section. And pressure groups, key players in prodding governments to enforce laws against corporations, need both the symbolism and the universalism of criminal law. Their ability to monitor performance could be affected, since it would be easier for both the government and the corporate sector to argue that, unlike criminal law, there is no public interest involved or public right to know in regulatory law. Moreover, their key lever, the continuing failure of regulatory agencies to comply with their official mandate to enforce the law, would be irretrievably weakened. Such groups derive their ideological power from the gap between what the law demands and what the agency actually does. The stronger and more universalistic the agency mandate, then, the greater the potential bargaining strength of proregulatory forces, the greater the potential to embarrass the regulatory agency, and the greater the chances of shaming the offending corporation. As Winter has recognized:

> Without the clear power and duties to interfere with private interests, the administrative agency would not have a position from which to barter effectively. If legal doctrine allowed clear cut rules to be discarded whenever an agency preferred non-enforcement . . . , the value of the legal rule as a bargaining chip would be diminished, for the regulatory process would begin with the assumption that full enforcement was not even a benchmark. (Winter 1985, pp. 240-241)

Such a shift would also affect the expectations of corporations, providing them with more excuses and increased time to delay. Let us not forget that corporate crime is very profitable, so the motivations for delay are strong. Moreover, corporations could protest any regulatory action on the grounds that it was precipitate and premature—they were going to cooperate, they would say, but they just were not allowed long enough to negotiate the terms. Adopting the cooperative model, then, will both undermine the power of the regulatory agency and legitimate this loss.

What we should not do, however, is much clearer than what we should do. Identifying the dead ends is easier than finding the throughways, if they even exist. Further analysis is required, despite the danger that it will substitute for action. We must look more skeptically at the potential of law to be effective in the regulatory process. How does this potential vary with different kinds of corporate crime? We can no longer assume that the many and varied behaviors proscribed under the label "corporate crime" will meet with the same degree of support from pressure groups, labor, social demo- cratic parties, and other proregulatory forces. Thus we cannot assume that enforcement strategies should be identical in detail and strength. We need to know what kinds of regulatory structure, what combinations of criminal and civil law, are most compatible with the exercise of proregulatory influence. And we need to continue documenting the shortcomings of existing regula- tory regimes as well as developing ideas and analyses that simultaneously keep the pressure on the state AND have the potential to make a real difference. This must be accompanied by an understanding of the sources of resistance that starts at the level of political economy. Effective reform is contingent on the power structure, and cannot be analyzed without taking it into account. Finally, we must explore the degree to which meaningful change can be achieved without a major shift in the economics and ideology of capitalism, as this appears unlikely barring a complete ecological collapse, one which affects developed countries as much as the Third World.

In the meantime, since securing even minimal regulatory effectiveness requires constant vigilance and political struggle, those who want effective control should look for ways to increase the power of pressure groups and focus media attention on the frequency (great) and the human consequences (immense) of corporate crime. This necessitates confronting prevailing cul- tural assumptions that attribute all social evils to the criminality and drug habits of the poor and powerless, and shifting the political spotlight onto those who do the most damage and cost the most lives. The result of continuing along our present path will be to undermine, not assist, the struggle for effective control of corporate crime.

NOTES

1. Dr. Dan Kirkwood, Robert Gordon Institute of Technology, Aberdeen, commenting on the Piper Alpha explosion that killed 166 men (*Toronto Globe and Mail* July 27, 1988, p. 1).

2. Report by R. Barber, one of Ontario's first factory inspectors (cited in Tucker 1987, p. 75).

3. The ideological basis of policy is clearly illustrated by the fact that the identical discovery that "nothing works" for either traditional or corporate crime led to diametrically opposite policy shifts. Increased punitiveness and criminalization was the solution prescribed for traditional lower-class criminality; but increased cooperativeness and the abandonment of criminalization was the remedy for corporate offenders!

4. It is unlikely that they would have been substantially more effective if they had marched to different drummers, although the potential of dissenters to effect change from the inside is not understood clearly. Indeed, Tucker (1987, pp. 43-44), in his study of enforcement of the Ontario Factory Act from 1888-1900, found that 30 of 35 charges laid were the work of one inspector who also was a former mechanic and union activist. An inspector who was a former manufacturer laid 4 charges over the 12-year period, and a "political appointee" laid 1. Perhaps this kind of microlevel factor needs to be examined further.

REFERENCES

Anderson, J. E. 1975. *Public Policy-Making*. New York: Praeger.

Bardach, E. and R. A. Kagan. 1982. *Going by the Book*. Philadelphia: Temple University Press.

Braithwaite, J. 1982. "Enforced Self-Regulation: A New Strategy for Corporate Crime Control." *Michigan Law Review* 80:1466-1507.

———. 1985a. "White Collar Crime." *Annual Review of Sociology* 11:1-25.

———. 1985b. *To Punish or Persuade*. Albany: State University of New York Press.

———. 1988. "Toward a Benign Big Gun Theory of Regulatory Power." Canberra: Australian National University, Australian Institute of Criminology.

Braithwaite, J. and B. Fisse. 1983. "Asbestos and Health: A Case of Informal Social Control." *Australian-New Zealand Journal of Criminology* 16:67-80.

Carson, W. G. 1970. "White Collar Crime and the Enforcement of Factory Legislation." *British Journal of Criminology* 10:383-398.

———. 1982. "Legal Control of Safety on British Offshore Oil Installations." In *White Collar and Economic Crime*, edited by P. Wickman and T. Dailey. Toronto: Lexington Books.

Clinard, M. B. and P. Yeager. 1980. *Corporate Crime*. New York: Free Press.

Cobb, R. W. and C. D. Elder. 1972. *Participation in Politics*. Boston: Allyn & Bacon.

Coffee, J. C. 1984. "Corporate Criminal Responsibility." Pp. 253-264 in *Encyclopedia of Crime and Justice*. Vol. 1, edited by S. Kadish. New York: Free Press.

Cohen, S. 1979. "The Punitive City: Notes on the Dispersal of Social Control." *Contemporary Crises* 3:339-363.

———. 1985. *Visions of Social Control*. Cambridge, U.K.: Polity Press.

Coleman, J. 1985. *The Criminal Elite*. New York: St. Martin.

Comack, E. 1988. "Law and Order Issues in the Canadian Context." Paper presented to the American Society of Criminology, Chicago, November.

388   CRIME & DELINQUENCY / JULY 1990

Downing, P. and K. Hanf. 1983. *International Comparisons in Implementing Pollution Control Laws.* Boston: Kluwer-Nijhoff.

Edelhertz, H. 1970. *The Nature, Impact and Prosecution of White-Collar Crime.* Washington, DC: U.S. Department of Justice, National Institute on Law Enforcement and Criminal Justice.

Elkins, J. R. 1976. "Decision-Making Models and the Control of Corporate Crime." *Hobart Law Journal* 85:1091-1129.

Fellmeth, R. 1973. "The Regulatory-Industrial Complex." In *Common and Corporate Accountability,* edited by R. Nader. New York: Harcourt Brace Jovanovich.

Fels, A. 1982. "The Political Economy of Regulation." *University of New South Wales Law Journal* 5:29-60.

Fisse, B. and J. Braithwaite. 1983. *The Impact of Publicity on Corporate Offenders.* Albany: State University of New York Press.

Foucault, M. 1979. *Discipline and Punish.* New York: Pantheon.

Galanter, M. 1974. "Why the Haves Come out Ahead: Speculations on the Limits of Legal Change." *Law & Society Review* 9:95-160.

Goff, C. and C. Reasons. 1978. *Corporate Crime in Canada.* Toronto: Prentice-Hall.

Grabosky, P. and J. Braithwaite. 1986. *Of Manners Gentle.* Melbourne: Oxford University Press.

Gunningham, N. 1974. *Pollution: Social Interest and the Law.* Oxford: Centre for Socio-Legal Studies, Oxford University.

―――. 1984. *Safeguarding the Worker.* Sydney: Law Book Company.

Hawkins, K. 1984. *Environment and Enforcement.* Oxford: Clarendon.

Hopkins, A. 1978. *Crime, Law and Business.* Canberra: Australian National University, Australian Institute of Criminology.

Horton, J. 1981. "The Rise of the Right: A Global View." *Crime and Social Justice* 15:7-17.

Jamieson, M. 1985. *Persuasion or Punishment.* Master's thesis, Oxford University, United Kingdom.

Kagan, R. 1978. *Regulatory Justice.* New York: Russell Sage.

King, D. K. 1985. "The Regulatory Use of the Criminal Sanction in Controlling Corporate Crime." Paper presented to the American Society of Criminology meetings, San Diego, November.

Levi, M. 1981. *The Phantom Capitalists.* London: Heinemann.

―――. 1984. "Giving Creditors the Business: The Criminal Law in Inaction." *International Journal of Sociology of Law* 12:312-333.

Lewis-Beck, M. S. and J. R. Alford. 1980. "Can Government Regulate Safety? The Coal Mine Example." *American Political Science Review* 74:745-781.

Long, S. 1979. "The Internal Revenue Service: Examining the Exercise of Discretion in Tax Enforcement." Paper presented to the Law and Society meetings, May.

Lynxwiler, J., N. Shover, and D. Clelland. 1984. "Determinants of Sanction Severity in a Regulatory Bureaucracy." Pp. 147-165 in *Corporations as Criminals,* edited by E. Hochstedler. Beverly Hills, Calif.: Sage.

Martinson, R. 1974. "What Works? Questions and Answers about Prison Reform." *The Public Interest* 35:22-54.

Meier, R. and J. P. Plumlee. 1978. "Regulatory Administration and Organizational Rigidity." *Western Political Quarterly* 31:80-95.

Meier, R. and J. F. Short. 1982. "The Consequences of White-Collar Crime." In *White-Collar Crime: An Agenda for Research,* edited by H. Edelhertz and T. Overcast. Toronto: D. C. Heath.

Melossi, D. 1980. "Strategies of Social Control in Capitalism: A Comment on Recent Work." *Contemporary Crises* 4:381-402.

Mitnick, B. M. 1980. *The Political Economy of Regulation*. New York: Columbia University Press.

Morgenstern, F. 1982. *Deterrence and Compensation*. Geneva: International Labor Organization.

Noll, R. 1978. *Reforming Regulation*. Washington, DC: Brookings.

Pearce, F. and S. Tombs. 1988. "Regulating Corporate Crime: The Case of Health and Safety." Presented to American Society of Criminology meeting, Chicago, November.

Peltzman, J. 1976. "Toward a More General Theory of Regulation." *Journal of Law and Economics* 19:211-240.

Rankin, E. and R. Brown. 1988. "The Treatment of Repeat Offenders under B. C.'s Occupational Health and Safety and Pollution Control Legislation." Presented to the Canadian Law & Society Association meeting, Windsor, June.

Reasons, C., W. Ross, and C. Patterson. 1981. *Assault on the Worker*. Toronto: Butterworth.

Sabatier, P. 1975. "Social Movements and Regulatory Agencies: Toward a More Adequate and Less Pessimistic Theory of Clientele Capture." *Policy Sciences* 6:301-341.

———. 1977. "Regulatory Policy-Making: Toward a Framework of Analysis." *Natural Resources Journal* 17:415-460.

Scholz, J. 1984a. "Deterrence, Cooperation, and the Ecology of Regulatory Enforcement." *Law & Society Review* 18:179-224.

———. 1984b. "Voluntary Compliance and Regulatory Enforcement." *Law and Policy* 6:385-404.

Shapiro, S. 1985. "The Road not Taken: The Elusive Path to Criminal Prosecution for White Collar Offenders." *Law & Society Review* 19.

Shover, N., D. A. Clelland, and J. Lynxwiler. 1986. *Enforcement or Negotiation: Constructing a Regulatory Bureaucracy*. Albany: State University of New York Press.

Smith, R. J. 1976. *The Occupational Health and Safety Act*. Washington, DC: American Enterprise Institute.

———. 1979. "The Impact of OSHA Inspections on Manufacturing Injury Rates." *Journal of Human Resources* 14:145-160.

Snider, L. 1978. "Corporate Crime in Canada: A Preliminary Report." *Canadian Journal of Criminology* 20:142-168.

———. 1985. "Legal Reform and Social Control: The Dangers of Abolishing Rape." *International Journal of the Sociology of Law* 13:337-356.

———. 1987. "Toward a Political Economy of Reform, Regulation, and Corporate Crime." *Law and Policy* 9:37-68.

Snider L. and W. G. West. 1980. "Social Control, Crime, and Conflict in Canada." In *Power and Change in Canada*, edited by R. J. Ossenberg. Toronto: McClelland and Stewart.

Stigler, G. 1975. *The Citizen and the State*. Chicago: University of Chicago Press.

Stone, C. 1975. *Where the Law Ends*. New York: Harper & Row.

Sutherland, E. H. [1938] 1977. "White Collar Criminality." Pp. 71-84 in *White Collar Crime*, edited by G. Geis and R. F. Meier. Beverly Hills, CA: Sage.

Thomas, J. 1982. "The Regulatory Role in the Containment of Corporate Illegality." In *White-Collar Crime: An Agenda for Research*, edited by H. Edelhertz and T. Overcast. Toronto: D. C. Heath.

Tucker, E. 1987. "Making the Workplace Safe in Capitalism: Enforcement of Factory Legislation in Nineteenth Century Ontario." Paper presented to the Canadian Law and Society Association meeting, Hamilton, June.

Walker, S. 1985. *Sense and Nonsense about Crime*. Monterey, CA: Brooks/Cole.

Watkins, J. C. 1977. "White Collar Crimes: Legal Sanctions and Social Control." *Crime and Delinquency* 23:290-303.

Whiting, B. J. 1980. "OSHA's Enforcement Policy." *Labor Law Journal* 31.

Winter, G. 1985. "Bartering Rationality in Regulation." *Law & Society Review* 19:219-250.

Yeager, P. C. 1986. "Managing Obstacles to Studying Corporate Offenses: An Optimistic Assessment." Paper presented to the American Society of Criminology meeting, Atlanta, November.

[18]

The State and White-Collar Crime: Saving the Savings and Loans

Kitty Calavita   Henry N. Pontell

We attempt to make sense of the law enforcement response to the savings and loan debacle and the larger pattern of white-collar crime enforcement of which it is a part. Drawing from government documents and in-depth interviews with federal regulators and enforcement officials, we argue that the current response to savings and loan fraud is unprecedented both in terms of the extensive resources committed and the prosecution of thousands of white-collar offenders. Pointing out that this at first seems inconsistent with the government's relative tolerance of corporate crime cited in other white-collar crime studies, we borrow from state theory to explain this "crackdown." By bringing together two traditions that have usually remained distinct—white-collar crime research and state theory—this analysis may contribute both to a better understanding of the government response to white-collar crime and to a more empirically grounded approach to the state.

In early 1989, news reports began to reveal evidence of widespread fraud in the U.S. savings and loan (S&L) industry, in what has turned out to be the costliest white-collar crime scandal in U.S. history.[1] Shortly after his election, President Bush announced a plan to bail out the crippled industry and investigate and prosecute thrift crime. Several months later, Congress passed the Financial Institutions Reform, Recovery and Enforcement Act of 1989 (FIRREA). This law authorized $75 million annually for three years to fund the Justice Department's efforts to prosecute financial fraud. The FBI budget for these cases went from less than $60 million for fiscal year 1990 to over $125 million in 1991, and FBI personnel dedicated to financial fraud almost doubled (U.S. Senate 1992:45). By 1992, over 800 savings

This research was supported by a grant from the Academic Senate, University of California, Irvine, and under Award #90-IJ-CX-0059 from the National Institute of Justice, Office of Justice Programs, U.S. Department of Justice. Points of view in this document are those of the authors and do not necessarily represent the official position of the U.S. Department of Justice. Address correspondence to Prof. Kitty Calavita, Criminology, Law and Society, School of Social Ecology, University of California, Irvine, CA 92717-5150.

[1] For a description of the epidemic of savings and loan fraud and the conditions that facilitated it, see Calavita & Pontell 1990, 1991.

and loan offenders had been convicted, with 77% receiving prison sentences (U.S. Department of Justice 1992b:66).

Edwin Sutherland in 1949 documented the pervasiveness of white-collar crime and highlighted the lenient treatment received by elite offenders compared to perpetrators of street crimes. Since Sutherland's lead, a vast literature has developed attesting to the differential treatment of white-collar criminals (Geis 1967; Carson 1970, 1982; Clinard et al. 1979; Clinard & Yeager 1980; Ermann & Lundman 1978, 1982; Barnett 1982; Levi 1984; Pearce & Tombs 1988; Snider 1978, 1991). Recently, however, a number of scholars have questioned the conventional wisdom that white-collar offenders are favored by the legal system (Katz 1980; Hagan & Nagel 1982; Hagan 1985; Wheeler & Rothman 1982; Wheeler et al. 1992). While the empirical and theoretical foci of these latter studies vary, they all argue that a crackdown on white-collar crime is underway.

The government effort to ferret out and prosecute S&L criminals seems inconsistent with the longstanding argument of legal favoritism of elite offenders, and might seem to substantiate these more recent arguments that white-collar criminals have been put on notice by an outraged public and "enterprising" law enforcement officials (Katz 1980:170–71). We argue here, however, that the issue is more complex than this "either/or" debate implies. Pointing out that the official response to white-collar crime is decidedly *selective* (e.g., regulators continue a policy of lenience toward violators of labor standards and occupational safety and health laws), we use the S&L case to explore the patterns of that response and the conditions under which it is likely to include a crackdown on corporate offenders.

In an effort to make sense of the enforcement response to the S&L debacle and the broader pattern of white-collar crime enforcement of which it is a part, we borrow a number of concepts from the state theory literature, thereby bringing together two traditions that have much in common but have largely remained distinct. While state theorists generally focus on the role of the state and public policy in *subsidizing* specific capitalists, or the capitalist class collectively, with favorable public policies, corporate crime scholars focus on government action (or inaction) in the *punishment* of capitalist actors. Yet, the way a state punishes (or does not punish) capitalist offenders must be related to the nature of the relationship between the state and capital and the degree to which the offenses in question jeopardize that relationship. This article represents an effort to synthesize the white-collar crime and state theory traditions in order to understand the U.S. government response to savings and loan crime, as well as the current selective crackdown on white-collar crime more generally.

We first provide a brief overview of the scholarship defining white-collar crime and locate thrift fraud within this context. We then outline the government reaction to thrift crime and pose alternative explanations for the crackdown, including the possibility that it reflects a growing intolerance of white-collar crime in the post-Watergate era. We further argue that the highly selective nature of the crackdown on white-collar crime suggests that the explanation must lie elsewhere. In searching for a viable explanation for the aggressive response to thrift fraud, we place it within the context of state theory, focusing on the notion of "relative autonomy" posited by structuralist theories of the state. We point out that the assertive posture of the government in pursuing thrift fraud—and financial crime more generally—seems compatible with the structuralist position that the state must work to preserve economic stability, and that in doing so it enjoys a measure of autonomy vis-à-vis individual elites. Having illustrated the utility of these structuralist insights for explaining the pattern of the response to thrift crime by the late 1980s, we turn next to the shortcomings of a pure structuralist model. In particular, we note the inadequacy of any model that attributes to the state a coherence of purpose and collective rationality that were conspicuously absent in the early (mis)handling of the thrift disaster. We argue here that the indecision and active struggle among policymakers and regulators during the mid-1980s over how to respond to early signs of thrift fraud reveal a state that neither is monolithic nor unilaterally enjoys relative autonomy. After offering some suggestions for an alternative synthetic model, we conclude that just as it is necessary to unpack "the state," so too the concept of corporate crime must be unpacked to reveal its various dimensions and its relationship to the modern state whose job it is to preserve the stability of the economic and financial system.

Our data come from a variety of sources, including government documents, congressional hearings and reports, and interviews with key policymakers, investigators, and regulators. The interviews with FBI investigators and officials in the Federal Deposit Insurance Corporation (since 1989, the thrift insurance agency), the Office of Thrift Supervision (the federal thrift regulatory agency since 1989), and the Resolution Trust Corporation (the new agency charged with managing and selling insolvent thrifts' assets), were tape-recorded and open-ended. They took place in Washington, DC, and in field offices in California, Texas, and Florida, and generally lasted between one and two hours, with some key respondents being interviewed several times over the course of two and a half years. Secondary sources and journalistic accounts of specific cases supplement the primary and archival material.

"White-Collar Crime" Revisited

Sutherland (1949:9) defined white-collar crime as "crime committed by a person of respectability and high social status in the course of his [*sic*] occupation." Recognizing that the concept includes a broad range of behaviors and motivations, later scholars have attempted further classification. One broad distinction is that between "corporate" or "organizational" crime which is committed by executives and managers acting as representatives of their institutions on behalf of those institutions versus white-collar "occupational" crime perpetrated by employees acting independently of their organizations and victimizing them for personal gain (Clinard & Quinney 1973; Coleman 1985; Hagan 1985; Schrager & Short 1978; Shapiro 1980; Wheeler & Rothman 1982).[2] There are a myriad of other ways of categorizing and labeling white-collar crime, and indeed some (e.g., Wheeler et al. 1982) include in the concept any crime committed by a white-collar individual, whether or not it occurs within the context of his or her occupation. The white-collar crime definitional debate is beyond the scope of this article and, in any case, has generally resulted in an intellectual cul-de-sac (see Geis 1992). For our purposes here, the important distinction is that between "corporate" and "occupational" crime, as defined above.

Following Sutherland, numerous researchers have found that corporate crimes are treated differently by law enforcement than are common street crimes. Clinard et al.'s (1979) study of legal actions taken against 582 of the largest corporations in the United States supports Sutherland's contention that not only is corporate crime extensive but law enforcement and regulatory systems tend not to take it very seriously. Case studies of specific industries and/or specific corporate violations corroborate these findings. Whether the focus is on the great electrical company conspiracy (Geis 1967), the Pinto case (Dowie 1979), the Firestone tire scandal (Coleman 1985), occupational safety and health violations (Carson 1970, 1982; Berman 1978; Calavita 1983), or environmental crimes (Gunningham 1974; Barnett 1982), a substantial literature documents the anemic legal response to corporate crime.

These empirical studies of corporate crime have focused primarily on the manufacturing sector. These *manufacturing* crimes are perpetrated for the purpose of maximizing corporate profits and/or cutting production costs and therefore are in a sense consistent with the logic of capital accumulation. Increasingly, however, a qualitatively different type of "corporate" crime has attracted headlines. As financial services replace industrial pro-

---

[2] It is of course possible for lower-level employees to commit occupational crime. Clinard & Quinney (1973), for example, point to a variety of occupational crimes by blue-collar workers, such as embezzlement and theft.

duction as the primary locus of economic activity in late capitalism, more corporate crime scandals involve *financial* fraud. Many of these crimes are distinct in important ways from the manufacturing crimes described above. Unlike corporate crimes in the manufacturing sector, financial fraud is often perpetrated by corporate executives for their own personal gain. More important, while manufacturing crimes tend to advance corporate profits and thus follow the logic of capital, financial fraud undermines that logic, jeopardizing the stability of the financial system and/or institutional survival.

Such financial frauds may thus be thought of as a hybrid. Like traditional corporate crime, the fraud is often carried out by management as part of company policy, not by isolated individuals acting independently of institutional prescriptions. Indeed, many thrift kingpins operated within institutions whose primary purpose was to provide a "cash cow" to management. Unlike traditional corporate crime, however, these financial frauds ultimately erode the viability of the corporation itself. In this sense, it is crime *by* the organization *against* the organization; or to use a variation of Wheeler and Rothman's (1982) conceptual scheme, the organization is both weapon *and* victim. Thus, these financial frauds combine aspects of both traditional "corporate" crime—in which the offenses are company policy and are committed via company transactions—and "occupational" crime perpetrated by individuals for personal gain, in which the institution itself is victimized.

While thrift fraud is unusual in its scope and impact, it is by no means unique in combining aspects of corporate and occupational crime. As we have shown elsewhere (Calavita & Pontell 1991), some insurance industry fraud is similar to this thrift fraud, as is much crime in other financial institutions, such as pension funds and credit unions. What these crimes have in common is that they are committed *by management, against the institution.* As we will see, the government response to the thrift crisis hinges in part on the peculiar nature of this hybrid form of corporate crime.

"Throw the Crooks in Jail": A Crackdown on White-Collar Crime?

In a speech to U.S. Attorneys in June 1990, President Bush promised, "We will not rest until the cheats and the chiselers and the charlatans [responsible for the S&L disaster] spend a large chunk of their lives behind the bars of a federal prison" (quoted in U.S. Department of Justice 1990:1). Announcing his plans for attacking financial institution fraud, the president was unequivocal: "[W]e aim for a simple, uncompromising position. Throw the crooks in jail" (quoted in U.S. House of Representatives 1990a: 128).

President Bush undoubtedly hoped to gain political mileage from an emphatic response to the worst financial fraud epidemic in U.S. history. However, this was not empty political rhetoric—at least not entirely. By 1989, both the legislative and executive branches were devoting considerable attention to savings and loan fraud. FIRREA allocated $225 million over three years to the Justice Department's financial fraud efforts. Almost immediately, FBI personnel assigned to financial fraud investigations climbed from 822 to 1,525. The total Department of Justice budget for financial institution fraud went from $80,845,000 to $212,236,000 (U.S. Senate 1992:45). The 1989 law also provided for increased penalties for financial institution crimes and extended the statute of limitations for such crimes from 5 to 10 years. The Comprehensive Thrift and Bank Fraud Prosecution and Taxpayer Recovery Act of 1990 raised maximum statutory penalties from 20 to 30 years in prison for a range of specific violations, reserving the most severe sanctions for "financial crime kingpins."

The number of prosecuted S&L offenders grew quickly. Major financial institution fraud investigations increased 54% from 1987 to 1991, when the FBI opened over 260 investigations every month. By early 1992, it had over 4,300 major financial fraud investigations underway, of which about 1,000 involved savings and loans (U.S. Senate 1992). From October 1988 to April 1992, more than 1,100 defendants were formally charged in "major" savings and loan cases,[3] and 839 were convicted (for completed prosecutions, the conviction rate was 92.6%). Of the 667 offenders who had been sentenced by the spring of 1992, 77% received a prison sentence (U.S. Department of Justice 1992b:64).

At no time in its history has the U.S. government allocated so many resources and concentrated so much of its law enforcement effort on pursuing white-collar criminals and sending them to prison.[4] The question is, Why? Two explanations come to mind. The first possibility is that this assault on financial fraud is

[3] "Major" cases are those in which "a) the amount of fraud or loss was $100,000 or more, or b) the defendant was an officer, director, or owner[of the S&L] . . ., or c) the schemes involved multiple borrowers in the same institution, or d) involves [sic] other major factors" (U.S. Department of Justice 1992a:9).

[4] The law enforcement response to the S&L crisis is of course not without its critics. Public interest groups as well as Congress, citing backlogs and unworked cases, have questioned the job the Justice Department is doing in prosecuting thrift offenders (see, e.g., U.S. House of Representatives 1990a; U.S. Senate 1992). Whether or not the Justice Department could pursue these cases more efficiently is beyond the scope of this article. White-collar crime cases are notoriously difficult to investigate and prosecute (Katz 1980; Braithwaite & Geis 1982). It is worth noting that S&L fraud cases are among the most difficult and time-consuming with which the FBI has ever had to deal, dependent as they often are on intricate financial schemes involving "daisy chains" of participants (personal interviews). The more important point here, however, is that the U.S. government has launched an unprecedented attack on this form of white-collar crime.

an indication of the erosion of official tolerance for white-collar crime postulated by a number of recent scholars. Katz (1980), for example, notes an increased emphasis on the criminal prosecution of business and political elites. Arguing that while earlier in this century journalists, populists, and other "lay catalysts" spearheaded the movement against business and political corruption, beginning in the 1970s prosecutors and public officials began to take the initiative, rendering the general public a "passive audience" (p. 169). Katz notes that the potential for *institutional* reform has been eroded by the "case" approach taken by law enforcement and that the movement against white-collar crime may be in decline since its peak in the 1970s. He nonetheless concludes that "some degree of institutionalization of the increased emphasis on white-collar crime has been achieved" (p. 178). Hagan (1985:286) similarly argues that in the post-Watergate era, the prosecution of white-collar and corporate crime has been stepped up. And Braithwaite and Geis (1982:292-93), on the eve of Ronald Reagan's presidency, observed that the post-Watergate era had seen a "surge of governmental . . . interest in corporate crime" and warned against reversing the trend.

While not distinguishing among different types of white-collar crimes, a number of empirical studies report an increased willingness to prosecute and sanction white-collar offenders in general. Focusing on prosecutorial patterns in the Southern District of New York from 1963 to 1976, Hagan and Nagel (1982) point to "proactive" policies, including an increase in resources for white-collar prosecutions and an "activist" approach to successful completion of these cases. According to this study, while there was a general tendency for white-collar offenders to receive favorable sentencing, this depended on the nature of the offense, with those convicted of mail fraud being most likely to be sent to prison (60%) and those convicted of illegal restraint of trade the least likely to be incarcerated (2.4%). Hagan and Palloni (1983) similarly report an increased tendency to sentence white-collar criminals to prison, albeit with relatively short sentences.

Wheeler, Weisburd, and Bode (1982) investigated eight types of white-collar crime in seven federal districts for the years 1976, 1977, and 1978 in order to determine the effect of a number of variables on white-collar sentencing. Surprisingly, they found that higher-status perpetrators of white-collar crime received prison sentences more often than did their lower-status counterparts.[5] Although they observe that in the aftermath of Watergate

---

[5] It is noteworthy that the Wheeler et al. study included few of what could be called "corporate" or "organizational" crimes and indeed contained a large contingent of very low-status violators, including significant numbers of the unemployed. Geis (1991) has suggested that the type of offenses and offenders included in this study do not fit particularly well Sutherland's original definition of "white collar crime."

judges may be sensitized to the seriousness of elite deviance, Wheeler et al. (p. 658) speculate that heavier penalties for higher-status individuals is not a new phenomenon but is "anchored in historical patterns that link greater social obligation with higher social status."

These arguments contesting the notion that white-collar criminals receive more lenient treatment are complicated by a number of issues. Some (e.g., Katz 1980; Hagan 1985) suggest, for example, that there has been a *shift* toward greater intolerance of white-collar crime since the Watergate revelations; others (such as Wheeler et al. 1982, who subtitle their article "Rhetoric and Reality") contend that the assumed favorable treatment of higher-status offenders has always been a myth. Further, to a large extent, the empirical studies focus on the status of the offenders rather than the nature of the offenses. Despite the fact that embedded in these data are revelations that certain offenses continue to be dealt with leniently and almost never result in prison sentences, the cumulative effect of this research has been to buttress the increasingly common refrain that we are witnessing a "crackdown on white collar crime."[6] The government reaction to thrift crime might, then, simply be part of a larger pattern of decreasing official tolerance for white-collar crime.

The second possible explanation for the vigorous response to thrift fraud is that the unprecedented epidemic of fraud has quite naturally required a corresponding, unprecedented response. There is, however, a common flaw in both of these explanations: The "crackdown" on white-collar crime is highly *selective*. While Congress, the Justice Department, and the thrift regulatory agencies take an aggressive approach to financial institution fraud, corporate and business crime in other sectors is virtually ignored. Further, the regulatory response to crime in these other sectors seems unrelated to the frequency or scale of the crimes involved. Since the Reagan administration began dismantling the Occupational Safety and Health Administration in the early 1980s (Calavita 1983), sanctions against employers who violate safety and health standards have plummeted. Despite the fact that hundreds of thousands of U.S. workers are killed and disabled annually from work-related accidents and illnesses, employers are rarely prosecuted criminally for safety and health violations. (The production of asbestos will result in 170,000 deaths from lung cancer and other related diseases; yet none of the corporate executives who deliberately concealed the dangers have been criminally charged.) The U.S. Food and Drug Administra-

---

6 Tillman and Pontell (1992) have recently contested this crackdown hypothesis. Presenting data on Medicaid provider fraud in California, they found that Medi-Cal offenders were less likely to be sentenced to prison than comparable street criminals, and conclude, "Our findings provide considerable support for the white-collar leniency thesis" (p. 423).

tion continues to be reluctant to recommend criminal prosecution of corporate executives who conceal the hazards of their products or deliberately fabricate data to attest to their safety (Coleman 1985:44–45). Indeed, if we focus on traditional forms of corporate crime in the manufacturing sector, there is no evidence of any crackdown. The point here is that if the aggressive response to thrift fraud were simply a reflection of a broader crackdown on white-collar crime or a straightforward response to the scale of thrift crime, then we would expect to see similar patterns in other sectors where regulatory violations are frequent and egregious. The laxity that characterizes much regulatory enforcement contrasts markedly with the aggressive response to thrift fraud, however, and suggests that the answer must lie elsewhere.

To understand the government response to thrift misconduct, particularly in conjunction with the lenient reaction to other regulatory violations, we need to examine the nature of the state itself and its relationship to the industrial and financial sectors it is charged with regulating.

A Structuralist Perspective on Regulatory Enforcement

Sociologists have long made a distinction between "social" regulations (such as occupational safety and health standards) which are aimed at controlling production processes, and "economic" regulations (such as insider trading restrictions) which regulate the market and stabilize the economy (Barnett 1981; Cranston 1982; Snider 1991; Stryker 1992; Yeager 1991). While the former protect workers and consumers against the excesses of capital—and tend to cut into profits—the latter regulate and stabilize the capital accumulation process and historically have been supported by affected industries.

This distinction is based on a structuralist approach to the state, which emphasizes the "objective relation" (Poulantzas 1969) between the state and capital (see also Althusser 1971; O'Connor 1973). This objective relation guarantees that the capitalist state will operate in the long-term interests of capitalists independent of their direct participation in the policymaking process or mobilization of resources. Central to this objective relation under capitalism, the state must promote capital accumulation since its own survival depends on tax revenues derived from successful profit-making activity, as well as the political stability that is contingent on economic growth. In addition, it must actively pursue "political integration" (Friedland et al. 1978), "legitimation" (O'Connor 1973), or "the cohesion of the social formation" (Poulantzas 1969) in the interest of political survival and the economic growth on which it depends. As O'Connor (1973) has pointed out in his seminal work on the capitalist state's fiscal crisis, the state's capital accumulation and legitimization functions are often mutually contradictory: efforts to promote and protect capital accumulation favor the capitalist class and may jeopardize the state's legitimacy by alienating the other classes who inevitably pay the price. From this perspective, state institutions must continually grapple with this contradiction and its various forms of fallout, which according to O'Connor is at the base of the state's "fiscal crisis."

In this structuralist rendition, the state enjoys "relative autonomy" in its efforts to realize these potentially contradictory functions. In direct contrast to the instrumentalist model espoused by Domhoff (1967, 1978) and others (Kolko 1963, 1965; Miliband 1969), structuralists argue that state managers are not captive to individual capitalist interests and indeed are capable of violating those interests in order to pursue the broader and more long-term interests of capital accumulation and political legitimacy. Nonetheless, its autonomy is "relative." While the state may be free from the manipulation of individual capitalists or even the business community as a whole, it is by no means autonomous from the structural requirements of the political economy within which it is embedded and which it must work to preserve (see Poulantzas 1969, 1973).

Most of the corporate crime literature that borrows from this structuralist perspective focuses on social—rather than economic—regulation. This literature addresses the generally lax enforcement of these regulations and ties that laxity to the capital accumulation function of the state and the perceived costs of interfering with profitable industry (Barnett 1979; Calavita 1983; Snider 1991; Yeager 1988). These scholars also note, however, that the legitimation mandate of the state periodically requires that it respond to political demands to shore up worker safety, reduce environmental hazards, or enforce labor standards. Thus, when there is a politically powerful working-class movement, or in the face of high public visibility of the social costs of nonenforcement, the state may mount correspondingly visible enforcement campaigns. The point is, however, that active enforcement of social regulation occurs primarily in response to public pressure and is usually short-lived, receding once political attention has shifted elsewhere and state legitimacy is no longer threatened. Whether the issue is occupational safety and health standards (Carson 1982; Walters 1985; Calavita 1986; Gunningham 1987; Tucker 1987), environmental regulation (Adler & Lord 1991; Barnett 1979, 1981; Yeager 1991), or U.S. Office of Surface Mining enforcement (Shover et al. 1986), empirical studies consistently confirm that social regulation ebbs and flows with public pressure; in the absence of such pressure and the related challenges to state legitimation, enforcement dwindles.[7]

In contrast, when the goal is economic regulation, the state tends to assume a more rigorous posture. Despite occasional protest from the individual capitalists at whom sanctions are directed, the state rather vigorously enforces regulations that stabilize the market and enhance economic viability. Unlike social regulations which are implemented primarily in response to on-again/off-again legitimation needs, economic regulations are integral to the capital accumulation process and are thus more consistently and urgently pursued (Barnett 1981; Snider 1991; Yeager 1991). While case studies are far fewer in this area, some excellent research has focused on the U.S. Securities and Exchange Commission (SEC). As Yeager (1986) and Shapiro (1984) have shown, while the SEC is by no means omnipotent in the face of its powerful Wall Street charges, nonetheless it rather routinely seeks criminal sanctions and stiff monetary fines for elite offenders.

Extensive comparative research documents this enforcement discrepancy. Clinard et al.'s (1979) comprehensive analysis of enforcement actions against the 582 largest corporations in the United States during 1975 and 1976 found a strong relationship between level of enforcement and type of violation. While over 96% of "manufacturing violations" (involving social regulations concerning such things as product safety and food and drug standards) were handled entirely at the administrative level, only 41.5% of "trade violations" (involving economic regulations controlling bid rigging and other unfair trade practices) were disposed of administratively. Further, while over 21% of trade violations were processed criminally, less than 1% of manufacturing violations were criminally processed, and *no* labor standard violations were prosecuted criminally. Clinard et al. (p. 147) conclude, "Corporate actions that directly harm the economy were more likely to receive the greater penalties, while those affecting consumer product quality were responded to with the least severe sanctions. Although over 85 percent of all sanctions were administrative in nature, those harming the economy were most likely to receive criminal penalties."

Surveying enforcement efforts across a variety of regulatory areas, Barnett (1981:17) similarly concludes that enforcement is directly correlated with whether the regulation in question pro-

---

[7] As Yeager (1991:28) points out, there may be cases in which social regulation and its enforcement are the product of "intraindustry competition" and the desire of some segments of capital to use regulations to enhance their own competitive edge. For example, Kolko (1963) demonstrates that the Meat Inspection Act of 1906 was spearheaded by large meatpackers to eliminate smaller companies that could not comply with the new social regulation of the industry. Far more common, however, is the scenario depicted above, in which social regulation is opposed by industry and enforced by the state primarily to further its legitimation needs.

tects or impedes capital accumulation. Regulations perceived as
"anticapital" received the least enforcement and those protecting
markets or economic stability elicited the most enforcement.

This empirical discrepancy in the enforcement of social and
economic regulations is consistent with the structuralist depiction of the state, and the concept of relative autonomy in particular. While social regulations potentially cut into profits and interfere with the capital accumulation process, the function of
economic regulations is to stabilize and shore up that process. In
pursuing this economic function, the state inevitably encounters
individual opposition and periodic attempts to neutralize enforcement, but overall its successes in this area dwarf its halting
efforts at social regulation.

In the next section, we draw from this structural analysis of
the state, and the distinction between social and economic regulation, to explain the vigorous response to thrift fraud by the late
1980s. As we will see, the pattern of that response confirms the
utility of these structuralist insights and seems to contradict competing models of public policy such as instrumentalism, plural-
ism, or public interest/consensus theory. Following this discussion, we turn to the limitations of a pure structuralist paradigm
for explaining the pattern of collusion and influence peddling
that characterized the early stages of the thrift crisis, then sketch
the outlines of a more synthetic approach to the state.

The Thrift Cleanup, Capital Accumulation, and Relative Autonomy

At first glance, the details of the crackdown on thrift fraud
seem to fit well with the structural model described above. Most
important, the law enforcement response is consistent with the
logic of the state's capital accumulation function and its relative
autonomy in realizing that function. For if we look at the pattern
of enforcement, we find that it varies with the degree to which
the fraud jeopardizes financial stability. It is noteworthy, for example, that priority is placed on financial institutions on the
verge of failure or already insolvent and in which fraud played a
significant role in the collapse.

The official definition of a "major case," or cases to which top
priority is assigned, refers to dollar losses, the role of insiders,
and the like (see note 3 above). Yet, government officials consistently specify another factor as among the most important ingredients: *whether the alleged fraud contributed to insolvency*. Ira
Raphaelson, at the time Special Counsel for Financial Fraud in
the Deputy Attorney General's Office, told a Senate subcommittee that cases are treated as "major" depending on dollar losses
and whether the fraud played a role in an institution's failure
(U.S. Senate 1992:10–11; emphasis added):

Senator Dixon: "How do you define a major case?"

Mr. Raphaelson: "If it involves an alleged loss of more than $100,000 or involves a failed institution."

Senator Dixon: "There are at least 4300 cases over $100,000?"

Mr. Raphaelson: "Or involving a failed institution, it might be less than $100,000. But *because it is linked to a failure, we still consider it a major case.*"

At the same hearing, Harold A. Valentine, Associate Director for General Government Programs of the U.S. General Accounting Office (U.S. Senate 1992:55), defined major cases as "those involving failed institutions or alleged losses of $100,000 or more." Referring to their prioritization of cases, as well as sentence severity, one FBI agent in Florida gave an example: "If you steal over $5 million and you make a bank fail, you've popped the bubble on the thermometer there!" (personal interview). The same Florida agent tied the influx of federal resources for financial fraud investigations to the economic importance of these cases. He explained that a few years ago:

We as financial crimes or financial institution fraud investigators were vying for manpower in this office along with [drugs and public corruption] squads. We had to share the white-collar crime staffing . . . with these people. *Now that we've had such dramatic increases in the number of failed institutions in the last year and a half, they're being investigated here and Congress has appropriated huge amounts of funds to target that.* (Emphasis added)

In addition to the "major case" specification, in June 1990 the Office of Thrift Supervision, the Resolution Trust Corporation, and the Federal Deposit Insurance Corporation developed a matrix with which to prioritize thrift fraud investigations and used the matrix to draw up a list of the "Top 100" thrift institutions to be investigated. Among the most important ingredients in this prioritization were the financial health of the institution, whether fraud had contributed to insolvency, and the economic effect on the larger community (personal interviews).

Enforcement statistics confirm these priorities. A General Accounting Office report (U.S. Senate 1992:8) reveals that of the approximately 1,000 major thrift cases under investigation in fiscal year 1991, *one-third* involved failed institutions, and the other two-thirds were for investigations of fraud that contributed to major losses. The Dallas Bank Fraud Task Force handles *only* failed financial institution fraud cases. Indeed, the task force was established in 1987 when it was brought to the attention of officials that 18 thrifts in the Dallas area were on the verge of collapse.

When alleged fraud does *not* result in demonstrable losses, no further investigation is pursued. In response to a query from Congress about criminal referrals made in connection with Silverado Savings and Loan, the Justice Department explained that one of the referrals in question was dropped: "This matter

involved no demonstrable loss; prosecution was declined in the
United States Attorney's Office, District of Colorado" (quoted in
U.S. House of Representatives 1990a:121).

The emphasis of the regulatory and law enforcement community is thus on fraud in failed, or failing, "problem" institutions in which the alleged fraud undermines the thrift's financial
health. This selective focus suggests that *the crackdown on financial
fraud represents less an effort to control crime per se than it is a desperate
effort to contain the damage in a fraud-ridden and ailing industry*.[8]
While crime in one financial institution might elicit relatively little concern, the epidemic of crime in the thrift industry in the
1980s threatened the survival of the industry itself and, indeed,
the stability of the whole financial system. The law enforcement
reaction was thus meant both to incapacitate the offenders and
as a deterrent to curb the epidemic of fraud. The unprecedented
crackdown on this form of white-collar crime conveyed the deterrent message that this fraud will be dealt with seriously; and defining fraud de facto as including only those activities that might
lead to insolvency highlights the "damage control" basis for this
crackdown. Together with the reregulation of thrifts under FIR-
REA, the aggressive prosecution of thousands of thrift offenders
was designed to stop the hemorrhage of public dollars and stabilize the industry.[9]

The General Accounting Office's Harold Valentine (U.S.
Senate 1992:19) called bank and thrift fraud and the financial
collapse to which they contributed "perhaps the most significant
financial crisis in this nation's history." The Justice Department
(1990:2) referred to it as "the unconscionable plundering of
America's financial institutions." A senior staff member of the
Senate Banking Committee explained the attention being given
to thrift fraud: "This industry is very close to the heart of the
American economy! We teetered on the edge of a major, major
problem here. . . . [W]e got a major problem, but we teetered on
the edge of a major collapse. . . . You know, all these [financial]
industries could bring down the whole economy" (personal interview).[10]

---

[8] A continuum of law enforcement motivations might be devised in which pure
"crime control" lies at one extreme and "damage control" at the other. Thus, victimless
crimes and statutory offenses are prosecuted to penalize the offender for having violated
the law: it is the *fact* of law violation in and of itself that is at issue in this kind of "crime
control." At the other extreme is "damage control," in which the primary motive for enforcement is to contain the effects of the violation. It follows that, as in the case of thrift
fraud prior to the 1980s, little response will be elicited in the absence of perceived effects
from the offense. Between these two extremes, there is considerable overlap and, it could
be argued, it is in this middle region that much day-to-day law enforcement lies.

[9] We are not suggesting here that an aggressive law enforcement response is the
most effective deterrent to fraud. (It might be argued that reversing the deregulation that
in the early 1980s set the stage for the fraud epidemic was the more potentially effective
deterrent strategy.) The point instead is to determine the motives for the crackdown.

[10] One official spoke of the "havoc ratio"—the amount of havoc that a given thrift
crime wreaks on the institution, the community, and the general economy. The reason

Bank and thrift fraud are of course not new. Investigators and regulators report that abuse by thrift insiders was frequent in the 1960s and 1970s but attracted little attention since the institutions were generally thriving (personal interview). One regulator who said that fraud has always existed in thrifts claimed that "[hot prices in real estate are] the only thing that pulled everybody's asses out for years" (personal interview). A staff member of the Senate Banking Committee explained it this way, "People basically bet on the come. If the market goes up, we all win. And if the market goes down, you begin to look back and see what corners were cut. But you don't look back if the market goes up" (personal interview). The current response to thrift fraud thus has less to do with punishing criminal activity per se than it does with preventing further damage to financial institutions that lie "close to the heart of the American economy."[11]

A number of studies have noted the role of regulatory agencies in minimizing uncertainty and risk and generally stabilizing the financial system. Shapiro's (1984) study of the Securities and Exchange Commission is exemplary. As Shapiro reports, SEC officials see their function as protecting the securities and exchange system rather than as its adversaries. Similarly, Reichman (1991) underlines the stabilizing effect of regulating risks in the stock market. Abolafia (1984) observes a similar dynamic in the commodities futures market, where regulations "structure anarchy." And Yeager (1986) draws attention to the fact that the Reagan administration, while virtually dismantling the worker safety and health system and eroding environmental protections, was relatively aggressive in pursuing insider trading and stock market fraud in an effort to restore confidence in the integrity of the market and encourage investment. As Snider (1991:224) explains, "Controlling this type of corporate crime turns out to be in the interests of the corporate sector overall, as well as being compatible with state objectives. Such laws protect the sanctity of the investment market, which is central to the ability of corporations to raise money by issuing shares."

The U.S. government's mission to salvage the thrift industry is consistent with this literature. And the mission is all the more

these crimes are so serious, she said, is that they have the potential to wreak havoc far beyond the millions that the offender actually steals. She explained, "Using a thrift to go on a shopping spree is a lot like a fellow who wants to rob a teller at a bank. . . . In order to get the $20,000 dollar cash drawer, he blows up the entire building" (personal interview).

11 It might be argued that the vigorous prosecution of thrift offenders has to do also with the fact that the "villains" are identifiable individuals, not corporations. This certainly makes prosecution and conviction easier. Nonetheless, it is also the case that in a number of notorious corporate crime scandals in the manufacturing sector—the great electrical company conspiracy comes to mind here—individual offenders have been identified as the responsible parties yet have received notoriously lenient treatment. The central ingredient here seems to be that in the thrift case, the institutions—and ultimately the industry—were victims, not beneficiaries, of the offenses.

urgent since this industry—and the capital it stands to lose—are government-insured. This, then, is an effort directed less at penalizing wrongdoers for their misdeeds than at limiting damage to the industry, preventing comparable damage in other financial sectors, and containing the hemorrhage of government-insured capital. An upper-echelon Washington official, when asked to comment on this interpretation, said simply, "You hit the nail right on the head" (personal interview).

The crackdown on thrift crime thus begins to make sense. As we have seen, savings and loan fraud is not new. What is new is the devastating effect it has had on the industry and the billions of dollars of government liability for losses. The need to contain the damage precipitated the unprecedented response and explains the priority accorded failed and failing institutions. So consistent is this pattern that the very criminality of an act is defined not only in terms of whether it violates the law but also in terms of the effect it has on an institution's financial health. Thus, a regulator explained that violations of bank statutes and agency regulations—such as misapplication of bank funds, violations of loan-to-one-borrower restrictions, and nominee loan schemes—are often treated by regulators as illegal *only* if they result in a loss for the institution. "If you're good for the money," he explained, referring to various types of loan fraud, "you're not defrauding the bank" (personal interview).

This pattern of the government response to thrift crime seems to confirm the utility of the structuralist model of the state, in particular, the notion of relative autonomy. Despite the vast resources available to these corporate offenders, an unprecedented campaign was launched to prosecute and penalize their frauds. Further, enforcement is focused on frauds that jeopardize the stability of the financial system. Thrift fraud was not taken seriously until it began to undermine one institution after another in the 1980s, and as we have seen, the current prosecutorial effort still aims only to curb fraud that causes demonstrable losses.

This pattern is inexplicable from a straightforward instrumentalist position, which would predict that these affluent offenders could shield themselves from prosecution and/or conviction by mobilizing their extensive resources. Neither is it explicable from a traditional interest group model, according to which public policy is the result of pressure from any of a plurality of special interests. The U.S. Savings and Loan League—the thrift industry's major association and during the 1980s one of the most successful lobbying groups in Washington—was certainly the most powerful political actor in this arena; yet it was incapable of derailing the Financial Institution Reform, Recovery, and Enforcement Act of 1989 and the enforcement campaign that it unleashed—a failure that triggered intense controversy and recriminations within the association (O'Connell 1992). Further, the *public's* knowledge of the scope of the thrift disaster was minimal before President Bush's announcement of the bailout and enforcement effort following the 1988 election. Media attention to the scandal quickly intensified, but only *after* the state response was well underway, suggesting that it was not public pressure that triggered the vigorous government reaction.[12] While this reaction is inexplicable from either an instrumentalist or an interest group model of public policy, it is consistent with the structuralist notion of the capital accumulation function of the state and its ability to sacrifice individual capitalists' interests to long-term economic survival.

Furthermore, these structuralist insights offer the only viable explanation for the pattern of the current crackdown on white-collar crime more generally. The increased intolerance of corporate crime noted by Katz (1980), Hagan (1985), and others is in fact a *selective* intolerance—directed at financial fraud and similar violations of economic regulations that undermine the stability and viability of the economic system. This intolerance of risky financial fraud, in combination with the absence of a corresponding response to traditional corporate crimes that violate social regulations, cannot be explained by instrumentalism or by any general theory of post-Watergate reformism. It is, however, precisely what structuralists would predict.

The Limitations of Structuralism

While the structural model of the state offers a viable explanation for the crackdown on thrift fraud beginning in the late 1980s, it contains notable empirical and theoretical limitations. Structuralists have been criticized for reifying structure and imbuing the state with the anthropomorphic ability to act, for depicting the state as monolithic, and for exaggerating its rationality (Block 1987; Chambliss & Seidman 1982; Skocpol & Finegold 1982; Calavita 1992).

At least as important here is a glaring empirical deficiency: The structural model by itself is unable to account for the early mishandling of the thrift crisis in the mid-1980s. In particular, it cannot explain the reluctance of many state actors to recognize widespread fraud in the S&L industry and to adopt a rigorous enforcement stance until the crisis was full blown. A close look at the way state managers responded—or failed to respond—to the

---

12 It has been consistently alleged that during the 1988 presidential campaign, both Michael Dukakis and George Bush deliberately avoided any discussion of the S&I. issue since both political parties shared responsibility for the disaster (Mayer 1990:260–61; Pilzer 1989:208–9; Waldman 1990:90). The dearth of news reports on the subject before the election is indeed striking, particularly in comparison to the rapid escalation of media attention beginning in 1989, suggesting that the candidates' strategy may have been successful in keeping the issue out of the public eye.

early stages of the thrift crisis reveals a state that is neither omniscient nor uniformly rational. Instead, it is comprised of real-life political actors with often disparate motives, whose various locations within the state expose them to conflicting demands and pressures. In this context, not only is relative autonomy historically and institutionally contingent but the structural imperatives of the state as guardian of the economic and political order may be fatally derailed.

An important dimension of the early response by state managers involved influence peddling by thrift owners and operators, particularly in the form of generous campaign contributions to key policymakers. Deregulation had expanded the opportunities for fraud at little risk, exacerbating the thrift crisis (see Calavita & Pontell 1990, 1991). Having set the stage for an epidemic of crime, policymakers were slow to limit the damage. The powerful and well-financed U.S. Savings and Loan League was a significant force behind the deregulation that provided the opportunities for fraud.[13] Financial pressure was then brought to bear by the operators of suspect institutions to avoid regulatory scrutiny and investigations of alleged fraud. A few examples will serve to clarify the mechanisms through which this pressure was exerted and its effect in temporarily shielding thrift offenders from prosecution.

Charles Keating, owner of Lincoln Savings and Loan in Irvine, California, contributed heavily to political candidates at the state and federal levels and to both political parties. In early 1987 Lincoln was investigated by the Federal Home Loan Bank (FHLB, the thrift regulatory agency at the time) in San Francisco for poor underwriting of loans and investment irregularities. In April 1987 Senator DeConcini called the chair of the Federal Home Loan Bank Board (FHLBB) in Washington, Ed Gray, to a now-infamous meeting in his office. Attending the meeting were Senators McCain, Glenn, and Cranston, all of whom had received hefty campaign contributions from Keating. The San Francisco regulators were soon summoned to another meeting with the senators, this time joined by Senator Riegle, who was to become chair of the Senate Banking Committee and who also had received generous donations from Keating. At this meeting, the senators—now known as the "Keating 5"—tried to persuade

---

13 Representative Fernand St Germain, Chair of the House Banking Committee at the time, spearheaded the 1980 increase in deposit insurance and sponsored the Garn–St Germain Act of 1982, which effectively deregulated the thrift industry. He was a major and frequent recipient of U.S. League of Savings and Loan largesse during this period. The Justice Department investigated connections between St Germain and the thrift lobby and concluded that there was "substantial evidence of serious and sustained misconduct" by St Germain in his relationship with the League. A House Ethics Committee came to the same conclusion. However, no formal prosecution was initiated, and in 1988 St Germain was voted out of office. He is currently a lobbyist for the thrift industry in Washington, DC (Jackson 1988; Pizzo et al. 1989).

the regulators of the financial health of Lincoln and the absence of any "smoking gun" to prove misconduct.[14] Later that summer, Ed Gray was replaced by M. Danny Wall as chair of the FHLBB, and the investigation of Lincoln was moved to Washington, DC, out of the hands of the "hostile" San Francisco regulators. Lincoln was not closed until two years later, a delay that cost the government an estimated $2 billion.

The Keating case is by far the most widely publicized instance of political influence peddling to stave off scrutiny of thrift fraud, but it is only part of a larger pattern. The connections between former House Speaker Jim Wright, Representative Tony Coelho, and thrift executives—detailed in the report of the Special Counsel in the House Ethics Committee investigation of Wright—are exemplary of this pattern (U.S. House of Representatives 1989). Such ties between key policymakers and the thrift industry were replicated throughout the country, most notably in California, Texas, Arkansas, and Florida, where thrift failures proliferated and losses soared.[15] One senior official in Florida reported that *all* the Florida thrifts that managed to stay open after insolvency did so with the help of their owners' and operators' well-placed political connections (personal interview). Pointing out that the relationship between massive campaign contributions and political intervention was not just a matter of elected officials watching out for their constituents, a senior regulator put it this way:

> It was always the worst S&Ls in America that were able to get dramatically more political intervention. The good guys could never get political muscle like this. Some of it makes sense, of course, because you have a bigger incentive [to make contributions] if you are a sleaze. . . . If you know you are engaged in fraud, what better return is there than a political contribution? (Personal interview)

The political patrons of thrift offenders were regularly confronted with evidence of their clients' misdeeds. During the two-hour meeting between San Francisco regulators and the Keating 5, regulators repeatedly explained the irregularities at Lincoln. Michael Patriarca, senior regulator with the San Francisco FHLB, finally told the group of resistant senators, "I've never seen any bank or S&L that's anything like this. . . . They . . . violate the law and regulations and common sense" (Pizzo et al. 1989:293). Several months later, the San Francisco regulators were barred from any further dealings with Lincoln.

---

[14] Field notes of meeting taken by William Black, San Francisco FHLB representative in attendance, reproduced in Pizzo et al. 1989:392–404.

[15] Senator David Pryor of Arkansas, a state with a per capita thrift failure rate among the highest in the country, put a hold on the FSLIC recapitalization bill in the Senate, informing Ed Gray that unless he "correct[ed] the abuses which have been taking place in Arkansas" (meaning regulatory activity, not savings and loan fraud), the bill would remain on hold (letter quoted in Mayer 1990:232).

In other instances, members of Congress actively chose not to hear evidence of wrongdoing. One regulator told of a meeting with House Speaker Jim Wright regarding Vernon Savings and Loan in Texas. As he remembers the meeting, "I got involved in attempting to defend the agency [the FHLB, in its actions against Vernon], and the Speaker went ballistic and started yelling. Thereafter . . . the Speaker's aides sought to get me fired" (personal interview). The same regulator was, without explanation, "disinvited" to testify before St Germain's House Banking Committee in 1987 on the subject of crime in the S&L industry. Having submitted his formal testimony 24 hours in advance as required, the regulator was met by House aides as he attempted to enter the hearing room and was bluntly told that his testimony was no longer needed (personal interviews).

A number of important points are clear from this brief look at the early stages of the thrift crisis. First, key policymakers were responsive to the demands of those with the resources to exert influence through the financing of electoral campaigns. This influence limited the ability of the state to react effectively to early warnings of a fraud epidemic and increased the scale of the debacle. The record of political access by individual executives at the expense of overall economic viability seems to contradict the structuralist depiction of the state as relatively autonomous and driven by the singular motive of preserving the economic order. Instead, it is more compatible with instrumentalist notions of a direct link between economic resources and political access and the reluctance of the state elite to take action that violates the interests of their benefactors.

Second, however, the specific *pattern* of influence peddling and the persistent and sometimes vitriolic struggle between members of Congress and regulators, together with the crackdown on thrift crime beginning in 1989, suggest a reality that is more complex than either the instrumentalist or structuralist models can account for by themselves. While the structural need to shore up financial stability precipitated the vigorous response to thrift crime, the clash in the mid-1980s between regulators and Congress (and, according to personal interviews, members of the White House staff as well) debunks the notion of a uniform state purpose. In addition, it suggests that relative autonomy is not necessarily a quality of the state as a whole but varies across the institutions that together compose the state, much as state-centered theorists Skocpol and Finegold (1982), Hooks (1990), and others (Krasner 1984; Rueschemeyer & Evans 1985) have maintained. Members of Congress, whose political careers depend on a steady influx of campaign funds, may be particularly susceptible to the demands of those with the resources to make large campaign contributions. Career civil servants in regulatory agencies, while certainly not immune to political pressures and financial temptation,[16] may for structural reasons be less susceptible to such pressures and periodically may take a more rigorous enforcement approach. Thus, not only does the record of the early response to thrift fraud reveal a state in which cooptation by private interests *exacerbated* the financial crisis, but also the struggle between politicians and regulators highlights the fragmentation of the state and the variable and contingent nature of state autonomy.

This account of the evolution of the thrift crisis suggests the need for a synthetic model of state action. As we have seen, while the state periodically is capable of concerted action in the interest of financial stability and to shore up government-insured capital, the real-life political actors who make up the state have their own political and career interests and are susceptible to a variety of external influences. The result is a shifting pattern of policies that reflect in varying degrees both individual influence and structural imperatives, capture, and autonomy.

Block (1987) is one of the few to attempt such a synthetic model, and his work may be of use here. Block (p. 84) starts from the premise that "state managers collectively are self-interested maximizers, interested in maximizing their power, prestige, and wealth." These state managers enjoy some autonomy and are capable of restricting the activities of even the dominant classes. This ability derives from the fact that the dominant classes are dependent on the state for a variety of essential services, including checking through regulation the excesses intrinsic to the capitalist economy.

While Block notes that the career and institutional interests of state managers are the immediate cause of policy outcomes, those interests are in turn linked to the "capitalist context." In describing this context, he notes both the structural dependence of the state on economic growth and the economic elite's ability to buy influence over policymakers and control the media, thereby integrating structuralist and instrumentalist approaches. He makes an important contribution to state theory, locating human agency between the structure of capitalism and individual

---

16 A vast literature documents the phenomenon of "captured" regulatory agencies (Lowi 1969; Cranston 1982; Snider 1991). The record of thrift regulation reveals several instances of regulator collusion with the thrift industry. For example, when the owner of Centennial Savings and Loan in Santa Rosa, CA, was questioned by examiners about his extravagant parties, excessive compensation and bonuses, and multiple land flips, he hired the deputy commissioner of the California Department of Savings and Loans, making him an executive vice-president and doubling his $40,000-a-year state salary. Similarly, Don Dixon at Vernon hired two senior officials from the Texas Savings and Loan Department in an effort to ward off investigation (personal interviews). Political appointee M. Danny Wall, Ed Gray's successor as head of FHLBB, had close connections to friends of the thrift industry in Congress and was largely responsible for postponing the closing down of Lincoln (personal interview). What is important here, however, is that over time thrift regulators seem to have been less compromised by thrift industry influence than Congress and more willing to take a rigorous regulatory stance.

policy outcomes, thus providing the missing causal link in the potentially teleological argument of structuralists.

What Block's synthetic approach fails to highlight is the *contradiction* between the structural function of state managers as guardians of economic and political stability and their simultaneous susceptibility to instrumental influence by economic elites that threatens to disrupt and occasionally—as in the S&L case—derail the collective endeavor. The way this contradiction is played out depends in part on the relative susceptibility of such instrumental influences through history and across state agencies. As we have seen here, thrift regulators in the mid-1980s seem to have experienced greater autonomy from the S&L industry than did Congress. In this context, the contradiction between structural imperatives and instrumental influences was manifest in the form of intrastate conflict, as regulators and Congress locked horns over regulatory enforcement.

To account for the intricacies of this case—and to advance state theory more generally—we need an inclusive and multifaceted approach, one that matches rather than conceals the complex face of empirical reality. Such an approach would at a minimum incorporate insights from the structuralist and instrumentalist traditions. It would perhaps start from a structuralist base, placing at the center of analysis structural imperatives and the objective relation between the state and capital. At the same time, however, it would recognize the very real instrumental economic influences on state actors and the ways in which they jeopardize structural imperatives.

Our study documents the limited utility of specific instrumentalist and structuralist concepts and has begun to sketch out in general terms the contours of a synthetic approach. While a single case study can reveal the limitations of prevailing models—and perhaps underscore their insights—it will take a collective, cumulative effort to construct adequate alternatives. This much is clear: If our models are to reflect the complexity of political reality, they must incorporate rather than exclude, integrate rather than draw boundaries.

Conclusion

We have argued here that the aggressive reaction to thrift fraud in the late 1980s is not indicative of a general crackdown on corporate crime, recently postulated by some white-collar crime scholars. The timing of the response, the almost exclusive focus on fraud that leads to institutional insolvency, and the selective nature of the crackdown—targeting financial fraud while virtually ignoring traditional corporate crime in the manufacturing sector—all suggest that it is not an increased intolerance of white-collar crime that motivates the reaction but a concern with economic stability.

To understand this government response, we draw on a number of concepts from the state theory literature. We demonstrate that a structural theory of the state provides the only viable explanation for the aggressive reaction to thrift fraud by the late 1980s. Nonetheless, the structuralist model, by itself, is inadequate to account for the mishandling of the early stages of the crisis. As we have seen, access to the levers of state power available to thrift executives with virtually unlimited funds provided by their savings and loan "money machines" initially shielded them from detection and sanctioning, in a scenario consistent with the instrumentalist model of the state and much of the corporate crime literature. This instrumentalist dynamic was in large part responsible for the reluctance of Congress and other key policymakers in the mid-1980s to recognize the scope of thrift fraud. But by the end of the decade, with the thrift industry decimated, the federal insurance agency bankrupt, the government tab mounting, and fears that other financial and economic sectors might be next, state managers launched an unparalleled, if belated, effort to contain the fraud and curb the damage.

This analysis highlights the importance of de-reifying the state, which is often presented in structuralist accounts as monolithic and displaying an anthropomorphic ability to act. In so doing, it has become clear that the political actors and agencies that make up the state neither act from a singular motive nor always act rationally to preserve the economic order. Indeed, in the early stages of the thrift crisis, state policy was in conspicuous disarray, with political actors in various institutional locations holding fast to their own particular agendas—agendas that in some cases substantially exacerbated the crisis. Thus, in unpacking the state, we see that both instrumentalists and structuralists oversimplify reality. Specifically, the relative autonomy of state agencies and their ability to deal rigorously with elite offenders is both historically and institutionally variable.

Such "state-centered" theorists as Skocpol and Finegold (1982), Hooks (1990), and others have already noted that state autonomy varies, with some state agencies being remarkably strong and capable of enforcing their own agendas, while others are relatively weak and pliable. What the savings and loan case illustrates is that an active struggle may ensue between those with instrumental connections to external interests and those in the state who are more insulated from those interests and may be in a better position to pursue collective goals. While in this case, members of Congress in the mid-1980s acted to neutralize regulators in the interest of their affluent benefactors, the battle lines are likely to shift with various issues and over time. Indeed, on some issues and in some contexts, it may be that regulatory agencies are more susceptible to "capture" than is Congress, although the latter's reliance on significant infusions of cash from affluent interests may predispose it to instrumental behavior.

Just as it is important to reexamine the monolithic concept of the state, the concept of corporate crime must be unpacked if we are to understand the pattern of the state's response to corporate offenders. To explain the current response to thrift fraud, side by side with the official tolerance for other corporate offenses, an important distinction was made here. White-collar crime research generally defines corporate crime as crime committed by corporate offenders *on behalf of the organization;* but thrift fraud *undermines* the financial viability of the institution and ultimately the industry itself. Thus, it is important to distinguish between traditional corporate crimes in the manufacturing sector that enhance profits at workers' or consumers' expense, and financial fraud that enriches individuals at the expense of the economic system. The state is likely to tolerate the former, taking action primarily in response to grassroots political demands and to shore up its own legitimacy, while treating the latter with more urgency.

The current response to thrift fraud makes sense within this context. As we have seen, the way the state punishes corporate offenders depends on the nature of the relationship between the state and capital at various points in time and across agencies, and the way the offenses in question jeopardize that relationship or undermine the economic process around which the relationship revolves. In attempting to explain the crackdown on financial fraud, we thus bring together two traditions that have remained relatively distinct—state theory and white-collar crime research. It is hoped that the analysis will contribute not just to a better understanding of the government response to white-collar crime but to a more integrated and empirically grounded approach to the state.

References

Abolafia, Mitchel Y. (1984) "Structured Anarchy: Formal Organization in the Commodities Futures Markets," in P. Adler & P. Adler, eds., *The Social Dynamics of Financial Markets*. Greenwich, CT: JAI Press.

Adler, Robert W., & Charles Lord (1991) "Environmental Crimes: Raising the Stakes," 59 *George Washington Law Rev.* 781.

Althusser, Louis (1971) *Lenin and Philosophy and Other Essays*. New York: Monthly Review Press.

Barnett, Harold (1979) "Wealth, Crime, and Capital Accumulation," 3 *Contemporary Crises* 171.

—— (1981) "Corporate Capitalism, Corporate Crime," 27 *Crime & Delinquency* 4 (Jan.).

—— (1982) "The Production of Corporate Crime in Corporate Capitalism," in P. Wickham & T. Dailey, eds., *White Collar and Economic Crime*. Lexington, MA: Lexington Books.

Berman, Daniel M. (1978) *Death on the Job: Occupational Health and Safety Struggles in the United States*. New York: Monthly Review Press.

Block, Fred (1987) *Revising State Theory: Essays in Politics and Postindustrialism*. Philadelphia: Temple Univ. Press.

Braithwaite, John, & Gilbert Geis (1982) "On Theory and Action for Corporate Crime Control," 28 *Crime & Delinquency* 292.

Calavita, Kitty (1983) "The Demise of the Occupational Safety and Health Administration: A Case Study in Symbolic Action," 30 *Social Problems* 437.

——— (1986) "Worker Safety, Law, and Social Change: The Italian Case," 20 *Law & Society Rev.* 189.

——— (1992) *Inside the State: The Bracero Program, Immigration, and the INS*. New York: Routledge, Chapman & Hall.

Calavita, Kitty, & Henry N. Pontell (1990) "'Heads I Win, Tails You Lose': Deregulation, Crime, and Crisis in the Savings and Loan Industry," 36 *Crime & Delinquency* 309.

——— (1991) "'Other People's Money' Revisited: Collective Embezzlement in the Savings and Loan and Insurance Industries," 38 *Social Problems* 94.

Carson, W. G. (1970) "White Collar Crime and the Enforcement of Factory Legislation," 10 *British J. of Criminology* 383.

——— (1982) "Legal Control of Safety on British Offshore Oil Installations," in P. Wickham & T. Dailey, eds., *White Collar and Economic Crime*. Lexington, MA: Lexington Books.

Chambliss, William J., & Robert Seidman (1982) *Law, Order, and Power*. Reading, MA: Addison-Wesley Publishing Co.

Clinard, Marsall B., & Richard Quinney (1973) *Criminal Behavior Systems*. 2d ed. New York: Holt, Rinehart & Winston.

Clinard, Marshall B., & Peter Yeager (1980) *Corporate Crime*. New York: Free Press.

Clinard, Marshall B., Peter C. Yeager, Jeanne Brissette, David Petrashek, & Elizabeth Harries (1979) *Illegal Corporate Behavior*. Washington, DC: National Institute of Law Enforcement & Criminal Justice, Department of Justice.

Coleman, James W. (1985) *The Criminal Elite: The Sociology of White Collar Crime*. New York: St. Martin's Press.

Cranston, R. (1982) "Regulation and Deregulation: General Issues," 5 *Univ. of New South Wales Law J.* 1.

Domhoff, G. William (1967) *Who Rules America?* Englewood Cliffs, NJ: Prentice-Hall.

——— (1978) *The Powers That Be*. New York: Random House.

Dowie, Mark (1979) "Pinto Madness," in J. Skolnick & E. Currie, eds., *Crisis in American Institutions*. 4th ed. Boston: Little, Brown.

Ermann, M. David., & Richard J. Lundman (1978) *Corporate and Governmental Deviance: Problems of Organizational Behavior in Contemporary Society*. New York: Oxford Univ. Press.

——— (1982) *Corporate Deviance*. New York: Holt, Rinehart & Winston.

Friedland, Roger, Frances Fox Piven, & Robert R. Alford (1978) "Political Conflict, Urban Structure, and the Fiscal Crisis," in D. Ashford, ed., *Comparing Public Policies: New Concepts and Methods*. Beverly Hills, CA: Sage Publications.

Geis, Gilbert (1967) "White Collar Crime: The Heavy Electrical Equipment Antitrust Cases of 1961," in M. Clinard & R. Quinney, *Criminal Behavior Systems: A Typology*. New York: Holt, Rinehart, & Winston.

——— (1991) "The Case Study Method in Sociological Criminology," in J. R. Feagin, A. M. Orum, & G. Sjoberg, eds., *A Case for the Case Study*. Chapel Hill: Univ. of North Carolina Press.

——— (1992) "White-Collar Crime: What Is It?" in K. Schlegel & D. Weisburd, *White Collar Crime Reconsidered*. Boston: Northeast University Press.

Prosecution in Common Law Jurisdictions

322   The State and White-Collar Crime

Gunningham, Neil (1974) *Pollution, Social Interest and the Law*. London: M. Robertson.

—— (1987) "Negotiated Non-Compliance: A Case Study of Regulatory Failure," 9 *Law & Policy* 69.

Hagan, John (1985) *Modern Criminology: Crime, Criminal Behavior, and Its Control*. New York: McGraw-Hill Book Co.

Hagan, John L., & Ilene H. Nagel (1982) "White-Collar Crime, White-Collar Time: The Sentencing of White-Collar Offenders in the Southern District of New York," 20 *American Criminal Law Rev.* 259.

Hagan, John, & Alberto Palloni (1983) "The Sentencing of White Collar Offenders before and after Watergate." Presented at American Sociological Association annual meeting, Detroit.

Hooks, Gregory (1990) "From an Autonomous to a Captured State Agency: The Decline of the New Deal in Agriculture," 55 *American Sociological Rev.* 29.

Jackson, Brooks (1988) *Honest Graft: Big Money and the American Political Process*. New York: Alfred A. Knopf.

Katz, Jack (1980) "The Social Movement against White-Collar Crime," 2 *Criminology Rev. Yearbook* 161.

Kolko, Gabriel (1963) *The Triumph of Conservatism*. New York: Free Press.

—— (1965) *Railroads and Regulations, 1877–1916*. Princeton, NJ: Princeton Univ. Press.

Krasner, Stephen D. (1984) "Approaches to the State: Alternative Conceptions and Historical Dynamics," 16 *Comparative Politics* 223.

Levi, Michael (1984) "Giving Creditors the Business: The Criminal Law in Inaction," 12 *International J. of the Sociology of Law* 321.

Lowi, Theodore J. (1969) *The End of Liberalism*. New York: W. W. Norton.

Mayer, Martin (1990) *The Greatest Ever Bank Robbery: The Collapse of the Savings and Loan Industry*. New York: Charles Scribners' Sons.

Miliband, Ralph (1969) *The State in Capitalist Society*. London: Weidenfield & Nicolson.

O'Connell, William B. (1992) *America's Money Trauma: How Washington Blunders Crippled the U.S. Financial System*. Winnetka, IL: Conversation Press.

O'Connor, James (1973) *The Fiscal Crisis of the State*. New York: St. Martin's Press.

Pearce, Frank, & S. Tombs (1988) "Regulating Corporate Crime: The Case of Health and Safety." Presented at American Society of Criminology annual meeting, Chicago.

Pilzer, Paul Zane (1989) *Other People's Money: The Inside Story of the S&L Mess*. New York: Simon & Schuster.

Pizzo, Stephen, Mary Fricker, & Paul Muolo (1989) *Inside Job: The Looting of America's Savings and Loans*. New York: McGraw-Hill Publishing Co.

Poulantzas, Nicos (1969) "The Problem of the Capitalist State," 58 *New Left Rev.* 67.

—— (1973) *Political Power and Social Classes*, trans. T. O'Ryan. London: New Left Books.

Reichman, Nancy (1991) "Regulating Risky Business: Dilemmas in Security Regulation," 13 *Law & Policy* 263.

Rueschemeyer, Dietrich, & Peter B. Evans (1985) "The State and Economic Transformation: Toward an Analysis of the Conditions Underlying Effective Intervention," in P. Evans, D. Rueschemeyer, & T. Skocpol, eds., *Bringing the State Back in*. New York: Cambridge Univ. Press.

Schrager, Laura Shill, & James F. Short, Jr. (1978) "Toward a Sociology of Organizational Crime," 25 *Social Problems* 407.

Shapiro, Susan (1980) *Thinking about White-Collar Crime: Matters of Conceptualization and Research*. Washington, DC: National Institute of Justice.

—— (1984) *Wayward Capitalist: Target of the Securities and Exchange Commission*. New Haven, CT: Yale Univ. Press.

Shover, Neal, Donald A. Clelland, & John Lynxwiler (1986) *Enforcement or Negotiation: Constructing a Regulatory Bureaucracy.* Albany: State Univ. of New York Press.

Skocpol, Theda, & Kenneth Finegold (1982) "State Capacity and Economic Intervention in the Early New Deal," 97 *Political Science Q.* 255.

Snider, Laureen (1978) "Corporate Crime and Canada: A Preliminary Report," 20 *Canadian J. of Criminology* 142.

―――― (1991) "The Regulatory Dance: Understanding Reform Processes in Corporate Crime," 19 *International J. of the Sociology of Law* 209.

Stryker, Robin (1992) "Government Regulation," in E. F. Borgatta & M. L. Borgatta, eds., 2 *Encyclopedia of Sociology.* New York: Macmillan Publishing Co.

Sutherland, Edwin H. (1949) *White Collar Crime.* New York: Dryden.

Tillman, Robert, & Henry N. Pontell (1992) "Is Justice 'Collar-Blind'? Punishing Medicaid Provider Fraud," 30 *Criminology* 547.

Tucker, Eric (1987) "Making the Workplace 'Safe' in Capitalism: The Enforcement of Factory Legislation in Nineteenth Century Ontario." Presented at Canadian Law & Society Association annual meeting, Hamilton, ON, 3–6 June.

U.S. Department of Justice (1990) *Attacking Savings and Loan Institution Fraud.* Report to the President. Washington, DC: U.S. Department of Justice.

―――― (1992a) *Attacking Financial Institution Fraud, Fiscal Year 1992 (First Quarterly Report).* Washington, DC: U.S. Department of Justice.

―――― (1992b) *Attacking Financial Institution Fraud, Fiscal Year 1992, Second Quarterly Report.* Washington, DC: U.S. Department of Justice.

U.S. House of Representatives (1987) *Adequacy of Federal Efforts to Combat Fraud, Abuse, and Misconduct in Federally Insured Financial Institutions.* Hearings before the Committee on Government Operations, Subcommittee on Commerce, Consumer, & Monetary Affairs, 19 Nov. 1987. 100th Cong., 1st sess.

―――― (1988) *Combatting Fraud, Abuse, and Misconduct in the Nation's Financial Institutions: Current Federal Efforts Are Inadequate.* House Report No. 100-1088, Committee on Government Operations. 100th Cong., 2d sess.

―――― (1989) *Report of the Special Outside Counsel in the Matter of Speaker James C. Wright, Jr.* Committee on Standards of Official Conduct. Washington, DC: GPO.

―――― (1990a) *When Are the Savings and Loan Crooks Going to Jail?* Hearing before the Subcommittee on Financial Institutions Supervision, Regulation & Insurance of the Committee on Banking, Finance & Urban Affairs, 28 June 1990. 101st Cong., 2d sess.

―――― (1990b) "Effectiveness of Law Enforcement against Financial Crime." Field Hearing before the Committee on Banking, Finance & Urban Affairs, Dallas, TX, 11 April 1990. 101st Cong., 2d sess.

U.S. Senate (1992) *Efforts to Combat Criminal Financial Institution Fraud.* Hearing before the Subcommittee on Consumer & Regulatory Affairs, Committee on Banking, Housing, & Urban Affairs, 6 Feb. 1992.

Waldman, Michael (1990) *Who Robbed America: A Citizen's Guide to the S&L Scandal.* New York: Random House.

Walters, Vivienne (1985) "The Politics of Occupational Health and Safety: Interviews with Workers' Health and Safety Representatives and Company Doctors," 22 *Canadian Rev. of Sociology & Anthropology* 97.

Wheeler, Stanton, & Mitchell Lewis Rothman (1982) "The Organization as Weapon in White-Collar Crime," 80 *Michigan Law Rev.* 1403.

Wheeler, Stanton, David Weisburd, & Nancy Bode (1982) "Sentencing the White-Collar Offender: Rhetoric and Reality," 47 *American Sociological Rev.* 641.

Yeager, Peter (1986) "Managing Obstacles to Studying Corporate Offences: An Optimistic Assessment." Presented at 1986 American Society of Criminology annual meetings, Atlanta.
—— (1988) "The Limits of Law: State Regulation of Private Enterprise." Presented at the 1988 American Society of Criminology annual meetings, Chicago.
—— (1991) *The Limits of Law: The Public Regulation of Private Pollution.* Cambridge: Cambridge Univ. Press.

Statutes Cited

Comprehensive Thrift and Bank Fraud Prosecution and Taxpayer Recovery Act of 1990.
Financial Institutions Reform, Recovery and Enforcement Act of 1989 (FIRREA).

[19]

Fiddling tax and benefits: inculpating the poor, exculpating the rich

Dee Cook

Introduction

The relationships between lawbreaking, wealth, poverty and culpability will be explored here by analysing judicial responses to the 'poor' who defraud the state by fiddling supplementary benefit (now income support)[1] and the relatively 'rich' who defraud the state by evading income tax.[2] The essence of these two forms of economic crime is very similar: making false statements to a government department – Inland Revenue or Department of Social Security (DSS) – to achieve illegal financial gain from the public purse. But the economic and social attributes of the typical offender are very different and this may, initially, seem to confirm the old adage that there is 'one law for the rich and another for the poor'.

Income inequality in itself is not, however, the *sole* factor determining the punishment of tax and benefit fraudsters. 'Taxpayers' and benefit 'claimants'. are categories which have been produced by particular histories, and historical discourses have made it possible to attribute entirely different motives to those who fiddle personal tax and those who fiddle social security payments. The comparative analysis which follows will, therefore, start by examining the origins of the contradictory discourses within which it is possible successfully to justify the crimes of those who fiddle taxes, and at the same time denounce the crimes of those who fiddle welfare benefits. It will be argued that such discourses still influence Inland Revenue and DSS policies on the regulation and prosecution of fraud, and are still reproduced in the sentences meted out by the courts. Consequently the ideological construction of 'taxpayer' and 'claimant' both informs and reproduces the unequal and inconsistent sentencing rationales which result in the rich and the poor 'paying' for their economic crimes by very different means.

The 'idle poor'

Historically the poor have been portrayed as idle, feckless and culpable:

> What encouragement have the poor to be industrious and frugal when
> they know for certain that should they increase their store it will be
> devoured by the drones, or what cause have they to fear when they are
> assured, that if by their indolence and extravagance, their drunkenness
> and vices, they shall be reduced to want, they shall be abundantly
> supplied?
>
> (Revd J. Townsend (1786) quoted in Fraser, 1973: 35)

This image, coupled with a powerful invocation of work-incentives, is also
evident in the assumption behind the 1834 Poor Law that 'every penny
bestowed that tends to render the condition of the pauper more eligible than
that of the independent worker, is a bounty on indolence and vice' (ibid.).
The discipline of the workhouse put into practice the Poor Law principles of
less eligibility and effort incentives, as they were designed to deter the
'undeserving' (the able-bodied unemployed) from entering and, hence, from
claiming poor relief.

History certainly repeats itself: these vocabularies and images are still
associated with the 'undeserving poor' in the later twentieth century. For
instance, in 1971 Conservative MP Rhodes Boyson wrote that the cosseting
welfare state made claimants like 'broiler hens' (rather than 'drones'), and he
continued,

> No one cares, no one bothers – why should they when the state spends
> all its energies taking money from the energetic, successful and thrifty
> to give to the idle, the failures and the feckless?
>
> (Boyson, 1971)

In the late 1980s such vocabularies and quasi-explanations for poverty and
economic dependence have become fused in the composite image of the
'benefit culture'. But the essential themes of idleness, fecklessness, culpability
and lack of work-incentives remain unchanged in two centuries. Moreover,
it is a short step, by implication or by design, to encompass 'fraud and abuse'
within the definition of the benefit culture itself and so effectively to link
claiming benefit with *scrounging* (undeservingly or fraudulently) from the
state. For instance, speaking at the 1988 Conservative party conference,
Social Security Secretary John Moore asked:

> It is right that an able-bodied adult can draw unemployment benefit
> simply by signing on once a fortnight without making any real effort to
> find work?

He went on to promise additional measures to ensure yet stricter availability-

Fiddling tax and benefits: inculpating the poor, exculpating the rich   111

for-work testing and announced that in 1988 £250 million had (allegedly) been 'saved' through the investigation of 'people cheating the benefit system' (*Guardian*, 13 October 1988). In a similar vein the Employment Secretary Norman Fowler warned, 'I give notice that we are not prepared to see taxpayers' money being used to finance the fraudulent'. But what of the great British taxpayers, in whose name the poor are so rigorously policed? As will be argued below, they are also on the fiddle, but are likely to be defrauding the state of far more revenue than are the 'idle poor', and receiving minimal sanction for so doing (Cook, 1989).

The hard-pressed taxpayer

Disraeli's comment that there were only two inevitabilities in life – death and taxation – illustrates a traditional British hatred of paying personal tax. Thus the image of taxation as a 'harsh inquisitorial system', coercing and interrogating taxpayers and demanding information, dominates the traditional 'old' view of tax (Sabine, 1966). A 'new' view which saw progressively graduated taxation, designed to serve public welfare, emerged in Lloyd George's 'People's Budget' and in post-1945 attitudes to social and economic reconstruction (ibid). But the old view of tax as an 'intolerable inquisition' remains ideologically powerful and sustains the image of the taxpayer as a victim of draconian state regulation:

> Taxation has no merit in itself. It is but a necessary evil and should be limited to the lowest level possible.
> (Boyson, 1978: 135)

> People trying to make a go of things get hounded by the taxman . . . the Inland Revenue is bashing the little man.
> (*The Times*, 22 June 1985)

These views on taxation inform the vocabularies of motive of those who fiddle their taxes and, when allied to criticisms of the progressive role of taxation, such views may justify illegal evasion in terms of a 'backdoor' tax revolt against the (mis)use of tax*payers*' money for subsidising 'tax-*consumers*' (Burton, 1985: 75). Tax avoidance and evasion can thus be constituted as 'heartening' evidence that the rich can save their wealth from their 'rapacious fellow citizens' (Shenfield, 1968: 26). Clearly such attitudes represent non-compliance to the letter and spirit of the tax laws as strategies for the accumulation of personal wealth. In essence this 'sporting' view of taxation depends on the assumption that 'There are *no* ethics in taxation. There is no moral law in taxation' (Houghton, 1977: 60). Yet issues of morality, culpability and criminality are uppermost when the poor use similar strategies to increase their incomes.

The hard-pressed taxpayer is ideologically constructed as a double victim: a victim of the state bureaucracy of taxation, and victim of the idle poor who are subsidized at the taxpayer's expense. Popular discourses about taxation therefore invariably impinge on issues concerning welfare provision, and so the imagery of the 'benefit culture' does surface in public rhetoric about tax. But it is the image and rhetoric of the 'enterprise culture' which currently dominates tax talk. The 'go-getting' society envisaged and promoted by the New Right demands low taxes, effort-incentives, high rewards, and the 'spur of poverty' for those who fail (Loney, 1986). Rates of tax adjudged to be 'high' are thus anathema to the enterprise culture, and the evasion of such taxes may be represented as in accordance with the spirit of 'enterprise'. Commenting on the growth of the illegal (and tax-free) hidden economy, Mrs Thatcher stated that it was 'big, flourishing, thriving' and meant that 'The enterprise is still there'. (ITV *Weekend World*, 17 November 1985). But when enterprise involves benefit claimants working 'on the side', both the individual's motivations and the economic and social consequences of the hidden economy are perceived very differently.

Givers to and takers from the state

Beneath the images of the idle poor and the hard-pressed taxpayer lie fundamental contradictions between the ideals of collectivism (realized through citizens willingly paying taxes to finance state welfare) and individualism (realized through the entrepreneurial spirit and the accumulation of personal wealth). If the latter perspective is adopted then tax revenues evaded are seen to belong to the *citizen*, who merely fails to pass them on to the over-regulating state. This view of the taxpayer as 'giver' to the state profoundly influences policy relating to the prosecution and punishment of tax fraudsters. If, by contrast, the former perspective is adopted, taxpayers who fiddle are seen as failing in their part of the citizenship bargain with the state, yet they still retain the economic status of 'givers'. But whichever perspective is adopted, the benefit *claimant* must always be constituted as a 'taker' from the state and, ultimately, from the taxpayer. The punishment of benefit fraudsters is rooted in their negative economic and social status as 'takers', echoing the eighteenth-century vocabulary of 'drones', updated in the 1980s rhetoric of the idle dependency of the benefits culture.

The unequal regulation, prosecution and sentencing of tax and social security fraud is therefore underpinned by a series of contradictory discourses concerning the status of tax and benefit fraudsters respectively: first, they may be differently regarded as givers to or takers from the state. Second, they may be perceived as the products of the contradictory cultures of enterprise or dependency. Third, they may be regarded as fiddling their own or someone else's money.

Fiddling tax and benefits: inculpating the poor, exculpating the rich   113

Prosecution and punishment: departmental policies

It is impossible to discuss the differential sentencing of tax and social security fraud without first examining the departmental policies which determine both investigatory practice and the official (and effective) rationales behind the decision to prosecute. These policies may involve the use (or misuse) of bargaining and non-prosecution strategies which are, officially, guided by the need to safeguard public funds and maintain departmental integrity, yet are effectively guided by deeper (and contradictory) political and ideological principles. When put into practice, the policies of the Revenue and DSS give rise to very different rates of prosecution, and very different modes of punishment, for the fraudsters involved.

Tax fraud
The Board of Inland Revenue summarizes its current prosecution policy as follows

> While the majority of investigations will lead to a financial settlement, the sanction of criminal prosecution remains for the most serious examples of the various classes of tax fraud. Generally a case will be considered for prosecution if it contains particularly serious features such as forgery or conspiracy, false declarations in investigations or where dishonesty by a tax adviser is involved.
> (Board of Inland Revenue, 1988)

Or, as one tax official succinctly put it to me,

> The first responsibility of the Revenue is to get money in and not to lock people up and prosecute them.

Enforcement policy is thus geared to securing the *compliance* of the taxpayer to the tax laws, and the Revenue regards this as best achieved through negotiation, bargaining and private financial settlement where tax is found to be owed (Keith Committee, 1983). If there is evidence of 'fraud, wilful default or neglect' on the part of a taxpayer, additional financial penalties (and interest on back taxes found to be due) may be imposed. Penalties are calculated as a percentage of tax unpaid and in strict law could be up to 200 per cent, though in practice the Revenue does not seek penalties exceeding 100 per cent (Inland Revenue 1987). This figure is further reduced in accordance with the degree of the taxpayer's co-operation, the gravity of the offence and fullness of voluntary disclosure made. Although compounded financial penalties are presented as a pragmatic response to the aims of collecting taxes, ensuring compliance and deterring tax fraud, they can be used only because tax fraudsters can literally 'pay' for their crimes. By contrast,

Few social security offenders have resources which would make it
practicable for the DHSS to apply such a remedy. The result is that,
while social security offenders who are prosecuted are publicly
identified in the courts and in the media, most tax offenders remain
unknown in the community.

                                                    (NACRO, 1986b: 89)

Prosecution is reserved only for a selection of the most 'heinous' cases of tax
fraud, yet the notion of a general deterrence is invoked in the assertion that
'it is the possibility of prosecution which prevents the spread of tax fraud to
unacceptable limits' (NACRO, 1986b: 378). It is a paradox that, on the one
hand, Revenue enforcement policy is directed to private financial settlement,
yet on the other hand we are asked to believe that the exemplary prosecution
of the *very few* (322 convictions in 1987/8) serves as an effective deterrent
against fraud, even when the *majority* of fraudsters enjoy negotiated private
justice!

Problems also emerge when analysing the practical outcome of Revenue
prosecution criteria: the Centre for Policy Studies commented, in evidence to
the Keith Committee (on the enforcement powers of the Revenue
Departments), that

> ease of presentation of the prosecution case has been a more important
> factor in the decision to prosecute than it should be. . . . a bigger
> proportion of the more socially harmful kinds of offences tends to be
> the subject of negotiated settlement.
>
>   (Keith Committee, 1983: 22.1.3)

And so, for instance, it is extremely difficult to prove that a businessman has
wilfully understated profits, but relatively easy to prove cases involving the
fraudulent misuse of tax exemption certificates (called '714's') in the
construction industry, or the theft of Inland Revenue cheques. Consequently
of the 322 convictions secured by the Revenue in 1987/8, 170 referred to
sub-contractors' exemption certificate frauds and 119 to the theft of Revenue
cheques (Board of Inland Revenue, 1988). Only twenty-four related to the
submission of false returns of income and accounts – that is, to offences
popularly regarded as income tax fraud! This disparity does, in part, arise
because 'the offences available to the Inland Revenue are ones which require
proof of *mens rea* in the form of dishonesty or intent to defraud' (Uglow,
1984: 130).

The offences which *are* prosecuted are thus not only those which are easier
to prove, but also the ones which usually equate with what is popularly
perceived as 'real crime' (that is akin to theft or forgery) and hence can be
easily represented as criminal and as *taking* from the state. By contrast, the
understatement of profits is not so readily equated with 'real crime': it may
be ambiguously portrayed as merely shrewd or shady business practice

Fiddling tax and benefits: inculpating the poor, exculpating the rich   115

(which is difficult to regulate, investigate and effectively sanction) and as, in essence, failing to pay *to* the state and taking from no one. Most of the offences which *are* prosecuted by the Revenue consequently involve 'crime' in the sense of 'taking' (not 'failing to pay') and are investigated by the police or the Board's Investigation Office, which approximates to the Revenue's 'police'. In these respects Revenue prosecution policy is not determined solely by the pragmatic goal of ensuring taxpayers' compliance and the effective collection of taxes: it is also shaped by ideological notions regarding what constitutes acceptable business practice (and acceptable levels of regulation), and by broader stereotypes of real"crime' and real criminals. Positive images of taxpayers, as entrepreneurial individuals who are the victims of state over-regulation, lie at the heart of the minimal prosecution of those who evade personal taxes.

Supplementary benefit fraud
Throughout the period of intense 'scroungerphobia' in the mid-1970s, DHSS enforcement policy rested on the principle that

> criminal prosecutions should take place . . . wherever the evidence is reasonably adequate to secure a conviction, and that the extenuating circumstances are a matter for the court rather than the prosecutor.
> (Fisher Committee, 1973: 205)

This policy of 'prosecution where appropriate' resulted in criminal proceedings being taken against 20,105 supplementary benefit claimants in 1980/81 (personal communication: DHSS, 1985). But, in accordance with the Thatcher government's emphasis on departmental cost-effectiveness, enforcement policy was reappraised and, following the Rayner team's inquiry in 1980, a 'non-prosecution policy' was adopted. Its aims were reiterated in 1983 (in the wake of the infamous 'Operation Major' anti-fraud swoop against homeless claimants in Oxford) by the then Secretary of State, Hugh Rossi. He stated

> I have taken the view that it is far more important and humane to check the abuse of the system when it is detected and to try to recover the money than to mount expensive prosecutions and to drag those individuals through the courts.
> (*Hansard*, 7 February 1983, col. 811)

On the face of it this non-prosecution policy is to be welcomed as it has certainly led to a reduction in claimants brought before the courts: in 1985/6 there were 8,902 supplementary benefit prosecutions compared with over 20,000 five years previously (personal communication: DHSS, 1988). But in practical terms the policy has several worrying aspects. First, the non-prosecution interview is geared to achieving 'benefit savings' by encouraging claimants suspected of fraud to withdraw their claim. Critics have argued that the Special Claims Control Units (SCCUs) set up in 1981 to spearhead this policy may have coerced claimants into forfeiting their claim to benefit in circumstances where there was insufficient evidence of fraud, and where a prosecution would certainly have failed (P. Moore, 1981; CPSA, 1984). Equally the *modus operandi* of SCCUs have been seen to involve intimidation,

> questionable interrogation techniques and unacceptable pressure to produce benefit savings, all in an atmosphere overcharged with the desire to meet targetted savings and root out fraud.
>
> (R. Smith, 1985: 118)

Mr Rossi's view of a 'humane' non-prosecution strategy is therefore highly questionable both in theory and in practice because cutting costs (incurred by prosecution itself), recovering money through benefit 'savings' and punishing 'scroungers' are the effective rationales underpinning DHSS enforcement policy in the 1980s. Consequently 'humanity' features in political rhetoric rather than in the practices of those handling cases of suspected fraud (Cook 1989; NACRO, 1986b; R. Smith, 1985; Beltram, 1984).

The key aims and methods of the DSS's current enforcement policy were amply demonstrated in television coverage showing examples of a non-prosecution strategy in action against unemployed claimants suspected of fraud. According to a Department of Employment official, the BBC *40 Minutes* programme *Dolebusters* (screened in October 1988) was 'a good picture of the work this team does' (*Tempo*, 1988). The investigations it screened were either based on anonymous tip-offs from members of the public, or adopted a proactive approach: targeting fraud-prone jobs (in, for instance, the building trade and taxi firms), the surveillance of claimants' vehicles for signs of work (tools, a bucket, a ladder . . .) or the scrutiny of the claimants themselves for 'dirty hands' (BBC, *Dolebusters*, October 1988). It is inconceivable that the great British taxpayer would be physically scrutinized and accused of fraud on the basis of clothing that was adjudged too smart for their declared salary level, yet this is the kind of intrusive regulation which is justified where the suspect is perceived as a *taker* from the public purse.

Also evident through this programme was the gross inequality in the respective rights of claimant and taxpayer accused of fraud: a taxpayer so accused would be encouraged to have a legal adviser present at interviews with Revenue staff, and interviews would be conducted in a manner reflecting departmental emphasis on the *rights* of the taxpayer (*Taxpayers' Charter*, 1986). By contrast, *Dolebusters* showed an unemployed man interviewed, under caution, in the back seat of an investigator's car, being told of his right to seek legal advice – a totally meaningless 'right' given the conditions of the interview.

Fiddling tax and benefits: inculpating the poor, exculpating the rich   117

Regardless of the merits or otherwise of any single case, what is at issue here is the morality of a non-prosecution policy which encourages claimants to withdraw their benefit claims 'or else'. First, the alleged 'evidence' on which they are so advised may be a malicious letter, anonymous telephone call or the fact that the claimant drives a van which contains a bucket! Clearly such evidence would be insufficient to mount a prosecution, yet is often used to 'persuade' claimants to 'sign off'. Second, claimants are thus 'paying' for alleged crimes (without being convicted), by forfeiting their entitlement to state benefits. The result may be 'benefit savings' for the Treasury, but it cannot be considered justice. In the words of one magistrate, the non-prosecution interview 'seems to have some elements of blackmail'. Third, the 'or else' alternative – the threat of prosecution – was *still* applied to over 9,000 supplementary benefit claimants in 1987/8, making a nonsense of the apparent policy rationales of 'humanity' and the desire not to 'drag individuals through the courts'. The outcome of a non-prosecution strategy is very different when applied to taxpayers who have failed to declare income: for them non-prosecution, financial penalty and private justice have positive advantages.

Paying the penalty

It is often alleged that tax fraudsters have already 'paid' for their offences, by repayment of taxes due and sometimes by additional financial penalty, and that prosecution would be both gratuitous and counter-productive. For this reason the taxpayer's ability to pay is in effect offered as a justification for an enforcement policy which 'spares the taxpayer's feelings' (Keith Committee 1983). But, at the same time, it is also argued that financial penalties *are* a form of punishment on a par with the punishments available under the criminal justice system: for instance, one accountant (also a magistrate) commented that a financial penalty was 'in effect a fine'. Another accountant/magistrate felt that penalties were an effective deterrent because 'very few people will offend twice'. Clearly then, there is a belief that individuals who repay evaded taxes have made reparation, and that if additional financial penalties are imposed, they have been *punished* too. Penalties are also justified as a practical means of fulfilling the Revenue's primary function – collecting tax – because *private* negotiations facilitate full disclosure and speedy settlement. But one senior Revenue official felt that although compliance may well be encouraged by settling 'out of court, as it were', there was a need to

> weigh up the relative value of publicity as a deterrent in relation to *lack* of publicity being helpful in a handful of cases.

He noted that 'publicity usually surrounds the "have-nots" getting caned, not the higher income groups'.

As already argued, taxpayers are in a position to be able to offer to 'pay for their crimes; benefit claimants are not. None the less, it should be stressed that wherever benefits are overpaid (for reasons other than 'official error'), claimants *are* required to pay (NACRO, 1986b). Current regulations state that where a claimant admits fraud, up to £6.80 per week may be deducted from future benefit payments until the debt to the DSS has been repaid (CPAG, 1988). It is difficult to see how benefit fraud is deterred by enforcement policies which may reduce a claimant's income to £6.80 below the poverty line and, if criminal proceedings are then taken, may possibly reduce that income still further through a fine. Ironically in such circumstances, fraud may become the only means of economic survival for some benefit claimants.

To summarize, there are several paradoxes within official discourses on Revenue and DSS enforcement policy. Both departments stress cost-effectiveness, the importance of safeguarding public funds and espouse non-prosecution policies. Yet in 1987/8 these policies resulted in only 322 Revenue prosecutions compared with 9,847 for supplementary benefit fraud (personal communication, DHSS, 1988; Board of Inland Revenue, 1988). In the same year the total yield from the Revenue's *compliance* activities was £2,013 million (Board of Inland Revenue, 1988), yet when Norman Fowler spoke of 'taxpayer's money being used to finance the fraudulent' (*Guardian*, 13 October 1988) he was speaking about unemployed benefit claimants who work on the side, not about the far more costly fiddles of the taxpayers themselves! More manpower and resources are directed against 'scroungers' than tax evaders despite the fact that tax fraud is of far greater magnitude (NACRO, 1986b; HC 102, 1983/4; Keith Committee 1983: 772). The official rhetoric of 'cost-effectiveness' and 'benefit savings' is therefore put into practice very selectively. As a result most taxpayers pay for defrauding the public purse through private financial settlement, yet thousands of benefit claimants each year pay twice – through reparation to the DSS and through sentences imposed by the courts.

Sentencing: the data

Having established that very few tax fraudsters are prosecuted, and that those who are prosecuted have often committed offences akin to theft (for instance, of Revenue cheques) and forgery (misuse of 714 exemption certificates), it follows that any analysis of the sentencing of tax evaders will be based on a very small number of cases. By contrast, there are thousands of prosecutions each year for supplementary benefit (now income support) fraud. But several difficulties arise when attempting to make sentencing comparisons as the relevant data are not comprehensive or complete. For instance, first, the Revenue and DSS do not publish information on sentencing, as this is seen to be the responsibility of the courts. Second, the

Fiddling tax and benefits: inculpating the poor, exculpating the rich 119

Home Office statistics, based on categories such as 'Revenue Law offences' and 'Social Security offences', make it impossible to distinguish, for instance, those tax and supplementary benefit fraudsters who have been prosecuted under other categories, such as the Theft Act. Third, the use of overall categories such as 'Social Security offence' conceals distinctions between contributory and non-contributory (means-tested) benefits. As a result, it is impossible to tell what benefit has been fiddled!

Despite many practical difficulties in obtaining precise comparable data, a NACRO Working Party reporting on *Enforcement of the Law Relating to Social Security* (1986b) did make specific comparisons with the enforcement of Revenue Laws. Evidence to the working party had stressed the use of 'harsher penalties against social security offences than against those infringing tax laws'. In relation to prosecutions mounted, the ratio of prosecutions brought for Revenue and Social Security offences respectively, was around 1:30 in 1984 (NACRO, 1986b: 69). Moreover, the report noted 'the relative severity of the custodial sentences in some cases, compared with sentences for comparably serious offences in spheres other than social security'. This observation was supported by unpublished DHSS figures which indicated that in 1984/5 433 unsuspended prison sentences were imposed for benefit frauds in England, Wales and Scotland (NACRO, 1986b: 76–7). The report concluded that

> Sometimes . . . the sentencing authority is influenced by the tendency
> . . . to attach a special kind of moral turpitude to people living on
> benefits.
>
> (NACRO, 1986b: 77)

This is certainly true of many of the sentencing discourses which will be discussed below.

The analysis which follows will be based upon official commentaries on criminal proceedings mounted by the Inland Revenue from 1982 to 1988,[3] details of 206 cases of supplementary benefit fraud heard in one magistrates' court in the Midlands from 1981 to 1987,[4] and media coverage of tax and supplementary benefit fraud cases. In relation to the latter, publicity is inextricably linked to the reporting of criminal proceedings in the courts, and if tax fraud cases do not reach the courts, then public awareness of the extent and costs of tax evasion will be minimal. By contrast, local newspapers reporting proceedings in magistrates' courts will cover many 'scrounger' stories, thereby reinforcing the belief that benefit fraud is the more widespread and poses the greater threat to the 'taxpayer' and hence to society. The media, therefore, not only reproduce the sentencing discourses of the courts, but also produce the ideological conditions and the vocabularies within which such discourses are sustained and justified (Golding and Middleton, 1982).

Sentencing: tax fraud

In July 1986 an unqualified accountant who, over a seven-year period, had concealed income amounting to £98,000 from the Inland Revenue, was reminded by the judge sentencing him that the Court of Appeal had ruled that those guilty of persistent dishonesty must expect a custodial sentence and a financial penalty. The accountant was sentenced to four months' imprisonment and fined £10,000 (personal communication, Association of Inspectors of Taxes (AIT), 1988). In June 1987 the joint owner of an Italian restaurant was sentenced to nine months' imprisonment for a £176,000 tax fraud. The judge commented that the defendants had engaged in 'a highly unsocial activity which worked to the disadvantage of all honest taxpayers and continued that 'the Courts have shown that immediate custodial sentences are required except in exceptional circumstances' (ibid).

On the face ot it, then, the sentencing of tax fraudsters should reflect the degree of economic and social harm the offences inflict on society and, if a persistent fraud is involved should result in financial penalty in addition to custody. However, in practice there are a variety of circumstances relating to the status of the offender and the extent of his/her admission of guilt which distorts the sentencing process. For instance, the restaurateur mentioned above had made a false declaration of 'full disclosure' following an earlier investigation in 1984. His failure to admit at the outset the full extent of his concealed income was an important factor affecting his relatively severe sentence. By contrast, two wholesale market traders who defrauded over £12,000 were fined £5,000 because they were first offenders, had made restitution to the Revenue and had co-operated with the investigation (ibid.). (But, as will be argued below, where supplementary benefit fraud is concerned, almost all offenders plead guilty, all are required to make restitution to the DSS, yet this does not similarly mitigate their sentences.)

In the case of Lester Piggott, Judge Farquason commented that if Piggott had fully disclosed details of his income to the Revenue, he might have found it possible to be 'lenient' with him (ibid.). This is remarkable in view of the scale of Piggott's offences (tax and interest in excess of £3 million owed) and their persistence (since initial investigations in 1981), yet demonstrates that even when tax fraudsters are recidivists, their offences may be largely mitigated by full admission of guilt and paying back the taxes defrauded. Mitigation may also arise from the 'status' of the offender himself, although in Piggott's case the vast amount he defrauded (and his failure to 'come clean' to the Revenue earlier) effectively ruled out any such mitigation for the 'housewives' choice' jockey. He was sentenced to three years in custody. However, others have successfully used their status in the community as mitigation: for example, the director of a dispensing chemists (who was also a Justice of the Peace!) was found guilty of submitting false trading accounts. Although over £28,000 had been defrauded, defence counsel argued against

Fiddling tax and benefits: inculpating the poor, exculpating the rich   121

a custodial sentence on the grounds that the director had paid back taxes owing, admitted his guilt and had served the community as a JP and a worker for charity. The judge took such 'work for the community' into account when suspending the nine months' custodial sentence, but ironically pointed out that 'tax evasion is effectively stealing from the community' (personal communication, AIT, 1988).

In a similar vein, it was pleaded that a chartered accountant, prosecuted in 1982 for falsifying accounts, 'had been a busy professional man, of high reputation in the community, who had now lost everything'. Clearly the magistrates who sentenced him to fines of £1,500 accepted that his 'career had been shattered' and that he had, in effect, already been punished through the social stigma of criminal proceedings (ibid.). This theme is found in the subsequent sentencing of many other tax fraudsters where, for instance, 'anxiety and general disgrace' or 'previous good character' is seen to justify a fine. But, in turn, the fine is seen as an available penalty because tax fraudsters can usually 'pay' for their crimes by this means. The notion that to come from a 'good' social background is in itself mitigation (because such offenders are seen to suffer loss of status through prosecution itself) is also evident in the case of two directors of an engineering company, who in 1983 had been found guilty of a £40,000 tax fraud. They were sentenced to pay £5,000 fines and their six months' custodial sentences were suspended, as the judge commented it was 'sad to see men of their background' involved in a persistent and substantial Revenue fraud (ibid.).

But some tax fraudsters may benefit from their relatively high social status and, where applicable, from their lack of financial means too: for instance, a partner in a firm of accountants who illegally transferred funds to offshore companies to evade UK taxes was given a nine months' suspended sentence because of his professional inexperience and the professional ruin which would follow the case. Yet the judge also accepted that the offender was 'virtually penniless' and so did not impose a fine or costs! (ibid.). By comparison, *all* benefit fraudsters suffer from being 'penniless', but this certainly does not exempt them from paying either fines or costs. But, as already argued, the taxpayer is regarded by definition a giver to the state, assumed to be guided by positive entrepreneurial values and to be essentially 'non-criminal' in terms of personal and social characteristics. These assumptions underpin both the minimal use of criminal sanction against tax fraudsters and the often compassionate views of sentencers.

Sentencing supplementary benefit fraud

In March 1987 Lord Lane heard six appeals from social security fraud offenders sentenced to over one year in custody, one of whom had been gaoled for thirty months! He said that

It is clear that in order to qualify for prosecution at all, offences must
be other than minor.

(*Guardian*, 25 March 1987)

He accordingly reduced their sentences to between four and six months. But
at the same time he dismissed other appeals by three 'drifters' who had used
false names to fiddle the DHSS: their custodial sentences, of three to four
years, were upheld. Even though it could be argued that such itinerant frauds
are premeditated and that these offenders 'make a business out of cheating
the public purse', it is difficult to justify sentences of three to four years while
those who make far more money at this 'business' (through tax fraud) are
sentenced so leniently.

In urging judges to reduce prison sentences for social security offences
Lord Lane argued that the element of 'deterrence' should not play a large part
in the sentencing of such cases (ibid.). But the magistrates who sentence the
vast majority of benefit fraudsters clearly think (and act) differently.
Magistrates I have spoken to see deterrence as the primary reason for
prosecution (a view echoed by some DHSS staff), but paradoxically one
magistrate still felt that 'It is true to say that we sometimes feel the offence to
have been trivial'. Another was under the misapprehension that the DHSS
'wouldn't probably prosecute if the claimant "coughed" at the interview
stage'. As the following observations of the sentencing of supplementary
benefit fraud indicate, the admission of guilt and the scale of the fraud cannot
account for the inconsistent (and contradictory) sentencing rationales
invoked for social security offenders.

First, to take the issue of guilt: of the 206 cases of supplementary benefit
fraud I have analysed, 191 (93 per cent) pleaded guilty and hence the
conviction rate was very high, with 201 claimants found guilty. Some
claimants are totally unprepared for the court proceedings which may follow
their admission of guilt: for instance, Barry had admitted doing casual work
'on the side' when he was visited by a DHSS official, but was unrepresented
in the magistrates' court, as were 43 per cent of my sample. (He had been told
that the case was unlikely to go to court!) It seems that the admission of guilt
plays no part in the DHSS decision to prosecute: such decisions are made
locally with a good deal of managerial discretion (NACRO, 1986b). This
may influence the second issue – the seriousness (or triviality) of cases
brought before the courts.

Lord Lane indicated that offences prosecuted 'must be other than trivial'
(*Guardian*, 25 March 1987): official guidelines suggested that a minimum of
£250 should have been defrauded. This figure seems extremely low in
relation to the scale which tax frauds have to reach in order to attract
prosecution but, even then, this minimum does not apply to fiddles involving
the alteration, theft or misuse of girocheques (ibid.). In practice, this means
that supplementary benefit claimants may be prosecuted for fiddling giros
worth less than, for example, the £70 which the Inland Revenue write-off as

Fiddling tax and benefits: inculpating the poor, exculpating the rich   123

'not worth recovery' from PAYE taxpayers. The scale of the fiddle does not always determine sentencing in such cases: for instance, four of the six immediate custodial sentences passed in one Midlands magistrates' court over my period of research (referred to in Table 6.1) were imposed for giro frauds. In one case the amount defrauded was only £67.10. Three suspended prison sentences were imposed for giro fiddles worth £63, £94 and £129· respectively. It is inconceivable that tax evasion resulting in losses to the Revenue of such small amounts would be considered worthy of prosecution, let alone a custodial sentence. Such sentences also belie the assumption that only 'serious' cases of benefit fraud are prosecuted. Although many giro frauds are considered closest to 'crime' in the sense that some involve forgery or theft, they are usually desperately crass frauds motivated by poverty, rather than organized frauds motivated by greed (Cook, 1989).

All supplementary benefit fraudsters I spoke to justified their crimes as their only available response to the situation of hopelessness, chronic poverty and degradation in which they found themselves (see Chapter 1 in this volume). Yet these justifications are not ones which can be successfully invoked in court. One magistrate I spoke to summarized a common view amongst sentencers: 'I don't want excuses', he said, and argued that offenders would do better to admit they are wrong and 'say sorry'. But this view may lead to harsh reactions towards those who do not (or cannot) play the game as magistrates wish. For example, Bert had worked 'on the side' as a building-site labourer while claiming benefit and was repaying the £572 he owed to the DHSS. Several factors may have been offered as mitigation: Bert told me that he had recently been separated from his wife and was attempting to 'set up home again'. He had difficulty paying for household goods and clothes, and still wanted to buy presents for his children. But when magistrates asked him if he had anything to say before sentence, Bert (who was unrepresented) shrugged his shoulders and said, 'It was one of those things, I suppose'. Not only were the magistrates unaware of his personal circumstances, but also they showed great displeasure at what they considered to be his flippant attitude, though like many poorer defendants, he was nervous and confused by the proceedings (Carlen, 1976; Crow and Simon, 1987). He was sentenced to pay fines of £180 (and costs).

As most benefit frauds are motivated by poverty, it is particularly inappropriate that the fine remains the most popular sentence for benefit fraud (Table 6.1). Despite a decline in the overall use of the fine as mass unemployment became a fact of economic and social life in the 1980s, NACRO found that courts were reluctant to modify their use of financial penalties in cases of social security fraud (Crow and Simon, 1987: 48).

The practical effects of imposing fines upon those least able to pay them was well demonstrated in the case of Jim, a father of three young children, who was prosecuted in 1986 for failing to declare his wife's part-time earnings. He had been overpaid £996 in benefits and this was being repaid to the DHSS by deductions of £1.65 per week from his supplementary

Table 6.1 The sentencing of 206 supplementary benefit fraud cases in one
Midlands magistrates' court October 1981 to August 1987

Sentence passed	Number of cases	(%)
Immediate custodial sentence	6	3.0
Suspended custodial sentence	11	5.4
Community service order	22	10.9
Probation order	26	12.9
Fine	82	40.8
Conditional discharge	54	27.0
Total	201	100.0

Note: Costs awarded to the DHSS in 156 cases (78 per cent).

benefit (as it had been agreed he could repay no more than this weekly
amount). He had accumulated debts exceeding £1,000 arising from loans,
clothing clubs and hire purchase payments and had seen his wife's earnings
as a way of paying off these debts. Ironically magistrates sentenced him to
pay fines totalling £210 (and costs!), at the rate of £3 per week and
commented that

> This country is fed up to the teeth with people like you scrounging from
> your fellow citizens.

Moreover, benefit fraud was said to be 'one of the worst forms of stealing
there is'. Privately, Jim's response to the sentence was to say that the
magistrate was 'on another planet to us' and, despairingly, he joked that

> Ah well, it's the red light under the porch now.

It is difficult to envisage any legal means by which he *could* pay such fines.

Jim's case is not untypical: most of the benefit fraudsters I observed in
court were in debt and found it impossible to make repayment of loans on
low and fixed levels of supplementary benefit. (Following the April 1988
changes which introduced income support and state-sponsored loans
through the Social Fund, it is likely that the material conditions of poverty
and debt which generate fraud are worsening for many claimants.)

In another case, Jeff (a father of three) had recently been made redundant
and his wife had taken a part-time cleaning job to clear debts (for 'clothing
clubs' and the purchase of a washing machine). Her earnings had totalled
£280 and at the time of the hearing this amount was being repaid to the
DHSS by deductions of £3 per week from his supplementary benefit. Jeff and
his wife were anxious and upset about the court case: they were first
offenders. The magistrate, however, considered Jeff's 'taking from the state'

Fiddling tax and benefits: inculpating the poor, exculpating the rich   125

as very serious because 'rules are to be kept' and imposed fines totalling £100 (and costs). It could be argued that the fines, to be repaid at the rate of £2 per week from benefits that were already £3 lower than the basic supplementary benefit level (because of repayment direct to the DHSS) were a very harsh sentence: guilt had been readily admitted, compensation was being paid, and the experience of being taken to court had already proved a harsh deterrent for Jeff and his wife. When compared to the negotiated private justice enjoyed by those who 'take from the state' through tax evasion, the sentence seems still less appropriate.

Although not demonstrated in Table 6.1, there has recently been a decline in the use of the fine for supplementary benefit offenders in the Midlands area I studied: for example, of those sentenced there between 1981 and 1983, 48 per cent were fined. But by 1986/7 this figure had fallen to 37 per cent, accompanied by an *increase* in the use of the conditional discharge. While this sentencing trend is to be welcomed, it does raise questions about the DHSS's prosecution policy. As NACRO has pointed out,

> The process of investigation, formal warning of the consequences of a further offence and recovery of the amount overpaid will usually be sufficient to chasten and deter.
>
> (NACRO, 1986b: 73)

If this is the case, prosecution (even if it results in a conditional discharge) can be seen as gratuitous. A fine can be seen as entirely counter-productive.

There is much inconsistency regarding what constitutes appropriate 'deterrence' for those who defraud the public purse. Tax evasion is seen as best deterred in part by the exemplary prosecution of a very few of the worst cases of tax 'crime', but largely by individuals' making private settlements with the Revenue (lack of publicity facilitating compliance to this end). Benefit fraud is seen as deterred through the fairly arbitrary prosecution of those whom local DHSS officials deem 'serious' fraudsters, with maximum publicity being sought. Yet DHSS staff, prosecuting solicitors and some magistrates *privately* admit that for benefit fraudsters such deterrence is ineffective. None the less, they justify both prosecution and (relatively harsh) sentences by the ritual invocation 'Well, you have to do *something* with them'. But this futile justification is not required for the majority of tax fraudsters who never appear in the courts: it seems that *nothing* needs to be done with them. Those who *do* appear in the courts do not attract the public villification that is reserved for the poor who defraud the public purse (Golding and Middleton, 1982). They are also well able to pay for their crimes by financial penalties and by loss of their social status – status which the poor do not possess and so cannot lose.

Doing something about the unequal punishment of tax and benefit fraud

In conclusion, I would argue that we *can* do something to reduce the injustices described here. First, more manpower and resources could be directed to the investigation and regulation of tax evasion. Currently, counter-evasion officers working in local tax offices yield fifteen times their own salaries in taxes recouped, and officers in Special Offices yield thirty-two times their salaries (Board of Inland Revenue 1988: 41). On grounds of cost-effectiveness alone, the government should be pressured to recruit more staff to regulate tax evasion than social security fraud. Second, on grounds of consistency and social justice, the prosecution polices of the DSS and Inland Revenue should be reviewed. If the DSS is really *serious* about its non-prosecution policy, then the claimant's rights should be safeguarded during 'non-prosecution interviews', and the number of prosecutions mounted by the DSS should still be greatly reduced. At the same time, the Revenue should consider the deterrent value of, first, mounting so few (and so selective) prosecutions, and second, of private financial settlements. The Keith Committee Report (1983) suggested that the names of tax defaulters should be published as a deterrent to fraud, a possibility which was again raised by NACRO (1986b). The Revenue remain squeamish about publishing the names of those individuals who are usually, after all, 'good upstanding citizens'! None the less, research has indicated that tax fraudsters are *more* likely to be deterred by the threat of adverse publicity than private settlement or, indeed, certain criminal sanctions: for instance, in a questionnaire survey of fifty-six executives, 'national publicity' of their offending was regarded as a more severe penalty than the imposition of either a £5,000 fine or a two-year suspended prison sentence (Levi, 1987: 321)! The option of deterrent publicity is one which could very easily be taken up, and which would stigmatize (and inflict an effective punishment on) tax evaders, without further increasing the prison population.

Social security fraud is one of the least deterrable crimes because it is generated by poverty. Tax evasion is, in theory, a very deterrable crime because it is motivated not by need but by greed. This simple observation is obscured by the historical legacy of imagery about the idle poor and the energetic, thrifty taxpayer, updated in the rhetoric of the enterprise and benefit cultures. Currently the poor 'pay' more, and more often, for defrauding the state than do the rich whose fiddles are far more costly. It is ironic that common-sense critiques of allegedly lenient sentences of poorer offenders often argue that poverty appears to license crime (see Chapter 1 in this volume). But, on the evidence of this chapter, I would argue that the reverse is true: poverty itself inculpates the poor, while wealth and 'enterprise' exculpates the rich.

Notes

1 The research on which most of this chapter is based was conducted before April

Fiddling tax and benefits: inculpating the poor, exculpating the rich   127

1988, and so the term 'supplementary benefit' will continue to be used wherever applicable. Income support, which replaced supplementary benefit following the April reforms, will be referred to only when discussing current enforcement policies or administrative regulations which differ from those in force at the time of my research. Also, since mid 1988, the social services department is DSS not DHSS.

2 The research which forms the core of this chapter aimed to compare the commission, regulation, investigation and punishment of supplementary benefit fraud and income tax fraud: the latter was restricted to enable a meaningful comparison between the experiences of *individual* claimants and taxpayers. For this reason large-scale corporate tax frauds are not dealt with here.

3 The Inland Revenue Staff Federation and Association of Inspectors of Taxes kindly provided me with details of prosecution policy and official commentaries on criminal proceedings. Although this information was already 'in the public domain', thanks are due to them for making the task of research easier for me.

4 Details of a sample of 206 supplementary benefit fraud cases heard in one magistrates' court in the Midlands refer to a period between 1981 and 1987. Information was collected on pleas, verdicts, representation, sentencing and the award of costs and compensation. In addition court proceedings were observed in several cases of benefit fraud and, wherever practical, I spoke to the fraudsters involved.

Bibliography

Beltram, G. (1984) *Testing the Safety Net,* London, Bedford Square Press and
     National Council for Voluntary Organzations.
Board of Inland Revenue (1988) *130th Annual Report,* Cm 529, London, HMSO.
Boyson, R. (1971) *Down With the Poor,* London, Churchill Press.
     (1978) *Centre Foreward: A Radical Conservative Programme, London,*
     Maurice Temple Smith.
Burton, J. (1985) *Why No Cuts?,* Hobart Paper no. 24, London, Institute of
     Economic Affairs.
Carlen, P. (1976) *Magistrates' Justice,* Oxford, Martin Robertson.
Cook, D. (1989) *Rich Law, Poor Law: Differential Responses to Tax and*
     Supplementary Benefit Fraud, Milton Keynes, Open University Press.
CPAG (1988) *National Welfare Benefits Handbook: 18th Edition,* 1988/9,
London, Child Poverty Action Group.
Crow, I. and Simon, F. (1987) *Unemployment and Magistrates' Courts,* London,
     NACRO.
Fisher Committee (1973) *Report of the Committee on Abuse of Social Security*
     Benefits, Cmnd 5228, London, HMSO.
Fraser, D. (1973) *The Evolution of the British Welfare State,* London, Macmillan.

Golding, P. and Middleton, S. (1982) *Images of Welfare,* Oxford, Martin
     Robertson.
Houghton, Lord (1977) 'Administration, politics and equity', in IEA, *The State of
     Taxation,* IEA Readings no. 16, London, Institute of Economic Affairs.
Inland Revenue (1987) Leaflet 73, *How Settlements are Negotiated,* London,
     HMSO.
Keith Committee (1983) *Report on the Enforcement Powers of the Revenue
     Departments,* Cmnd 8822, London, HMSO.
Levi, M. (1987) *Regulating Fraud: White-Collar Crime and the Criminal Process,*
     London, Tavistock.
Loney, M. (1986) *The Politics of Greed,* London, Pluto Press.
Moore, P. (1981) 'Scroungermania again at the DHSS', *New Society* 22, January:
     138-9.
NACRO. (1986b) *Enforcement of the Law Relating to Social Security,* London.
Sabine, B.E.V. (1966) *A History of Income Tax,* London, Allen & Unwin.
Shenfield, A.A. (1968) *The Political Economy of Tax Avoidance,* IEA Occasional
     Paper no. 24, London, Institute of Economic Affairs.
Smith, R. (1985) 'Who's fiddling?', in S. Ward (ed.) *DHSS in Crisis,* London,
     Child Poverty Action Group.
Taxpayers' Charter (1986) London, Board of Inland Revenue/HM Customs and
     Excise.
Tempo (1988) Department of Employment Group Staff Newspaper November.
Uglow, S. (1984) 'Defrauding the public purse', *Criminal Law Review* March,
     128-41.

[20]

Variations in Regulatory Enforcement Styles

BRIDGET M. HUTTER*

This paper examines intra- and inter-agency variations in the enforcement styles of three regulatory inspectorates in Great Britain. It is argued that the accommodative approach typically associated with regulatory enforcement is not a homogeneous and uniform concept, rather it embraces a range of strategies. These are described and a variety of organisational, social and political factors are considered as explanations of the variations which arise.

I. INTRODUCTION

The question of how regulatory officials use the law and what they aim to achieve in so doing was the starting point of many early studies of regulatory enforcement. Authors such as Carson (1970), Cranston (1978), Hawkins (1984), Kagan (1978) and Richardson *et al.* (1983) all sought to understand how the law and the criminal sanction are used to control business and industrial activities. Each of these studies identified the adoption of common enforcement practices by officials from a variety of backgrounds. Enforcement of the law, it was argued, did not simply refer to legal action; rather there is a wide array of informal enforcement techniques used by all enforcement officials but coming into prominence in the regulatory arena. Such techniques include education, advice, persuasion and negotiation.

In order to enhance our understanding of law enforcement, a binary model of enforcement has been adopted by some researchers. Both models are used by all enforcement officials on occasions but, as we will see, some tend to identify more closely with one enforcement style than the other. The enforcement style approximating that which is most often favoured by regulatory officials is variously referred to as the accommodative (Richardson *et al.*, 1983; Hutter, 1988) or compliance (Hawkins, 1984; Reiss, 1984) model of enforcement. Securing compliance is its main objective, both through the remedy of existing problems and, above all, the prevention of others. The preferred methods to achieve these ends are co-operative and conciliatory. So where compliance is less than complete, and there is good reason for it being incomplete, persuasion, negotiation and education are

---

* Some of the research described in this paper was carried out with the support of the Health and Safety Executive. I am grateful to Keith Hawkins and Bob Kagan for their comments on earlier drafts of this paper. The views expressed herein are, of course, those of the author.

ISSN 0265–8240 $3.00

154   *LAW & POLICY   April 1989*

the primary enforcement methods. Accordingly, compliance is not necessarily regarded as being immediately achievable; rather it may be seen as a long-term aim. The use of formal legal methods, especially prosecution, is regarded as a last resort, something to be avoided unless all else fails to secure compliance. Indeed, the importance of legal methods lies in the mystique surrounding their threatened or possible use rather than their actual use (see Hawkins, 1984, Chapter 6).

This model of enforcement is often contrasted with another termed the 'deterrence' model by Reiss (1984) and the sanctioning strategy by Hawkins (1984). This is a penal style of enforcement which accords prosecution an important role. Indeed, the number of prosecutions initiated may be regarded as a sign of success and taken as an indicator of the job being done. While Hawkins and Reiss argue that the methods preferred in such a model are penal and adversarial, they do not agree about the objectives of such an approach. Reiss clearly regards deterrence and compliance systems as ". . . oriented towards preventing the occurrence of violations" (1984, p. 24) whereas Hawkins would not attribute the sanctioning model such a narrow objective. Rather, he argues, that the sanctioning model may have a variety of objectives ranging from pure retribution to utilitarian aims. Moreover, the objectives of prosecution may differ within an organization, with those at the top, for example, emphasising general deterrence and those at field-level holding punitive aims.[1]

While studies generally associate regulatory enforcement with the accommodative style and the sanctioning style with the police, it was always emphasised that in reality all enforcement agencies would use both styles, albeit with different levels of commitment. This said, it remains the case that the majority of studies, especially the earliest ones, identified the accommodative style as characteristic of most regulatory agencies. The first studies to document any significant deviation from this pattern were of American regulatory agencies in the 1970s. Kelman's study of occupational safety agencies in Sweden and America, described inter-agency variations (1981). Shover *et al.*'s study of the Office of Surface Mining in America (1982) examined intra-agency variation, revealing even more patently the role of the environment within which enforcement takes place. Kelman and Shover *et al.* both describe agencies which adopted enforcement strategies that more closely approached the sanctioning model.

My research into the law enforcement procedures of Environmental Health Officers in Great Britain mapped out further evidence of intra-agency variations in enforcement strategies, leading me to refine the binary model of enforcement (Hutter, 1988). In this paper, I want to present evidence of differences in approach by way of a brief outline of the findings of this study, and by then relating them to a subsequent examination I have undertaken into inter-agency variations, namely the enforcement of the law by Factory and Industrial Air Pollution Inspectors in Great Britain (see Centre for Socio-Legal Studies, 1983). Then I will go on to discuss some of

Hutter REGULATORY ENFORCEMENT STYLES 155

the factors which may account for variations in the enforcement styles discerned.

II. TWO "COMPLIANCE" STRATEGIES

Environmental Health Officers are local government employees charged with undertaking local authority responsibilities for the enforcement of environmental health legislation in Great Britain. Their primary tasks are wide-ranging, and relate to housing, food, diseases, air pollution, noise and working conditions. They are therefore responsible for maintaining and improving the quality of the immediate environment. Most local authorities in Great Britain employ an environmental health department to undertake these tasks. In all cases, the department is accountable to, and, as a minimum, subject to the control of the local council.

The fact that EHOs are locally based and controlled gives the researcher rich opportunities for gaining some insight into how the law is interpreted and enforced in different political and social settings. Four sample departments were selected for investigation. They differed in a number of important respects, such as the wealth of the areas within which they were located; levels of urbanisation and industrial activity; the predominant type of environmental health problem present; and the internal organisation of the department. A variety of research methods were employed, including three months in each department accompanying inspectors in the course of their working day, a documentary survey, and interviews in each department.[2]

The comparative approach did prove fruitful, for while all of the sample departments worked within a framework of enforcement approximating the compliance as opposed to the sanctioning model, two distinct strategies *within* the broad approach of compliance strategy emerged from this research. These I have termed the persuasive and the insistent strategies.

A. THE PERSUASIVE AND INSISTENT STRATEGIES

The persuasive and insistent strategies both share the common objective of securing compliance, as opposed to effecting retribution, but they differ about the stringency of the means to these ends. The *persuasive* approach epitomises the accommodative approach adopted by so many regulatory agencies. The range of tactics favoured by those adhering to such a strategy are informal. Officials educate, persuade, coax and cajole offenders into complying with the law. They explain what the law demands and the reasons for legislative requirements. They discuss how improvements can best be attained. Patience and understanding underpin the whole strategy, which is regarded as an open-ended and long-term venture. This strategy approximates Braithwaite, Walker and Grabosky's notion of the Diagnostic Inspectorate (1987).

156   *LAW & POLICY   April 1989*

The *insistent* strategy is less benevolent and less flexible than the persuasive approach. There are fairly clearly defined limits to the tolerance of officials adhering to this strategy. They are not prepared to spend a long time patiently cajoling offenders into compliance and they expect a fairly prompt response to their requests. When this is not forthcoming, these officials will automatically increase the pressure to comply. They will readily initiate legal action to effect their objectives should they encounter overt resistance to their requests. However, it is important to stress that the ultimate objective of these enforcement moves is to gain compliance, not to effect retribution. As Braithwaite, Walker and Grabosky (1987) note, there is an important and empirically significant middle ground between the sanctioning and compliance models identified in the binary model of enforcement. The insistent strategy forms part of this middle ground, which includes the "Token Enforcers" described by Braithwaite *et al.* and Bardach and Kagan's ideal of 'flexible enforcement,' wherein officials are flexible both in their interpretation of the rules and in their readiness to use legal coercion. The differences between the persuasive and insistent strategies concerning rule-interpretation in many respects mirror their varying propensities to use legal coercion; those who are most flexible in their interpretation of the law are also more inclined to be flexible in their readiness to apply legal sanctions.

The insistent strategy differs from the sanctioning model of enforcement both with regard to its objectives and methods. Its aims, as noted above, are precisely the same as those adhering to the persuasive strategy, namely to secure compliance. An illustration is offered by the use environmental health departments make of Improvement Notices, which are legal documents requiring compliance within a specified period of time and stating explicitly that failure to do so may result in prosecution. While departments approximating the insistent strategy would more readily serve these legal notices than those favouring the persuasive strategy, their actions in the case of non-compliance with a notice are similar. In all departments, non-compliance with a notice was likely to lead to the initiation of court proceedings. Likewise, they would all adopt the common practice of terminating these proceedings if the offender remedied the problem before the hearing. None of these Departments would want to punish an offender simply for failing to comply within the expiry period of a notice. The intention of any threatened legal action is to effect an improvement or remedy; once this has been achieved, any impending prosecution becomes redundant. This may be contrasted with the behaviour of the inspectors of the Occupational Health and Safety Administration (OSHA) in America, who Kelman (1984: 102) described as imposing fines even if the offense is corrected in the presence of the official.

The legal actions employed under the insistent strategy are by no means as immediate as in the sanctioning model. Kelman (1981: 181) explains that OSHA officials could and did impose fines the first time they discovered an

Hutter REGULATORY ENFORCEMENT STYLES 157

offense. In a similar vein, Shover, Clelland and Lynxwiler (1982: 212) identified one region of the Office of Surface Mining in America which believed in the literal application of rules as well as automatic and uniform penalties against violations. Again, this is a markedly more severe approach than the insistent strategy, which grants officials discretion to use informal enforcement techniques. Inspectors are encouraged to make their own decisions about interpreting situations and how best to tackle them. But while these inspectors are not expected to effect improvements and remedies immediately, neither are they expected to permit non-compliance for extended periods of time, something which would be tolerated by the persuasive strategy.

These models of the persuasive and insistent strategies pertain not only to differences between environmental health departments, but also help to describe and explain differences of approach between the Factory and Industrial Air Pollution Inspectorates.[3] At the time I undertook my research (April 1983–April 1987), both of these Inspectorates formed part of the Health and Safety Executive in Britain.[4] Both are well established. The Factory Inspectorate was created in 1833 and the Industrial Air Pollution Inspectorate (originally known as the Alkali Inspectorate) in 1863. The Factory Inspectorate is responsible for the health and safety of workers in such places as factories, refineries and construction sites, and the Industrial Air Pollution Inspectorate is concerned with the quality of air and the control of environmental pollution. The Factory and Industrial Air Pollution Inspectorates are Central Government agencies, in comparison to EHOs, who are the responsibility of local government. The remit of EHOs coincides with both of these central agencies. The essential difference between them centres on the severity of the problems dealt with. Factory and Industrial Air Pollution Inspectors generally handle the most serious health and safety and environmental pollution problems, while EHOs are responsible for the multitude of less serious matters in these areas.

B. THE EMPIRICAL EVIDENCE

Prosecution records provide crude indicators of a propensity to avoid or to favour legal enforcement methods. There are, of course, problems in taking prosecution at face value as evidence of variations in strategies. To some extent, these figures reflect the size of the agency's jurisdiction and the potential number of prosecutable offences coming to light in each area.

In the case of environmental health departments, the propensity to initiate legal action can be suggested by relating the number of prosecutions initiated by each of the four sample departments to the total number of food premises in each local authority. Food and food hygiene offenses are selected because the complaints records of the sample departments do not reveal any major differences with respect to the severity of the offenses committed. Rather they show that the types of offenses being dealt with are

158   *LAW & POLICY   April 1989*

fairly similar, for example, foreign bodies in food, dirty milk bottles, unfit food, or unsanitary and infested food premises.

It is difficult to claim that any one area had premises which were any better or worse than any other, so I assume for the purposes of argument that we can regard any differences in frequency of offending between areas as insignificant. In this case we find that there is a marked difference in propensity to initiate legal action (see Table 1).

Table 1. The Probability of a Food Premise being Prosecuted by
Departments A, B, C and D, 1977–79

Dept.	Probability of Prosecution		
	1977	1978	1979
A	1:1327	—	1:332
B	1: 171	1:257	1:147
C	1: 66	1: 47	1: 88
D	1: 35	1: 42	1: 68

Source: Departmental records

The corresponding figures for the Factory and Industrial Air Pollution Inspectorates are given in Table 2 which relates prosecutions to the number of premises regulated by these Inspectorates. It should be emphasised, however, that this still provides us with only a crude indicator of Inspectorate activity.

Table 2. The Probability of a Premise being Prosecuted by the Factory
Inspectorate and Industrial Air Pollution Inspectorate 1983–85

Inspectorate	Probability of Prosecution		
	1983	1984	1985
Factory	1:326	1: 351	1: 364
Industrial Air Pollution	1:975*	1:1975	1:1978

Source: Agency Records
 * Excluding the prosecution of illegal cable burners (see Table 4), who do not have premises.

C. A MATTER OF PHILOSOPHY

Debates about the stringency with which the law should be enforced are not just the concern of academics but can be found in professional journals, within departments and inspectorates, and between individual inspectors. In May 1979, for instance, the magazine *Municipal Engineering* contained correspondence concerning the enforcement of the Food Hygiene (General) Regulations, 1979. An Environmental Health Officer from the Bromley

Environmental Health Department wrote to the magazine calling for the 'consistent application' of these Regulations through legal enforcement. In response to this, an officer from Kyle and Carrick District Council wrote to the magazine claiming that it would be a 'retrograde step' to prosecute every time an immediate response is not forthcoming from an offender. A few months earlier the journal of the Institution of Environmental Health Officers, *Environmental Health*, carried a report on the publication of *Health and Safety Statistics 1976* which noted, '. . . that the enforcement notice procedures had been used by Her Majesty's Factory Inspectors on many more occasions than in the local authorities', commenting that:

> ". . . most progress made by district councils in raising standards has been achieved by informal means. As in other aspects of environment, it is the informal approach which invariably produces the best and more permanent result." (*Environmental Health*, March 1979).

The same debates emerged at a departmental level. As I moved between environmental health departments while undertaking my fieldwork, it was often remarked that I must be finding substantial differences between areas. Officers often chose to work in authorities which employed their preferred enforcement strategy and those adhering to one approach could be extremely critical of those taking a different view. Persuasive strategy officers criticized counterparts in insistent strategy departments for trying to be policemen or for acting like "little Hitlers". Conversely, they were themselves criticized for being "softies" or "country bumpkins". This latter characterisation perhaps derives from the fact that, in my sample at least, EHOs adhering to the persuasive strategy were from the least urbanised and least industrialised areas.

D. THE FACTORY INSPECTORATE AND THE INSISTENT STRATEGY

Debates about the enforcement approach that should be adopted are a fundamental part of early Factory Inspectorate history. Bartrip and Fenn, referring to the early history of this Inspectorate, (c1837–1846) explain that:

> "Within the inspectorate there were those who favoured an enforcement policy weighted towards conflict and prosecution, and those who were sympathetic towards an approach emphasizing co-operation and persuasion" (1983: 213).

The tensions between the two strategies were heightened in the 1859–78 period, argue these authors, when the Inspectorate was organised under two joint Chief Inspectors who held very different views about enforcement practice. One, Alexander Redgrave, regarded prosecution as a last resort, whereas the other, Robert Baker, ". . . almost gloried in it" (Bartrip and Fenn, 1983: 215). The two men also held very different evidentiary requirements for prosecution, with Redgrave only prosecuting when there was a high chance of conviction. Redgrave's strategy eventually dominated the

160   *LAW & POLICY*   *April 1989*

Inspectorate,[5] but it should not be gleaned from this discussion either that Baker totally rejected the accommodative style or that Redgrave never prosecuted. Bartrip and Fenn note that ". . . both men recognized the necessity and value of a conciliatory approach to their work" (Ibid).

Redgrave's conciliatory approach is also favoured by the present day Factory Inspectorate. The Chief Inspector's Annual Report for 1985, for example, states:

> "Advice, encouragement and enforcement are essential elements of the Inspectorate's work" (HSE, 1986: 3).

> "The informal procedures, verbal advice and written advice are those which are used in the vast majority of cases" (ibid, p. 36).

These statements are supported by various studies of this Inspectorate. M. Jamieson found that:

> ". . . the 'advisor' image of inspector was the dominant model for a sizeable proportion of the Inspectorate" (1985: 111).

Carson's (1970) findings accord with this, and so do my own.

During 1984–1986 I accompanied 33 factory inspectors on their visits to a total of 111 sites. The dominant enforcement style was undoubtedly accommodative, but it was closer to the insistent strategy than the persuasive approach. While all inspectors tended to use informal procedures in the first instance, they would have no hesitation about invoking legal sanctions should they fail to secure compliance. That was not usually necessary, however. The 1985 Chief Inspector's Report estimates that "In less than one in every 25 visits does the need for enforcement by prosecution or formal notice arise" (HSE, 1986: 8). My observations would again accord with this, with the additional qualification that the most frequently used legal method is the enforcement notice. Of the 111 Factory Inspectorate visits I accompanied, none resulted in prosecution. In six cases, improvement notices were served; in some cases more than one notice was served on an employer. The fact that Factory Inspectors are prepared to consider legal action even this often, however, is in marked contrast to the persuasive strategy. And so is the Factory Inspector's observed tendency to enter any situation thinking in terms of potential evidential requirements.

The subject of prosecution, in fact, often enters Factory Inspector's conversations, although Inspectors do not all hold homogeneous views. One section of the Inspectorate seems more prosecution-oriented than the majority. Some of these views are influenced by task. Factory Inspectors working in construction groups, for example, tend to be more inclined to prosecute than their colleagues elsewhere (see also Jamieson, 1985: 147). A small proportion (6 of 33) of Factory Inspectors felt the need to impress upon me that while prosecution may be much talked about by some of their colleagues, it is not an everyday—or even every week—occurrence for most inspectors. One inspector commented that prosecution constitutes a very,

Hutter REGULATORY ENFORCEMENT STYLES 161

very small part of their work, adding that in his opinion ". . . too many people talk about prosecution being the be-all and end-all of their work". Another described prosecution and enforcement notices as "helpful but not normal tools of enforcement." And several said that they would prosecute if all else failed but they would consider that in having to prosecute they too had failed.

E. INDUSTRIAL AIR POLLUTION INSPECTORS AND THE PERSUASIVE STRATEGY

The view of the Factory Inspectors may be contrasted with those of Industrial Air Pollution Inspectors, whose enforcement approach most closely resembles the persuasive approach. In the 1981 Annual Report it is explained that:

> ". . . discussion, persuasion and co-operation leading to mutually agreed solutions, are preferred to coercion. In consequence, the inspectorate has made only limited use of the full enforcement powers" (HSE, 1982: 17).

Persuasion is a key word in describing this inspectorate's enforcement approach. Prosecution does not really form part of their everyday vocabulary. Indeed, legal action of any kind is regarded negatively and as a sign of failure.

These characteristics are partly attributable to one of the central legislative concepts in environmental control, namely that of 'best practicable means', which suggests that standards should be adapted to individual works and revised to reflect changes either in technical ability or in environmental needs. Responsibility for determining these matters lies with the Inspectorate, which negotiates standards with industry and with individual worksites. Factory Inspectors, by contrast, traditionally have worked with legislation which more often specifies standards, leaving less scope for negotiation than does the concept 'best practicable means'. Moreover, as I will discuss later, Factory Inspectors generally have less opportunity to regularly visit premises and forge long-standing relationships with those they regulate.

As with the Factory Inspectorate, the enforcement style adopted by the Industrial Air Pollution Inspectorate is well-established historically. The first "Alkali Inspector" was Dr. Robert Angus Smith, described by Ashby and Anderson, in their history of air pollution control, as the person who ". . . moulded the Alkali Inspectorate into the shape it still possesses today" (1981: 24). This 'shape' relies on negotiation, persuasion and trust, an approach which was itself moulded by the difficulties placed in the way of these early Inspectors (ibid). The Inspectorate's policy of working closely with industry was subject to criticism in these early years. The public, Dr. Smith wrote ". . . are continually confusing or attempting to confound our duties with those of the police . . . The Government Inspectors have been more as teachers raising up the standard of labour in the works" (Ashby and Anderson, 1981: 29). Similar criticism has been directed to the Inspec-

162   *LAW & POLICY   April 1989*

torate in more recent years, especially in the 1974 Social Audit Report, but the Inspectorate has stuck by its policy, which it believes has produced noticeable long-term improvements.

F. ORGANIZATIONAL CONTROLS

Adherence to a given enforcement philosophy is built into each agency's organization in a number of ways. Expectations are made very clear to officers/inspectors by a combination of superior and peer group pressure. Selection of cases for legal action is formally controlled through hierarchical review by progressively senior officers. In those agencies which discourage formal legal action, the majority, if not all, of the prosecutions recommended by the individual officer are simply rejected. So control by persuasion is chosen almost by default, as the officer new to the organization, who may favour prosecution, eventually ceases to select it as a plausible enforcement method. In agencies favouring accommodative techniques, a powerful method of control over individual officers is the notion that anyone who needs to resort to formal enforcement matters has failed in his job—as Richardson (1983: 185) reminds us, most officers want to be regarded as 'good' at their job and avoid disapproval.

In agencies adhering to the insistent strategy, the number of cases forwarded for possible legal action may be taken as a measure of work completed. So those officers who do not recommend cases for formal action are easily spotted; if persistently failing to recommend formal action, they may be formally reprimanded and accused of not pulling their weight within the department. Several cases of officers being reprimanded for these reasons came to my attention when undertaking fieldwork into Environmental Health Departments C and D. Where the insistent strategy is adopted, however, there are organizationally-set limits on the extent to which such legal methods should be employed. Officers are not expected to be zealous in their use of the law, but are required to prosecute no more than once or twice a year, on the assumption that in any one workload there will be only a small proportion of cases where informal methods are never going to succeed. Such cases typically involve serious, persistent or blatant offending. When officers come across these cases, they are expected to act formally, rather than carry on in the hope that informal methods will eventually succeed.

In three of the four environmental health departments studied, cases under consideration for legal action were subject to approval not just by senior officers but also by the elected local council's environmental health committee (see Hutter, 1988). In the fourth department, the council had delegated the authority to make these decisions to the Chief Environmental Health Officer. The Industrial Air Pollution Inspectorate operates a very centralized system, as all cases intended for legal action must first be approved by the headquarters organization. The Factory Inspectorate, however, operates a much more decentralized system; only those cases which are unusual or have attracted great public attention are referred to the very top of the organization for approval. This is not to suggest, however, that individual inspectors' decisions are final, since decisions to initiate legal action are always subject to the approval of immediate superiors even in routine cases. It is perhaps significant that it is those agencies and departments in which control of this kind is most decentralized that the insistent strategy prevails.

An officer's peer group represents another major source of conformity (Blau, 1963; Hill, 1972). The individual who deviates from agency strategies may be persuaded to feel that he has let down his colleagues by not presenting a uniform approach to the public. He may be subject to negative evaluations of his work and, because of his implicit challenge to the strategies and procedures of his colleagues, is likely to elicit some hostility at work. Such methods are most effective when the working day is structured around morning and late afternoon visits to the office. So while superiors learn of an officer's activities through reports of visits, expense claims and the like, colleagues hear about each other's work through informal chit-chat in the office. Where deviation from the general approach to work is apparent, supervisors may even instigate peer group pressure to conform. In the inspectorates examined, Industrial Air Pollution Inspectors are the least amenable to this form of control, as they come into less contact with colleagues during a normal working week. Because of the low numbers of inspectors based in each district office (usually two and at most three) and the large physical districts covered by these inspectors, they cannot always make daily visits to the office.

The tendency of staff to adhere to the enforcement style preferred by the agency for which they work is perhaps not surprising. In his study of American forest rangers, Kaufman (1960) explains that there are a number of conditions which promote identification of members with an organization. For example, all organizations will try to recruit people whom they believe will conform with the organization's policy. Once members have joined, there will be varying degrees of supervision over their activities and training about how to undertake one's new job. Moreover, once an individual has joined an organization, his or her position, welfare and future will be related to those of colleagues and superiors. It should not be forgotten, of course, that organizations can offer rewards to those who conform in the form of promotions.

III. WHAT ACCOUNTS FOR VARIATIONS IN ENFORCEMENT STYLE?

Data collected from the study of these three different agencies suggest a complex of factors which lead to variations in enforcement strategy. The case of Environmental Health Officers is especially revealing, as it involves

164 *LAW & POLICY   April 1989*

members of one profession, enforcing the same legislation, but working in different areas of the country and subject to varying political control.

A. ORGANIZATIONAL FACTORS

Enforcement practices are sensitive to organizational resources available to the agency—particularly the department's budget and staff numbers, viewed in relation to the number and complexity of environmental problems encountered. In my samples, those adhering to the persuasive strategy had greater organizational resources than those who favoured the insistent strategy. Not only were their jurisdictions smaller, but Environmental Health Departments A and B were not faced with any particularly serious environmental health problems, since a comparatively high proportion of the regulated in these areas maintained reasonable standards. Hence, officers in these Departments did not have to devote a large proportion of their time to bringing premises up to the basic minimum standards. Conversely, in Departments C and D, which were characterised by the insistent strategy, resources had to be devoted to a larger number of more severe environmental health problems, especially in the area of housing, to bringing many more businesses up to acceptable minimum standards, and to combatting widespread ignorance about minimum standards.

The Factory and Industrial Air Pollution Inspectorates also differ with respect to resources. As we can see from Table 3, whereas the ratio of field Factory Inspectors to premises regulated is 1:747, it is just 1:68 for Industrial Air Pollution Inspectors. Quite clearly, this gives the latter a much greater opportunity to revisit premises and, since the enterprises they regulate have less chance of avoiding detection of violations, to effect a remedy by means of persuasion.

Table 3. Comparison of Factory Inspectorate and Industrial Air
Pollution Inspectorate Resources in 1987

	Factory Inspectorate	Industrial Air Pollution Inspectorate
No. of HQ Inspectors	24	8
No. of Field Inspectors	538	29
No. of premises regulated	401,836	1,986

Source: HSE Records

Contradictory interpretations can be placed upon the relationship between resources and prosecution. It may be argued, for instance, that if agency resources are tight and felt to be inadequate to deal with the problems to be tackled, then there will be pressure to employ formal-legal procedures. A Chief Officer of an environmental health department explained in a public document that "One of the most distressing aspects" of a shortage of experienced staff was "the lack of time" that could be spent by officers educating the regulated at their place of work. "This", he wrote, "is likely to result in the increasing need to resort to the use of statutory enforcement powers through court proceedings in future years". Shover *et al.* (1982) came across similar arguments in their study of the Office of Surface Mining in America, namely that scarce opportunities for negotiation with the many small strip mining companies in Appalachia was one of the factors which led the Eastern office of this agency to adopt a prosecution-oriented strategy in the early 1970s.

Such observations appear to conflict with the arguments forwarded by economists, who argue that prosecution costs may lead agencies with insufficient resources to *avoid* legal action (see Bartrip and Fenn, 1980; Veljanovski, 1983). Clearly, the cost of prosecuting will constrain all enforcement agencies from acting formally against a *large* proportion of violations—although financial cost may not be the only or the prime consideration. Most of those I spoke to would agree that prosecution is expensive, but those adhering to the insistent strategy argue that there comes a point when it is less costly than repeated visits to offenders, particularly those who persistently display little inclination to improve. There are a number of strands to such an argument. One is that there are some offenders for whom education and negotations are only cost-effective if the momentum can be maintained through frequent visits from officers. Thus, if the agency has insufficient resources to keep such momentum going, then it may be less costly to prosecute than to 'waste' money on the few educational visits that can be managed. Secondly, the agency may consider that prosecution, even if costly, is rendered cost-effective through its deterrent effects on other offenders. These debates about the role of resources in determining enforcement strategy emphasize that the selection of particular enforcement strategies is not the result of one, but a variety of factors. It is not resources alone that determine policy. The way in which they are used is determined by the interplay between their availability and other influences.

B. POLITICAL FACTORS

Another set of factors which help to explain variations center on what may be loosely termed the political context of enforcement. The degree of public awareness and concern about regulatory problems fall into this category. In general, the activities undertaken by the enforcement officials discussed in this paper arouse very little public or political interest. It is only occasionally, in cases of serious incidents or accidents, that their work attracts media publicity. For Environmental Health Officers, such events may be a serious outbreak of food poisoning, or overcrowded housing, highlighted by a death in a fire. Severe injuries or death sustained at work may bring Factory Inspectors into public profile, as in the case of the June 1974 explosion at a chemical works in Flixborough, in which there were multiple fatalities and over 100 injuries. A major environmental incident in which there is wide-spread complaint, temporary evacuation, or visible damage to vegetation is necessary before the Industrial Air Pollution Inspectorate is mentioned by the press to any great extent. But in the main, the routine work of these agencies does not cause a lot of public or political excitement, and this may help explain why all of these agencies generally favour an accommodative rather than sanctioning style of enforcement (see Hutter, 1988).

This said, it could be expected that visible differences in the severity of the regulatory problems encountered would be reflected in enforcement approach. This seems to hold true for the environmental health departments examined, where the more urbanized the local authority, the more stringent the enforcement strategy seems to be. In local authorities which have a high concentration of rented accommodation and a close proximity of industry and housing, environmental health problems are likely to be immediately visible. As a consequence, their political salience is heightened and there will probably be greater public and local council pressure upon the environmental health department to be seen doing something substantive. This is particularly the case because departmental concern for organizational self-preservation is greatest in these areas. Since the 1972 Local Government Act, which released local authorities from their statutory obligation to appoint environmental health officers, urban environmental health departments have felt threatened, especially where a large part of the department's resources are devoted to housing problems. Officers worry that their other functions are not fully appreciated by the local council and that the department's functions will be taken over by another department whose primary responsibility is not environmental health. Consequently, these departments are eager to display that they are doing a worthwhile job. They are quick to point out that they serve notices and prosecute, as tangible evidence of their 'hard' work, particularly when they compile annual reports and report their activities to the council.[6]

Again, these findings accord with those of Shover *et al.* (1982), who cite varying degrees of public concern as one of the explanations for the adoption of radically different enforcement strategies by different regions in the Office of Surface Mining. Likewise, Bardach and Kagan (1982: 207–8) explain how regulatory agencies are influenced by political and media considerations, sometimes using legalistic enforcement tactics as a defence against public allegations of complacency. The opposite enforcement style may develop when regulatory offenses cause no serious political or media disquiet. Gunningham (1987), for example, demonstrates how low visibility occupational health hazards may be overlooked by the agency in the absence of public or labour union concern. He describes how the New South Wales Mines Inspectorate failed to prosecute regulatory violations in a remote and unprofitable asbestos mine in Baryugil, where some 100 aborigines either died or became seriously ill from exposure to asbestos dust.

Hutter REGULATORY ENFORCEMENT STYLES 167

In the case of environmental health departments, there is also direct political control of the agency and formal, institutionalized channels for the local population to communicate its feelings, namely through the environmental health committee of the locally elected council. As far as I can tell, each of the councils which controlled the departments in my sample played its part in determining policies and guiding strategy decisions. Indeed, at a most fundamental level, decisions about the stringency with which the law should be enforced are left to the deliberations of the Chief Environmental Health Officer in conjunction with local government.

All of the councils in my sample took an active part in discussing and forming policies. Three councils (those which controlled Departments A, B and C) charged their environmental health committees with the duty of approving or rejecting the service of notices or initiation of court proceedings proposed by the environmental health department. The Chief Officer of Department D did not have to consult the council before taking legal action but he did have to be sensitive to its wishes. Of the other three departments, Department C was the only one to keep complete centralized records of council decisions. These records reveal that the council's environmental health committee only selectively approved the Department's recommendations for prosecution. For example, in 1978, 24 out of 80 cases recommended by the Department for prosecution were rejected by the committee. On the other hand, in 1979, none of the 39 cases brought to the Committee's attention were prevented from continuing through the legal process. The differences in the proportion of cases approved reflects a change in the composition of the Committee following the local elections in 1979. These figures also reveal how the Department tried to adjust to the views of the Committee: in 1979 it recommended 50 per cent fewer cases for prosecution than it had in 1978.

The four environmental health departments I researched covered the range of political opinion in Britain. Department A was subject to a powerful Conservative council and it served a traditionally Tory area. Department D was employed by a Labour council with a strong majority. Departments B and C were in marginal constituencies. At the time of my research, Department B was subject to a marginal Conservative council and Department C was subject to a marginal Labour council. Reviewing the data in Table 1, it appears, as one might predict, that the probability of prosecution is lower where a Conservative council is in power.

I am reluctant to conclude, however, that varying political pressures have a consistent effect on how the environmental health committee and the enforcement officers respond to environmental health problems. This is partly because environmental health appears to be of relatively little political importance, whichever party is in power. Moreover, those enforcement officers who worked in the politically marginal constituencies could not with any certainty predict how a change in the political composition of the council would affect their work. Department B offers an example. At the time of my fieldwork, the Conservative council in power was attempting

168   *LAW & POLICY   April 1989*

to force the Department to *increase* its use of formal methods (Hutter, 1988: 145). While they were not demanding a radical shift in strategy, they were not supporting the tendency suggested by Table 1's prosecution figures, that is, that a Conservative majority would produce a disinclination to prosecute.

This seems to contrast with the American situation, where one study found that OSHA offices were more severe, in terms of their prosecution policies, in states where elected government officials were Democrats (Scholz and Feng Heng Wei, 1986). Indeed, in *all* of the British cases, the environmental health committees served to *reduce* the number of prosecutions. Why British environmental health committees should want to guard against the environmental health department's powers to prosecute is not entirely clear. Undoubtedly part of the explanation lies with the moral ambiguity which seems to surround the employment of the criminal law as a method of regulating business (see Hawkins, 1984; Hutter, 1988; Justice, 1980; Kadish, 1963).

In the case of Departments A and B, we are reliant upon officers' accounts of their relationship with their employers. In Department A, all officers were quite certain that the council was against the use of formal methods. In fact, several officers who had quite recently joined the Department told me of instances when their recommendations for prosecution had been rejected by the council or they had been reprimanded for threatening to take legal action against local businesses. In Department B there was also an understanding, of apparently long-standing, that the local council discouraged legal action. But this case is interesting because Department B has been subject to a succession of councils of varying political persuasions. While officers maintained that each of these councils accepted, if not encouraged, the adoption of the informal-educative strategy, it was quite clear that there were occasions when they were asked to adopt a more stringent approach with respect to particular offenses. For instance, at the time of my fieldwork, the council, which held a small Conservative majority, was attempting, as noted above, to force the Department to increase its use of formal methods in the case of food and food hygiene offenses.[7] This was being met with some resistance, particularly from junior officers. They were reluctant to disturb their good relationship with local retailers, particularly since this reorientation in strategy would, in all probability, last for only as long as this council held onto its slender majority.

Unfortunately, the size of my sample was not large enough to trace any firm relationship between enforcement styles and the political environments within which departments operated. But the strength and stability of the local council does appear to be related to the degree to which its environmental health department adheres to its selected enforcement strategy. In my sample, Departments A and D were both controlled by long-standing councils which held strong majorities, whereas Departments B and C both experienced fairly frequent changes in the political make-up of their controlling councils.[8]

These factors do not help much in understanding why Factory and Industrial Air Pollution Inspectors adopt varying strategies from each other. While public concern explains why Factory Inspectors are prepared to favour a severe approach in specific cases, it does not account for their adherence to the insistent strategy. Arguably environmental pollution attracts much more public concern than many of the problems dealt with by the Factory Inspectorate, but neither this nor fierce criticism of their approach has caused the Industrial Air Pollution Inspectorate to change from the persuasive strategy. Neither of these Inspectorates is subject to direct political control, although both have obviously been subject to the financial strictures imposed by the central Government in recent years and have experienced investigations into their efficiency and effectiveness (see Hutter and Manning, forthcoming). Nonetheless, this is qualitatively different from the type of political control exercised by the local authorities over environmental health departments. Indeed, the absence of such control in the cases of the Factory and Industrial Air Pollution Inspectorates perhaps serves to underline its influence when it is present elsewhere.

C. SOCIAL FACTORS: RELATIONAL DISTANCE AND FREQUENCY OF INTERACTION

A more important explanation of the approaches adopted by different agencies centers on the nature of their relationship with the regulated. In the case of Environmental Health Officers, geographical proximity is important. The degree to which officers are integrated into the locality they serve affects not only their personal inclination to adopt either informal or formal techniques but also influences officers' assumptions about the population they control. Those who operate in a small and fairly close-knit community generally know the people they are dealing with, and they fear that the positive outcomes of legal action may be outweighed by its negative effects—both in terms of their working relationships and their social interactions with the regulated and their families. Officers working in these smaller environments typically assume that they are dealing with good, respectable people who are in need of education and advice.

Conversely, those working in large conurbations adopt a more suspicious attitude. They are less likely to be acquainted with those they regulate, do not fear to the same extent the negative consequences of legal action, and are likely to adopt a cynical and less charitable view of the regulated. Not knowing the regulated well, the location and incidence of rule-breaking may be less predictable. These factors combine to suggest more frequent recourse to formal enforcement methods.

These findings support Black's "relational distance" hypothesis: "The greater the relational distance between the parties to a dispute, the more likely is law to be used to settle the dispute" (1980: 49). They also are in line with studies of the police, which suggest that less punitive methods of enforcement tend to be employed in stable, homogeneous areas (Banton, 1964; Cain, 1973; Whyte, 1945). In larger and more anonymous social settings, enforcement officials are policing a population of strangers, so must judge people on more objective, legal and universalistic criteria than their rural counterparts, who are more likely to be able to evaluate the situation in the light of particularistic knowledge. The degree to which enforcement officials are integrated into the community they serve also seems to be one of the mechanisms whereby they learn of acceptable and 'normal' methods of handling deviance and transgressions within a particular social setting.

Of course, there are circumstances other than geographical and social proximity which allow enforcement officials to gain a closer and more individual relationship with the regulated. Shover *et al.* (1982), for instance, identify organizational reasons for regional variations between different offices of the Office of Surface Mining. In the area adopting an accommodative approach, inspectors were given individual assignments to particular mines, whereas enforcement was less personalized and considerably more stringent in the area where inspectors were assigned to geographical areas. Opportunities for closer co-operation between enforcement officials and the regulated are also afforded when the population subject to control is small and closely defined. Of significance here seems to be the frequency with which inspectors interact with those they regulate, the suggestion being that the greater the frequency of interaction, the less the inclination to resort to formal legal methods (see Scholz, 1984).

These factors were well understood by both Factory and Industrial Air Pollution Inspectors, as many of those I accompanied explained both their own enforcement strategy and those of other inspectors in terms of their relationship with the regulated. Industrial Air Pollution Inspectors, for example, explained that they know the people they work with very well and are able to visit them frequently and "keep business on its toes". They often contrasted their own positions with that of Factory Inspectors who, as I suggested earlier, have many more premises to regulate per field-level inspector.

Further evidence that the existence of a relationship with the regulated is important in determining enforcement strategy is furnished by an examination of who is prosecuted. For instance, many of the prosecutions initiated by Industrial Air Pollution Inspectors pre-1984 were against Metal Recovery works, especially illegal cable burners (see Table 4).[9] While these Inspectors would react stringently and immediately against any unregistered business operating without pollution arrestment equipment, it is also noteworthy that illegal cable burners tended to be unknown to Inspectors. Moreover, they were often transitory operations, so inspectors had to act quickly and had no opportunity to establish long-term relationships. Similarly, Factory

Hutter REGULATORY ENFORCEMENT STYLES 171

Inspectors working in the Construction Industry Groups tended to be more sanctioning than many of their colleagues. Again, they are often dealing with transitory operations, whose operators often are unknown to them.[10] Moreover, even if it were possible to persuade these offenders to remedy problems, it is highly unlikely that inspectors would be able to check that improvements had been effected, given the short duration of many construction jobs.

Table 4. Industrial Air Pollution Inspectorate Prosecutions, 1978–83

Prosecutions Heard	Year					
	1978	1979	1980	1981	1982	1983
Metal Recovery Works	8	5	10	17	n.a.	15
Total Number	13	7	10	15	n.a.	17

Source: Annual Reports.

IV. CONCLUSION

In this paper, I have sought to demonstrate that the accommodative approach typically associated with regulatory enforcement is not a homogenous and uniform concept. Instead, it is one which embraces a range of enforcement strategies which vary in the degree to which officials are committed to principles of negotiation and the avoidance of legal action, even though such principles may underpin their fundamental orientation. Thus in three different inspectorates in England and Wales, intra- and inter-agency variations have been identified.

A range of factors have been considered—including organizational, political and social factors—that cause agencies to moderate or exaggerate their commitment to either an accommodative or sanctioning approach. The social context of enforcement emerges as an especially important influence, for it may affect perceptions of the severity of offenses, attitudes to offenders, and the accompanying presence or absence of public concern about offenses. Similar factors cause individual inspectors/officers to select and move between strategies.

Of particular importance seems to be the relationship between the enforcement official and the regulated. In this respect, the research lends some support to Black's relational distance hypothesis and Scholz's suggestion that the frequency of interaction between enforcement officials and those they regulate influences enforcement style. But it should be remembered that the factors identified all interact with each other to determine enforcement style. For example, the resources available to an agency will determine how frequently an inspector can visit premises. This, in turn,

172 *LAW & POLICY* April 1989

will influence the relationship between an official and those he or she regulates which, as we have seen, will be a contributory factor in determining enforcement style. Further in-depth comparative work should increase our understanding of the 'middle ground' lying between the accommodative or compliance model of enforcement and the sanctioning or deterrence model identified by early studies of regulatory enforcement.

BRIDGET HUTTER *is a Research Fellow at the Centre for Socio-Legal Studies, University of Oxford. Her recent research has addressed the question of compliance in health and safety and environmental regulation in Great Britain and the impact of these regulations upon industry. She is the author of* The Reasonable Arm of The Law? *(Clarendon Press, Oxford, 1988).*

NOTES

1. Hawkins, unpublished research.
2. Full details of this research can be found in Hutter, 1988.
3. See Centre for Socio-Legal Studies, 1983, for details of this research. It should be noted that the Railway Inspectorate was also studied as part of this research but in order not to confuse this discussion, I have not included details of their approach in this paper.
4. The Industrial Air Pollution Inspectorate has now returned to the auspices of the Department of Environment to be part of a new Pollution Inspectorate.
5. The reasons for this are discussed by Bartrip and Fenn, 1983; Carson, 1974; and Martin, 1983.
6. As is the case with much regulatory activity, there are difficulties in measuring the amount of work undertaken by environmental health officers and its effectiveness. They are dealing with the quality of life and many of the problems they encounter are continuous; they are not always dealing with discrete events but with matters of habit.
7. The reason for this appears to originate from a desire to improve facilities which were particularly important to the town in its capacity as a tourist attraction.
8. At the time of my fieldwork, Department A was in a Conservative stronghold and Department D in a strongly Labour area. Department B was subject to a council with a small Conservative majority and Department C was controlled by a marginal labour council.
9. As a result of amendments to section 78 of the Control of Pollution Act in the Health and Safety (Emissions into the Atmosphere) Regulations 1983 this Inspectorate ceased to be responsible for itinerant cable burners.
10. Kagan (1984) makes a similar observation in his discussion of why the police seem more punitive than regulatory officials.

REFERENCES

ASHBY, E. and M. ANDERSON (1981) *The Politics of Clean Air*. Oxford: Clarendon Press.

BANTON, M. (1964) *The Policeman in the Community*. London: Tavistock.

BARDACH, E. and R. A. KAGAN (1982) *Going by the Book: The Problem of Regulatory Unreasonableness*. Philadelphia: Temple University Press.

Hutter REGULATORY ENFORCEMENT STYLES 173

BARTRIP, P. W. J. and P. T. FENN (1980) "The Administration of Safety: The Enforcement Policy of the Early Factory Inspectorate," 1844–64. *Public Administration* 58: 87–102.

BARTRIP, P. W. J. and P. T. FENN (1983) "The Evolution of Regulatory Style in the Nineteenth Century British Factory Inspectorate," *Journal of Law and Society* 10: 2.

BLACK, D. (1980) *The Manners and Customs of the Police*. New York: Academic Press.

BLAU, P. M. (1963) *The Dynamics of Bureaucracy*. Chicago: The University of Chicago Press.

BRAITHWAITE, J., J. WALKER and P. GRABOSKY (1987) "An Enforcement Taxonomy of Regulatory Agencies," *Law and Policy* 9: 323–350.

CAIN, M. (1973) *Society and the Policeman's Role*. London: Routledge & Kegan Paul.

CARSON, W. G. (1970) "White Collar Crime and the Enforcement of Factory Legislation," *British Journal of Criminology* 10: 383–398.

CARSON, W. G. (1974) "Symbolic and Instrumental Dimensions of Early Factory Legislation: A Case Study in the Social Origins of Criminal Law," in R. Hood (ed.) *Crime, Criminology and Public Policy*. London: Heinemann.

CENTRE FOR SOCIO-LEGAL STUDIES (1983) *An Agenda for Socio-Legal Research into the Regulation of Health and Safety at Work*. Oxford: Centre for Socio-Legal Studies.

CRANSTON, R. (1978) *Consumers and the Law*. London: Weidenfeld & Nicholson.

GUNNINGHAM, N. (1987) "Negotiated Non-Compliance: A Case Study of Regulatory Failure," *Law and Policy* 9: 69–95.

HAWKINS, K. (1984) *Environment and Enforcement: Regulation and Social Definition of Pollution*. Oxford: Clarendon Press.

HSE (1982) *Industrial Air Pollution 1981*. London: HMSO.

HSE (1986) *Report by HM Chief Inspector of Factories 1985*. London: HMSO.

HILL, M. J. (1972) *The Sociology of Public Administration*. London: Weidenfeld and Nicolson.

HUTTER, B. M. (1988) *The Reasonable Arm of the Law?: The Law Enforcement Procedures of Environmental Health Officers*. Oxford: Clarendon Press.

HUTTER, B. M. and P. K. MANNING (forthcoming) "The Contexts of Regulation."

JAMIESON, M. (1985) "Persuasion or Punishment: the Enforcement of Health and Safety at Work Legislation by the British Factory Inspectorate," M.Litt. dissertation, University of Oxford.

JUSTICE (1980) *Breaking the Rules*. London: Justice.

KADISH, S. H. (1963) "Some Observations on the Use of Criminal Sanctions in Enforcing Economic Regulations," *University of Chicago Law Review* 30: 423–49.

KAGAN, R. A. (1978) *Regulatory Justice*. New York: Russell Sage Foundation.

KAGAN, R. A. (1984) "On Regulatory Inspectors and Police," in K. Hawkins and J. M. Thomas (eds.) *Enforcing Regulation*. Boston: Kluwer-Nijhoff.

KAUFMAN, H. (1960) *The Forest Ranger: A Study in Administrative Behaviour*. Baltimore: John Hopkins University Press.

KELMAN, S. (1981) *Regulating America, Regulating Sweden: A Comparative Study of Occupational Safety and Health Policy*. Cambridge, Mass.: MIT Press.

KELMAN, S. (1984) "Enforcement of Occupational Safety and Health Regulations: Comparison of Swedish and American Practices," in K. Hawkins and J. Thomas (eds.) *Enforcing Regulation*. Boston: Kluwer-Nijhoff.

MARTIN, B. (1983) "The Development of the Factory Office up to 1878: Administrative Evolution and the Establishment of a Regulatory Style in the Early Factory

174 *LAW & POLICY* April 1989

Inspectorate," paper presented to 'Regulation in Britain: A Conference', Trinity College, Oxford University, September 1985.

REISS, A. (1984) "Selecting Strategies of Social Control over Organizational Life," in K. Hawkins and J. Thomas (eds.) *Enforcing Regulation.* Boston: Kluwer-Nijhoff.

RICHARDSON, G. M., A. I. OGUS and P. BURROWS (1983) *Policing Pollution: A Study of Regulation and Enforcement.* Oxford: Clarendon Press.

SCHOLZ, J. T. (1984) "Co-operation, Deterrence and the Ecology of Regulatory Enforcement," *Law and Society Review* 18: 179–224.

SCHOLZ, J. T. and H. W. FENG (1986) "Regulatory Enforcement in a Federalist System," *American Political Science Journal* 80: 1249ff.

SHOVER, N., D. CLELLAND and J. LYNXWILER (1982) *Constructing a Regulatory Bureaucracy: The Office of Surface Mining Reclamation and Enforcement.* Washington DC: National Institute of Justice.

SOCIAL AUDIT (1974) *The Alkali Inspectorate: The Control of Industrial Air Pollution.* London: Social Audit.

VELJANOVSKI, C. G. (1983) "Regulatory Enforcement: An Economic Study of the British Factory Inspectorate," *Law and Policy Quarterly* 5: 75–96.

WHYTE, W. F. (1945) *Street Corner Society.* Chicago: The University of Chicago Press.

[21]

JOURNAL OF LAW AND SOCIETY
VOLUME 15, NUMBER 1, SPRING 1988
0263-323X $3.00

Law, Policy, and Legal Avoidance:
Can Law Effectively Implement Egalitarian Policies?

DOREEN McBARNET*

This special issue of the journal tackles the question of law, democracy, and social justice: to what extent do legal forms and institutions help or hinder the implementation of egalitarian policies? Can legal regulation effectively promote social justice and democracy?

The effectiveness of the regulation of business has been the subject of extensive socio-legal research and analysis. Laws have been introduced ostensibly to provide individual rights for the less powerful in society or to protect collective interests against the absolute rights of property or the absolute right of business to pursue profit maximisation. Health and safety codes, pollution regulations, rent control, and anti-discrimination legislation are good examples. Yet research on the effectiveness of the regulation of business has not been optimistic. Although the tendency to critical assessment in the social sciences may often *under*play the measure of real progress achieved by legal reform, it is nonetheless the case that research has tended to highlight the limitations of regulation rather than its success.

The failure of egalitarian regulation has been largely ascribed to four factors: the failure of the law makers, the failure of the law enforcers, the failure of the drafters, and the failure of the whole cumbersome apparatus of law itself, destined always to lag behind dynamic business.

Those who make the law have been criticised for succumbing to powerful lobbies and fatally weakening legislation as a result, or for being necessarily a "captive state" by virtue of social networks, economic powerplay, or the blackmail of multinational business able to threaten to damage the economy by turning elsewhere if regulation is overdone. The substance of the law itself is thus often seen as an inadequate compromise riddled with exemptions and loopholes and lacking the teeth to give it any chance of effectiveness.

This in turn affects the enforcers. What can they do with inadequate powers? How successful can bluff be against sophisticated violators?

*Centre for Socio-Legal Studies, Wolfson College, Oxford OX2 6UD, England.

This paper draws on the research of the author and Graham Mansfield in a project funded by the E.S.R.C. on tax evasion and avoidance.

Enforcers also are seen as "captured". There is a trade between regulators and regulated; regulators are often insiders from the regulated industry. Organisational pressures intrude. There are too few enforcers, too many people and organisations to be policed. Negotiation, compromise, and underenforcement result.

At a more technical level the drafter is blamed. How can law be implemented effectively when it is overcomplex, unclear, and riddled with loopholes? At the most general level of all is the notion of lag: law is just too slow to keep up with the pace of changing economic reality.[1]

But there is another problem which has been ignored in the analysis of why egalitarian regulation fails – not how the law makers *make* law, not how the regulators *enforce* it, but how those on the receiving end *use* and manipulate it. Political lobbying over the content of law is one way in which the potentially regulated can actively influence the effectiveness of law. But the active role of those subject to regulation does not stop with the passing of an Act. Rather, legal techniques are brought into play to create strategies for weakening the law by legally *avoiding* it. Even if one could imagine a legislature so committed to egalitarian policies that it would not compromise in its law-making, armed with an enforcement agency with the commitment and powers fully to control violations, effective regulation may meet yet another barrier.

Enforcers cannot enforce laws unless they are violated. What regulation studies have underplayed is the extent to which the regulated do not violate but merely avoid the law. Responses to law are not just a matter of breaking it (crime) and obeying it (compliance). It is also possible to use legal techniques to achieve non-compliance with the *intent* of the law without technically violating its *content*. The law is not broken but it is, nonetheless, entirely ineffective in achieving its aims. *Despite* the legislature, *despite* the enforcers, law becomes merely symbolic.

This focus requires re-examination of the two other factors conventionally blamed for the failure of regulation: drafting skills and time lag. Faulty, hasty, and excessively complex drafting may well create problems for regulators. But much of the complexity of law and the convoluted style of its wording is not the cause but the result of avoidance. Specific devices to avoid law result in more law and more verbose law in the attempt to close the loophole. As for the notion of lag – the inevitable inability of the rusty apparatus of law to keep up with thrusting dynamic business practice – it may also confuse cause and effect. It may be less a matter of law lagging behind business practice than business practice quite deliberately moving out of reach of law. Regulation is not so much lingering behind business practice as a major motivation for its change. Business adapts to law not necessarily by complying with its aims, but by changing to keep outside its ambit. Those allegedly subject to the law can turn the law upon itself and render it ineffective.

AVOIDANCE IN ACTION: TAX AVOIDANCE

Consider two examples of avoidance in action – tax avoidance and the avoidance of rent regulations. Both are particularly relevant to the issue of law and social justice in that they are attempts to use law to limit absolute private property rights. Taxation impinges on private property rights for the *collective* 'good', rent legislation impinges on private property rights in order to establish counter-rights for *individuals* in a less powerful market situation. To the extent to which the tax system claims to be progressive (perhaps less and less), tax law is also aimed at the redistribution of private wealth.

But the world of taxation is riddled with avoidance devices. Indeed, there is a whole sophisticated tax avoidance industry specialising in the creation, marketing, and dissemination of legal methods to minimise or avoid tax. Take capital gains tax, for example. In 1965 the Labour Chancellor of the Exchequer introduced capital gains tax in the interests of greater equity. It was to be an effective tax on the rich, "an attempt to make speculators, property developers and well-advised financiers pay a fair share of tax on their profits".[2] But creating effective law that impinges on the interests of the "well-advised" is a difficult task. Being well-advised includes being well-advised on how to avoid tax. Capital gains tax has been successfully avoided over the years by a series of devices which have rendered it "the most legalistic and least cost-effective major tax in the Government's armoury" according to specialist commentators.[3]

One can, of course, avoid tax simply by taking property out of the jurisdiction altogether by going off shore to one tax haven or another. Or, indeed, one can evade tax by criminal action, by simply not disclosing assets – the world of secret money, numbered Swiss bank accounts and safe deposits. But there is the less drastic option – though it involves transaction costs – of taking advantage of one device or another to *avoid* the law in a way which may break the spirit but does not break the letter of the law, and thus leaves the avoider immune from either the necessity of compliance with the law or the risk of punishment. Specific devices popular at various stages over recent years have included such esoteric-sounding but utterly routine methods as 'bed and breakfasting' for avoiding capital gains tax on shares; 'bondwashing' for avoiding tax on gilts; or, on a rather different tack, 'offshore rollup funds' for 'legally laundering' income into capital to take advantage of the differentials in tax rates between the two.

Bed and breakfasting traditionally refers to a way of creating artificial capital losses to set against real capital gains and thus reduce or totally avoid paying capital gains tax. This involves taking shares which are currently at a lower value than when they were purchased, and which the owner actually intends to continue to hold in the hope that they will rise in value again. In the meantime the shareholder can crystallise the paper loss by selling the shares one evening and buying them back (by pre-arrangement with the dealer) the next morning. As long as they are out of the shareholder's hands for 'bed and breakfast' the paper loss will count against real gains and avoid tax. The introduction of indexation meant that a loss in relation to index-linked value

115

(even though there was none in relation to actual cost) could be crystallised in this way too. This method is continually practised on a large scale, seen as "a staple of investment practice",[4] and indeed was widely recommended as a way of cutting the real costs of the Stock Exchange's 'Black Monday' in October.[5]

Bondwashing and offshore rollups use the law by manipulating the legal definition of income and capital. Bondwashing, in addition, depends on two exemptions: the exemption of government bonds (gilts) from capital gains tax if held for over a year, and the tax-exempt status of particular categories of investment and market actors, notably pension funds and market jobbers.[5]

Gilts realise income twice a year with a dividend. The practice was to sell the gilt, just before the next dividend was due for a price which reflected the value of the coming dividend. The dividend would have been subject to income tax but, by selling the gilt at a value that included the dividend rather than actually realising the dividend, the dividend value became a capital gain rather than income. The capital gain was exempt from tax. The security was sold to a tax-exempt organisation which took the income without paying tax and resold the security so that the process could begin again. Therefore no tax was paid at all.

Offshore rollup funds enjoyed a heyday in 1983-4, when some £2,000,000,000 was invested in them. Again, the interest (subject to income tax) on deposited funds was 'converted' into capital by taking it to a fund off shore (out of United Kingdom jurisdiction), 'rolling up' the interest due by adding it to the capital sum and re-importing the money as capital rather than income. At the time, higher rate income tax was seventy-five per cent compared to thirty per cent capital gains tax, so that for the higher rate taxpayers who normally used this device the tax savings were enormous.

Tax avoidance schemes attained a certain notoriety as employed by the Rossminster Group in the 1970s. For example, a major specific capital gain, perhaps resulting from a once-only transaction such as the sale of land for development, would be offset by a paper loss artificially created by a paper marketed scheme. These schemes were often inordinately complex, using devices relating to several areas of law – for example, different corporate entities constructed solely for the purpose of playing some role in the scheme, trusts, charities, and offshore elements. Financial transactions never intended to be fulfilled would cancel each other out in substance but in legal form would stand to create a situation where effectively 'nothing' became $+x -x$. A positive paper gain was created but fell into an exempt category, and was therefore irrelevant. A corresponding paper loss was left and this could be used against the gain in the real world which the scheme was designed to offset.[6]

All of these devices have now provoked legal action of some sort in an effort to control them. But many standard devices also have long histories of such attempts to control them without great success. The specific form of the device aimed at by the law may cease to be used, only to give rise to another remarkably similar but formally different method which technically escapes the law. Bed and breakfasting, for example, was the subject of regulatory measures in 1982. But it merely became 'weekending'. Instead of one

116

transaction, there were two, carefully timed to fall into two accounting periods and thus avoid the rules. Old-style bed and breakfasting is in fact legal again. Bondwashing has been the subject of regular legislation and litigation since 1927 and has featured in every Finance Act since 1965. Its history demonstrates sixty years of careful adaptation of the device to meet new controls without essentially losing its effect. The announcement on 15 September 1983 that offshore rollup funds were to be subject to new methods of assessment was followed in the financial press within two days by advertisements for rollup alternatives, at least some of which have proved effective.

What we are seeing here is a positive and manipulative response to the attempts by law both to establish measures geared to greater social equity and to make those measures effective. Both types of law have met with active avoidance techniques which undercut the law by technically legal means.

Such techniques, though perhaps most notable and blatant in the area of tax, crop up across the range of law. Rent legislation can be taken as another example.

AVOIDANCE TECHNIQUES AND THE RENT ACTS

Nelken's study of landlords, law, and crime describes the harassment techniques used by landlords to exploit tenants despite the legal rights established by the Rent Act 1965. He points to the scope provided by the Act, which sought to "encourage as a priority 'freely negotiated' agreements between landlord and tenant",[7] and underlines that many of the methods used by landlords, such as 'winkling' (offering financial inducements to leave tenancies) were quite legal. Therefore, the substance of the law is seen as allowing, whether by policy or by silence, the practices which made it ineffective.

It is vital to recognise that the ineffectiveness of regulation is often written into the law itself.[8] But the law has also been used, in much more subtle and technical ways, in an endeavour to create loopholes where there is no positive policy encouragement at all. In short, even where the law-makers do positively seek to make law unambivalently effective, legal avoidance techniques can be brought into play to try to undermine it. The crucial technique is the manipulation of definitions. Exceptions to rules seem to be inevitable on equity grounds. Yet, as soon as an exception is recognised in law, the way is open for those whose activities the law is seeking to bring within the ambit of its control to redefine those activities to fall within the exempt category. Just as in tax law a more favourable rate of capital tax over income tax has spawned devices to redefine income as capital, so the distinction between tenants and licensees created the "potential for wholesale avoidance" of the Rent Acts by redefining ordinary tenancies in terms of licences.[9] Indeed, precedents soon became available for "judge-proof licences", achieved, for example, by renting through a company specially created for the purpose with memor-

117

andum and articles of association which permitted the company only to licence and not to lease. By definition, anyone renting accommodation from the company could be only a licensee and not a tenant.[10]

Likewise, exemptions in the Rent Acts for holiday lettings or lettings with board led to a rash of "holiday lettings in sunny Kilburn"[11] or the provision of board "consisting perhaps merely of a sandwich".[12]

To some extent judges do look through the legal form of the activity to its substance. For example, in an effort to uphold the spirit rather than the letter of the law, the judges in *Street v Mountford*[13] and *Ramsay v I.R.C.*[14] recognised the need to look through the form of devices to their substance, and see them as merely means of evading the Rent Act in the former and taxation in the latter case.

But as new criteria are established for what *is* acceptable, devices are adapted to fit these criteria and stay on the right side of the fence between illegitimate and legitimate practices. The emphasis in tax law on a need for commercial purposes as well as merely tax avoidance if transactions are to be held to result in reduced tax has, for example, led to tax planners advocating that commercial purposes should be built into schemes. Regulation founders on adaptation.

Legal avoidance techniques are routine and permeate the range of law. Current research on insolvency law shows how financial institutions have constructed devices to secure priority for their claims over the scarce resources of insolvent companies.[15] In the face of statutory attempts to ensure basic equality among creditors, or indeed priority for particularly weak creditors such as employees, devices such as the floating charge have been adopted to keep lenders in the most powerful position. Even in areas such as health and safety regulation one can see examples of avoidance in action. For example, Braithwaite's study of multinational pharmaceutical companies mentions in passing a company in the United States of America involved in its eleventh lawsuit over a drug declared by the enforcement agencies to be in contravention of the Food and Drugs Act. Each time the drug was banned its ingredients were minutely adapted to make up a "new" drug, and it was marketed until successfully challenged again.[16]

What makes avoidance possible? To understand this we must look at the role of the legal profession and the nature of law itself.

THE ROLE OF THE LEGAL PROFESSION IN AVOIDANCE

Research on the legal profession has tended to focus on access to it rather than what it actually does. Lawyers offer two classes of service – off-the-peg and tailor-made, or routine and creative. Access is a vital aspect of the issue of legal avoidance, but it is not so much access to lawyers as access to the *creative* role of lawyers that is at issue. Lawyers are not simply means to the implementation of statutory or other ready-made rights, but creators of legal techniques, definitions, and devices. Indeed, far from being means to the implementation of rights, it is lawyers who create the devices which *obviate* them and render them ineffective.

The legal profession, in short, is as much geared to the avoidance of law as it is to its implementation. Nelken, observing the legal advice necessary for some of the Rent Act avoidance strategies he describes, sees them originating in the readiness of "tame solicitors, barristers" and others to participate in shady dealings.[17] But avoidance is not just the prerogative of a few marginal "tame" members of the legal profession: it is a normal, routine part of the legal profession's role. Indeed, it is the creative side of the lawyer's job that is its most prestigious aspect and attracts the highest fees.

It is important to give due emphasis to the active and creative role of lawyers in working *against* the spirit of the law. There is little point in merely laying the blame for loopholes in the law at the door of the legislators and those who draft the law. Exemptions or faulty drafting may provide scope for legal creativity – these may leave the chink open for the thin end of the wedge. But it takes the active hammering of the profession to split the law apart. Lawyers may not, of course, see themselves as working against the spirit of the law. Their role is merely to interpret, apply, and work with the law as best they can in the light of their client's interests – any client's interests. But the nature of law allows considerable scope for legal creativity, and the nature of access to the law means that that creativity is more likely to be used to avoid than to implement egalitarian law. So long as there is unequal access to the creative role of lawyers, avoidance techniques are bound to be available only to those with the resources to buy legal expertise to tailor-make law to fit their own interests.

If, then, law tends to be less than effective in promoting egalitarianism, it is not simply because it is handed over on a plate by pre-determined structures, by a captive state, or by incompetent drafting. It is because of the *post hoc* creative work upon the law by the legal profession on a day-to-day, pragmatic basis to meet the interests of clients who can afford to buy its services in creating or avoiding law.[18]

AVOIDANCE AND THE NATURE OF LAW

How can the law be used to avoid the law? This may seem rather a contradiction in terms. But law is a multifaceted phenomenon and one facet can often be used to contradict another. Within the concept of law we can distinguish the ideology *of* law (as in the rule of law), legal ideology (the ideas expressed in law), legal policy (the purpose of law), the *content* of law (the actual wording of statutes and cases), legal forms and institutions, the legal professions, and legal techniques.[19]

Avoidance devices use the legal *techniques* of the legal *profession* to work on the *content* of statutes and cases, to produce a method of literally complying with the words of the law while nonetheless defeating its purpose. This is done in a way which meets the requirements of the *forms* and procedures of law,

119

may even use the *institutions* of law for endorsement, and justifies the whole process via the *ideology* of the rule of law.

This special issue of the journal is not just about law and social policy, but also about democracy. The ideology of the rule of law in a democratic state requires that citizens be governed according to law, not by the whim of governors. Law should therefore be pre-stated, not *post hoc*. This, of course, assumes a degree of certainty in the content of law which is, in fact, elusive. It is elusive because the content of law cannot include every possible variant which it is intended to cover, or would be intended to cover if it had been foreseen. Indeed, one of the reasons every variant cannot be foreseen is that, in order to create a legal loophole, a good deal of legal brainpower is being put into *finding* a variant – however outlandish – which has *not* been foreseen.

Law seems to fall between two stools. In attempting to formulate effective regulations it can either be very general or very specific. In either case the rule of law can be called on to criticise and undermine it. If it is very general it necessarily operates with wide discretion in its application and this is resisted and lobbied against in the name of the rule of law. If it is specific, the very fact that it specifies the circumstances in which it should apply leaves it open, again in the name of the rule of law, to circumvention by carefully defining one's activities to fall outside its ambit.

Much law in Britain has tended to the latter approach – to literal interpretation and to only literal compliance – and thus to avoidance. Indeed, when in *Ramsay v I.R.C.* the judges abandoned literalism and looked through formal compliance to the substance of the activities involved, this resulted in something of a furore, with explicit criticism in the name of the rule of law. For example, a long-running series of letters in the press saw the "new approach" as "usurping the authority of Parliament", "infringing the provisions of the European Convention for the Protection of Human Rights"[20] and as a "clear infringement of individual freedom and a support for the state".[21]

The ideology of law can, in short, be called upon both to lobby against or challenge broadly framed law and to justify using the forms, techniques, and institutions of law to defeat its more specific content and purpose. And, although the rule of law has been looked to as a source of support for the underdogs of society,[22] in fact it is much more accessible to the top dogs of society with the resources to articulate and use it.

CONCLUSION: LAW AND AVOIDANCE

Law is, in its nature, multifaceted, contradictory, and manipulable, and it is the legal profession's role to take maximum advantage of the contradictions to manipulate the law in the interests of its clients. As the law, the legal profession, and access to both stand, it is hard to see how avoidance can be avoided. One problem is unequal resources; the other is endemic in the tensions and contradictions within the law itself.

Before the inevitability of avoidance is assumed, however, much more detailed analysis of law and its avoidance across a range of areas and styles of jurisdiction is necessary. As well as degrees of success and failure, it may be that there are areas where avoidance has *not* succeeded. It may be that some regulatory approaches are more effective in limiting avoidance than others. For example, one argument in response to avoidance of the law is to call for laws framed in terms of general principles and purposes and for wide discretion in their application.

But perhaps a word of caution is necessary here. For these are the very approaches which those who call for effective regulation of the rich criticise in the law governing the poor. Too much discretion, too little accountability in welfare law or policing, for example, are criticised precisely in the name of the rule of law. Those anxious to tackle the issue of whether the institutions of law in Britain today can foster egalitarian regulation *and* democracy are faced with the fundamental question of what is *law*? How far down the road to discretion can law go and still be *law*?

NOTES AND REFERENCES

1   J. Braithwaite, *Inegalitarian Consequences of Egalitarian Reforms to Control Corporate Crime* (1980); C. Stone, *Where the Law Ends: the Social Control of Corporate Behaviour* (1975).
2   *Financial Times*, 2 May 1985.
3   id.
4   *Financial Times*, 20 April 1982.
5   *Financial Times*, 30 October 1987.
6   G. Mansfield, "Techniques of Tax Avoidance" presented at the Law and Society Association Conference, Washington, 1987.
7   D. Nelken, *The Limits of the Legal Process* (1983) p. 56.
8   D. McBarnet, *Conviction* (1981).
9   D. Yates and A. J. Hawkins, *Landlord and Tenant Law* (2nd ed. 1986). See also J. Farrand and A. Arden, *Rents Acts and Regulations* (2nd ed. 1981); J. T. Farrand "Rent Act Roundup" (1978) 42 *Conveyancer* p. 379; M. Haley, "Avoiding the Rent Act: *Street v Mountford* and Beyond" (1985) 135 *New Law J.* p. 1053.
10   J. E. Adams, "Licences Made Easy" (1976) 40 *Conveyancer* p. 5.
11   Shelter Housing Aid Centre, *Annual Report 1974-75* (1975).
12   *R. v Battersea etc. Rent Tribunal ex p. Parikh* [1957] 1 W.L.R. 410.
13   [1982] 2 W.L.R. 877.
14   [1981] S.T.C. 714.
15   D. McBarnet and C. J. Whelan, "The Development of Priority in Insolvency" presented at the Law and Society Association Conference, Washington, 1987.
16   J. Braithwaite, *Corporate Crime in the Pharmaceutical Industry* (1984).
17   D. Nelken, op. cit., n. 7, p. 56.
18   D. McBarnet, "Law and Capital in the Role of Legal Form and Legal Action" (1984) 12 *International J. Sociology of Law* p. 233.
19   D. McBarnet and H. F. Moorhouse, "Business Law and Business Ideology" (an unpublished paper presented at the Social Stratification Seminar, Cambridge, 1977, and liberally used in *Economy and Society* (1984; eds. D. Sugarman and G. R. Rubin) pp. 49 and passim).
20   *Financial Times*, 5 July 1984.
21   *Times*, 3 March 1984.
22   E. P. Thompson, *Whigs and Hunters* (1975).

Name Index